Peter Berger
Subaltern Sovereigns

Religion and Society

Edited by
Gustavo Benavides, Frank J. Korom,
Karen Ruffle and Kocku von Stuckrad

Volume 66

Peter Berger
Subaltern Sovereigns

Rituals of Rule and Regeneration
in Highland Odisha, India

DE GRUYTER

This book has been published open access with the support of the Open Access Book Fund of the University of Groningen.

ISBN 978-3-11-221618-7
e-ISBN (PDF) 978-3-11-045883-1
e-ISBN (EPUB) 978-3-11-045872-5
ISSN 1437-5370
DOI https://doi.org/10.1515/9783110458831

This work is licensed under the Creative Commons Attribution-NoDerivs 4.0 International License. For details go to https://creativecommons.org/licenses/by-nd/4.0/.

Library of Congress Control Number: 2022950212

Bibliographic information published by the Deutsche Nationalbibliothek
The Deutsche Nationalbibliothek lists this publication in the Deutsche Nationalbibliografie; detailed bibliographic data are available on the Internet at http://dnb.dnb.de.

© 2025 the author(s), published by Walter de Gruyter GmbH, Berlin/Boston
This volume is text- and page-identical with the hardback published in 2023.
The book is published open access at www.degruyter.com.

Typesetting: Integra Software Services Pvt. Ltd.
Printing and binding: CPI books GmbH, Leck

www.degruyter.com

In memory of Georg Pfeffer

Preface

This book has been long in the making. The description and analysis of the festivals in Chapters 6 to 9 – the Ganga Puja, Nandi Porbo, Bali Jatra and the Go'ter – are based on long-term ethnographic fieldwork I conducted between 1999 and 2003 in the context of my PhD research that was part of the Orissa Research Project, funded by the German Research Foundation (DFG). Accordingly, most of the support that I acknowledged in the preface of my earlier book (Berger 2015) has also been crucial for this one.

Georg Pfeffer has introduced me to Odisha and to the Adivasi cultures of Central India in particular. Without his academic insights, example and personal encouragement this book could not have been written. He died in 2020 and this book is dedicated to the memory of this great scholar of tribal India. Equally vital for this project was the cooperation, support and often genuine interest I have experienced when working with the different local communities over the years, especially with the Gutob and Ollar Gadaba, Parenga, Joria, Mali and Dombo. Some persons and places will be mentioned in the pages that follow (in some cases I use pseudonyms) but I want to express my deep gratitude to all people I worked with in the field, for allowing me to experience and document those festivals and to stay in their villages, and for sharing some of their views and knowledge with me. Amrei Volkmann stayed with me in the field for seven months and we attended most of the festivals discussed here together. Her presence also enabled the documentation of different perspectives, for instance, when she accompanied the buffalo-bringing group from Gudapada to the village of the Go'ter hosts (Ponosguda), while I recorded the parallel events going on in that village. Without her support over the decades I could not have pursued my academic work the way I did. I am also indebted to Manto Pradhan, my former research assistant, whose dedication during my earlier fieldwork significantly increased the quality of my ethnographic work and understanding. Also D.K. Behera, P.K. Nayak and M.D Hussain supported my ethnographic research in very important ways.

I had the idea of this book in my mind for many years when I was finally able to get back to my ethnographic material and start writing in 2015. I am grateful to Frank Heidemann for inviting me to Munich for a fellowship that allowed me to focus on nothing else for a while, and to the wonderful staff of the Center for Advanced Studies (CAS) in Munich, for their support and good company. The intention was to complete the manuscript during a visiting professorship at the Indian Institute of Technology in New Delhi in 2020/21, an equally privileged academic place as the CAS, as I know from many visits. The Covid-19 pandemic prevented that from actually happening but I thank Sarbeswar Sahoo and the Department for Humanities and Social Sciences for the invitation. In this situation, my own faculty, the faculty of Theology and Religious Studies of the University of Groningen, facilitated the completion of the manuscript by granting me a sabbatical. I thank the faculty also for financially supporting the language editing of the manuscript.

Various colleagues have contributed to the book in different ways. I am especially grateful to Roland Hardenberg, for our friendship, intellectual exchange and close cooperation over the years. He supported the writing of this book in various ways, through many conversations, reading of the manuscript or by providing some of his own unpublished ethnographic material to be included in this book. The different (NWO and DFG funded) research projects we are currently leading (together with René Cappers) on cereal cultures in Odisha I hope will further contribute to the ethnography of the region, which also was Georg Pfeffer's primary concern. In turn, I would be happy if this book would be of some value to our PhD students who are currently working with the Parenga, Joria, Didayi, Sora and others. Chris Gregory is another scholar whose support, critical comments and inspiration has been very important and much appreciated, ever since we first met in 2004. As with comments generally, I do not always heed all of his advice, so the result obviously is my sole responsibility. I also thank Elena Mucciarelli for commenting on parts of the manuscript, Sophia Schäfer for conversations about the history of Christianity in Koraput, Peter Bisschop for suggesting relevant literature, René Cappers and Sonja Filatova for checking botanical terms and Pascal Jouquet and Ajay K. Harit for discussing termites with me and sharing some of their knowledge about these fascinating creatures. This may also be the appropriate place to acknowledge the work of Thomas Malten (Malten n.d.) on the Desia language. On the basis of Mahapatra (1985), Gustafsson (1989) and his own work in Koraput he compiled a Desia dictionary in the form of a searchable PDF file, which was extremely useful during my research.

I also want to thank the following persons and institutions: The Frobenius-Institute recently digitized and archived more than 3000 photographs I took during my fieldwork, some of which are included in this book. I am grateful to Peter Steigerwald for his excellent work in digitizing all these images. Hence for all the photographs printed here (except where noted) the reference is: copyright Peter Berger / source Frobenius-Institute. Philipp Gries prepared the wonderful maps and SOAS granted permission to include one of von Fürer-Haimendorf's photographs here. Oxford University Press (India) permitted to reprint of some the myths Verrier Elwin had collected (published in Elwin 1950, 1954) and the Institute of Indian Studies (University of Groningen) was so kind to pay their bill. The University Translation and Correction Service (UVC) of the University of Groningen was in charge of the language editing. At De Gruyter I want to thank Katrin Mittmann and Aaron Sanborn-Overby for their support and professional cooperation. I am grateful to Igor Blumer for compiling the index.

Contents

Preface —— VII

1 Introduction: A Proverb and Its Protagonists, Their Rituals and the Region —— 1
    1.1 The Region —— 4
    1.2 Tribal Central India as a Culture Area and Its Subregions —— 8
    1.3 Indian "Tribes" —— 14
    1.4 Tribal Society and Kingship —— 17
    1.5 Historicity and Temporality —— 19
    1.6 The Argument and the Chapters —— 29

Part One: Kings, Subjects and Subaltern Sovereigns

2 Some Pan-Indian Ideas about Kingship —— 43
    2.1 Varna, Ashrama, Purushartha —— 44
    2.2 King, Earth, Fertility —— 49
    2.3 Good Kings, Bad Kings and the Idea of "Barbarians" as the Repugnant Other —— 53
    2.4 The Ontology of Kings —— 59

3 Indigenous Views on Kingship —— 64
    3.1 Kings and Subjects in Tribal Myths —— 68
    3.2 Kingship in Dongria Kond Myth and Ritual —— 90
    3.3 Tribal and Pan-Indian Ideas of Kingship: Summary and Comparison —— 101

4 Kings and Tribes: History and Models of Their Relationships —— 108
    4.1 From the Eastern Gangas to the Kings of Nandapur/Jeypore —— 108
    4.2 Modalities of the King/Tribes Relationship —— 119
    4.3 Hierarchical Opposition and Shared Responsibility of Royal and Tribal Sacrificers —— 137
    4.4 Conclusion —— 144

Part Two: **Proverbial Performances**

5 Royal Rituals in Comparative Perspective: The King's Dasara — 155
    5.1   Dasara in Bastar — 159
    5.2   Analysis and Discussion — 170
    5.3   Dasara in the Nandapur/Jeypore Kingdom — 177
    5.4   Analysis and Discussion — 187
    5.5   Dasara Celebrations in Villages — 191
    5.6   Analysis and Discussion — 206
    5.7   Dasara in Mysore and Puri — 208
    5.8   Conclusion — 212

6 Rituals of Rice and Rebellion: The Ganga Festival of the Joria — 218
    6.1   Two Different Cultivation Systems — 220
    6.2   The Joria — 223
    6.3   The Ganga Festival — 227
    6.4   Discussion and Interpretation — 260

7 Of Millet and Mounds: The Nandi Festival of the Joria — 270
    7.1   The Nandi Festival — 270
    7.2   Discussion and Interpretation — 293

8 A Festival of "Flowers:" The Bali Jatra of the Mali — 312
    8.1   Bima: Rain, Wind and Agriculture — 314
    8.2   The Bali Jatra Epic — 318
    8.3   Interlude: Affinal Gifts and Rice — 319
    8.4   The Bali Jatra in Komra — 322
    8.5   Discussion and Interpretation: Affinity and Kingship — 346

9 Transformations of the Dead: The Go'ter of the Gadaba — 356
    9.1   The Gadaba — 357
    9.2   Embodiments of the Dead — 360
    9.3   Exchanges and Replacements — 367
    9.4   Go'ter in the Dry Fields — 375
    9.5   Discussion and Interpretation: Death and Regeneration — 383

10 Conclusion: Navigating Life — 396

Appendix 1: Glossary of local terms (including botanical names) —— 405

Appendix 2: Myths —— 413

Appendix 3: Nandi song (*Nandi git*) —— 437

Bibliography —— 441

List of Tables —— 461

List of Maps —— 463

List of Photos —— 465

Index —— 467

1 Introduction: A Proverb and Its Protagonists, Their Rituals and the Region

Raja Dasara, Joria Nandi, Mali Bali, Gadaba Go'ter. This short proverb presents four doublets, each one consisting of a social category, mentioned first, followed by an associated ritual: the Dasara festival of the king (*raja*), the "sand" (Bali) festival of a community of horticulturalists called Mali, and two rituals associated with cultivating communities: the Nandi of the Joria and the Go'ter of the Gadaba. On one level, therefore, the aphorism identifies social categories through signature rituals. The Gadaba are famous in the region for their Go'ter ritual as are the Joria for their Nandi festival. On another level, the saying contrasts as much as it relates rulers and ruled. It gives precedence to the king by mentioning him and his festival first, followed by his subjects (*porja*) and their rituals. It seems that the expression epitomizes a ritual polity, one in which sovereign and subalterns are integrated through the rituals with which each of them is identified. The aim of this book is to understand these rituals, each on its own terms and in relation to the others. As will be seen, the ruled are not only subordinate beneficiaries of a sacrificial state represented by the king, as the latter equally depends on the sacrificial power of his subjects, who are, in this sense, subaltern sovereigns.[1]

---

[1] My use of the terms "subaltern" and "sovereignty" will become evident in the course of the book. A short comment may nevertheless be apposite already at this stage. I employ "subaltern" as an equivalent to the word *porja*, how it is used locally, that is in the region of the former Nandapur/Jeypore kingdom. In that sense, *porja* designates both "subjects" of the king and certain "tribal communities" of the region. In particular, *porja* thus indicates a relationship between subjects/tribal communities and the king (the *porja/raja* relationship), represented in particular in rituals and myths. When I speak of the subaltern point of view, or use similar expressions, I am referring to the ideas and perspectives of the indigenous communities. Hence I do not use the word in the general sense, for instance as defined by Ranajit Guha (1988, 35), as "a name for the general attribute of subordination in South Asian society whether this is expressed in terms of class, caste, age, gender and office or in any other way." The terms "subaltern" and "subalternity" have been widely applied to designate various aspects and conditions of subordination (see Berger 2012; Novetzke & Patton 2008; Salah 2014).

Likewise, I employ the notion of "sovereignty" not as it is commonly used in political theory, where the relationships between rulers and rules are first of all related to the modern (Western) state and the ways in which the latter enforces and legitimizes its monopoly of physical force, jurisdiction and legislation (see Delcourt 2007). Rather, I aim to uncover local understandings of sovereignty and in this case, in contrast to the categories of subaltern/ *porja*, sovereignty is not an approximate translation of an indigenous category. In local terms sovereignty describes a semantic field that is much broader than the political domain as it is commonly considered. Many years back, Geertz (1980, 135) already outlined with regard to the

I heard this proverb for the first time shortly after I had started my long-term ethnographic research on the ritual system of the Gadaba in January 1999. The Go'ter ritual of this ethnic group that inhabits part of the plateau of the Koraput district in the south of the Indian state of Odisha had been well studied, comparatively speaking, especially by my teacher Georg Pfeffer, who had taken me to the tribal area of Koraput for the first time three years before. Except for this ritual and the Gadaba (Gutob) kinship terminology, however, not much was known about this community, and I intended to contextualize the Go'ter in the ritual system as a whole. While I thus focused on the Gadaba during this research period of almost two years, I was acutely aware that they formed a part of a much more comprehensive regional society. This awareness also stemmed from the work of Georg Pfeffer (e.g., 1997), who had long stressed the cultural unity of the various communities of the region, irrespective of them being classified as "tribe" or "caste" by the Indian administration. Accordingly, I included as much comparative ethnographic evidence as I could in what was to become my PhD thesis in order to understand Gadaba rituals and society as part of a larger framework (Berger 2015).

After I had encountered the proverb in the field, it became clear to me that documenting those rituals would significantly enlarge my comparative perspective. At the time, neither the Nandi nor the "sand" festival of the Mali had been described in the ethnographic literature and I had no clue what those rituals were about. However, I decided that I would try to document them should I get the chance. The Dasara of the king was a thing of the past, or so I thought, but hoped that the others were still performed. The first opportunity came in January 2000. Through a Joria ritual specialist (*dissari*) who I had met in the Gutob Gadaba village of Gorihanjar, I learned that the Joria perform not only the Nandi but also a twin ritual called Ganga Puja. While the other rituals had not yet been described, the latter had not even been mentioned: neither was it referred to in the local

---

traditional Balinese state such "an alternate conception of what politics is about and what power comes to." The case discussed in this book might be regarded as a variant of biopolitics, but not in the Foucauldian sense of the problem of how the state can regulate and influence individual bodies and pleasures; it is not about population management (see Means 2022; Mendieta 2014). The power over life (well-being and wealth) that is at stake here does not only concern human life but the flow of life in general, including plants, animals and people. It is also distinctive in other ways. First, both rulers (kings) and rules (*niam*) are divinely instituted and motivated; second, the principal mode of sovereignty is sacrifice; third, the ruled are as much involved in biopolitics (read: sacrifice) as the rulers, sacrificial sovereignty is shared among *raja* and *porja*. Therefore, the kingdom as a whole is a sacrificial polity, which is exactly what the proverb under discussion epitomizes; and, finally, this polity includes human and non-human sovereigns, human society is conceptualized as part of what Sahlins (2017) calls a "cosmic polity."

aphorism nor in the academic literature. Together with my partner, Amrei Volkmann, and two Gadaba friends from my host village of Gudapada, who had also never seen the Ganga Puja before, we went to the Joria village to attend the festival. It was a bewildering experience. The performances featured stilt dances and ritual animals and it was quite different from anything I had seen thus far in Gadaba villages. What was it all about?

A month later I spent several days on my own in the same village to witness the Nandi festival. As I had learned by then, both rituals are always celebrated together in successive months and for three years in a row. A year later, we had the chance to record the Ganga Puja in much more detail in another Joria village, the village of the *dissari*. In retrospect, I think that I have been very fortunate, as we also attended much of the "sand" festival hosted by a Parenga village and witnessed a Go'ter ritual in detail, also from a perspective that had hitherto not been documented – from the viewpoint of the hosts' affines.

While I was enthusiastic about the chance to document much of the subaltern rituals of the proverb, at the same time, it was a sobering experience. My initial plan was to study the Gadaba rituals, and I had to accept that dealing with the Nandi, Ganga Puja and Bali Jatra was far beyond the confines of my PhD thesis. Moreover, it was clear to me that I had a sketchy idea of those rituals at best. Much like Karl Gustav Izikowitz (1969), who was the first to document the Go'ter ritual in the 1950s, my understanding of these complex and elaborate rituals was very limited. All of the festivals have a core ritual period of about ten days, preceded by many ritual activities in the previous weeks, even months. While each of them was about cereals – finger millet (Nandi, Go'ter), rice (Ganga Puja) and wheat (Bali Jatra) – they seemed to deal with many other things as well. I had only documented part of the activities and was also lacking general in-depth ethnographic knowledge about the Joria and Mali and, in the case of the Bali Jatra specifically, of the oral epic that seemed to be so relevant to the ritual. It was thus clear at the time that I had to postpone the task of dealing comparatively with the rituals. When I submitted my PhD thesis in 2004 – only published in English over ten years later (Berger 2015) – I could do no more than mention the proverb, adding in a footnote that I had documented the rituals and expressing my hope that such a project could be taken up some time later, also because colleagues had by then started their fieldwork with the Mali and Joria, and thus more ethnographic data on the communities and their festivals might be available in the future.[2]

---

[2] I wrote: "I had the opportunity to witness significant portions of the *bali jatra* in a village dominated by Parenga. I was able to document the *nandi* festival and the associated, entirely

Though I did not anticipate that it would take nearly twenty more years, I had been correct in assuming that the work of my colleagues would be crucial in taking on this project. Tina Otten and Raphaël Rousseleau subsequently published their work on the Bali Jatra and the Joria, respectively, and their contributions indeed turned out to be very important for this book. In fact, it was not only their work, as I soon came to realize when I actually returned to my material and started writing this book in 2015. Much of the work done by Indologists, historians and anthropologists working in the Orissa Research Project (1999–2005), in the context of which my own PhD research was conducted, and of other colleagues working in the wider region, also turned out to be vital. What everybody knows, proved to be true once more: academic work is a collective effort.

1.1 The Region

The aphorism identifies the signature ritual of a king and those of his subjects, or rather, of some of the communities inhabiting the kingdom. Formerly, the seat of the king was Nandapur, which today is a small town located in the middle of a plateau in the mountain range called the Eastern Ghats. The communities mentioned in the proverb – Gadaba, Joria and Mali – live in the immediate vicinity of the former capital, to which they still refer as the "navel place" (*bumli jaga*), where the king was born.

The region of my immediate concern is the area of this former kingdom, keeping in mind that, usually, Indian kingdoms did not have definitely determined boundaries (e.g., Shulman 1989, 21). In its later form, after the capital had shifted to Jeypore, the kingdom was more or less coterminous with the Koraput District, one of the founding districts when the state of Odisha ("Orissa" up to 2011) was established in 1936. Almost the size of Belgium, Koraput was one of the largest districts in India before it was subdivided into four districts in 1992, namely Koraput, Rayagada, Nabrangpur and Malkangiri. Nandapur and Jeypore both lie in the present Koraput District.

Although it has been stated that the "term 'Eastern Ghats' is honoured by time but by nothing else," suggesting "an entirely non-existent homogeneity"

---

unknown, *ganga* ritual in two Joria villages. Although a comprehensive comparison of the major rituals of different tribes in the Koraput district is overdue, these data will not play a role in this study. Since my colleague Tina Otten is working on the *bali jatra* of the Mali, and another Parisian colleague, Raphaël Rousseleau, is engaged in ethnographic research among the Joria, a better overview of the connections among the individual rituals will perhaps become possible in the future." (Berger 2015, 305–06, fn. 132).

(Spate 1960, 679), the mountain range in the middle of which Nandapur lies stretches continuously for some 350 kilometers from the south-west to the north-east, roughly parallel to the coast line of the Bay of Bengal (see Map 2). Its southern tip is cut through by the Godavari River, which flows into the sea soon afterwards. The width of this mountain range varies, being about 90 kilometers at its widest point. Coming from the coast, the mountains rise steeply and the Nandapur plateau is about 900 meters above sea level. This tableland is covered with countless hills and ranges some of which rise up to 1500 meters. To the west, the mountains drop down to a 600 meter plateau in one continuous line of hills that diagonally traverses the undivided Koraput District. Jeypore lies right at the foot of the 900 meter plateau on the 600 meter plateau, which extends westwards becoming the Bastar plateau, now part of Chhattisgarh state (Gregory 2013). Bastar used to be an even larger district than undivided Koraput and was also a former kingdom, with Jagdalpur as its capital. Again, like Koraput, Bastar has been, and still is, an area populated by various tribal communities, some of which live in higher mountain regions such as the Abujhmar Hills (Grigson 1991). In 1999, Bastar was also subdivided into several districts. While focusing on Koraput and the former Nandapur/Jeypore kingdom, I will frequently refer to Bastar in the chapters that follow.

Countless rivers originate in the Eastern Ghats, three of which deserve mention here, the Indrawati, the Kolab and the Machkund, all tributaries of the Godavari River, the mythical origin of the Gadaba. The Indrawati originates in the Kalahandi District, north of Koraput, and flows down the 900 meter plateau westward into Bastar, passing Jagdalpur. It drains the Bastar plateau and flows into the Godavari. The Kolab River has its source in the Koraput District itself and also drains westward, leaving the 900 meter plateau close to Jeypore, in the vicinity of a Joria village called Ponosput Bagra, which we will encounter again in Chapter 5. It then makes a sharp turn to the north before turning south again, and it is called Sabari when it joins the Godavari. The Machkund River, finally, originates in the part of the Eastern Ghats that today belongs to Andhra Pradesh and, for some distance, it marks the border between that state and Odisha. Right in the area of the Gutob Gadaba, the river turns sharply and flows south-westward, dropping down into a deep and narrow valley as the impressive Duduma Waterfall, which is mentioned in many local myths. Running through the steep valley, it passes by Bondo villages on its true right side and Didayi villages on its true left side and continues its lengthwise journey through the mountain range for some 130 kilometers before it leaves the hills, soon to join (as Sileru) the Sabari near the village of Motu.

In the twentieth century, all three rivers have seen major changes, as massive dams have been built for hydro-electric projects (the Balimela, Jalaput and

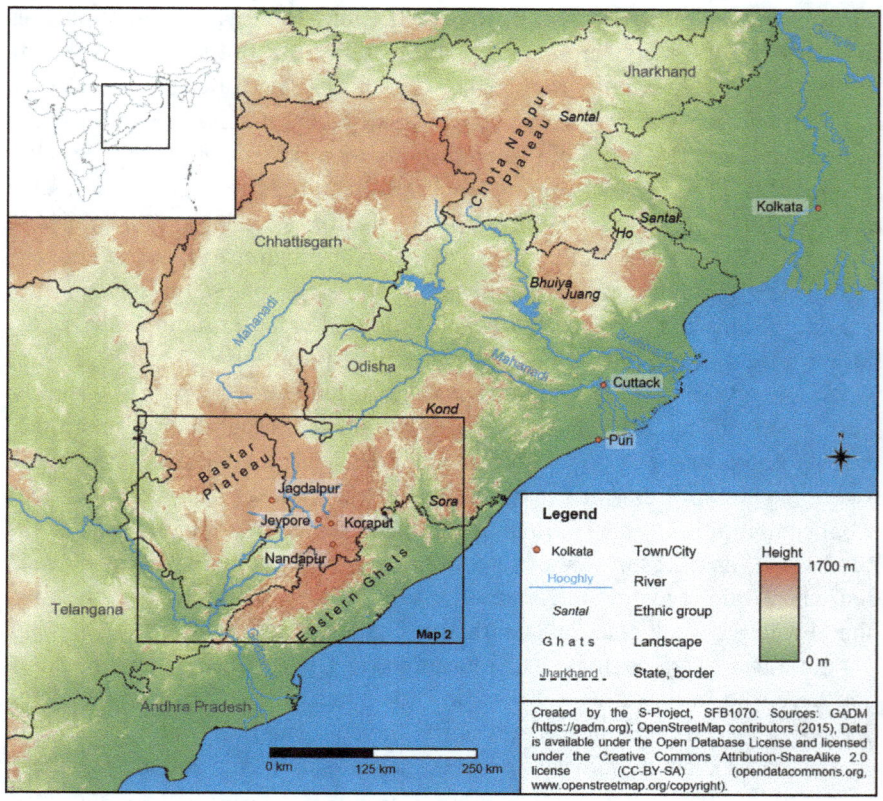

Map 1: Odisha in Central India

Kolab Reservoirs can be seen in Map 3). The rushing waters of the Duduma Fall have been reduced to a trickle, as most of the water is diverted. Rich in minerals, the region, which was until recently considered by some to be "probably the most jungly of all India" (Spate 1960, 680), has become an industrial hotspot in the last decades, to the detriment of the environment and its inhabitants (Borde 2021; Mishra 2002; Padel 2009, 315–39; Padel & Das 2006; Padhi and Sadangi 2020; Stanley 1996; Vyasulu 1985). These projects also changed the social composition of these places and led to an influx of "lowlanders" to the hills.

The Machkund power project, located in the Gutob Gadaba area, was planned before independence but only constructed afterwards. With its completion, lowlanders from Andhra Pradesh and Odisha moved to the newly established settlement to take up their much desired permanent jobs in the government project. In addition to these project employees, other people also came who, while not

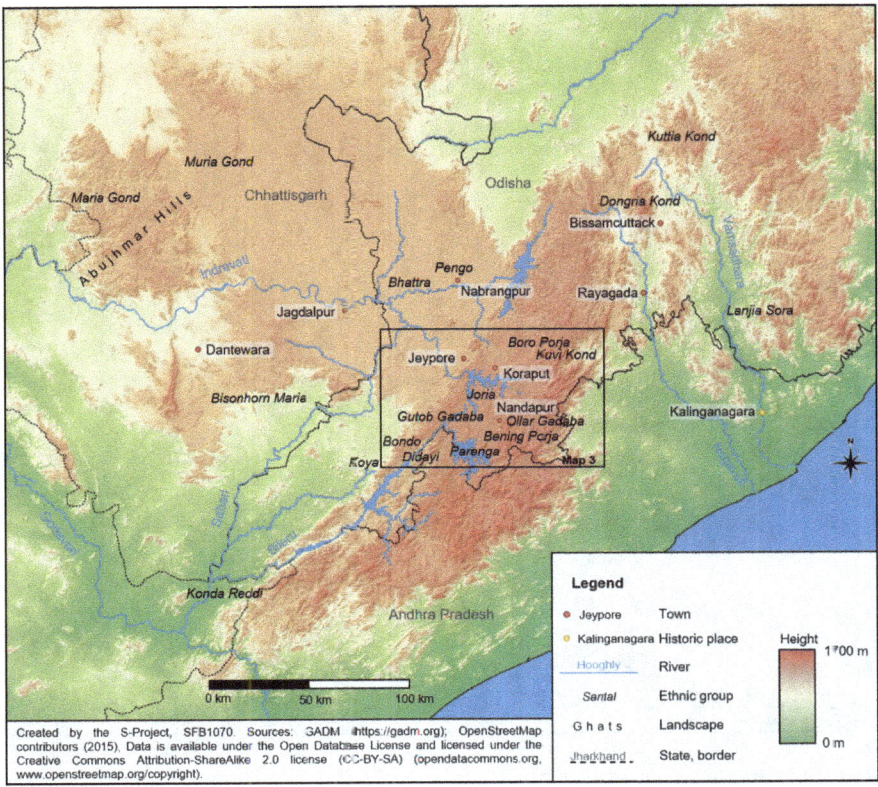

Map 2: The Eastern Ghats and the Bastar Plateau

employed in the "Power House," provided infrastructure: barber shops, restaurants, laundries, school teachers and shop keepers. I came to know the settlement quite well in 1996, when I spent two months there and lived in one of the project quarters, regularly visiting a Gadaba village from there. What struck me at the time was that life on this little "island" was totally disconnected from its surroundings. Even most of the people who had been born in the project settlement had never set foot in a tribal village, just a twenty minute walk away. As Christian Strümpell (2008) discovered, the lowlanders conceived of this place as a polluted "outside," no matter how long they had lived in the hills, and they still regarded the villages from which they originally came as "inside," although by then they had actually become strangers to them. Caste rules applied to the "inside" only and the lowland immigrants thus lived in a state of continuous liminality.

North-east of the massif on which Nandapur is located, and adjacent to it, lies another range of hills stretching from the former little kingdom of Parlakimedi

1 Introduction: A Proverb and Its Protagonists, Their Rituals and the Region

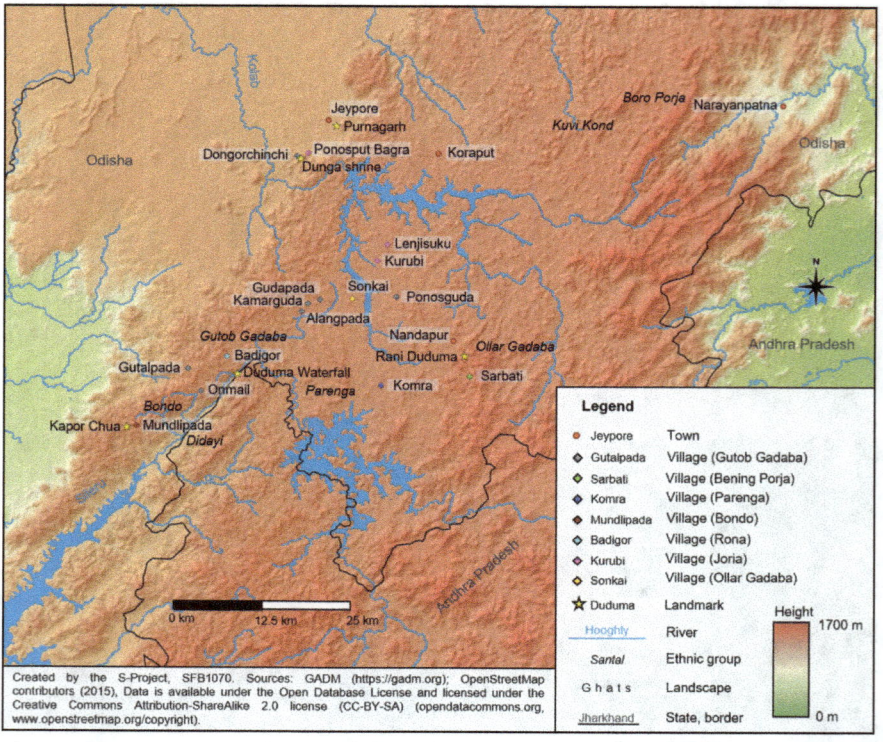

Map 3: The Nandapur/Jeypore Region

(see Berkemer 2004) – today on the border of Andhra Pradesh and Odisha – northwards up to the Mahanadi River, the "Great River" of Odisha that flows from west to east and roughly divides the state into a southern and northern half (see Map 1). These hills are mostly inhabited by Sora and Kond communities. North of the Mahanadi lies the great Chota Nagpur plateau, which makes up most of the present-day district of Jharkhand (Carrin 2013) and extends to the Ganges. Among the indigenous people of this area are the Oraon, Munda, Ho and Santal.

1.2 Tribal Central India as a Culture Area and Its Subregions

Geographical and ecological features obviously have an impact on the possibilities for communication between local communities and on their movements. Anthropologists have long identified regions inhabited by presumably historically related communities that share cultural, social or political patterns, often notwithstanding a great linguistic diversity. Despite these shared family resemblances, the communities of such regions also show significant cultural differences and variations. Accordingly, the identification of such regions of cultural commonalities-cum-distinctiveness was and is an important heuristic tool for comparison (Gingrich & Fox 2002; Holy 1987), and irrespective of the many problems in defining "regions" (for India see Sopher 1980; Vora & Feldhaus 2006), anthropologists have contextualized the ethnographies of specific localities in their wider region of interest, which often also cut across national boundaries. For instance, in his work on the Native American communities of California, Kroeber (1925, 898–918) early on distinguished different "culture areas" in the wider region, tracing the diffusion of cultural elements. The notion of "culture area," he wrote, was unfortunate in the sense that it stressed the geographical area, while what was actually the focus of attention should be "cultural content" (Kroeber 1939, 2). Also, as early as 1935, J.P.B. de Josslelin de Jong (1977) outlined his view of how to understand Indonesia and the Malay archipelago as a "Field of Ethnological Study," tracing variations in structures of descent and intermarriage. This approach was subsequently applied and further developed by various scholars (e.g., Barraud & Platenkamp 1990). Whether in Amazonia (Viveiros de Castro 1998) or highland Papua New Guinea (Rubel & Rosman 1978), South Africa (Kuper, 1982, 2002) or the Southeast Asian highland region called Zomia (Scott 2009), scholars have compared institutions, practices and ideas across their region of concern, with some success. Such comparisons also highlighted certain distinctive cultural facts and features in a given region, such as, respectively, perspectivism, competitive exchanges, the structure of the homestead or cherished statelessness.[3]

---

[3] Methodologically, the work of Claude Lévi-Strauss (e.g. 1986) fundamentally advanced such comparative efforts through his study of mythology. Lévi-Strauss moved away from diffusionist assumptions of historical distributions of cultural traits to an analysis of structural transformations that did not assume an "original myth" in any chronological sense, but compared all variants of one myth and related myths in a culture area. Moreover and significantly, cultural ideas may manifest in different cultural domains and transformations may therefore also be traced across articulations of myth, ritual or architecture, among other forms of cultural expression. While Lévi-Strauss occasionally also compared obviously unrelated myths, he left no doubt, as Michael Oppitz (1975, 218) pointed out, that the comparative study of myth should take place within the limits of history and geography. However, while such "controlled comparison" (Eggan 1954) came to be the standard method in anthropology, sometimes "uncontrolled comparison" (Sahlins 1963, 235) also merited insights.

More than any other anthropologist working in the region, Georg Pfeffer[4] was devoted to the comparative study of Central Indian tribal societies, or "Middle India," as he usually called it (see also Carrin and Rousseleau 2021; Parkin 1992). Pfeffer demonstrated this in his early work on *Status and Affinity in Middle India* (1982) through to his last book entitled *Henry Lewis Morgan's Comparisons* (2019). His comparative efforts had multiple levels and took different directions. He wanted to grasp the commonalities and variations of the tribal communities of Middle India, many of which he had visited in his numerous ethnographic field trips since the 1970s. Moreover, his intimate knowledge of Hindu religion and society – he had previously conducted long-term fieldwork with sweepers of Punjab and the Sasan Brahmans of Puri – led him to repeatedly stress the differences between Hindu and tribal cultures in India, despite their many historical connections.[5] Finally, because of his general theoretical interest in kinship studies, he was of the opinion that Middle Indian ethnography had something to contribute to anthropology in general. Accordingly, he compared relationship terminologies, social structures and worldviews of Central India with other regions, such as indigenous North and South America or Australia (Pfeffer 2004, 2016, 2019).

For the purposes of this book, Pfeffer's identification of different subregions within the wider culture area of Central India – the geographical region I have outlined above – is particularly important. In a seminal contribution that initiated a series of volumes on tribal studies that he co-edited with Deepak Kumar Behera (Pfeffer 1997, see also 2009, 2019, 135–63), Pfeffer outlined the general features that all or most Central Indian tribal communities share, while also distinguishing different "complexes." Among the commonalties, Pfeffer particularly mentions enduring structures of affinity and descent (clanship), seniority as an ordering principle and the social category of "client."

Most tribes recognize totemic exogamous categories of patrilineal descent, but in contrast to the Hindu plains, pedigrees are irrelevant, with the clans having no "depth" but rather being horizontally opposed to each other:

> clans differ from those of Indian upper castes (. . .) or from those of the Nuer (. . .) [on Nuer descent and time-reckoning, see below], in that they lack a concept of lineal ramification involving elaborate pedigrees. Though its representatives may perform ritual functions within a village [such as the *sisa* or *pujari* I will repeatedly mention in later

---

[4] Georg Pfeffer died in 2020. For an appraisal of his life and work see the obituary written by Roland Hardenberg and myself (Berger and Hardenberg 2021).
[5] Pfeffer is not the only one who sees tribal societies as different from Hindu religion and culture in significant ways, see, for instance, Berger (2016b), Hardenberg (2010), Parkin (1992, 222), Vitebsky (2013, 120).

chapters], a clan is primarily a sociocentric category of affinal exchange and *never* a corporate group involved in any kind of action (Pfeffer 2019, 98).

Affinity is recognized as a crucial value but, in contrast to North and South Indian patterns, affinity in tribal Central India is collective and enduring, it diachronically unites social wholes, usually villages. While Central Indian affinity entails symmetric matrimonial exchange, hierarchy is not absent, and status differences that are recognized between bride-giving and bride-taking groups shift temporarily, which Pfeffer called an "oscillating hierarchy" (2004, 404). Like affinity, the value of seniority is ubiquitous in Central India, and at various levels of the social structure "elder" segments are opposed to "younger" ones. Also, tribal communities as a whole are related as elder and younger "brothers" throughout the region, such as the Ho and Munda in Chota Nagpur or the Parenga and Gadaba in Koraput, a feature that is also regularly mentioned in local myths (e.g., M14).

One common feature that Pfeffer stresses is the interdependent relation between tribal cultivators and their non-cultivating "clients," called Dombo (or Dom) in some regions and Panc in others. These "clients" are musicians who play at life-cycle rituals and during village festivals and who, in addition, used to be weavers. As petty traders, they act as economic middle-men between the village and the weekly markets. Both regionally and in the academic literature generally, they are represented as disreputable money-lenders and exploiters of the tribes (e.g., Elwin 1950, 1; Fürer-Haimendorf 1943; Niggemeyer 1964b; Vitebsky 2017a; see Waak et al. 1994, 28–33). Pfeffer (1997, 7–11), in contrast, argues that they are, and probably have long been, an integral part of local tribal society, in economic, social and religious terms, irrespective of the fact that they are not classified as a "scheduled tribe" by the government but as a "scheduled caste." The work of Roland Hardenberg among the Dongria Kond (2017a, 2018a, 52–139) and my own work with the Gadaba (e.g., Berger 2002, 60–63, 2015) has confirmed many of Pfeffer's arguments. In the Niamgiri Hills that the Dongria inhabit, the Dombo are the only other resident community. Also, in the case of the Gadaba, the relationship to the Dombo must be very old. Although several other non-cultivating communities are found in Gadaba villages, the Gadaba only have a word for the Dombo in their own Gutob language (Goren). The Dombo will be repeatedly mentioned in the pages that follow. In local myths as well as in the Ganga Puja of the Joria, it is mostly the disreputable and corrupt representation of the community that is foregrounded.

In addition to such commonalities among the Central Indian tribes "as a unit," Pfeffer distinguishes cultural subregions or "complexes," namely the Kond Complex, the Sora Complex, the Gond Complex, the Chota Nagpur Complex and the Koraput Complex (Pfeffer 1997, 2009, 2019). In the cases of Chota Nagpur and Koraput, specific tribal groups are not mentioned, as in the other cases, as many communities constitute those culture areas. However, the other complexes are also not homogeneous. For instance, different tribal segments – Dongria Kond, Kuttia Kond, Kuvi Kond – constitute the larger Kond tribal category of more than one million people. The same is true for the Gond and the Sora. Especially in Bastar, the situation is very similar to Koraput in that it is quite a plural society (S. Gell 1992, 14; Grigson 1991, 37). The variations across these different complexes can be illustrated by the example of clanship.

As mentioned above, most tribes distinguish and oppose totemic unilineal exogamous descent categories, which we may call "clans." The clans are crucial for distinguishing "brothers" from marriageable "others." The specifics vary between the different complexes. For example, the different Kond groups feature territorial clans, in the sense that villages of one clan are only found in a certain territory belonging to that particular clan. With regard to several of the tribes of Koraput, the link between descent and territory is not absent, but different, as I found out. The clans are not territorially structured as among the Kond, and different clans of the same community are found next to each other. The decisive territorial units in this case are the villages, which have a specific descent-cum-territorial identity; this is why I have called them "village clans" (Berger 2015, 102–8). Among the Gond, the situation is different again, as many Gond tribes cluster brother-clans into exogamous units known as phratries. This has, for instance, been described for the Koya of Malkangiri by Ulrich Demmer (2009). The Sora, most notably studied by Piers Vitebsky (1993, 2017a), are unique in this regard as they do not feature clans in this sense at all (Suryanarayan 2009). Such commonalities and variations can be found in many domains, with myth and ritual being of particular relevance to this book.

Linguistically, Central India shows a great diversity, and for many indigenous people it is common to speak two or more languages. Three of the four language families present in India can be found in this region. Gond and Kond tribes speak languages belonging to the Dravidian family (Steever 2019); the Sora, and many communities of the Chota Nagpur Plateau (e.g., the Ho, Santal, Kharia and Munda), speak Munda tongues belonging to the Austroasiatic family (Anderson 2008), thus with clear linguistic ties to Southeast Asia. In his important comparative work, Robert Parkin (1992) focused in particular on these tribal groups. All three language families are found in Koraput, and the case of the Gadaba illustrates the social proximity of the different languages.

Members of the junior segment of the Gadaba speak a Dravidian language (Ollari), while the neighboring senior Gadaba are one of the communities (like the Bondo, Didayi and Parenga) that speak a Munda language (Gutob). Both of them, like all tribes in Koraput, speak an Indo-European Odia dialect (formerly written Oriya) called Desia as a *lingua franca* (Gustafsson 1989; Mahapatra 1985). Mahapatra (1985, 7) assumes that the Nandapur region is the "focal area" of this Desia language.[6] Gudapada, my host Gadaba village, is a Gutob village. For an unknown number of generations, Ollar Gadaba, who came originally from the village of Mundagor, have lived in Gudapada as the internal affines of the local Gutob "earth people." In addition to Desia, these Ollar Gadaba speak Gutob and are no longer competent in Ollari. When an Ollar Gadaba marries into a Gutob village, the person usually learns the new language as well. However, many tribal tongues, for instance Ollari, are endangered languages that are rarely spoken today.

As this book is about the festivals of the former Nandapur/Jeypore kingdom, the "Koraput Complex" provides the primary focus of my comparisons and discussions. However, frequent references will also be made to the Sora and the Kond, especially the Dongria Kond, who inhabit the Niamgiri Hills on the north-eastern margins of undivided Koraput. The latter had a king of their own who was a vassal of the Maharaja of Jeypore. Because of the many similarities and intensive historical connections between Jeypore and Bastar, I will also often relate to the ethnography of that region and the "Gond Complex." I will not at this point summarize the main features of Koraput, some salient characteristics of which have already been mentioned. In the chapters that follow, I will introduce particular communities in more detail and also discuss specific aspects of the region, such as its political history in Chapter 4 and its specific agricultural characteristics in Chapter 6.

It is sufficient to mention for now that the plateau features a number of cultivating tribal communities. Those that I will refer to most frequently are the Ollar and Gutob Gadaba, the Bondo, Parenga and Joria. In addition, numerous communities populate the plateau and often live in the same villages as the tribal cultivators (Berger 2002; Senapati and Sahu 1966, 79–154; Waak et al. 1994, 21–44). I have previously called them "'non-ST' Desia" (Berger 2002) as they are not recognized as "scheduled tribes" or "ST" by the administration. Among them are the horticulturalists (Mali), potters (Kumar), blacksmiths (Kamar), herders (Goudo), liquor distillers (Sundi), Rona (former royal militia) and, in almost every village, the Dombo. The Rona are an exception insofar as they are also cultivators and landowners, or *roit*. Most of these non-ST Desia are probably later

---

[6] "Nandapur may be treated as the focal area of the dialect. This place was the main centre of culture in the Koraput region since the 14th century A.D. when the Silavamsi kings first established their capital at Nandapur. (. . .) Hence, Desia spoken in and around Nandapur seems to be the real form of the dialect" (Mahapatra 1985, 7).

immigrants into the hills, a view which also corresponds with local narratives. In the early days, as a Gadaba myth (M1) narrates, there were no Rona, Mali, Goudo or Brahmins. However, when such immigration historically occurred is entirely obscure. In any case, they are an integral part of the socio-cultural configuration of the region, even though they are not considered to be "tribes."

1.3 Indian "Tribes"

In India, more than 100 million people are classified as "tribes" and are listed as such in the decennial surveys. According to the 2011 Census, they constituted 8.6% of the total population (Ministry of Tribal Affairs 2013, 1). Politically, this classification – as well as the associated benefits provided by the government – is disputed and this has regularly led to conflicts. From an academic viewpoint, this administrative categorization makes little sense. Criteria for "tribal" status such as "primitive traits" or "backwardness" (Ministry of Tribal Affairs 2013, 1) hardly qualify as academic. Moreover, sociological categories of "tribe," "caste" and "class" are all mixed together in the administrative classification of "Scheduled Tribes," "Scheduled Castes" and "Other Backward Classes." The same community may be classified as a "tribe" in one district and as a "caste" in another, or its categorization may change from one census to the next. In short, the administrative labels are relatively random from an academic perspective.

Furthermore, the term "tribe" is contested in academia and arguments for or against the use of the term have been articulated for a long time (e.g., Beteille 1977, 1991; Hardenberg 2018a, Pfeffer 2002; Skoda 2005, 49–61, Weisgrau 2013). The alternative term "Adivasi," meaning "original inhabitant," is widely used in India, also partly by the people themselves, and in the academic literature. Similarly, in scholarly works, the expression "indigenous people" is often used, for instance in the recently published *Brill's Encyclopedia of the Religions of the Indigenous People of South Asia* (Carrin et al. 2021; Carrin 2021). While this may seem to be a good solution, the question of indigeneity in India is most likely no less problematic than the term "tribe."

I agree with Viveiros de Castro that we should be cautious of abandoning our analytical categories all too quickly before we know how to properly replace them, leading to "wishful unthinking" (Viveiros de Castro 1998, 470). The decisive point is whether a certain concept or any particular contrast – such as "tribal" vs. "Hindu" – is in some way heuristically meaningful and helps to understand a complex reality. My approach is twofold, distinguishing an analytical and a local level. First of all, it is vital to pay attention to local categories and understand their semantics. In the chapters that follow, I will deal with many such local ideas, which often entail oppositions. For instance, the "king" (*raja*) is contrasted to the "subject" (*porja*), "earth people" (*matia*) to "late comers" (*upria*), the "lowlands" (*tolrasi*) to the "uplands" (*uporasi*), "people" of the plateau or "land" (Desia) to "hill dwellers" (Dongria) or "elder brothers" (*boro bai*) are contrasted with "younger brothers" (*sano bai*). Many of these concepts are relational and their meaning may shift according to context. *Porja* means "subject," but it also refers to specific local communities, such as the Boro ("senior") Porja who are "cultivators" (*roit*). *Bai* may denote an actual "brother," any male member of the same clan, irrespective of whether the person belongs to the same community or not, or it may refer to local communities as a whole. Frequent mention will be made of the "twelve brothers" (*baro bai*) in the following pages, which refers to the different local communities and their mythical origin, but alternatively also to Gadaba society as a totality. It is thus important that such terms are understood in their particular context.

The second aspect of my approach is more abstract, analytical and comparative. Based on the local categories and documented practices and institutions on the ground, generalizations and comparisons can be made. This is a very common method, of course, and widely applied. Consider, for instance, what Chris Fuller wrote with regard to the use of the term "Hinduism:"

> Anthropological or sociological analysis abstracts from empirical data and also attempts to make them intelligible by using concepts and deploying generalizations that are formulated comparatively and rarely correspond precisely to indigenous categories in any particular society. That "Hinduism" is not a traditional, indigenous category (. . .) in no way nullifies an analysis that demonstrates that Hinduism is a relatively coherent and distinctive system founded on common structures of relationships. (Fuller 1992, 10)

In the same way, I have compared Hindu and Gadaba death rituals and showed that despite significant similarities (e.g., in the making and consumption of temporary "bodies" of the deceased) the relationships involved differ fundamentally, articulating contrasting values. In the case of the Gadaba, relationships of exchange in the context of death are symmetrical and reciprocal. Groups of external clan brothers mutually take care of the removal, consumption and replacement of the liminal dead. This final phase of these death rituals will be discussed in detail in Chapter 9. The clear referent of the ritual is society, constituted by relationships of brotherhood and affinity. Because of the dominant value of ritual purity, such an exchange is unthinkable in the Hindu context, where pollution and "sin" are passed on and "digested" in one direction only. While ancestors also play a role in Hindu death rituals, the ultimate value here is liberation (Berger 2016b, Parry 1994). Despite the great diversity of tribal and Hindu death rituals in

India, similar patterns and contrasts can be identified in other cases (e.g., Behera 2010, Reichel 2009, 2017, Vitebsky 1993, 2017a; de Maaker 2016).

The concept of tribe can thus be used as a sociological ideal type to contrast with other societal forms. In several works, Pfeffer (2002b, 2003; see Berger & Sahoo 2020, 29–36) has argued for such a use, contrasting tribes with gathering-hunting bands and peasants. These types are not only different from each other in terms of modes of subsistence but also with regard to social morphology and ideology. Gatherer-hunters with immediate return economies (Woodburn 1982) mostly feature community structures in flux, with highly variable and changeable conglomerates of individuals with no enduring patterns of kinship. In contrast to relationships of reciprocity that create debt, relationships of sharing (imposed or demanded) do not create dependence on specific others and work as a leveling mechanism that undermines attempts at status differentiation and property accumulation. This corresponds to the dominant values of equality and individualism of such societies. In the case of India, Nurid Bird-David and Ulrich Demmer have shown that the South Indian gathering-hunting community called Nayaka or Jenu Kurumba contrasts with tribal cultivators. As Bird-David pointed out, the Nayaka conceptualize the "forest as parent," thus in kinship terms as a "giving environment" (Bird-David 1990, 190), of which they are part and with respect to which they display a strong ethic of sharing.[7] Comparing the Jenu Kurumba to the Koya tribal cultivators of Malkangiri District, Demmer argued that both communities conceptualize society in different ways. As with other tribal communities in Central India, the Koya imagine their society as kinship based, a "group model of society" (Demmer 2009, 278), while the Jenu Kurumba community envision society as a process of negotiation between individuals.

Like gatherer-hunting bands, tribes are acephalous, without centralized institutions of power – there is no monopoly of force. However, tribal society is composed, structured and imagined differently. Society is constituted in a segmentary way, consisting of enduring kinship-based collective units of the same type on different levels of the social structure (Sahlins 1968), which are integrated by exchange relationships. Society is conceptualized as a totality, which is not unfrequently equated with humanity in tribal self-designations.[8] Peasants form a partial society in a different way to gatherer-hunting bands (Wolf

---

7 See Mummidi (2021) for a recent criticism of Bird-David's arguments, with reference to her own fieldwork among the Konda Reddi.

8 For instance the Bondo speak of themselves as Remo ("man", "human") (Elwin 1950, 1) and the Dongria as Kuang ("men," "human being")(Hardenberg 2018a, 3); many Gond communities described themselves as Koitor (S. Gell 1992, 15), the Ho as "men" (Ho) (Reichel 2020, 351) or the Santal as Hor Hopon or "sons of man" (Schulte-Droesch 2018, 365).

1966). While the latter are part of the environment and do not constitute an imagined societal whole on their own, and group membership is not a major issue, peasants are part of encompassing, centralized and hierarchical sociopolitical orders, with an elaborated division of labor, effective system of taxation and a proper monopoly on force.

1.4 Tribal Society and Kingship

There seems to be a contradiction here. If the proverb with which this book is concerned deals with a "king" and his "subjects," how can those subjects constitute, or be understood as, a "tribal society"? Are not "tribes" precisely composed of those who do not recognize any centralized political power? Those who excel in the *Art of Not Being Governed* (Scott 2009)? On the one hand, it could be said that the system of taxation in the hills has not been very effective; that the royal administration actually was poorly developed and had little impact on tribal lives; that kings did not really have armies worth the name and certainly did not have a monopoly on force in this sense or direct control over their subjects; in other words, that the royal polity was rather flat. This seemed to have been the case. In January 1867, John Shortt (1868, 281) made a "rapid tour through Jeypore" just four years after the British had assumed direct administration of it and reported:

> This province is now divided into six regular districts, in addition to a wild tract in the south, scarcely explored, and inhabited by a rude barbarous [sic] class of people, over whom the rajah has no control, although they are attached to him, and owe him military service when called upon. They pay no tribute, but, during the feast termed "Dusserah," they bring him annually as offerings some of the products of their districts. (Shortt 1868, 264)

Gadaba, Bondo, Parenga and others were thus not "governed" by the king of Jeypore, but "attached to him," which manifested especially during Dasara, when they provided gifts to the king as *raja beti*.

Perhaps even more important than the actual lack of control, on the other hand, is the tribal perception of the king. Rather than speaking of the king and his subjects, from the tribal perspective in any case, one should speak of the tribes and their king. Despite their independence, they acknowledge the king, want a king, even need a king. Why is this the case? Why are they "attached to him"? It is because, from the tribal perspective, the king is first of all a metasacrificer and the kingdom a sacrificial polity. When the king stops sacrificing, the earth goddess becomes angry and the well-being of all is at stake, as Birsa Sisa, a Gadaba from Gudapada, told me vividly (see Chapter 3). Kings and subjects are complementary sacrificers, contributing to the flow of life from their global and local vantage points. In Chapter 4, I will discuss in some detail the different ways the relationship between kings and tribes has been depicted by various scholars. There are very few who have seriously dealt with the tribal perspective on this issue and this book hopes to make a contribution in this regard. As I will repeatedly demonstrate in the pages that follow, while the tribal cultivators acknowledge and require the king as sacrificer, they also consider themselves to be sacrificial sovereigns, albeit on a different level.

The beginnings of this argument concerning the sacrificial sovereignty of the tribal people of Koraput go back to an early article of mine that was published twenty years ago (Berger 2002). I had noticed during my fieldwork with the Gadaba that two overlapping hierarchies were operating on the 900 meter plateau: a regional one and a local one. In the regional hierarchy, the Gadaba and other tribal cultivators – Bondo, Didayi, Parenga, Joria, to name a few – are in the middle of a threefold hierarchy. Above them are communities such as the Mali or Rona, which distinguish themselves by lowland status criteria, namely by not eating beef, abstaining from liquor and wearing the sacred thread. Below the tribal cultivators are, especially, the Dombo, who are petty traders, musicians and, formerly, weavers. In fact, not much distinguishes the Gadaba from the Dombo in terms of life-style, except that the former are the cultivators and the latter their clients.

Exactly this status as cultivator (*roit*) is crucial and the decisive criterion for the local hierarchy. Villages are commonly populated by tribal cultivators and representatives of other communities (gardeners, blacksmiths, potters, herders) that rank above or below them in the regional hierarchy. In the village context, however, all non-cultivating communities rank below the original tribal inhabitants of the village. As "earth people" (*matia*), the latter cultivate the fields and are the village sacrificers, and this aspect makes them superior or "senior" (*boro*) to all other communities that may reside in the village as "junior" (*sano*) "late comers" (*upria*). Late comers, whether the regionally senior herders (Goudo) or the junior Dombo, receive a share of the harvest, but they have to pay "respect" (*manti*) to the earth people in the context of the sacrifice to the village earth goddess (*hundi*). Moreover, Gadaba or Joria earth people are not "village kings" in the sense that they would replicate the "power" of the king on the local level, as in the model of the dominant caste (Berger 2002, 2015, 160–66; see Skoda 2005 chapter 4). They are sacrificers, and in this sense they are sovereigns of life like their king.

It is this status of subaltern sovereignty that is articulated, manifested and enacted in the festivals that are discussed in this book, local rituals that are in some way about kingship and about kings. Nonetheless, as will become clear, the relationship between kings and tribal subjects is not always without tension. Quite the contrary, on the level of both myth and ritual, ambiguities and contestations abound. The discussion of tribal myths in Chapter 3 reveals two different ways of dealing with the conundrum of "tribal kingship." One set of myths uses the idiom of brotherhood to rationalize the distinction between king and subjects. The younger brother manages to accomplish a "royal" task – such as mounting a horse – and becomes king, while the elder brother fails and thus becomes "subject." Other myths narrate a rebellion against a wicked king, a Dom King, who is killed and replaced by a proper forest king.

Whether in tacit or explicit ways, rebellion is the topic of several rituals that will be discussed. The Ganga festival of the Joria (Chapter 6) enacts the mythical rebellion against the Dom King, while the Go'ter ritual of the Gadaba (Chapter 9) does not so much discuss kingship as dramatically demonstrates the *unruliness* of the tribal subjects. These themes and patterns are also clearly present beyond the confines of Koraput. In my interpretation of the coronation rituals in Keonjhar (Chapter 4), the tribal Bhuiya are both elevated and subjugated during the process because of their ambiguous status from the perspective of the king, who recognizes them as subjects and as sacrificial sovereigns at the same time. The result is a dynamic of hierarchical encompassment that assigns global sovereignty to the king in this particular context. During the Dasara festival in Bastar (Chapter 5), just after his re-enthronement, the tribal subjects abduct their king and take him into the forest, thus claiming him as their own, only to accompany him back to the capital later in an effervescent procession. The combination of "tribal society" and "kingship" – including tribalized kings and subaltern sovereigns – is thus not a conceptual impossibility but is at the heart of the rituals to be discussed and a variant of the "original political society" (Sahlins 2017).

1.5 Historicity and Temporality

The proverb *Raja Dasara, Joria Nandi, Mali Bali Gadaba Go'ter* suggests a ritual polity, identifying a king, his subjects and their signature festivals. In turn, several of these festivals refer to kings and kingship, some more explicitly than others. Dasara is obviously about a king, his court and his subjects, while the Ganga festival of the Joria also clearly enacts a competitive relationship between royal and subaltern elements of the polity, referring to myths about a wicked Dom ruler who is killed by a rebellious tribal jungle boy-cum-king. A host of other local stories narrate the establishment of kingship and the co-creation of kings and subjects. The epic related to the Bali Jatra also tells the story of kings, their marriages, sacrifice and the establishment of a palace. Yet, what is the temporality of all this, of the proverb, the festivals and the stories? Are they to be understood as indigenous comments on the past; the proverb as indexical of a former kingdom; the rituals as enactments of earlier events; and the stories expressions of a collective memory or oral "history"? Although I summarize what is known of the Nandapur/Jeypore kingdom and the relationships between kings and tribal subjects in Chapter 4, it is not my concern in this book to find traces in either rituals or myths of what presumably "really happened." I primarily understand the festivals as manifestations of values that have a time dimension; or, inversely, they articulate temporalities that at the same time are an expression of values.

In this regard it may be useful – at least as a kind of working definition – to distinguish historicity from temporality, as Michael Heckenberger (2007) suggests. Historicity refers to indigenous views of the past that are articulated in discourse. Temporality pertains to non-discursive notions of time that are implicit in what people do: how they shape and are engaged with their environment, that is, their social, religious and material world. Time, in this sense, is part of the habitus; it is "felt," not reflected upon (Heckenberger 2007, 286). Both dimensions are closely interconnected, I would say, as the way life is lived influences how people talk about time, and vice versa, time discourse influences practice – time "felt" and time conceptualized and verbalized are interdependent. Moreover, and significantly, in understanding indigenous historicity and temporality and the "shaping" of the world, we must acknowledge that agency is not only, and perhaps not even primarily, assigned to human beings but to all kinds of non-human (meta) persons (Fausto and Heckenberger 2007, 14; Sahlins 2017). This may be one principal difference between European understandings of history and its documentation (historiography), where society is regarded as the relatively random outcome of an aggregate of multiple and dynamic interactions of human hands and minds through time; dynamics that coagulate in events that cause other events.

The following discussion will be particularly based on my ethnography of the Gadaba,[9] but the ideas and practices mentioned – or very similar ones – are likely to have a more general currency, certainly among the other Desia communities of Koraput, but probably in tribal Central India beyond this region. The first thing to be stressed is that there is a multiplicity of connected conceptualizations of time; forms of time-reckoning that have been described by terms

---

[9] Although historicity and temporalities have been discussed in my extensive description and analysis of Gadaba society and religion, I have not often explicitly addressed the topic (see Berger 2015, xvii, 338, fn. 185).

such as linear, oscillating and cyclical (A. Gell 1992; Leach 1977, 1991). Both in the discourse about the past and in their socio-ritual practices, the Gadaba demonstrate a complete disinterest in ordering events – births, deaths, accidents, illnesses, droughts – in a linear, chronological manner that identifies absolute points in time. When they refer to a certain event, they do so in a relational way, similarly to the Santal, as has been described by Marine Carrin (2002, 153), "'my mother fell ill on the eve of Sohrae, the cattle festival'." The actual year such a festival took place would soon be forgotten among the Gadaba. When Gadaba talk about time, they do so in an explicitly "flat" way, contrasting "now" (*ebe*) and "then" or "before" (*age, purberu*) and "people of now" (*ebro lok*) from "people of then, before" (*agtu lok, purberu lok*).[10] *Age* and *poche* are used both as a temporal (before/after) and spatial (in front/behind) contrast, in the same way as *tole* (before/below) and *upore* (after/above).

As soon as events can no longer be connected to a specific biographical memory, they merge with an undifferentiated past that has little or no depth. One example of such time-talk is Birsa Sisa's statement – to which I will return later (e.g., Chapter 3) – about the king and the human sacrifices he used to sponsor, and the time now, when this is no longer the case, leading to all kinds of "illnesses." What is also conspicuously absent are references to the future. As cultivators, they of course anticipate, for instance, a future harvest, and they speak of the "next year" (*aiba borso*). Linguistically, people could speak of *aiba somoi* or the "coming time" or *aiba din*, the "coming day/time" and accordingly of *aiba din lok*, "people of the future." However, I have not heard anyone using such expressions and there are no references to such expressions to be found in either of the two excellent dictionaries on the Desia language (Gustafsson 1989; Mahapatra 1985). "The future," it seems, does not constitute a conceptual temporal entity that would equal the contrasting categories of the "then" and the "now."

This opposition of past and present does not mean that there is an unbridgeable gap between them, that the "then" has no influence on the "now," quite the contrary. In significant ways, the past is eternally present. This is particularly so with the crucial idea of the socio-cosmic order called *niam*.[11] This concept is particularly applied in contexts of ritual and intermarriage. Someone

---

10 Speaking about "today" or the "present time" people would also speak of *aji kali* ("today time") and they also refer to the past as *purberu* ("before") or *adi din* ("ancient times"), whereby "day"(*din*) is used as reference to time in general. Ancestors are also referred to as *purberu lok*, "people from before." Gustafsson (1989, 1022–26) provides several time expressions in Desia.

11 With reference to the Dongria Kond, Hardenberg (2018a, 1 fn.1) defines *niam* in the following way: "The word *niam* means "moral law" and describes actions considered to be in accordance with the rules and traditions laid down by the gods."

would say, for example, that it is not *niam* that no music accompanies a certain ritual occasion; or that cows still have to be sacrificed during particular festivals because it is *niam*, even though today very few people eat beef. Ignoring *niam* leads to severe consequences, including blindness, vomiting blood and madness, among other possibilities. *Niam* is considered to have been instituted by the gods in the past and since then has remained in effect in its own right and unchanging. In a society without writing and without specialists who are considered custodians of *niam*, knowledge of these rules is generalized and, in practice, this means that what *niam* is has probably, to a certain degree, always been negotiated. An imagined continuity has thus been upheld, even though it is likely that changes have been incorporated without acknowledging them as such. Clearly, what is valued is not change but continuity (Berger 2017). This view of the past is thus an example of "prescriptive" structures – those that "assimilate circumstances to themselves" (Sahlins 1985, xii). The Sora offer another example of this form of historicity. Personal experiences of illness and death are collectivized and in a way taken out of time:

> Whatever the circumstances of your death, a way will be found to connect it causally to people who have died previously and to make it seem similar to their death. In this way, the specific, individual circumstances of each event are reduced to generic patterns. This is a technique of time-structuring which draws all contingent experience into patterns of repetition. (Vitebsky 2013, 126)

Such a notion of the past is also materially manifested in the center of every Gadaba village. The assemblage of upright and flat stone slabs (*sadar*) represents the collectivity of the village ancestors, linked to the local representation of the earth goddess, whose stone shrine (*hundi*) is found opposite the *sadar*. People who die are made to merge with the ancestors and each generation is represented by one set of stones (see Chapter 9). However, after they are erected, these stones lose their specific identity and it is irrelevant which set represents which generation. The only two stones that are remembered and which receive sacrificial blood in the context of annual rituals are those that are considered to have been erected first, at the "time the village sat down" (*ga bosilabele*). Quite literally, therefore, the "now" opposes the "before" when the living villagers squat on the stones representing a collective and undifferentiated ancestral past to discuss their contemporary village affairs. However, the past not only *opposes* the present – and consequently the ancestor stones the living – as the ancestors and the living are also *united* in the idea of a continuous local brotherhood of the "earth people" (*matia*). Again, the close cultural proximity of Gadaba and Sora becomes evident in this aspect of their "megalithic culture." The stones that the Sora erect for their dead also soon lose any connection to specific people; instead, they signify "togetherness in the undifferentiated solidarity of the patrilineage" (Vitebsky 2013, 120).

Despite such material imaginations of a continuous undifferentiated past reaching into the present, many local myths do describe various stages in the creation and transformation of local society: how god (Maphru) tricked the original brother/sister pair into copulating and becoming husband and wife, giving birth to the twelve tribes of the region; how an elder brother failed and a younger brother succeeded to accomplish certain tasks that turned the latter into the king and the former into the subject; and how the Gadaba came from the Godavari River to the Nandapur region and the ritual confederation of "twelve brothers" was established though sacrifice. Certain stories deal with more recent processes and events and conceive of these changes through mythological frames, a feature Sahlins (1985, 54) called "mytho-praxis." There are narratives describing how "high castes" have become the intermediate layer between the former close and dual relationship between king (younger brother) and subjects (elder brother), a process that – if it occurred in this way – must have taken place centuries back, before the advent of the British; how sahibs, government and police have come to trouble the locals (M15); and how the king allowed land to be taken away by the government to build a Power House, thereby putting an end to the era of kingship (M3).

As both the "eternal past" of the ancestral materiality of the megalithic platforms and the mythological transformations show, temporality is fundamentally related to the social structure of a society; it is a function of the quality of social relationships (Vitebsky 2013). This has already been aptly demonstrated by Evans-Pritchard's (1969, 104–8) work on the Nuer of Eastern Africa. The coordination of social relationships between groups and individuals are expressions of "structural time." On the one hand, Nuer distinguish age sets, seven of which are in existence at any given time; on the other hand, relationships are defined in relation to a common ancestor, that is, in relation to the past. The "structural distance" between two living individuals is thus determined with reference to a closer or more distant earlier time. However, the Gadaba and most tribal communities of Central India, as I have mentioned above, do not reckon descent in this diachronic way – ancestors are opposed *en bloc* to the living and are not used to structure the relationships between the latter. Localized clans are opposed to each other "horizontally" and the diachronic dimension is the result of repeated exchanges between local groups, often villages. The temporality of such exchanges can be described as oscillation. In the case of the Gadaba, women given in marriage and the dead given during death rituals (Chapter 9) constitute such oscillating movements.

Such exchanges are one of the ways that the equivalence of alternate generations is expressed, a feature that also entails a time dimension. Symmetric (though delayed) exchange and consumption of the dead between two agnatic villages, and the repeated exchange ("cross-cousin marriage") of "daughter sisters" (*ji bouni*) between two affinal villages, actually result in an identification of alternate generations, as I have described in greater detail elsewhere:

> the movements of the agnatic and affinal processes of exchange – the path of the buffaloes and the path of the brides – are fundamentally analogous. Both elements extend across generations and oscillate between groups in a rhythm that structurally equates alternate generations. (Berger 2015, 352)

Such an equivalence is compounded by ideas of reincarnation, whereby the life-force (*jibon*) of a person is reborn in his or her grandparental generation and the kinship terminology, which equates (though neither completely nor systematically) some kin terms for alternate generations and thus equates "odd" and "even" levels. The Juang are the most explicit example of this "circular model," and their terminology opposes siblings, grandparents and grandchildren, on the one hand, and parents and children on the other (Pfeffer 2004, 390; 1994a; McDougal 1963). As Robert Parkin concludes in his comparative study of Central Indian tribes,[12] "there are really only two generations recognized in these societies. These generations perpetually revolve around and replace one another (. . .)" (Parkin 1992, 216). Like the symmetric transactions between villages, adjacent generations engage in a mutual and unending exchange.[13] The structural time of the Gadaba and other Central Indian tribal communities is thus not a "projection into the past," as described by Evans-Pritchard for the Nuer (1969, 108), but a constant oscillation of past and present, which, in effect, amounts to their equation and a timeless continuity, as in case of the local earth people mentioned above.

---

12 His comparative analysis focusses on tribes speaking Munda languages. However, he makes it amply clear that language is not the decisive criterion. For instance, when he writes: "This means that (. . .) we cannot speak of a distinct 'Munda kinship model': too much is shared by the Munda and their Dravidian and Indo-European neighbours (alliance, kinship terminology, reincarnation, descent, inheritance, village structure (. . .)" (Parkin 1992, 218–19).
13 The constitution of Central Indian tribal society thus resembles sociological types such as the Australian four-section systems, that is, two horizontal affinal sets that engage in matrimonial exchange and two vertical generation sets that practice "child exchange" (Allen 2000, 71). Parkin writes: "Comparison between India and Australia are nothing new, though they have been criticized in recent years, especially in Dumont's dismissal (. . .) of Radcliffe-Brown's attempts to compare Australian and south Indian societies (. . .). However, in *central* India circumstances are different, and it is here, if anywhere, that comparisons with Australia are feasible" (Parkin 1992, 218; see also Pfeffer 1994a, 2004, 399–402).

The Sora likewise clearly articulate this idea in their death rituals. Their extensive dialogues ultimately aim at transforming the dangerous dead – who represent a particular illness category and strive to inflict the experience of their own suffering on the living – into benevolent ancestors. The dead person is "redeemed" from a precarious status to merge with the ancestors in the underworld. The chants of the ancestor-men, which are part of the efforts of redeeming the dead person, also convey this idea of permanence: "fathers – fellow-Ancestors; today – now, Sunday – Monday, Tuesday – Friday [i.e. every day]." The ethnographer who acted as an ancestor-man himself, comments: "the temporality of this act [of transformation] is complex, and the expressions meaning 'now' or 'today' signify not only the day in question but also a continual time, a perpetual present: now and always" (Vitebsky 2013, 124).

When we documented the Ganga Puja of the Joria and realized that certain ritual actors embodied royal soldiers fighting against "low-caste" subjects, in a clear reference to the myth of the wicked Dom King, we wondered if the festival was a reference to the past in some way. In conversations with various Joria afterwards, it became clear, however, that they were not referring to historical kings or events such as a war or rebellion (see Chapter 6); that the festival was not about "the past" in that sense at all (see Bird-David 2004). What our Joria interlocutors said about their festival echoed what I had earlier heard Gadaba saying about *niam*. The festival (sacrifice) had been given to them by the King God and they perform it unchanged. All elements of the festival are expressions of divine will and form, and performance of the festival in the way stipulated by *niam* is crucial to its efficacy. Violating this would be to invite disaster (*bipod*).

As I see it, the temporalities of the subaltern festivals discussed in this book are instances of conflated time, a continuous now, or – which amounts to the same thing – an eternal before, as described above. Ritual performances are understood as manifestations of timeless *niam* and therefore enable humans to benefit from the divine powers that instituted the festivals and *niam* in the first place. However, humans neither claim to know much about divine temporalities nor of the whereabouts of gods. What the rituals aim to effect is to engage in tangible relationships with metapersons in the *here and now*; a synchorization as much as a synchronization. Such festivals are thus instances of conjuncture of human and divine time and space, opportunities to temporarily merge the three worlds that are locally distinguished. Gods move "down" from the upper world and ancestors climb "up" from the underworld to the middle world, where humans mostly live short and precarious lives. In the liminal space that the festivals provide and the ritual aggregation they bring about, ancestors and gods eat, drink and dance with humans, whose bodies they sometimes inhabit – they "play" (see Chapter 6). While gods and the dead are in some ways always present in human houses, villages and the landscape, these rituals enable effervescent moments of most intensive and intimate contact that facilitates fundamental transformations and regeneration (see Conclusion).[14]

While this interpretation may seem acceptable, it should be remembered that the dynamics of the festivals discussed bring into play different and more complex ritual temporalities. To take the Go'ter of the Gadaba as an example (see Chapter 9). When someone dies, he or she is first pushed back into the past, so to speak, made to leave the community of the living and to join the undifferentiated ancestors. Of course, the deceased is still very much part of the "now" (as I mentioned above, the dead/ancestors are also conceived to be co-present), but he or she is also linked to ancestors that are associated with the "before." As in the case of a newborn child, their status in this regard is ambivalent. Even after the first three stages of death rituals have been completed, the status of the dead is still ambiguous and the process not consummated. During the last phase, the dead are brought back into the now, the time-space of the living, they are provided with new bodies (of water buffaloes) and again enjoy the company and consolation of their relatives for some time. The living buffalo-dead are then taken away by external clan brothers who ingest and thus assimilate them. However, they are also replaced by stone slabs now representing the permanent ancestors (e.g., at the *sadar*), eternally present in the megalithic structures.

Thus far, we are dealing with the interplay between before and now and the "eternal past." However, the ritual also implicitly projects into the future. Some of the buffalo-dead are killed in the dry fields, their blood vitalizing the fields on which, soon after, finger millet will grow; a food source of "life" (*jibon*) for the living (Berger 2018). While not verbally conceptualized, the ritual dynamics thus extend into the future, insofar as the dead nourish the living in the time to come. The Go'ter constitutes a past in the present that sustains the future.[15]

While events can be appropriated into local mytho-logics or prescriptive conceptualizations of the socio-ritual order (*niam*), as described above, indigenous cosmologies obviously can and do fundamentally change, as do understandings

---

14 Similarly, Nurit Bird-David (2004) described for the Nayaka of South India that in their trance performances, when the dead speak with the living, the aim is not to reconstruct a narrative of the past as such but to interact with the dead and to maintain the relationships with them. Only via these relationships do the Nayaka learn selectively about the past about which they do not bother as such.

15 As in case of the Gadaba, and very similar to them as I will discuss later in more detail (Chapter 9), the Sora also combine different, eternal linear and cyclic temporalities. Next to the "perpetual present" of the ancestors, ancestral elements are passed on through the generations. On the one hand the dead pass on their names, but they also nurture the living "by putting their soul-force into the grain which the living eat" (Vitebsky 2013, 122).

of the past and, with this, local identities (e.g., Robbins 2004). The nineteenth century brought new forms of historiography and historicism to India, which put many local social and ethnic identities into new historical contexts (Malinar 2007, 15–18). As Marine Carrin, the foremost ethnographer of the Santal,[16] probably the largest indigenous community of India, wrote about the impact of the Santal Rebellion (Hul) in the middle of the nineteenth century: "The time of the Hul marks a break in Santal thought as they suddenly feel the need to produce a historical consciousness to be able to chase the *dikus* (outsiders) who exploit them but also to build a Santal identity" (Carrin 2002, 154). Barbara Lotz also described the Hul as "one of the most important turning points in more recent collective memory" (Lotz 2007, 239).

Certain Santal rebels who fought against their exploitation by Hindu overlords and the East India Company emerged as divinely inspired heroes who would restore Santal Raj (Santal "rule"). This rebellion led, on the one hand, to a refined process of identity formation but, on the other, also shaped the image of the Santal as maintained by administrators and academics. After numerous works on Santal culture, history and myths were published in the aftermath of the rebellion, the Santal took the self-conscious process of culture work into their own hands. From the 1930s onward, Rogunath Murmu, a Santal teacher, writer and intellectual, (re)invented a Santal script (Ol Chiki), which he claimed was an original script that had been lost, in order to create cultural self-esteem and a shared identity for a community of many millions of people dispersed over a vast territory (Lotz 2007). From the middle of the twentieth century, this cultural movement turned into, or was complemented by, a political one, as Santal and other tribes of the region promoted an "Adivasi state," which ultimately came into existence in 2000, when Jharkhand was founded (Carrin 2013).

The Desia of Koraput did not experience anything comparable to the Santal and were rather in the backwaters of colonial interventions. As John Shortt wrote in 1868:

> For many years Jeypore was scarcely known to Europeans; and although the criminal and judicial control was in the hands of the British Government, it was scarcely exercised till within the last few years; and it was only in 1856 that the province was, for the first time, visited by C. W. Reade, Esq., the then governor's agent at Vizagapatam, since which time the successors of Mr. Reade make annual visits, and spend from two to three months in the province. (Shortt 1868, 280–81)

North of Koraput, roughly between the rivers Nagavali and Mahanadi, the situation was quite different. In the hills inhabited by Kuttia Kond, the British had

---

16 For a recent ethnography on the Santal see the monograph by Lea Schulte-Droesch (2018).

discovered the practice of human sacrifice, which they violently suppressed for several decades from the 1830s onward, leading to armed resistance by the Kond (Padel 2009, 8–10). However, no colonial interventions or rebellions[17] are reported among the Desia of the Koraput plateau, the area around Nandapur, which remained, in this sense, a remote area. Another consequence of this is that while the British officers Campbell and Macpherson produced detailed and valuable ethnographic descriptions of the Kond of the nineteenth century, no comparable documents are available for the Desia of Koraput. What we have are general and impressionistic descriptions, such as those by Shortt (1868), Carmichael (1869) and Thurston (1909a–c), which are not based on a close and long-term acquaintance with any particular community.

The political identities of the tribal communities are still in a nascent state. It was only in 2010 that I noticed that a "Gadaba society" (Gadaba Samaj) had just been established, but most Gadaba I asked about this had not yet heard of it at the time. Equally, movements that had an influence on other parts of Odisha seem to have had little or no impact on Koraput. Otto Waak, when discussing the status of the Dombo, noted that the devotional movement of Chaitanya (sixteenth century) left no trace in the region, nor did the reform movements of the nineteenth century. He adds that "critical and educated Indians [sic]" ("aufgeklärte Inder") such as Nehru "obviously did not exist here" (Waak et al. 1994, 32–33; translation PB).

Missionary activities also had a rather slow start and limited success in the region.[18] The Breklum Mission was established in Jeypore and Koraput town in the early 1880s but with little success at first. Around the turn of the century, the number of converts increased significantly, but it was almost exclusively members of the Dombo community who found the new faith attractive (Waak et al. 1994, 206). In 1909, a branch was established in Nandapur and here too converts were usually Dombo. In 1911, the missionary Edlef Sell reported that two Gadaba had been baptized (Waak et al. 1994, 242). In 1914, the Christian community in Koraput (probably the town and surrounding villages) had 2,470 members and 770 aspirants for baptism (called "catechumen"). In Nandapur, the numbers were 629 and 690 respectively (Waak et al. 1994, 203–4).

When I started my initial fieldwork in the mid-1990s Christianity played a very marginal role. The only village where I encountered a substantial number of Christians was Komra, where we documented the Bali Jatra (Chapter 8). About

---

17 In Chapter 4 I will discuss a rebellion that allegedly has occurred in the fifteenth century, triggered by a dynastic change in the Nandapur kingdom.
18 On the Protestant churches in Jeypore and Koraput see Kosala (1981) and Schäfer (forthcoming).

40 Dombo households were Christians, but at the time, I did not inquire further about them. Given the proximity to Nandapur, it could well be that they were descendants of those who had earlier been converted by Breklum missionaries. In the 1970s, some Gadaba had become Seventh Day Adventists and I encountered a few of them in one or two villages of the Gutob Gadaba. A Hindu reform movement that came to the region about the same time – called Mahima Dharma in the region of its origin (Dhenkanal District of Odisha) and Olek Dormo among the Desia (Guzy 2007) – had a more widespread influence. In most Gadaba villages one finds a few people who have adopted this lifestyle (Berger 2020). Mention may also be made of reform initiatives by the Congress Party in the 1940s (Fürer-Haimendorf 1943, 153, fn. 2). However, none of the above-mentioned influences have yet led to a radical change as has been described with reference to the Santal, or, closer to the Desia and more recently, with regard to the Sora, who radically shed their former animist religion and embraced Christianity. This not only led to an abandonment of their dialogues with the dead, but also to new conceptualizations of time (Vitebsky 2013, 2017a).

In summary, the fundamental transformations of identities and temporalities witnessed by some indigenous communities of Central India, which had often been triggered by encounters in the nineteenth century, did not occur in the same way in Koraput. Of course, there have been changes among the Desia as well, and I have discussed some of the recent dynamics elsewhere (Berger 2014, 2015, xiii–xix, 2020). However, the present book is not about change but focuses on ideas and practices that have presumably been constant for some time. The ethnographic present of my description of the subaltern festivals (Nandi Porbo, Ganga Puja, Bali Jatra and Go'ter) is approximately the year 2000, the time around which I documented them. As far as the Dasara festival of the king is concerned, I rely on other people's descriptions, for instance with reference to Bastar. It is quite notable that, despite many political changes, Dasara celebrations in Jagdalpur show a remarkable continuity throughout the twentieth century.

1.6 The Argument and the Chapters

I have already indicated some aspects of my argument in this book. Here, I will summarize it briefly. While studies on kingship in India abound, little attention has thus far been paid to the conceptualizations of the king and kingship by the tribal communities of Central India. The proverb and the proverbial performances it refers to are an invitation to reconsider this and to approach the "indigenous view of kingship" as it is expressed in the festivals concerned, as well as in local myths. The principal question is: What constitutes sovereignty from the indigenous perspective? As I have pointed out previously (Berger 2002), from the local point of view it is the faculty of being sacrificers that establishes the senior status of the founders of a village, the "earth people." It is through sacrifice that *niam* is manifested – the divine rule as instituted by god (Maphru), or, as he is also often described, the King God (Raja Maphru) – and well-being in a general sense is ensured; the well-being of people, of animals and of crops. Sovereignty, then, is about the ability to navigate the flow of life through sacrifices to the earth goddess in particular, as stipulated by *niam*; it is a sacrificial sovereignty, a sovereignty of life. Regeneration is inevitably linked to the proper socio-ritual order (*niam*), or rule in this sense.

In the eyes of the indigenous communities of Koraput, the king is first of all such a sacrificial sovereign – a metasacrificer who performs at the global level (the kingdom) what his subjects perform at the local level (their villages). Born from the "navel place," the king ensures regeneration and generalized well-being through sacrifice, and human sacrifice in particular, the ultimate gift to the earth goddess. As Birsa Sisa said (see Chapter 3), today "they have entirely stopped [performing these sacrifices] (. . .). On this account, the earth goddess (Dorti Mata) has become somewhat angry (. . .) and for this reason, illnesses are now breaking out all over the world." A bad king is one who neglects his sacrificial responsibility and, accordingly, rebelling against a bad king and his negative fertility is a way to promote regeneration and well-being. Significantly, the tribal cultivators regard themselves as co-responsible in the pursuit of regeneration. Also, when they come to the capital to celebrate the royal Dasara, they do so not as passive, awestruck spectators of royal glory, worshippers of the king on whose sacrificial performance they entirely depend. They flood into the capital, enacting their role as sacrificial sovereigns and claiming their independence; they demonstrate their pivotal role as earth creatures in performing various forms of sacrifice and engaging in effervescent and at times violent "play" (*kel*), simultaneously showing their "political muscle," as Alfred Gell (1997, 436) put it.

It is in this field of sacrifice and regeneration that indigenous ideas of sovereignty correspond to, and have perhaps historically co-evolved, with more widespread pan-Indian Hindu ideas of the king as sponsor of sacrifices and the "husband of the earth." There are good reasons to believe that the jungle kings were also not only driven by political calculus – that is, intending to control the tribal communities as best as they could, legitimizing their rule by adopting tribal deities and performing sacrifices – but genuinely valued the indigenous people in their role as sacrificers and earth creatures, those with a fundamental connection to local divine powers (Schnepel 2002, 253). At the same time, however, the kings – and their Brahmans – also strove to assert their superiority as sacrificers, which resulted in the dynamics of hierarchical oppositions between king and subjects in the course of royal festivals, as mentioned above.

In a nutshell, this is the argument that I will pursue in the course of this book. Each of the proverbial festivals, in its own way, addresses the question, perhaps one should say the conundrum, of subaltern sovereignty and the connection between rule and regeneration. However, I do not intend to reduce the festivals to mere "cases" or illustrations of my argument. As I indicated above, the ethnographic study of most of these festivals is in its infancy, and although I will relate the festivals to the question of subaltern sovereignty, I will allow the rituals to speak for themselves. These are very complex festivals, displaying many facets, and they are open to various interpretations and perspectives.

The book is divided into two parts. The first part aims to provide a basis for the subsequent discussion of the five proverbial performances in part two. In **Chapter 2,** I start by outlining some Hindu ideas about kings and kingship that have been very widespread in India. Obviously, such ideas are connected to specific periods, people and places but my aim is not to provide a history of kingship in India but to identify a few themes that resonate with, or can be compared or contrasted to, the indigenous view of kingship that I will try to unravel in the chapters that follow. I will discuss ideas that link the king to the earth, even see him as a "husband of the earth" who induces her to provide well-being for all. Closely associated with this idea of regeneration and provider of fertility are ideas about good and bad kings. The myth about the wicked King Vena is particularly instructive and will be discussed in some detail, also because it is an elite rationalization of the existence of "barbarians" – how indigenous peoples used to be depicted – and of their marginal place in social, moral and spatial terms. One version of this myth has been collected directly in the area of my concern, the Jeypore kingdom, and explicitly links the sacrifice of King Vena and the accidental production of a "monster" to the tribal communities of the region.

The final section of the chapter examines kings and their subjects as part of the hierarchical chain of being, a notion which is closely associated with the hierarchical worldview of the Vena story. This ontological scheme – manifest in multiple forms, such as temple structure or ritual process – employs an imagery of centricity, where "radiant energy" (*tejas*) (Inden 1998, 71) of the god and the divine king diffuses outward to the less valued center, and to the "barbarians" at the far end. Agents with different bio-moral qualities can and must engage differentially with the center and also profit from their participation in a graded manner. On the margins, it seems, the passive recipients of *tejas* dwell who have little to offer in return.

Chapter 3 reverses the perspective and looks at kingship from the point of view of the indigenous subjects. The first part of the chapter is devoted to the analysis of a number of myths, among which I distinguish two types: the brotherhood stories and the Dom Raja myths. The brotherhood stories narrate how god initiated the creation of king and subjects, giving two brothers a certain task (mounting a horse). The younger brother succeeds and becomes king, the elder fails and becomes subject. Notably, the brotherhood stories make use of elite codes that are reminiscent of the Vena myth and representations of tribes as "barbarians." Through alimentary (eating beef, raw meat, cannibalism), matrimonial (marrying a princess or demoness) and political codes (mounting a horse, carrying loads), a contrast between civilized (younger brother) and wild (elder brother) is established, the latter being negatively valued. The tribes of the region derive from the elder brother(s). The Dom Raja stories, by contrast, are subaltern narratives that do not employ elite status codes. In these stories, a forest-born boy-cum-king (the Bening Raja) secretly follows his adoptive father to the royal capital as he wants to pay tribute to the king, who happens to be a wicked Dom King. The boy greets the Dom King with his feet and in the resulting battle kills him with forest weapons and takes his place. In these stories, the Bening Raja has an autochthonous origin and the mode of assuming office is rebellion. Moreover, no contrast between wild and civilized is articulated and the forest is valued as powerful and providing.

In the second part of the chapter, I focus on one community in particular, the Dongria Kond, and examine their ideas of kingship as articulated in myth and ritual. The ritual discussed is the "buffalo sacrifice" that came to replace human sacrifice. I focus, in particular, on sacrificial objects closely associated with kingship and the clan territory and how sacrifice to the earth ensures generalized well-being: plentiful children, successful hunting, abundant crops and human health. In the conclusion to this chapter, I discuss indigenous notions of sovereignty that I infer from the myths and rituals and compare Hindu and tribal views of kingship.

Chapter 4 is also divided into two sections. The first sketches the political history of the Jeypore/Nandapur kingdom, summarizing the available historical sources. I briefly discuss the sequence of major kingdoms on the coast, such as the dynasty of the Eastern Gangas (*c.* 500–1000 CE), the Imperial Gangas (1112–1434 CE) and the Sun Dynasty (1434–1590), as well as their relationship (as far as it is known) to the Nandapur jungle kingdom in the hills. Of special interest are two dynastic changes that occurred within a few years in the fifteenth century. On the coast, the Imperial Gangas were succeeded by the Sun Dynasty, while a dynasty of the same name (i.e., Sun Dynasty or Suryavamshi) replaced the Stone Dynasty in Nandapur that presumably had come into existence sometime in the thirteenth century. The relationship between these parallel dynastic changes is unclear and many hypotheses have been ventured. Various sources, among them the chronicles of the royal family of Jeypore, narrate that the dynastic change in Nandapur did not occur smoothly and that tribal subjects are said to have risen against the first king of the Sun Dynasty (Vinayaka), who claimed the throne of the former Stone Kings. Burkhart Schnepel and Raphaël Rousseleau have attempted to uncover the historical dimensions of this story and Rousseleau also draws a significant comparison with these narrations (and allegedly historical events) and the Dom Raja myth mentioned above, which is common in the region.

My interest does not so much concern the extent to which these stories relate to actual historical events but rather whether and how they might be related to and find expression in the festivals under discussion. As it happens, the local community (Benek or Bening Porja) where I recorded one version of the Dom Raja story (M5) is associated by Rousseleau with those who have in the past rebelled against Vinayaka, the first Sun King, because of their allegiance to the Stone Dynasty. However, the Bening also had certain ritual privileges under the succeeding Sun Kings. As such, they were received by the king during Dasara, bringing the first paddy harvested in the kingdom from their villages. These villages are located near a place that figures prominently in many regional myths, the Queens Fall (Rani Duduma) and the rocks that bear the marks of a mortar (Kotni Mala). Here, the mythical jungle boy who overthrew the Dom King was born. In the myth I recorded in a Bening village (M5), the speaker identifies the Bening as foster parents of the jungle boy, who is referred to as Bening Raja and Silputi Raja, thus "Stone Place" (*silputi*) King, possibly an allusion to the Stone Dynasty (Silavamshi). Furthermore, the Bening are considered to be a section of the Joria, the community who performs the Ganga Puja, which enacts the Dom Raja myth in a refracted manner and is all about rice and rebellion. I will return to this configuration of myth, ritual, the Joria/Bening and kingship in Chapter 5 when dealing with Dasara, and again in Chapter 6, when I discuss the Ganga festival in detail.

In the second part of Chapter 4, I examine various scholarly representations of the historical relationships between kings and tribes in Central India. For the purpose of discussion, I distinguish five different modalities of the king/tribe relationship, which I critically investigate. While some authors demonstrate a rather unilateral view of the king/tribe relationship, seeing the influence mainly flowing in one direction, most scholars propose understandings of the relationship that entail some sort of interdependence and mutual integration. Consequently, I deal with those approaches in more detail and further develop my argument in relation to their work. In particular, the coronation ceremony of the king of Keonjhar and the Konto Kuari festival of the Bhuiya demonstrate an understanding of kings and tribes as co-sacrificers, and the hierarchical dynamics between them in the course of the rituals are the result of this perception and the interplay of royal and tribal sovereignty.

The second part of the book commences with my discussion of Dasara in **Chapter 5**, the first of the proverbial performances. As the successor to earlier public royal festivals, Dasara probably made its first appearance around the fifteenth century and soon became one of the most important royal rituals in many parts of India, regenerating the king and his realm. Based on the work of Indologists and historians, I start out identifying four key elements of Dasara: the goddess, the king, the community and the theme of regeneration – of turning death into life, or the conquest of death. Subsequently, I discuss Dasara comparatively at various levels. I start out with the festival as it has been observed in the jungle kingdom of Bastar, as detailed descriptions of the festival in Jagdalpur throughout the twentieth century are available. My analysis of Dasara in Bastar focuses on four aspects: the germination of cereals, the role of the local (tribal) goddess called Maoli – who is closely associated with the process of renewal and the sacrificial death of the king – the function of the tribal participants as sacrificers and, finally, the role of tumultuous events and indigenous notions of "play."

From Bastar, I turn towards the Jeypore kingdom and discuss the little that we know about the Dasara festival as celebrated in the towns of Jeypore and Nandapur. There is one relatively detailed description of an episode of Dasara as performed at the margins of the Jeypore kingdom that provides important clues as far as the tribal participation in the festival is concerned. As part of his own celebration of Dasara, the king of Bissamcuttack, vassal to the Maharaja of Jeypore, held a sacrificial festival that accorded a crucial ritual role to the Dongria Kond.

Then I take stock again, comparing Bastar and Jeypore, especially with regard to the dimensions of tribal participation in Dasara, the relationship between king and tribal subjects and the meaning of collective, partly ferocious effervescent events. I argue that these performances are not only intended to demonstrate tribal political independence or to "obstruct the state," as Alfred Gell (1997) argued, but that they are a vital dimension of sacrificial sovereignty in the religious sense, entailing ideas of regeneration and the navigation of life and death.

In the next section of Chapter 5, I change the perspective and deal with Dasara rituals as they are performed in different villages of the region. In Gutob Gadaba and Dongria villages, Dasara rituals are of minor importance in the annual ritual cycle. In both cases, no explicit connection to the king is discernable and another common feature is that the festivals concern the margins of the village and its protection from outside. The situation is different in the Rona village of Badigor, formerly the place of the *mutadar*, who locally represented the king in this remote corner of the Jeypore kingdom. The Dasara ritual here seems to replicate the performances in the capital, with a buffalo being sacrificed for Boirobi, with clear references to Shiva. Significantly, the sacrificer of the buffalo is a Gadaba, not a Rona. The next example again provides a different picture and concerns the Joria village of Ponosput Bagra, close to Jeypore town, and its relationship with the royal capital. Scholars have often described processes of appropriation of tribal deities by kings and we have such a case here. Today, the Joria still sacrifice a buffalo during Dasara at a Durga shrine on top of the hill behind their village. However, they narrate how this fierce human-eating goddess was taken, domesticated and transformed by the king in the past, when a shrine for the goddess (then renamed Kalika) was built in the Purnagarh, the "Old Fort" that was established in the seventeenth century when the capital was moved to Jeypore.

As a last comparative step, I look at two examples of the festival in classical Hindu kingdoms, those of Mysore and Puri. In the conclusion to this chapter, I argue that Dasara festivals in the jungle kingdoms of Jeypore and Bastar can be regarded as distinctive. Their distinctiveness derives first of all from the nature of the involvement of the community. For South Indian Hindu kingdoms, Burton Stein (1983), for instance, outlines how the community is constituted by the reverence expressed by the participating public vis-à-vis the king and the goddess, the people thus sharing in their royal-cum-divine power, similar to the idea of "radiant energy," as described by Inden (1998, 71). By contrast, the tribal population that pours into the royal capital bringing their local deities along, do not come merely to worship the king and his goddess but as ritual actors on their own terms, as co-sacrificers. These special forms of tribal participation have certain implications and consequences that I further discuss in the conclusion to this chapter.

While Dasara in jungle kingdoms may thus be regarded as distinctive, they are not unique on a pan-Indian level. "Tribal" participation in royal cults is not an uncommon feature, even in those royal polities that are not considered jungle kingdoms. Classical normative Hindu texts (Kane 1974) stipulate that a "tribal festival" should be part of the celebration of Navaratra, which displays many features discussed previously with reference to Bastar and Jeypore. Puri is another case in point. Although "tribes" are conspicuously absent during the Dasara festival, it is well known that the god Jagannatha has a "tribal" heritage and the "tribal" temple priests (Daita) perform ritual roles involving killing and renewal that are reminiscent of the sacrificial function of the indigenous population in the jungle kingdoms.

Chapter 6 deals with the first subaltern festival, but one that is left unmentioned in the proverb, the Ganga Puja of the Joria. As cereals play a crucial role in all the local rituals that are subsequently discussed, I first outline the main agricultural features of the region. Indigenous cultivators of the plateau – such as the Joria and Gadaba – grow two staple crops that they consider in complementary and contrastive terms – paddy and finger millet. After introducing the Joria community, I turn to the Ganga Puja, a festival which deals with the cultivation of wet rice in many ways. Its second most notable feature is the fact that throughout the ten days of the festival a certain number of Joria villagers enact roles associated with the former royal polity of Nandapur; some "become" Dom, others Ghasi, yet others Paik. Moreover, there is a competition and tension between the low-status Dom and Ghasi, on the one hand, and the royal soldiers (Paik), on the other, which fully erupts on the last day of the festival after all of the groups have accompanied the procession of the Ganga deities (clay pots and oil lamps) for days. On the last night of the festival, a stilt dance takes place, during which the deities inhabit the bodies of the stilt dancers (belonging to the group of Paik) and make them walk. After the stilt dance, the festival stipulates that a fight takes place between the Dom/Ghasi and the Paik. In the analysis of the festival, I focus on three aspects. First, I discuss the conspicuous relationship between the Ganga festival and the stories about the Dom Raja; second, I try to approach the local perceptions about what is going on during the festival, what the nature of the deities and the performances are and how the ritual form complying to the socio-cosmic order (*niam*) facilities well-being in a general sense; and, finally, I examine the relationship between two aspects that are continuously present during the ritual: "dance" (*nat*) and "play" (*kel*).

The Nandi festival, performed a month after the Ganga Puja, is a celebration of finger millet. As I discuss in **Chapter 7**, the most conspicuous aspect of this festival and at the same time its greatest conundrum is the relationship between finger millet, on the one hand, and termites, their eggs and their mound, on the other. Another remarkable feature is an elaborate mural that is painted in the Nandi house over many hours, accompanied by the invocation of deities. Two icons are made from earth and eggs taken out of a termite mound and then placed in a basket on top of millet cakes and millet grain, with everything being placed in front of the mural (called "sky wall" in the Nandi song) depicting the moon, sun, stars and divine "pathways." Like the Ganga divinities, the Nandi deity is then also taken in procession through the village, throughout which songs are sung that refer to the deity as Earth Beauty Dust Beauty (Mati Sundori Duri Sundori) and urge her to move on.

My analysis of the festival first tries to unravel the connection between the termite mound and finger millet. After introducing some scientific facts about the particular species of termites involved (*Odontotermes obesus*), I discuss the local meanings of termites and the mound, again especially with reference to myths. The latter make it plain that termites are associated with "life" and "wealth" of different kinds, including coins and grain. In one story, millet grain is first transformed into earth, then into termites. Ultimately, I argue that millet and termites are considered as corresponding and equivalent to each other. A decisive clue to understanding the connection between earth and grain comes from a Pengo myth (M8) that identifies the Earth Beauty Dust Beauty as a female shaman who applies agricultural tools to the earth itself, "grinding earth" (*mati*) and "pounding dust" (*duri*). Moreover, she turns out to be the provider of the knowledge of cultivation and hunting. As termite mounds are considered a "gate to the underworld" in many parts of India (König 1984), I subsequently investigate the connection between the dead and grain, a link that is very obvious among the Gadaba and Sora and also present, though in less elaborate ways, among the Joria. Taking a comparative perspective, I finally discuss the mural as a kind of house, a dwelling place for the gods who come down to the middle world as much as the dead "climb up."

The theme of cereals and regeneration is also central to the festival discussed in **Chapter 8**, the "sand" festival of the Mali. Surprisingly, the most important cereal is wheat, which is not commonly grown in the region. Although the Bali Jatra is the signature festival of the Mali, many other communities perform it. In the case I discuss, it was performed in a Parenga village, where the original hosts of the festival were Rona. As in the case of the previous festivals, local narratives are also crucial here. During the first phase of the festival, the oral epic is sung intermittently over weeks by female specialists (*gurumai*). The second phase of some ten days then constitutes the climax of the festival. Before I describe the festival as we observed it in the village of Komra, I first outline some of the main features of one of the main characters of the epic and the performance, the group of Bima and their connection with rain, storm and agriculture. That the male Bima are important in the story should not belie the fact that the Bali Jatra is a festival of "flowers" dominated by women. Accordingly, the Bima should first of all be understood as maternal uncles, they are the brothers of a sister. Moreover, at least from the perspective of the Pengo and Dongria, the Bima are not the brothers of just any sister, but of the earth goddess. In my interpretation of the epic as it was documented by Tina Otten, the Bima make three subsequent affinal gifts: sisters in marriage, tools for and knowledge of cultivation and, finally, rice itself.

The last phase of the festival begins with the preparation of the Bali deity (an earthen pot, a winnowing fan and a bow) and the fetching of "sand" in baskets from the paddy fields by all the women of the village. Seeds of wheat are sown into the sand by each individual household and by the *gurumai*, whose basket is then placed in the Bali temple. The Mali only make an appearance to paint the mural that depicts scenes of the epic and shows all the gods that will enter the temple in the séances called "trance dance" during the night. At the end of the festival, the baskets of wheat seedlings are brought out of the individual houses and the temple and taken back to the paddy fields, where the sand is returned and the seedlings distributed as Bali "flowers" to create or maintain ritual friendships.

My analysis of the Bali Jatra focuses on two aspects of the festival – affinity and kingship. As I mentioned above, affinity is a crucial value in tribal Central India and the other side of clanship or "brotherhood." The communities of the region contrast "brothers" (of the same clan) with marriageable "others" (of a different clan), and this ubiquitous classification is applied not only to human groups but to other relationships as well, including those with crops and fields, at least in the case of the Gadaba. Most generally, affinity concerns those modes of relatedness that are vital for the regeneration of life. Among the various metaphors that are used to signify such relationships (such as cattle and milk) are "flowers," and in many ways the Bali Jatra is a festival about "flowers" (seeds and seedlings), performed by "flowers" (women). The connection to kingship is apparent in different ways, both in the epic and in the performance. Furthermore, the king of Jeypore used to perform the Bali Jatra before celebrating Dasara and, significantly, as Tina Otten discovered, he first received the Bali "flowers" from the representatives of various villages, before exchanging them with people of his court. This may be understood as an act of worship by the subjects, an establishment of a bond with their king. However, it can also be read in a different way. That the king first received the auspicious results and the token of successful sacrifices and trance dances from the villagers and the *gurumai*, amounts, in my view, to an acknowledgment of the status of his subjects as sacrificial sovereigns.

The Go'ter ritual of the Gadaba, which I discuss in **Chapter 9**, is unusual in comparison with the other festivals in at least two ways. Like the Nandi festival, no explicit link to kingship is discernible in the Go'ter. However, not only kings are conspicuously absent from the Go'ter but also gods, which is unlike any other festival discussed in this book. Moreover, the Go'ter is not a ritual concerning the annual cycle but the life-cycle; it is the final death ritual. Put very briefly, during the Go'ter a local group of brothers temporarily bring back to life those who have died since the previous occasion, providing the dead with new bodies they can inhabit – the bodies of living water buffaloes. After the buffalo-dead have been fed and feasted for some days, clan brothers from different villages take them away, replacing them with stone slabs at different megalithic assemblages in the hosts' village. In this way, the liminal dead are transformed into permanent ancestors.

Initially, I focus on two aspects, the different embodiments of the dead during the Go'ter (buffalo, stone and branch bodies) and the dense web of agnatic and affinal relationships these rituals spin between villages. I then analyze the climactic sequence of the ritual, which involves the arrival of buffalo-dead from other villages, which are then killed in a special manner in the dry fields, their bellies being slit open by a crowd and the intestines torn out of the still living animal. It is this practice that gives the ritual its name – "tearing" (*go'ter, jur*). Based on the most detailed description of a particular occasion that is provided by Karl Gustav Izikowitz (1969), I concentrate on three aspects of the performance: the relationship between the killing and crops, the role of the hosts' affines and the meaning of the ritual ferocity displayed.

The ritual stipulates a specific location of the killing, namely the dry fields, where, most prominently, finger millet is grown. As I demonstrate, the Go'ter not only transforms the dead but also – by means of a "human sacrifice" – nurtures the living. Being killed on the dry fields, the dead revitalize the fields on which the next generation of millet plants will grow shortly after, facilitating the growth of a crop that is closely associated with "life" from a Gadaba perspective. The Go'ter ritual thus traverses and connects different forms of being – human, animal, earth and plant. The affines of the group of brothers who sponsor the ritual are crucial, because they alone provide the particular category of buffaloes that are killed in the dry fields. As I have also argued in relation to the Bali Jatra, processes of regeneration often depend on affinal involvement and contributions.

Finally, I understand the ritual ferocity in two complementary ways. On the one hand, both the violence toward the sacrificial animal and between actors is part of the generative performance of subaltern sacrificial sovereignty; a ferocious assertion of life by shedding blood and defeating death by not fearing it. We encountered such behavior, sometimes conceptualized as "play," in several of the festivals discussed in this book. In the case of the Dongria, these performances even have the same name as the Gadaba death ritual; their buffalo sacrifices are referred to as "tearing" (*jur*). On the other hand, the Go'ter may also be understood as a political message of unruliness, perhaps formerly addressed to the king in Nandapur, and as such an "art of not being governed" (Scott 2009).

Part One: **Kings, Subjects and Subaltern Sovereigns**

2 Some Pan-Indian Ideas about Kingship

As an institution and idea, kingship has occupied a vital place in Indian society and religion from Vedic times – at least since the so-called Aryans settled in the Ganges Valley some three thousand years ago – down to the present day. While the new Indian constitution abolished kingship after Independence, the nascent nation chose as its emblem Ashoka's Lion Capital, its wheel figuring prominently on the Indian flag; thus, a reference to the first, and one of the few, pan-Indian kingdoms and a reminder of "righteous rule." However, kingship not only remained part of the national imagery, and was also not restricted to politics. In all its many dimensions and manifestations, society in India was imbued with the idea of kingship, and its religions were saturated with, if not at least informed by, notions of royal leadership, and this has also not changed. Today, ex-kings, or their descendants, engage in politics and try to capitalize on primordial loyalties (Skoda 2008) and public figures ritually sweep the chariots of deities, as kings still do (Hardenberg 2008). Moreover, the idea of kingship is found in all corners, including among Indian tribal communities, who mostly lived on the margins of earlier kingdoms and whose actual integration into the administrative systems of kings was partial at best.

If kingship in India has existed for, say, 3,000 years, it is evident that we cannot speak of the same set of ideas or a constant political format. Obviously, many transformations occurred (e.g., Heesterman 1985), and kingship always looked different depending on the region or the – societal or academic – perspective (Ali 2011). As Jan Gonda (1957b, 158) wrote, "'the king' could mean something quite different to a soldier, a peasant, a brahman, or a courtier.' One of the questions this book tries to address is what the king means to the indigenous population, the *porja* or "subjects," in highland South Odisha.

The various festivals that are at the heart of this book all deal with kings and kingship, albeit in different ways, and not very explicitly in all cases. In order to grasp the tribal point of view of kingship, which will be the aim of the next chapter, I first want to outline some of the main ideas about kings and kingship that have had wide currency in many parts of India for a very long time. In this way, the indigenous conceptions of kingship can be related to these more general themes, some of which also return at the local level, although in adapted and indigenized forms. Needless to say, I do not intend to deal with the pan-Indian ideas of kingship in any exhaustive manner here, and this chapter will not offer anything new to the indologist, who may want to move on to the next chapter straight away.

Kingship cannot be understood in isolation, as notions of kingship are part of a complex conceptual latticework whose gradual development through Indian history is mainly accessible through an enormous textual corpus; texts that, in their nature, form and aims, display a great variety. Although these texts show what kingship ought to be rather than what it actually was, they obviously correspond to a social and religious reality on the ground, and they have responded to and informed practices and policies as much as contributed to further philosophical discourse. What has been said about the perspectival and transformative nature of kingship above is certainly also valid for this ideological framework as a whole. There is no rigid system of ideas, no single view of Hindu kingship (cf., Heesterman 1985, chapter 8); rather, we are dealing with relational ideas whose meanings and emphasis shift as the composition and constitution of the framework changes according to particular contexts and specific philosophical and religious traditions. Nevertheless, there are certain common ingredients in this grid of collective representations that have informed the idea of kingship; obviously so, as the latter was part of this ideational framework from early on.

2.1 Varna, Ashrama, Purushartha

One important dimension of this framework that is mentioned in the tenth book of the *Rig Veda* (RV 10.90[1]) concerns the *varna* – four categories or classes that constitute a holistic vision of society and its interdependent hierarchical parts. The mythical origin of these classes illustrates the paradigmatic act in Vedic society, namely sacrifice. They are the result of the self-sacrifice of the cosmic man (*purusha*, see also, the *Laws of Manu/Manusmriti* chapter 1, 31), who divided up his body: out of his mouth came the Brahmans (priests); from his arms originated the Kshatriyas (warriors, *rajanyah* in RV 10.90.12); from his thighs the Vaishya (people); and from his feet the Shudras (servants). Obviously, each part contributed to the whole, but being linked to different corporal (and hence social) locations, their contributions were also different. The division of labor, referring to religion, rule, subsistence and service, as well as mutual duties was often formulated in pairs with regard to teaching, protection, sacrifice and gift-giving (Biardeau 1982, 78). In fact, it has been argued that the four categories themselves should also not be understood as a linear hierarchical order but as a series of increasingly inclusive oppositions (Dumont 1980, 66f).

---

[1] See for instance: http://gretil.sub.uni-goettingen.de/gretil/corpustei/transformations/html/sa_Rgveda-edAufrecht.htm.

The first three *varna* are regarded as "twice-born," as their male members receive initiation and have access to the sacred texts of the Veda, in opposition to the Shudra, who are excluded from the study of the Veda and the performance of Vedic sacrifice. The Vaisha, as peasants and traders, are opposed to the "two forces" that, according to the *Laws of Manu* (part of the *Dharmashasta* literature), are destined to rule over "all creatures" (Dumont 1980, 72). This latter opposition of Brahmans and Kshatriya is crucial. They are not only opposed but also closely associated and mutually dependent on each other. The category of Kshatriya not only refers to the warrior but to the king in particular. He dominates in terms of power and wealth, and must protect the Brahman and sustain him, offering gifts to him. The Brahman is superior in religious terms, being the only one who may teach the Veda, with the other classes being receivers of this sacred knowledge. Hence, the "mouth" of *purusha* is an appropriate place of origin for the Brahman category, as it was not so much a matter of reading the texts but reciting them, while the "arms" for the Kshatriya are befitting, as they execute legitimate force (*danda*) and grant protection. Along with the pairs of teaching/being taught, giving/receiving gifts, providing/receiving protection, the key activity they contributed to in complementary ways was sacrificing, with the king sponsoring the sacrifices (as *yajamana*) and the Brahman conducting them. It was through their joint cooperation in the performance of sacrifices that the order of the kingdom and the order of the cosmos were maintained, thus *dharma* in a general and most encompassing sense. The performance of the *varna*-specific duties was the specific *dharma* (*svadharma*) of the members of a particular class.

Around the middle of the first millennium BCE, the advent of a new figure on the religious landscape complicated this simple binary of Brahman and king, and it forever changed Vedic religion, gradually transforming it into what later came to be known as Hinduism, predicated on the creative tension between society and salvation. The renouncer (*sannyasin*) challenged everything that the Brahman and the king stood for, the order which was maintained through their sacrifices, and instead proclaimed the aim of individual liberation (*moksha*) as superior (see Olivelle 2003). The renouncer triggered a "revolution of values" (Smith 1990) that did not lead to the abolition of hierarchy, but changed the principles on which this hierarchy was based: from the martial values of the Vedic Kshatriyas, – the "law of the fishes" based on strength and violence – to a situation where violence in relation to the *ahimsa* ("noninjury") doctrine was regarded as problematic. With regard to the nature of kingship, Daud Ali (2011, 94) describes this situation as a shift from "agonistic" to "irenic" values of kingship. The king was no longer the eater of the weak but he who guaranteed the peaceful order of his kingdom, with the help of and dependent on the Brahman. The

Brahmans, appropriating ascetic values, built their new identity and legitimacy on non-violence and purity, vegetarianism being one expression of this development (Smith 1990). Ideal Brahmanhood came to be defined in soteriological terms, the values of the renouncer meaning that those Brahmans who were the least involved with the world and society were considered superior and those like the priest, working for and dependent on others, inferior; in other words, autonomy came to signify superiority (Fuller 1992, 18; Heesterman 1985, chapter 1; Parry 1994, 266f):

> While the superior can pretend to autonomy, the inferior is dependent on the superior to make safe, auspicious and beneficent its *own* powers and capacities – a rule which applies as much to kings in relation to Brahmans as it does to women in relation to men. (Parry 1994, 267)

Positioning themselves in relation to the new values of renunciation – with the Brahmans thinking for both their own class as well as for the king in the texts they composed – resulted in paradoxes and contradictions for both. For the Brahmans, it effected a fundamental ambiguity of being "both inside and outside the world" (Parry 1994, 269), with this ambivalence being evident for instance with regard to meat consumption and sacrifice, as illustrated in the *Laws of Manu* (see Berger 2011). For the Kshatriya, a direct relatedness to transcendental values was perhaps even more difficult establish. How are non-violence and liberation supposed to fit with the function of the king, where violence and concern for the world are part of his *svadharma*? Nevertheless, kings and renouncers were not simply diametrically opposed, as there was also a conceptual overlap with regard to certain ideas – crucial throughout this book – to which I will turn shortly, namely those related to regeneration and fertility.

Closely connected to the conceptual relationship between the roles of Brahman, king and renouncer are the Brahmanical theories of life stages (*ashrama*) and the "goals of man" (*purusharta*). Both schemes show the intellectual appropriation of ascetic ideas by Brahman thinkers. The goals consist of a core group: the triple group (*trivarga*) of *dharma* (cosmic order, duty), *artha* (aim, material wealth) and *kama* (desire, pleasure), to which the fourth, *moksha* (liberation), was added. As with the relationship between king, Brahman and renouncer, Malamoud (1982, 41) stresses that the goals of man represent a "revolving hierarchy" depending on the viewpoint taken. *Dharma*, it may be argued, is superior to the other two *trivarga* goals, as it is independent of them and *artha* and *kama* are mere instruments of *dharma*. In the *Arthashastra*,[2] it is stated, unsurprisingly,

---

[2] This "Treatise on Success" (*arthashastra*) is an ancient Sanskrit text concerned with governance, military strategy and politics that is often associated with the author called Kautilya.

that *artha* is the root of both *kama* and *dharma* (Malamoud 1982, 40). Much depends on whether the goals of life are referred to in their specific or general dimension. Undoubtedly, as mentioned above, it is the function of Brahman and king to maintain the cosmic order and *dharma* in this general sense (the specific sense being the particular duties) appears to be superior to all other aims. However, this is an "aim" after all, which is the general meaning of *artha* (the specific one being interest in material wealth) and, in this sense, "all the purusharthas are arthas" (Malamoud 1982, 44–45). Moreover, no aim can be reached without desire, which motivates action, and hence, the faculty of desire is the basis of any action. But, of course, both desire and wealth outside *dharma* are fruitless, and so on. The *trivarga* form a totality, perhaps even representing "an exhaustive list of all possible 'motives'"[3] (Malamoud 1982, 40 n. 17), at least for man in the world, who should strive toward the realization of all three aims.

The link between *varna* and the *purusharta* is obvious. The *svadharma* of the Brahmans is equivalent to *dharma* in general, one reason why members of this *varna* claim superiority, which is usually granted to them as far as religion is concerned. Yet, again, there is no single, uncontested or absolute hierarchy (Malamoud 1982, 50; Burghart 1978). The *svadharma* of the king – *rajadharma* (cf. Derrett 1976) – is *artha*, he has to seek prosperity for the sake of the people in his kingdom (*rashtra*): "the production and circulation of material wealth is the object of political acts on the part of the king, whose ultimate aim is to reign over men" (Malamoud 1982, 52). The condition for prosperity is a safe environment; hence, the protection of the people of his realm is a crucial part of *rajadharma*, and the king is able to provide protection because of his strength and power, which is in turn based on his support of Brahmans and deities.

The text has been composed over a period of time, probably starting in the second century BCE (see Kautilya 1992; 2013).

3 Malamoud's statement is based on the correspondence between the three goals of life of the *trivarga* and the theory of the three strands of *Samkhya* philosophy that has been very influential in many Hindu traditions. Briefly (cf. Inden 2006, 216f; see below), all matter is a combination of three qualities, *sattva* (goodness, true knowledge, brightness) being the highest, *tamas* (inert badness, darkness, ignorance) the lowest. Significantly, each of the two is empowered by *rajas*, the intermediate quality of "restless activity" and "passionate energy" (Inden 2006, 216). Malamoud mentions the association of *sattva* with *dharma*, *tamas* with *kama* and *rajas* with *artha*. But one can easily also see a correspondence between *sattva* and the Brahman, *tamas* and the low strata (excluded from true knowledge) and *rajas* and the *kshatriya* or king. In the latter case already the word *rajas* suggests a relation to *raja* and the description of this middle strand (energy, activity, the color red, will) seems to confirm this. If the goals thus correspond to the *gunas* that define all there is and can be they are indeed exhaustive. But it also shows that the ideas of kingship are fundamental in many ways.

> His power ought to overflow. Consequently, the 'increaser of his friends' should bestow gifts; being a dispenser of bounty, he should delight and gratify his subjects: the title *raja* is in a significant way often derived from *raj- ranj-* in the sense of 'to make glad, to delight'. (Gonda 1956a, 48)

Also, the original meaning of the root of the word *raja* is, according to Jan Gonda, related to the function of protection, *raj* in his "opinion originally expressed the idea of 'stretching (out), stretching oneself out,' the king being the one who 'stretched himself out and protected (other men) under his powerful arms'" (1957b, 143).

While the king's primary domain is thus *artha*, he is also related to *dharma* and *kama*. As mentioned above, he must maintain the cosmic order through sacrifices, with the help of the Brahmans, but he also surveys the hierarchical order of society and enables his subjects to realize their *svadharma*; protection, wealth and order being different aspects of the same thing. However, *kama*, desire in general and sexual pleasure in particular, is also associated with the function of kingship. Hunting, drinking and sex are part of a king's profile. Yet, a king has to observe *niti*, the "art of conducting oneself" (Biardeau 1995, 53), and a king who puts his own desire before that of others in his realm is a failure. Exactly because it is the king who is allowed to engage in pleasures, "it is the Kshatriya whom the texts warn against excessive attachment to kama" (Malamoud 1982, 51).

This leads me to the king's relationship to the goal of liberation and the system of life stages. Starting from the premise that a kingless country is destined to sink into lawlessness and chaos[4] – even a bad king being better than no king at all (e.g., Derrett 1976, 608) – it is not surprising that kings were not encouraged to seek personal liberation but to perform their duties as described above. The *ashrama* system, outlining the ideal stages of life, in particular for the Brahman, but also for all twice-born *varnas* more generally,[5] suggests that the initial period of studentship (where *dharma* is predominant and *artha* and *kama* more or less precluded; Malamoud 1982, 52) is followed by a period of being a householder that includes the establishment of a family and the procreation of children, particularly sons that are necessary for ancestor worship and death rituals for the parents. This phase corresponds closely to the royal function, as a balance of the *trivarga* is needed, and *artha* is stated as an explicit goal, in contrast to all other stages of life. The last two stages show the influence of ascetic values that have

---

[4] As it is stated in the Ramayana: "if there is no king who separates good and bad, this world is wrapped in darkness, so that nobody can know what to do" (Gonda 1956a, 71).
[5] This scheme of life-stages underwent significant transformations. In its original form, established around the fourth century BCE, it provided four different ways a religious life could be lived and did not include the idea of a succession of life-stages (Olivelle 2003, 277–80).

been included in the Brahmanical perspective. After an intermediate period of forest dweller, when the duties of a householder have been fulfilled and suspended, the person becomes a renouncer, theoretically dead to society, pursuing the final goal of liberation. A king may not seek renunciation while in office, and a legitimate heir is not supposed to strive for *moksha* either, before having fulfilled his duty as king.

Fundamental disorder (*adharma*) is the result of members of a *varna* consistently violating their *svadharma*, even if with the best of intentions. Biardeau (1982) illustrates this in her analysis of some aspects of the Mahabharata. Two heroes of the epic, Bhisma and Drona, were certainly virtuous, but as the former was a prince who renounced his duties as householder and the latter a warlike Brahman, they contributed to an *adharmic* situation that, in the end, could only result in a disastrous battle, bringing about the end of the epoch and the start of the Black Age. Also, on the Pandava side, as Biradeau argues, only Arjuna emerged as the ideal king, though his elder brothers, Yudhisthira and Bhima, were the more obvious candidates. However, it was Arjuna (after being convinced by Krishna) who finally faced his duties as Kshatriya and embraced *artha*, whereas Yudhisthira promoted *moksha* and Bhima *kama*, the latter being excessively violent and corrupting *niti*, the proper conduct of warriors. War, as Arjuna is taught by Krishna, is itself a form of sacrifice thus befitting a Kshatriya as *yajamana*. The battle aimed at the protection of the people and general welfare; key duties of a king as stressed above. Arjuna could not flee from his obligations, "a king, by virtue of being a king, has to get his hand dirty [read: bloody]" (Biardeau 1995, 58). By following his *svadharma*, Arjuna also served the values his elder brothers represent, *moksha* and *kama*. Moreover, through the idea of *bhakti* (devotion), salvation became generalized and accessible to all (Biardeau 1982, 96f). In this way, a king – Arjuna as devotee of Krishna – can also strive for *moksha* without abandoning his duties in the world.

2.2 King, Earth, Fertility

Approaching the relationship between king and the earth, we briefly have to consider the relationship between kings and deities more generally, a topic to which I will return in the last section of this chapter and repeatedly throughout this book. Classical Sanskrit literature stresses the divine nature of kings.[6] As

---

[6] But there are views to the contrary, of course. Thus Ali (2011, 91) argues that the king in Vedic times was not regarded as divine but as paradigmatic sacrificer.

such, it is said in the *Laws of Manu* (*Manusmriti* 7.5): "Because a king is made from particles of these lords of the gods, therefore he surpasses all living beings in brilliant energy." Similarly, Gonda (1956a, 59) states:

> In examining the status of the ancient Indian king from the religious point of view we should never forget that he is called and considered a *deva*, that is to say, not God, the sole Eternal Lord and Creator of all things, nor his Son or representative, but one of a class of powerful beings, regarded as possessing supernormal faculties and as controlling a department of nature or activity in the human sphere. King Pariksit, the Atharvaveda for instance states, was "a god among men."

However, such "gods among men" were and still are not so uncommon in India. Arthur L. Basham – who also described the king as "evidently the fellow of the gods, if not a god himself" (1971, 83) – commented that divinity "was cheap in ancient India. (. . .) If the king was a god on earth he was only one among many (. . .)" (1971, 88). Similarly, Chris Fuller argues that one characteristic of contemporary Hinduism is the porous dividing line between the human and the divine. The very practice of worship (*puja*) brings about an identification of worshipper and deity. Moreover, humans claiming to be gods are nothing unusual in the context of "Hinduism's fluid polytheism" (Fuller 1992, 31).

The appropriation or sharing of royal and divine status is mutual and, accordingly, we not only find divine kings but also royal gods. Paradigmatic kings, such as Indra or Rama, are perhaps the most popular among the latter but there are many other examples. William Sax, for instance, describes in detail how gods compete over territory and people like kings in contemporary Garhwal, in particular in the context of ritual processions (Sax 2002, chapter 6). The royal status of the god Karna not only becomes apparent in his function as ruler over a territory and its people but also as he administers justice and distributes wealth like a king. Moreover, he has the ability to bring rain. This, Sax (2002, 173) writes, "is perhaps the most widely recognized characteristic of divine kingship cross-culturally, and is certainly prominent in the Hindu tradition." It is to this role of the kings as agents of regeneration and their relationship to the earth that I will now turn to in a bit more detail.

Making the earth fertile is one of the foremost duties of the king, who "causes her [the earth] to give what is desired by any class of beings" (Gonda 1957b, 151; cf. 1956b, 154). Duncan Derrett (1959) and Minoru Hara (1973) paid particular attention to kingship in connection to fertility, sexuality and manliness. The latter stressed the king's role as "husband of the earth" (*mahi pati*) and argued "that the earth (*mahi*) is the wife of a king who rules over it, and that [a] conjugal relation between *mani-*, the earth, and the king, who rules the earth, can be discerned" (Hara 1973, 98). Being married to the king, the earth would even pass through all the stages of womanhood, from a bride – the king being her suitor – to a married woman giving birth, to a widow after her royal husband's death.[7]

Derrett more specifically distinguished three roles of the king in relation to the earth: 1) as "maintainer of the earth" (*bhu barana*), 2) as "protector of the earth" (*bhu palana*) and 3) as "enjoyer of the earth" (*bhu bhojana*). The notion of "protector" corresponds with a key function of a king that we have already encountered in general. As maintainer, a king provides rain, through sacrifices but also "good government" (Derrett 1959, 111; cf. Gonda 1956a, 42f). Like Indra – the king of gods – a king is regarded as "rainer" and rain (*retas*, "rainwater") also has the meaning of semen, which "*satisfies*" the earth (Derrett 1959, 118). The root of the word "to rain" (*vrish*), Derrett (1959, 119) states further, "has a most ancient duality of meaning: it suggests the pouring or scattering of generative fluid."

Textual evidence thus makes it quite clear that the "enjoyment" of the earth is also of a physical, sexual kind. On the one hand, this imagery is violent as far as conquest is concerned (e.g., speaking of "rape" when taking a city, Derrett 1959, 112) but, on the other hand, the appropriate treatment of the earth as wife, according to *dharma*, is also stressed (Derrett 1959, 113). Significantly, ideas concerning the king-earth relationship go beyond being mere illustrations or metaphors, also entailing the legal rights of a king as far as the products of the earth are concerned:

> Brahma arranged that the king was (. . .) the owner of all wealth and specially (wealth) that is inside the earth (. . .,) the *bhartir* ('husband', 'maintainor', 'master', 'lord') is he, <videlicet> the 'overlord of the gods' (i.e. Indra). Thus the labour of the *prajah* was his to tax, whether by forced labour or otherwise. (Derrett 1959, 114)

Hence, from the special relationship between king and earth – a "king's ultimate lordship of the soil" (1959, 115) – resulted in the right of the king to receive levies from all those who lived from the earth (Gonda 1956a, 46). He had a right to labor and to the products of the earth and could confiscate land as punishment. However, as Derrett stresses, the king should not be the enjoyer of his subjects and under normal conditions the relationship between king and subjects was one of mutual support: "It is only if they [the subjects] stop 'feeding' him, or fail in their duty, or he is overcome with greed, that the relationship breaks down, and he 'preys upon' them" (Derrett 1959, 117). The sexual potency of a king is

---

7 See also the description and analysis of medieval rituals of affusion (*abhiseka*) by Ronald Inden, in which the new king is also daubed with different kinds of earth that are connected to his different body parts (1998, 61f).

frequently stressed, he being a "bull among men" (Derrett 1959, 119). A king's "necessary qualification" (Derrett 1959, 119) is signified by the harem, and the idea of an unmanly king is obviously repugnant. A king's virility also translates into the military domain: "A lord of the earth who is not intent on conquest is as blameworthy as the effeminate husband of a woman" (Hara 1973, 105).

Returning to the relationship between king and renouncer, it is particularly with regard to this dimension of fertility and generative power that the conceptualizations of both overlap.[8] As Derrett (1959, 119) points out, both the king and the *sannyasin* are associated with an abundance of semen, and both should not die a natural death. Underlying this overlap is a complex of ideas related to sacrifice, heat (*tapas*) and transformation, a form of "cooking" (Malamoud 1996). Similar to the householder maintaining the sacrificial fire in his house, the king is the patron and sponsor of sacrifices. Turning his back on the world, the renouncer cannot escape the field of sacrifice, Malamoud states, but can only change his position in relation to it. Through his austerities, the renouncer internalizes the sacrificial fire and creates the heat that, on the one hand, transforms him in the desired direction of liberation and, on the other hand, creates a powerful generative energy that can be of use in this world. Not spilling semen – like Shiva, the divine ascetic par excellence, whose symbol is the phallus or *linga* – is part of ascetic practice and this internal transformational process. Parry (1994, 259f) also provides evidence with regard to his ethnography in Banares, revealing that the power of the Aghori ascetic, often manifested in either curse or blessing, is connected in particular to reproduction and fertility. Due to a curse of an Aghori, the royal line did not produce any male heirs and as soon as the curse was lifted the queen conceived a son. Moreover, in order to beget children, Hindus and Muslims bathe next to the tank where the founder of the sect, Kina Ram, practiced austerities. The bodily fluids of Aghori, in general, are "charged with special potency" (Parry 1994, 260).

Being related to the sacrificial process in different ways, then, both the king, as "rainer," and the ascetic are associated with generative powers and

---

[8] But there are more correspondences between king and renouncer as William Sax (2002, chapter 6), for instance, points out with regard to the royal god Karna in Garhwal, who has already been mentioned above. Karna assumes the role of a king but he is also considered as ascetic, being morally superior vis-à-vis other deities, and as he is associated with special powers that enable him to function as oracle but also to inflict illnesses or madness on opponents. More generally, Sax argues that the much debated roles of king, renouncer and Brahman should be understood as contextual "relational strategies" (Sax 2002, 185), rather than fixed identities. Combining features of all three roles, Karna is a case in point. Also the old traditions of warrior ascetics are an example of the combinations of the roles of the renouncer and the military function of the Kshatriya (see Hausner 2007, 78–89).

fertility, the former also making use of the power of the latter, who is indifferent to the world. How both are supposed to end their lives is connected to the same complex of ideas. A king should die in battle, which is conceived of as sacrifice and associated with heat, while the ascetic will have formally concluded his death rituals before his actual death, as part of his initiation into the status of renouncer. He may die as a consequence of ascetic practices – Derrett (1959, 119) writes, the *sannyasi* "should be buried alive or drowned, starve themselves to death" – but, in any case, the ascetic is not cremated, as the final transformation has already been accomplished.

2.3 Good Kings, Bad Kings and the Idea of "Barbarians" as the Repugnant Other

Even though it is commonly said that a corrupt king is better than no king – which would mean anarchy – the texts are also quite clear about what "bad" kingship is and what its consequences are. Given the stress on order and protection that I have outlined above, it is no surprise that a bad king is one who upsets order, misuses his power and neglects his duties to his subjects, the gods and the Brahmans; in short, one who ignores *rajadharma*. In contrast to righteous rule that guarantees fertility and plenty, drought, famine and barrenness, or simply destruction, are the consequences of bad rule (Gonda 1956a, 43). A king who thus violates his office must inevitably face the consequences of his wicked actions, for which no sacrifice can possibly atone (Derrett 1976, 606). Moreover, he is likely to be murdered: "An unrighteous and vicious king, however mighty an emperor, is sure either to be killed by his infuriated subjects or subjugated by his enemies" (Kautilya 1992, 121; *Arthashastra* 6.1.15–18). Regicide is thus the direct result of the situation (Shah 1982, 64). People, also Brahmans, are even encouraged to put an end to his rule violently, "to put him to death as if he were a mad dog" (Gonda 1956a, 69).

The theme of the bad king is elaborately expressed in the pan-Indian myths about King Vena. This story is relevant to my discussion of the tribal view of kingship, as will become apparent in the next chapter. My description here refers mainly to the work of Ronald Inden (2006, chapter 9) and, to a lesser extent, Wendy Doniger (1980, chapter 11). As Doniger (1980, 329) points out, this story has been told and retold in many different versions, from the Vedas down to devotional literature, and can be read in different ways.[9] Most obviously, it

---

9 Inden mostly focuses on the *Puranas*, especially the *Vishnudharmottara*.

discusses kingship, subjecthood and related questions of morality; that is, questions of good and evil.

Things had already gone wrong in the ancestry of Vena, as his maternal grandfather was *mrityu* or "death" and Vena was thus wicked from the start. Violent toward children and cruel in hunting, Vena violated *dharma* early on. As the king, he mixed classes and castes so as to produce degraded offspring (Doniger 1980, 324, 327). Moreover, he adhered to a radical doctrine (its followers being called "sensationalists") that accepted only those phenomena directly accessible to the senses and hence questioned the validity of the Veda, the existence of gods, and thus the daily business of the Brahmans. Being the king, this was not a personal opinion but state doctrine, a state should be "an actualization of the chosen ontology" (Inden 2006, 225). Consequently, Vena ordered that the sacrifices to the non-existent Vishnu should be offered to him instead.

The Brahmans first tried to persuade the king, pointing to the consequences in very clear words, even threatening him, but to no avail. Then they informed Vishnu about their plan to kill Vena because of his transgressions and asked for divine support. The Brahmans requested that the act of killing should also directly lead to the generation of a new king "for the welfare of the people" (Inden 2006, 231). Motivated by divine anger, the Brahmans killed Vena with a special sacrificial grass (*kusa*), to which *mantras* had been applied. Immediately thereafter, the Brahmans moved Vena's left leg back and forth, "as though trying to start a fire" (Inden 2006, 232) and a new creature came into being: short, ugly, dark, terrible to look at, representing Vena's sins and evilness. The Brahmans instructed the creature to "sit down" (*nishida*) and as a result he became Nishada, representing the evil in all beings and the ancestors of the barbarians or *mlecchas*, in particular (Thapar 1971, 422). Hardly satisfied with this result, the sages rotated the right arm in the same way and Vishnu appeared in the form of a man who was called Prithu, "the broad one" (Inden 2006, 233). With him, righteous kingship on earth was established. Barrenness and famine came to end as Prithu pursued the earth with bow and arrows. She turned into a cow and asked not to be killed (or, alternatively, fled to Brahma who mediated and made Prithu into the protector of the earth, Gonda 1957b, 127), to which Prithu consented, and thereupon the cow provided all that was necessary for all classes of beings (Doniger 1980, 321). The earth herself was called *prithivi* after him (Gonda 1957b, 127; Inden 2006, 234).

Among the many noteworthy aspects of this myth – Inden focuses on the idea of evil in general, and Doniger on the parent/child relationship – I want to point out two things in particular. First, the special relationship between king and earth is again stressed; the latter is even named after Prithu and domesticated by him, providing all the necessary wealth. Second, the myth provides the rationale for a social hierarchy that is political, moral and geographical or spatial at the same time. Vena's generative sacrifice – for that is what it is, with the arm/leg being rotated "as if to start a fire" – creates a division between a ruling class and a class of subjects, those who "sit down," that is to say, who obey. Those in the superior category are "honorable," they are Aryans who are morally superior, stemming from the right upper part of Vena's body. They are also superordinate in economic terms, being cultivators. Nishada, originating from the left, lower part of the body, is the opposite – black, wicked, representing the inferior section of the population: "*a son named Barbarian, from whom were descended various foreign tribes*" (Doniger 1980, 327). The descendants of Nishada – the Nishada class being the result of cross-*varna* matrimonial relations, thus the "mixing" of which Vena was accused in Brahmanical theory (Tambiah 1985, chapter 6) – are the savage, non-Aryan hunters from the forests of the Vindhya Mountains (or, alternatively, untouchable fishermen). Moreover, as a result of their corrupted heritage, they engage in disreputable practices associated with death and dirt. Spatially, while the descendants of Prithu make up the royal center, those of Nishada constitute the subordinate tribal periphery (Inden 2006, 34f): "Vaishnava ideology conceived of the *dharma*, the Order that the kings and peoples of India were supposed to build and maintain, as a hierarchy of contrasting, relatively good and bad zones, inhabited by relatively good and bad people" (Inden 2006, 235).

Speaking about king and kingdom therefore also means speaking about center and periphery. The periphery may consist of other rival kingdoms, and I will return to this "horizontal" aspect in the next section. Here, relying mostly on Romila Thapar (1971) and Aloka Parasher (1991, esp. chapter 6), I will continue to discuss the other dimension of the periphery, as perceived from the center, the "wild hill tribes" inhabiting the margins. One term that has been used to describe such communities has just been introduced, Nishada (Parasher 1991, 197–202), a notion that is already found in the Vedic literature, alongside other designations of otherness that I will briefly discuss here. However, whatever the terms, a few aspects are shared by all these representations, and they have also been fairly constant throughout the texts dealing with them. First, these descriptions have been based on little knowledge about such communities and this is no doubt grounded in the lack of interest in associating with them (Thapar 1971, 436). Second, the texts mostly express a radical opposition and strict separation of the self-designated "nobles," Aryans, and later the associated Brahmanical tradition, and the others, called Nishada or by other names. However, on the ground, interaction, mutual influence and integration also occurred. Third, with a few exceptions perhaps (Parasher 1991, 197), the descriptions of these people are negative, and various Brahmanical models tried to rationalize their inferiority, the story of Vena being one prominent example of this. The basis of this negative view lies in the question of control, or the lack of it. As long as these communities resisted Brahmanical domination, as long as economic or political integration proved difficult or impossible; in other words, as long as they refused to "sit down," they were depicted as the degenerated Nishada of the Vena story.

This latter aspect is evident with regard to the descriptions of the Nishada early on, as Thapar (1971, 422) observes: "References to the four *varnas* in Vedic literature includes mention of the Nishada who appear to have been a non-Aryan tribe who succeeded in remaining outside Aryan control but had a low status of ritual ranking." What the term Nishada shares with several others – like Sabara – is that it is used in both a general and a specific way: generically, to denominate all those "wild tribes" outside the Aryan cultural and political sphere; but also apparently as a designation for a particular community inhabiting the hills of Central India.[10] Particular to the category of Nishada is that the term is used for an occupational caste of fishermen as well as for an "alien tribe" (even cannibals) (Parasher 1991, 200).[11] Parasher suggests that this might be related to a transitory process, in which the Nishada were integrated into the Brahmanical system, as usual at a low rank. However, as she states that "the Nishadas continued to form a peripheral culture outside the Brahmanical dominance" (Parasher 1991, 200), it seems as if only a part of the community was integrated, while other segments resisted. However, perhaps it was a different community altogether and obviously these categories must be handled with much care, as they have neither been used with much consistency or accuracy, nor can we assume one continuous meaning of these terms throughout the centuries, or, for that matter, a completely constant ethnic composition through time.

Two terms that are common in the *Rig Veda* and which are often used interchangeably to signify others are Dasas and Dasyus, those who spoke unintelligible languages, were "flat-nosed" and associated with demons. Most interesting is that they apparently were not "poor savages" but wealthy ones. As Parasher points out, we do not know what their wealth consisted of, only that it came from the plains and mountains, but it was clear that the Aryans wanted to get

---

10 Parasher discusses several specific cases in detail: the Kirata (1991, 187–91), the Sabara and Pulinda (191–96), the Nishada (1991, 197–202), Pundra (1991, 202–6) and Andhra (1991, 206–10).

11 In some cases "tribes" seem to have been clearly distinguished from "castes." The fifths century text called *Amarakosa*, for instance, lists those communities designated as "mleccha jati" and contrasts them to communities generally referred to as Candala, a common term for untouchable communities, also in *The Laws of Manu* (Parasher 1991, 195).

hold of it, and apparently with little success initially, as they called upon Indra to help them defeat the Dasyus (Parasher 1991, 182–85).

The most well-known term for "barbarians," which is largely equivalent in meaning to Nishada as a generic concept, is *mleccha*, the word appearing for the first time in the *Satapatha Brahmanas* (800–500 BCE).[12] Like the other terms, *mleccha* has been used widely and in a variety of ways. In some cases, it referred to border areas, to people outside the nucleus of Brahmanical centers of influence who were not "hill tribes" but rather communities similar to the Aryans. Often, however, the term was used to designate hill and forest people. Again, language was the initial criterion of difference – Sanskrit being much more than merely a language for the "Aryans" – *mlech* meaning "to speak indistinctly" (Parasher 1991, 46). As mentioned above, *mlecchas* were regarded with contempt, being culturally outside the *varnashramadharma* system and politically independent. Up to around the fifth century CE, Brahmanical culture and influence did not make much progress in the hills of Central and Eastern India (Thapar 1971, 416; Parasher 1991, 205, 209). Brahmanical doctrines tried to explain the existence of *mlecchas* by way of mixing of *varnas* (cf. Tambiah 1985, chapter 6) – of which king Vena was accused – which was largely a theoretical exercise with little relationship to realities on the ground (Parasher 1991, 185), or as result of the disobedience of the sons of Visvamitra, whose descendants the *mlecchas* supposedly were.

In addition to these rationalizations, there was also a rather pragmatic attitude toward these communities. Kautilya, for instance, pointed to the strategic advantage of "keeping the forest tribes happy" (Thapar 1971, 418), because in this way they could be involved in military campaigns or at least would refrain from plundering. Moreover, Thapar outlines two successive ways *mlecchas* were integrated into the Brahmanical order. On the one hand (between the first century BCE and fourth century CE), *mleccha* communities that rose to political power were integrated as "degenerate kshatriyas" (*vratya kshatriya*); that is, Kshatriya, who, because of some ritual negligence, drew the ire of the Brahmans and lost their original status (Thapar 1971, 419). Later (ninth century CE onward), on the other hand, dynasties with *mleccha* backgrounds established themselves and adopted a new strategy. With the help of Brahmans – who profited from the system of land grants – they constructed royal genealogies that provided them with the necessary legitimation.

---

[12] See Bhattacharya (2020a) for a critical discussion of the term *mleccha* and the arguments of Thapar and Parasher.

Thapar makes another important point that brings us back to the topic of kingship more specifically and to a theme that will be discussed in detail later, the integration of tribal cults into Hindu cultural traditions. She writes that *mleccha* fertility cults and those regarding the mother goddess especially – various forms of the Devi – began to play a significant role in Hinduism from the fifth century CE onward (Thapar 1971, 433). However, as I have pointed out above, the king was closely associated with and responsible for the earth, its fecundity and fruit, so this dimension could hardly have been a new aspect. Accordingly, Derrett (1976, 605) argues that Hinduism inherited from Vedic religion a ritual division of labor, with the Brahmans dealing with the Vedic gods, while the kings are crucially related to the chthonic deities. In this sense, tribal religions did not introduce fertility rituals and the worship of the earth as a divine being, but rather this is essentially the field where ideologies and practices met and overlapped. As will become clear later, ideas and practices concerning the earth are one decisive reason why kings played an important role in the imagination of tribal communities and, conversely, tribal ideas and cults resonated very well with Hindu ideas of kingship.

In conclusion to this section discussing good and bad kings and their relationship to "barbarians," one version of the Vena story (M24) that was unearthed by Raphaël Rousseleau (2008, 63; 2010b, 44) in the "manual" of D.F. Carmichael (1869, 75) should be mentioned. It was recorded by Lieutenant J. Macdonald Smith, who was Assistant Agent to the Governor of Jeypore in the 1880s (Thurston 1909a, 160), and thus in the exact area with which this book is concerned. This version is notable insofar as it actually connects the pan-Indian Vena story with the local tribal set-up of the Jeypore kingdom. Thus, here we encounter not only references to generic terms such as Nishadas discussed above, but also some of the actual communities populating the area, which are represented as descendants of King Vena. It "may be convenient," Carmichael (1869, 75) writes, "to give in this place the generally received opinion of the Natives here, as to the origin of these wild races:"

> A certain king in Hindustan, named Vena, dying without heirs, the Rishis or Sages, by the power of incantations pronounced over a jar of oil, which they stirred about with the thigh-bone of the deceased monarch, endeavoured to create a proper successor. The being they summoned into existence was, however, a monster rather than a man, and they forthwith exiled him to the south of the Vindhya mountains, where he became sovereign of the hill tracts. His name was NISHADA; he had five sons, GAITA, MUKA, MANYA, KONDA and KODU, and from intermarriages between the descendants of these brothers, the following castes were formed – Koya, Chanchu, Savara, Yarakala, Maddu, Basa, Rona, Gonda, Jodiya, Pangu, Nogala, Bottada and Bonka.

Noteworthy in this version is the fact that Nishada is not only a monster, which is congruent with the versions I have discussed above, but also a king, a mountain king, perhaps in contrast to the valley king, north of the Vindhyas, the good king who is not mentioned in this story. In particular, it is important that some of the tribal communities of the area are mentioned, some of which will reappear in the pages below: the Koya, Chenchu, Rona, Joria, Pengo, Bhattra (Bottada) and Bonda (Bonka).

King Vena is not mentioned in any of the myths collected by Elwin (1954; 1991a) or which I recorded, and I think Rousseleau (2010b, 44) is right when he says that this version probably comes from a scribe in the royal capital of Jeypore. Several tribal myths, to which I will return in detail in the next chapter, do deal with a wicked king, but he is framed in local terms as Dom King.

2.4 The Ontology of Kings

The idea of kingship is linked to various cosmological notions and philosophies. One influential set of ideas is also known as the theory of the three "strands" (*guna*). A basic premise is that "the cosmos was thought to be a living thing. The primordial stuff of which it was made [called *prakriti*] was conceived of not as mere physical matter but as a kind of ever-changing protoplasm" (Inden 2006, 216; see Marriott 1989; Marriott and Inden 1977).[13] Significantly, this cosmic protoplasm constitutes the cosmos not in a homogenous way but in a differential manner that results in a hierarchical chain of being. Everything is a combination of three strands (*guna*) that determine the physical form, the intellectual or internal capacity and the moral quality of the form of being: *sattva* (whiteness, lightness, transparency, goodness, knowledge), *rajas* (activity, energy, heat, will) and *tamas* (darkness, heaviness, opaqueness, badness, ignorance). The middle strand, *rajas*, is the activating principle that combines with the other two. When *sattva* combines and dominates *rajas*, the result is a being of "luminous power/will" or "radiant energy" (*tejas*) (Inden 1998, 71), "the power of gods and men to do good, their power to uphold Dharma, cosmo-moral order" (Inden 2006, 218, cf. 261).[14] The combination of *tamas* with *rajas*, in contrast, means that darkness and ignorance become a powerful force: "the power used by demons, atheists, and barbarians to mislead and overwhelm men" (Inden 2006, 219). This theory of bio-

---

13 I rely mainly on the work of Ronald Inden in this section. He is especially concerned with Pancaratra Vaishnavism, referring to the *Vishnudharmottara Purana* in particular.
14 Thus *tejas* is closely related to the notions of power (*shakti*; Wadley 1977) and auspiciousness (*subha*; Hardenberg 2008; Marglin 1985).

moral substance – of which the Vena story obviously is one manifestation – thus presents a contrast between the civilized and the uncivilized; those who uphold the socio-cosmic order, like the king, and those who threaten it, like the barbarians. There is no doubt, moreover, about how to deal with the latter: "the demon or barbarian either submits or is slain" (Inden 2006, 222).

As the beings populating this living cosmos are malleable, actions and, in particular, ritual action, result in ontological transformations. Bio-moral qualities can thus be differentially transferred from gods to kings and to normal humans. A paramount king (or king of kings) is thus imbued with *tejas* by being ritually bathed with water that is infused with Vishnu's *tejas* in the context of a ritual bath (*rajyabhisheka*) that is regularly repeated (Inden 2006, 261f; 1998).[15] The deity is made immanent in the king and other beings of the king's realm can then participate in the "luminous power/will" thus achieved: "The paramount king embodied Vishnu in himself and his court and his kingdom, all of whom shared, albeit it differentially, in the well-being and prosperity that the manifestation of Vishnu brought" (Inden 2006, 264).

One expression of his power as a paramount king (*cakravartin*), or king of kings – the public recognition of it and the possibility of the people sharing in his *tejas* – took the form of annual royal processions, when the king, his court and a portable image of Vishnu moved through his realm conquering the "four quarters" (*digvijaya*). Such ritual processions could turn into military campaigns should the king face any resistance, but they should culminate in the building of a temple in honor of the cosmic overlord, Vishnu. As the king shared in the divine *tejas*, so did the people by worshipping the king and the deity: "through participation in the life of the king of kings and Vishnu [the 'people'] *raised themselves above* the everyday, moving closer to heaven and release from life in the world" (Inden 2006, 268).

Crucial to this cosmology of kingship were thus notions of centricity and radiation that exemplified and manifested the Hindu chain of being. Kautilya's notion of the royal polity as having "seven limbs" (*saptanga*), with the king's body in the center, from which *tejas* was disseminated, is one example of this idea (Inden 2006, 263).[16] This corresponds to the contrast between civilized and

---

15 Also in contemporary Odisha the royal coronation crucially involves the sprinkling of water that, accompanied by *mantras*, "transforms the king into a god" (Marglin 1985, 159) or a "walking incarnation of the god" (Hardenberg 2008, 96; my translation).
16 Inden elsewhere mentions a somewhat different setup: 1. Lord or Master (king); 2. Companions and officials; 3. Royal capital; 4. Countryside; 5. Royal revenue or treasure; 6. Army and 7. Allies (Inden 2006, 132). The main source is Kautilya, the author of the *Arthashastra*, the art of statecraft (Kautilya 6.1.15–18, 1992, 121).

uncivilized spaces mentioned above, as the civilized royal center is engulfed by citizens and the periphery populated by barbarians. This centralized structure was manifested in royal performances that made use of emblems of royalty such as elephants and horses, but also turbans, umbrellas, fly-whisks, swords, shoes and the crown (Gonda 1956b, 122). Examples of such performances in Vedic times include the installation ceremony (*rajasuya*) and the horse sacrifice (*ashvamedha*) (Heesterman 1985, chapter 8). The descriptions of these performances in the Brahmanical literature were, of course, as normative as Kautilya's ideal kingdom.

One such performance, the court assembly – which was also a crucial part of the Dasara festival to be discussed in detail in Chapter 5 – is described by Ronald Inden (2006, chapter 5) with reference to a dynasty of Western India from the twelfth century (the Caulukya of Gujarat). Kingdoms, Inden argues, did not exist loosely side by side but were integrated into a hierarchy of kings, or a ranking of kings, great kings and the king of kings, those at the top obtaining obedience from all and having no overlord themselves. During the court assembly, these relationships became manifest:

> They [the assemblies] were total representations of the hierarchy of kingship considered to embrace the entire earth and made clear and visible at one time and place. (. . .) [They were] also an enactment of *rajadharma*, the set of relations that kings were ordered to have among themselves (Inden 2006, 134, 149).

While not all of the details that the text elaborates on concern me here, what is important is that the different elements were ordered spatially in relation to the king at the center on his lion throne. Proximity and smaller numbers indicated closeness and superiority. Thus, along with army commanders (*dandanayaka*), marshals, councilors and other officers, there were four lords of provincial kingdoms (the number always distributed equally on all four sides of the throne), eight provincial lords and then different levels of vassal kings (*samanta*) of neighboring kingdoms. The latter are called "lords of the marshes" by Inden and included 16 high lords of the marshes, 32 common and 64 lesser ones. The numbers make clear that an ideal order is represented, as the reality would unlikely mirror the hierarchy so neatly (Inden 2006, 137ff). The actions that are mentioned in the text are also significant. All participants prostrate (*pranama*) themselves before the king before they assume their particular spatial position in relation to him. That is, they indicate their submission by placing their heads at the feet of the king (in contrast to the jungle boy who greeted the Dom Raja with his feet, but this is for the next chapter). Other important ingredients of the assemblies are fights and contests between animals and between humans and an inspection of the army (Inden 2006, 138).

The hierarchical and centralized structure manifesting the chain of being could be found in ritual performances as described, but also in the construction of temples, the structure of temple worship and the hierarchies of deities. Temple constructions were part of royal policies, the ritual and the military aspects complementing each other (Fuller 1992) and often going hand in hand, as in the royal processions across the kingdom mentioned above. With regard to the eighth to twelfth centuries,[17] Inden argues, temples "were structures which powerful kings constituted as icons of the Hindu chain of being" (Inden 2006, 192). For example, having assumed the position of paramount king after his "conquest of the quarters," Muktapida Lalitatitya (eighth century CE) built temple complexes for his new capital, whose structural layout hierarchically orders categories of people (Inden 2006, 193). Only Brahmans (Satavas, who cared for the central image of Vishnu), the "most perfect men in the ontological scale" (Inden 2006, 207), were allowed into the inner sanctum, while the paramount king, his ministers and relatives had access to the middle temple, and normal subjects had to be content with visiting the outer precincts.

Accordingly, the rewards of their religious actions, their "fruits," were hierarchized as well. The Satavas who worshipped Vishnu in the sanctum could expect liberation at the end of their lives, which meant union with their deity, "spatially conceived of as the highest 'place' in the Hindu chain of being" (Inden 2006, 206). While the paramount king, if all goes well, could be reborn as Satava Brahman, his subjects – "but visitors to the temple" (Inden 2006, 207) – could be reborn as beings who visited the middle temple. The centralized order manifesting the chain of being was thus a redundant structure, ranking forms of being in space and time. Forms of life closer to the center were of a more refined bio-moral substance (of higher purity, power or auspiciousness) and as such closer to liberation as well.

The power and sovereignty of the king is thus derived from the fact that he is a divine king, a metaperson embodying the power (*tejas*) of gods and who is therefore able to provide order and well-being for all, even though, as we have seen, the soteriological "fruits" were not the same for all but different according to their inherent qualities. As Inden (2006, 152–53) writes:

> Finally, the great king on his lion-throne was himself an iconic realization of the *Purusha*, the Cosmic Man, the Personal Absolute, Shiva, the Cosmic Overlord. (. . .) Those who worshipped the image or sign of the Cosmic Overlord, who "shared in" his being, were called his *bhaktas*. Those who assembled around the lion-throne to do homage to the

---

[17] More particularly, the Karkota Empire of Kashmir and King Muktapida Lalitatitya of the eighth century CE.

overlord of the earth were also – the same word is used – his *bhaktas*, those who shared in his kingship, those who were, as we would say, "loyal" to him. The idea of the king of kings as a hypostasis of cosmo-moral order on earth was, thus, no figure of speech. He did indeed embrace within his persona, himself together with his domains, the entire earth as an ordered, integrated totality.

What Inden indicates here is that the king was worshipped like a god and that through this worship devotees could participate in what he represented.[18] Moreover, this *likeness* was no mere metaphor, rather the king shared in the divine being, he was an expression of it. The term "hypostasis," which is also used in Christian theology to denote one specific form (in the trinity) of the undivided God, seems to suggest that the king was a particular manifestation of a general divine nature, a realization of a divine order that he had to maintain at the same time. This is one explanation as to why "kinglessness" means anarchy and why "bad" kings are unacceptable, considered an appearance of the demonic within the divine.

---

[18] While Inden here stresses that his subjects share in his being, in another article concerned with medieval royal installation rituals of affusion (*abhiseka*), he also notes a more reciprocal aspect of the relationship between king and his subjects. During the installation ceremony the king is repeatedly bathed, at one moment also by the "whole world" (*sarva-loka*), including women and ordinary persons (1998, 68f) who thus transfer "royal authority to the king" (1998, 77), which the king subsequently reciprocates by distributing wealth and by redistributing royal authority.

3 Indigenous Views on Kingship

We are the kings. (Samo Sisa, Gudapada)

The Hill Bhuiya "boldly aver that the country belongs to them. They assert that the Raja is their creation, and that the prerogative of installing every new Raja on his accession is theirs, and theirs alone." (Dalton 1872, 142, quoted from McDougal 1963, 7)

They [the Dongria Kond] are not to be ruled but they themselves are the rulers (. . .). (Nayak 1989, 184)

It is maintained by our informants that the presence of Narangi Jani is essential on the occasion of the coronation of the Raja (of Jeypore), for he enjoys (what a Pengo asserted) the right of *Singhasan Mati* ["earth lion-seat"]. (Thusu 1977, 14)

When approaching tribal views on kingship one cannot rely on a huge corpus of written documents, which are largely non-existent, but must depend on ethnographic accounts, including oral history, rituals and stories. What they reveal is that tribal identity in the region is articulated relationally, just as much between different tribal groups, for instance with regard to the seniority of local communities, as in relation to the king, and thus, as "subject" or *porja*. Often this identity is formulated in relation to Dasara, the royal festival at which delegations of tribal communities paid homage to the king.

When ethnographer K. N. Thusu conducted research around 1970 among the Pengo – who live in the area around Nowrangpur, north of the royal capital of Jeypore – informants responded to his inquiries about their past with the following proverb (Thusu 1977, 12):

Pengo Poraja,
Andkuria Dombo,
Kaunsalya Gaudo,
Peeta Bhatra,
Toibadi Baja,
Taleboshe Raja

While some elements of the saying are obscure to me,[1] it is clear that – much like in the aphorism with which this book is concerned – a number of communities of this particular sub-region of the kingdom are related to the *raja*. This concerns tribal cultivators (Bhatra and Pengo) and service communities (Dombo, Goudo). Moreover, special reference seems to be made to Dasara. "Toibadi Baja" refers to

---

[1] Especially the words Andkuria, Kaunsalya, Peeta are unclear. Neither the author nor his informants do provide much information on the meaning of the proverb.

the music (*baja*) of particular drums (*toibadi*) that the Pengo played during the Dasara procession in Jeypore (Thusu 1977, 14). Like the Bhuiya of Keonjhar, the Pengo interlocutors of Thusu claimed that they helped the king establish his rule in the Nandapur/Jeypore kingdom long ago and would therefore have the particular and rightful role during the coronation of the king of sitting on a throne called *singhasan mati* (literally "lion-seat earth"). The last line of the saying might refer to this aspect, as *taleboshe* means to "sit down," which is a metaphor for settling down and establishing a place; here, establishing the kingdom.

About the same distance from Jeypore as the Pengo, only up on the plateau to the south of the town, similar ideas are found among the Gutob Gadaba. Memories about the former kings and relations with them were faint when I started my ethnographic fieldwork some 50 years after independence in the 1990s. Older Gadaba who I questioned on this topic vaguely recalled the *raja beti* in the month of *dosra*. At that time, a delegation from the village, led by the *naik* (headman), walked the 30 kilometers, as the crow flies, down the hills to attend the Dasara festivities. Because it was his duty to feed the delegation during this trip, the *naik* had been granted a special paddy field, the *naik bera*, which it is still called today. However, that was about as much as I could gather about those bygone days of the king.

The idea of kingship, however, seemed to be omnipresent. In 2010, I accompanied a group of young Gadaba women and some other men – villagers, musicians and local administrators – to the Adivasi Mela, the Tribal Fair in the state capital of Bhubaneswar, where the government annually invites the "62 tribal groups of Odisha" to perform dances on stage, present food and build "traditional" huts in the fairground (Berger 2014). When I later asked the young women what they thought about the whole event, they did not have much to say, being rather overwhelmed by their new experiences in the capital and the traumatic trip back to Koraput in extremely overcrowded trains (which I did not dare enter). However, one older woman, Suborna Sisa, aged perhaps 45 at the time, thought for a moment and then said it would be just like *raja beti*, only that in earlier times the king called them to Jeypore, while now the government (*sorkar*) called them to Bhubaneswar to dance. This perception of continuity seems to be well founded. Indeed, around 1940, Gadaba and members of other tribes danced in front of the king during the "gala show" at the Jeypore Dasara (Sahu 1942, 35). Even earlier, in the 1870s, the British official, W. W. Hunter, visiting the *raja* of Dhenkhanal, recalled that "around noon (. . .) arrived a band of jungle people, whose national dance the Maharaja wished to show me" (quoted in Elwin 1948, 12).

However, even in this case, the duty toward the king did not consist in merely paying a visit during Dasara and dancing and drumming in the procession. Kings in Jeypore, and perhaps earlier at Nandapur also, used the tribal communities as a labor resource. In the 1960s, the Ollar Gadaba east of Nandapur still remembered well the forced labor they were required to do during the period before independence – sometimes with payment, sometimes without – such as carrying loads for the king and minor landlords (probably *mutadar*), or carrying those people themselves on palanquins (Thusu and Jha 1972, 74).

The Bondo, some 50 kilometers due south-west of Jeypore, also made their way down to the capital during Dasara. Based on his research in the 1940s, Verrier Elwin raised a number of significant points with regard to their relationship to the king of Jeypore. He writes that the "people are singularly loyal to their ruler, and the fulfilment of their duties to him and his officials is one of the virtues that is regularly impressed on young people" (Elwin 1950, 4f). As such, it may not be surprising that in the context of marriage – an ultimate question of *niam* or divine rule – reference is made to the king among the Bondo. Before leaving for the bride's village, a man of the delegation performs a short speech-cum-invocation that starts with the sentence: "Giving honour to the Maharaja we live in his kingdom" (Elwin 1950, 97).

Particularly noteworthy is the Bondo's partial replication of the centralized royal order, a feature that seems to be unique in the region. Whereas the Gadaba villages are not ranked (nor are those of the Pengo, Parenga, Didaye or Joria), the Bondo village of Mundlipada is the center of the "bara-jangar group," according to Elwin – that is, of twelve (*baro*) villages thought to be the original Bondo settlements. Not only do the Bondo bring gifts to the king of Jeypore during Dasara, but the village headman (*naik*) of Mundlipada, "subsidized and supported in his position by the Maharaja" (Elwin 1950, 6), also receives gifts ("tribute") three times a year from the headmen of the other villages.

Moreover, there is a ritual connection between the *bara-jangar* villages and the royal capital. While some other Bondo villages are not involved in this, the *bara-jangar* villages are ritually united in the worship of Pat Khanda Mahaprabhu, located in a shrine on a hillside above Mundlipada that includes a banyan tree in which a sacred sword (*kanda*) is hidden. With the headmen of the other *bara-jangar* villages attending, the sword is brought out and worshipped, and the blood of the sacrificed fowl is poured over it. Elwin (1950, 5) states that this sword is clearly connected to the royal court in Jeypore, as such swords would also be honored there; which is in fact the case. Also, the accompanying invocation leaves no doubt about the connection to kings. Notably, the invocation refers to Nandapur, the earlier seat of the king, which still has primacy of place in the regional imagination of kingship: "O Nandapur Mahaprabhu, O Pat Khanda Birkam, O Budha Bhairo of Nandapur (. . .). O Pat Khanda Mahaprabhu, let the kingdom, earth and country be well" (1950, 147). As Elwin rightly points out, Birkam (Vikrama) and Bhairo (Bhairava) were names of the kings in Nandapur and

Jeypore. However, it is not clear if the invocation actually refers to human kings at all. I would interpret "Nandapur Mahaprabhu" as the mythical King God (Raja Maphru), who is said to have been born in Nandapur (see M12), which is therefore referred to as "navel place" (*bumli jaga*) still today. "Pat Khanda Birkam" may refer to the sword that is worshipped in Nandapur during Dasara and "Budha Bhairo" certainly indicates a shrine (of which Elwin probably was unaware), where sacrifices also take place during the latter festival (see Chapter 5). This temple is located just outside Nandapur at the foot of the legendary Kotni Mala Hills that will figure repeatedly in the present chapter.

Especially significant is the combination, or almost fusion, of royal and divine significations, with Nandapur Mahaprabhu referring to a royal god and Pat Khanda Birkam to a divine king. What we have here is a congruence of local and global metapersons: royal gods in Bondo villages and the former royal capital. Perhaps it is no wonder, then, that among the Bondo, the *barajangar* group – ritually united by the Pat Khanda Mahaprabhu sacrifice – is also "the most devoted to the Maharaja," according to Elwin (1950, 6). Pat Kanda is also a major deity in the villages of other tribal groups of the region and is associated with the sun-moon deity (Sī Arke in Gutob and Remo) or Dorom, in contrast to the earth (Bosmoti). However, a sword is not worshipped, nor to be found, in any such places known to me. Nonetheless, the name might suggest an association of the deity with kingship or, in other words, another variant of the idea of royal divinity and divine rule or *niam*.

The connection between kingship, the tempers of deities and sacrifice was also crucial in statements by my Gadaba interlocutors. When discussing the performance of village sacrifices with Birsa Sisa,[2] a Gadaba of Gudapada, back in 2000, he became annoyed by the fact that some of the village sacrifices had been abandoned, and said:

> They have entirely stopped [performing some of the sacrifices] – stopped. On this account, the earth goddess (Dorti Mata) has become somewhat angry, has become angry, and for this reason, illnesses (*rogo*) are now breaking out all over the world (*dunia*), you know? For her, blood is not enough [. . .].

He then lowered his voice and continued:

> Listen, in Nandapur they've sacrificed a buffalo, sacrificed a sheep, sacrificed a human being (*loko*), in Nandapur, in the *dosra* month. In Jeypore they've sacrificed a sheep,

---

2 In my earlier monograph (where I also mentioned this statement and provided the Desia transcription as well), I used the pseudonym Buda Sisa for Birsa Sisa (Berger 2015, 113–14). I lived in his household during the first phase of my fieldwork in Gudapada. He died about ten years ago.

sacrificed a buffalo, sacrificed a human being. But now they don't sacrifice any more human beings, don't sacrifice any buffaloes, and don't sacrifice any sheep: what are [they] doing? They do coconuts, this and that.

This statement raises a number of truly fundamental points, and I will return to it again repeatedly in the pages that follow. Birsa made it clear that he considered it the responsibility of the kings in Nandapur and Jeypore to sacrifice, even to provide human sacrifices for the earth goddess, who demands blood or becomes angry, producing "illnesses." Today, Birsa concluded, this is no longer done and coconuts would certainly not do the job.

Alongside such valuable comments from the oral history of the region, we should also devote our attention to those discursive and performative cultural forms that especially entail ideas about sovereignty, if we are to better understand the tribal view of kingship. In this chapter and in most of the others, the focus will therefore be on myth and ritual in particular.

3.1 Kings and Subjects in Tribal Myths

Verrier Elwin produced a great collection of Central Indian tribal myths filling two volumes (Elwin 1954, 1991a [1949]), but he apparently did not consider the topic of kingship to be of particular importance. In both volumes, neither the extensive index of "mythological motifs" nor the "general index" contain entries on kingship or kings. In the myths he collected (locally called "stories," *katani*), however, the motif of kingship is very prominent and also in those stories I recorded more than half a century later.[3]

Elwin makes the important observation that, except "in a few instances, the Gadaba stories might just as well be Parenga, or – with the change of a few names – the Koya stories might be Didayi" (1954, ix). Indeed, the same motifs are found in various transformations in diverse myths narrated by different tribal communities. Moreover, Joria tell stories about the origin of the Gadaba cloth, or the Gadaba about the origin of the Tiger clan among the Bondo (see Elwin 1954, xxxiv). Thus, the "stories come from the village rather than from the individual," as Elwin (1954, xi) rightly remarks (adding that excellent

---

[3] Elwin recorded the myths between 1941 and 1951; I collected the stories between 1999 and 2016. Elwin recorded Koya, Didayi and Gadaba stories in the respective tribal languages, Bondo, Joria and Parenga in Oriya (that is, probably the highland dialect of that language, called Desia), "for the narrators were all bilingual" as he says (Elwin 1954, x). He also shared his method of translating the stories on the spot. In contrast, I have recorded the stories first (always in Desia) and translated them later, with the support of others (see appendix).

storytellers could not be found in the region), and, furthermore, they do not even originate from individual tribal communities. Rather, they "travel" in the region and, like the clan system (Pfeffer 1997), all communities share them. Hence, when I speak, for example, of a "Bondo myth" in the following, I merely want to indicate that the story was narrated to the ethnographer by members of this community.

The Creation of Kings and Subjects: The "Brotherhood" Stories

In the following, I will start by quoting one myth in full, which happens to be a Gadaba story from the region where I worked most. However, for reasons I have just outlined, this is not why I chose to start with this one as a sort of reference myth. Rather, this story introduces a number of themes relevant to my discussion in this chapter, such as the role of a horse, of carrying loads, of food and of marriage. In fact, these four themes are two sets of complementary codes selectively used in a large number of myths that deal with how social categories (in particular king and tribes) are created, related and transformed. Marriage and food constitute one complementary set. Both are closely associated with each other from the local point of view as highly generative and efficacious processes which lead to a change in status (Berger 2015, see M13[4]). The other set concerns the question of who carries and who is carried; it is about power. Humans either carry loads on their back (for themselves or for others) or are themselves carried by a horse.[5]

I will first outline the different themes and the dimensions of creation, relation and transformation with regard to the present myth. In a second step, I will deal with them comparatively, by referring to three other myths from the region. Mostly, I will refer to myths from the Jeypore/Nandapur region, sometimes referring to relevant aspects of myths from beyond this core area. For convenience sake, I have made a selection of especially relevant myths that are quoted in full in the appendix, for the other stories, the reader can consult the respective sources.

In the village of Guneipada, in the middle of the Gutob Gadaba region, Elwin recorded the following story (subsequently referred to as M1):

---

4 The demoness in M13 only agrees to marry the elder brother if he too eats her food, raw meat.
5 Carrying is an expression of senior status in ritual contexts. For instance are the dignitaries of the "earth people," the dominant group in the village, carried on the shoulders of the "late comers" in the context of the sacrifice for Pat Kanda (see photograph in Berger 2015, 380).

The twelve Gadaba brothers were born on the banks of the Godaveri River. One day they went to hunt in the forest, and as they went the eldest brother felt very thirsty. The youngest brother was carrying a gourd full of millet-gruel in a carrying-stick. The eldest brother sat down and began to drink some of the gruel. The other ten brothers went on, leaving these two behind. They presently came to a sago palm and drank the juice.

Meanwhile a horse, sent by Mahaprabhu, came to where the eldest and youngest brothers were sitting. The eldest brother caught it but when he tried to mount it the horse attacked him. He said to the youngest boy, 'Put the gruel down for a moment and hold the horse for me. I will go and get a bamboo ladder and will mount with that.' The youngest boy held the horse and the other went to find a bamboo for a ladder.

But while he was away the youngest boy got onto the horse and galloped away. When the eldest brother returned to the place there was no horse and no brother. So he picked up the carrying-stick with the gruel and followed the marks of the horse's feet. The other ten brothers joined him and they all went along after the horse's tracks to the Jeypore Hills. But the youngest boy got there first and became the Raja of the place.

When the eldest brother arrived with his load and the people heard what had happened they called him Bhoi [carrier] Gadaba. The youngest brother married the daughter of the Raja of Jeypore. But they could not find a wife for the eldest brother. He sent his sepoys [soldiers] to find a wife and they went to the Godaveri River. There they found a girl called Tarki Asurin [demoness]. They tried to catch her but she bit them. At last however they held her down and making holes in her ears, tied her with long strips of *siari* creeper [*Bauhinia vahlii*], and so took her to the Raja. The eldest brother married her, and gave her golden rings in place of the creeper with which they had tied her ears. After a time the girl longed for the jungle and ran away to the hills. The eldest brother followed for love of her. He was the first Asur [demon] Gadaba.

Formerly the Gadabas used to carry loads of food for the Raja and so they were Bhoi Gadabas. In those days there were no Ronas, Malis, Gaurs, Brahmins. But in these days the Raja only takes food from the high castes; he will no more eat from the hands of Gadabas.

Then ten other brothers were named Kond, Bondo, Didayi, Jhoria, Parenga, Konda Dora, Holar, Pengu, Chileri, and Maria. (Elwin 1954, 519f)

This story narrates a transformation of society. The tribal order of the twelve brothers changes into a royal polity. Significantly, the first transformation is divinely motivated. Mahaprabhu – or just Maphru, as he is commonly referred to – is generally seen as the creator god who installed the socio-cosmic order of *niam*. Here, he sends a horse[6] and thus triggers a new royal order. There is another social transformation mentioned at the end of the story in a kind of additional comment: the existence of a new layer of society, the "high-caste" late

---

[6] See Lydia Icke-Schwalbe (1968) for a comparative investigation on the meaning of the horse in myths and cults among different tribal communities of Central India. She points out that, next to being a symbol of kingship and rule, the horse is also associated with fertility, at least among the Gond (1968, 16f); two elements that are also the core of the Vedic horse sacrifice (*ashvamedha*).

comers who take the middle position between the king and the tribes. We are not informed about how, from where or why they came. Moreover, this new change is not divinely motivated and it may be inferred that it is thus less radical and less relevant than the first.

The social transformation in time – twelve brothers > (tribal) subjects/(tribal) king (two layers) > (tribal) subjects/high castes/(tribal) king (three layers) – is related to a spatial contrast between three places. The twelve brothers are born at the Godaveri – the river that cuts through the southern extension of the Eastern Ghats creating a deep valley – and they migrate to the royal capital of Jeypore, a little less than 200 kilometers due north. The third location is not referred to explicitly, as it is the current settlement area of the Gadaba and as such self-evident to the speaker as the plateau between Jeypore and the Godaveri, although much closer to the former.

In a preliminary analysis of the myth and in approaching the tribal ideas of kingship, I want to look at the crucial codes mentioned above: food and marriage, the horse and the issue of mounting it. To begin with, I want to relate them to the tribal order of kinship. The feudal polity is obviously hierarchical, starting with the king, followed by Brahmans, other service castes such as gardeners (Mali) and herders (Goudo), then soldiers (*sepoys*) and another group serving the king as soldiers, the Rona. However, the original tribal order is also not "egalitarian." It is structured by seniority and the dominating kinship idiom is that of relative brotherhood. Even though power is not institutionally centralized among the tribal communities of the plateau, an elder brother has authority, certainly among the Gadaba, as I came to know during my fieldwork, and if told to do something the younger brother will usually obey (see M11, M13).[7]

In the story, this situation is clearly articulated in terms of the codes mentioned. It is the younger brother who carries the millet gruel and the elder who consumes it. The younger brother is told to hold the horse and he does. The tribal pattern of seniority is reversed when the younger brother manages to mount the horse and thus acquires the means of power, the horse representing royal supremacy and political leadership. With this, the elder brother finds himself in the role of carrier of food to be consumed by the "king," his younger brother, no longer the other way around. That the elder brother becomes *porja* (subject) is left implicit in this story.

Mounting the horse is only one of the means by which the younger brother became king, or perhaps rather was qualified to become king (because in this way, he "got there first"), the other is marriage. Obviously, a king was already

---

[7] This does not preclude that on other occasions adult brothers fight physically.

ruling in Jeypore, whose daughter the younger brother marries. Subsequently, the new king uses his staff to find a bride for his own elder brother, which turns out to be a difficult task. He sends his soldiers to find and tame a demoness, a jungle creature coming from the Godaveri, like the twelve brothers themselves. The soldiers domesticate her and back in the capital she is somewhat civilized, as the *siardi* creepers (*Bauhinia vahlii*) are exchanged for golden earrings. However, this civilizing effort does not last long and she returns to the forest with the elder brother following, both of them being the ancestors of the "demon" Gadaba.

The myth thus constructs a sharp contrast between the wild and the civilized, including people, places and practices, marriage being only one way of expressing this opposition. The forest or jungle, forest people (the brothers), hunting, palm juice and millet gruel, *siardi* creeper and, in particular, the biting demoness are all representations of the wild, in contrast to the royal town of Jeypore, golden earrings, an army, a princess and a horse.

The other brothers are the ancestors of the other tribal groups, now subjects, which are then "named," and thus given an explicit identity after their younger brother has been established as the king. The list provided offers a quite accurate representation of the tribal composition of the area: Kond, Bondo, Didayi, Joria (Jhoria), Ollar (Holar), Parenga and Pengo (Pengu), which are all tribes of the region.[8] It is noteworthy that this story makes an explicit contrast between tribal cultivators and the "high caste" late comers: the gardeners, herders, priests and royal soldiers. In other stories (e.g. M12, M3) that narrate the origin of the different communities of the region they are often mixed. Regionally, however, there is in fact a clear distinction that is recognized between the tribal cultivators and the non-cultivating groups that have specific occupations (Berger 2002) which corresponds with the description in this myth. The difference between the tribal brothers and the late comers is articulated with regard to commensality. Earlier, the tribes could share food with the younger brother, even after he became king; thus, he was still considered one of them. With a tone of resentment, it is observed that this situation changed with the coming of the high castes, which alienated the king from his tribal brothers, from whom he no longer accepted food.[9]

This co-creation of king and subjects is discussed in a number of other myths, three of which I want to draw on here for comparison (M11, M13, M15). Each of them makes use of only a selection of the four codes mentioned and

---

[8] The Maria are found somewhat further away in Bastar; what Chileri refers to is unclear.
[9] What the story is not mentioning is that members of all four communities (Rona, Mali, Goudo, Brahman) also do not accept food from any of the tribal communities mentioned.

leaves one or more out: M11 leaves out marriage, M13 the horse, and M15 food and the issue of carrying loads. However, each myth introduces a new dimension as well.

M11, collected in a Didayi village, uses three codes to establish a threefold hierarchy, adding a new social category – that of the Dom or Dombo, who rank below the cultivating tribal communities in the local hierarchy (Berger 2002). The first man and woman – the ubiquitous incestuous sibling pair who are turned into spouses by divine intervention (see M12) – had three sons. In the course of the story, the younger son does not eat beef and manages to ride a horse. Status here seems to be directly linked to power. Immediately after the feast of beef, which the younger brother avoids, the mother asks her sons to mount a horse and only the non-beef-eater manages to accomplish the task. Having assumed the role of power, the younger son then introduces the next criterion of carrying loads. The middle son had consumed beef and could not mount the horse, but he does manage to carry the load as ordered by the younger brother. Failing in every task – having not only eaten beef but actually killed the cow – the eldest brother is scolded by the younger: "You don't know how to ride a horse (. . .) and you cannot even carry a load." Their parents then decide that their younger son will be king, their middle one Didayi Porja and their oldest Dom.

To explain the creation of subjects and king, M13 especially draws on the complementary alimentary and matrimonial codes. This story was recorded in the Joria village of (Lenji) Sukku, some 15 kilometers north of Nandapur, where I documented the Nandi and Ganga festivals (see Chapters 6 & 7) some 60 years later. A striking new feature of this myth is music. The two brothers know how to play instruments well, to such an extent that animals and humans start dancing when they hear them. Obviously this "sweet music" is not merely entertainment but a means of attraction (people/animals are drawn in), enchantment (they forget their everyday affairs and dance) and control (even dangerous creatures can then be approached and dealt with). In my discussions of Dasara, the "gods market" in Bastar (Chapter 5) or the festivals of the Joria, I will return to the sound dimensions of the rituals, which are a sonic form of divine empowerment.

Here, the brothers make use of their music to approach two women in their search for brides. The younger one is pretty, the elder ugly, having long teeth, nose and hair, as well as huge ears. Enchanted by the music, the ugly woman is tamed in the manner we have already encountered in M1, her huge ears are pierced and she is tied with *siardi* creepers. In addition, a certain kind of wood is tied to her back, which is an indication of the way Gadaba used to wear their waist cloth (*kisalo'*), which distinguished the women from all others in the region (see photo 9.1). As soon as the brothers stop playing music the two women refuse to comply and resist them. Only by means of starvation are they made to agree to marriage. The elder, ugly woman, in turn, forces the elder brother to eat her kind of food, namely raw meat. Quite clearly, she is a demoness as in M1 (without being named as such), she is aggressive, wild and ugly. This is made more than explicit by unmasking her as a cannibal. Through another, even more violent act (cutting off her ears and knocking out her teeth), the elder brother domesticates her and takes her to the Duduma Waterfall, where their descendants now live – the Gadaba and Parenga. Meanwhile, the younger brother and his wife commence the "race of kings," among them the "Maharaja of Jeypore."

The third story (M15) comes from a Koya village, further south. Like M11, the myth is concerned with the offspring of the original incestuous couple, here two sons and two daughters, and as in M1 a horse is made by Deur (another name for the sky god, Dorom or Mahaprabhu, etc.) to be mounted. However, the motive for this action is much more explicit in this story: there is no hierarchy among the communities, there is no leader, and general anarchy prevails ("everyone does according to his own mind"). The status of king and subject is not merely an effect of the action of mounting a horse or failing to do so, as the god clearly articulates what is at stake before the attempt is made: "Whichever of you two boys can mount and ride this horse will be Raja, the other will be Poroja." Two more features of M15 are noteworthy. First, the younger sister also mounts the horse and rides "round the world" with the younger brother looking for a place to settle, while the elder brother carries their loads for them. At the selected location ("Mahul-lakta Hill"[10]) they marry – thus repeating the original incest – and become "Raja-Rani."

The second new feature is a comment on the royal administration, a somewhat bleak note at the end of the story. In M1, we encountered the king's soldiers (*sepoys*), who searched, found and overwhelmed the demoness. M15 distinguishes more roles and is much more negative about their effect on the people: "Bhima [the younger brother, now king] made Amins [revenue officials] and guards and police. Very soon the police and Amins began to trouble the people and everyone was afraid of them." In contrast to the soldiers in M1, these troublesome representatives of the state have no function in the generation of the category of subject but are rather described as some sort of unintended negative consequence, a pestilence on the people that was created by the younger brother once he became king. From the perspective of the subjects, it seems it was not a good idea of their younger brother to bring them into

---

10 I am not aware that this name refers to a actual geographical location. *Mahul* is the name of the flower from which the popular liquor is distilled. *Lakta* refers to "matted" hair and thus indicates asceticism. Both may signify a forested place.

existence. This aspect foreshadows the topic of the wicked king, the Dom King, to which I will turn shortly.

The three myths also provide more spatial coordinates, by elaborating the geographical code. While M1 introduced the forested banks of the Godavari, the capital of Jeypore, and a further unspecified area where the Gadaba then lived (and still do today), M11 introduced the Machkund River – also a "jungle" area – at whose banks the Didayi settle, and north/east (and upstream) of which the Gutob Gadaba and Parenga villages are also to be found (i.e. the area left unspecified in M1).

The narrative of M13 unfolds between two famous waterfalls in the area, though only one of them is mentioned explicitly. It starts with the Kotni Mala Hill, where two brothers live. This hill, where marks can be seen in a rock that resemble those of a mortar (*kurni*), lies just south-east of Nandapur, with the Rani Duduma (Queens Fall, also "Queen-Gorge-Mother," *rani-jol-ma*, see M3) adjacent to it. Both hill and waterfall implicate each other and figure prominently in many myths, often being jointly referred to as Kotni Mala, Bet Jola[11] ("Mortar Creepers, Hunting Gorge," see M3, M4; thus the name combines the two main modes of subsistence called *beto-taso*, hunting [*bet*] and cultivation [*tas*]). The story ends about 30 kilometers to the west at an impressive waterfall,[12] simply called Duduma ("Waterfall"), where the Machkund River drops more than 160 meters (Senapati and Sahu 1966, 13) and continues its course at the bottom of a steep valley toward the Didayi and Bondo area.

On the basis of the four myths discussed thus far we can say that, from the local perspective, the institution of the king – and hence the *raja/porja* relationship – is established by divine intervention and with the aim of creating order. While the subjects are granted senior status in local terms, it is the younger brother who accomplishes the task that qualifies him to become king. What further distinguishes the *porja* from the *raja* is their connection to the wild, which is

---

11 *Jola* means ravine, gorge; but also spring, moat or bog (see Gustafsson 1989, 208; Mahapatra 1985, 221). Rousseleau translates "*mal*" with mountain, not with creeper (and Kotni Mal hence as "Mont du mortier," 2008, 192). *Mal* also means (flower) "garland" and may be understood as a reference to rice (see Chapter 8); which obviously also would make sense in connection with the mortar.

12 Not only Adivasis consider this to be a divine place. Also members of the Brekhum mission, visiting the waterfall in 1882, were obviously overwhelmed by it, writing: "Anbetend stehen wir vor der Erhabenheit dieser Natur, der Schöpfung des Allmächtigen, stille" (quoted in Waak et al. 1994, 2–3; approximately in English: "In adoration we stand before the majesty of nature, the creation of the Almighty, silent"). Already 20 years ago it had become a popular picnic spot for middle class Hindus on holiday trips.

articulated in culinary and matrimonial terms especially, but also in spatial terms, contrasting forest and royal capital.

The creation of a royal polity constituted by tribal brotherhood, with the subjects sharing their food with their fraternal king, turns out not to be enduring or, in other words, turns out to have certain undesirable side effects. The polity does not remain a dyadic *raja/porja* order. Instead, other people come in, the "high castes" that rob the tribes of their commensal relationship with the king, and, perhaps worse, policemen, guards and tax collectors also arrive, implying control, exploitation and servitude, as well as causing trouble and fear. Other myths also point to this dimension; for example, a story collected among the Bondo (M17) describes how the king of Jeypore dreamt of the birth of the most important Bondo deity, the above-mentioned Pat Kanda Mahaprabhu. Sending his men to Bondo territory to worship the god had the effect of all Bondo taking flight, as they were afraid that they would not cope with the demands of their visitors. However, the king's men "chased" them and brought them back, and a number of administrative-cum-service duties that catered to the needs of the officials were then established, alongside sacrificer and headmen, such as carrying baggage, fetching water and taking reports to the police. M17 presents this administrative intervention in a matter-of-fact, less agitated way than M15.

Also, another story (M19) starts out by saying that Mahaprabhu sent the *raja*, the government and the sahibs "to rule over mankind" and because people were afraid, they lived peacefully, which probably means to say, they obeyed. The story then takes an ironic twist, as the god decides to create order among animals as well, creating two kinds of monkeys and a dog, and assigning them the positions of Sahib-Raja, Police and Reserve Police, respectively. The chatter of the monkeys, according to the story's ending, would be equivalent to making a report to the police. In any case, whether in a fearful or humorous way, the stories clearly articulate the downsides of being a subject.

With regard to the rationale of becoming a subject, two things are particularly noteworthy in the myths discussed thus far. One is the issue of beef-eating. When I started my fieldwork in the mid-1990s, many of the Gadaba men and women ate beef, and cattle sacrifices were a regular feature in life-cycle and annual rituals. However, there was certainly a discourse that indicated that beef-eating and cattle sacrifices were potentially problematic. Some people did not eat beef and others – Birsa, for instance – only cooked beef outside but not inside the house. State institutions had a clear stance on it. When I was married (the passive form is quite suitable here) in the Gadaba village in 2000 (Berger 2015, 531f), the police warned me not to sacrifice cattle, as would traditionally have been the case (they tolerated cattle sacrifices by the locals which they knew took place). Some children also told me that they had received a beating at school, as a classmate had leaked to the Hindu teacher that beef had been consumed at home (Berger 2014). A footnote from Elwin (with reference to a Bondo myth) indicates that this was not a recent situation.

> All the tribesmen used to keep cattle for agriculture, sacrifice and food. Under Hindu influence many of them have ceased to kill cows openly even for sacrifice, though the practice continues secretly and most tribesmen do not hesitate to eat the flesh of a cow which has been killed accidentally or by a wild animal. The custom is so firmly established in the mythology that it is hard for the people to believe that beef-eating is wicked as their Hindu neighbours say it is. (Elwin 1954, 358, fn.1)

At the time of my research, cattle were not sacrificed secretly but in public ceremonies. Also, I do not think that in the 1990s, or at the time of Elwin's research, locals regarded their beef consumption as wicked or that eating beef (or not) would be "one of their major ethical preoccupations," as Elwin (1954, L) claims. Rather, beef-eating has been, probably for a long time, a distinctive status criterion in the region. All those "high castes" mentioned in M1 (Rona, Mali, Goudo, Brahmins; the latter not found in villages, but only in towns such as Nandapur) abstain from eating beef, and some from pork as well (Berger 2002, 69), and they wear the Hindu sacred thread as a sign of their regional higher status. The myths thus recognize beef-eating as a status indicator, as part of the alimentary code, although among the Adivasis, I doubt it was a matter of ethics. At the same time, the myths do contain a moral dimension, even though their narrators would not subscribe to it. M11 significantly makes a distinction between those who do not eat beef (the future king), those who do (the future tribal subjects) and those who are the lowest because they actually killed the cow.[13] It thus seems that the tribal myths have incorporated external elements of a Hindu discourse and valuations that mark beef-eaters as lowly; hence, their status as subjects.[14]

The other noteworthy issue, related to the previous one, is the role of demons, who are usually female. In M1 and M13 (see also M2), the tribal subjects – in particular, the Gadaba and Parenga – are said to be the descendants of the union of a demoness and an elder brother. This immediately triggers the association with the Vena story discussed in the previous chapter, where the first

---

13 Unlike in the plains, Gadaba do not leave the business of killing a cow to the Dombo, but do it themselves (speaking of the situation twenty years ago).
14 This motif is also to be found among the Kuttia Kond. Niggemeyer (1964a, 222f) recorded a myth in which the younger brother, after having consumed goat, chicken and dove meat is able to ride the horse and subsequently becomes king, while the elder brother had eaten meat of the pig, buffalo and cow, failed to climb the horse and becomes Kond.

creature resulting from the sacrifice of the wicked king is an ugly being "from whom were descended various foreign tribes" (Doniger 1980, 327) – an ugly creature, subject to his "younger brother," the king. It seems that the tribal myths are an indigenized version of the pan-Indian Vena story (see Rousseleau 2010b). As in the case of beef-eating and cattle sacrifice, they seem to have accepted and appropriated external criteria for the explanation of their own status as subjects. However, in contrast to beef, the tribes of the region do have a moral stance on "demons," perhaps the most vicious of whom are Soni and, particularly, Rau (Rahu). At least as far as the Gadaba are concerned, these creatures stand outside the moral order of *niam*, which is based on relationships of reciprocity. Like the police – as has been pointed out to me repeatedly, echoing the attitude of fear articulated in M15 and M17 discussed above – demons always take by force and never give; they practice what Sahlins (1965, 147f) called "negative reciprocity."

In his analysis of elite and subaltern versions of the myths about Rahu – the demon of eclipse – and their relation to the Dom community, Ranajit Guha (1985) deals with exactly this problem. Why do subaltern communities rationalize their own low status using external Brahmanical norms such as beef-eating (riding a horse being another instance)? For Guha, relationships of dominance and oppression are encoded in myths – or religion more generally – and subaltern mythology deals with this situation in ambivalent ways. On the one hand, they internalize their debasement, for example by accepting Brahmanical status-criteria of beef-eating or elite representations of tribal communities as descendants of demons. On the other hand, subaltern myths also document defiance and subversion. This would also, Guha argues, entail an "alternative morality" (1985, 12) that endorses banditry or the wicked king Vena as forms of resistance. Without discussing his arguments further here, it can be said that the myths of the Koraput region that I deal with in this chapter, may also be seen to show such ambivalence. In the creation of kingship, the low, wild, demon-like status of the subjects is accepted as vital, as we have seen, quite similar to the Vena story. However, there are other tribal myths that elaborate the indigenous view on what constitutes a bad king, a Dom King, a king from the lowest level of Desia society. These myths provide another model of the creation of kingship, one in which sovereignty is framed differently, not in relation to beef-eating or horse-riding, but in terms of wilderness and rebellion. In order to define the tribal view of a bad king, however, it is also necessary to summarize what the myths say about the normal behavior of good kings. What makes a proper king? What are his qualities?

Good and Bad Kings: The Dom Raja Stories

Proper kings do two things, they host sacrifices and create order. Mahaprabhu is himself the creator of divine order, of *niam*. He created affinity out of consanguinity – spouses out of siblings – and from the primordial union sprang the tribes of the region. However, he wants more order among humans and thus initiates kingship. Like the divine order of *niam*, which finds articulation and application especially in the domain of ritual conduct (Gadaba also speak of *niti niam*), the royal order is foremost a ritual order. That is to say, sacrifice and order are two sides of the same coin. This is a very common experience for all Desia during festivals, as the social composition of a village and the seniority of its segments become manifest in sacrificial performances, when body parts of the animal victim, as well as the spatial and temporal set-up, are related to the status of the participants, in contrast to those who may not participate in the performance at all.

A festival often referred to in the myths, which is similarly about order and sacrifice, is the royal Dasara. One dimension of Dasara is the payment of tribute (*beti*), which is given by delegations of tribal communities to the king in Jeypore. A Bondo myth (M20) describes how a boy who brought a goat, rice and two rupees to the king as a tribute was called "Mandhara – giver of *man*, honor." Yet clearly, hosting Dasara is not merely the king's right and a means to receive tribute, but his duty as well, which is linked to the performance of sacrifices, especially human sacrifices. Thus, reminiscent of the Gadaba Birsa Sisa, quoted earlier, who stressed the role of (human) sacrifices in Nandapur and Jeypore, a story from the Ollar Gadaba (M2) states that after the younger brother became king, he started performing Dasara and sacrificing humans. Another myth I recorded (M7), narrates that, at the time of Dasara, a hill deity regularly caught young girls who were dancing and consumed them. The deity was overpowered and brought to the king of Jeypore – to Purnagarh (the "Old Fort") – and handed over to him. The people then started sacrificing buffaloes – surrogate victims for humans – at the time of Dasara.[15] Here, the king prevents irregular, random killing of humans and through his power is able to tame the deity and transform the relation of predation into one of regular worship.

---

[15] The narrators of the story did not mention a name of a deity, just used the generic term *maphru* (god). However, the place on top of the hill pertaining to the village of Ponosput-Bagra (where the Joria are considered as "earth people" and are the sacrificers), where they sacrifice the buffaloes, is (at least nowadays) a Durga shrine. In Purnagad, south-east of Jeypore, about 6 km away from the hill-shrine, the Kalika temple is supposedly the place (both on account of the Joria and the Brahman temple priest) where the dangerous deity had been installed.

Several myths refer to human sacrifice without mentioning Dasara. A Parenga story (Elwin 1954, 269f) narrates how Bhima Raja (Bhima being associated with rain in the region; I will discuss this figure in more detail in relation to the Bali Jatra in Chapter 8) attempted to build a tank[16] but the water always drained away. Ultimately, the youngest daughter of Megh ("cloud") Raja, called Jalkamni, is sacrificed: "Bhima Raja (. . .) made a pit into the tank and cut the girl's throat above it" (Elwin 1954, 270) and her blood turned into water. "Since then Jalkamni has lived in the world and rain has fallen," the story closes.[17] During the most important village festival of the region (Chait Porbo), a Joria story (M16) recounts how a shaman is searching for plantain leaves to sacrifice to Pat Deota, who is equipped with the royal symbols of horse and sword.[18] The earth goddess (here, Thakurani) is willing to provide them if the shaman sacrifices his daughter, adding that should it be done his daughter "will live in the houses of Government and great Rajas." In the end, the shaman sacrifices his daughter and from "her blood sprang up plantain trees." Somewhat further away from the region of my immediate concern, in the Kalahandi district of Odisha, a Kond story also deals with Bhima Raja and his Rani. After constructing fields, he had no seed and so sacrificed his middle son "and sprinkled his blood all over the soil. From the boy's blood every kind of grain sprang up" (Elwin 1954, 164f).

Some of these above-mentioned stories refer to human kings, the others to royal deities. M7 and M20 mention earlier human kings in their specific locations, or capitals: Nandapur, Jeypore and Purnagarh (in Jeypore). The Parenga, Joria (M16) and Kond myths deal with royal gods. In either case, however, whether human king or divine god, the connection to (human) sacrifice is explicit. In two of the stories, the kings/gods actually perform it, while in the other story, the sacrificial victim is said to henceforth live in the houses of kings and rulers. Significantly, it seems to be the earth, in particular, that receives human sacrifices – either the earth goddess demands it directly and the human is sacrificed at her shrine, or the victim's blood is poured into a pit or sprinkled over the earth. Also noteworthy is the generative power of blood, its potential to give new life. Blood

---

[16] There are no tanks in the tribal villages of the region. However, kings are known for building tanks (e.g. Conzelmann 2010).
[17] Jalkamni (Kamni) is the water deity among the Gadaba and Bondo, especially associated with the rivers in which the paddy fields are constructed.
[18] In a Parenga story Pat Deota – equivalent to Pat Khanda Mahaprabhu – is also referred to as "raja of the gods" (Elwin 1954, 590) and the Bondo myth (M17) quoted above establishes a very close relationship between this deity and the king in Jeypore who dreams of the god's birth and sends his men to worship him.

turns into water that will then make the plants grow, it transforms into trees or into seeds, a theme we will revisit when discussing the Go'ter ritual of the Gadaba (Chapter 9). A good king, in summary, constitutes order by sacrificing, especially at Dasara. If he does not perform sacrifices, as Birsa Sisa described, the earth goddess becomes angry, and that means the opposite of fecundity and well-being, illness. Through the offering of blood to the earth – of human blood in particular – the king generates fertility in the form of water, trees and seeds.

A king must care for the land with respect to its fertility, but also in terms of its availability for the subjects. This point is brought home by a myth (M3) I was told by a Dombo in the Gadaba village of Onmail, close to a settlement and site of a hydro-electric project that makes use of water from the Machkund River. The project was planned before Independence (see Stanley 1996; Strümpell 2008) but only completed afterwards. Even though Elwin claims that there are no remarkable storytellers in Koraput, in this notable narration, the storyteller starts off in a completely conventional way, combining various traditional motifs (the primordial incest from which the tribes sprang; the hunting sequence at the Queens Fall; the birth of the king in Navel Pit Nandapur), but ends with a surprising critique: the king allowed the modern Indian State to take the land away from the tribal inhabitants, who lost all rights to what was turned into government land. Thus the story ends:

> Now, what did the king do? "Give us one foot of land" they came to ask from the king. One foot [of land] they said but turned the whole place into a government settlement. Made the settlement, one piece of land of the waterfall, they build the Power House, cut the [Duduma] waterfall. (. . .) [King] gave one piece [of land], [but] the government (*sorkar*) took everything now. [It] fell into the hand of the government. Alas (*are!*), the king has no land, the Porja have no peace (*santi*). The government keeps all the fields. Like that, all over the place the king lost [all things], the children of that womb [presumably the offspring of the incestuous sibling pair, the 12 tribes] were true and the senior people too, old king lost the country, the era of the king is gone. (M3)

What this story thus laments is the failure of the king to maintain order, in the sense of watching over his land on which his subjects depend. This was not only the end of peace for the tribal cultivators, but the end of kingship as well. Let me now turn from this negligent king to the bad king, the Dom Raja.

The myths I collected, as well as those recorded by Elwin, all assume the existence of a Dom King but do not explain how he came to power. However, in the Koraput District Gazetteer from 1945, R.C.S. Bell (1945, 80; see Rousseleau and Behera 2002/3, 58f) mentions a "tradition in the Agency" that does provide a story of Dom usurpation.

> A tradition in the Agency, current among others besides the Dombs, has it that the Panos of Ghumsur in Ganjam district proved themselves so obnoxious to the people by their criminal habits that the Raja issued an order that any Pano should be killed wherever he should be found. In fear of this edict the men of the tribe scattered and some of them sought refuge in the hills of Jeypore. Soon after their arrival one of their number succeeded by a trick in inducing the Kondhs of the locality to accept him as their king. Observing that the Kondhs were in the habit of worshipping a certain *bija* tree [*Pterocarpus marsupium*] this man concealed himself in the tree and suddenly leapt from it when the Kondhs were performing their devotions, announcing that he had been sent to them to be their king. Simultaneously he summoned some of his fellow-refugees who had concealed themselves nearby and declared that they were his retinue. The Kondhs believed that a king had been given to them by the tree as a reward for their devotions and accepted the ruler thus sent to them. They built forts for him at a number of places, of which the remains of one near Sembliguda are still clearly visible and are known locally as the 'Domb fort'. A period of terror and anarchy followed during which the Raja and his followers came to be called 'Dumbas' or 'devils', which name was later changed to 'Domb'. (M23)

I will not discuss this story here, which probably was not recorded in a tribal village but in Jeypore; rather, I will focus on the Dom Raja stories, as they are common in the region, dealing with the downfall of this king. The figure of the Dom King is mentioned in a number of myths, two of which I collected – one among the Gutob Gadaba in Gudapada, one among the Bening Porja of the village of Sarbati.[19] I will follow the same procedure as above, first quoting this latter story as a reference myth (M5) in full, then complementing it in my analysis with relevant dimensions of its variants. The Bening Porja are a particularly small community, living beside the Queens Fall mentioned above, only a few kilometers from Nandapur. They are said to have had a particular kind of relationship to the king, as will be further discussed in the next chapter.[20]

> Well, there is a village named Sapuram. Gorua Dokra and Moti Dokri of the Bening community, two people, lived in this Sapuram village. These people lived by collecting roots and fruits. Well, Dom King lived then, named Nono Muni, one Dom lived, Moon Sage (Chandra Muni) Dom, in this interior. By doing the work of a messenger/ambassador (*rajdut*) he became king. When he lived, our Bening people took no lease of land, we did not

---

19 Raphaël Rousseleau (2008, 2010b; Rousseleau and Behera 2002/3) also discusses the topic of the Dom Raja. He is mainly interested in the relationship between this myth and the actual history of the Jeypore Kingdom and argues that the myth mirrors the history of the Silavamshi and Suryavamshi dynasties and the shift from the former to the latter. I am more concerned with the Dom Raja stories in relation to other tribal myths and ritual performances as described and analyzed in Chapter 6. But I will deal with some aspects of the history of the king/ tribes relationships in the next chapter.
20 Rousseleau and Behera (2002/3, 61) refer to them as Benek Porja and argue: "we can maintain that the actual Benek Paraja are directly related to the more ancient royal dynasty historically documented in Nandapur."

do any agriculture then. Not doing agriculture they did collect roots (*pit* tubers, *Dioscorea bulbifera*) and honey and gave them as tax. Later, a jug (*mota*) with stone rice (*gora chaul*) they give as tax. At the time Gorua Dokra [and] Moti Dokri, these people lived and went digging for roots. That way, the Lizard Stone Maggot Spring way (Tendka Pakane Khira Jhola) they went. Carrying a net they went to Kitlum Mali near Pool Crab Mountain (Kundi Kakda Parbat). There Raja was born, Bening Raja, Stone Place (Silputi) Raja. The tiger (*bag*) watched and the deer (*katra*) fed it with milk (*dud*) during the day. ([the narrator explaining] We are Desia people, we don't know milk (*kir*), we say *dud* ["mother's milk"]). These people [Gorua Dokra and Moti Dokri] they went for searching for food. They heard the child cry and as they approached the tiger and deer withdrew. They took the child, carrying it while digging for roots. Then they went to Earth Deity Spring (Jakor[21] Jola), from there to King Spring (Raja Jola) and it became evening. They stayed there and in the morning went back to Sapuram. There they lived, taking care of the boy, feeding him with tubers and fruits; the boy grew up.

At the time to pay tax, the old man thought: "the Dom [king] does not know I have a son, I am childless, I hide him from the king." The youth saw that he was preparing a stalk of bananas, *pit* tubers, honey and other things and asked, "Where are you going, father?" – "I will bring this as tax to the king's house," the old man said. – "I will also come along," the boy said. But the old man answered, "No, my child, if you come, there will be destruction (*nosto*). I have told that I have no child, I am sterile from beginning. If you will go there, the king will kill us." The boy remained silent. But he followed his father secretly through the bushes. When he arrived he explained, "Hiding, hiding I arrived, father." – "Well then," the old man said, "salute the king." And after he said that Bening Dokra [the old man] saluted the king. Then the royal boy (*raja pila*, i.e. son of the old couple) greeted with his feet. "You are greeting with your feet?" the Dom said, and took his weapon (*nalibeti*) to kill him. The Bening boy fled into the forest, came to Hunting Spring (Bet Jola) and told a bamboo bush, "Make me a shield (*chitki pairi*) and a bamboo sword (*komtri kanda*)." The wheel (*chakra*) was created and the *komtri* sword was made, the bamboo sword. With it he went to war and killed the Dom king. After he killed the king all works were finished and he kept the sword. This sword became Potangi Pat Kanda. The sheath still is in Nandapur. That is the story. [The narrator then immediately added] Well, these people when they bring Nandi sing this song, I sing you a piece: "Don't go here, don't go there, the black sword is there (*enke no ja tenke no ja kanda kalu oche*), don't go there, don't go there face/honey [?] is there (*tenke no ja tenke no ja mu bilu oche*).

This myth discusses three actors and their relationship: the old Bening couple, the Dom King and the boy, who also turns out to be a king. Many stories of the region begin with an old childless couple who live by gathering and fishing, thus at a time before agriculture. Obviously, these are forest people and, accordingly, they give forest products as tax to the Dom King. Later, after having begun agricultural practices, they provide him with bad quality rice, full of

---

21 Jakor is the name of a deity associated with the earth in Gadaba (and other Desia) villages (Berger 2015, 120, 404–09). This deity is possibly related to the local representation of the earth goddess called *jakeri* among the Dongria Kond (Hardenberg 2018a, 47, 625; see below).

stones, which may be interpreted as a tentative sign of resistance against the Dom King. The narrative only reveals a few details about the latter, namely that he was an envoy, perhaps of some other king from a different place, before becoming king himself. Moreover, he is twice referred to as a sage. Taken together this might indicate that he was originally an outsider.

The other king of the story, the boy, is clearly a forest creature, as can be seen from his place of birth, his name and his upbringing. The place, Kitnum Mali, probably refers to Kotni Mala, the rocks near Queens Fall, which show signs of being a huge mortar, mentioned in M13. The designation Pool Crab Mountain might also relate to this spot, with its combination of waterfall and hill. In any case, Hunting Spring (Bet Jola) does refer to this place – Kotni Mala, Bet Jola being the standard expression for this particular combination of rocks and waterfall – to which the young man goes (returns) to receive the weapons. While the name Bening Raja refers to his later forest parents and the community of the same name, Silputi Raja translates as "Stone Place King" and might signify his mountainous place of birth (in addition to a possible reference to the Stone Dynasty (Silavamshi) of Nandapur from the thirteenth century, as Rousseleau (2008, 2010b) would argue). Especially evident is the forest nature of the king as he is also nursed by a deer and protected by a tiger before he is adopted by gathering and fishing forest people – the Bening couple.

After the sequence dealing with the king's birth and adoption, the second part is about Dasara and the fight with the Dom King. Because the boy (Bening Raja) has been kept secret, he is told to stay home while the old man goes to pay his dues to the Dom Raja. Perhaps the old couple had recognized in their foster child a rival king from the start and feared bloodshed. However, the boy does not obey and follows the old man. Whether intentionally or out of ignorance, it is not clear, but when facing the Dom Raja he does not properly acknowledge the status of the king. An illegitimate king – a Dom King – is greeted in an inverse manner, with the feet: a low status king being saluted with a low status body part. The reaction of the thus insulted Dom King is violent and the response of the Bening King again testifies to his forest nature: he escapes into the forest and is supported once more by forest creatures, not animals this time, but a bamboo tree at the Queens Fall, which provides the Bening Raja with forest weapons. By no means inferior tools, the Bening King slays the Dom King with these weapons, and so becomes the new king, while his sword receives a new name[22] that is reminiscent of the name for a major celestial deity (Pat Kanda). It thus becomes an object of worship, part of which is still said to be in

---

22 Potangi is a town 25 kilometers east of Nandapur, the area of the Ollar Gadaba.

Nandapur.²³ The narrator of the story directly links the sword of this myth to the Nandi festival of the Joria, to which I will return in Chapter 7.

In several important ways, this myth contrasts with the brotherhood stories I discussed above. The first aspect to mention is the autochthonous creation of the Bening Raja, autochthonous in the strict sense, as he is born from the earth (at Kitlum Mali, "Pool Crab Mountain") on his own, without intervention. Other myths also mention that the king or King God was born from the earth. M3 narrates the birth of the king at Kotni Mala, after the queen had left (jumping into the waterfall): "Then the king was born there. Navel Pit King's house is in Nandapur. There you find *nal bumii* (navel pit), Kotni Mala, Bet Jola." M12 starts with the birth: "At Nandapur, King God (Raja Maphru) was born on a hillock, in the forest. He came out there, was born there." Thus he "came out" of the earth, notably in the forest, near hills and water. This autochthonous origin of the king contrasts with the creation of kingship as the result of a divine quest for order and as a consequence of the accomplishment of some divinely inspired task, such as riding a horse. The Bening Raja is simply born a king.

However, although born a king, and this is the second aspect, the Bening Raja does not automatically assume office but has to overthrow and kill the Dom Raja. In contrast to M1, where the younger brother marries the king's daughter to become the new king of Jeypore, Bening Raja has to rebel against and fight the Dom Raja. The third aspect is that this story of the Dom Raja establishes kingship without hierarchy. The codes that distinguish status in the brotherhood myths – of carrying loads, eating beef, riding a horse or marriage – are absent and, accordingly, we find no seniority between brothers or communities, nor do we encounter the topics of debasement, of incompetent carriers, wicked beefeaters or ugly demon brides. The rule of the Bening Raja does not involve inferior, humiliated subjects, at least not in this story. While the brotherhood stories assert a tribal king by denigrating the tribal subjects, the Dom Raja myth is truly subaltern and neither relies on elite status codes nor on hierarchy. Quite the contrary, the motif of humiliation is inverted in the Dom Raja stories, as it is the Dom King who is debased by being greeted with the feet by the jungle boy. Finally, what should be stressed is the positive valuation of the forest and all forest creatures. Whereas in M1 and M13, the forest is connoted with demonesses that are wild, aggressive and ugly, the Dom Raja story depicts the forest as providing, protective and powerful.

---

23 The story does not make it explicit where the capital of the Dom King lies, but it seems to have been Nandapur, as the sheath of the sword is still there.

Five other myths deal with or mention the Dom Raja. Four were collected in tribal villages (M6, M9, M14, M18; two Gadaba and two Parenga), the fifth (M23) comes from Bell (1945), the first part of which I have already mentioned in explaining how the Dom King came to power. However, this myth, albeit only briefly, also mentions the downfall of the Dom King. Four of these myths confirm the basic message of M5, and they also add more details and actually provide some clues about what makes the Dom Raja a bad king. One of them (M14) holds some surprises.

M6 has the same structure as M5 discussed above, the birth of the boy king and his adoption by the old couple in the first part, then the fight and victory over the Dom King in the second. In this version, however, both the Dom King and the boy are verbally more explicit. The Dom Raja actually demands tax from the couple ("Will you bring it or not?"), perhaps indicating a threat; while the boy not only greets the Dom Raja with his feet but challenges him verbally, saying: "Which *raja*? Tell! I bid salute with my feet, quickly I will [sit] where you are sitting now. (. . .) How big are you, how big am I?" Not only is the oral threat more explicit in M6, the destruction due to the war is also more disastrous, as the earth is "spun around" (*buligala pruthi*); the "earth is finished" (*pruthi sarigala*); and the "country is finished" (*des sarigala*). In particular, the royal capital seems to have been destroyed ("Earth destroyed, where many [*lake*, 100,000] kings reigned") and the number of subjects decreased ("here at Nandapur the *porja* decreased, but there you have a lot of place") and the palace is shifted from Nandapur to Jeypore. The myth may thus actually provide a rationale for the historical shift of the royal capital, stressing at the end the pivotal and unique role of the new *raja* in hosting Dasara in Jeypore.

In two stories, we are given some hints about the bad behavior of the Dom King and how it contrasts with the proper conduct of a good king as outlined above. Instead of providing grain, especially through the performance of human sacrifice, the Dom Raja steals or withholds it. At a divine feast, as a Parenga story narrates (M9), the earth goddess ate so much that she vomited and seven girls and five boys were born from her vomit: seven kinds of grain (among them rice and finger millet) and five different pulses (e.g. black gram), respectively. After the gods sent the grain and pulses to the Middle World to feed humans, the Dom Raja wanted to take the seven sisters as his wives, so caught and kept them in a "pit" and imprisoned their brothers. Two gods (the by now well-known Dharmo Mahaprabhu and Pat Deota, alias Pat Kanda, actually all variants of the sky god) then conquer the Dom fort as kings, as they "got onto a horse" first, beheading the Dom Raja and freeing the sisters and brothers, thus providing humanity with grain and pulses again. The king gods thus actually sacrificed the Dom King, while the people – so the story ends – still sacrifice to the stone head of the Dom Raja to procure rainfall.

Given the above identification of the grains as daughters of the earth goddess, it is quite clear that this is what another Gadaba story (M18) indicates when speaking of the "young and beautiful daughter" of Mother Earth, without explicitly mentioning that this refers to cereals. Also in this story, the Dom Raja wants to marry her and tries to take her by force. This time it is not deities but other kinds of seeds that rescue her. The young woman throws castor seeds at the king, which turn into bees and drive the Dom Raja and his army away.

The Dom Raja story provided by Bell (M23) also repeats the general narrative of the boy found in the forest, who is nursed by an animal (although it is not a wild animal, but a goat) and raised by foster parents. However, details of how the boy overthrows the Dom Raja are not provided, and the story jumps directly to the moment when the boy establishes a new kingdom in Narayanapatnam, which was later moved to Nandapur. What is special in this version is that it is the only one that mentions the later succession of kings. It recounts how a descendant of the boy had no sons and due to divine intervention decided to give his daughter to "a certain youth who had come to his kingdom," also through divine initiative. The current royal family of Jeypore would be their descendants. This may thus refer to the dynastic change from the Stone to the Sun Dynasty, which I will discuss in the next chapter.

As I argued above, the Dom Raja story (M5) can be contrasted with the various versions of the brotherhood narratives, with the former involving the autochthonous creation of kingship, the acquisition of rule via rebellion, and the absence of hierarchy and the use of elite codes for making status distinctions, as well as a positive valuation of the forest, which is unconnected to debased demon qualities. However, a fourth Dom Raja story (M14) recorded in a Parenga village actually presents a combination of the two types of myths, plus a shot of Ramayana. The first half of the story is about the birth of the future rebel king and how he overthrows the Dom Raja. In the second half, the seniority of brotherhood is, as we know already, turned into the distinction between the king (younger brother) and his subjects, Gadaba and Parenga being the descendants of the elder brother. While this myth thus maintains the topos of rebellion as a means to assume the throne, two aspects stand in contrast to the reference Dom Raja story (M5) discussed above (hierarchy and the origin of kingship), and another is ambivalent (the valuation of the forest).

The rebel king is not earth-born in this myth (M14) but is the offspring of a noteworthy union between a merchant's "lovely daughter" and two deities, Rama and Lakshman, well know from the Ramayana epic. While in some stories the king seemed to be human and in others divine, this myth presents a hybrid king, half human, half divine. After the seduction by the two gods, the daughter (while she is not called Sita in the myth, she also disappears into the earth like the Ramayana heroine[24]) first gives birth to twins, two boys who become separated, and later a girl. The younger son is found and raised by an old foraging childless couple in the forest – here called Beng Raja and Rani – and later becomes the slayer of the Dom Raja and the new king. While the general outline of the Dom Raja story is thus the same, the rebel king clearly is not autochthonous but an outsider (as both his merchant grandfather and his divine fathers come from elsewhere).

The hierarchy established in M14 between the younger and elder brothers is very similar to the other myths around this theme (M1, M11, M13, M15). After the younger brother kills the Dom Raja and becomes king, he finds his elder brother again and makes him his carrier. As in M1, the younger brother then tries to find a bride for the elder and finds their sister, the female child of the merchant's daughter and Rama and Lakshman. She displays many of the attributes of a demoness (aggressive, cannibalistic) and had previously already been tamed by her father gods in the usual manner (*siardi* ropes through the ears and a "stone" around the waist, referring to the *kisalo'* cloth). The elder brother and his new wife – a variant of the original incest – soon return to the forest and become the ancestors of the Gadaba (elder brother) and Parenga (younger brother).

The valuation of the forest is ambivalent in the myth, as it is both protective, as in M5, perhaps even nurturing, but also associated with a demon-like creature, as in M1. The twin brothers are taken into the "jungle" after their birth and the younger one is left under a sacred fig tree (*pipal, Ficus religiosa*), the elder under a sago tree (*Caryota urens*). Here, the aspect of feeding is not made explicit, but obviously, the trees protect (and perhaps feed[25]) the infants in a similar way to the deer and tiger in M5. At the same time, however, in M14, the forest is associated with the demon sister of the twins, who persuades her elder brother and new husband to return to the jungle.

M14 thus represents an intermediate type, between the Dom Raja stories of M5 and M6 and the various brotherhood myths. The throne is assumed by rebellion, but the *raja/porja* distinction is the consequence of establishing a new royal order, including the debasement of the tribal subject, although in an

---

24 After disappearing in the earth she re-surfaces at Kappor Chua, a place that has been mentioned in several myths before. Elwin (1954, 386) explains that this is a "sacred grove and spring" near Mundlipada, the main Bondo village, where Sita is supposed to have bathed. In the myth (M14) she is bathed there by Lakshman.
25 In another Bondo story (Elwin 1954, 185f) deserted twins are nurtured and raised by a sago palm under which they lie ("drinking, drinking they grew up," 1954, 185).

attenuated form: the demoness is not called as such and even though she is dangerous and a cannibal, she is at least not said to be ugly. The valuation of the forest and the origin of the king might be related. Perhaps there is some consistency in the boy king not being presented as autochthonous but as an outsider, and the forest having an ambivalent value. The contrasting features of the brotherhood myths, the Dom Raja stories and the intermediate form are summarized in the table below.

Table 1: Comparison of "Brotherhood" and Dom Raja Stories

	Brotherhood Stories (M 11, 12, 13, 15)	Intermediate Form (M 14)	Dom Raja Stories (M 5, 6)
Origin of king	Divine intervention	From outside	Earth-born
Acquisition of rule	Solve task	Rebellion	Rebellion
Hierarchy (elite codes)	+	+	-
Debasement of tribes	+	+	-
Debasement of king	-	+	+
Valuation of forest	-	- +	+

What the various Dom Raja myths do not explain is why the Dom King is a Dom. Dombo, as they are called in the region (also Harijan, Goren by the Gutob Gadaba), were weavers[26] and they are still petty traders and musicians today among the Desia, but no trace of these activities can be found in the stories. As the position of village herald is always assumed by a Dombo, the description of the Dom Raja as a former envoy might be regarded as an indication of local practice. It is more likely, however, that the Dom Raja stories are part of a discourse that regards Dombo as disreputable. Such representations are to be found locally, as well as in the literature. Due to their role in trade and as intermediaries in market transactions (e.g., the purchase of cattle), Dombo have the local reputation of being rascals, likely to cheat you if you do not watch out. Moreover, they have a low regional status and the tribal cultivators do not, as a rule, dine or intermarry with them.

However, this is only one side of the story, and in my experience many Desia have very close and amicable relationships with Dombo, even ritually being their *tsoru* brothers (Berger 2015). Despite some exceptions (Berger 2015; Hardenberg 2017, 2018a; Pfeffer 1994b, 1997), the colonial and academic literature

---

[26] Dombo were still weaving in the village of Gudapada during my initial fieldwork beginning 1999, already then a rarity. But they discontinued the practice soon afterwards.

echoes the pejorative side of the Dombo representations. As such, they are described as deceiving "Domb tricksters," with a "hereditary aptitude for theft" (Bell 1945, 62, 79), infiltrators into the hills (Fürer-Haimendorf 1943, 151, fn. 1), "degraded missionaries of a lofty faith" (Elwin 1950, 21), as the "criminal population of the district" (Somasundaram 1949, 38), or as having a "rogue" or "devilish" character (Sahu 1942, 95). Vitebsky (2017a) also has few positive things to say about this group – called Pano in the Sora area, as among the Kond – and much like Niggemeyer (1964b), he stresses their corrupt and exploitative activities as disadvantageous to the tribal population. Rather than mirroring the actual role of Dombo in Desia society, I would argue, the Dom Raja myths return to these motives of greed, fraud and corruption that abound locally as well as in the literature. M23 is a case in point as a Dom succeeded in becoming the king of Jeypore because of treachery and the "criminal habits" associated with this community.

I now turn to the Dongria Kond, an indigenous community that will be discussed repeatedly in this book. Their case is especially discussed here as excellent ethnographic descriptions are available and ideas of kingship figure very prominently in their cosmology, myths and rituals.

3.2 Kingship in Dongria Kond Myth and Ritual

The Dongria Kond or "Hill" Kond live in a clearly circumscribed area called the Niamgiri Hills. These steep hills, which rise up to 1500 meters from the surrounding plains of about 400 meters, lie at the margin of the core region with which this book is mainly concerned. Today, they belong to the Rayagada District but they pertain to the greater Koraput area and were previously part of that district (until 1992). At the foot of the hills lies the town of Bissamcuttack, where earlier the Thatraja resided, a vassal king who owed allegiance to the Maharaja of Jeypore about 120 kilometers away across the Koraput Plateau. Such a vassal king had certain responsibilities:

> On behalf of the Jeypore maharaja, the *thatraja*[27] of Bissamcuttack ruled over the Dongria Kondh, the highlanders, as well as the plainsmen of three taluks. Besides the collection of land revenue from the tenants, the special duty of *thatraja* was to secure 500 soldiers, *paikas*, for the protection of the great zamindary in time of war or rebellion. (Nayak 1989, 180)

Thus, the Dongria had their "own king" close at hand. Ethnographically they are well documented. Prasanna Kumar Nayak's work, from which I quoted

---

[27] *That* refers to a battalion of 5000 soldiers, as Nayak explains (1989, 180).

above, especially focuses on Dongria feuding (1989, see also 2021). With regard to the Dongria myths, I rely on the work of Jena et al. (2002). My most important source is the comprehensive ethnography of Roland Hardenberg (2018a), who examined and analyzed their buffalo sacrifice in great detail. As Hardenberg points out, kingship is an idiom of superiority, both socially and cosmologically, and his ethnography shows that it is also a relational idiom.[28] The Dongria proudly refer to themselves – perhaps reminiscent of the Bondo attitude toward the king of Jeypore – as "children of the king" (*raja mila*, 2018a, 74) and, in turn, regard themselves as kings vis-à-vis their Dombo clients, their "subjects" (*praja*), the only other community living in the hills alongside the Dongria. In this context, a Dom Raja as encountered in the Desia myths above would be a clear inversion of the situation as seen by the Dongria.

The notion of superiority or, more specifically, sovereignty is also cosmologically embedded. The superior male "deity" (*penu*) is called Dharmuraja, the sun god and father of the Dongria, who is also (at least sometimes) considered to be the husband of the earth goddess (Dharni). Dharmuraja chose Niamraja – the "king of moral rules" (*niam*) – to rule over the Dongria. Niamraja is the supreme mountain deity of the Dongria and resides in the highest peak of the area, the "mountain of rules"[29] (*niamgiri*), which also designates the entire area inhabited by the Dongria. According to Hardenberg, it is the male deities in particular who bring knowledge and rules to humans, the Dongria, and who are therefore considered kings.

The creation of both the sun god and Niamraja is narrated in origin myths collected by Jena et al. (2002) that I summarize here.[30] As has become apparent in the various myths I have discussed above, many different names and versions of deities' names circulate, in addition to the different ways ethnographers choose to write those names. Thus, Dharmuraja (as spelled by Hardenberg) is equivalent to Dharmaraja, Dharam Devata or Mahapuru (Jena et al. 2002, 136) and to Mahaprabhu, Dorom, Pat Deota, Pat Kanda (among others) mentioned above, all related to the sky god (sun or sun/moon), in contrast to the earth goddess (variously called Bosmati, Thakurani, etc., here Dharni).

---

28 Also Hardenberg (2018a, 74, fn. 8) observed what has been repeatedly noted in the discussion of tribal myth: "When talking about the raja Dongria are never quite specific about whether they mean the gods who are represented as kings or the kings living in the palaces in the plains."
29 The word *giri* is translated as "path" (e.g. Hardenberg 2018a, 326) as well as "hill" (Jena et al. 2002, 12).
30 The narratives collected by Jena et al. are of amazing detail, compared to those collected by Elwin or myself on the Koraput plateau.

The creation of the sun god king: Dharamraja (Jena et al. 2002, 136–43) (M21)

The first creature Jamarani, the "ancestral mother of the Dongria" (133), together with Sita Penu, goddess of wealth, created *raitos* or cultivators inside the earth, in complete darkness; thereafter animals and plants. But the *raitos* demanded more human beings to be created. "She [Jamarani] explained that such a large number of human beings would require a king who would be responsible for the people's welfare and could act as a mediator between the people and *jamarani*, the supreme creator." (136) But finally Jamarani agreed, called all the gods in order to create a king together. A figure was made from clay in the shape of a human body but it was not completed, the limbs were lacking. Jamarani gave life to the figure and put it in a bamboo cradle. A fly pointed out to Jamarani that putting the figure into a cradle would not be sufficient, the fly said to Jamarani: "You have formed a figure and kept it in the open: how do you expect it to become active or later to produce offspring of its own? It would be better to protect the figure by keeping it in an earthen pot. Only by doing so will it become active after some time and can procreate" (137). Jamarani did as suggested and after some days different types of deities emerged from the pot. Jamarani also gave birth to different kinds of people, "scheduled castes" such as Hadi or Ghasi and "pure castes" such as Paika and Brahmans. But as a king had still not being created the people urged Jamarani again: "if you do not give us a king we will not be able to live in this darkness for long, and peace and harmony will not last. Since it was you who created us, it is you who are obliged to save our lives. We cannot move in this darkness, and we need a king who will bring us light" (138).

Jamarani then sought the help of her assistants (Alleni and Jateni) who went to the river deity Gangi Penu for help. Gangi Penu instructed the assistants how to sacrifice for her (the proper sacrificial offering being a pig) and to take sand from the bottom of the river and grind it. When the assistants showed the grinded sand to Gangi Penu it was found to be still too coarse and they threw it away. The sand was swallowed by a swan who laid an egg on the bank of a river. Jamarani asked her assistants to search for the swan that was finally found. The egg was placed in an earthen pot made by potters, three more pots being placed on each side of the pot containing the egg. Jamarani proclaimed that the king who would bring light would emerge from the pot.

Then sun god (Dharam Devata, Dharamraja) was born from the egg. However, no one – neither gods nor humans – had witnessed the event as all were asleep. With one exception. As it turned out, only a Harijan boy had witnessed the sun god's birth. The other deities became angry that is was a Harijan boy who was the only witness and "slashed his body to pieces" (141). Dharmaraja was shocked by this cruel action and granted the Harijan boy a privilege, saying to him: "You will be the one who can watch me performing my ablutions, or bathing, who will be able to see me picking up my sword, raising my umbrella over my head and placing myself on the throne, with my crown on, to rule over the people" (141). After some hesitation, because she first considered the sun god to be still too young to rule, "jamarani put royal robes on the sun god, and gave him a sword, hat and shoes to wear. When he walked out of the darkness, light filled every place he crossed and the people were overjoyed for having been redeemed from the darkness by their king, Dharmaraja" (142).

Then the people emerged from the belly of the earth through a crack, the Adivasi [Dongria] being the first to emerge from it. They divided themselves into clans (*kuda*) established a shrine for the earth deity (*dharani vali*) and each one selected a certain territory for settlement.

In contrast to the stories discussed above, this myth (M21) has a cosmogonic character. Moreover, the king that this myth deals with is clearly a divine, not a human, king. While this story discusses other significant aspects, I want to focus here on the process of the creation of king and subjects and on the relationship between the two.

Two female deities are crucial for the creation of the god king and humans – with the help of other gods (and "assistants"). Jamarani (also called Jaura Penu, Hardenberg 2018a, 613) is the female version of Jomraja, the god of life and death of the Gadaba and other Desia. However, there is another goddess involved, Sita Penu or Sita Penu Lahi Penu as she is also called. She is the goddess of "wealth" and "rice" (both called *lahi*), rice being the highest form of "life" (*jiu, jela*) and, consistent with similar ideas I have described above, this rice-wealth goddess is also considered the daughter of the earth deity (Dharni) (Hardenberg 2018a, 37f, 611f). The existence of the earth is already taken for granted and she is not herself created; rather, crops, animals and cultivators are generated by this divine pair. The need for a king is articulated by Jamarani as well as by humans. The former stresses that the king's role is to be the provider of human welfare and a mediator between humans and gods (hence his role in sacrifices), while the latter focus on the royal function of maintaining peace and harmony and leading the people out of the earth, where they are still contained.

The creation process described proceeds in two steps and entails what might be called multiple intericrity. Creation is achieved through a redundancy of containments, many of which have an earthly aspect. Significant too are the materials of creation. In the first step, an incomplete clay figure is put into an earthen pot as a procreative and activating device, generating different kinds of people, not tribal cultivators (*raitos*) such as the Dongria, who were created earlier, but low (Hadi, probably Dombo, and Ghasi) and high castes (Brahmans and Paik). In the second step of creation, the sun god Dharmaraja is not made from clay but from coarse sand, contained successively by a swan, an egg and an earthen pot. While high and low castes are the result of a failed attempt to create a king with an incomplete effigy (reminiscent of the Vena story), a king finally emerges from a perfectly complete form, an egg. All creatures, it is clear, humans and king gods, are of earthly matter and generated through repeated chthonic containment.

After Dharmaraja has been born from the egg, he still needs to become king, which means he has to be recognized as the king by his subjects and has not yet been instated. However, after his birth there is a complete lack of acknowledgement as all humans are asleep; everyone, except a Harijan boy (thus a Dombo), who was the only witness. He is then killed in a way that resembles the Meria sacrifice or the buffalo sacrifices, which the Dongria still practice today, by hacking the victim to pieces. The Dombo earlier provided, and still provide, the sacrificial victims; here, the boy himself becomes the victim of divine violence. Dharmaraja intervenes, resurrects the boy and turns him into a proper subject, as he is allowed to "watch" the royal performance, handling his various royal insignia. Thus, he makes himself king by creating a subject who acknowledges (watches) his role as king. This is then confirmed by Jamarani, who consecrates him as king, providing Dharmaraja with royal objects.

In the final sequence, Dharmaraja assumes his role as sun king and leads the people out of the darkness of the earth's womb into the sunlight. It is not the high or low castes, but the Adivasi cultivators, the first to be created by the two goddesses, who confirm their precedence by emerging from the earth first. They immediately establish the core elements of their existence, the trio consisting of clanship, territory and sacrifices to the earth goddess. While the unspecified gods had sacrificed the Harijan boy, Dharmuraja made him his subject. As soon as the Adivasi emerge from the earth, they start sacrificing. Subjects are thus distinguished from sacrificial victims, the former sacrificing surrogate victims to the earth, from which they originate.

This myth is different from both types discussed above. Neither a task (such as carrying loads or riding a horse) nor a lowly practice (such as eating beef or marrying a demoness) create the division between king and subject, as in the brotherhood stories. While a hierarchy is created, it is based on a different criterion – precedence (cultivators are created first, emerge first). There is, interestingly, also an element of external moral standards with regard to violence. That Dharmuraja is shocked by the way the Harijan boy is killed hardly mirrors the Dongria point of view, as this is the way they kill sacrificial victims during the buffalo sacrifice. It may thus represent a lowland or colonial perspective. However, while this external sentiment results in the creation of subjects, the moral transgression is not performed by the low status categories (e.g., the Harijan boy) but by the gods.

Similar to the brotherhood stories, three levels of subjects are distinguished: Adivasi cultivators, "high castes" and "low castes," and as is common from the village perspective, in contrast to the regional perspective, it is the Adivasi cultivators who have – as earth people and sacrificers – the highest local status (Berger 2002). The Dongria myth (M21) only has one aspect in common with the Dom Raja stories (there is no rebellion and no mention of a forest), namely, the autochthonous creation of the god-king. Like all other creatures, Dharmaraja is earth-born. However, unlike M5 and M6, the creation is not unmotivated, it does not happen for no reason, but is the result of both divine and human requests. In contrast to the brotherhood stories and similar to the Dom Raja myths (M5, M6), this Dongria story does not employ elite status criteria that lead to the selection of the king or to his legitimation.

While the cosmogonic Jamarani-Dharmaraja story (M21) thus lacks most of the themes and codes of the brotherhood and Dom Raja stories, these are employed in a sequel myth (M22) that narrates how Dharmaraja installs another king, who is closer to the people than the sun. Again, I present a summary of Jena et al. (2002, 159–61).

> Dharam Devata [Dharmaraja] wanted a king to rule the people on earth and called all gods and also humans for a meeting. It was planned to test the powers of the future king. The task for the candidate would be to exactly determine the number of seeds contained in a cucumber and pumpkin.
>
> At the time the wicked king Biribija ruled over another country. Of his seven sons he loved the first six but he and his elder sons despised the youngest. The latter, in turn was critical of his father's unrighteous rule and the wicked actions of his elder brothers. The king prohibited the youngest son to go to the meeting called for by Dharam Devata, while his elder sons went there to meet the test. Being sons of a king they were honorably received in Dharam Devata's court. But while they failed the test the youngest – who had secretly followed and mixed with the common people – new the answer and was made king of the earth by Dharam Devata. "The people were satisfied that they had been given a wise king and dharam devata named him Niyam; with his title (raja) added to this name, he was known among his people as Niyamaraja" (160).
>
> Frustrated by their defeat, the six brothers tried to trick their younger brother into eating beef but Niamraja read their intentions and refused to accept the meat that was offered to him. Dharam Devata acknowledged his faultlessness and instructed him how to rule and to take care of the welfare of his people. Moreover, he should also regularly inform him about the events in his kingdom. Provided will all sorts of seeds – and taking Sita Penu with him – the new king reached his kingdom: "When Niyamraja reached the earth, it was devoid of hills, but a mere wish on his part caused hills and mountains of various shapes and sizes to emerge. He manifested himself in the form of a great hill and his people had already begun to regard him as king of the hills. Thus he became the king of the hill gods and chose the highest peak as his abode, the Niyamgiri or Niyam Hill, from where he could observe his people. Today, an entire range of hills bears his name" (161).

Like the Parenga story about Rama, Lakshman and the merchant's daughter (M14), this second Dongria myth (M22) is a combination and variant of the brotherhood and Dom Raja stories and also adds new dimensions.

A wicked king also figures prominently in this myth, although he is not called Dom King but "Black Gram Seed" (Biribija), the color obviously representing his evilness. He is not a local but comes from "another country." One element the story shares with the Dom Raja myths (M5 and M6) is that the would-be king goes to the "meeting" secretly and that he rebels against the wicked king. Admittedly, "criticizing" a bad king is not the same as killing him, but both are forms of opposition, even if on a different scale, and they demonstrate the righteousness of the new king. The positive valuation of the hill-cum-forest is evident in the fact that this is the very form of the new king, Niamraja, the forested mountain called Niamgiri, "path/mountain of moral rules," towering over the area at 1500 meters. The feature of the autochthonous origin of the new king is ambiguous. While he is clearly a prince of a foreign country, when he "reached the earth" he manifests himself as the highest peak. Thus, while he is not from the place, he becomes the very environment the Dongria inhabit.

Equivalent to the brotherhood stories, a task needs to be performed, but this task is not related to performances of sovereignty and servitude (horse riding/carrying loads) but to cultivator's knowledge (the number of seeds). However, this second Dongria myth (M22) also employs elite status codes (beef-eating) to underline the immorality of the elder brothers and the virtuousness and cleverness of the younger.

A new feature of the second Dongria myth (M22) is the relevance of knowledge linked to *niam* (the wise king named Niam), a feature that is particularly related to male gods, as I mentioned above; this knowledge, moreover, is directly linked to Dongria livelihood. Also, the gift that Niamraja brings from Dharmaraja is related to cultivation, as he provides the Dongria with seeds and wealth in the form of the goddess Sita Penu Lahi Penu. Dharmaraja and Niamraja are thus related in a way that is reminiscent of the relationship between the Jeypore Maharaja and his vassal king in Bissamcuttack. The superior sun god is far away, while Niamraja is very close to the Dongria and is asked to provide "information" to Dharmaraja about what is going on in his domain.

I will now turn to the material and performative representations of this cosmology in the village lay-out and the rituals of the buffalo sacrifice. In this context, the two male deities, the sun god and the god of the mountain, often merge.

Kingship, Village Space and the Buffalo Sacrifice

Implicit reference to the Meria sacrifice is made twice in the Dongria myth (M21) concerned with the creation of the first king, Dharmaraja – the killing of the Harijan/Dombo boy and the establishment of a shrine for Dharni –, while it is not mentioned at all in the story of the selection of Niamraja (M22). In the creation myth, it was Dharmaraja who made possible the populating of the land, the foundation of clan territories and the worship of the earth deity, such that the connections between sacrifices to the earth goddess, the rule of the sun god (and his vassal king Niamraja) and clan territory are quite explicit. The sacrifices of today, generally called "buffalo sacrifice" (Kodru Parbu) – and perhaps previous human sacrifices as well – make the connections between land, clan, sacrifice (stressed at the end of M21) and kingship even more explicit. Accordingly, one of Hardenberg's chapters dealing with certain aspects of the buffalo sacrifice is called "Clan land and rulership: The umbrella (*satara bonda*) of the king" (2018a, 510–16). Most conspicuous in this context are sacred objects – ritual knife and umbrella – that circulate through the region of a clan in the rhythm of buffalo sacrifices held in one or another of its villages, thus constituting an agnatic ritual unit and territory called *muta*. "The connection," Hardenberg (2018a, 513) writes, "between these two ritual objects and the clan is so strong that people define a *muta* by saying that it consists of those villages sharing the same 'knife and umbrella' (*suri bonda*)."

When a village decides to perform the buffalo sacrifice, the sacred objects – many of them made from iron and some associated with former human sacrifices – are brought to the hosting village. Among these objects is the knife (*suri*) with which a ritual specialist later pierces the victim – tethered to a pole in front of a hut representing the earth goddess – through a hole from within this hut in a crucial symbolic act of ritual killing (2018a, 517). The other object, on which I want to focus here, is the *satara bonda*, the object with the highest status in the whole ritual associated with the sun god (2018a, 602). It is a small round metal object made from iron or brass that is fixed as the pinnacle of a long bamboo pole. It is an "umbrella" (*satara*) and is also referred to as the umbrella deity (Satara Penu). Other objects considered by the Dongria to relate to kings are attached to this pole, such as iron arrows and peacock feathers. During a buffalo sacrifice, there are two such umbrella poles, a junior one representing the village territory, which accordingly never leaves the locality, and a senior one representing the clan territory (*muta*), which circulates with the knife (together *suri bonda*) in the rhythm of the buffalo sacrifice. This senior one is identified with Niamraja, who is said to reside in the object during the ritual. Dongria hold that these *bonda* were given to them by the kings. Hardenberg stresses, however, that it is not clear whether they refer to human or divine kings, as any great (mountain) god is also considered a king and addressed accordingly as *raja* (2018a, 515, 596).

The core events of the buffalo sacrifice extend over three days, from Friday to Sunday. Friday is considered the day "the umbrella will stand" (2018a, 542f), and the erection of the pole is the main event of that day, during which reference to the king is most explicit. As the place where the *bonda* is erected is of crucial significance, I will briefly point out the main features of the sacred geography of a Dongria village as described by Hardenberg (see 2018a, 32, 427f). As in all Kond settlements, Dongria houses are arranged in two, more or less curved rows creating an oval open space in between which opens toward the east (including south) and west (including north). In the center of a Dongria village, only a few meters away from each other, are two complementary stone constructions, *jakeri* and *koteiwali*. *Jakeri* are the stones locally representing the earth goddess (Dharni) that are, although in the center of the village, relatively oriented toward the west. *Koteiwali*, represented by a menhir and oriented toward the east, is her husband, and the father of the Dongria (2018a, 432). He signifies the male principle and the sun in relation to the earth (2018a, 48, 476), is considered the male founding deity of the village (2018a, 337), represents the mountain gods and Niamraja in particular (2018a, 125, 382) and he is associated with rule but also with war (2018a, 559). We can thus clearly recognize the cosmology of the myths described above – in particular, the opposition of earth and sun god – in this spatial layout, noting that Dharmaraja and Niamraja merge as male gods embodied in the *koteiwali*.

These opposing structures of the earth goddess and her husband are further elaborated during the buffalo sacrifice (2018a, 478). A hut (*dharni kudi*) is constructed, either around or near the *jakeri* stones, and a sacrificial post (*bisimunda*) is erected in front of it (2018a, 468f). Symmetrically, for her husband, a wall (*palawara*) is built behind the menhir representing *koteiwali*, and a sacrificial post (*panikimunda*) is erected in front of the stones (2018a, 455). Moving from west to east, one thus finds the hut of the earth goddess with the *jakeri* stones, the sacrificial post of Dharni, the sacrificial post of *koteiwali*, his menhir and the wall. The two sacrificial posts of these two ensembles hence face each other (2018a, 425).

The ritual actions that focus on the *bonda* as representations of kingship and Niamraja occur on the first of the three main days of the festival and involve trance, procession and sacrifice (2018a, 542f). In one buffalo sacrifice described by Hardenberg, shamans (*bejuni*) surrounded by the other villagers danced in front of the bamboo poles in the fashion of divine kings (*rajanga*) and of Niamraja, the "king of gods" (2018a, 548), in particular. Raising their right fists rhythmically, the shamans moved a few steps in one direction and then turned back again, these actions signifying war and victory (Hardenberg personal communication). Cloths were then tied around the shamans' heads in the form of turbans, a common sign across the region that the ritual medium is ready to receive gods inside his or her body, in this case Niamraja. The youngest of the shamans jumped onto the sacrificial bamboo pole next to the *bonda* and climbed halfway up, about two to three meters. After shaking wildly, she climbed down again, fell unconscious and was taken care of by villagers. After her, the two other shamans climbed the pole in a similar fashion. According to Hardenberg, the shamans bring Niamraja down into the village in this way.

The bamboo pole with the *bonda* was later untied from the wall of *koteiwali* and carried through the village. Being received like a guest in every house, white cloths were tied to the pole and sacrificial offerings were made, with blood smeared onto the pole. After this tour around the village, the *bonda* was returned to the *koteiwali*, attached to the wall again and the main sacrifice of that day took place. A white ram was sacrificed in the Dongria way, that is, hacked to pieces amidst the shouts and whistles of the men, and its head then tied to the *bonda*. The divine king of the Dongria was worshipped in this manner on the first main day of the Kodru Parbu. The main buffalo sacrifice that gives the festival its name takes place on the final day, and is dedicated to his wife, the earth goddess. On the evening of this first day, the attention already shifts from the male god to the goddess and the iron tools associated with her, especially the ceremonial axe (*tangi*) (2018a, 551f). As these subsequent rituals do not have explicit links to kings and kingship, I will not discuss them further here.

Society is thus constituted in the context of sacrifice. To be more precise, the "unity of the clan is (. . .) defined in relation to the sacrifice of the earth goddess" (Hardenberg 2018a, 583). Yet, the purpose of the sacrifice is not only to reassert collective identity but to regenerate well-being in an encompassing sense, which the Dongria formulate in the words *nehi ane*, "it will be good" or "it will be right" (2018a, 606). Hardenberg quotes a striking passage from Macpherson that illustrates this notion. Here, the earth goddess herself gives clear instructions on how to perform the sacrifice and what the benefits of the action will be: "let each man place a shred of the flesh [of the human victim] in his fields, in his grain store, and in his yard (. . .).[31] Then see how many children will be born to you, how much game will be yours, what crops, how few will die. All things will become right" (Hardenberg 2013a, 606; Macpherson 1865, 122f).

In this exchange of life for life, kingship plays an important role in the form of ritual objects that are crucial for the sacrificial performance and which link territory, gods and clanship. The objects are either closely associated with deities or directly represent them at certain moments in the festival: especially the ceremonial axe (*tangi*), on the one hand, and the ritual knife and the brass pinnacle or umbrella, together referred to as *suri bonda*, on the other. The axe is associated with the earth goddess and the locality of the village, which it does not leave, while the *suri bonda* represent the sun god and Niamraja in particular, defining the clan (2018a, 224, 513) and circulating within its territory, the *muta*. Said to have been formerly given to them by the king, these objects are

---

[31] The Dongria no longer bury the meat, but place it near the *dharni kudi*, though other Kond groups have been reported to still bury the flesh. Also with regard to the Go'ter of the Gadaba (Chapter 9) other ethnographers have stated that the flesh of a particular buffalo (representing a revived deceased human person) is buried, while I could not confirm this practice during my fieldwork.

woven into the socio-ritual fabric of Dongria society, from the clan as a whole to the individual villages, to the local lineages and individual houses that are the keepers of these valued objects.

There can therefore be no doubt about the crucial significance of royal symbols in the most important festival of the Dongria. The question of whether the *muta*, in the sacrificial sense, corresponds to the unit of the same name in the former royal administration, or whether the organization of Dongria villages into *muta*, perhaps even the associated buffalo (former human) sacrifices themselves, had at some point been established by kings, is very difficult to answer. On the basis of his ethnography, Hardenberg (2018a, 584, 596f) argues that the *muta* of the Dongria is first of all a ritual unit of agnates sacrificing to the earth goddess and is not defined by "any central agency from outside" (2018a, 584). In this sense, the *muta* would clearly be different from the administrative unit and might have preceded the latter. Hardenberg concludes that the two systems – administrative and sacrificial – overlapped but "one was not derived from the other" (2018a, 599).

It is indeed difficult to imagine that the sacrificial system of the Dongria was at some point established by some human king. These practices are most likely not the result of acts of royal will, and the sacrifice functions – and probably did so in the past – perfectly without any royal ingredients. While the rituals thus work well without human kings, it is evident that Dongria cosmology imagines humans to be ruled by king-gods. The buffalo sacrifice clearly is a local practice, but one which human kings of the past possibly found suitable to adapt to and to link up with (a possibility I will again consider in Chapter 9). As paradigmatic sacrificers themselves, kings were conversant with the language of sacrifice and could thus legitimate their claims to supremacy by involving themselves in local rituals. Conversely, the Dongria practice in this way was able to include and refer to a powerful outsider. The buffalo sacrifice and the royal Dasara can hence be understood as complementary sacrificial systems operating on different levels. Whereas the buffalo sacrifice constitutes Dongria society and the different segmentary levels from *muta* down to the individual house, the royal Dasara adds the global framework, integrating the Dongria into the sacrificial polity. These speculations of a historical nature, however, will not concern me here further, but will be the topic of the next chapter, after which I will take a closer look at the Dasara festival. Nevertheless, the Dongria case, which demonstrates a particular pervasion of ideas of kingship with regard to cosmology, myth and ritual, strongly suggests such correspondences.

3.3 Tribal and Pan-Indian Ideas of Kingship: Summary and Comparison

Local ideas of kingship are deeply embedded in indigenous worldviews. Accordingly, these ideas about kingship speak to and are informed by the key values that govern such worldviews, values such as kinship and seniority; the former especially in the form of brotherhood, the default mode of human existence from the highland perspective (Berger 2018), the latter as the indigenous articulation of hierarchy as value (Pfeffer 1997).

The tribal ontology of kings is closely related to the indigenous notion of sovereignty. In general, gods and humans are seen as distinct but not altogether different forms of being. In the Dongria creation myth (M21), for instance, the sun god and humans both emerge from the earth. Gods are obviously more powerful than humans and, consequently, as recipients and performers respectively both are differentially related to sacrifice. Especially in the ritual context of trance and possession – moments of ritual aggregation – divine powers and human bodies merge (see Otten & Skoda 2014; or with regard to the dead, Vitebsky 1993). In the case of the king, the human/divine distinction is also not always so clear, and the idea of kingship relates to human, divine or hybrid beings. The brotherhood stories seem to identify the king as a human ruler, but the earth-born creature of the Dom Raja stories that overthrows the wicked king rather seems to be divine, like the King God (Raja Maphru) that emerges from the "navel place" Nandapur or at Kotni Mala in other myths (M3, M12). The Dongria creation myth (M21) – and many other references to metapersons as kings (e.g., among the Desia, Jomraja, giving and taking the bodies of humans at birth/death) – understands the god to be a king. In the subsequent Dongria myth (M22), the situation is ambiguous. The wicked king Black Gram Seed rules over "another country" and it is not clear if he is human or divine. After his youngest son successfully accomplishes the task set out for him, however, he "reached the earth" as Niamraja – obviously a king-god – and manifests himself as the mountain. The buffalo sacrifice of the Dongria corresponds to these narratives. Niamraja is the divine mountain, but he also takes the shape of knives or metal "umbrellas" (reminiscent, perhaps, of the Pat Kanda (sword) of the Bondo) or the stones of *koteiwali*. We are thus speaking of an animist view of kingship, where select aspects of nature or material objects are regarded as non-human royal metapersons. This leads us to the question concerning what sovereignty means from the indigenous point of view.

Sovereignty, from this perspective, clearly is not about ruling people, conquering or demarcating a territory. It concerns the ability to regulate and govern the flow of life and, hence, to ensure well-being in an encompassing sense, including progeny, fertility and the health of humans, plants and animals.

This, of course, closely aligns with A.M. Hocart, who argued that the germ of sovereignty lies in the control of the flow of life, guaranteeing the good life in an all-inclusive sense (e.g., Hocart 1970, 30–40). The Dongria articulate this idea in their concept of *nehi ane*, "it will be good," "it will be right" (Hardenberg 2018a, 606); the Gadaba in the notion of *bol soman*. *Bol* means "good" and "well." *Soman* has a variety of meanings that capture the encompassing nature of the "goodness" that is at stake: it means equal, balanced, even, alike, but also exact and complete (Gustafsson 1989, 525; Mahapatra 1985, 278). Thus *soman korbar*, "to make even," means to rectify something, to make something good, or complete that which was wrong or broken. Both concepts also entail a normative and moral dimension: "rightness" or the proper way things should be done in order to be "good." Consequently, they also refer to *niam*, the socio-cosmic order or "moral law" (Hardenberg 2018a, 352) that is particularly manifest in ritual. Well-being and order (*niam*) go together.

For the Dongria, *lahi* is a notion that is closely related to well-being and means both "wealth" and "rice" (including little millet), the latter being the daughter (Lahi Penu) of the earth goddess and the highest form of "life" (*jiu, jela*; *jibon* in Desia). The connection to sacrifice as the regulation of the flow of life is obvious. Kings are sovereigns, as they guarantee well-being through the circulation of life in sacrifices. When the Dongria perform the buffalo sacrifice or the Gadaba the Go'ter, they, like kings, also navigate the flow of life, but on another level, not of the "country" (*des*) or "kingdom" (*raj rasi*) but on the level of clan territory (*muta*) or village (*ga, nayu, ungom*). It is a form of subaltern sovereignty. The flow of life that guarantees well-being is a shared responsibility of both the elder and the younger brother.[32] Accordingly, M2 ends after the younger brother becomes king: "The king started with the Dasara festival, the Gadaba Porja started the Go'ter. The king sacrifices humans during Dasara, Gadaba sacrifice the buffaloes. The Joria do the Nandi."

Analyzing the myths, I have focused in particular on the way social categories are created, related and transformed, especially the categories of king and subject. Subjects, moreover, have turned out not to be reducible to a homogenous category: the myths outline three layers of society – low castes, tribal cultivators, high castes – that correspond to the empirical reality I documented among the Desia (Berger 2002). Significantly, while the tribal cultivators acknowledge the senior status of communities such as the Mali, Rona or Paik at a

---

[32] Because sovereignty is about well-being through sacrifice, the keepers of the most important royal objects among the Dongria are the priests (*jani*) not the headmen (*naika*) and their function is ritual, not political.

regional level, locally – that is, in their villages – they claim and are acknowledged to be superior because of their status as "earth people" (*matia*), due to their sacrificial sovereignty. Unlike a dominant caste in the plains, replicating the domain of Kshatriya power on the village level, the tribal cultivators are senior only in terms of sacrifice and their vital relationship to the earth that guarantees the well-being of all village inhabitants, whether tribal cultivators or not. It is for this reason that, in Gadaba villages, the non-cultivators who receive a share of the harvest show "respect" (*manti*) to the earth people in the context of the sacrifice to the local earth goddess (*hundi*) (Berger 2002; 2015, 164f), in the same way as the Bondo boy in M20 was a giver of "honor" (*mandhara*) when he brought the gifts to the king during Dasara. It is not political power but sacrificial sovereignty that is honored here.

It is perhaps this aspect that one of my Gadaba friends, Samo Sisa, of the village of Gudapada, referred to when he stated "we are the kings." The context of this remark was the constant conflicts he had with his father, which occasionally erupted into physical violence. We, the younger generation, are the kings now, and the older generation, now grandfathers, are subject to our rule. At the time, I thought he was referring to the physical strength, virility and dominance of the younger men. However, most likely, Samo was referring to the autonomy of his generation, which pivots around the complex of land and sacrifice. It is the young married men who cultivate the land and are thus responsible for the necessary sacrifices.

On the level of ritual, which often closely corresponds to the myths, one pattern is clearly discernable. It is the sun – or both the sun and moon in the case of the Gadaba and Bondo – that is conceptualized as celestial king-god and locally represented in shrines that make a reference to kingship. While the shrine of the Sun Moon deity (Si Arke) has various names among the Gadaba, the one most commonly used is Pat Kanda, thus referring to the "main sword." However, in none of the Pat Kanda shrines that I saw was an actual sword to be found. Nor did people state that there used to be one. While explicit reference to kingship is here only made with regard to the name, Elwin (1950, 145f) states in relation to the Bondo that the main Pat Kanda shrine in Mundlipada actually contained a sword that was worshipped (see Nayak 2013). Also, among the Dongria, the *koteiwali* is explicitly linked both to kingship (also with regard to sacred metal objects) and the sun god. In all cases, the shrines referring to the celestial king-gods are contrasted with and linked to the shrine of the earth deity, generally considered to be the wife of the celestial king-god, hence also a queen, although this is mostly not stressed (the names Jamarani, "queen of life and death,"[33] and Takurani, "ruling queen," being an exception). The reference to kingship is most explicit with regard to the male sun-moon deities, who have numerous names (Sī Arke, Pat Kanda, Mahaprabhu, Pat Deota, Dharmuraja, etc.), but all share one feature: they are considered to have constituted the divine socio-cosmic order, referred to as *niam*.

Among the myths that deal with kingship, I have identified two types, the "brotherhood" myths and the Dom Raja stories, as well as intermediate forms combining elements of both. In the brotherhood myths, kingship is established out of the tribal agnatic unit by divine intervention motivated by a quest for order. Status and the aptitude to rule are tested, with the result that the younger brother becomes king and the elder brother subject. On the one hand, this may be perceived as a reversal, as now the younger brother commands the elder, the opposite of everyday experience. However, it can also be understood, on the other hand, as an articulation of the local seniority of tribes as earth people and sacrificers, as outlined above, complementing the global sovereignty of the king.

Noteworthy in this process of the creation of a royal polity in the brotherhood stories (and also in the intermediate forms) is the prominence of external criteria of assessment with regard to status and eligibility for sovereignty, as well as the debasement of the elder brother, the subject. Underlying both, I would argue, is the opposition of wild versus civilized, which finds expression in alimentary (beef-eating, eating of raw meat, cannibalism vs. refraining from those practices), matrimonial (marrying an ugly, fierce demoness vs. marrying a princess), political (carrying loads vs. riding a horse) and geographical (forest vs. royal capital) codes that devalue the wild in contrast to the civilized. The wild turns out to be of lower status and powerless, with the tribal subjects (explicitly Gadaba and Parenga) conceived as the descendants of the elder brother and a non-human demoness. This powerlessness is also in evidence with regard to some unintended consequences of the creation of the royal polity and the emergence of certain functionaries of the royal organization. Being alienated through high-caste intervention from their king, who no longer shares their food, or troubled and exploited by tax officials and the police, the tribal subjects cannot do anything about it, with the best option being to flee.

The Dom Raja stories invert the valuation of the wild, of the forest and its creatures, depicting it as protective, providing and powerful. Given this view of the wild, the king is no longer the result of actions defined by the external status criteria of the royal organization – hierarchy or seniority being conspicuously

---

[33] Compare Jena et al. (2002, 363): "Jamarani: The deity who created the entire Dongria world (goddess of life and death)."

absent – or tasks to be accomplished, but is an earth-born forest creature, and the mode of assuming office is rebellion. First, the forest king greets the Dom King with his feet and when the latter then attacks, the former overthrows him with his powerful forest weapons. In one version, the force of the battle is such that the capital is destroyed and shifted to Jeypore, where the king established Dasara, assuming his sacrificial responsibility with regard to the quest for life.

Following Ranajit Guha (1985), the brotherhood stories can be seen as ambivalent with regard to their definition of kingship and subjecthood. They do claim the tribal descent of the king but, while granting them senior status, they debase the subjects by relying on external values, portraying the tribal communities as of low, wild and demonic ancestry. As such, these stories subscribe to an elite representation of kings and tribes, the view of Brahmans and Kshatriyas, corresponding to the message of the King Vena story. The Dom Raja myths, by contrast, are subaltern narratives of sovereignty, not only independent of external moral valuations, but powerful and rebellious. The ambiguity is also visible in the intermediate versions that combine elements of the brotherhood stories with those of the Dom Raja myths.

What both tribal and Hindu views of kingship share is that the king, as divine being or metaperson, is the provider of well-being and order through sacrifice. Both speak the same language of sacrifice centering on the flow of life, especially with regard to the fertility of the earth, which may include sexual connotations and the idea of kings being husbands of the earth. In this sense, tribal and Hindu worldviews overlap and speak to each other, and it is this intersection, most likely, that historically enabled the various ritual relationships between kings and tribes that are the topic of the next chapter. They contrast, however, on a number of accounts, notably with regard to the character of their animist ontologies and the nature of subjecthood.

While both tribal and Hindu ontologies view the cosmos as animated, in the latter view life is ranked according to a chain of being, whereas in the former, there is only one kind of life. Hindu ontology represents what Sahlins (2014, 282), discussing and adapting Descola's (2013) ontological schemes, calls "hierarchical animism," while the tribal ontology might best be described as a combination of "classical" and "segmentary animism" (Sahlins 2014; see Arhem and Sprenger 2016; Hardenberg 2021 Vitebsky 2017b).

Hindu forms of life are ranked according to the theory of the "strands" (*guna*), or similar ideas, which entails that they have different physical, intellectual and moral properties. Ultimately, everything is created from a kind of cosmic protoplasm that is unstructured and universal, but in its concrete existence, being is always ranked. Moreover, this hierarchy of being has a soteriological dimension, where those who are most refined have the greatest chance of release from the circle of rebirths. In contrast, in tribal ontologies, the same kind of life animates plants, animals and humans, perhaps even gods. In the ritual cycle of the Gadaba, human life is transformed into animal life, which in turn is transformed into plants, which feed human beings (Berger 2003, 2018; Hardenberg 2021). All life is of the same nature. The life-force that animates human beings circulates through the generations, but there are no moral qualities attached to it, nor can it be refined in subsequent rebirths, attaining liberation at some stage.

The hierarchy of the Hindu chain of being is manifested in concentric structures: the palace, the temple, the chariot (e.g., during the Car Festival of Jagannath; see Hardenberg 2008, 2011), the kingdom. All of them order beings according to their bio-moral qualities. Humans can share or participate in the radiant energy (*tejas*) of the king according to their proximity or distance from the center. The royal-divine power of the king is disseminated from the midpoint toward the periphery. Modes of participating in the king's *tejas* (or power, *shakti*, or auspiciousness, *subha*) focus on worshipping him when he moves from his center in a procession through his kingdom. This mode of partaking in divine energy is different from the tribal technique, in which possession is central in moments of ritual aggregation. The divine, conceptualized as king, is directly made present in the bodies of humans. Moreover, when this happens, all people profit equally from the divine presence, not in a graded manner according to status. Even though the Gadaba do conceptualize the former capital as "navel-place," where the King God came into existence, images of centricity and center-persons are largely absent. Also, the ritual media, whose bodies the deities temporarily inhabit, or the specialists who perform the sacrifices, are not "sacred," they are not deities themselves. This stands in contrast to *gurus* or ascetics in the Hindu context (Bailey 1981; Berger 2020). The flow of life does not depend on center-places or center-persons, although the king in the capital contributes to it on the global level. The tribal mode of participation in the power of non-human metapersons is instantiation, the making present of the powers themselves, not radiation of the power from the center.[34]

---

[34] This may also be the reason why, among the Muria, the appointed royal official (*majhi*) in a district (*pargana*) had no authority and did not, in the view of the tribals, partake in the royalty of the king. As Simeran Gell writes (1992, 10): "The kingship was absolute; it could not be confounded with its representations, and the attributes that characterized it could not be affixed, in howsoever diluted a form, on to those who were said to 'stand' for the King." This corresponds with the situation in Keonjhar where *sardars* were appointed by the king as representatives of clusters of villages called *pirh*. McDougal (1963, 61) reports that a *sardar* had "virtually no authority" vis-à-vis the other Juang.

3.3 Tribal and Pan-Indian Ideas of Kingship: Summary and Comparison — 107

The valuation of center and periphery in the Hindu perspective has a direct consequence for the nature of subjects. Normal subject-householders may approach the outer space of a temple and thus are included differentially in the worship of the king or god, but they are merely "visitors" (Inden 2006, 207). Even further away from the center are demons or barbarians. It is significant that the Hindu texts regularly equate barbarians with demons, and it is likely, though impossible to prove, that the brotherhood stories here have appropriated a pan-Indian topos, which leads to the mentioned ambiguity with which the *raja-porja* relationships are expressed. On the basis of the evidence presented here, and more will follow in subsequent chapters, it is clear that the indigenous comminities do not consider themselves to be subordinate visitors to the royal-cum-ritual center. The attitudes expressed in the epigraphs to this chapter make this quite clear. Moreover, Dongria myth and rituals exemplify how they see themselves – first and foremost as sacrificers. Clanship, territory (earth) and sacrifice constitute their very humanity. When Dongria and other tribal delegations went to the capital during Dasara, they did not perceive themselves to be visitors, mere witnesses to the royal grandeur. They acknowledged the king as a metasacrificer and regarded themselves as linked to him as co-sacrificers – as subaltern sovereigns.[35]

---

35 Another example that stresses the crucial significance of the tribal identity as sacrificers is provided by Simeran Gell (1992, 9) with regard to the Muria of Bastar. In the region of her fieldwork, the earth-priest (*gaitc*) was at the same time the *majhi* of the area, formally an official appointed by the king. Gell writes that he "did not stress his Majhi-hood, but rather his position as *gaita* (earth-priest) of his village and it was obvious that he regarded this office as conferring much greater prestige than his Majh-ship."

4 Kings and Tribes: History and Models of Their Relationships

4.1 From the Eastern Gangas to the Kings of Nandapur/Jeypore

Throughout much of Indian history the subcontinent was scattered with kingdoms, great, small and very small. "On the eve of independence in 1947," Chris Fuller (1992, 106) writes, "there were 565 kingdoms or 'princely states' in the Indian subcontinent, which were not under direct British rule." Thus, every few kilometers one encountered someone who claimed to be a king of some sort. The larger kingdoms, some of which managed to establish suzerainty over vast areas, or almost pan-Indian rule, were found in the plains and fertile river valleys, while those of the hilly hinterland were usually much smaller. No matter how big or small, however, all of them found themselves in a dynamic network of rising and falling, expanding and contracting kingdoms. In this sense, even the great kings had to share their sovereignty, as they had to acknowledge overlords, grant considerable autonomy to their civil-cum-military functionaries (*nayakas*) in provinces at some distance from their capital, and often maintained precarious relations with their vassal kings on the periphery of their kingdoms. Moreover, unruly vassals strove to become independent and to subjugate other kings in their turn, or they were challenged by other upstart princes or overambitious *nayakas* (see Berkemer 1993, 143f; Berkemer 2001; Berkemer and Frenz 2003; Kulke 1997; Schnepel 2002).

Significantly, this dynamic of rivalry, conquest and defeat involved the religious domain as much as it relied on military power. As the rulers were regarded as god-kings and warfare itself as a kind of sacrifice (Fuller 1992, 125), it is unsurprising that the construction of temples or the patronage of deities were key in establishing, maintaining and legitimizing rule. This dynamic involving "ritual politics" worked in two dimensions, as Hermann Kulke (1979, 3) has pointed out. Horizontally, a king had to keep an eye on other rulers, close and distant; vertically, a sovereign had to be accepted and supported by the population. Where a Hindu king ruled over a non-Hindu tribal population, this vertical dimension took a particular shape. It is with such "jungle kingdoms," as Burkhart Schnepel (2002, 135; 1995, 147) called the little kingdoms of the forested, hilly and inaccessible hinterland inhabited by tribal communities, that I am concerned with here in particular. Schnepel developed his concept of jungle kings with reference to the Jeypore kingdom, and as such his work will be especially relevant here.

Even though it was "off the beaten track," the Jeypore kingdom was part of the dynamic network of near and far kings and belonged to the region called Kalinga, comprising especially the coastal area between the rivers Mahanadi and Godavari. This region was conquered by Ashoka in 261 BCE and the bloodshed of this war is said to have turned him into a supporter of Buddhism. In his 13th rock edict, he addresses the "forest dwellers" (*atavi, atavika*) and warns them to give up their crimes and follow his ideals, which Kulke (1979, 7) takes as a sign that he regarded the tribes at the fringes of his empire as dangerous enemies.[1] The famous Gupta king Samudragupta also crossed this area in the course of his military campaign against the south in the fourth century CE, and he obviously encountered resistance from local chiefdoms, among them a certain "tiger king" in the "great woodland," supposedly referring to the area of Kalahandi-Koraput (Kulke 1979, 9).

When the Gupta dynasty collapsed, a new royal dynasty referred to as "Eastern Gangas" established itself around 500–550 CE, on the doorstep of the area I am concerned with. About 130 kilometers east of Nandapur as the crow flies, down the Eastern Ghats, on the banks of the Vamshadhara River (literally "preserver of the dynasty," Kulke 1979, 12), the Ganga kings ruled in their capital of Kalinganagara, which is probably Mukhalingam in today's Andhra Pradesh. For about half a millennium, this "petty local dynasty" (Majumdar 1996, 28) ruled its small kingdom of central Kalinga, squeezed in between the kingdom of Kongoda of the Shailodbhava dynasty in the north and the Eastern Calukyas to the south, who assumed suzerainty over the Eastern Gangas in the ninth century and the latter lost their sovereignty a century later (Berkemer 2001). It is important to mention the Eastern Gangas here, as the highland of the later Nandapur/Jeypore polity was explicitly part of this kingdom and was referred to as Tri-Kalinga, the "wild region covered with hills and forests" (Majumdar 1996, 19; see Kornel and Gamang 2010).

The Gangas had their own impressive comeback, however. Coming from the heartland of the former Ganga kingdom around Kalinganagara in about 1112 CE, the Ganga king Codaganga defeated the Somavamsi kings, who had come from Daksina Kosala to West Odisha and had extended their kingdom down the Mahanadi to include coastal Orissa in the early tenth century (Kulke 1979, 13). Codaganga thus managed to unite the area of central Orissa, known as Utkal, with Kalinga and established the rule of the "Imperial Gangas," which dominated the vast region between the Ganges and Godavari for several centuries. As Kalinganagara was now at the margins of his new empire, Codaganga

---

[1] For a criticism of this position see Oberdiek (1991, 95).

moved his capital to Cuttack in the Mahanadi delta and also built the Jagannath temple in Puri around 1135, an example of the ritual politics mentioned above, to legitimize his rule in the new area (Kulke 1979, 20, 41–47). His successors called themselves Gajapati, "Lord of the Elephants," a royal title that all subsequent dynasties patronizing the Jagannath temple have adopted down to the present day (Hardenberg 2008; Kulke 1979, 58f).

It was a *nayaka* from Kalinga – a local administrator-potentate who was supposed to rule the southern domain of the kingdom on behalf of the Ganga King in Cuttack – who finally put an end to the Ganga dynasty, which had been declining in power for a while. These *nayakas* were far more powerful than being mere representatives of the central king. Schnepel assumes that they had "quasi-royal status" (Schnepel 2002, 99). It was one such *nayaka* called Kapilendra who usurped the Ganga throne in 1434 and established the new Suryavamshi or Sun Dynasty. This lasted until 1590, when the Kings of Khurda came to power under Moghul suzerainty, until their influence was limited to being Kings of Puri under the British Raj (Hardenberg 2008).

Away from the main centers of power on the coast, yet not unconnected to them, a new kingdom was established in the thirteenth century in the heart of the Eastern Ghats, with Nandapur as its capital. One may wonder why anyone would want to establish a kingdom up there in an inaccessible area affected by malaria and inhabited by people who knew how to defend themselves. However, this place lay on an ancient trade route from the coast across the mountains to central India, which may have been an incentive (Rousseleau 2008, 205, fn. 14; Schnepel 2002, 153, fn. 37). Not much is known about its origin,[2] but the kings referred to themselves as the Stone Dynasty (Silavamshi) and were (as the region called Tri-Kalinga), under the influence of Ganga rule until the power of the latter declined and the Silavamshis declared themselves independent from their Gajapati overlords on the coast (Schnepel 2002, 101).

It is striking that in the middle of the fifteenth century we see a parallel dynastic change, one, already mentioned, among the imperial Gajapatis on the plains, and the other in the Nandapur kingdom in the hills. Only nine years after Kapilendra assumed the Gajapati throne in Cuttack, the Silavamshi dynasty in Nandapur also came to an end, in 1443, and a new Suryavamshi dynasty was established, thus bearing the same title as the new Gajapati rulers at the coast. However, the Suryavamshis of the hills lasted much longer than

---

[2] Senapati and Sahu (1966, 57) claim that it was founded by a branch of the Central Indian Sailavamsi Dynasty who migrated to the Koraput region.

those of the plains, until 1952, when the Orissa Estate Abolition Act brought a formal end to all of the kingdoms in the state (Thusu & Jha 1972, 69).

The origin of the Suryavamshi kings of Nandapur is mysterious. Several different stories and theories exist, some of which are based on royal family chronicles. Nirlamani Senapati and Nabin Kumar Sahu (1966, 58f) present a number of versions in the Koraput District Gazetteer. The first theory assumes that the new Suryavamshi kings in Nandapur were of Rajput descent, while a second claims that the last Silavamshi ruler in Nandapur – Pratapa Ganga Raju – gave his daughter to a prince from Jammu and Kashmir and the new dynasty was thus established. A third version, based on Ganga family chronicles, holds that after being defeated by Kapilendra, the eldest son of the last Ganga king (Bhanu Deo IV) founded a new kingdom in the south (at Gudari, near Gunpur), which subsequently assumed sovereignty over Nandapur. However, how this could have led to a change to the Suryavamshi dynasty is obscure. A fourth theory argues that the Nandapur Suryavamshis are the descendants of a servant of the Gajapati in Cuttack, who bestowed Nandapur on him as a principality and also gave him his daughter to marry. Senapati and Sahu offer a fifth version and maintain that, after assuming power, Kapilendra conferred the Nandapur kingdom on a family member and thus established a Suryavamshi branch there.

After summarizing these different versions of the dynastic change from the Stone to the Sun Dynasty, Senapati and Sahu (1966, 59) mention an episode that refers to the period after the new king, Vinayaka, assumed power in Nandapur. Its source is not specified and the authors do not further comment on it. It tells first how Vinayaka had married the daughter (Lilavati) of the last Silavamshi ruler and assumed office as king. "It is said," the story continues,

> that at the beginning Vinayaka Deo was not recognized as a ruler by a section of people who overthrew his rule and at that critical period he was helped by an influential merchant named Lobinia to recover his possession. The merchant prince offered him a large army of cavalry and infantry and also 10,000 cattle for transport, and with this help Vinayaka Deo reoccupied Nandapur and suppressed the turbulent enemies.

A very similar story is provided by Kumar Bidyadhan Singh Deo (quoting Vadivelu 1915), a member of the royal Jeypore family, in his work, *Nandapur: A Forsaken Kingdom* (1939, 9f). Here, the narrative is linked to the second theory of dynastic change mentioned above, thus providing the connection with a prince from Jammu and Kashmir.[3] While on pilgrimage to Benares, the said prince,

---

3 It is likely that the versions of Senapati and Sahu and Singh Deo are from the same source, namely Vadivelu (1915). Senapati and Sahu refer to this text as basis for the second theory mentioned above and Singh Deo as source for the story that links the Kashmir heritage to the

Vinayaka Deo, received divine instruction to go to Nandapur, being promised "both sovereignty and happiness." Thus he went as instructed and arrived at the Sarveswara temple in Nandapur (which actually existed, as the photographs provided by Singh Deo show), where he sought the support of the deity. This deity, in turn, appeared in a dream of the king of Nandapur advising him to give his only daughter to a Kashmir prince, who would be staying in his temple. Thus, it happened that the king took:

> the Prince to his palace, made him his son-in-law, and entrusted to him the government of his kingdom. Vinayaka Deo continued to rule over his country for some time but troubles soon arose and, unable to overcome them, he repaired to his native country of Jammu. On the way he came by an unexpected God-sent help from a very rich and influential merchant named Lobinia, who placed at his disposal a large army of cavalry and infantry with 10,000 cattle for transport. With this equipment Vinayakasingh Deo returned to Nandapur, put down the turbulent elements there, and placed himself firmly on the throne. In token of his gratitude to the merchant prince whose help was most opportune, Vinayakasingh Deo used for his signature Chatuni (a rope intended by the merchants for tying cattle). (Vadivelu, quoted in Singh Deo 1939, 10)

For Burkhart Schnepel, who discusses the different versions presented here in detail and rejects all of the above-mentioned explanations for various reasons, the link to the merchant is crucial. While he warns us against "overstretching the historicity" of the story above and argues that one "should take seriously the social logic of the family chronicle" (2002, 152), he is nevertheless convinced of the historical basis of this narrative. As Nandapur was located on an ancient trade route, he assumes the former presence "of warrior merchants, who knew how to secure their caravans and local bases along the trade routes in military style" (2002, 153). Moreover, he argues that the Vinayaka legend would confirm the political involvement of the powerful merchants in the Nandapur region. Rather than being merely helped by a merchant after his failed attempt at rule, Schnepel assumes that Vinayaka had not only been assisted by the merchant when he faced a crisis but had previously established this support, which could be relied on in such times. Ultimately, Vinayaka could have been a warrior merchant himself, a powerful outsider well acquainted with local conditions. This would also explain why the new king used a merchant symbol as his royal signature (2002, 154).

What I find particularly striking in the two passages quoted above is the apparent armed resistance against the new king, whom "a section of the population" did "not recognize" and so "overthrew his rule." Other sources quoted by

---

sequence of rebellion and support from the merchant. It is evident that their descriptions are very similar even in details and formulations.

Schnepel specify who these people were. The royal chronicles of the Jeypore family also describe the same situation, in which the king is supported by the merchant Labani: "The king revealed the seditious activities of his tribal subjects [to Labani] and sought the help of the merchant" (Sarma, quoted in Schnepel 2002, 154). In the previous chapter, I described different versions of a story in which a king is rejected, fought against and finally overthrown, namely the stories of the Dom Raja. The jungle-born boy greets him with his feet and thus articulates his "non-recognition," and he fights the king with his forest weapons, overthrows him and appropriates the throne. Obviously, Vinayaka regained power and here the Dom Raja story does not match the Vinayaka narrative, but otherwise the parallels are conspicuous. The Dom or Dombo are petty traders in the region and their notorious reputation stems from this fact, and not from their other occupations as weavers and musicians. Could it be that the Dom Raja is a local representation of the "warrior merchant" that Schnepel identified?

Raphaël Rousseleau (2008, 2010b; Rousseleau and Behera 2002/3) was the first to point out significant correspondences between the story of Vinayaka and the Dom King and also argues that they relate to historical facts. He mainly relies on the Dom Raja story mentioned by Bell (1945, 80; M23), which he says originated about 100 kilometers north of Nandapur (2008, 203), and complements it with variants he himself recorded.[4] Rousseleau distinguishes three sequences in Bell's version that would correspond to historical sequences: 1. The appropriation of power by the Dom King; 2. Rebellion against the Dom King by the young boy from the forest, who subsequently becomes king, and the beginning of the Silavamshi dynasty; 3. Establishment of the Suryavamshi dynasty by a "certain youth who had come to his [the Silavamshi ruler's] kingdom" (Bell 1945, 80), namely Vinayaka. With regard to the third sequence and the establishment of the Suryavamshi dynasty, suffice it to say here that Rousseleau (2008, 207f) supports Schnepel's interpretation of Vinayaka as a "warrior merchant" (either himself a merchant or an ally of one) who married a Silavamshi princess to legitimize his rule. Instead, I want to focus on his arguments with regard to the establishment of the Silavamshi dynasty, the second sequence.

Rousseleau argues that the mythical forest boy refers to the founder of the Silavamshi dynasty and supports this in two ways. First, he sees a correspondence between the name of the dynasty, the "Stone" dynasty and the fact that in the myth the boy is said to have been born from a rock (and the motive of the navel being kept within the hillock). Rousseleau does not specify to which version he is referring, and Bell's version does not mention this aspect, but the

---

4 The stories he collected are unfortunately not provided in his book, only referred to.

myths I collected seem to support his argument. The king is said to have been born at (or from) a rock with marks of a mortar, Kotni Mala (M3), which is mentioned in the same breath as the Queens Fall (Rani Duduma) in many stories. This is probably the place that the Dom Raja story (M5) refers to as "Crab Pool Hill." This version makes the connection between the boy and the Silavamshi dynasty explicit, as the boy is also referred to as Silputi Raja, which translates as Stone Crack King, thus the king coming forth from a crack in a stone. The second piece of evidence that Rousseleau presents refers to an unspecified narrative in which a blood stained sword is washed in a reservoir before flying eastward to the town of Pottangi, the area of the Ollar Gadaba. Myth M5, that I recorded, also states that the bamboo sword of the forest boy became Pottangi Pat Kanda (Great Sword [of] Pottangi). This motive, Rousseleau (2008, 209f) argues, correlates with an inscription of the last Silavamshi king, which also refers to a sword that is washed in the sea.

Another strand of Rousseleau's argument deals with the role and identity of the old foster parents of the forest-boy-cum-king. According to his sources, they are called Benek Raja and Benek Rani, which would be a transfigured form of Vinayaka (2008, 201f). Furthermore, one section of the Joria community call themselves Benek Porja (who I came to know as Bening Porja[5]), today inhabiting a few villages close to Nandapur, in the hills in the vicinity of the Kotni Mala rock and the Queens Fall. They regard themselves as the descendants of the mythical foster parents and therefore maintained a special relationship with the kings of Nandapur and Jeypore. Rousseleau's interlocutors mentioned a few noteworthy details in this respect. He was told that they were granted land by the king and also enjoyed certain ritual privileges, among which, two are particularly important for my present discussion. They were the first to sow paddy in the whole kingdom, and during Dasara they brought rice from the Kotni Mala rock and water from the Queens Fall to the king in Jeypore (and perhaps earlier to Nandapur?). Thus, both the Silavamshi king and the Benek Porja are closely related to this particular location of the Kotni Mala rock and the waterfall. Moreover, the latter are said to not be allowed to go near the "throne of the 32 steps"[6] in Nandapur, because this is the "navel place," where the umbilical cord of the first Silavamshi king would have been buried (Rousseleau 2008, 93, 198f).

---

5 I visited one village called Sarbati, where I recorded M5. My interlocutor rather pronounced the name of his ethnic group Bening, which also appears in the myth (Bening *raja*). It is clear, however, that this is the same group. M14 speaks about Beng *raja* and *rani*.
6 Singh Deo provides a photograph (1939, 8).

As descendants of the foster parents of the first Silavamshi ruler, the Benek Porja did have a tense relationship with the succeeding Suryavamshi kings.[7] Rousseleau reports that members of the royal dynasty of Jeypore would not stand directly opposite any Benek Porja, and that the latter actually waged war against the Suryavamshi kings of Jeypore. Obviously, Rousseleau concludes, the Benek Porja regarded the Silavamshi kings as more legitimate rulers and supported them against the Suryavamshi usurpers (Rousseleau 2008, 210).

I have discussed Rousseleau's data and his arguments in some detail here for two reasons. First, like the ethnohistorical work of Schnepel, his work adds to the historical understanding of the Nandapur/Jeypore kings, even though I am in no position to judge the validity of their historical arguments. As I am dealing in the first place with tribal ideas about kingship as articulated in ritual and myth, I am much more interested in what Schnepel calls the "social logic" of this material, or what I would rather call the ritual and socio-cosmic logic. This is the second reason why the work of Schnepel and Rousseleau is relevant here, as they contribute to the understanding of this domain, which is obviously entangled with and a refraction of "history" as well. Before I conclude the historical overview of kingship and outline the different models of the king/tribe relationship in the next section, I want to stress a few aspects of the data and arguments expressed here that will be relevant to later chapters.

Were the Benek Porja that particular "section of people," the "turbulent elements" and those "seditious (...) tribal subjects" mentioned in the accounts quoted above, who rose against and overthrew Vinayaka's rule when he first tried to establish it? Given the comments of the Benek today claiming that they were opposed to and even waged war against the Jeypore *raja*, it seems clear that, whatever the historical facts, this community identifies with the rebels of the past in connection to the Vinayaka story, the Dom Raja foundation myth of the Silavamshi kings and the sacred geography of Nandapur, Kotni Mala and Rani Duduma in particular. However, their relationship to the Jeypore kings seems to have been ambivalent. On the one hand, they fought the Suryavamshi usurpers; on the other hand, they apparently kept their ritual privileges under the Jeypore kings and received land grants, or could at least keep the land given to them earlier. This may be explained by the fact that the Benek community, in their role as foster parents, also indirectly "contributed" to the Suryavamshi dynasty, as Vinayaka married a Silavamshi princess to lay the foundation of the Suryavamshi dynasty.

---

7 One may wonder, however, why they should then adopt the name of the founder of the Suryavamshi dynasty, Vinayaka/Benek.

It is significant that the Benek Porja are a section of the Joria, because it is this community that actually performs this mytho-history of the Dom Raja during their Ganga festival, as I will discuss in detail in Chapter 6. This festival is the most elaborated rice festival I know of in the area and also includes the ritual initiation of the rice cultivation cycle. This aligns well with the Benek's claim that they were the first to sow paddy in the region. The other element of the Ganga festival is the enactment of a pre-colonial polity, in fact a partial and refracted performance of the Dom Raja myth, including a rebellion. As the analysis of the myths in the previous chapter showed, fighting the Dom King and promoting the growth of grain are two sides of the same coin. Thus, in the Ganga festival, fertility, rice and rebellion also merge, as in the case of the Benek Porja, who fight the king at times but initiate the paddy cycle every year.

Another pertinent question is: Why is the Dom King a Dom and what is his relationship with the warrior merchant who helps Vinayaka establish his rule? I have argued above that the Dom Raja stories reiterate the general regional stereotypes of the Dom as greedy and corrupt. The myths dealing with the Dom Raja represent him as the inverse of a proper king, with the Dom Raja stealing or withholding grain rather than providing fertility by hosting (human) sacrifices. Therefore, I do not think that one can argue that the Dom King is actually identical to the merchant who helps Vinayaka simply because the Dom are also traders; in other words, that the Dom are the local representation of the merchant. Rather, it is the cultural logic that depicts the bad Dom King (negative fertility) as the counter-image of a good king (positive fertility).

Moreover, I would argue that it is precisely the tribal cultural logic that does equate them in myth and ritual. Whether the forest boy fights and overthrows the Dom King or the "tribal subjects" rebel against and initially overthrow the merchant king Vinayaka comes down to the same thing from the tribal perspective. The structure and values are redundant and it is in this sense that the Dom Raja and the merchant king are identical. In both cases, the paradigmatic righteous king is the earth-born king; the tribal forest king in contrast to vicious and corrupt kings from the outside. This is what the Joria enact in the Ganga festival, which combines rice and rebellion; they perform their subaltern sovereignty and promote fertility as local sacrificers by fighting the Dom King, who is a caricature of the proper sacrificer king. Concluding this section, let me now return to the historical development of the Nandapur/Jeypore kingdom before discussing the different kinds of king/tribe relationship in the next.

After the establishment of the new Sun Dynasty in Nandapur in the fifteenth century, the usual dynamics of (ritual) politics continued, that is, kings trying to remain autonomous from higher ranking kings while making or keeping other rulers dependent as vassals. Let me give one concrete example of each, starting with the former, concerning the relationship of the sons of the two founders of the Sun Dynasties on the coast and in the hills. Gajapati Kapilendra was succeeded by Purushottama, who intended to extend his kingdom southwards and fought against the Vijayanagara Empire (which dominated south India from about the middle of the fourteenth until the middle of the seventeenth century). By this time, Vinayaka had been succeeded by his son Viyaya Chandra in Nandapur, who supported the Gajapati king in his southern quest. As the Jeypore version of the Kanchi-Kaveri legend outlines, however, this support soon transformed into a demonstration of autonomy by the jungle king from the hills. While Purushottama was returning from his military expedition in 1479, his army is said to have become lost in the hills of the Nandapur kingdom and Viyaya Chandra took the opportunity to ambush the army of his overlord and steal, not only an elephant from the supposed "Lord of the Elephants" (Gajapati), but also a golden image of Durga, Kanaka Durga, which was installed as the state deity in Nandapur (Schnepel 2002, 159f; Senapati & Sahu 1966, 59).

In addition to dealing with the Gajapati overlord, the kings of Nandapur/Jeypore had to deal with a number of smaller kingdoms that they sought to maintain as vassal kings. Thusu and Jha (1972, 71f) list a number of chiefdoms who were at some point vassals of the king of Jeypore, among them Bobbili and Salur, east of Nandapur at the foot of the hills, and Kotapat, about 40 kilometers north-west of Jeypore, which was ceded to the Jeypore Maharaja by the king of Bastar for military support received in the eighteenth century. An example of the often precarious relationship between the king of Jeypore and his vassal kings is discussed in detail by Schnepel (2002 chapter 4), who considers the relationship between the Jeypore king and the figure of the Thatraja of Bissamcuttack. This place and its king were mentioned in the previous chapter, as it lies at the foot of the Niamgiri Hills, inhabited by the Dongria Kond. Bissamcuttack is quite far from Jeypore, in the north-east corner of the kingdom, some 120 kilometers across the Eastern Ghats as the crow flies, which is perhaps one reason why the vassal king thought he could permit himself some disobedience vis-à-vis his overlord. Another reason might be that the incident Schnepel discusses occurred in the context of the British Raj, when the king of Jeypore had ceded his power to the new colonial rulers. However, it is likely that similar skirmishes had also ensued earlier in history. The arena of the clash and challenge was Dasara, the royal festival that will be discussed in detail in the next chapter. Clearly, this festival was crucial for both vertical and horizontal legitimation. According to Schnepel (2002, 186), the basis of the conflict concerned the kind of services expected by the Jeypore king and the status granted to the Thatraja, either as an independent zamindari or as a dependent fiefdom. Among the regular services expected were the provision of some 700 Paik foot soldiers when needed and the regular appearance and show of deference at Dasara. It was this latter symbolic subjugation that the Thatraja rejected by not showing up during Dasara in 1876, the exact year in which the new successor to the throne of Bissamcuttack should have been appointed by the king in Jeypore.

This kind of politico-ritual dynamic of contestation between superior and inferior kings probably occurred throughout the existence of the Suryavamshi *rajas* in the hills, who also shifted their capital according to the circumstances of the moment. I have spoken of the Nandapur/Jeypore kingdom at times, as these two places have been the most important seats of the kings. However, there have also been other capitals intermittently. At the beginning of the sixteenth century the Muslim Golconda kings established their sultanate, and it was in the year of the death of the Suryavamshi ruler Viswanatha Deo, in 1571, that Nandapur was actually occupied by the Golconda Shah, with Viswanatha's son Balram Deo admitting defeat and paying tribute to the new overlord. Nandapur was consequently included in what was called Chicacole, the most northern of the northern Circas.

It was around this time, under Viswanatha, that the capital was moved away from the Golconda rulers, from Nandapur to Rayagada in the valley of the Nagavali River, about 100 kilometers to the north-east and some 700 meters lower than the plateau of the Eastern Ghats. The capital was shifted back to Nandapur at some point and then moved again during the reign of Vira Vikrama Deo in the middle of the seventeenth century; this time, to Jeypore, less than 40 kilometers to the north-west, 300 meters lower, at the foot of the high plateau. At the time, the Golkonda Sultanate was still in power and expanding, so again this shift might be connected to the threat from that side. Shortly afterwards, however, the Moghuls overthrew the Golconda Sultanate, in 1687, and Nandapur became part of the dominion of the Nizam of Hyderabad, who first ruled on behalf of the Moghuls and later, around 1724, achieved independence. Due to quarrels about succession within the royal family, the capital was again shifted temporarily (between 1711 and 1752) to Naranyanpatnam, again across the Eastern Ghats, some 60 kilometers away at the foot of the hills, before it returned to Jeypore once again.

All the while, Nandapur had remained the ritual center of the kingdom, where the golden Durga was kept as a state deity and where new kings were installed. It was Vikrama Deo I (1758–81) who completely and finally shifted the capital, including the goddess, to Jeypore. At that time, the British East India Company had already entered the hinterland. In 1765, the Moghuls granted the latter the Northern Circas, as the British had defeated the French and, in 1775, British forces actually occupied Jeypore. Despite this, civil and criminal justice remained in the hands of the king until the British took over direct administration in 1863. However, the British colonialists soon found Jeypore – around this time a town of 6,689 inhabitants, according to Francis (1907, 261) – to be an unpleasant place to live, and in the 1870s they moved their headquarters up to Koraput on the 900 meter plateau, hoping for a healthier climate. A few years later, when the Breklum mission established a missionary station there in 1882, the tribal village of "old-Koraput" numbered some 200 people and the "new-Koraput" of the British administration some 700 inhabitants (Waak et al. 1994, 199). Koraput town also remained the regional administrative center when the new state of Orissa was founded in 1936 and the Jeypore zamindari became a thing of the past (Behuria 1965, 53–73; Bell 1945, 22f, 166; Schnepel 1995; Schnepel 2002, 165, 265f; Senapati & Sahu 1966, 60–76; Thusu & Jha 1972, 69f, 140f).

4.2 Modalities of the King/Tribes Relationship

Data on the actual historical relationships between kings and tribes is scarce, open to various interpretations and limited in scope. Royal inscriptions, such as Ashoka's rock edicts or on copper plates, are brief and often vague. Dynastic chronicles are usually not concerned with elaborating on relationships with the indigenous population, and if they were mentioned it was in the context of political claims and efforts of legitimization, an instance being the mention of the "seditious activities of his tribal subjects" in the Jeypore family chronicles quoted above. Singh Deo's (1939) account of Nandapur and the Nandapur kingdom is also silent on the issue of local communities. Archaeological evidence is scarce and descriptions from outsiders based on actual observations are few. From the side of the tribal subjects, we have memories and oral histories, such as those with which I started the previous chapter, and myths that deal with kingship, which might be used as historical indicators with all due care, as do Schnepel and Rousseleau. Also, rituals are important in this regard, especially Dasara, with which the next chapter will be concerned, as they actually involve interactions between the king, the court and the tribal subjects that are, at least to some extent, historically documented. Nevertheless, every statement about the historical relationships between kings and tribes can only be an approximation.

One thing is well documented, however, namely that the British colonial administration fundamentally transformed the relationship between tribes and the state in many places. Motivated by Victorian aesthetics and morals, as well as economic-cum-political aims, British intervention policies took various forms. They forced the Juang women to abandon their leaf dresses, for example, and famously fought against the Meria sacrifices of the Kond. In particular, they regulated access to and use of tribal land and in this way targeted the economic and religious base of tribal society. They also interfered in the succession of *rajas* in many places. Accordingly, tribal rebellions and insurgencies were common among the Kond, Koya, Santal, Gond, Bhuiya and others, and we have to assume quite different relationships between tribes and state in the pre-colonial setting compared to the context of the British Raj (S. Gell 1992; McDougal 1963; Padel 2009; Pfeffer 2014; Sundar 2007; Thusu & Jha, 1972).

On the basis of the material available, different scholars have depicted the historical relationships between kings and tribes in various ways.[8] In the remainder of this chapter, I will outline five different modalities of the representation of the king/tribe relationship. My aim here is not to pigeonhole scholars, which would be difficult in any case, as an author might argue in favor of several of the models discussed below. Moreover, the different modalities are not completely exclusive but often overlap and correspond. It is likely that different aspects of the king/tribe relationship were prominent in different contexts and at different points in history. Also, of course, I do not wish to claim that other models of the *raja/porja* relationship might not be identified. The heuristic purpose is to outline, contrast and compare the different ways kings have related to tribes and vice versa, in order to be able to identify references to such patterns in the festivals that will be discussed and analyzed later. The five relationship models distinguished are: 1. Interdependence & tribal autonomy; 2. Cultural hegemony of kingship; 3. Rajput role model; 4. Power & authority from below and, 5. Models of mutual integration.

Interdependence and Tribal Autonomy

The work of Simeran Gell[9] (1992) and Robert S. Anderson and Walter Huber (1988) on Bastar and that of Charles W. McDougal (1963) on the Hill Juang of

---

8 In the context of a research internship I supervised in 2020, Sagnik Bhattacharya, a student of history, wrote two papers in which he investigates the relationships between the state and indigenous communities in India, with a special focus on Eastern India. In one paper (Bhattacharya 2020a) he focusses on Sanskrit texts and discusses the transformation from the representation of *mlecchas* as complete ontological others (in the *Dharmashastras*) to a strategy of their "utilitarian inclusion" at a later stage (as evident in the *Mahabharata*). The second paper (Bhattacharya 2020b) deals with the Mughal and colonial period and explores the Santal and Kond rebellions as reactions to colonial interventions that fundamentally changed former relationships between indigenous communities and the state.
9 Based on the work of Joshi (1967), Simeran Gell (1992, 4) also mentions integration at the level of the pantheon, namely the Hinduization of the tribal goddess Danteswari, which was turned

Keonjhar can be considered exemplars of the first model. They stress three aspects: (1) independence in practical terms, (2) a relationship of reciprocity between king and tribal subjects, and (3) symbolic integration, a shared ideology.

All of these authors emphasize the first aspect of tribal autonomy in the pre-colonial situation. Anderson and Huber (1988, 33) sketch a "process of monarchical development" in Bastar, in which they distinguish three phases. After the Kakatiyas of Warrangal fled from the Moghuls to establish a "kingdom in the jungle" (Anderson & Huber 1988, 33), the first stage of their rule was characterized by a weak center, which was "structurally congruent with tribal polity" (Anderson & Huber 1988, 33). Thus, the new kings adapted to tribal patterns first, before, in the second phase, establishing themselves in the center in the more pan-Indian classical fashion of Hindu kingship; for instance, by importing Brahmans from Orissa. The third phase, finally, consisted in the implementation of a royal administration between court and village mainly for the purpose of revenue collection. This led to a division into a Hindu center and a tribal periphery with a high degree of independence. Anderson and Huber (1988, 34) write that aside "from the occasional visitations of representatives from the loosely structured royal revenue administration, tribal socioeconomic organization was autonomous." Similarly, Simeran Gell stresses the "freedom that the Muria enjoyed under the traditional kingly regime," and continues: "As it was the kingship was notable for its unimportance so far as any practical consequences in the lives of the tribals were concerned. It (. . .) was regarded as completely irrelevant to everyday life and economy" (1992, 10).

McDougal presents the same picture for Keonjhar, as the "Juang were for the most part ignored and allowed to conduct their affairs without interference" by a pre-colonial state that "exercised little administration of the Juang hills" (1963, 9, 60). The situation seems to have been the same in the Koraput District and the former Jeypore kingdom:

> Strictly speaking the relation between the landholder who was the Maharaja of Jeypore and his tenants may be said to have been non-existent as the ordinary ryot in the district seldom came into contact with even the higher estate officials and never with the Maharaja. Difficulty of communication is no doubt one reason for this. Another reason seems to be the considerable indifference of the estate to the welfare of the ryots (Behuria 1965, 78)

---

into the tutelary deity of the state, with the king being the incarnation of the goddess, and other tribal gods being integrated into a divine hierarchy. This aspect, which is only briefly referred to by Gell and not further elaborated, is the core of what I called models of mutual integration that emphasize the appropriation of tribal religion by kings (thus Hinduization), and, conversely the influence of tribal cultural patterns on the royal order (Tribalization).

Hence, especially in economic and everyday terms, the tribes were independent from the king, while the relationship is also described as reciprocal and interdependent. Annual payment of tribute and occasional supply of labor from the tribal side were reciprocated by the king with a policy of non-interference in internal matters, arbitration of conflicts and the "highly valued benedictions of protection and prosperity of their [the tribal people's] god-kings" (Anderson & Huber 1988, 34). The same situation was found in Keonjhar, where the king recognized the tribal right to land, granted the right to deal with internal matters autonomously and settled disputes in return for tribute, labor and homage. This reciprocity was also expressed ceremoniously at Dasara, when king and tribal representatives exchanged greetings and gifts (McDougal 1963, 7, 61).

It was particularly in the sphere of ritual where the royal and tribal worlds met, overlapped and were partly integrated, and where the relationship between king and tribes was expressed. "On a symbolic and ceremonial level," Anderson and Huber (1988, 34) write, "in terms of a certain sharing of rituals and ideology – most significantly the divinity of the king – monarchy and tribal culture were tightly fused" (1988, 34; see Gell 1992, 4, 10). Dasara, discussed in detail in the next chapter, was a crucial occasion in this regard. It was the moment when disputes could be brought before the king and, especially, it was the time to represent social units and their relationships in sacrificial terms. During this time, representatives of village clusters – called *parganas* in Bastar, *pirh* in Keonjhar and *muta* in the Nandapur/Jeypore kingdom – and their wider delegations went to the capital to pay homage to the king. Similar to the situation of the Dongria Kond and their king in Bissamcuttack (Nayak 1989, 123f, 180f), McDougal (1963, 364–68) describes how the delegations, led by the head (*sardar*) of the village cluster (*pirh*), made their appearance in the capital. Representatives from every village of the cluster joined the delegation, each village taking two goats, along with turmeric, pulses and vegetables, which they handed over to the royal officials. The biggest goat was returned to the Juang as a whole, which they sacrificed in a special ritual for the well-being of the king (a parallel event also being performed by the other major tribal group of he region, the Bhuiya). Significantly, ritual elders from all Juang villages participated, and McDougal stresses that this was the only occasion where such high-level ritual cooperation with the maximum number of participants took place. Although the details of this ceremony are not provided, it seems that the Juang sacrificed and ate the goat on behalf of the Juang community as a whole and in addition to this each *pirh* received the carcass of one buffalo, which was cooked and consumed by the respective group of villages. The sacrificial performances at Dasara not only expressed the relationship between king and subjects but ritually constituted the tribal communities as totalities in distinction to others

(Juang, Bhuiya), as well as internally, in terms of the various village clusters. McDougal thus concludes:

> The rituals of kingship provide occasions when the tribal identity of the Juang in relation to other groups in the regional social structure is given formal expression. They also serve to integrate the Juang into the larger polity: representatives of all different types of groups in the region, racial [sic], linguistic, occupational, and religious, meet together for a common purpose. The Dasara festival is the only occasion when representatives from all Juang villages in Keonjhar participate jointly in the performance of a ritual. (McDougal 1963, 368)

It is thus the ritual domain that constitutes relational tribal identities, vis-à-vis the king and other communities.

While he thereby recognized the importance of the king and Dasara with regard to the articulation of tribal identity, McDougal does not regard the organization of Juang villages into clusters (*pirhs*) as an invention of the royal administration. While the office of the *sardar*, as head of the cluster, was given the role of revenue collection by the king, McDougal considers it to have been a prior traditional Juang institution (1963, 59). Equally, Hardenberg argues that the *muta* – as village clusters are called among the Dongria (see previous chapter) – cannot be reduced to their probably later administrative function but were a crucial dimension of the indigenous socio-ritual organization, here connected to the buffalo sacrifice (2018a, 584; see also Parkin 1992, 95).[10] This view contrasts markedly with the model of the king/tribe relationship that assumes a fundamental and formative impact of royal institutions on tribal organization and culture.

Cultural Hegemony of Hindu Kingship

The cultural hegemony of kingship is asserted in particular by Raphaël Rousseleau and, in an extenuated form, by Prasanna K. Nayak, whose work on the Dongria Kond I have referred to previously. Like McDougal, in a section entitled "Regional polity: zamindar king's authority," Nayak describes the ritual relationships between the Dongria and the king of Bissamcuttack at Dasara but also notes the political interference of the king and his administration in the interior hills. The *mondal*, Dongria who were appointed by the king as heads of a cluster of villages (*muta*), had a prominent role in the royal administration of the Niamgiri Hills. In

---

10 Also the village confederations (*bar*) of the Hill Bhuyia had first of all socio-ritual functions (Roy 1935, 93–98).

contrast to what Simeran Gell (1992, 9f) says about the *majhi* in Bastar, Nayak describes the *mondal* as powerful in certain respects. They had the power of arbitration in conflicts and could impose fines on villagers. However, Nayak (1989, 181) also notes that "the law and order problem inside the hill country was ultimately controlled by the king and particularly by the junior representatives, the *amins* [revenue collectors] and the *paikas* [soldiers]." The exercise of royal control and power was, according to Nayak, not merely a royal fantasy but actually experienced by the otherwise bellicose Dongria: "the authority of the king was so much felt by the Dongria Khonds themselves that at the sight of the *paikas* they used to become docile" (Nayak 1989, 182). These *paik* toured the Niamgiri Hills at times on behalf of the king, either when a "law and order" problem was at stake or in the case of the king calling for a meeting.

Alongside an interest in "law and order," the king of Bissamcuttack had an interest in maintaining ritual relationships with the Dongria as well, which were especially articulated during Dasara. As this is one example I will discuss in the next chapter, I only want to mention in passing here that five different Dongria clans sacrificed buffaloes provided by lowland royal administrators (*talukdars* and *patras*) – or by the Thatraja himself[11] – at five different temples in Bissamcuttack. The priests (*jani*) of the Dongria selected and sacrificed the animals, and the events were supervised by the *mondal* of the respective village cluster, which corresponded with a clan territory. Important for the present discussion is that those involved in the proceedings received gifts (colored saris) as well as land grants and, therefore, Nayak supposes that the royal organization had an impact on local economic differences (property in land): the "relative economic differentiation (. . .) may be partly but surely attributed to the king's discretion and discrepancy in his patronage" (1989, 181).

Nayak concludes the section by arguing that, alongside the authority of the king over the Dongria,

> the control exercised by the king and the king's men over many aspects of their sociocultural, religious and economic life, was remarkable. And on the basis of a further detailed study, it could be safely said that the retention of a number of traditional customs,

---

11 Nayak (1989, 123) mentions that the Thatraja used to sponsor the buffalo sacrifices performed by the Dongria at the Niamraja shrine in Bissamcuttack twice a year; whether this included Dasara is not clear from his description. Schnepel (2002, 289), however, specifies that it was the Thatraja who sponsored the five buffaloes the Dongria sacrificed during Dasara. The earliest description of the occasion we have states that it was the "Jeypore Samasthanam" (Sahu 1942, 179) who sponsored the buffaloes, which I think refers to a royal representative or to the Thatraja himself.

practices, beliefs, ideas and activities of the Dongria Kondh was partly but significantly the contribution of the king of Bissamcuttack and his administration. (Nayak 1989, 182)

In contrast to authors who stress the autonomy of the tribal population vis-à-vis the king, Nayak thus emphasizes the actual authority of the king over the hill areas and his far-reaching control over many aspects of their lives, which was not merely restricted to occasional labor, tax collection and the annual ritual articulation of homage. Moreover, the royal order, he claims, had a certain preserving function with respect to traditional Dongria culture. Significantly, however, Nayak speaks of "retention" and does not regard the Dongria practices and institutions as derived from the royal order. Rousseleau goes a step further in this direction.

For a very long time, Rousseleau argues, at least since the fourteenth century, the tribes of the Koraput plateau around Nandapur, and the Joria in particular, were exposed to a Hindu political and ritual organization, which led the royal Hindu order to have a significant impact on tribal ideas and institutions. Kingship here is regarded as a mediating institution that fundamentally transformed tribal culture and organization to such an extent that the latter is undistinguishable from pan-Indian Brahmanical patterns. In his understanding, Kshatriyaization – a term coined by Kulke (2001) – refers to the process in which local ritual practices are adapted to Brahmanical sacrificial regulations via the royal framework and thereby domesticated (Rousseleau 2008, 273); Kshatriyaization is thus a mode of Hinduization. Rousseleau "insist[s] on" the "hegemonic position" of the royal order in a political and cultural sense (2012, 138). Accordingly, tribal festivals, rituals, deities and ritual specialists must be understood in terms of the "kingdom frame" (2012).

At the very core of the annual festivals in the villages of the region, and across the different tribal communities, lies a sacrificial pattern that involves the distinction of two ritual roles: the sacrificer (*pujari*) and the ritual cook (*randari*) and the production and consumption of sacrificial food called *tsoru* in Desia or *go'yang* in Gutob. While this *tsoru* complex is present among the different communities of the region, it is absolutely vital and highly elaborated among the Gadaba – it epitomizes their society (Berger 2015). According to Rousseleau, all this must be understood in Brahmanical terms: the word *caru*, for instance, is of Sanskrit origin and the Brahmanas also mention the ritual relationship between *pujari* and ritual cook (2012, 146). Ultimately, he argues, the social units referring to sacred and secular status (see Pfeffer 1997) must also be seen in the light of the royal Hindu model.

> Conformément à notre analyse des titres villageois en termes de charges sacrificielles, l'examen des racines du *soru* nous mène encore une fois à une conclusion très proche de celle d'Hocart, selon laquelle le processus dit d'hindouisation recouvre essentiellement l'adoption de prescriptions brahmaniques relatives au rituel sacrificiel. Ces prescriptions comprennent (. . .) une spécialisation de lignages villageois dans des charges rituelles, et participent d'un processus de *distinction* du lignage sacrifiant sur le modèle royal. (Rousseleau 2008, 273)[12]

One of the most important festivals of the region is the Chait Porbo (April festival), often referred to as the "Spring Festival." I have described and analyzed this festival in detail, including how it involves the two most important and complementary village deities, the shrine of the earth deity in the village center (*hundi*) and the shrine of the Sun Moon deity, referred to by various names (Dorom, Gumang, "senior house," Pat Kanda), outside the village proper (Berger 2015, 368–400, 445–74; see Otten 2000/2001).[13] According to Rousseleau, Chait Porbo must be regarded as "a kind of village *Dasara*" (2012, 145), as during one ritual, the village sacrificer (*pujari*) stands on the *hundi* shrine before the sacrifice and is then doused with water from a clay pot by a woman. This, Rousseleau holds, would be like an *abisheka*, the ritual bathing that is part of a royal consecration. The *hundi pujari* would thus "not only [be] the patron of sacrifice and owner of the land, but also, through these roles, a kind of king of the village" (2012, 146).[14]

The deity Pat Kanda, Rousseleau argues, is also derived from the royal pattern. As Pat Kanda literally means the "main sword" there seems to be an obvious connection to the king and to the goddess Durga. From a historical perspective, it might be argued that the kings formerly conferred swords (*kanda*) – as royal insignia – on the heads of the *muta* (village clusters). These *muta* were important administrative links between king and villages and also significant units in the processions of the people from the villages to the capital during Dasara. Pat Kanda then "was imposed progressively from the *mutha* to the village level" (2012, 147f).

---

12 "Conform to our analysis of village titles in terms of the tasks related to sacrifice, the study of the roots of *soru* leads us once again to a conclusion very close to that of Hocart, according to which the process called Hinduization essentially covers the adoption of Brahmanical rules related to the sacrificial rite. These prescriptions include (. . .) a specialization of the village lineages in ritual tasks and participate in a process of *distinction* of the sacrificial lineages from the royal model."(translation PB, with the help of https://www.deepl.com/translator, based on the German translation by Benedikt Pontzen (Rousseleau 2010a)).
13 Both my ethnography and my analysis present a different picture than put forward by Rousseleau but these differences, while considerable and relevant, are not further discussed here.
14 It is unclear to me how this can be explained within the logic of the Hindu model, as the *pujari* is said to be sacrificer, thus assuming the role of the Brahman and king at the same time.

While Rousseleau does not claim that tribal institutions were actually invented or brought into existence by kings and the royal administration, he holds that the royal-cum-Brahmanical model fundamentally transformed tribal institutions, rituals and ideas. In my view, this boils down to denying any tribal cultural autonomy, as everything is understood in pan-Indian Hindu terms. Perhaps this is the reason that Rousseleau speaks of "tribal society" and "Hindu castes hierarchy," as "we used to call" them, as obsolete analytical categories (2012, 134). For him, they turn out to be the same, mediated and integrated by the royal culture machine, the "kingdom frame" as cultural grinder. Accordingly, Rousseleau concludes, becoming a *porja*, subject, "marks the end of real autonomy. We have seen how a royal pattern influenced the festivals of the Joria Poraja society, and, from this example of cultural hegemony, we can suppose that other elements affected and consequently also changed their society" (2012, 150f). How the agency of the subjects could be involved in this process is not so clear. Formulations like "cultural hegemony" or the notion of cults being "imposed" suggest, rather, a top-down transference of Hindu patterns.

Rajput Role Model

The aspects of agency and motivation are very explicit and prominent in the work of Surajit Sinha (1997 [1962]), who argues that many tribes of Central India imitated the Rajput role model of north-western India. As such, he also concedes a significant influence of royal patterns on tribal organization and culture, like Rousseleau, but in his version of the king/tribe relationship, the tribal communities are the driving force in the process, not mere recipients of a hegemonic pan-Indian culture.

Concerned with the process of state formation in Central India, Sinha discovered that many of the presumably egalitarian, lineage-based tribal communities had intensive and long-standing relationships with feudalistic states, some of which were mentioned in the previous section. Based on his long-term fieldwork among the Bhumij, formerly associated with the kingdom of Barabhum in what is today West Bengal, and, in a comparison, including Gond, Raj-Gond, Munda in other parts of Central India, his intention was to discern the process of what he calls "Rajputization of the tribes" (1997, 305). He claims to have found "aristocratic moods" (1997, 304) on all levels of society, from kings to chiefs, from village headman to the plain cultivator, all striving to socially upgrade in the Rajput model, which was their template for action and revision of their lifestyle. This included a certain Rajput chivalry, patronizing deities such as Durga, the employment of Brahmans where possible, and the invention of genealogies, as well as Brahmanical rites of passage, wearing a sacred thread indicating "twice-born" status and preferably intermarrying with families of recognized Rajput or Kshatriya rank. Moreover, this model also entailed that certain practices should be avoided, such as manual labor, drinking, eating chicken, widow remarriage and allowing women their usual autonomy, such as visiting markets or group dancing; in other words, many elements that are commonly recognized as part of processes of Sanskritization, a term made popular by Srinivas (see Ikegame 2013b).

This process had a number of social and cultural consequences – it resulted in a system that had a "feudalistic superstructure with a tribal base" (1997, 334) and led to the development of ranked social classes in previously egalitarian tribal social orders. Moreover, while the Rajput model is ubiquitous, these Central Indian polities were different from the major early lowland Hindu kingdoms, as the "tribal-derived states" (1997, 336) did not develop elaborate administrative and military systems.

While Sinha stresses the motivation from below to strive to imitate the Rajput model, he, significantly, understands Rajputization as a dynamic, bilateral process. Hence, the tribal egalitarian order not only became stratified, with village headmen adopting a presumably Kshatriya lifestyle, but the king also had a strategic interest in taking tribal cults seriously and patronizing them: "in his eagerness for social upgrading the raja could not ignore the tribal gods and rituals and the associated priesthood" (1997, 321). Part of the dynamic was thus a "universalization" of the local tribal culture, which increased and "upgraded" the importance of local cults, leading to patronization by the king, which might include the building of a temple in a tribal sacred grove. In this way, the king assumed an essential role in the tribal religious world.

> There was a widespread belief in Barabhum that the raja ruled on behalf of the god Brindabanchand and goddess Koteswari and as such the raja shared in the divinity. The human congregation in Barabhum was thus bound by a moral order of shared sacred ideas and sentiments with the raja as the pivot. (Sinha 1997, 319)

This is a very similar view to that of Simeran Gell, Anderson and Huber, who stressed the fusion of king and tribal worlds in the religious domain. Moreover, the dialectic between royal Hindu cults and tribal rituals and their mutual influence is similar to and the core of the integration model. Sinha's work thus foreshadows much of the arguments of later scholars, such as Kulke and Schnepel, whose arguments concerning the king/tribe relationship will be discussed in the last section of this chapter.

Although it was perhaps not so rare that *rajas*, especially little kings, actually had a tribal heritage, a special case, also briefly discussed by Sinha, are the

Gond kingdoms of Central India, also referred to as Gondwana. Four different kingdoms[15] of explicitly tribal origin dominated much of Central India for about four centuries (fourteenth to eighteenth century) (Bhukya 2013) and one of the Gond communities still carries the royal reference in its name, the Raj Gonds. Christoph von Fürer-Haimendorf has done long-term research on the Raj Gonds of Adilabad in particular, the most northern district of the newly formed state of Telangana, some 400 kilometers west of Jeypore.

Without referring to Sinha, he also tentatively formulates a Rajput role-model hypothesis (Fürer-Haimendorf and Fürer-Haimendorf 1979, 122–51). While the Gonds of Bastar maintain the usual segmentary tribal organization, the Raj Gond actually combine two systems, a hierarchical one based on aristocratic lineages and clans, with territorial and political implications, as well as an egalitarian one based on segmentary clans and phratries, mainly concerned with kinship and the clan cult. Like Sinha, Fürer-Haimendorf argues that the Gond *rajas* imitated a Rajput/Kshatriya model by building forts and palaces, performing the Dasara festival – where the king gave a feast and received tribute – and adopting royal symbols, such as flags, to be paraded during Dasara, as well as ritual weapons and fly whisks. Aristocratic status can be claimed by all members of the king's patrilineage and this lineage holds juridical power in a certain territory. An important ritual function of the king was the removal of ritual pollution (*tapu*) as a result of transgressions. During Dasara, the king would prepare a certain chalk powder (*vibhuti*) that was crucial for the ritual reintegration of previously excommunicated persons. However, while the king thus had a certain ritual function during Dasara, especially in the context of these purification rituals, it was precisely his involvement in the latter that prevented full participation in the highly significant cult of Persa Pen, the clan god. Because of an association with ritual pollution, no king could ever act as a priest for the clan-god cult. This clearly shows the relative distinctiveness of the two systems described by Fürer-Haimendorf. Despite the aristocratic lineages and kingship, Gond society was still characterized by a strong egalitarian sentiment and a stress on equal brotherhood. Accordingly, when the king participated in clan rituals, he did so as one among many.

As to the genesis of this dual system, Fürer-Haimendorf briefly ventures the hypothesis that originally each clan inhabited a separate territory and that within each clan sacred and secular leadership was divided between different

---

[15] The four kingdoms were Garha in the north, Deoghar and Kherla in the center and Chanda in the south. They covered a region which lies today across eastern Maharashtra, southeastern Madhya Pradesh, Western Chhattisgarh and Telangana.

lineages. Through contact with Rajput and other Hindu princes, the secular heads assumed the *raja* style and claimed aristocratic status (1979, 148f). Thus, in the case of the Gond, the Rajput role-model also mainly characterized the relationship between (Hindu) kings and tribes, with the notable feature that the kings themselves were tribesmen.

Power & Authority from Below

The imitation of royal Hindu patterns grants a kind of follower agency to tribal communities, perhaps involving a process of humiliation of some sort: the experience of a powerful cultural other and subsequently the desire to change one's identity accordingly (Sahlins 2005). It takes quite a different understanding of the king/tribe relationship to attribute a politically more self-assertive and a culturally more self-confident attitude to the tribal communities, in addition to the ability for strategic camouflage. Alfred Gell and Uwe Skoda assume such a position, albeit with different emphases.

With regard to the relationship between the tribal communities of Bastar and their king in Jagdalpur, Alfred Gell (1997) states that the former enjoyed a high degree of independence and lack of exploitation by the state, which was a two-dimensional kingdom. That is, as Sinha also pointed out, the kingdom lacked an elaborate administration, so that basically there was no intervening layer between the king and his subjects. It was exactly the absence of such a revenue-extracting administrative layer that guaranteed tribal freedom and economic autonomy. The crucial point is that, according to Gell, the tribal subjects were very aware of this situation and highly inventive in devising mechanisms to maintain that favorable condition. The strategic repertoire mainly consisted in the skilled exercise of impression management during Dasara and a forceful statement of their view that nothing should stand between them and their king in various tribal rebellions. In fact, Gell argues, Dasara and the rebellions were "parallel mechanisms" (1997, 436), the former being as political as the latter were ritualized.

During Dasara, representations of subalterns and sovereigns were enacted by the tribal communities. Portraying a self-image of wildness and as being "too primitive to be governed," through their worship of the god-king the tribal subjects created the public representation of the *raja* as all powerful, thereby obscuring the actual "power-vacuum" (1997, 436). It was not only that the king in fact had no real power over the tribal population, as the Gond also made Dasara a demonstration of their own power, appearing in the capital in large numbers, armed, united and in a kind of effervescent mood that would make any ruler uncomfortable (see Berger 2016a). This dimension of tribal power was also enacted ritually, as the king was abducted and made one of their own through commensality. Even though Dasara thus conveyed a rather ambiguous message, the *raja*, according to Gell, understood the message – a kind of open secret – all too well. While I will discuss the details of Gell's analysis of Dasara in the next chapter, the function of the festival from the tribal perspective and the king/tribe relationship is thus clear: "exalting the king and obstructing the state" as the felicitous title of the article goes. This royal ritual, Gell (1997, 449) concludes, did not enhance the power of the rulers, but of the ruled.

At the other end of Odisha, seen from Jeypore, the *raja* of the kingdom of Bonai also maintained a special relationship with his tribal subjects, particularly the Bhuiya. Based on local texts on the history of this kingdom and its royal family, as well as on oral history and documents concerning the rituals of coronation, Uwe Skoda argues that the king of Bonai acknowledged the "authority of the soil" that the Bhuiya represented (2012, 118). Insofar as little kings had to participate in the sovereignty of their overlords, which consisted, in equal measure, of military power and privileged access to the state deity, Skoda points out that Bonai conforms to the descriptions of little kingdoms discussed by Cohn, Stein and Dirks.[16] In the case of Bonai, this meant that the kings were part of the Garhjat states affiliated to the superior Gajapati ruler and his Jagannath cult. While the Bonai kings often tried to contest the superiority of the Gajapatis, they desired direct access to the "Lord of the Universe," that is, Jagannath.

Skoda argues that this picture is incomplete as far as Bonai goes, as the king also depended on authority from below. Local narratives show how the newly arrived stranger-king needed the help of local people and local deities to establish his rule in the first place. In the story, a local, and apparently a Bhuiya, helps the king to kill local chiefs and subsequently becomes subordinate zamindar (*samanto*) in the new kingdom. In one version of the text, he is called Matiswar, "lord of the soil" (2012, 113). This special relationship between king and the Bhuiya is expressed during both Dasara and the coronation rituals. In the latter, the king – identified with a local form of Shiva, Baneshwar ("Lord of the Forest"), on whose behalf he rules – has to sit on the lap of the Bhuiya chief and receives a *tika* (a mark on the forehead) from him, with earth taken from the shrine of his own tutelary deity. Also, during Dasara, while the king rejects the *samanto*'s claim to be *diwan* (minister), he grants him certain honors, such as allowing him to enter via the Big Gate and rising from his throne in his presence (although not moving toward him). As a former outsider,

---

16 See a detailed discussion of their work in relation to Odisha in Skoda and Otten (2013).

the king thus acknowledges the autochthonous status of the Bhuiya, their special relationship to the soil and his need to share in their authority. Skoda thus also stresses the importance of the authority and power from below, taking a step beyond Alfred Gell, in that he also outlines the king's need to share in the authority of the soil, and it is exactly this dependence that constitutes the power of the Bhuiya.

However, Skoda does not elaborate much on how this authority of the soil is constituted, nor does he clearly outline what he means by "power" and "authority." For example, he writes that the "Raja also depended upon the regalia and symbols of office and power from below," especially the mark of earth (*tika*) on the king's forehead, and further states that the "relation between the Raja and Samanto – in power as in authority – seemed to be balanced well into the twentieth century" (2012, 119). How power is similar to or different from authority is not specified. Is power meant here in the same way it is used by Gell, as the actual force demonstrated by the Gond during Dasara, and does authority relate more to the domain of ritual? This remains unclear. Equally, where does the authority of the soil come from and how is it characterized? Is it just because the Bhuiya are the first settlers and in this sense "earth people," as their name suggests? Or is there more to the connection with the earth?

One can infer from the conclusion that the "authority" of the soil is above all of a ritual nature, as Skoda states, with regard to the relationship of the little kings to their superiors (referring to the work of Cohn and Stein), that the former "share the authority or ritual sovereignty of the overlords" (Skoda 2012, 126). Accordingly, the authority from below would also be based on ritual and on a relationship to a deity. On the one hand, this connection becomes explicit when the Bhuiya chief takes earth from his shrine to mark the king's forehead during his coronation and, on the other hand, the ritual sovereignty is expressed in the prerogative of the Bhuiya to act as temple priests of the god Baneshwar, the tutelary deity of the king.

In my view, Skoda's important argument concerning the "authority of the soil" is therefore closely aligned to what I argued in the previous chapter. However, I placed more emphasis on the actual ritual actions of the tribal participants, especially on the sacrificial dimension, and also elaborated on what can be called a sacrificial ontology. Subaltern sovereignty finds its expression in sacrifice and is grounded in their earth nature. "Gutob" or "Bhuiya" are not only community labels but refer to an ontology in which they are constituted as "earth creatures," where autochthony is a paramount value and brotherhood closely connected to it. M21 makes this point very clearly, as it describes how the Dongria emerged from the belly of the earth and immediately established themselves as sacrificers to the earth in a certain clan territory. Likewise, as I will show in Chapter 9, the Go'ter of the Gadaba stresses the ontological connections between earth (and cereals) and humans. It is from their earthhood that their sacrificial seniority derives, which concerns their ability to navigate the flow of life and well-being – the tribal view of sovereignty. This local sovereignty of the autochthonous "earth people" – Lords of the Soil in this sense – is acknowledged by "late comers," as I have described previously (Berger 2002), as well as by the king, as I think the Bhuiya example also makes clear.[17]

Models of Mutual Integration

Most authors who have been concerned with the relationship between kings and tribes have proposed some kind of model of integration. While Rousseleau's view of Hindu cultural hegemony can be read as a variant of one-way, "top-down" integration, most scholars recognize a dynamic of mutuality. For example, Anderson and Huber (model one) argued for a cultural synthesis in the symbolic (ritual and myth) domain of kingship and an adaptation of tribal patterns in the process of kingdom formation, while Sinha identified processes of Rajputization as much as a universalization of tribal culture. While the aspect of integration is thus present to some extent in most, if not all, models, the authors discussed in this section deal most explicitly with this aspect of mutual influence, adaptation and appropriation. Nevertheless, the scholars do not present the processes of integration in a uniform way, but have different emphases and view this dynamic from different perspectives.

Indoctrination and Integration

Another pioneer in the study of the relationship between kings and tribes, historian Hermann Kulke, early on criticized ideas of Hinduization as often being too one-sided and instead stressed the mutuality of the process (e.g., 1979, 18). Despite thus acknowledging a two-sided dynamic, Kulke nevertheless – probably

---

[17] Nandini Sundar (2007, 45) is also more explicit than Skoda concerning what the special relationship to the earth consists in. She writes on the relation of the tribal people of Bastar to the earth: "In the cultural logic through which people depict their past, the right to cultivate, and the demarcation of village boundaries rested not on written title deeds but upon 'permission from the Earth', of course as interpreted by the founding lineage and the mediums. Claims to political authority were derived from religious authority, which in turn depended on one's powers of intermediation with the earth."

due to the sources that he used – viewed this process from the perspective and rationale of the king. In his endeavor to establish, maintain and possibly extend his rule, a king required legitimation in two dimensions, as I briefly noted above: horizontally in relation to other *rajas*, vertically in relation to his subjects. With regard to the latter, the kings employed a twofold strategy, indoctrinating the tribal subjects, on the one hand, and integrating them, on the other. As carriers of pan-Indian Hindu culture, Brahmans were crucial with regard to the former, for codifying worship and deities according to textual standards and for culturally "developing" the regions in which they received land donations. In addition to other techniques of integration – such as the assimilation of tribal communities into the lower ranks of a local caste hierarchy or making them part of the royal militia, which was essential for the integration of the tribes, especially in the early phases of the development of a kingdom – the royal patronage of tribal cults was vital. Not only did the kings acknowledge the authority of tribal deities, but in the process of state formation the kings also adopted the tribal gods and, more often, goddesses, as their own tutelary deities, transforming local worship into state cult (Kulke 1978a, 1978b, 1979, 1997). The story of the Bonai *raja* becoming a representative of Baneshwara is one example.

Another case of royal patronage of tribal cults mentioned by Kulke concerns the Eastern Gangas, discussed in the previous section. Inscriptions narrate that the founder of the dynasty climbed the highest mountain of the region, Mahendragiri, and received the royal regalia, and thus the legitimate right to rule, from the residing Sora deity that he worshipped. That this rule was not only established by patronizing tribal cults but also by military means may be inferred from the fact that the inscription then recounts that the king killed the Sora chief before he conquered Kalinga. In any case, the local god remained the family deity of the Ganga kings for many centuries (until the thirteenth century), even after a new state deity had been established in Kalinganagara and the capital was shifted to Cuttack (Kulke 1979, 19f).

Shared Worldview and Tribal Need for a Mediator and Husband of the Earth

These arguments concerning the integration of tribes and tribal cults into Hindu royal polities were further developed by Burkhart Schnepel. He not only provided more examples of royal patronage of tribal goddesses (Schnepel 1995, 2002, 2005) but also added new dimensions and perspectives; especially, the significance of the religious dimension from the perspective of the king and the tribal views of the processes of integration.

One example of royal patronage within the Jeypore Kingdom was the case of Bissamcuttack, the capital of the Thatraja, located at the foot of the Niamgiri Hills and inhabited by the Dongria Kond (Schnepel 2002, 243–54; Nayak 1989, 123f, 180). Above, I discussed the precarious relationship this king had with his overlord in Jeypore. Like the king in Nandapur, the Thatraja is said to have performed human sacrifices in the past. Moreover, he patronized a number of local deities in the capital, among them Markama, the tutelary deity of the town, with the priests being recruited from the Paik community, the militia of the king. The Dongria and their most important deity, Niamraja, the "King of Rules," were also included in the framework of royal patronage. All Dongria worship this deity as part of the buffalo sacrifice in the hills, described in the previous chapter (Hardenberg 2018a), and a certain clan does so in the original cave of the deity. However, a temple for Niamraja was also built in Bissamcuttack by the Thatraja, and earlier the Dongria worshipped in the Niamraja temple twice a year, receiving a buffalo from the king, which they sacrificed and jointly consumed. Thus, we see a pattern very similar to the Juang and their king in Keonjhar discussed above.

Significantly, Schnepel argues that the integration of the tribal cult by the *raja* not only helped the king legitimize his rule but that both sides also profited from this and perceived it in a religious sense. The king established himself as the foremost patron of the sacrifice to the earth and as such as the lord or husband of the earth (*bhupati*). He assumed this role not only due to strategic calculus but out of a genuine belief in the powers of the autochthonous deities. Both the king and the tribal subjects regarded his role as sacrificer as crucial for the flow of life and general well-being (Schnepel 2002, 252f).

Schnepel specifically discusses the indigenous perspective in a relatively recent article (Schnepel 2014). Dealing with different examples of indigenous communities from Odisha, he argues that tribal communities valued kings, kingship and royal authority. Despite their acephalous social organization, he claims that the concept of kingship was not altogether alien to them but that "royal themes in mythology and ritual did genuinely exist among the tribes" (2014, 251). Royal and tribal ideologies therefore offered certain possibilities of contact and overlap. Moreover, confirming the evidence from the Dongria and from Bastar, Schnepel maintains that the tribes wanted a king and were concerned with royal succession, not least because they strove to share in his royal dignity. Complementing Kulke, Schnepel emphasizes that the interest in mutuality was two-sided and even though the motivations were not identical on both sides, there was a considerable ideological overlap that unified kings and subjects. This space of overlap was expressed as well as constituted in ritual.

The case of the Bhuiya of Keonjhar and their former role in the installation of the king is discussed by Schnepel in detail to make this point (2014, 247–53).[18]

The installation ceremony for the king in Keonjhar is clearly an example of the integration of Hindu kingship and indigenous culture. As described by Dalton in 1872 (see Roy 1935, 118–28), Brahmanical rites frame the whole ceremony, which nevertheless also involves a crucial tribal component. This complementarity is also visible insofar as Brahmans spatially oppose the Bhuiya in the seating arrangement in the throne room. At some point, the king re-enters the hall "riding" on the back of a Bhuiya chief, the "horse" behaving wildly as it carries the king into the hall. Then, as discussed by Skoda, and mentioned above, the king dismounts his carrier and sits on a Bhuiya's lap, his human throne. Subsequently, 36 Bhuiya chiefs[19] receive imitations of royal insignia (umbrella, sword) and the king receives a mark on his forehead (*tika*) from one Bhuiya chief. The king then symbolically sacrifices one Bhuiya with his sword, after which he again leaves the hall on his "horse." On the next day, Bhuiya chiefs assemble again to pay homage to the king, bringing gifts and prostrating themselves, the *raja* placing his foot on their foreheads.

According to Schnepel, the ritual is conspicuously ambiguous as it involves, on the one hand, aspects that clearly mark the high status of the Bhuiya, such as their right to bear the insignia of the king and to give *tika* to the king, hence as installers of the king. On the other hand, the ceremony entails very explicit signs of tribal submission, such as performing as a horse, being sacrificed by the king and prostration in front of him. Schnepel (2014, 252f) tries to explain this by arguing that the Bhuiya are superior to the king before his coronation but show submission afterwards, and he holds that the ceremony expresses a "dialectical relationship" of mutual obedience (2014, 253).

Another puzzle is how to interpret the scene in which the king sits on the lap of a Bhuiya, who thus appears to be a human throne. As Schnepel sees it, this puts the king in a junior position to the Bhuiya, comparable to the relationship of son to father. Moreover, during his field visits to Keonjhar, Schnepel and his colleagues noted that during Bhuiya weddings the groom sits on the lap of his father. This would suggest that the coronation is actually also a kind of marriage. Schnepel (2014, 253) concludes:

---

18 Next to earlier sources such as Roy (1935), who discussed still earlier sources like Dalton from 1872, Schnepel's arguments are also based on his own ethnographic research in the early 1990s.
19 If we follow Roy's description, these "chiefs" were probably village headmen.

But whom does the king marry? I would like to suggest here that the bride can be none other than Thakurani, the personified and deified earth of the Bhuiya country. During the rite of installation, as is stressed in Roy's account, Thakurani was represented by an earthen vessel filled with water which was placed next to the king-to-be and object of *puja* veneration. Some of the Bhuiyas' most important roles in this installation ceremony thus symbolically express the king's status as the husband of the (Bhuiya) earth. The subsequent (symbolic) human sacrifice of a chief to the earth sealed, sanctified, and celebrated this connubial relationship. This, then, appears to be a final reason (besides the various political, religious, social, and economic ones which have already been mentioned) why the *adivasis* of Orissa (sometimes) wanted a king: they needed husbands and patrons for their earth goddesses in order to tame their wild and terrible sides (when unmarried) and to ensure the fertility and well-being of kings and subjects alike.

There is then some evidence that, as far as their indigeneity and autochthoneity are concerned, tribal societies do not stand on their own. Even in their own imaginations, politics and rituals, tribals themselves feel that the close relationship to *their* earth needs to be mediated through a king (...) to whom to marry their earth goddess in order to make the land, as well as its animals and human beings, fertile and prosperous.

Here, Schnepel rightly stresses the crucial role of the king as sacrificer from the tribal perspective, guaranteeing generalized well-being and fertility. This position was also clearly articulated by my Gadaba interlocutor, Birsa Sisa, quoted previously, who said that the earth goddess becomes angry if kings stop sacrificing humans, buffaloes and sheep. I think that the interpretation of the king as husband of the earth also correctly represents the indigenous cultural logic that relates death, regeneration and sacrifice – the general flow of life – to marriage, and it also mirrors how deities are perceived to be related on a local level. Tribal cosmologies conceptualize the sun or sun-moon deity as king and oppose it to the earth goddess. As such, Gadaba contrast Dorom or Sĩ Arke (Sun Moon) to Bosmoti (earth goddess), manifesting this complementary opposition in the layout of their villages, with the shrine of the latter inside (*hundi*) and the shrine of the former outside the village proper (Pat Kanda). Likewise, the Dongria contrast Dharmaraja/Niamraja (sky god) with Dharni (earth goddess) and manifest these deities in their villages as *koteiwali* and *jakeri*, respectively. Both Gadaba and Dongria conceive of the relation between sky and earth deities as that of husband and wife. But there is more to be said about the royal installation ritual in Keonjhar and Schnepel's interpretation.

4.3 Hierarchical Opposition and Shared Responsibility of Royal and Tribal Sacrificers

While Schnepel correctly interprets the tribal view of the king as sacrificer in relation to the earth, in my view he fails to fully understand the status of the tribes as subaltern sovereigns. They are not merely "makers and installers of kings" (2014, 252), but they are also kings because of their own role as mediators of and sacrificers for the earth; as earth-beings and earth-kings. The data discussed by Schnepel makes more sense when seen in this way. The Thatraja in Bissamcuttack gave a buffalo to the Dongria in order to sacrifice to Niamraja, not simply as a gift or a provision for a feast, but as acknowledgement of their role as sacrificers. Not only do the tribes want to "share in royal sovereignty" (2014, 251) but the king likewise depended on this subaltern sovereignty to participate in the *sacrificial* "authority from below."

This also explains the ambiguity in the coronation ceremony of the *raja* of Keonjhar, which Schnepel rightly identified but inadequately interpreted. The Bhuiya are not elevated in status before the coronation and then subjugated afterwards. If that was the case, why would the Bhuiya chief play the role of the horse also before the coronation? Rather, throughout the ritual, a tension is articulated between the acknowledgement of the Bhuiya as kings (receiving royal insignia) and as subjects (carrying the king like a horse, reminiscent of the brotherhood stories discussed in Chapter 3) at the same time, thus the apparent paradox of subaltern sovereignty. In the context of royal coronation, the sovereignty of the Hindu king must be represented as dominant and encompassing. Accordingly, Brahmanical rites frame the whole ceremony, and the fact that the Bhuiyas only receive imitations of royal symbols may be seen in this way. The king is represented as the superior, global and encompassing sacrificial sovereign of the state, and the Bhuiya as subaltern sovereigns. The ongoing tension is thus the result of the dynamic in the hierarchical opposition of royal and tribal sacrificial sovereignty played out in the ritual.

In his own observations of the coronation ritual of Keonjhar some 60 years after Dalton, Roy (1935, 118–23)[20] provides further important evidence that supports my argument for the acknowledgement of the sacrificial role of the Bhuiya and of the complementary, yet hierarchical, status of king and tribe as co-sacrificers. The first significant indicator is the fact that the king sits on the lap of what Roy (1935, 199) described as a "Bhuiya officiant," thus a priest. It is the status of Bhuiya sacrificer that is crucial to the making of a king. Even more important is a second aspect. In the coronation rite, the king and a Bhuiya co-perform the paradigmatic type of sacrifice; namely, a symbolic human sacrifice. Dalton (in Roy 1935, 125f) notes in this regard, "that in former days there was no fiction in this part of the ceremony." In Roy's description, the *raja* is first

---

[20] Schnepel (2014, 250) also mentions some of these aspects, without drawing conclusions from them, however.

handed a sword by a Bhuiya headman (from a certain village) with the title Rona ("warrior"), who authorizes the king to kill human beings, that is, to perform human sacrifices. First the king touches the neck of the human victim ("Meriah") twice with the sword, and then the Bhuiya headman repeats the action. The "tension" – that is, the dynamic of the hierarchical opposition of the complementary roles of sacrificer-king and sacrificer-subject – is very explicit in this sequence. The king receives both the weapon for the sacrifice and the verbal permission to sacrifice from the Bhuiya and he is thus clearly dependent on him, deriving his sacrificial authority from his tribal subject. However, he is the first to sacrifice, with the Bhuiya only coming second. The dynamic of this sequence thus expresses a kind of alternating disequilibrium within a few blinks of the eye, with the question of status being left open (compare Heidemann 2010). Only the general framing of the rite in Brahmanical terms indicates the superiority of Hindu kingship and the encompassment of the subaltern sovereigns.

This status dynamic is compounded when we look at the victim, who notably is a Kond. I would argue that this underlines the relational and contextual status of sacrificial sovereignty. In their own territory, the Kond are sacrificers and used to procure victims from outside of their community; here, they provide the victims. Similarly, on their own territory and in their villages, the Bhuiya, Gadaba, Joria and Dongria are not encompassed, or inferior sacrificers, as they are in the context of royal rituals in the capital. Locally, they enjoy superior status and are "honored" as sacrificers and earth people (Berger 2002), and as such they perform the Nandi, Ganga and Go'ter festivals, which are discussed in subsequent chapters.

While the hierarchical relations between royal and tribal sacrificers thus shift and are contextual, there seems to be a general difference between king and earth people, which is precisely why the Bhuiya and other tribal subjects want a king. Schnepel makes an important point when he mentions in the quote above that in addition to guaranteeing well-being, the king tames the "wild and terrible sides" of deities. Indeed, it is the *shakti* of the *raja* as metasacrificer that distinguishes him from the tribal earth creatures and sacrificers for the earth; that is, from the subaltern sovereigns. This is the message of M7, which I collected near Jeypore. This myth narrates how the tribal villagers could not deal with a human-eating goddess and how the king of Jeypore tamed her by building a temple: "they caught her, bind her and took her to the house of the king. Otherwise the whole village would have been gone, empty. They took her to Purnagarh, called the king and handed her over." Today, the villagers still sacrifice buffaloes to the goddess on top of their hill during Dasara, but it was the king who was able to pacify the fierce and dangerous deity in the capital. Both the sacrificial complementarity and differential *shakti* of king and tribal subjects become evident in this instance.

Let me return to the coronation ritual for the king of Keonjhar once more. The description given by Roy and the earlier observations of Dalton both present another important feature that is reminiscent of the Dom Raja stories I discussed in the previous chapter; namely, the connection between kingship and forest. In contrast to the brotherhood myths, which present the forest as primitive and demonic, the Dom Raja stories depict the forest as a powerful place. The righteous boy-king is born in the forest and with the help of forest weapons is able to slay the Dom King and install himself as ruler. Likewise, in the coronation ceremony in Keonjhar, references to the "jungle" abound, especially with regard to forest creepers (Roy 1935, 120f, 125). The king is provided with a crown made from creepers, he is fanned with a whisk made from creepers – the same plants (*siardi*) that are used in the brotherhood myths to tame and tie up the demonic tribal women – and an umbrella made from creepers is held over his head. Clearly, the tribals are represented in the coronation ritual as sacrificers and forest people, both aspects and qualities which the king requires in assuming kingship and becoming a sacrificer himself.

Roy put forward his own early version of an integration model with regard to his research among the Bhuiya of the Bonai kingdom. In a section entitled "Influence of Religion on Social Integration" (1935, 104–17), he advances a hypothesis with regard to the king's participation in the Konto Kuari festival of the Bhuiya, suggesting that it would provide insights into similar ancient processes of mutual integration between "Aryan immigrants into India" and the "non-Aryan population;" this would be a politics of conciliation that enabled the immigrants to deal with the "masses of non-Aryan population." The former would have imposed some of their ancient culture on the latter, thus leading to an "Aryanization of the aborigines," while this process also entailed a mixing of "Indo-Aryan" with the "animistic religion of the indigenous population," leading to the "amalgam" of the present Hindu pantheon (1935, 116f). I imagine that the language of the time immediately creates some distrust in the contemporary reader, but a little refashioning in more modern terminology might make this argument seem more acceptable. However, irrespective of modern or anachronistic terminology, rather than overemphasizing these remarks, I want to highlight some of the elements of this festival described by Roy in detail, as they are relevant to the discussion of the relationship between kings and tribes.

Roy's data on the Konto Kuari festival[21] brings out four interrelated aspects in particular: 1) the joint sacrificial responsibility of king and Bhuiya for the well-being of the country and, at the same time, again; 2) demonstrates the

---

[21] In Uwe Skoda's (2015) discussion, the Konto Kuari festival is part of Dasara, this is, however, not evident from Roy's earlier description.

dynamics of hierarchy between king and tribal subjects; 3) this is also articulated in the dual nature of the deity itself, which comes out of the earth, yet is of a royal nature, like the forest boy of the Dom Raja story; and 4) finally, the data emphasizes the sociological function of the festival, actually constituting tribes as wholes and as part of the larger royal polity, including the capital, the town with its castes and the palace.

According to Roy, the festival was a relatively recent innovation, and had only been performed for some 30 years at the time he was writing. At the center of the festival is an unspecified iron object that has been accidentally dug out of the earth in the hills and is kept in a secret place by a Bhuiya priest (*dihuri*) of the village of Jolo. As among many tribes of the region, the Bhuiya distinguish sacred from secular leadership (the secular leader being called *naek* or *padhan*), the ritual dignitary being senior to the secular one (Roy 1935, 81; see Berger 2015; Pfeffer 1997). The festival, which occurred once a year in September/October, started when the *dihuri* of Jolo visited the *raja* at his fort in Bonai (Bonaigarh), receiving from him an earthen vessel filled with unhusked rice, turmeric and vermillion. Back at home, the *dihuri* performed the first offering to the deity (the iron object, referred to as "image" by Roy (1935, 106)) with these ingredients, which set in motion a long sequence of sacrifices. Kept in a bamboo box, the deity went on a tour through tribal villages, going from house to house receiving sacrificial offerings.

After days of touring villages in a procession accompanied by music, on the evening of the sixth day, an earth shrine was erected at the roadside near a village, in the vicinity of Bonaigarh. A canopy was prepared to host the *raja* and members of his family, and when they arrived the *dihuri* approached the king with the image and greeted him. A standardized verbal exchange followed, the *dihuri* inquiring about the health and welfare of the king, the queen, their children and servants, their elephants and horses, land and earth (*prithivi*). After affirming that all was well, the *raja* in turn asked about the welfare of the priest and his children and the Hill Bhuiya generally. The *dihuri* then put the image on a cloth held by the king, which was then placed on a small silver throne. Thus handing over the deity, the *dihuri* said: "Here is your deity (Deota); we kept it in the hills. Examine and see if the image is broken or intact" (Roy 1935, 110). After affirming that everything was in order, the image was passed to a priest of the king (*amat*), who also officiated for the family deities of the king. He put the image on its throne on the earthen altar and worshipped it, also offering two goats. Afterwards, villagers came to make offerings.

Subsequently, the image was carried into Bonai town, where it was worshipped by different castes and was finally installed in a newly prepared shed on the palace grounds. The next day, the sacrifice of a sheep and a goat followed, after which the king carried the image into the interior of the palace, where family members offered it sweets. On an interior veranda of the palace, the *amat* then bathed the image and offered at least one buffalo, one sheep and sixteen or more goats. Then the journey of the deity continued via the room where the state umbrella was kept, to houses of royal family members, to other residents of Bonaigarh and finally to the house of the *amat*, who handed the image back to the *dihuri* of Jolo. The Bhuiya priest then sacrificed on behalf of an "untouchable" Pano, who received this honor because his ancestor was said to have originally found the image.

After another tour through nearly a dozen villages in the company of Bhuiya headmen, the image finally returned to the village of Jolo, where it was first put into a tree in the "jungle" and then placed inside the house of the *dihuri*. Roy describes a massive presence of the Hill Bhuiya on this occasion, in fact "all Pauri [Hill] Bhuiyas of the country" (Roy 1935, 114) had come to offer sacrifices, performed by the *dihuri*. After the feast, when everyone had left, the *dihuri* took the image back to its secret place.

Like the installation ritual for the king of Keonjhar, the Konto Kuari festival clearly documents the sacrificial co-responsibility of king and Bhuiya. As the *dihuri* put it when handing over the deity to the king, it is "his deity," but the Bhuiya are its caretakers and "keep it in the hills." The image travels through the kingdom, traversing its different realms geographically, socially and politically, from hill villages to the capital on the Brahmani River, across the different communities, and from the forest realm of the subjects (the image kept in tree in the "jungle") to the center of the kingdom (palace and the room of the state umbrella). Clearly, the polity is united in the ritual process and the king and his priests, as well as the Bhuiya, co-perform the festival. The king provides objects signifying fertility (earthen pot, rice), which the *dihuri* uses for his first offering, followed by numerous sacrifices in Bhuiya villages. However, the offerings of the king are also substantial, as his *amat* sacrifices one or more buffaloes and sheep and sixteen or more goats.

Most intriguing and relevant is the dialogue between the king and the *dihuri* when they first meet, inquiring reciprocally about each other's well-being both individually and collectively. I have encountered this kind of generalized well-being – also documented by other ethnographers, among the Kond and Bondo, for instance (Elwin 1950, 147; Fürer-Haimendorf 1943, 168; Hardenberg 2018a, 606; Macpherson 1865, 122f) – in invocations of the Gadaba to their deities, as mentioned in the previous chapter (Berger 2015, 58f), when everything, humans, animals and earth, are included in the quest for life. This is truly significant as it points toward a notion of fertility linked to ideas of shared being between earth, people, plants and animals, something to which I will return when discussing the *go'ter* ritual of the Gadaba. Perhaps even more than the complementary sacrificial practices themselves, this dialogue shows the shared concern for well-being and fertility of king and tribe.

While they thus share this goal and jointly participate, the tension in status and the hierarchical shifts I have indicated above are also clearly discernable in this festival. In a kind of inversion of the structure of the coronation ritual in Keonjhar, both the spatial movement of the image in the Konto Kuari festival and the ritual sequence suggest that the Bhuiya encompass the royal domain in this festival. The image moves from the hills to the capital in the plains and back into the hills, where it is kept by the Bhuiya. In the middle of the ritual process, this Bhuiya dominance is temporarily suspended, when the image is handed to the *raja* and seated on the throne; that is, when the royal dimension of the deity becomes explicit. Then, the king (the *amat* on his behalf) sacrifices first and only afterwards the "men of surrounding villages" (1935, 111), whether Bhuiya or not, is not specified. I would argue that – despite the sacrificial complementarity and encompassment of the king in the ritual process as a whole – here the principal difference between king and tribes I indicated above also becomes apparent: the *raja* as powerful metaperson, in contrast to subaltern earth creatures. This is the reason why the deity belongs to the *raja* as the *dihuri* tells the king: because the deity is itself a king. Accordingly, the image is treated like a king and placed on a throne. However, the deity itself is, like the Bhuiya, an earth-creature and hence the Bhuiya are its custodians.

Finally, the Konto Kuari festival demonstrates the same sociological potential as was reported with regard to Dasara: it constitutes, distinguishes and integrates tribal communities. Like the Juang and the Dongria, the Hill Bhuiya knew no chiefs or political leadership, as Roy points out. The village confederations (*bar*) were about joint worship and rituals of reintegration after someone was excommunicated because of a transgression. As with the Juang *pirh* or the Dongria *muta*, there was no higher level of socio-ritual organization among the Bhuiya than the *bar*. Only in relation to the king, in contexts such as Dasara or the Konto Kuari festival, were tribes actually constituted as totalities. Both McDougal (1963, 364–68) and Nayak (1989, 123f) describe how the Juang and the Dongria, respectively, are both represented as a totality in the sacrificial context of Dasara, and they stress, like Roy, the massive presence of the tribal communities in terms of numbers. It is thus fair to assume that this is a more general feature, namely that, somewhat paradoxically perhaps, the tribes constituted empirical units only in relation to the king, when they were integrated into the larger polity and distinguished from each other, as much as from Hindu castes. The "kingdom frame," to put it in Rousseleau's terms, did not create tribal institutions, but it relationally constituted tribes empirically in ritual representations of the royal polity.

4.4 Conclusion

In the first section of this chapter, the history of the Nandapur/Jeypore kingdom was embedded in the political dynamics of the wider region. This included the constant competition between rulers of different orders, superior overlords and dependent vassal *rajas*. These political dynamics were also the reason why the capital was shifted from Nandapur to Jeypore in the seventeenth century and intermittently to other places as well. One coastal dynasty was particularly important, namely the Ganga kings, who first ruled Kalinga (today Andhra Pradesh) for roughly 500 years, from 500 CE onwards. After a period of decline in power they then managed to extend their kingdom northwards to include the Mahanadi delta and the region then known as Utkal, which later came to be called Orissa. Under the name Trikalinga, the hill region of Koraput was part of the Ganga kingdom, where at least from the thirteenth century onward the Silavamshi kings established their rule in Nandapur on the plateau of the Eastern Ghats. In the fifteenth century, we see a striking parallel dynastic change among the great Gajapati kings in the Mahanadi delta as well as in Nandapur. Within the short span of nine years, the previous dynasties were replaced by rulers of the Suryavamshi or Sun Dynasty, first in Cuttack, then in Nandapur. The situation on the coast is quite well understood by historians, but what happened in Nandapur?

There are various hypotheses and stories concerning this dynastic change. The first Suryavamshi ruler in Nandapur was Vinakak, and some narrations mention that he faced trouble from the tribal population, which did not acknowledge his rule and rebelled against him. Only with the help of a wealthy and influential merchant could the unrest be put down and his rule restored. After contemplating the various scenarios and sources (such as local royal family chronicles), Burkhart Schnepel (2002) comes to the conclusion that Vinayak might have relied on the power of merchants or have even been a warrior-merchant himself. Nandapur was located on an ancient caravan route from the coast across the Eastern Ghats to Central India, and Vinayaka used the symbol of the merchant as his royal signature. This suggests that Vinayaka was an outsider and perhaps a merchant as well.

Like Schnepel, Raphaël Rousseleau (2002/3, 2008, 2010b) also uses local narratives, including the Dom Raja story that I discussed in detail in the previous chapter, to unearth the history of the Nandapur kingdom. Relying particularly on the version presented by Bell (1945; M22), he argues that the story of the jungle-boy who overthrew the Dom King refers to the founder of the Silavamshi dynasty. Moreover, Rousseleau identifies the descendants of the old foster-parents of the boy as a section of the Joria living close to Nandapur near the mythical sites of the Kotni Mala rocks and the Queens Fall (Rani Duduma). The Benek (or Bening), Rousseleau claims, self-identify as the descendants of the old couple, and they pointed out to him certain privileges they had enjoyed during the time of the kings of Jeypore, and possibly earlier as well, when the capital was still in Nandapur. One privilege was that they annually sowed the first rice in the whole kingdom; another was that they brought water and plants from the Kotni Mala rocks and the adjoining waterfall to the capital during Dasara. The Benek also report that they sometimes had a tense relationship and even rebelled against the Suryavamshi kings in the past, thus testifying to their particular tie to the previous Silavamshi kings that they had "brought up."

Whatever the validity of Rousseleau's historical argument – I am more concerned with the tribal collective representations of kingship as expressed in myth and ritual than with the actual history of the kingdom – his findings are highly relevant with regard to the indigenous ideas I aim to understand. As such, it is not so important if the Benek were historically those "turbulent elements" fighting against the first Suryavamshi ruler named Vinayak – obviously in their eyes an illegitimate and external usurper of the throne of the autochthonous Silavamshi king – but it is significant that they identify with those rebels of the past and that they are said to have been later granted the privilege of initiating the rice cultivation cycle. This is important because these two aspects, rice and rebellion, are vital in the Ganga festival of the Joria – the community to which the Benek belong – which I will discuss in detail in Chapter 6. From the point of view of indigenous cultural logic, rice and rebellion are closely related. To fight the Dom King is to promote fertility, in the same way as supporting a good king-cum-sacrificer is to guarantee abundance. The analysis of the Dom Raja story in the previous chapter made clear that the Dom Raja is a "bad" king, above all because he represents negative fertility, as he steals or withholds seeds. It is thus no wonder, then, that the Ganga festival, which actually initiates the rice cultivation cycle, celebrates rice as much as it enacts the rebellion against the Dom King.

In the second section of this chapter, I discussed the different ways the king/tribe relationship has been represented. The different modalities of the relationship that I distinguished on the basis of scholarly work on Central India show distinctive features as well as commonalities. They are similar insofar as all of the scholars discussed in the second section of the chapter argue for some kind of process of integration between kingship and the tribal population. However, the intention of comparing and contrasting these various approaches was to highlight significant differences and to understand various dimensions of this complex relationship throughout history. The approaches were distinctive especially with regard to the viewpoint assumed; that is, whether the relationship was perceived mainly from the perspectives of kings, tribes or both. Naturally, these viewpoints were to a large extent limited and enabled by the material that was the basis for the investigation. The direction of the flow of influence ("upward" or "downward" or mutual) and the motivations and agency ascribed to the actors were often correlated to the chosen perspective (and, hence, to the data under consideration). Finally, another aspect that we have to keep in mind when assessing these different modalities, which is again dependent on the historical or ethnographic data available, is that the scholars focused on different domains of social life, on politics and social structure, on ritual and religion or on everyday life and modes of livelihood.

Two rather opposing approaches are those of Rousseleau and Alfred Gell. Both stress a relatively unidirectional flow of influence, but in different directions, and they ascribed agency to one side in particular. Focusing on ritual and religion, Rousseleau assumes a top-down influence of the royal Hindu model with little or no agency attributed to the *porja*. Gell, by contrast, sees all the volition with the tribes, who used ritual ultimately for political purposes, to keep the state undeveloped. While displaying tribal ferocity and royal grandeur, it was actually the state that was primitive and powerless. In his Rajput model, Sinha also generally perceives the relationship from below and grants the tribes agency, but he assumes that their only motivation is to become kinglike themselves. Obviously, models that perceive the relationship either from the royal or subaltern perspective have their shortcomings, as both kings and tribes would have had their own interests and means to influence the relationship or to avoid it.

While I grouped Skoda in the same model, there are relevant differences when compared to Gell. Skoda argues for "authority from below" but from above, as it were; that is, taking the king's perspective. It is not the tribes who recognize their own power and subversively communicate this via rebellions and rituals, as Gell argues, but the king, who cannot but take note of the authority of the tribes and thus has to act accordingly. Again, this point of view is unsurprising given Skoda's sources. However, in contrast to both Rousseleau and Gell, he does not claim a unidirectional influence but clearly is concerned with the mutuality of the relationship, even if, much like Kulke, he perceives it mainly from above.

In fact, most scholars assumed some mutual influence and a process of integration. While Kulke seems to view the relationship mainly from the perspective of the kings and their political interests, the other scholars discussed try to understand the relationship between kings and tribes from below as much as from above. Schnepel stresses the king's genuine belief in the power of tribal deities and the tribes' desire for a king so they can share in his royal dignity and use his power of mediation with regard to their earth goddess.

Simeran Gell, McDougal and Anderson and Huber, the authors whose approach I have described as "interdependence and tribal autonomy," have a different view from those stressing mutual integration. While Anderson and Huber, for instance, speak of a fusion of the tribal and royal cultural worlds in the sphere of religion, like Simeran Gell and McDougal, they stress the cultural autonomy of the tribes, and implicitly also that of the Hindu kings. During the third phase in the development of the Bastar kingdom, as distinguished by Anderson and Huber, they do not see a cultural integration of kingship and tribal subjects but two explicitly distinct spheres, a Hindu center and a tribal periphery. This is similar to the positions of Fürer-Haimendorf and Sinha, who document two parallel systems, co-existing but not necessarily mixing: the tribal, segmentary structure and the feudal hierarchical structure. The distinctiveness of these systems is well illustrated by Fürer-Haimendorf. As he points out, the aristocratic status of the king and his lineage were irrelevant as far as the clan cult was concerned, as in this respect the king was just one of many and the ideology of brotherhood prevailed. The king's involvement in rituals of purification even prevented his full participation in the clan cult. Thus, we have two worlds interacting but remaining separate and distinctive.

In my view, it is important to assume the possibility of a kind of "fusion," which would be a process different from integration in the sense of assimilation, adoption or appropriation, whether by the king assimilating tribal cults or by the tribal imitation of a royal lifestyle. Taking the views of Alfred Gell, Anderson and Huber further, I would understand fusion here as the overlap of two worlds that show something like an elective affinity in a certain domain. Clearly, this would be the sphere of religion and, in my view, ideas concerning the sacrificial flow of life in particular. Without denying that processes of integration in any of the forms discussed above may have been crucial to the relationship between kings and tribes, I would argue that it was above all the understanding of sacrifice and regeneration – of sovereignty in the sense of controlling the flow of life – that resonated between Hindu kings and tribes. This enabled a complementarity and interdependence between two corresponding forms of sacrificial sovereignty, one from above and one from below, one royal and global, the other tribal and local. Obviously, it is impossible to prove that this was at any point the actual historical situation and it would be naïve to assume that exactly the same process occurred everywhere in Central India. Moreover, the dynamics of elective affinity and integration do not theoretically exclude each other and may well be a historical possibility, namely an "original" elective affinity of sacrificial worldviews that subsequently co-evolved and mutually influenced each other.

It is this understanding of the king/tribe relationship as an elective affinity between two worldviews of sacrificial regeneration that is the basis of the criticism I have articulated with regard to some of the arguments put forward by the scholars discussed above, notably Rousseleau, Skoda and Schnepel. While Rousseleau's research is both important and original, I do not agree with some of his interpretations. I regard his views concerning the "cultural hegemony" of Hindu kingship as problematic, as this denies any autonomy to tribal worldviews and practices as well as indigenous agency. This interpretation – which too often primarily relies on superficial correspondences, such as linguistic similarities – is difficult to maintain given the ethnographic facts presented by numerous scholars, including myself elsewhere and in this book.

If my reading of his argument is correct, then Skoda significantly complements Alfred Gell's view concerning the "power from below." Rather than demonstrating the tribal power to keep relations in the state horizontal, Skoda argues that, with regard to the kingdom of Bonai, the king acknowledged, in fact depended on, the "Lords of the Earth." While Skoda does not sufficiently emphasize the nature of Bhuiya authority, nor does he clearly distinguish authority from power, it can be assumed that he understands power as actual force (e.g., in military terms) and authority as located more in the field of ritual. If that is the case, then his material documenting the view from above, as well as his interpretation, support the argument I am developing in this book – namely of subaltern sovereignty – from another angle.

Schnepel's work, especially the "tribal view" presented in his more recent contribution (Schnepel 2014), is also crucial with regard to the ideas discussed here. However, I have again offered a complementary and partly alternative reading of the material. Both of my main criticisms, additions and adjustments, concern the status of the Bhuiya in relation to the king. Schnepel rightly identifies the role of the king as sacrificial guarantor of fertility and well-being from the tribal perspective. This is confirmed in numerous ways by the rituals and myths discussed in the previous chapter and the statements of my Gadaba interlocutors. What Schnepel fails to see, in my view, or in any case insufficiently foregrounds, is the sacrificial role of the tribes, in his case the Bhuiya. In the sacrificial sense that is the basis of the indigenous notion of sovereignty, the Bhuiya are not only "earth beings" but also kings, contributing to regeneration and the flow of life; they are not merely "installers of kings" who want to share in royal dignity. The reverse is also evident: the king depends on the tribes in their capacities as sacrificers, and in this sense on their "authority from below."

As soon as this is acknowledged, the "ambiguity" of the status of the Bhuiya in the coronation ritual can also be adequately explained, namely as derived from their status as subaltern sovereigns. That the Bhuiya are represented as "horses" at one moment and offered imitations of royal insignia at another, in my view, testifies precisely to their seemingly paradoxical status as both subjects and (sacrificial) sovereigns. The tension articulated in the ritual should be understood as a dynamic hierarchical opposition in Dumont's (2013) sense, which shifts throughout the ritual process. As it is a coronation ritual, the court strives to represent the *raja*'s sovereignty as paramount and accordingly the whole ceremony is encompassed by Brahmanical rites. However, the Bhuiya are accepted as co-sacrificers in the crucial moments of the ritual. This is evident from the fact that it is a priest, that is, a sacrificer, on whose lap the king is seated as a "human throne." Even more important is the interaction between king and Bhuiya headman during the symbolic human sacrifice, which perhaps was not only symbolic in the past, as Dalton suggests. The king first receives his sacrificial legitimation from the Bhuiya, who hands him the sword, and then king and Bhuiya co-perform the sacrifice, the king "striking" first, the Bhuiya second.

The complementary sacrificial roles of king and Bhuiya and the fluctuating hierarchical opposition between royal and tribal sovereignty is also strongly present in the Konto Kuari festival that was documented in detail by Roy. Compared to the coronation ritual, in the context of this festival, the hierarchical relation between Bhuiya and king seems to be reversed, as the tribal sacrifices actually encompass the royal rites, with the festival proceeding from the Bhuyia hills, through tribal villages, down to the capital and back up to the hills and into the "jungle." In my view, the most striking scene occurs in the middle of the festival, in a liminal space on a roadside near Bonaigarh, when the Bhuiya priest and king meet. Two things are asserted in this moment. First, the sacrificial co-responsibility of Bhuiya and king with regard to generalized well-being is articulated in a standardized dialogue concerning the health and well-being of animals, people and the earth. Second, even though the ritual movement of the festival as a whole signifies the encompassing of the royal component through the tribal performance, the king asserts his superiority as global sacrificer in this moment. The Bhuiya hand over the deity to the king, stating that it is "his" deity – a deity that is of a royal nature, as it is placed on a throne: a divine king like the human *raja*. While this is not explicitly stated, perhaps king and deity are identified, like Danteswari with the king of Bastar, a fusion of royal deity and divine king. Mirroring the sacrificial sequence during the coronation ritual, the superiority of the king is also made explicit in this moment, as the king's priest sacrifices first followed by "the villagers."

This close association, sometimes perhaps even identification, between king and deity and the divine nature of kingship is one reason that, despite the tension, the shifting hierarchical opposition between tribal and royal sacrificers, there is a principal difference perceived by the tribes between their king as sacrificial metaperson and themselves, as earth born but definitely human sacrificers. Because of this, the king is able to domesticate fierce human-eating deities, as is narrated in a story (M7) I recorded, and he is also able to care for the regeneration and well-being of the kingdom as a whole, on a global level, while the subaltern sovereigns navigate the flow of life locally, on their territory.

Finally, there is an important sociological dimension resulting from the relationship between kings and tribes. Most tribes of Central India, certainly those that are a part of the Nandapur/Jeypore kingdom, rarely aggregate beyond the level of the village, with the most inclusive unit being the village cluster, which has various names (*bar*, *pirh*, *muta*) depending on the region and serving social-cum-ritual functions – such as reintegration after excommunication or sacrifice – but not political purposes. It is therefore also problematic to describe the "headmen" of such units as "chiefs," as it was not a question of political leadership. The village "headmen" were petty chiefs at best. Tribal identity was thus sociologically grounded in the village or clan territory, not beyond. People calling themselves something like "earth creatures," such as the Bhuiya or Gutob (Gadaba), or simply "human," such as the Kuang (Dongria), Remo (Bondo) or Hor (Santal), never assembled as a unit of joint action. However, in distinction to gathering-hunting bands (Pfeffer 2002; 2016; Demmer 2009), these communities entertained an idea of themselves as social wholes. In the case of the Gadaba, as in many other communities in Central India, this ideal unit is related to the number twelve, signifying a totality; hence, the "twelve brothers" are ubiquitous. The Gadaba complement this agnatic whole with an affinal component, making it twelve-plus-one. Only in the case of severe crisis does this idea of Gadaba society as a totality actually materialize ritually (Berger 2015, 299–304). This sociological feature of tribes has already been pointed out by Marshall Sahlins, namely that in a segmentary order, the highest levels are the weakest, are poorly defined and functionally irrelevant. Empirically, in fact, tribes would even merge into one another at the borders of their territory. Accordingly, rarely "united politically, often not definable with precision, the 'tribe' may be beset with a crisis of identity" (Sahlins 1968, 16).

It is here that the king comes in. As documented with regard to the Dongria, Bhuiya and Juang and most explicitly stated by McDougal (1963, 368) quoted above, tribal communities actually took shape as totalities vis-à-vis the king, especially during Dasara. The massive tribal presence also referred to by Alfred Gell, therefore, probably not only had the purpose of intimidating the king but also of performing and enacting collective identities. It was in relation to the king in the center – the "navel place," as it is also called by tribes such as the Joria and Gadaba – that non-centralized segmentary tribal identities were constituted, distinguished (from other tribes and the castes of the town) and integrated into the royal polity. The proverb, *Raja Dasara, Joria Nandi, Mali Bali, Gadaba Go'ter*, is another instance of precisely this point.

This function of the king in the ritual constitution of tribal collective identities may have also had its repercussions at the level of ideas. The Gadaba, in any case, make reference to the king in their notion of "twelve-plus-one," mentioned above, as they speak of *baro bai tero gadi*, which I have usually translated as "twelve brothers, thirteen seats." However, this "seat" is obviously the seat of the king, the throne. Thus, kingship is an important element in the imagination of the Gadaba of their society as a totality.

Part Two: **Proverbial Performances**

5 Royal Rituals in Comparative Perspective: The King's Dasara

In this chapter, I turn to Dasara, the first festival mentioned in the regional proverb, with the further specification that it is the "King's Dasara" (*Raja Dasara*). The aphorism thus already identifies one of its most conspicuous features: it is a royal ritual of and about kings and kingship. It is and has been celebrated all over India in the lunar month of *asvina* (mid-September/mid-October) and is known under many different names, including Dasara ("Tenth"), Navaratra ("Nine Nights") and Mahanavami (the "Great Nine-Day" festival), among others.

In a recent contribution, Bihani Sarkar (2020) outlines the historical development of the festival and states that its origins are difficult to determine with certainty, suggesting that diverse traditions have probably contributed to its formation, not least indigenous practices centered on the worship of goddesses. This, then, is the second general feature of the festival, the focus on Devi worship. More specifically, it is the relationship between kings and goddesses that is crucial in all manifestations of Dasara. As far as origins are concerned, also Burton Stein (1983) has pointed to multiple influences. In his view, the Mahanavami festival, which was first reported on, at least in South India, in the early fifteenth century CE, took the place of royal public rituals that were performed up to and including the Gupta period (which ended in the sixth century CE), notably the famous horse sacrifice (*asvamedha*). These rituals aimed at the general regeneration of sacred royal power so that the king could act according to *rajadharma*, providing protection and bountifulness to the people of his domain. Arguing against juridical interpretations of kingship articulated in the *Dharmashastra* texts, which regarded kings more as politicians and power pragmatists than sacred personae, Stein argues that the Mahanavami festival fulfilled general purposes similar to the earlier performances of divine kings, regenerating the king and his realm in this general sense.

Despite its somewhat elusive nature due to the heterogeneous origins of the festival, Dasara is coherent in its basic features and has also shown a remarkable persistence. For South India, Stein (1983, 84) notes that the "continuity of major elements of the Mahanavami over several centuries is impressive," and he argues that the structure of the sixteenth-century performance of the Vijayanagara kings and the festival of the late nineteenth century are so similar that one description can be used to complement the other.

There seems to be a general consensus among scholars concerning the major elements of Dasara celebrations (see also Fuller 1992; Hardenberg 2008; Simmons et al. 2018). I have already mentioned the two most crucial features, the goddess and the king, and as a corollary, horses, swords and warfare. Both king and goddess are related via a third element – that of turning death into life, in other words, sacrifice. For Sarkar (2020), it is the goddess in her various manifestations that provides coherence to the festival as a whole. The Devi integrates heterogeneous traditions (Brahmanical, local) included in the festival and unites everything under one common theme, that of the conquest of death, which is narrated in the mythologies concerning her victory over demons which is performed in the rituals.

> The charismatic heart of this ceremony was the Goddess herself: elusive because she integrated the essences of other goddesses, and yet powerfully coherent. Her coherence came from a representation of death, and the ceremony became an enactment of her triumph over death. The buffalo, a *vahana* [vehicle] of Yama, was a symbol of death. Durga's slaying the buffalo symbolized both her mastery over and her association with death and danger. (Sarkar 2020, 341)

Furthermore, Stein emphasizes the complementarity of kings and deities in medieval South Indian conceptions of sovereignty: "the sovereignty of neither is complete; the sovereignty of both, together, is perfect" (1983, 89). Sovereignty is thus constituted by combining powerful humans and gods. Moreover, this structure is pervasive and found on every level of society, from the kingdom to the village and clan, down to the household. In each case, we find this complementary form of human/divine sovereignty.

Stein develops his argument further and includes what I here consider the fourth element of the festival – along with king, goddess and sacrifice – namely, the community: "Those who fall under the sovereignty of both kings (. . .) and gods comprise a community of reverence or worship (. . .)" (1983, 89). A community is created and united in the worship of human and divine powers on different levels. The "realm itself," Stein (1983, 89) continues:

> was defined by the worship of the king and his tutelary deity as in the *Mahanavami* or *Navaratri*. Worship is constitutive of (it establishes or creates) community; the sovereignty of great humans (fathers, clan heads, kings) and gods is realized in worship events, or ritual performances, of a public kind in which all of any corporate whole (family or kingdom) express membership (. . .).

The integrative function of Dasara in social and ritual terms has likewise been stressed by other scholars (e.g., Sarkar 2020) and I referred to this aspect in the conclusion of the previous chapter. In addition, the examples that will be discussed below amply demonstrate this aspect. Here, I want to draw attention to one particular aspect of Stein's argument, namely the nature and scope of this "sharing" in sovereignty and the role of the community. According to Stein, subjects – and I refer to the level of the kingdom here – worship or "revere" the king and his goddess and thereby benefit from their "perfect sovereignty" in terms of protection and fertility. They are "co-sharers" in royal/divine sovereignty insofar as they are beneficiaries of its power, but not in the sense that they also hold some kind of power themselves. While they participate in worship, it seems the subjects have nothing to contribute in terms of sovereignty themselves. These powerless beneficiaries, while active in reverence and worship, seem to be passive in this sense.

The notion of sovereignty that comes to the fore in the Dasara rituals of "jungle kingdoms" is different at least in one important aspect: the involvement of tribal communities and their deities in the ritual proceedings. As such, with regard to his analysis of Dasara in the kingdom of Bonai, Uwe Skoda has rightly emphasized that one should speak of a triangle of "the Raja, the Adibasis and the goddess(es)" (2015, 100). The plural with regard to the last element, the goddess, is important, as tribal goddesses are included in the festival, alongside other deities, especially the tutelary deities of the kings. In Bonai, the Bhuiya hand over their goddess (Kant Kumari) to the king to be worshipped by his priest in the context of Dasara, before she is handed back to the Bhuiya, who return with her to the hills. The Bhuiya community, Skoda (2015, 82) writes, "which is believed to be autochthonous in the area, is powerful and represents authority over the soil."

This is a very important observation, but as I argued in the last chapter – also in relation to Skoda's work –, I think the nature of tribal sovereignty needs to be further specified. What has become explicit in my analysis of the coronation ceremony of the king in Keonjhar (and my comments on Schnepel's interpretation) and of the Konto Kuari festival of the Bhuiya of Bonai, exactly the ritual Skoda is referring to,[1] is the tribal participants' role as co-sacrificers. In contrast, Skoda's description suggests a relatively passive role for the Bhuiya in the Dasara rituals,[2] with the Bhuiya bringing the deity down from the hills and handing her over to the king and his priests but then having nothing further to contribute until the goddess is returned to them. True, while the king and his priests keep custody of the tribal goddess the Bhuiya do not sacrifice to her. However, literally hundreds of sacrifices are performed by the Bhuiya, in countless villages, before

---

1 In his description of the Konto Kuari festival, Roy (1935) does not mention any connection to Dasara.
2 Skoda's description here perhaps somewhat echoes the perspective of the royal chronicles of Bonai, depicting a frightened Bhuiya who left the goddess behind because he thought the king was after him to kill him. The king and his men first searched for the Bhuiya but when he could not be found, the king handed the goddess over to his priest (Skoda 2015, 89). The sacrificial agency of the Bhuiya is downplayed here.

and after the period of royal worship of the goddess. In particular, the whole ritual sequence ends with a collective sacrificial feast in which "sacrifices [are] brought by all the Pauri Bhuiyas of the country" and "offered by the Dihuri [Bhuiya priest] to the goddess" (Roy 1935, 114). Moreover, Roy notes (1935, 117) that three to four generations before he observed the festival, the royal officiant (*amat*) sacrificing to the goddess was a Bhuiya priest, an aspect also noted by Skoda. Thus, I would argue, before, after and during the royal sequence of the festival, the active participation of the Bhuiya as sacrificers is vital. Beyond the fact of the appropriation of a tribal deity by a king, what is at stake here and what is crucial to the festival is the sacrificial sovereignty of the subalterns. Only this aspect makes "perfect sovereignty," to use Stein's words. This chapter demonstrates to what extent this argument of tribal sacrificial sovereignty can be substantiated with regard to the Dasara performances in the region of my immediate concern.

In order to understand the structure and meanings of Dasara in the former Jeypore kingdom, and to be able to assess what, if anything, is specific to those celebrations, I will engage in a comparison of Dasara, as celebrated in the adjacent jungle kingdom of Bastar.[3] I start with Bastar because these rituals have been most thoroughly described over a period of a century, whereas the data available on the Jeypore/Nandapur kingdom is unfortunately incomplete and sketchy. Starting with Bastar will enable me to complement the data available on Jeypore and to make sense of Dasara comparatively.

While I do not claim that the festival was performed identically in both kingdoms, the basis for such a comparison could not be sounder and similarities between the two jungle kingdoms of Jeypore and Bastar have also previously been noted (e.g., A. Gell 1997, 437; Rousseleau 2008, 217f). The geographic, social and cultural conditions in which the kingdoms and the Dasara festival are embedded are indeed very similar. Bastar and Jeypore are part of the historical region called Dandakaranya, which extends over the three modern states of Chhattisgarh, Odisha and Andhra Pradesh (Das et al. 2020, 259; Gregory 2004; Otten 2014). Like Jeypore, Jagdalpur also lies on a plateau populated by numerous tribal communities belonging to the general local category of *koitor* – "humans," as the Gond call themselves. Among them are Dorla, Dhurwa, Maria and Muria – and non-cultivating indigenous "caste" groups such as gardeners, potters, weavers and blacksmiths. Like the Dongria Kond, who practice shifting cultivation in the steeper Niamgiri Hills, the Hill Maria live in the remoter Abujhmar Hills. Tribal communities are ranked according to seniority, as Pfeffer (1997) has documented

---

3 On the anthropology of Bastar see the overview by Chris Gregory (2013) and his monograph (Gregory 1997).

for tribal Central India generally, and the social structure likewise collectively contrasts agnates or "brothers" with affines, as is the case in Koraput. Whereas the vassal king in Bissamcuttack was more than 180 kilometers away by road from his overlord in Jeypore, Jagdalpur, the capital of Bastar, is less than half the distance, and connected to Jeypore by ancient trade routes. Accordingly, the historical relationships between the two kingdoms, either of a supportive or competitive nature, have been numerous (see Anderson & Huber 1988, 27f; Francis 1907, 274; S. Gell 1992; Grigson 1991; Sundar 2007, 12f, 44 fn. 41; Thusu 1968).

This chapter proceeds by first discussing Dasara as celebrated in Bastar and then comparing it to other descriptions of the festivals, as celebrated in the former Jeypore kingdom, including Nandapur, the first capital, and Bissamcuttack, the location of an erstwhile vassal of the Jeypore Maharaja. I then shift the perspective and look at Dasara celebrations as performed in different villages in the (former) Jeypore kingdom, notably the performances of the Gadaba, Rona, Dongria and Joria. Finally, I broaden my scope of comparison again by taking the Dasara celebrations of two former Hindu empires into account, those of the Gajapati ("Lord of the Elephants") in Puri and the king of Mysore, before I conclude the chapter by outlining the distinctive patterns and characteristic features of Dasara in the jungle kingdoms.

5.1 Dasara in Bastar

The Goddesses

Like Dasara festivals in other parts of India, in Bastar female goddesses are also at the center of ritual activities that (re)constitute kingship and the relationship between king and subjects, capital and villages. Of the many goddesses that are worshipped, two stand out, Danteswari and Maoli (variously written Mauli, Mavli, etc.). Their identities and their relationship with each other, as well as their connection to Durga and other deities, are complex and ambivalent. They are defined in relation to a set of oppositions such as foreign/local, Hindu/tribal and elite/subaltern. Given this complexity, it may be best to start with what is relevant to the festival and at the same time unequivocal – the locations of the goddesses.

In addition to the many Danteswari village shrines, this goddess is worshipped in two main temples that are at the heart of Dasara proceedings. One is located in the palace compound itself, in the center of Jagdalpur, the former capital of the kings of Bastar. The other shrine is found in a place called Dantewara, about 90 kilometers west of Jagdalpur. The name of the place immediately makes the connection to the goddess clear, and numerous local oral traditions tell variations of the story of how Danteswari helped to establish the Kakatiya dynasty in Bastar, which was founded in the fifteenth century. Ever since, Danteswari has been the tutelary deity of the kings of Jagdalpur. At the time, so the narrative goes, King Annam Deo was fleeing from Warrangal to evade Muslim armies, some 200 kilometers due southwest of Dantewara. Danteswari offered her help to the king, saying she would walk behind him and protect him. He was not to look back but could rely on the tinkling of her anklets to reassure him of her presence throughout the journey. When crossing a river, however, she sank so deep that the sound of her anklets was muffled and the king turned around to see if she was still there. Furious about the lack of trust, the deity refused to go any further and thus her shrine came to be established at the confluence of Shankhini and Dankini rivers and Dantewara came into existence (Glasfurd 1862; Gregory n.d.). Today, it is considered to be the main shrine of Danteswari.

Another important location to be mentioned is the temple of the goddess Maoli, the "ancient village goddess of Jagdalpur" (Mallebrein 1996, 499), just opposite the palace in Jagdalpur. What, however, is the identity of Maoli in relation to Danteswari? Before the Kakatiyas established their rule and made Danteswari their family deity and the superior goddess of the state, another "Snake Dynasty" (Nagavamshi) is said to have ruled parts of Bastar. This dynasty worshipped the goddess Manikeswari, a transfiguration and appropriation of tribal village cults of Maoli. It may be that the local Maoli cults were Hinduized as Manikeswari – a deity popular in Odisha – by the Nagavamshis and then, in a second step, when Danteswari was established by the Kakatiyas, made into one of her "32 sisters" (Mallebrein 1996, 489). Maoli, meaning "mother" (Sundar 2007, 64), would thus be the local tribal goddess, while Danteswari would have come from elsewhere, established by the Kakatiya kings. These kings widely promoted Danteswari worship and established temples throughout their region of influence, with the deities worshipped as village deities (also often just called Mata, "mother"). Nevertheless, they also integrated Maoli into their cult, especially the women of the royal family of the Kakatiya dynasty, who were attached to Maoli (Mallebrein 1996; Sundar 2007, 61f).[4]

---

[4] Harihar Vaishnav and Chris Gregory (Gregory n.d., 43ff) recorded a local myth (*kahani*) in Kondagaon, northwest of Jagdalpur, that narrates the origin of Maoli worship. It is relevant also, as it makes an explicit connection to the goddess' fight against wicked kings. In short, a baby was nursed by a banyan tree, adopted by a barren woman who raised her as her own child. Growing up the girl would teach others in religious and moral matters and ended up repeatedly fighting immoral kings. Being caught off-guard, while performing a fire sacrifice, the king and his soldiers attacked the girl and her followers and in order to prevent bloodshed

From the village perspective, as well as during Dasara, Maoli's superior status has been noted by several scholars. Sundar stresses the importance of Maoli, noting that: "while the festival is seen as dedicated to Danteswari, Manikeswari or Mawli is acknowledged in every ritual of Dussehra" (Sundar 2007, 64). Katherine Hacker (2014, 215) also maintains that Maoli is considered "older and thus senior" to Danteswari, which becomes apparent during Dasara because the Dasara rituals spatially proceed from Danteswari's temple to that of Maoli. Discussing village festivals in Bastar which feature the manifestation of numerous deities through possession, Nicolas Prévôt (2014, 243) observes that Maoli Mata is "the most important and most auspicious goddess [and] always precedes the others" in the "play of the gods," to which I will return below.

As discussed in the previous chapter when dealing with the various modes of relationships between king and tribes, complex interactions between royal deities and village gods and goddesses are likely to have occurred throughout the centuries. While Mallebrein (1996, 489) stresses the Hinduization of tribal goddesses such as Maoli and Manikeswari, Nandini Sundar (2007, 62f) understands the process as "mutual appropriation" and "endless mimesis" between rulers and tribals. Both Gregory (n.d.) and Alfred Gell (1997) point out competing and partly antagonistic views of the same deity. While, from the elite perspective of the king and his Brahmans, Danteswari might be framed as Durga, the tribals see her as a manifestation of their village deities, whom the king would thus effectively be worshipping. This tribalization of the royal family deity would also be visible in the form that the goddess chose to manifest herself, namely in the distinctive local idiom of possession (Gell 1997, 437f). I think it is important to consider the point that royal and tribal participants had overlapping but not entirely similar representations and understandings of the goddesses and their worship. Moreover, caution is needed to avoid putting too much emphasis on the names of deities. Based on my experience among the Gadaba, one and the same deity can actually be referred to by multiple names by the same group of people. For example, the village deity of Pat Kanda, is also referred to as Gumang or senior house, while the earth goddess is called Dorti Mata and Bosmoti, among other names. What actually defines a deity is its relationship to others, for example, the celestial sun-moon deity in opposition to the earth.

---

the girl sacrificed herself by jumping into the fire pit. Subsequently, the people called her Maybali ("mother sacrifice"), Mabali, Mavli and began worshipping her.

The Dasara Festival

We have at our disposal descriptions of the Dasara proceedings from the beginning to the end of the twentieth century. Two of them (Marten 1912; Majumdar 1939) deal with Dasara before independence, when the king still held office, while the other two (Mallebrein 1996; Sarkar and Dasgupta 1996) documented the festival in the 1990s. While the contributions differ in their focus on certain aspects of the festival, a basic structure clearly emerges and has remained constant throughout the century (see Sundar 2007, 67).[5] Other contributions will also be relevant in various ways. Alfred Gell (1997) does not provide more data on Dasara, but in my view presents the most sophisticated and stimulating interpretation of the rituals.[6] Nandini Sundar (2007) is not primarily concerned with the rituals as such, but her important work offers a historical contextualization of Dasara, as well as some additional details on the performances in 1992.

After the violent death of Raja Pravir Chandra Bhanjdeo in 1966, the role of the king during the festival has been taken over by government representatives (such as the District Collector), the priest of the Danteswari temple in Jagdalpur and the royal family priest. The sources dealing with Dasara in the 1990s specified the occasions when the king should have performed a ritual but someone else acted in his stead. It is certainly significant to study who replaced the king in these rituals and how this changed the performance. However, this is not very relevant for my purposes. As I am interested in the ideas that become manifest in the rituals in the representations of kinship and the relationships between king and subjects (and their deities), I will focus on the role of the king and leave such substitutions unmentioned in the following. The description I present below is thus not an account of a Dasara festival of any particular year, but rather presents the general structure of the performance as I infer it from the various specific descriptions from the twentieth century.

Ritual Space-Time

The ritual movements in space and time – of (meta) persons and (meta) objects – provide the basic structure of the festival. Similar to village festivals such as Chait Porbo, which I have discussed in detail elsewhere (Berger 2015), Dasara is first confined to one location, the town of Jagdalpur, but then opens

---

5 See also Naidu (1975). For a popular description see Kriti (2018).
6 For a critique of Gell's argument see Sundar (2001).

up to "guests" from outside and subsequently transgresses the boundaries of the capital itself. Also similar to Chait Porbo, certain partly overlapping periods characterize the ritual temporality of Dasara. I would like to distinguish four such timelines, all of which are initiated on the first day of Dasara. 1) With the abdication of the king, a ritual stand-in is installed for nine days. This substitute displays a number of peculiar features and is accompanied by a sword, as a symbol of rule, and his state is synchronized with the growth of seeds sown on the first day, which are to germinate throughout this period. 2) The second timeline regards the presence of external deities in the capital and is constituted by two overlapping periods. On the eighth day, village deities from all over the region arrive in Jagdalpur accompanied by delegations from the respective locations. Once all are assembled, Danteswari arrives from Dantewara on day nine. After the renewal of kingship is accomplished, the village deities are the first to leave on the thirteenth or fourteenth day, after which Danteswari of Dantewara returns to her place in Jagdalpur. 3) The presence of the deities is vital for the renewal of kingship and the third timeline is concerned with the status of the king. After his abdication on the first day, he worships various deities on his daily round in his chariot. Only after the external deities have arrived (and after the "human sacrifice" of the stand-in) can he be re-enthroned on the tenth day. This is followed by a remarkable sequel, namely the abduction of the king by his tribal subjects, who take him out of Jagdalpur and into the "forest," only to return the king triumphantly to his capital afterwards. 4) All of these events – the king's abdication, his re-enthronement, his abduction and return – are temporally encompassed by the worship of a weaver deity in her shrine on the outskirts of the town, without whose permission it is impossible to conduct the festival.

The Consent of the Weaver Goddess (Kachin Devi)

Dasara commences on the new moon and proceeds throughout the bright half of the month of *asvina* (September/October).[7] The first act of worship is addressed to a weaver goddess called Kachin Devi. Her temple is about one kilometer from the palace, formerly on the outskirts of the town. The goddess is said to have once helped the king to fight the Marathas, thus earning his devotion, while another story narrates how the weaver priest of the goddess and his wife offered themselves as human sacrifices so that the palace could be built (Mallebrein 1996, 496).

---

[7] On the timing of the festival see Mallebrein (1996, 492), Marten (1912, 84), Sarkar and Dasgupta (1996, 111) and Scialpi (1986, 109 fn. 14).

People assemble at the palace, especially weavers, and among them also ritual media (*gunia*) – "under the influence of local spirits" (Marten 1912, 84) – who are venerated. Together with the king, who is seated on an elephant, they proceed to the Kachin Devi temple, where a pre-pubescent weaver girl is led out of the temple to circumambulate a swing, the seat of which is made from branches of the *bel* tree (*Aegle marmelos*), which has sharp thorns. After the circumambulation, possessed by the goddess, the girl is handed a stick, which represents a sword, and a shield. She then engages in a mock fight with a man, who is said to be either from the caste of Mahar or of oil-pressers (Teli). Subsequently, the girl is laid over the thorny seat of the swing and moved to and fro. The king instructs his priest to ask the goddess if Dasara can be safely performed with her consent. The girl takes a garland of flowers from her neck and passes it to the king's *pujari*, signaling the agreement and protection of the goddess. The king then returns to the palace, while the weaver girl stays at the temple for the duration of the festival.

Abdication and Replacement of the King

In the presence of the king, the *diwan* and other officials, the Brahman *pandits* announce the program of the festival in the Durbar hall on the evening of the first day. The first major event is the abdication and transformation of the king and his replacement. The *raja* hands over the control of the state to his *diwan* and immediately assumes the "garb of an ascetic" (Majumdar 1939, 159). He is smeared with sandalwood paste and a number of restrictions are placed on him: he must walk barefoot, he is not allowed to use vehicles for transport (except during his chariot processions), he has to sleep on the floor, his turban is removed and replaced by a wreath of flowers and he is not allowed to receive or give salutations.

A man is then installed as a stand-in for the king. He is selected from the members of the Halba caste (Jogi subcaste) and consecrated and enthroned in a very specific way. In the middle of the Durbar hall a pit has been dug, which is about one meter wide, two meters long and 30 centimeters deep, with the long side being oriented in a west-east direction. The man sits in the western end of the pit, facing east,[8] and on a heap of ashes covered with a cloth, his legs stretched out. His upper body rests on a vertical plank, another horizontal plank

---

[8] The *Dharmashastras* specify that the victim sacrificed for Durga or Bhairava should face east or north while being killed (Kane 1974, 166).

is fixed over his thighs and the man is "thus fastened down to the throne" (Marten 1912, 85) and unable to get up from this position. In front of the man, objects are placed in the eastern end of the pit: a sword,[9] consecrated water and grains of wheat, which are sown in the pit. Severe restrictions on movement and consumption are in place until the ninth day. He is not allowed to move and he also has to fast, only being allowed to drink some milk and eat some plantains. This man is described as an ascetic, or ruling ascetic, "Jogiraj" (Marten 1912, 85), and devotee, but also as a "victim." In fact, Marten (1912, 84) states that he was "no doubt till comparatively lately finally sacrificed." At the time Marten wrote, the Halba man, once released, was allowed to loot the bazaar without consequences. The king and his stand-in are thus both in exceptional transitional states and, significantly, they may never see each other.

Chariot Processions

For the next six days, the main activity is the procession of the four-wheeled chariot around the palace compound where the temples are located. The king first worships Maoli (Mallebrein 1996, 499; Marten 1912, 85), then other deities (Kalanki, Rama, Jagannatha) and subsequently ascends the chariot, where he holds the umbrella of Danteswari. The chariot is pulled by people of the Maria tribal group, taking a rectangular tour around the palace compound before ending at the Lion Gate of the palace after about three and a half hours. Here, female attendants perform *arti* over the king, waving lights over his head and body. He then descends from the chariot and goes to the Danteswari temple, where he worships the goddess and the arms he is carrying: a bow and arrows and a dagger. On the seventh day, the king worships the *bel* tree after completion of the chariot procession. This is the same tree from which the seat of the swing was made on the first day.

The Arrival of the Village Deities and the Night Sacrifice

The eighth day sees the arrival in huge numbers of all the village gods of the region, in the forms of silver umbrellas or long bamboo poles (*lat*) with conic brass tops or flags attached to them, carried by the respective village delegations, who all witness extensive sacrifices of goats, buffaloes (or, as a substitute,

---

9 The sword of Danteswari, according to Mallebrein (1996, 499).

pumpkins[10]) and catfish (*mongri*). There are no chariot processions on the eighth and ninth days and the proceedings only start late in the evening with the "night sacrifice" (*nisha yatra*). As to the locations of the sacrifices, the accounts differ. Marten (1912) states that the king first visits the Maoli temple and attends the sacrifices performed there and then proceeds to a garden where the sacrifices continue until dawn. Mallebrein (1996) describes a procession to the Bhadrakali temple in 1993, where Maoli and Bhadrakali are worshipped and six goats sacrificed. Upon its return to the palace compound, the procession stops at the Maoli temple where two more goats are sacrificed, before the procession finally moves on to the Danteswari temple, where more sacrifices of goats, pigeons, catfish and pumpkins (buffaloes) follow. These observations generally correspond with the description given by Sarkar and Dasgupta (1996), also based on witnessing the festival in the 1990s, but who add that the procession first visits the Khemeswar temple at the former boundary of Jagdalpur, before returning to the palace and the Danteswari temple via a stop at the Maoli shrine.

Release of the Stand-In and Reception of Danteswari from Dantewara

On the next day, the period of the Nine Nights (Navaratra) ends. The two most important events of this ninth day are the release of the stand-in and the reception of Danteswari, who arrives from Dantewara. In the evening, the king proceeds to the Maoli shrine to worship. Around the same time, his stand-in ends his period of austerities and he is given the sword of Danteswari and the sprouts of wheat that have germinated in front of him over the last nine days. After the sacrifice of a goat in the pit where he had been sitting (Mallebrein 1996, 503), the *jogi* also goes to the Maoli temple – screened from the view of others, especially the king – where he hands the sprouts and the sword to the priest of the temple and is then released.

Later in the evening, at the entrance to the town, which is about a kilometer from the palace, the great reception takes place. This is a meeting of people as much as a meeting of deities. The king proceeds to this spot barefoot, accompanied by members of his court, the goddess Danteswari from the Jagdalpur temple and her priest, who carries her umbrella and sword, as well as the

---

10 Already Marten (1912, 83) mentions the use of pumpkins as replacement for animal sacrifices and adds that they actually represent human victims. See Mallebrein (2007) on recent discussions about and examples of substituting pumpkins for animal victims.

numerous village delegations all carrying their deities. Danteswari from Dantewara also does not come on her own. Represented by her silver umbrella and her *doli* (swing) – her seat from her permanent temple in Dantewara – she is carried in a palanquin. Other villagers, among them Muria and Maria Gond, accompany her with their deities. The meeting is described as an effervescent moment, full of music and the singing and shouting of hundreds of people. It is an unruly scene of dance and play, with the police kept busy trying to "control the mob" (Sarkar and Dasgupta 1996, 118). Along with her priest,[11] the king carries the palanquin of Danteswari (from Dantewara) back to the palace, where her *doli* is placed in the Durbar hall and blessed food (*prasad*) from Dantewara is distributed. The Brahmans also decide the time at which the king should resume office on the following day. Later, Danteswari's *doli* is taken to the Maoli temple (Marten 1912, 86). This last element of the performance may provide an indication of the significance of the name of the ritual meeting of the deities, which is called Maoli Padghav,[12] the "reception of/by Maoli." To begin with, it seems unclear why Maoli should be referred to, as the performance basically consists in the meeting of two manifestations of Danteswari in the presence of a host of other village deities, certainly also Danteswaris and Maolis among them. That Danteswari of Dantewara is brought to the Maoli temple at the end of the day may be an indication that it is this local deity who is, above all, receiving the important guest from outside.

Re-Enthronement of the King

The tenth day, which gives the whole festival its name, sees the re-enthronement of the king and a massive procession in the eight-wheeled Great Chariot, the *bara rath*. In the morning, the king first worships Danteswari and then "the idol of Mawali [Moali] called Manikeshwari" (Marten 1912, 86) is brought into the Durbar hall and seated on a throne called *patsinhasan*, the "main lion-seat." Brahmans

---

[11] Sundar (2007, 64) notes that the priests of all temples in Jagdalpur used to be of tribal or low-caste background until recently and have been replaced by Brahmans "within the living memory of people." It can thus be assumed that the priest of Danteswari of Dantewara is or was of tribal background as well. In any case, Danteswari is brought to Jagdalpur on her palanquin along with many other local village deities and accompanied by Maria and Muria (Mallebrein 1996, 497, 503).
[12] The expression is alternatively written Mawli Pargao or Mavli Parhgav, among other variants.

announce the time when the king will resume his function as head of state, which will then be announced by the beating of drums.

In the afternoon, the king is again brought to the Durbar hall in a closed palanquin. Inside the hall he is also screened from view, now once more in his full dress with ornaments, signifying his royal office. He leaves the Durbar hall and ascends the *bara rath*, which also carries the emblems of Danteswari. Only the Dandami Maria have the privilege of pulling the Great Chariot on this occasion, which makes two rounds of its usual rectangular route. This occasion is again marked by a maximum presence of people, in particular from the tribes of the region. While Marten (1912, 86) speaks of a "most animated" scene, Mallebrein (1996, 504) describes a "degree of disorder (. . .) because the Maria, when pulling the chariot, become boisterous and attack everyone coming in their way." In the evening, after the completion of the procession, the king returns to the Durbar hall and is re-enthroned by Brahmans. Female attendants perform *arti*, first over the emblems of Danteswari seated on a separate throne, then over the king, who sits in front of a golden throne. Subsequently, the Durbar hall is opened to the public and the king and his officials receive their subjects.

Abduction of the King by Tribal Subjects

After the re-enthronement of the king, one might suppose that the festival is over. However, a remarkable sequel testifies to the "jungle" aspect of this kingdom and the relevance of the tribal population to the constitution of kingship or, in other words, their position as subaltern sovereigns.

The *diwan* of the kingdom described the proceedings at the beginning of the twentieth century as follows (Marten 1912, 86). In the early morning of the eleventh day, the king was "stolen" by Muria and taken in a palanquin to an encampment outside Jagdalpur, about three kilometers to the east. There he received gifts of wild animals, birds and money from his subjects, notably from representatives of all communities. In the evening, the Great Chariot, which had apparently been taken to the same place, was dragged back to town. This procession had certain peculiar features. The king was dressed in a yellow robe, carried bow and arrows and sat on a swing that was suspended from the roof of the chariot. Huge crowds accompanied the chariot as it was pulled in the direction of the town. Buffaloes were sacrificed in front of the chariot. It is noted that until the end of the nineteenth century these animals were simply thrown in front of the *rath* and crushed to death. Reaching an open space east of the town, the atmosphere – a "babel of sound" (Marten 1912, 86) – was reported to be wild: "Bands of Murias armed with bows and arrows rush about the midst the crowd shrieking out their war cries and every now and then capturing men to help to drag the Rath along" (Marten 1912, 86). After arriving at the Lion Gate of the palace, women again performed *arti*, the king descended from the chariot and then proceeded to the Danteswari temple, where he prostrated himself in front of the goddess. He then returned to the palace, sat on his throne and worshipped his "emblems of war" (Marten 1912, 86).

Descriptions from the 1990s (Mallebrein 1996; Sarkar and Dasgupta 1996; see also Naidu 1975, 84) highlight that the *bara rath* is stolen and taken to a grove outside Jagdalpur, a place called Kumbarkot. There, the king participates in *nayakhana*, the ritual eating of the first crops of the new season. Temporary huts are constructed from branches of the *bel* tree and the two Danteswaris (from Dantewara and from Jagdalpur) are put inside one of them. The goddesses also share in the consumption of the rice from the new harvest. Crowds of people assemble, along with their deities, many being possessed by them, and during the procession back to Jagdalpur there are numerous sacrifices of goats and pumpkins (substituting buffaloes).

It is clear that the basic structure of this sequence of the Dasara festival has also remained fairly constant throughout the twentieth century and upto the present (see Kriti 2018). The king is forced into the forest, where he has to share the new crops with his tribal subjects. He is thus "tribalized," as Alfred Gell (1997, 442) puts it.

Sacrifice to Kachin Devi and Release of the Weaver Girl

The twelfth day accomplishes another closure, with the king proceeding to the Kachin temple in the morning to sacrifice to the goddess whose permission to perform the festival he had sought on the first day. The weaver girl who has embodied the goddess is also present and is released from her duties after the performance of the ritual. The second event of that day is the Manjhi Durbar, the reception of village headmen by the king in the Durbar hall. During this reception, they can raise and discuss problems of their villages, receive honors from the king and bring gifts (natural produce, money) in return.

Farewell to Village Deities and Danteswari from Dantewara

The remaining days of the festival are devoted to the worship and the bidding of farewell to the deities from outside Jagdalpur. All of the village deities that have visited the capital for the festival move in procession to the Ganga Munda tank,[13] which must have been located on the outskirts of Jagdalpur before Independence. This procession, which occurs on the thirteenth or fourteenth day, is also known as Kutumb Yatra, referring to a local kinship group and thus to the ritual for the village deities. Members of the royal family – in earlier times, most likely the king as well – worship the village deities, who then return to their home locations with their delegations. Finally, on the last day of the festival, Danteswari from Dantewara receives the last sacrifices and departs in a palanquin for her home temple.

5.2 Analysis and Discussion

Before I continue with the description of Dasara in the Jeypore kingdom, a few key aspects of the festival performed in Bastar that I consider particularly important should be summarized and discussed. In many ways, my own interpretation corresponds to that put forward by Alfred Gell (1997), who based his analysis on the early descriptions by Marten and Majumdar. However, I would like to stress certain features to which Gell paid little or no attention, namely: (1) the germination of cereals, (2) the role of the goddess Maoli, (3) tribes as sacrificers and, finally, (4) the meaning of the tumultuous collective events over the course of the festival.

The period of the first nine days had at its core the ritual identification of the king with the ascetic. Restrictions of diet and movement apply to both, albeit they are more severe for the ascetic. Their status is reminiscent of the liminal period after a death, as described by Hertz (1960), where the mourner shares the fate of the deceased's body and soul. However, it is even more appropriate to regard this period as preparation for a sacrifice, the human sacrifice of the *jogi*, as a substitute for the king, whom he shall never meet during the period. Consequently, Gell (1997, 440) makes his "bow to Frazer" here ("if only in passing"), pointing to the theme of the death and rebirth of the king, "mirroring the cycle of natural fertility." The re-enthronement of the king on the tenth day of Dasara can indeed be regarded as a rebirth. However, perhaps Gell's bow to Frazer is a little bit too flimsy, as the latter probably would have paid more attention than Gell to those aspects of Dasara – notably, the ritual germination of plants – that connect divine kingship with general growth, fecundity and the forces of the earth (see de Heusch 1997).

---

[13] Majumdar (1939, 166) notes that this farewell ceremony was conducted under a Banyan tree not far from the palace.

Not only is the ascetic linked to the king as his stand-in victim during the first nine days, this period is also synchronized with the growth of cereals. As mentioned, the sword of Danteswari and consecrated water are placed in front of the *jogi*, who is fastened to his "throne," and seeds of wheat are sown, which germinate during this period. These germinating seeds – in relation to the sacrifice (human or other) to the goddess – are not a minor detail in my view but are fundamental to the cultural logic that informs the narratives and practices with which this book as a whole is concerned – the flow of life through sacrifice. I would argue that the first nine-day period establishes this vital connection between king as sacrificer and victim, the goddess (sword) and the growth of wheat. More so than Gell, Mallebrein (1996, 492) emphasizes this aspect of fertility and points out that Dasara is celebrated at a time after the monsoon, when the first crops have already been harvested. In connection to the harvests, she briefly mentions a celebration in which the goddess is worshipped in the form of a water-filled clay pot and grain seeds are sown and left to germinate for nine days, as in Dasara.[14]

Although the worship of the weaver goddess Kachin Devi encompasses the Dasara rituals as a whole in important ways, Danteswari and Maoli are at the center of the proceedings. In contrast to Danteswari – the tutelary deity of the Kakatiya kings who comes from outside – Maoli is the local deity, especially associated with tribal village cults. While in the general hierarchy of state goddesses Danteswari is superior, Maoli can claim precedence as the original goddess of the locality. In this sense, Danteswari and Maoli may also be seen to mirror the relationship between the king and the tribal population, which entails a similar apparent ambiguity in terms of status, as I have described above with regard to the relationship between king and Bhuyia during the coronation ritual in Keonjhar. While the tribes are subordinate to the king as subjects, as sacrificers they are also connected to the earth and the locality. Maoli's primordial status is recognized in different ways during Dasara. During the days of the chariot procession, the king worships her first and Maoli receives numerous offerings on the eighth night, during which there are massive numbers of sacrifices. Moreover, on the morning of the re-enthronement of the king, the idol of Maoli (Manikeswari) is placed on the main Lion Seat in the Durbar hall, thus the "superior" throne. The king and Danteswari are seated on separate thrones in the course of Dasara.

Two other aspects are particularly important for understanding Maoli's status as the primary local goddess. First, she appears to act as the host of Danteswari from Dantewara. She welcomes the goddess from outside on the ninth day,

---

[14] It is not clear who celebrates and where, presumably these are tribal village rituals.

as the name of this sequence of Dasara indicates – Maoli Padghav, "reception by Maoli"[15] – and the swing of Danteswari is brought to the Maoli shrine at the end of the day, confirming Hacker's (2014) point that spatially the rituals end at the Maoli temple. Second, Maoli is especially connected to the sacrificial process involving king, stand-in and cereals. At the end of the nine-day period in which the king, the ascetic, wheat and Danteswari's sword are correlated, the persons and objects arrive at Maoli's temple. Both *raja* and *jogi* report to Maoli, where the ascetic hands over the wheat sprouts and Danteswari's sword and then departs.[16] The process of sacrificial death and rebirth, which is a precondition for the re-enthronement of the king – and consequently the well-being of land and people – is closely connected to the local goddess. Ultimately, it is through the powers of both goddesses that this renewal is possible, as the king only resumes his office after Danteswari has arrived from Dantewara. The king and subjects are complementary in a similar way. It is not only the king, as sacrificer (and victim), who is essential for the sacrificial regeneration of kingship and his realm, but also his subjects.

As far as the role of the tribal population is concerned, Gell focuses on the sequence of the king's abduction, no doubt a very special and significant part of Dasara in Bastar. By taking the king into their habitat, the forest, and providing him with their food, the tribes – representatives from all communities – stress that he is *their* king.[17] Moreover, Muria, Maria and other communities host the king, much like – if my interpretation is correct – Maoli hosts Danteswari from Dantewara. What Gell overlooks, or in any case does not pay attention to, is the sacrificial role of the tribal population. On the eighth day, tribal people pour into Jagdalpur in great numbers, bringing their village deities with them, who undoubtedly receive sacrifices. Who sacrifices all the buffaloes, goats and catfish over the course of the night of sacrifice that follows? Who sacrifices buffaloes or, earlier, threw them in front of the Great Chariot when the king returns from the forest after his abduction? The otherwise detailed descriptions that we have do not specify this, but it is most likely that this was not

---

15 *Padghav* derives from Sanskrit *pratigraha* meaning "reception, receiving." Grammatically, Maoli *padghav* could mean both "reception of Maoli" or "reception by Maoli" (thanks to Arlo Griffiths for pointing this out to me). However, "reception of Maoli" would not make sense, as obviously it is Danteswari who is received.

16 Marten (1912) and Mallebrein (1996) state that king and *jogi* visit the Maoli temple; according to Majumdar (1939) the *jogi* worships in the Danteswari temple and is then set free. Sarkar and Dasgupta (1996) do not mention at all that the *jogi* visits a temple at this stage.

17 This is reminiscent to the myth (M1) discussed in Chapter 3, in which the Gadaba lament that the king no longer eats from their hands.

done by the Brahman priests, who were introduced to the court from Odisha from the fifteenth century onwards (Hacker 2014, 195, fn. 197). Also, as Sundar (2007, 64) notes, the priest of the Danteswari temple used to be a Dhurwa, as other temples were also looked after by low-caste or tribal people until a few decades ago. In summary, the massive tribal presence in Jagdalpur not only has the political function of keeping the state "flat" and the king close to the tribal subjects, as Gell argues. I would think that as sacrificers the tribes are also indispensable, as are their deities. "'[T]he people' are 'the Raja'" (Gell 1997, 445) not because the tribal population substitutes the king in his role as devotee, as Gell puts it, but because, just like the king, they are pivotal sacrificers during Dasara.

My last point concerns the riotous scenes of collective excitement that are a recurrent feature of Dasara. They occur after the tribal population has poured into the capital on the eighth day of the festival to attend (and probably to perform) the major sacrifices during the subsequent night. All observers have described these scenes of dancing, the playing of music and possession, but they also noted the ferocity of the participants, or the display of fierceness at certain moments in the proceedings, such as in the context of the reception of Danteswari from Dantewara, or during the procession with the Great Chariot after the king has been re-enthroned on the tenth day, and on the way back to the capital, after the king has been captured by the tribal population. It is not difficult to identify those situations as liminal moments: the tribal gathering with their deities after their arrival in Jagdalpur, a meeting on the outskirts of the town when Danteswari is welcomed, the procession after the rebirth of the king and his first appearance in public, and the procession back to the palace, between forest and capital. Observers have described these scenes in different terms, such as "disorder," "animated" or a "babel of sound." They have pointed to the shrieking of "war cries" and people being "captured" by the Muria who were pulling the chariot, and the police having difficulty in trying to "control the mob." It is obvious, I think, that these scenes are not spontaneous but as much a performative part of the festival as the buffalo sacrifices, the *jogi* stand-in or the sprouting wheat. The question is how to make sense of them.

Alfred Gell also noted the moments when there was a mass presence of the tribal population in the capital, "forming a great multitude who were both armed (with axes bows and arrows) and in a very excitable condition" (1997, 436). Elsewhere in the same article, he writes (Gell 1997, 445): "Here was a kingdom (. . .) which every year subjected its capital to a vast influx of excitable, armed tribal people in the grip of politico-religious effervescence motivated by forces well beyond the scope of civilized rationality." While Gell thus seems to suggest that the motivation of tribal participants was, at least in part, religious, he interprets these events in purely political terms. For him, the tribes were showing their "political muscle" (1997, 436) and would "indirectly" make an impression on and intimidate those supposed to rule them (1997, 445). Gell argues therefore that, while not necessarily intended by the tribal actors, this political coercion would, nevertheless, be the outcome of such collective action. Gell is probably right in assuming this effect on the king, his retinue and the poorly developed administration. I would argue, however, that there is another dimension to those unruly collective events. They are part of the ritual process and belong to a set of phenomena that I have described elsewhere as systemic effervescence (Berger 2016a), which assumes the local form of "play" here. Understanding the nature of this "play" is vital to comprehending the indigenous logic that makes these disruptive scenes a fundamental and integral part of Dasara.

Important cues for my argument again come from Alfred Gell who, in another contribution (Gell 1980), is explicitly concerned with Muria religion; however, he does not link his discussion of Dasara to this earlier work. In the latter, Gell argues that religious performances of the Muria center on different forms of distorting one's sense of equilibrium, or "equilibrium play" (Gell 1980, 232), when the sense of balance is intentionally challenged, manipulated or disrupted. This is done through swinging, carrying long bamboo poles that keep the carrier off-balance, or by dancing with the *anga*, a wooden frame representing a clan god, which is carried by a group of men. In the course of the dance, the god seemingly imposes his own will on the men's movements. Possession is another form of equilibrium play, as here the human body alone is the "horse" on which the deity "rides." Significantly, equilibrium play is a technique for both humans and deities. For gods and goddesses, it is a way to engage with the world of humans, to enjoy physical presence in the world and the vertiginous pleasures that come with bodily movement. For the Muria, in turn, it is the most important and most direct way to experience their gods and to have access to them. Through such play, human and divine worlds merge.

The festivals Gell is concerned with are, consequently, called "god playing" (Pen Kasana). They take place at the end of the dry season (May/June) and last for about two weeks. Numerous deities visit the villages and animate the wooden frames of the *anga*, the bamboo poles (*lath*) or the bodies of a ritual medium (*siraha* or *sirha*). The young men who dance with the *anga* are not possessed but are nevertheless "outside themselves," Gell argues, as the deities impose their will on the movement of the frame in a "whirling and plunging dance of the utmost ferocity" (Gell 1980, 225). This testifies to the general implications of equilibrium play that Gell notes. It involves the idea of danger and potential physical harm, as participants transcend the normal modes of bodily movement and endurance, "skill, courage and sang-froid are called for" (Gell 1980, 232). Moreover, in the case of the Muria, this altered condition or dislocation is not merely the state of possessed mediums or individual dancers who happen to carry an *anga*. Gell stresses the "total community participation" and that the "transformation (. . .) affects the community as a whole during the festival time" (Gell 1980, 223). This becomes particularly explicit with regard to dancing and singing, when the many bodies of the participants strive toward "complete unanimity" (Gell 1980, 223).

The reference to singing and dancing indicates the significance of an aspect of such festivals that is not discussed by Gell. Fortunately, we do have an important contribution by Nicolas Prévôt (2014), who devotes his attention to this dimension, namely music. As an ethnomusicologist, Prévôt conducted his fieldwork in Bastar 25 years after Alfred Gell and found very similar ideas and practices in his study of the Dev Bajar, the festivals called "gods-market." These events take place at different times of the year at villages that feature a weekly market. One deity of the location is honored with a sacrifice, with many others invited to join the event as guests. The highpoint is the "play of the gods" (Dev Khel), when the various deities take possession of their ritual media (*sirha*) and demand that their signature tune be played by the musicians. The gods are present in multiple ways, as objects (e.g., instruments, flag poles, *anga*) and human bodies, but particularly also as music. Being both a gift to the deity and the divine sound-form, music pervades the whole area, thus radiating divine *shakti*, as the musicians explained to the ethnographer. The atmosphere is also unruly in sonic terms, as various ensembles play different god tunes at the same time (with various possessions occurring simultaneously), while horns are blown and gongs beaten continuously. This "sound abundance" (Prévôt 2014, 240) is the desired result, as it indexes auspicious divine abundance.

Prévôt's contribution confirms some of Gell's arguments, for example, with regard to the collective nature of the play at hand. While deities "ride" their specific medium, in principle anyone can become possessed and all participants can become players and are affected by the event and the music. In addition, Gell relates the abundant consumption of liquor in the secular and religious life of the Muria, like the inclination to equilibrium play, to the "profound cultural preoccupation with dizziness" (Gell 1980, 239). While hardly anyone can fail to notice the social and religious dimensions of alcohol consumption among tribal communities in Central India, Prévôt outlines a much more specific argument about the correspondence between drunkenness, possession and spirits in the context of the gods-markets.

The play of the gods during the Dev Bajar is often disrupted by drunken men who are, or pretend to be, possessed by spirits; not by specific deities, as are the *sirha* (who are not supposed to drink during the performance), but by unspecified ghosts (*bhut*) or ancestors (*duma*). Accordingly, the drunkards (*matwar*) are considered "trouble makers" or nuisances, and if things go too far they are removed by others, which may cause fights. At the same time, as a kind of "unavowed value" (Moyer 2015), the performances of the drunkards are considered to be an integral part of the proceedings. Whether or not their possession is considered to be genuine by the other participants, the drunkards represent and embody this alternative set of metapersons – not gods, but the dead, and the general category of malicious spirits. As such, drunkards and spirits are a matter of "danger and respect" (Prévôt 2014, 235) as well. Drunkenness means being infused by the "essence of the ancestors" (Prévôt 2014, 244) and is thus an alternative form of possession. Significantly, drunkards and ancestors are identical musically, as the "drunkard tune" and the "ancestor tune" are one and the same. In summary, the drunkards are a disturbing and dangerous, but vital element of the *dev bajar*, during which the gods embodied by *sirha* are in the foreground, while the ambivalent and precarious relationships to the dead are, nevertheless, also acknowledged.

In my view, the tumultuous scenes during Dasara, the Gods Market and the Gods Playing[18] are the same kinds of events, very similar in ritual structure, in the techniques involved, in the values expressed and in the intended aims. In these events that are prescribed by the ritual structure, exceptional emotional states are generated, which are "trans-sentient," to use Piers Vitebsky's term (Vitebsky 1993, 255). The "playing" is an example of systemic collective effervescence (Berger 2016a), and I want to highlight two of its general features here – abundance and dislocation.

Everything seems to be present in plentitude during such events. The "sound abundance" mentioned by Prévôt – or the "babel of sound," as an early observer of Dasara described it – is accompanied and complemented by a profusion of objects, of human bodies dancing and being possessed, of animal bodies being sacrificed, of liquor being consumed and, not least, of deities and other metapersons. Abundance seems to be the dominant aesthetic form and the desired outcome at the same time. The techniques and manifestations of dislocation are also in abundance. In a multitude of ways, individual actors strive to transcend themselves, to transgress the borders between human and divine, to let go, to lose control. It is through compound abundance of visual, sonic, psychic and somatic sensations that these different forms of effervescent dislocation become possible in the first place. In turn, they mutually enhance

---

[18] I have not discussed here the Mandai, the spring festival celebrated in Bastar villages that corresponds to the autumnal Dasara. It also features a "play of the gods" and has been described by Hacker (2014).

each other: dancing and singing in unison; moving in and out of possession and trances; sacrificing animals; or watching them being sacrificed or crushed under the wheels of the king's chariot.

Ferocity is an important element in these effervescent practices, as part of the *anga* dances, but also in the display of strength or actual fighting. Fierceness and recklessness are an essential part of the play; it is a demonstration of power. However, this is not the 'political muscle" Gell referred to in his analysis of Dasara, but the manifestation and dissemination of power enabled by the divine presence; a general diffusion of *shakti* through play. It is a celebration of life by offering life in sacrifices, but also through not fearing harm or death in ferocious play. Dasara in Bastar is not unique in this regard, as the discussion of the Dev Bajar and Pen Karsana shows. Subaltern effervescence – including abundance and ferocity enabling the different forms of dislocation – is also crucial to Dasara in Jeypore, to which I will now turn, as it is to those tribal festivals that I will discuss in later chapters.

5.3 Dasara in the Nandapur/Jeypore Kingdom

Dasara in Jeypore

Dasara has been the main royal ritual in the kingdom since the fifteenth century; thus, since the time when the festival was first documented in South India (Stein 1983) and when Danteswari was established as the tutelary deity of the Jagdalpur kings. It is also about the time that the image of Kanaka Durga – the "golden" Durga – is said to have been stolen from the Gajapati ruler Purushottama by the Nandapur king. According to the royal Jeypore chronicles, Purushottama returned from a successful military campaign in the south and was traversing the Jeypore hills when the then ruler of Nandapur (Vijaya Chandra) ambushed the troops of the Gajapati and took the image from them to make it the main goddess of the Nandapur kingdom and the center of the Dasara celebrations. The goddess – supposed to have received human sacrifices during Dasara until the middle of the nineteenth century – stayed in Nandapur long after the capital had shifted to other locations. While the capital had already shifted to Jeypore (to the Old Fort) a century before, the goddess was only later moved to a temple in the new palace compound in Jeypore, built after the Old Fort had been destroyed by the British in 1775 (Schnepel 2002, 159f, 265, 267f). By the end of the last millennium, the Dasara festival had lost its significance and participation was low (Schnepel 2002, 276, fn. 31). More recently, however, there have been attempts to revive Dasara again (Rath 2014). Tina Otten (2009, 46) mentions that delegations from 60 villages came to Jeypore with their *lathi* gods in 2004.

In comparison to the detailed descriptions of the Dasara proceedings in Bastar, data on Jeypore is meagre. Data is thin on Jeypore itself, and the scattered remarks mostly ignore the involvement of the tribal subjects in the festival. However, we do have a description of a ritual sequel to Dasara – the Juro festival – performed in the vassal kingdom of Bissamcuttack (part of the Jeypore kingdom) and observed around 1940 and 1991, which is highly relevant to an understanding of the tribal participation in the Dasara ceremonies of the region. In the following, I will first describe what is known about Dasara in Jeypore, then move to Nandapur, on which we have some information thanks to the work of Raphaël Rousseleau and, finally, I will describe the Juro festival in Bissamcuttack. This section again closes with a discussion of those aspects I consider particularly pertinent with respect to the preceding description and interpretation of Dasara in Bastar.

Although there is some ambiguity regarding the days of the performances, the accounts generally describe the same sequence of events of the Dasara proceedings. On the first day (New Moon), Kanaka Durga, represented by a sword called Pat Kanda (the Great Sword), is taken to the east gate of the palace in a palanquin and worshipped there. Opposite the sword sits a *jogi* ascetic. He is not supposed to eat or drink until he is released after nine days (Crooke 1915; Sahu 1942, 35). Rousseleau (2008, 84) states that this man is supposed to come from Nandapur, and Fawcett's account (referred to in Crooke 1915, 34), from about 1885, specifies that the man is kept in a cage-like box, "representing the victim for sacrifice."

The connection to human sacrifice becomes more evident when the details of the sacrifice of goats and sheep are taken into account. Fawcett (in Crooke 1915) states that on the ninth day – when the ascetic is released – a black ram is completely covered in a cloth, its head shaved and rubbed with saffron water before being beheaded. After the sacrifice, the ascetic is set free and must depart immediately. In connection to Dasara in Jeypore, Thurston (1909a, 379) also mentions that a ram is washed and clad in a cloth "after the manner of a human being" and adds that it is fastened in a sitting position before being beheaded. Moreover, sacrifices of goats and sheep continue for several days, at least during the first seven days of Dasara, and those victims are decorated with flowers, which – like the ascetic – should come from Nandapur and are called "*meriah pushpa*" (Francis 1907, 263); thus, flowers (*phuspa*) representing a human victim (*meriah*).

More sacrifices follow, especially on the day of the "great offerings" (*boro uppano*), when buffaloes are also ritually killed, along with goats and sheep.[19] Tribal delegations probably arrive in Jeypore on that day, carrying flag poles representing their local deities (Sahu 1942, 25). Dressed in white and sitting on his white throne, the king holds an internal Durbar for people from the court, also receiving gifts (*bhet*). After the king, the queen does likewise. This is followed by the day of the "small offerings" (*sano uppano*),[20] when the king sits on his scarlet throne and receives dignitaries from his kingdom, such as *inamdars*, *mutadars* and vassal *rajas*, who pay their respects and receive a turban from the king in return (Francis 1907, 263; Rousseleau 2008, 85). Most likely, it was on this day that Dasara *beti* was also offered to the *raja* by the tribal representatives.

The last day features the great procession from the palace along the main street of Jeypore to the Dasara ground to the north. Sahu's description only focuses on the last day of the festival occurring in 1942.[21] From "all parts of Jeypore," he writes, "people have thronged in their thousands" (Sahu 1942, 33). "They have come with their banners, their drums and flutes and various other musical instruments. Hundreds of ceremonies have gone on for the past seven days and ceremony after ceremony is going on" (Sahu 1942, 33). Unfortunately, he does not describe a single one of the many rituals, but we may assume that they also involve worship of the tribal deities that have been brought into the town and include tribal participation in the sacrifices.

Amidst crowds of tribal people, "hundreds of flag-bearers" (Sahu 1942, 34) and the king seated on an elephant, Kanaka Durga, in her manifestation of the Great Sword, is taken to the Dasara ground to be worshipped by the king. Sahu notes that "hundreds of swordsmen carrying unsheathed swords" participated in the procession, which also figured "sword play" and "mock fights" (Sahu 1942, 34). Despite the fighting spirit thus demonstrated and police being present only in low numbers,[22] Sahu stresses the peaceful nature of the festival, "to the credit of the people" (1942, 34).

---

19 On 14th day according to Francis (1907, 263), on 7th day according to Rousseleau (2008, 85).
20 On the 16th day according to Francis (1907, 263), on the 8th day according to Rousseleau (2008, 85).
21 Sahu does not specify to which year his description related. He does mention, however, that the last day of Dasara fell on October 18 and that the festival went on for seven days before that last day (Sahu 1942, 33). Given that Dasara always commences after the New Moon of *aswino* (*dosra*) that would make it likely that the year he observed the festival was 1942. In 1942 the New Moon was on October 10.
22 Sahu speaks of 32 policemen (1942, 34).

Once the procession has reached the Dasara ground, music and dancing continue: "The whole night the aboriginals are going on with their rhythmic dances," Sahu observes and wonders, "what frenzy has caught them" (1942, 35). Around midnight, he managed to get away in a car, remarking that the *brinjal* ceremony had not yet started. In this part of the festival, a *brinjal* is fastened to a long bamboo pole and an arrow shooting contest takes place. At some point, the dancing ceases (based on my experience from village festivals, probably not long before dawn), the goddess returns to her temple and the festival comes to an end (Francis 1907, 263; Rousseleau 2008, 80f; Sahu 1942, 34f).

The great procession of the last day can only commence, however, after the delegation from the original capital of Nandapur has arrived carrying their banners on long bamboo poles. Moreover, the eldest of the Benek (Bening) Porja community is received by the king and brings him the first paddy of the whole kingdom from the fields adjacent to the Kotni Mala rocks and the Queens Waterfall (Rani Duduma). The rice is first offered to Kanaka Durga, then consumed by members of the royal family as part of the Nuakhia festival; the first ceremonial consumption of crops (Rath 2014, 16;[23] Rousseleau 2008, 93, 198f).

Dasara in Nandapur

A "great sword" (Pat Kanda) is also at the center of worship in Nandapur. According to Rousseleau (2008, 188), this sword is not associated with Durga, but with the fierce form of Shiva called Bhairava, the "fear-inducing one." On the basis of my own research among the Gutob Gadaba, I can add that from the village perspective the gender of the deity is not always that clear, nor necessarily considered relevant.[24] Each Gadaba village maintains a shrine for Pat Kanda (also called Gumang), which is normally considered the "senior house" and contrasted with the *hundi* shrine of the village goddess in the village center. In addition to a couple of other standard village deities, only a few villages feature

---

[23] With regard to the information concerning the consumption of the new rice from the Kotni Mala Hills as Nuakhia by the royal family, Rath refers to the following source that was not at my disposal: Vyasakabi Fakir Mohan (n.d.) *Cultural Heritage of Odisha, Koraput District*. Bhubaneswar: Smruti Sansad.
[24] Compare Thusu and Jha (1972, 103) who write with regard to the Ollar Gadaba: "it is not possible for our informants to mention specifically the sex of these deities (. . .)," referring to the village deities called Jhankir, Ganga and Nandi.

shrines for Boiro or Boirobi, names that are mostly used interchangeably. Every other year, a buffalo is sacrificed to Boiro in these places, normally in November (*diali*),[25] although in one case in April (*chait*).[26] In all of the cases I documented, however, the instrument of sacrifice – either an axe (*tangi*) or a machete (*gagra*) – was referred to and worshipped as Durga, while the shrine was referred to as Boiro(bi) (Berger 2015, 120f, 426f). It is also noteworthy that Boiro(bi) is the only deity among the Gadaba that receives buffalo sacrifices in the context of the annual cycle (Berger 2015, 112f). Otherwise buffaloes are only ritually killed in the final death ritual, to which I will turn in Chapter 9.

The Dasara festival in Nandapur commences on the first day with the priest of the "Old Bhairava" (Budha Bhairava) – a member of the Yogi caste – requesting a flag on a long bamboo pole and a goat for sacrifice from the Revenue Inspector who assumes the royal function and is the patron of the festival.[27] The priest takes the sword called Pat Kanda, which represents Bhairava, from his own house and brings it to the Bhairavi Temple, which lies at the foot of the Kotni Mala Hill, southeast of the small town. There the goat is sacrificed and some parts of the victim are attached to the top of the bamboo pole. Rousseleau states that until 1955 a member of another Yogi family sat in front of the sword during the festival (2008, 189).

After this first goat sacrifice, a procession visits several other shrines before finally arriving at the temple of Bhandarghariani, a goddess of the royal treasury,[28] in a building that now houses the Block Office.[29] A goat sacrifice also takes place here and the flag pole provided by the Revenue Inspector remains there until the end of the festival. An important aspect of this first day is the arrival of a delegation of Kond and Dora tribesmen from the village of Kondra. They receive three flagpoles from the Revenue Inspector and return to their village, reappearing on the eighth day.

---

25 In the villages of Gorihanjar, Alangpada, Raipada, Guneipada and Deulpada. In the last two villages the Boiro shrine is considered as the "senior house." Gadaba of Gorihanjar told me that the god came from Nandapur and also referred to him as *luar pakna* (iron stone) or *mongni* (meaning unclear) *pakna*.
26 In the village of Auripada.
27 It is not entirely clear from Rousseleau's account, to which time his description of the Dasara festival refers. It seems though that he has observed the festival during his ethnographic fieldwork in the early 2000s.
28 *Bandagor* means store-room.
29 Blocks are administrative units into which districts (such as the Koraput District) subdivide; the Block Office thus is the administrative headquarter of a block.

After nine different deities[30] have received offerings of coconuts on the fifth day, the eighth day sees the reappearance of the tribal delegation. The villagers of Kondra return to Nandapur with their banners and a goat for sacrifice, beating drums and accompanied by people from other tribal villages. The inhabitants of Nandapur also join in when the nine deities again receive sacrifices, this time piglets and fowl. At the Bhairava temple, two goats are sacrificed for the "Old Bhairava," along with other offerings. One goat is given by the people of Kondra, the other by the Revenue Inspector.

The names of the two men who perform as sacrificers on these occasions are instructive, as are the details of the sacrifice. The first is a Rona called *cheli kata dora* or *merya dora*, the second a Ghasi who is called *mundchina*. Dora is a title common among the Rona (Berger 2002, 65), the first name translating as the "Dora who sacrifices the goat." His other name clearly refers to the victim (*meria*) of human sacrifices. Rousseleau (2008, 190f) translates the name of the Ghasi sacrificer as "manipulator of the head." *China*, however, also means "scar" and more generally "sign" and may thus also be interpreted as that which stands for the head (*mund*), thus possibly the animal head being the sign of, or standing for, the human head. Also, the way the two goats are sacrificed clearly refers to the imagery of human sacrifice, as already encountered in the descriptions of the Jeypore Dasara: the animals are clad in white cloths and a barber cuts a tuft of hair from their heads. While the heads of the victims are buried under a stone, the people of Kondra receive the body of their goat for consumption, while the Ghasi takes the other one.

The procession then continues to the Thakurani temple, which is the main temple of the town located in the center of Nandapur. A goat sponsored by the people of Nandapur is sacrificed there before moving to the next stop at the throne hillock, the remains of the former palace and the throne with "32 steps." The procession ends back at the former treasury, the Block Office, and a sacrifice for Bhandarghariani concludes the day. On the ninth day, the Kondra delegation earlier proceeded to Jeypore, carrying their banners with parts of the sacrificial victims tied to the top to initiate the Dasara procession there (Rousseleau 2008, 191).

On the tenth day, the Pat Kanda sword is taken back to the house of the priest, with the deity receiving the sacrificial offering of a goat – sponsored by the Revenue Inspector – on the threshold of the house. In the evening, the animal market of Nandapur is the main location. The Pat Kanda sword is brought

---

[30] Rousseleau mentions the following nine deities: Duar Suni, Garbha Nishani, Budha Bhairava, Vetal Bhairava, Matta Bhairava, Vana Durga, Bhandaghariani, Thakurani and the goddess of the throne (no original name mentioned) (Rousseleau 2008, 190).

to the market in a palanquin and the bamboo pole that was left at the Block Office is also taken there. Another goat is sacrificed to the deity, again financed by the Revenue Inspector, and then the sword is taken back to the priest's house. After the end of the Dasara festival proper, the ceremonial consumption of the first grain (Nuakhai) takes places. As described above, the first paddy of the region, from the Kotni Mala Hill, had in previous times been brought to the king of Jeypore for consumption (Rousseleau 2008, 191f).

Juro Festival in Bissamcuttack

As mentioned in the previous chapter, the That Raja of Bissamcuttack, located in the northeast of the Jeypore kingdom, was a vassal of the Jeypore ruler and, as Schnepel (2002, 285f) points out, was ambitious as well. He did not always show his face as he was supposed to during the Jeypore Dasara, thereby paying respect to the Maharaja, but preferred to celebrate his own Dasara instead, supposedly including human sacrifices until 1854 (Sahu 1942, 178; since then buffaloes). Here, I am not interested in the political dimensions or the "horizontal" relationships between the rulers but in the tribal participation in the Dasara festival of Bissamcuttack, that is, in the role of the Dongria Kond in particular. While the descriptions of the Jeypore festival tell us very little about this aspect, the case of the festival of the That Raja may give an indication of the nature of the tribal involvement in Jeypore as well. In addition to Schnepel (2002) and Nayak (1989), my main source for the description of the Juro festival is Lakshmi Narayan Sahu, who joined the Servants of India Society in 1917 and lived at the "Jeypore Estate" for three years (around 1940), apparently as a protégé of the king (Sahu 1942, 2). While Sahu's description of the Jeypore Dasara festival is short and impressionistic, his documentation of the Juro festival is surprisingly detailed (Sahu 1942, 178–83). The author leaves no doubt that he considered the practices to be "inhuman and barbarous" (Sahu 1942, 182) and "hoped that the hill tribes will be prevailed upon to give up all their tribal festivals which make a shameless exhibition of cruelty" (Sahu 1942, 183).

Sahu translates *juro* as "snatching," which refers to the practice of taking flesh from the sacrificial victim while it is still alive and standing.

> It is their belief that it is more meritorious to snatch away flesh from the buffalo while it is standing and alive than to snatch away flesh from the dead buffalo after it falls on the ground and therefore every one [sic] in his excitement would be very eager to avail himself of the first opportunity to snatch away flesh from the victim (. . .). (Sahu 1942, 180)

Sahu refers to the Vizagapatam District Gazetteer, who had observed that the tribal priest used to strike the first blow, after which the crowd took over:

> the *pujari* used to give the animal the first blow and then followed the 'Juro') [sic] when the bloodthirsty excited Dongoria Kandhas, in their frenzy, rush in with their tangis [axes], axes, knives and *palaka lathis* [sticks] and attack the poor animal from all sides and snatch away portions of flesh from the living animal. Within a few minutes the animal falls to the ground and is hacked to pieces. (. . .). (Sahu 1942, 180f)

While Hardenberg does not mention the term *juro*, he describes exactly the same proceedings in the context of the buffalo sacrifices in the Niamgiri Hills at the beginning of this century (Hardenberg 2018a, 567f). In most cases Hardenberg observed, the proper time for the sacrifice, determined by the ritual specialists, was never reached, and the animal was killed before the scheduled hour in an unexpected move by a group of intoxicated men or an individual. The person who strikes the first blow – in Hardenberg's description, the symbolic killing is also supposed to be done by a ritual specialist – is a *bira*, a "hero" (Hardenberg 2018a, 567). However, he lives dangerously and may require protection from the police against retaliations by the hosts and the "protectors" (*mudrenga*) of their buffalo.

In the context of the Dasara festival reported by Sahu, the "Jeypore Samasthanam" (Sahu 1942, 179) sponsored several buffaloes to be sacrificed by Dongria Kond to different deities in Nandapur. Sahu might refer to the Jeypore king here or perhaps one of his representatives. Possibly, Jeypore Samasthanam signifies the That Raja, the representative of the Jeypore king in Bissamcuttack. This would be in line with Schnepel's description, who states that the buffaloes are sponsored by the That Raja (2002, 289). Notably, the Dongria sacrificers (*jani*) received rent-free land from the Jeypore Samasthanam for their services.

According to Sahu, the first and most important deity was Niamraja ("held in highest esteem," Sahu 1942, 180), followed by Thakurani, Durga and Markama, the tutelary deity of the That Raja (thus, comparable with Kanaka Durga in Jeypore, Budha Bhairava in Nandapur and Danteswari in Jagdalpur).[31] Sahu provides a list of villages that were responsible for the sacrifice to the respective deities. The assigning of buffaloes to villages was based on the territorial clans (*muta*). In the Niamgiri Hills, the buffalo sacrifices were (and are) also performed successively by villages belonging to the same territorial clan. Nayak (1989, 180) specifies that the priests (*jani*) of the following five territorial clans were responsible for the sacrifices during Dasara: *nisika, wadeka, sikoka, kadraka* and *pusika*.

---

31 Nayak's (1989, 180) account slightly differs, as he refers to the following five deities receiving the sacrifice: Niamraja, Markama, Durga, Thakurani and Bhairab.

As Sahu describes it, the Dongria Kond (and the Dombo *barik*) appeared in great numbers in the streets of Bissamcuttack, arriving from villages near and far (between 8 and 24 km distance from Bissamcuttack), counting some 500 in total. This is a considerable number, keeping in mind that Bissamcuttack at the time was "a village with 1,961 inhabitants" (Bell 1945, 159). Before the Dongria started out from their villages, the men drank the locally produced liquor from the *mohua* flower as well as locally produced millet-based "beer" (called *landa* and *pendom*). In addition, on their way to the town, they stopped at liquor shops (*arracks*), so they were quite drunk when they arrived in Bissamcuttack at around 9 pm in the evening on the ninth day of the Dasara festival, where they "pass the whole night, singing and dancing in the streets in different batches" (Sahu 1942, 179). The first ritual to be performed was the Raja Bali, the King's Sacrifice, around midnight. As it was a "regular" sacrifice for Durga, no *juro* was involved and the victim was decapitated. With this sacrifice, the worship of the ninth day ended.

Only on the tenth day, Dasara proper (*vijaya dasami*), did the Juro festival commence. In the early morning, Dongria from the nearest villages arrived and all Dongria groups then fetched water from a tank, in the form of a procession accompanied by music. The first animal for Niamraja was then brought by the *daffadar* (a military rank) and the Dombo *barik* and tied up with ropes. While the Dongria *jani* invoked the deity, the Dongria men danced wildly around the buffalo, with the noisy and tumultuous atmosphere often making the animal nervous and difficult to control. After the *jani* ended his invocation, the victim was killed in the *juro* fashion described above, and then, successively, the three buffaloes for the other deities.

Around noon, the Juro performances were over and sacrificial commensality followed. The Dongria men met their women and other relatives on the outskirts of the town, and while the meat was prepared and cooked more drinking and dancing occurred, before the people sat down to their meals. Later that day, the Dombo *barik* and the Dongria headmen (*samanthas*) visited the local "Samasthanam Office" and were received by the *amin* who was given *beti* from the Dongria and caste Hindus. This also included small amounts of money (*beti salami*, "gifts of greeting"), which was collected by the Dongria and handed over to the *amin*. In return, the Dongria village headmen received red cloth. This transaction ended the Juro festival.

The data presented by Schnepel, based on his observation of Dasara in Bissamcuttack in 1991 and an interview with the priest of the Markama temple, confirms this general pattern of the proceedings. However, he adds a few details and the days differ in comparison with Sahu's account 50 years earlier. Schnepel writes that during the seventh night of Dasara, three swords representing the deities Niamraja, Markama and Bhairava were specifically worshipped and that the Dongria Kond had arrived in the town on the eighth day. The largest group among them carried a white umbrella (*chattra*) that they had taken from the temple of Niamraja in the Niamgiri Hills. In Schnepel's account, the buffalo for Niamraja is also the first to be killed in the *juro* way. However, before the respective group hacked the victim to pieces, the Paik priest of the Niamraja temple in Bissamcuttack touched the animal with the sword representing Niamraja. Then the Juro sacrifice to Markama, Durga and Thakurani followed. Finally, a buffalo was killed for Bhairava by the lowland or Desia Kond, not in the *juro* manner, but by beheading the victim. On the ninth day, the Dongria Kond went to the palace to present *beti* to the That Raja, the headmen receiving red cloth in return (Schnepel 2002, 289f).

Schnepel does not mention the other dimension of ritual ferocity – in addition to the *juro* manner in which the animals are killed – namely, the fighting among the Dongria Kond themselves, which occurred before, during and after the festival on the way back to their villages, according to the description by Sahu (such ritualized competitive violence was also observed by Hardenberg (2018a) sixty years later with regard to the buffalo sacrifices in the Niamgiri Hills). He reports that smoldering village conflicts generally flare up during the festival and that fighting, murder and "general rioting" (Sahu 1942, 182) were common. As this was a regular feature, police arrangements[32] were made during Dasara to prevent that from happening, not always with success. In one case, although the police protected the buffalo that was sacrificed to Durga in the *juro* way, other Dongria villagers broke through the police cordon and tried to snatch flesh from the buffalo, which resulted in "bleeding injuries" (Sahu 1942, 182). Nayak, whose monograph focuses on collective violence between Dongria groups, also describes (based on police reports) how violence erupted between two groups during Dasara in 1966 because of a controversy over bridewealth payments. Dancing on the streets of Bissamcuttack – intoxicated and armed – the two groups concerned first abused each other verbally, then physical violence broke out and one Dongria "was hacked into three pieces just in front of the police station" (Nayak 1989, 77). Fearing police action, the Dongria then made a quick departure.

In this particular case of the Juro festival in Bissamcuttack, and among the Dongria Kond generally, sacrificial ferocity and social violence go together, an

---

[32] This is similar to the Go'ter of the Gadaba (see Chapter 9). Also in this context police is generally present to prevent violence between participants (here not between local groups but individuals).

aspect that can also be observed in the Go'ter ritual of the Gadaba (see Chapter 9). Apparently without being aware of Sahu's description, Nayak also mentions the *juro* practice among the Dongria Kond during Dasara. He comments that "presently" – Nayak started his fieldwork in 1975 – the Dongria dance and sing during Dasara in Bissamcuttack "as if [it] was their own festival" (Nayak 1989, 184), and he adds:

> They are not to be ruled but they themselves are the rulers incognito being the descendants of the legendary king the Niamraje. As such, they do not believe in any other kingship and the zamindar kings of the plains were treated at par with their status. (. . .) The Oriya term *paraja*, meaning "subjects", often attributed to them is a misnomer since they accept the attribution only with indignation. The Dongria were presenting the king with gifts and momentoes in recognition of their greater friendship with him, who in lieu of it gave one new cloth as headgear to each of the leaders representing the clans. (Nayak 1989, 184)

In other words, the Dongria were asserting their pivotal role as sacrificers and at the same time were declaring and demonstrating that they "are not to be ruled," and thus, their political independence. All of this was occurring in the context of a festival that supposedly celebrates and brings about the renewal of kingship. Thus, this also seems to be a case of "exalting the king and obstructing the state," as Alfred Gell (1997) observed in Bastar; except that the Dongria do not seem to have exalted the king very much.

5.4 Analysis and Discussion

A comparison of the Dasara festivals of the kingdoms of Bastar and Jeypore – the latter including the former capital of Nandapur and the vassal state of Bissamcuttack – reveals a close similarity between the rituals in the two jungle kingdoms and a resemblance of them both with the general pan-Indian features of Dasara I highlighted in the introduction to this chapter. Based in particular on the work of Sarkar and Stein, I stressed the four elements of the king, the goddess, sacrifice and community. All of these elements are found in the Dasara proceedings of Bastar and Jeypore; however, most, perhaps all of them, take a particular form.

Among the conspicuous articulations of Dasara in the jungle kingdoms are the identification of the king with his ascetic stand-in and the imagery (perhaps former practice) of human sacrifice with regard to the latter.[33] The ritual performances in

---

[33] The identification of king and ascetic stand-in is found in three cases (Jagdalpur, Jeypore and Nandapur); only the material of Bissamcuttack does not mention it. The data on all four

Bastar and Jeypore are explicit on the point that it is the ascetic substitute of the king who is (symbolically) sacrificed at the end of the nine-day period, which starts with the king's abdication and ends before his re-enthronement on the tenth day. The severe austerities and restrictions on consumption and movement of the victim-to-be indicate that the person sitting in the pit in front of the goddess (sword) and the sprouting seeds (in the Bastar case) is already quasi-dead. The germination of the seeds in front of the ascetic makes the life-enhancing function of the human sacrifice particularly palpable.

The Dasara celebrations of Bastar and Jeypore are not only special with regard to the sacrificial imagery of the ritual killing of humans and of the royal stand-in, in particular. The other key dimension to be noted is the role of the tribal people as sacrificers. Most of those who reported on the events remarked on the massive tribal presence and the number of local deities the tribal visitors brought to the capital, but they rarely touched on the details of who sacrificed all the animals. Yet, there can be little doubt that most of the animal sacrifices would have been conducted by ritual specialists (the *sisa, pujari, jani, palas* etc.) of the various tribal communities, from among whom, until recently at least, the priests of the temples were also recruited. The mention of a Pengo *jani* without whose sacrifices Dasara and other festivals in Jeypore could not take place may be a case in point. Thusu's Pengo interlocutors even claimed that the "ritual offerings" of their *jani* came first on such occasions (Thusu 1977, 14)

With the example of Bissamcuttack we do have an explicit and relatively detailed account of the crucial sacrificial role of the Dongria, despite learning little about the other aspects of Dasara in this vassal kingdom. The role of the Dongria during Dasara highlights, on the one hand, the contextual superiority of the tribal deity, as Niamraja is brought down from the Dongria hills and is the first to receive a sacrifice. The hierarchical relationship between Markama, the tutelary goddess of the That Raja in Bissamcuttack, and Niamraja is thus reminiscent of the relationship between Danteswari and Maoli in Bastar, in the sense that the local (tribal) goddess receives recognition and is accorded superior status at certain moments of the festival, although not generally. On the other hand, the pivotal role of the Dongria as sacrificers is made explicit. They not only sacrifice to their own deity but also to Markama, Durga and Thakurani. Moreover, they perform the sacrifices in the iconic *juro* manner that is particularly associated with the Dongria. The sacrificial ferocity seems to be an important factor, although it

---

cases makes references to human sacrifice, either through ritual practice, terminology of sacrificial victims or through statements that suggest that humans used to be sacrificed in the past.

is abhorred by the reformer Sahu. It is *vital* in the strict sense of the term, that is, life-enhancing.

The communal aspect of Dasara mentioned in the introduction is also shaped idiosyncratically in Bastar and Jeypore. The sacrificial function of the tribes and their mass presence in the capital already entails a communal dimension, of course. Beyond that, I would like to stress, first, the particular commensal relationship that is expressed and re-constituted between king and his tribal subjects. Abducting the king, taking him into the forest and thus "tribalizing" him, is a very special way of forging that relationship, and perhaps unique to Bastar. However, the dimension of commensality between *raja* and *porja* and the consumption of "first crops" (Nuakhai) that was also part of the king's abduction to the forest – especially as reported in the descriptions of Dasara in Bastar from the 1990s – is a feature that is also found in Jeypore and Nandapur. In all cases, the tribal population provides the king with food, thus emphasizing their equal status, their commonality and their brotherhood. The reference myth (M1) with which I started my analysis of the mythical expressions of the king/tribe relationship (Chapter 3) ended with a deterioration in the commensal bond between the elder and younger brother, altered by the influx of "castes," in contrast to the primordial situation: "In those days there were no Ronas, Malis, Gaurs, Brahmins. But in these days the Raja only takes food from the high castes; he will no more eat from the hands of Gadabas." During Dasara, however, the rituals stress that this commensal relationship remains unbroken.

The second communal aspect concerns the effervescent assemblies that are so conspicuous in the context of Bastar, where Dasara is only one occasion when the more frequent and generalized play of the gods occurs, in which the tribal groups of that region engage. This concerns a type of collective action that involves various dimensions of abundance and practices of dislocation, including dance, song, intoxication, possession and sacrifice. Ferocity, recklessness and a readiness for violence are constitutive of these practices and, as I have argued, are an expression of a particular kind of divinely inspired power – of *shakti*. This form of play is not confined to Bastar but, in quite similar forms, is also a crucial element in the festivals of the Jeypore kingdom, Dasara included. Again, the data from Jeypore and Nandapur is meagre in this regard and we can only make an informed guess that the processions that Sahu observed, which involved "sword play" and "mock fights," were events of a similar nature.

The involvement of the Dongria Kond and their important role in the Dasara proceedings of Bissamcuttack are a clearer case in point. Although, as far as we know, the Dongria do not conceptualize their practices as "play," I would argue that their Juro sacrifices and the regular violence among them are similar kinds of action. The buffalo sacrifices, both in the hills and the town, are accompanied by possession and intoxication, dance and music, the display of ferocity and actual violence, and the ritual killing of animals and fights between men, sometimes including homicide. The sacrificial ferocity is vital and generative; it is crucial for the fertility of the earth and a demonstration of the sacrificial power and sovereignty of the Dongria. Offering life and not fearing injuries or death constitutes an important aspect of the local male habitus, and the social violence between individual men or groups of them is a related practice. Fighting, even killing men in outbursts of violence is another way to manifest male virility, not only in a sexual sense but in a general sense of being generative. The fighting is also about the management of life and is productive of social relationships that are alternative forms of interaction alongside intermarriage and collective ritual events such as the buffalo sacrifice. The involvement of the Dongria in the Dasara festival, both the sacrifices and the social violence (the latter being probably as ambivalently valued as the drunkards in the "gods-market" described by Prévôt (2014) mentioned above), are thus forms of play that contribute to the regenerating capacity of the festival as a whole and manifest the *shakti* of the tribal participants and their claim to be subaltern sovereigns – sovereigns of life and death.

The Go'ter ritual of the Gadaba and the Ganga festival of the Joria, linked to Dasara in the proverb, also entail this kind of play where collective effervescence, abundance and dislocation, violence and ferocity, possession and music, all combined, constitute such generalized regenerative events. In the case of the Joria, this is also explicitly conceptualized as "play" (*kel*), whereas the Gadaba refer to rituals such as the Go'ter as "work" (*kam*), thereby also expressing the social obligations that come with hosting such events. In both cases, as well as in the Bali Jatra of the Mali, one aspect is very prominent – the cultivation of cereals. This is equally important in the Dasara festival of Bastar, but not to the same degree in the Dasara proceedings in the Jeypore kingdom, at least to the extent we know about it on the basis of the available data. In Bastar, the nine-day period during which the king's duties are suspended and at the end of which his substitute is (symbolically) sacrificed, was synchronized with the growth of wheat. Nothing similar was reported by the sources on Jeypore, Nandapur or Bissamcuttack, although cereals were important in the form of the first crops of rice as a gift and as the basis of commensality between king and tribes. This dimension of cereal cultivation will be of special importance in my analysis of the tribal festivals to which the proverb refers. Moreover, sprouting seeds are also a feature of some of the Dasara festivals as performed in the villages of the region, to which I now turn.

In the next step of my comparison I thus want to change the perspective on Dasara, moving from the towns and royal capitals to the tribal villages. What happens in the tribal villages and is there any consistency discernable in the village celebrations of different communities? I will start with a brief description of the performances I observed in the Gadaba village of Gudapada and the rituals of the Dongria Kond documented by Roland Hardenberg. Subsequently, I will outline the proceedings in a Rona village that previously had a special relationship to the king of Jeypore and, finally, I will look at tribal villages in the vicinity of Jeypore at the foot of the 900 meter plateau.

5.5 Dasara Celebrations in Villages

The indigenous population of the hills does not call the month when Dasara is celebrated *aswina*, but it is the festival itself that gives this month its name of *dosra*. However, for most Adivasis, this does not mean that Dasara plays a major role in the annual ritual cycle of the villages. As will be seen, the performances that have been observed in various tribal communities over the past decades are short and simple and probably have been so in the past. Writing in the early 1940s, Sahu comments in his overview of "The Annual Cycle of the Hill Tribes:"

> Mandia [finger millet] flowers, and bears seed in this month [*aswina/dosra*]. Then Dasara comes. They have a one day *puja* in this month. In this puja, they eat cucumber and other fruits, sacrifice goats on the roads, make their houses neat and tidy. The village headmen near about Jeypore take Dasara bheti to the palace. The usual bheti is a rupee in return for which they receive clothes. Some villages have been given flags; some are white, some red and these represent the local goddesses of their villages. They all pour into Jeypore from all directions in processional marches. The Naika, Barika and some other prominent people from every village go to Jeypore on this festive occasion. (Sahu 1942, 25)

What especially characterized Dasara from the village perspective was *dosra beti*, the paying of homage and tribute to the king in Jeypore, a theme that also returns repeatedly in the myths I have discussed above and which is still vivid in the memory of the people. Delegations from villages, the village headmen and the *barik* in particular, proceeded to the capital to bring gifts, but they also took their own deities and sacrificed on behalf of the king. For many delegations, this was a major endeavor and took several days, as the groups had to walk many kilometers to reach Jeypore. The people from Badigor, for example, whose buffalo sacrifice I will describe shortly, had to walk more than 60 kilometers to arrive at the king's palace.

The ethnographic accounts on the region also testify to the relative insignificance of Dasara rituals in tribal villages; it was at best a "one day *puja*," as Sahu writes. Some accounts, for example, on the Pengo Porja (Thusu 1977) or the Ollar Gadaba (Thusu and Jha 1972) do not mention Dasara rituals at all. Banerjee (1969, 98, 100) remarks that the Kuvi Kond of the village of Kuttinga, 70 kilometers across the plateau from Jeypore as the crow flies, brought turmeric and pepper to the king before 1952 as part of *dosra beti*, but had abandoned the village rituals at the time of her research in the mid-1960s. As far as the Didayi are concerned, Guha et al. (1970) do not mention Dasara village rituals in their monograph; however, the villagers of Kassamput, on the Machkund River, did tell Markus Ockert (1988) – a student of Georg Pfeffer – that they would sacrifice a cock to Iswar (Shiva) and to the earth goddess at the *hundi* shrine and an egg to Brehuning, who every other year would receive a pig as well. As far as the Bonda are concerned, Elwin reports that the headmen of the twelve villages (the *bara-jangar* group that I mentioned in chapter 3) assembled during Dasara (1950, 149).

Dasara in the Gadaba Village of Gudapada

In 1999, I observed the ritual activities in and around the Gadaba village of Gudapada on Dasara proper, that is, the tenth day of the lunar month of *dosra* (see Berger 2015, 418). In the annual village cycle, this ritual lies at the beginning of the harvest activities. As soon as the rains cease, the dry rice is harvested and it is in this period that the *dosra* rituals occur. In 1999, these rituals were performed on October 19 and about a week later the village *pujari* performed the Mandara, the ritual measuring of rice and millet that initiates the harvest activities and also indexes the agricultural year (Berger 2015, 420f). A year before, the *pujari* had sealed crop seeds inside his mud veranda and these were now taken out and inspected. If unharmed, it is an auspicious sign for the coming year. New seeds then replace the old and are sealed up for the coming year.

In the generally unremarkable Dasara rituals in Gudapada, three things stand out: first, nearly all sacrifices take place on the paths leading out of the villages; second, the ubiquitous offerings of catfish (*mangur mach*; caught in the rivers) and cucumber (*kakri*), which are rarely offered in other contexts; and, third, ritual healers undertake sacrifices for their "medicine" and ritual weapons. It may be noted that two aspects correspond to Sahu's description recounted above – the sacrifices on the paths and the consumption of cucumber.

Dasara is clearly not specifically a "Gadaba ritual," and households from all communities performed sacrifices on the paths at various times. As is common, the *pujari* of the village initiated the ritual with a *matam* sacrifice, that is, with an offering for the village as a whole. In the morning, he took his utensils and, on the path leading to the Pat Kanda shrine, outside the village, he first offered a catfish, then a cucumber and finally a coconut. He also offered husked rice from the previous year. Dasara partly has the function of a new crop ritual, as men are not supposed to eat the cucumbers that grow in their gardens before the performance of it. After the pujari completed his work, all households worshipped on the paths closest to their part of the village.

The blacksmith also sacrificed catfish and cucumber in his smithy. In addition, he offered a cock or a pig in alternate years. The Dombo and the Goudo offered catfish and cucumber, and if someone had earlier made an oath (*mansik*), cocks could also be sacrificed. Healers (*gunia, dissari*) of the village are the only people I know of who performed rituals inside their houses. A week before, they collected all kinds of branches, thorns, herbs and plants in the surrounding hills. All these items are collectively called "medicine" (*oso, sindrong*) and are used in healing rituals. The *dissari* called this performance of collecting the medicine *dosra marmardi*, perhaps reminiscent of the "slaying" (*mardini*) of the demon by Durga. Similarly, the healers use these medicines to fight all kinds of evil influences.

During the performance I attended, the healer sacrificed seven catfish, letting their blood drop on his medicine and his iron weapon (*jupan*), thereby enlivening both. I could not understand much of the invocations he mumbled, but a word that was frequently evoked was Nandapur, and Durga was also mentioned. Thus, the connection to the king and the goddess was possibly very much on the mind of the healer during the performance. Wherever I went in the following days – I visited the Gadaba villages of Gorihanjar, Galaguda, Kamarguda and Jalahanjar – the paths around the villages were littered with the signs of the same sacrifices.

Boirobi Puja in the Rona Village of Badigor

A week before the Dasara rituals in Gudapada, I observed the celebrations in the Rona village of Badigor, which lies in the western part of the Gutob Gadaba area close to the Duduma waterfall. At the time, the village had some 60 Rona houses and about half as many of the Dombo community. Of the different status categories common among the Rona (see Berger 2002, 65; Otten 2006), *pujari, dolpoti, dora* and *patro* were found in the village. The *mutadar* of the region used to be recruited from the members of the last group and during the time of my fieldwork a certain Kesebo Patro was still legendary for his many wives and great influence. He was said to have earlier collected tax (*sistu*) in the Bonda area for the king of Jeypore. The event was referred to as Boirobi

Puja, but in fact the festival included a whole series of sacrifices in a number of places in and around the village, with the ritual for Boirobi only being the last and most important one and thus iconic for the whole event. Unlike most village shrines, the Boirobi (here, explicitly a goddess) of Badigor was famous beyond the boundary of the village, and people came from places nearby on Tuesdays and Fridays to sacrifice and redeem vows (*mansik*) they had made.

On the third day of the month of *dosra* (October 12, 1999), about fifteen Gadaba men from the neighboring village of Ochengpada arrived in Badigor. They belonged to the *sisa*[34] status category – from which the sacrificers are normally recruited within a village – and they performed most of the animal sacrifices during the Boirobi festival, especially the buffalo sacrifice at the end. In addition to the Dombo musicians from the village, the other ritual actors were the *pujari*, the *patro* and the *dora*, all from the Rona community. The *patro*, from the family of the former *mutadars*, had sponsored the buffalo, the *pujari* invoked deities and performed *puja* but did not kill animals, while the *dora* sacrificed goats and chickens alongside the Gadaba *sisa*.[35] Important ritual objects were kept in the house of the *pujari*, and these accompanied the procession from one shrine to the next. They consisted of a bunch of peacock feathers, with which the *pujari* touched the victims before they were sacrificed, and two five-meter long bamboo poles, to which a white banner (*jenda*) was attached. They were of a deep brown color and obviously old. Without asking, I was told that they were from the "time of the king" (*raja bela*). I think it is likely that in the days of the king a delegation from Badigor, including the *mutadar*, took these poles to Jeypore during Dasara, but I did not inquire about this at the time.

In contrast to the Dasara rituals performed in Gudapada, the Boirobi Puja was a nightly affair and the *jatra* started only after nightfall, around 7 pm, in the house of the sponsor, the *patro*. As I have seen in other Rona villages, the Rona houses were surrounded by high mud walls, which created spacious yards. The yard of the *patro* also featured a *tulsi* plant on a platform, above which, for the occasion, a wooden structure (*chamda*) had been erected: four wooden posts with a roof made from leafy branches. At nearly all of the shrines that were visited during the subsequent procession, *chamda* of different sizes had been erected. Shortly after the Gadaba from Ochengpada had arrived, the

---

34 I use lower case letters (*sisa*) when referring to the general status category or to the ritual specialist recruited from this category and upper case letters (Sisa) when I refer to a specific local group.
35 It was said that he only killed the cock for the earth goddess at the *hundi* shrine during Chait Porbo.

Dombo musicians appeared in the yard of the *patro* and started beating their drums and playing the *moiri*.

The procession commenced from the house of the *patro* and first stopped briefly by a river to offer an egg. It then proceeded up a hill to a place called Tikrapada, perhaps a former village settlement.[35] Below the *chamda*, the *sisa* offered an egg and sacrificed a young chicken, after which everybody went to the house of the *pujari*. There, the bamboo poles were taken out of the house and the women of the household washed the feet of the carriers and of the Gadaba sacrificer, the *sisa*. The men also received *tika* from the women, who placed husked rice on their feet, knees, shoulders and foreheads. Subsequently, the procession moved to Ganga Gudi, a shrine for a goddess on the village border. Only men participated in the procession, while the women stood on the side of the street in front of their houses with smoking incense (*dupo*). A banyan tree surrounded by a wall made from piled-up stones constituted the Ganga shrine (*gudi*). In front of the entrance to the stone circle, a *chamda* had been erected; here, an egg was offered. The bamboo poles were leant against the tree and the peacock feathers also placed inside the shrine, at first covered with a white cloth. The *pujari* touched the animals with the feathers, lit incense and offered a coconut, then let the Gadaba *sisa* do the rest. He killed a white cock and a black goat. The latter had been sponsored by the Dombo of the village, who, along with the musicians, stayed outside the wall.

After the sacrifice, the procession moved back into the village – guided by the light of a gas lamp – to a concrete building referred to as *mandap* ("platform") opposite the assembly platform (*sadar*), also made of cement. Inside the small house a *chamda* had again been erected and the ritual sequence was also similar. The *pujari* touched the victims with the peacock feathers, the *sisa* killed a white cock and the *dora* killed a black goat.

The next stop was made at a place along the mud road leading out of the village called *duma bhuta*, literally the "bush (*bhuta*) of the dead (*duma*)." It consisted of an upright megalith at the foot of a tree. A small *chamda* had also been erected here and the *pujari* offered an egg and left small leaf-cups with sprouts of rice and black gram (*biri*). Animals were only sacrificed again at the next stop, the place of a former weekly market (*hato poda*), which had recently been abandoned. The *chamda* at the feet of the banyan tree there was about one meter high. The flag poles were leant against the tree, another egg offered and sprouts left below the *chamda* again among the roots of the tree. The *dora*

---

36 Also the old *hundi* shrine of Badigor still lies at the top of a hill and old people remembered that the village site was shifted when they had been children.

sacrificed a white cock, the *pujari* touched a brown goat with the peacock feathers, after which the *sisa* killed the animal.

Now the final destination, the Boirobi shrine, was approached, but first the sacrificial animals had to be collected from the house of the *patro*, so the whole procession returned to his yard. There, the buffalo and two rams were washed, and the buffalo was also dressed with a white cloth and adorned with flowers. The *patro* briefly led the animals into his house and back again into the yard, where the buffalo was worshipped by another *patro*; the old man prostrating himself in front of the animal. The animals were once more consecrated in the house of the *pujari* and then the procession finally moved to the Boirobi shrine outside the village.

This shrine was much more impressive than any of the structures that the procession had previously visited. In the center stood a huge banyan tree that overshadowed two concentric stone circles made from piled-up stones that had been built up around it, each with an entrance made from upright stone slabs. The inner circle featured a low solid shrine about 70 centimeters in height constructed at the foot of the tree from bricks and cement. Its small front opening was closed with a stone. The opening was just big enough for the earthen pot that was inside to fit through, which was said to contain an old iron chain. Beside the shrine, an iron trident had been planted in the earth. I was able to see all of the details more clearly in the light of the next day, when I was also allowed to take photographs.

Only the main actors were admitted to the inner stone circle: the *pujari*, who opened the shrine, the *patro*, the *sisa* and the *dora*. The two bamboo poles and peacock feathers were placed next to the shrine. Other men, women and children, and also the Dombo musicians, were crowded inside the outer stone circle around the huge aerial roots of the tree. The first two hours after the procession had arrived at the Boirobi shrine were occupied with *manasik puja*, that is, the fulfilment of vows made by individuals for various reasons. Men and women passed through their sacrificial items to be offered to the goddess. The *pujari* cracked open coconuts, while the *sisa* and *dora* sacrificed cocks, around 20 in total. All the while, the Dombo musicians kept playing. One woman danced ecstatically and briefly sat in the fire that the Dombo drummers maintained to tighten the skins of their drums.

It was around midnight when the two rams and the buffalo were finally brought before the shrine in the inner stone circle, after which they were taken back to the outer ring, as the space in the interior was too narrow to perform the sacrifices there. The two rams were touched with the peacock feathers by the *pujari* and then killed by the *sisa*, while the *dora* held them tight with a stick and a rope. The buffalo was tied to a smaller tree trunk and worshipped before being sacrificed. First, the pujari knelt in front of the animal and touched its hooves, and then the *sisa* also knelt in front of it and touched the forehead of the animal with his own. Then, he beheaded the animal with three strokes. The head was immediately placed in front of the opening of the shrine, the buffalo looking toward the clay pot inside. As soon as the buffalo was beheaded, people dispersed.

Only a few people – among them *pujari*, *patro*, *dora* and *sisa*, all men – went to the shrine the next morning, at around 7 am. The bamboo poles and the head had been left in front of the shrine. As I had also been told on other occasions, it is an auspicious sign if the head remains untouched and unaffected by other animals, whether ants or others, during the night and this was indeed the case. *Pujari* and *dora* performed a *puja* and the latter sacrificed a brown cock before the *pujari* closed the opening to the shrine with the stone and the buffalo head was removed. The men then returned to the village, taking the bamboo poles back to the house of the *pujari*. The Gadaba cut up and cooked the head of the buffalo (and the liver) in the Dombo part of the village. Rona generally do not eat the meat of pig, buffalo or cow. As only three Gadaba had remained in Badigor over night, they ate some of it and took the rest back to their village. Meanwhile, the Dombo cut up the body of the buffalo and arranged raw and cooked portions to be distributed later to neighboring villages.

Dasara Rituals among the Dongria Kond

Two years later, Roland Hardenberg observed the Dasara rituals in the Niamgiri Hills.[37] Among the Dongria, it is not catfish and cucumber that are offered but bananas, which are central to the festival. Humans give bananas to each other as gifts, as well as to the gods and the dead. The rituals do not demonstrate any explicit link to the king or kingship, but certainly there is a connection to a goddess, to the dead and to buffalo sacrifice.

On the second day of the lunar month of *dosra* (October 19, 2001), three days before the festival called Dasara Puja, Dongria households ripened banana stalks in front of their houses, in earthen ovens they had constructed for the occasion. After two days, the ripe bananas were dug out again. On that day (October 21), a buffalo was sacrificed, a collective ritual for the dead (*mahane*), in which all households were supposed to participate. The collective nature of the

---

[37] I am grateful to Roland Hardenberg for providing me with his unpublished material (field notes) on this festival.

performance also became evident in the distribution of the buffalo. All of the houses received portions of cooked and raw meat, all of the men received cooked meat "on their hand" and every woman and girl was given a small bowl of meat.

During the morning of the day of the Dasara Puja (October 22), the female village shaman (*bejuni*) and her assistant (*gurumeni*) visited each house and worshipped the house deities, represented either by stones or wooden posts. Banana stalks were hung above the deities, the gods were invoked and offered fruits, and then the people who were present ate some bananas, leaving the peelings as offerings at the stalk. Before noon, young men went from house to house with a winnowing fan to collect unhusked rice, bananas and money, beating drums and singing as they moved through the village. The rice was kept for a later feast, the money used to buy liquor. At the same time, the *bejuni* and the *gurumeni* sat next to the shrine of the earth goddess (*dharni*), with two baskets and a winnowing fan in front of them. Women from all households came and placed leaf-cups with cooked meat (presumably also buffalo meat from the day before) and rice in one basket and bananas in the other. Husked rice was put into the winnowing fan.[38]

When the baskets were filled, *bejuni* and *gurumeni* took them to a shrine, called *yatra kudi* ("festival house"), on the western border of the village (see map in Hardenberg 2018a, 32). Festivals, Hardenberg summarizes, generally invite gods or the dead into the village in the first phase and then send the visitors away again in the second phase, or they "throw them out," as the Dongria put it bluntly (Hardenberg 2018a, 318). This second phase of the rituals usually ends with a procession to the *yatra kudi*. The shrine is the location of a goddess referred to as Aji Budi ("old woman") or Thakurani ("ruling goddess"), who is venerated, needed and feared at the same time. She is feared because she can inflict illness and she is venerated as well as needed as she protects the village from evil forces in this transitional space. The location of the shrine is no coincidence, as the space west of the village is associated with dangerous influences (Hardenberg 2018a, 317f). The cremation ground of the Dongria is only a little further along the path outside the village.

Once *bejuni* and *gurumeni* arrived at the shrine, they attached bananas to its wooden frame and placed two leaves in front of it. The basket containing the food offerings from all of the women of the village was unpacked and a small portion from each individual bowl that the women had previously brought to the *dharni* was placed on the leaves. In this way, all households offered food to

---

38 Bananas were also hung at the *koteiwali* (by the senior *member*), the male deity, father of the Dongria and husband of the earth goddess.

the goddess. The offerings contained cooked meat, rice and vegetable broth. A banana stalk was also placed in front of the shrine. Then followed offerings for the deceased, whereby those who had died a "good" death (*mahane*) were distinguished from the dangerous ones who had died a "bad" death (*marha*), such as being killed by a tiger or falling from a tree. Small leaf-cups for the *mahane* containing cooked rice and bananas were placed on the ground further west of the shrine, in the direction of the cremation ground. The dangerous *marha*, by contrast, received meat, cooked rice, vegetable broth, husked rice and bananas, being served even further down the path to the west. The spatial orientation here obviously indexes the character of the beings worshipped: *mahane* protect the living but sometimes may also make them ill; however, nothing good is expected from the *marha*, who are thus provided with food further west and farther away from the village. After the goddess and the dead had received their share, the living ate. Among those present were also women and children.

Gadaba and Joria Villages Close to Jeypore

In 2016, I visited some Gadaba and Joria villages close to Jeypore for the first time. For many years, I had passed them by on my way from the town when heading up to the 900 meter plateau, and for a long time I did not even know that Gadaba and Joria lived there. I had often noticed a small shrine along the main road only a few kilometers from Jeypore. The two lions in front of the small square temple made it appear to be a Hindu shrine for Durga. As it turned out, it was only a satellite temple of the main Durga shrine on top of a hill that rises more than 200 meters just behind the temple. While a Gadaba acted as *pujari* in the roadside temple, a Joria *jani* was the sacrificer at the original location of the goddess on top of the hill. I accompanied the *jani* one Tuesday – the usual visiting day for worshippers at the shrine – and we climbed the hill for about 40 minutes before reaching the site. With us was a man of the Kumar (potter) community from the village of Peta, on the plateau. Obviously not used to climbing hills, he was sweating profusely, unlike the *jani*, who jumped from stone to stone with ease.

The shrine on top of the hill basically looked like thousands of hill shrines in the region. It had a low circular wall of piled-up stones with an opening marked by two upright stone slabs; inside the circle, two stones represented the deity. What made it different from the normal hill shrines that I have seen on the plateau were the Hindu paraphernalia. As in case of the roadside shrine, the entrance to the stone circle was protected by lions on each side and, beside the stones, the shrine also included numerous tridents, an icon of Durga riding a tiger, numerous pictures of the goddess and big brass bells. The shrine had no roof, but a red cloth covered the space above the stone circle. The whole area, shaded by many trees and, especially, big *siardi* creepers, featured countless sacred places and many stones and trees showed marks of worship. The *jani* cleaned and worshipped all of those places before sacrificing to Durga on behalf of his Kumar client and others who came later. The story that surrounds this place again demonstrates that the fates of the goddess, the king and the tribes are closely entangled. While the descriptions of Dasara discussed above did not mention tribal participation during Dasara in the town of Jeypore, this case helps to complement the picture.

When the capital was shifted to Jeypore in the seventeenth century, its original center was what is today known as the "Old Fort" (Purnagarh), which is now in the southeastern part of the town at the foot of the forested Nakti hill. Originally, it was more "a strategic jungle fortress than a palace" (Schnepel 2002, 268), allowing a quick retreat into the hills, if necessary. Because Vikram Deo I campaigned against the colonial power, this fort was destroyed by the British in 1775 in a punitive action.[39] The new palace was only built after Vikram's son (Ramachandra Deo II) had established good relations with the British (Schnepel 2002, 265–69). The most important deity of the new capital was initially not Kanaka Durga, the goddess that the Nandapur king had allegedly captured from the Gajapati and made his tutelary deity. At first, she remained in Nandapur and was only later taken to Jeypore and installed in a temple in the newly built palace compound. Originally, the most important deity was Kalika, whose temple was located in the Old Fort and is still there in this part of the town today.[40] Her story is another example of the often documented process through which kings adopted, patronized and Hinduized a tribal deity.

In my analysis of tribal myths, I have already referred to a story (M7) told to us by a group of people, especially a Gadaba woman, in the village of Ponosput Bagra, the Joria village from where the *jani* of the hill-top shrine is recruited. The story describes how the fierce goddess could not be controlled by the villagers themselves, as she regularly took away (and killed) girls. The people therefore handed her over to the king, who installed her in his fort, constructing a temple for her at Purnagarh. I was told variants of this story in conversations with various people in the Gadaba village of Dongorchinchi and the Joria village of Ponosput Bagra (both villages lie at the foot of the hill that houses

---

39 Described in detail by Bell (1945).
40 Indrajeet Mohanty (2013, 71) writes about Jeypore: "Till today a temple dedicated to a tribal goddess in the old fortress is the center of rituals."

the original shrine). I will summarize what Bolram Gadaba, the *pujari* of the roadside temple, told us.⁴¹

The goddess, Bolram Gadaba said, could not be satisfied, no matter how much they gave her, including human lives. The king then took her and made her his great goddess (*bor devi*), the major goddess of Jeypore. However, installing (*tapni*) her was not an easy task. No one could face the goddess and look into her eyes. The priest would only sit at the side of the shrine during worship. When they installed her, they tied up the goddess completely. Her head was moving around and when it turned to one side they fixed her in place with "nails" (*konta*, "thorns"), in her feet and her hands. It was only because she was thus fixed that the king could keep her, and she was also called the Great Fear-Inducing-One (Maha Boyonkoro). Today, her head is still somewhat turned to the side, but it is said that in the Dark Age it straightened due to her will. Even with the goddess thus tied and fixed, she still roamed around in the shape of a young woman (*somari tota*) or "white daughter" (*duba jio*) at the foot of the Nakti hill. Moreover, when the king installed her in the Old Fort, the goddess received a new name.⁴² As Bolram Gadaba stated, she is like Danteswari, in fact, she is an incarnation of that goddess.

When we⁴³ visited the Kalika temple in the Old Fort, the Brahman priest immediately recognized the story that the villagers of Ponosput Bagra had told us. He said that the goddess had wanted to give a sign (*china*) of her presence to the villagers. Therefore, she entered a young girl (*kumari*) and took her away and the girl died. However, he then gave the story another twist, pointing out the incompetence of the villagers in hosting the deity and her explicit wish to be taken by the king. The goddess appeared to the king in a dream and told him that the people would not worship her properly and asked him to take her to his palace. At that time, the Brahman continued, Purnagarh was the fort of the kingdom. With regard to the Joria from Ponosput Bagra,⁴⁴ he said that they were the "laborers" of the goddess. At first I did not understand the English word he used, so he specified, "we call it *betia*," thus referring to those who pay tribute (*beti*) to the king. The *betia* would come to the temple twice a year

---

41 I was accompanied by Manto Pradhan at the time.
42 This re-naming of deities is a common aspect of the Hinduization of tribal deities. In the myth (M7) referred above, the people present just spoke about "deity" (*maphru*), but the deity was also referred to as Durga both in her shrines at the road-side and on the hill. Kalika became the name of the goddess once installed in the Old Fort.
43 I was accompanied by Tuna Takri.
44 He referred to them as "Gadaba," probably not knowing or caring much about the differences between the tribal groups of the region.

in the month of *chait* and during Dasara. However, they would not perform *puja* and would not be allowed near the goddess. He added that his own family had long been responsible for the worship.

This passive view of the Joria was contradicted by the priest of the roadside Durga shrine, Bolram Gadaba. Without the *jani* of Ponosput Bagra, he said, the Brahman could not enter the temple, as she was the goddess of the "*jani* house" (*jani gor*). During the worship, it would be the *jani* who would go into the sanctum first, before the Brahman, he added. Then, he made an interesting comparison. It would be like the Gupteshwar temple, the regionally famous "hidden Siva" in a cave near the border between Bastar and Jeypore. This would be a Dhurwa goddess and therefore they would do the *puja* there. The god would be happy with the Dhurwa.

I was not present during Dasara in Jeypore or in the villages of Dongorchinchi or Ponosput Bagra, so I cannot provide a description of the actual proceedings as celebrated today. I was told that earlier, when countless goats and buffaloes were sacrificed in the palace for the goddess, that there used to be village delegations to Jeypore and all the "goddess poles" (*debi latimon*) would come to Jeypore. However, such delegations and "pole offerings" (*lati bog*) no longer take place, at least not coming from their villages. The hill goddess, by contrast, still receives buffalo sacrifices. Moreover, as the goddess was born on the hill – the hill being her "womb" (*pete*) – the buffalo sacrifice at the hill shrine during Dasara precedes the worship of Kalika in the temple at Purnagarh.

A Gadaba woman told me that the buffalo sacrifice on the hill would occur on the eighth day of Dasara, when the villagers take the buffalo up the hill with a flag pole, which they do not take to Jeypore.[45] The worship of Kalika in the Old Fort would only take place on the tenth day of Dasara. Irrespective of the question if these are the actual days on which the sacrifices take place, what is clear is that the Joria and Gadaba living at the foot of the hill claim a clear precedence of their goddess and their sacrificial rites, which was not contested by the Brahman temple priest of Kalika.

Thanks to a contribution by Eberhard Fischer and Dinanath Pathy (2002), we have additional information about the Kalika temple. The authors were not concerned with rituals, indigenous religion or the Dasara celebrations but were interested in the many murals of the Devi on the outside of the temple walls, along a roofed veranda that is found on all sides of the building. The text deals with the murals as they found them between 1979 and 1990 but also mentions

---

[45] There would be no point of taking the flag-pole, as the goddess (Kalika) is already there, in Jeypore, Bolram Gadaba explained.

the drawings kept by the family of artists, which served as templates for the murals. Obviously, they were impressed by what they saw, as they wrote:

> We know of no other traditional Indian temple that features such a variety of Sakti images on its walls. Upon closer inspection we realized that they display two sets of goddesses: (1) Dasa Mahavidya, i.e. the ten great goddesses and (2) Nava Durga, i.e. the nine forms of Durga (Fischer & Pathy 2002, 148).

They provide numerous images and photographs of the temple, the murals and the drawings, along with a map of the building. What interests me here, in particular, are those parts of the article that provide additional clues about ritual activities and the goddess, the history of the temple and the involvement of the tribal population.

The text supports the claim of Bolram Gadaba, mentioned above, that the Joria were (perhaps still are) the priests of the temple. While Fischer and Pathy do not mention a Brahman priest, they note that the "temple is looked after by a Jani, a priest of local origin who is a farmer by the family name of Raut" (2002, 143). While no explicit reference is made to the Joria community, we can assume that the *jani*[46] who the researchers met came from the Joria village of Ponosput Bagra, and possibly from the same family I met in 2016.[47] Moreover, the *jani* who Fischer and Pathy encountered claimed that his family had been the custodian of the temple for many years. As an inscription documents, the temple had been built on behalf of the king of Jeypore, replacing an older construction with mud walls and a thatched roof. According to the *jani*, who was about 60 years old when Fischer and Pathy talked to him in 1990, his father had told him that a young boy was sacrificed when the new temple was built.

The theme of human sacrifice also figures in the sketches of the artists, along with many other "bloody" themes and images. One of the drawings shows Manikasri or Manikesvari, about to sacrifice a child (Fischer & Pathy 2002, 156, figure 8a). The goddess keeps tight hold of the child, grabbing it by the hair and holding its arm while lifting her sword ready to strike with her right hand and holding in her left hand what appears to be a bowl to collect the blood. The authors assume that this image, along with several others, was originally painted as a mural on the southwest wall of the temple (2002, 151). That

---

46 *Jani* is the name of a status category from which sacrificers (*jani*) are recruited, similar to the *sisa* category among the Gadaba that provides the sacrificers. The title *jani* is also common among the Kond.
47 As far as the family name is concerned I assume that this information is based on a misunderstanding. Perhaps the *jani* said that he was a farmer and landholder (*roit*) and this was then assumed to be his family name.

sacrifice was an important practice in this temple can also be deduced from the presence of a sacrificial platform (*shakti-pitha*) on its eastern side. If all the doors in the walls that separate the sanctum of Kalika from the platform were open, the goddess could actually watch the sacrificial performances; in the past, probably sacrifices of buffaloes. However, as Fischer and Pathy (2002, 140) describe, the sanctum of Kalika usually remains closed, as "no one dares to open the doors to her shrine" and daily offerings of flowers are placed in front of the closed door. The authors classify the stone icon of Kalika as a version of Daksina Kali, who stands on top of a prostrate Siva, but they do not provide a photograph of the *murti*, perhaps because they could not enter the sanctum.

When I visited the shrine, the door to the sanctum was open but I was not allowed to go near it or to take a photograph, so I could only look from a distance. Bolram Gadaba also stated that the *jani* and the Brahman priest actually enter the sanctum during worship. In his popular booklet on Dasara in Jeypore, Paresh Rath (2014, 35) provides a photograph of the goddess, in which the lower part of her body is covered with a red cloth, such that if she stands on top of Shiva, this is not visible. The icon is made from black stone and, as Bolram Gadaba described, the head of the goddess is turned sideways, toward her right side.[48]

Obviously, we do not know exactly when the Gadaba and Joria villages near Jeypore were established. Given the megalithic structures that I saw in the villages of Dongorchinchi and Ponosput Bagra, it is clear that these settlements have been there a long time. The Gadaba in Dongorchinchi said – as they say on the plateau – that the king was born in Nandapur and then came to Jeypore. It is likely that these villages were founded in the course of this transfer, thus perhaps in the seventeenth century, when the Old Fort was established as the new capital.[49] The Gadaba in Dongorchinchi said that their ancestors came

---

48 In a second sanctum a form of Kali called Tara is worshipped. Her icon has obviously been redefined in the course of history, as the authors say it would be an image of a Jaina Tirthankara (Risabhanatha) from the twelfth century (Fischer and Pathy 2002, 140–43). The authors also provide a photograph of this image (2002, 155, fig. 6).

49 Burrow and Bhattacharya (1962, 46) mention a royal policy of Viswambara Deo I, king of Jeypore from 1672–76, who "encouraged people to make settlements in the plains" (Singh Deo in Burrow and Bhattacharya 1962, 46). The authors speculate that this might also explain the settlement of Ollar Gadaba in the plains around Salur (today Andhra Pradesh). However, it might also refer to the area around Jeypore town. The Vizagapatam District Singh Deo is referring to (in the quote provided by Burrow and Bhattacharya) in colonial times comprised the Jeypore presidency and the coastal area now belonging to Andhra Pradesh and was bordered by the Ganjam District in the north and the Godavari District in the south. The page reference Burrow and Bhattacharya provide seems to be incorrect and the quote is not to be found in the copy of Singh Deo (1939) at my disposal.

from the plateau to do *beti* for the king. Thus, they would be "*raja* Gadaba" and their villages *raja ga*, "king's villages." An old Gadaba interlocutor recalled that his father had carried the king in a palanquin. Eighteen people would have carried the king, taking him wherever he wanted to go, for example to Jagdalpur.

This task of carrying the king became iconic for the Gadaba, who have also been referred to as Bhoi Gadaba, that is, "carrier" Gadaba, and they have even been employed in this task at other courts, for instance in Jagdalpur or Bobbili. They used to be recruited for other work as well, such as thatching roofs. Whoever served the king in this way did not have to pay tax, I have been told. Moreover, the Gadaba and Joria not only served the king by thatching roofs or cutting wood, but also performed the ritual work of worship and sacrifice. While we do not know how the Gadaba or Joria used to be involved in the Dasara celebrations in Jeypore, the story of Kalika shows that tribal goddesses were crucial to the festival. Significantly, it was not only the tribal goddess who was important and powerful, supporting the king and his realm, but also the tribes. They were (still are?) the necessary mediators of their goddess and sacrificers at their hill-shrine and inside the Old Fort at the Kalika temple; perhaps they were also involved in the cult of Kanaka Durga later, after the goddess had been established in the new palace in Jeypore.

The villages of Dongorchinchi and Ponosput Bagra look like the villages on the plateau and their inhabitants perform the same annual festivals – such as Chait Porbo – as do all Desia. However, there are a few differences. As the name Bolram Gadaba suggests, people do not carry their status category (*kuda*) as part of their name. On the plateau, he would call himself Bolram Munduli or Bolram Sisa. The clan names have also been Hinduized in the two villages. The Cobra clan (*hantal, ontal*) is call *nag*, the Tiger clan (*killo*) *bag* and the Monkey clan (*golori*) has become *hanuman*. No Gadaba I met in these villages was able to speak Gutob or Ollari anymore. Moreover, when they migrated down from the 900 meter plateau and established the villages near Jeypore, the Gadaba and Joria also seem to have left behind their signature rituals, the Nandi and the Go'ter. People know of these festivals, although few seem to have ever attended them, and according to people's memory, they have never been performed in Dongorchinchi or Ponosput Bagra. Certainly, as far as the former is concerned, there are no megalithic structures in the village that suggest a performance of the Go'ter in the past. This may indicate that the proverb connecting Dasara with the Go'ter, Nandi and Bali, the festivals that will be discussed in subsequent chapters, originated during the reign of the Nandapur kings – those earth-born kings who figure in the myths, and were said to have performed human sacrifices. The kings of Jeypore, although in need of subaltern deities and

5.6 Analysis and Discussion

Dasara holds an important place in the year for the villagers from the Dongria, Gadaba, Joria and Rona communities. This is not necessarily because this festival would be a major ritual occasion in their villages, but because it provides the name of the month, which is called *aswina* in other places. This is the month of *raja beti*, of paying tribute to the king, and therefore it is an important time to re-constitute and display the relationship between *raja* and *porja*. This, then, is the common feature of Dasara for all villages, whereas the concrete rituals take diverse forms, especially in those instances where an explicit relationship to the king and the capital is absent. For those villages that had a special relationship to the king, the local Dasara festival was of greater importance than it was to others, for whom it was and still is a village ritual of relatively little significance.

Gadaba and Dongria celebrate Dasara on a minor scale, in one-day festivals that show no explicit connection to the king, and in the case of the Gadaba, they barely entail a communal dimension.[50] What both share is that their offerings and sacrifices (which are of a very different nature: catfish and cucumber vs. buffalo and bananas) concern the protection of the villages and, accordingly, take place on the margins of the settlements. Another related, common feature is the reference to goddesses and defense against dangerous forces; although, in the case of the Gadaba, this is a little less apparent. While the sacrifices conducted by the village sacrificers and the individual households do not explicitly refer to a goddess and do not directly entail a defensive dimension, for those ritual specialists whose task it is to fight off demons and angry spirits, Dasara is the moment to rearm themselves and to seek Durga's support in the context of the rituals. In sacrificing at the *yatra kudi*, the Dongria combine both aspects – the protection of the village and defense against evil forces from outside – especially the dangerous dead. Although a goddess, supportive but also feared, is worshipped, it is not the goddess who receives the buffalo sacrifice in the first place. She receives gifts of bananas and meat from the sacrifice that

---

50 The offerings of bananas by and among the Dongria could be a reference to *raja beti* though, as banana stalks were previously also among the products that were taken to the capital, as is also mentioned in one of the myths (M5) I discuss in Chapter 3.

has originally been offered collectively to the benevolent dead the day before. This buffalo sacrifice is thus connected to Dasara and the worship of the goddess but is different from those buffalo sacrifices that are explicitly dedicated to Durga (or other manifestations of the Devi) and which take place during Dasara proper, as in the case of the Rona of Badigor.

Both the Rona, who are relatively far away from the capital on the 900 meter plateau, and the Joria in the immediate vicinity of Jeypore did have a special connection to the king and, accordingly, Dasara still plays a greater role in their village rituals, including a buffalo sacrifice to a goddess. The *mutadar* of Badigor represented the king in this remote area close to the Bondo villages, and their buffalo sacrifice for Boirobi, with explicit references to Shiva, perhaps replicates the sacrifices that were previously performed in the capital. Noticeable again is the tribal role of sacrificer. While the different ritual specialists of the Rona have a vital role in the rituals, invoking the deities, consecrating the animals and also killing them (symbolically in the case of the buffalo and literally in the case of the other animals), it is clear that the function of the Gadaba as sacrificers of the buffalo is indispensable.

This pivotal role of tribal sacrificers is also evident in the relationship between the king and his goddesses in Jeypore and the Joria and their local hill deity close by. While the Brahman priest of the Kalika temple may have denied the significance of the Joria in the temple – even though evidence suggest that the Joria have, until very recently, if not still today, participated in the worship of the goddess – he acknowledged the precedence of the hill goddess, who still receives buffaloes as offerings from the Joria during Dasara.

The example of Kalika also shows that the pattern which can be discerned in Bastar, the hierarchical relationship between a royal tutelary deity (Danteswari) and local goddesses (Maoli), is a more general feature. As I pointed out with reference to the participation of the Dongria in the Dasara rituals in Bissamcuttack, the relation between Markama and Niamraja may be of a similar nature. In the case of Kalika, this also seems to be the same configuration: Kalika was transformed – a literally domesticated and appropriated tribal deity – and installed in the Old Fort before Kanaka Durga was transferred to the new palace in Jeypore, and she is still accorded a high status in the pantheon of the town. However, it is impossible to say whether Kalika is also considered superior to Kanaka Durga in certain moments of the Dasara ritual, as in the case of Maoli in Bastar, for the data available allows no conclusion to be drawn in this regard.

I want to make three more comments on the role of human sacrifice, cereals and play in the context of the village Dasara described above. It is noticeable that there was very little in terms of effervescent assemblies or play in the Dasara village performances. True, there was one instance of possession and sitting in the fire during the Boirobi Puja in Badigor, and it is likely that the buffalo sacrifice to the Hill Durga by the Joria involves more such effervescent scenes, as we encountered in Bastar. However, apart from these instances, the rituals of the Dongria and Gadaba – usually known for their rowdy and lively performances – were remarkably calm, minimalist and controlled. Such forms of play were not involved in the rather insignificant local Dasara festival but do find expression in other rituals that are more crucial for the communities concerned; such as the buffalo sacrifice (Kodru Parbu, formerly Meria) of the Dongria, the Go'ter of the Gadaba, the Bali Jatra of the Mali or the Ganga Puja of the Joria.

In contrast to the dimension of effervescent play, cereals and the imagery of human sacrifice both emerged in the village performances. Sprouts of rice and black gram were left at several sacrificial locations during the Boirobi Puja in Badigor, although I cannot say how long the seeds were allowed to germinate or where; that is, whether there are more similarities to the sprouting of wheat in the Bastar Dasara. Nonetheless, it is clear that the germination of seeds in the context of Dasara is a recurrent theme, as is human sacrifice. This motif emerged repeatedly, such as in the myth about the fierce Hill Durga capturing girls, before being tamed by the king; in the murals and drawings of the Kalika temple; and in the narratives of a boy having been sacrificed to exactly this deity at the foundation of the new building. Moreover, while the participants of the Boirobi Puja did not specify the meaning or purpose of the iron chains inside the clay pot in the interior of the little shrine, an association with the imagery of human sacrifice cannot be ruled out. Iron implements are generally associated with Durga in the region, and certainly among the Kond, such tools used in the context of buffalo sacrifices are still connected by the participants with the time of human sacrifices (Hardenberg 2014, 291; 2018a, 501f, 543f; Pfeffer 2009, 244).

5.7 Dasara in Mysore and Puri

To conclude this comparison of Dasara celebrations and put the rituals of the jungle kingdoms of Bastar and Jeypore into perspective, I will now, albeit briefly, look at Dasara as performed in Mysore and Puri. The kings of these realms are successors to the rulers of past Hindu empires of considerable influence. The Mysore kingdom emerged out of the great Vijayanagara empire in South India, while the king of Puri is heir to the former Gajapati rulers, the Imperial Gangas and the subsequent Suryavamshi kings with their capital in Cuttack, Odisha. These kingdoms had great political ambitions and military success during certain phases of their existence and were neither jungle nor little kingdoms, as defined by (ethno)historians (see Berkemer and Frenz 2003). With regard to Mysore, I will mainly rely on the description of C. Hayavadana Rao (1936), based on his observations from the 1930s, complemented by some more recent contributions (Ikegame 2013a; Scalpi 1936; Simmons 2018). As far as Puri is concerned, I will base my summary on the ethnographic work of Frédédique Apffel Marglin (1985) and Roland Hardenberg (2008), who did their fieldwork in the mid-1970s and 1990s respectively.

Mysore Dasara lasts for ten days and commences with the building of a platform on which an image of Durga is placed on a seat with the lion symbol. Then, one Brahman is selected, who performs Vedic sacrifices (*homa*) for Durga for nine days. He is initiated, "invested with the vow of performance (*diksha*)" (Rao 1936, 13), and a silk thread is tied around his wrist symbolizing his particular status. He should not move any distance from the place and must remain pure in "thought, word and deed" (Rao 1936, 14). At the same time, the king invokes his tutelary deity, Chamundeswari, and a silk thread is also tied around his wrist, after which the *puja* to the throne is performed and he then mounts the throne. Aya Ikegame (2013a, 147f) specifies that both the king and the queen receive these silk threads around their wrists and also mentions further restrictions that apply to the king. He cannot leave the palace for nine days and his special status is signified by particular clothes (made from unstitched silk) and dietary restrictions. Ikegame (2013a, 148) writes that

> (. . .) he is a prisoner captured in the ritual or, if we are allowed to go further, what he experiences is a temporal death in order to maintain his pure status. (. . .) He has to abandon any worldly desire (. . .). He has to sacrifice himself, both practically and ritually.

The state sword, which is worshipped during the first nine days of the festival, is brought out of the sanctum of the palace and placed next to the king in the Durbar hall. The first day ends with a Durbar and performances by wrestlers and "feats of arms" (Rao 1936, 22). This Durbar is repeated every evening, up to and including the eighth day, on which Durga's slaying of the demon is celebrated.

On the ninth day, the period of *diksha* ends and the Brahman removes the silken thread and can resume his normal life. After the worship of all kinds of instruments (including horses) a fire sacrifice for Chandi takes place and the king (and queen, according to Ikegame) then takes off his thread, which ends the vow and his special status. On the final, tenth day, the king worships the state arms and, taking them along, then proceeds to a platform with a *banni* tree (*Prosopis cineraria*), where wrestling matches are performed. In the afternoon, he reviews his troops and worships the tree, which in former times initiated the military season. The king then returns to the palace with his state arms.

The participation of the population is also of note. Rao describes the square in front of the palace as a "sea of human faces" (Rao 1936, 23) on the evening of the ninth day. During the festival, "thousands are fed" (Rao 1936, 24) and "large crowds" (Rao 1936, 27) assemble to watch the Durbar and associated performances of acrobats and wrestlers. The city is, Rao concludes, "one mass of humanity, peaceful and orderly" (Rao 1936, 28).

The Gajapati of Puri no longer has an empire or a people to rule, but he still plays an important role in the rituals of the palace and the Jagannath temple (Hardenberg 2008, 2011). As Marglin (1985, 166f) points out, in Puri, the Durga Puja and Dasara are separate but related festivals and continue for sixteen days, in both the Jagannath temple and the palace. At the center of the Durga Puja is the tutelary deity of the king, Kanaka Durga, who is housed in the palace. Nevertheless, the goddess Bimala is also central to the rituals in the Jagannath temple. On the first day, Kanaka Durga is moved to a pavilion in the palace compound for the duration of the festival and proceeds from there daily in a procession to the "Dasara Field" on the main road, where she is worshipped. Until the 1970s, she also received animal sacrifices on the eighth and ninth days of the Durga Puja, but this practice has been discontinued. Only Bimala still receives bloody offerings.

For Dasara proper, a sand platform is erected in the palace compound close to the pavilion where Kanaka Durga has been installed. A circle of leaves on the platform represents the ten directions. At the throne, Brahmins prepare and worship a container called the "increaser vessel" and the king and queen are later sprinkled with water from this container. The Brahmins also touch the king and queen with a number of auspicious objects, among them earth and seeds. The king then proceeds to the sand platform to worship weapons, before moving to the pavilion of Kanaka Durga where he receives a *sari* from Jagannath, the ultimate ruler, which is tied around his head. Back at the sand platform, the king then shoots arrows in ten directions, thereby conquering them. Then, the king watches dance performances in the audience hall and the last ritual of the day is the procession of the images of Jagannath, Durga and Madhaba on a chariot to the "Dasara Field" (Marglin 1985, 167f).

Puri features two kings, the human king in the palace and the superior, royal god ("Ruler of the World") in the Jagannath temple. Accordingly, the Dasara rituals are performed with regard to both kings in both locations. Certainly nowadays, with the human king now longer actually ruling but being restricted to a ritual function, the rituals in the temple are of much greater importance, involve more public participation and are more elaborate (Hardenberg, personal communication). While the sequences of some of the palace rituals have changed and others have been integrated or abandoned, Hardenberg (2008) reports that the main elements of the rituals he witnessed are still the same, compared to Marglin's earlier descriptions. He argues that the aspects of statehood have come to be less significant but that sacrifice, the war against evil (demons) and the regeneration of the cosmos remain the key features of the Durga Puja and Dasara, in which the king, empowered by Durga's *shakti*, plays a crucial role (Hardenberg 2008, 217f).

The Dasara performances in Mysore and Puri conform to the general pan-Indian pattern of Dasara, as could be expected, even though, in these particular instances, some aspects are foregrounded, others less emphasized. Goddesses, the king and sacrifices are crucial in both examples, while the elaboration of the communal dimension of the festival differs. In Puri, at least today, the palace rituals take place without much public participation,[51] while in Mysore in the 1930s, a massive crowd assembled at certain moments of the festival. In conspicuous contrast to the festivals in the jungle kingdoms, however, these large gatherings of people were "peaceful and orderly." Apart from wrestling and dance shows performed by specialists for the king and the public, the dimension of collective play and ferocious rowdy crowds seems to be absent from the festivals in Mysore and Puri.

Some of the features of Dasara as celebrated in Bastar and the Jeypore kingdoms are also to be found in the proceedings in Mysore and Puri. In Mysore, the king (and the queen) passes through a liminal period during the first nine days of the festival. Here, the king is not associated with an ascetic but with a Brahman, who takes a vow and performs fire sacrifices throughout the period. However, the symbolism seems to be the same, as normal rule is suspended and both the king and the Brahman face restrictions that signify their exceptional status. No such transitory phase seems to occur in Puri, but we know of similar expressions of liminality from other classical Hindu kingdoms. In Mewar (Rajasthan), for instance, the king handed over the state sword to the Raj Jogi, who returned it on the ninth day of Navaratri (Fuller 1992, 111f). While the symbolism of human sacrifice is much less pronounced than in Bastar or Jeypore, Ikegame states that in Mysore the king faces a temporal death and has to sacrifice himself.

The dimension of cereal growth is also detectable in Mysore and Puri, albeit indirectly and it is not very pronounced. In Puri, the king and queen are touched with various auspicious objects, among them earth and seeds from the "increaser vessel," while in the Mysore rituals, no such thing is reported. However, Simmons notes a relevant comment from the family chronicles of the

---

51 But the temple rituals are, as mentioned, very important and attract many people. Also each neighborhood in Puri celebrates Dasara (Hardenberg 2008, personal communication).

Wodeyar dynasty of Mysore, which took over from the Vijanagara kings at the beginning of the seventeenth century. After "his first Dasara, Raja Wodeyar built a palace in front of the Rangasvami temple in Srirangapattana in what was formerly a field of millet, and from that time onward the Wodeyar darbar continued to grow as had the millet" (Simmons 2018, 72). While Simmons regards this statement as mere "poetic simile" (ibid.), I think it is significant with regard to the ascribed general regenerative potential of Dasara that such a direct link between the performance of the festival, the growth of cereals and kingship is made.

5.8 Conclusion

While the Dasara performances of Mysore and Puri exhibit some relevant overlap with the festivals in the jungle kingdoms, in my view, the latter – despite the variations in the rituals of Bastar and Jeypore (including Nandapur and Bissamcuttack) – nevertheless show a distinctive pattern. This pattern is the direct result of the vital and massive tribal participation in the Dasara festivals, a dimension which is lacking in Mysore and Puri. Significantly, the tribes are crucial participants and ritual actors, not merely awed on-lookers, spectators of royal glory or passive recipients of royal *tejas*.

This tribal participation has various implications and consequences. First of all, it implies the tribal function of sacrificer and the associated hierarchical relationship between royal and tribal deities. Another corollary is the communal dimension, which includes effervescent and partly ferocious play, as well as communion between king and tribes. However, the communal dimension not only includes the relationship between king and tribes. As has been observed repeatedly by ethnographers with regard to the Dongria Kond, Bhuiya and Juang, the Dasara festival (or the Konto Kuari festival in the case of the Bhuiya) is the only instance when tribes manifest themselves as relational totalities. While the ritual integration of social units does not normally go beyond the levels of the village, the territorial clan or a group of associated villages (*muta*, *pirh*, etc.), in the context of Dasara, tribal collective identities become manifest in relation to the king and in relation to each other. As Ronald Inden (2006, 149) noted with regard to medieval court assemblies, such events were enactments of relationships within the kingdoms and between greater and lesser kings. The enactments of collective tribal identities and their relation to the king in jungle kingdoms pivoted around the performance of sacrifices. It was through sacrificing that communities enacted their collective identity.

Irrespective of the numerous and by no means insignificant variations and details, the general picture that emerges from this comparative analysis of Dasara in the jungle kingdoms thus reveals the above mentioned interrelated aspects (tribal participation, *raja/porja* relationship and homologous relations between deities, enactment of tribal identities) that all pertain to the logic of sacrifice. They are all also related to the main aim of Dasara in the jungle kingdoms, from the perspective of the tribal population in any case, which is not primarily military in nature, but procreative, and concerns general well-being (for instance, conceptualized as *bol soman* or *nehi ane* by the Gadaba and Dongria, respectively) and the growth of cereals in particular.

Sacrifice and well-being in the general sense, and with regard to the fertility of the earth in particular, is also the prevalent theme of the tribal myths discussed in Chapter 3. Myths and Dasara rituals closely correspond with each other. The myths vividly stress the connection between "good" kingship, sacrificial (human) blood, and rain and the growth of plants and cereals. Significantly, elder brother and younger brother have a shared sacrificial responsibility, and the king celebrates Dasara on the global scale, while the tribes perform their local festivals such as Nandi and Go'ter. The brotherhood stories describe the co-creation of kings and tribes and stress the brotherhood between *raja* and *porja*, while the Dasara rituals confirm and reconstitute this relationship through the abduction of the king, who is taken to the forest, or through the commensality of "first fruits."

The obnoxious intermediate layer of high castes, policemen and administrators, which interrupts the immediacy of the king/tribe relationship in some of the myths, is not ritually represented during Dasara. While the Brahmans perform their part in the festival, the tribal participants arrive in the towns and seem to play their own part unhindered and unmediated by high castes and administrators. However, it seems that Brahmans have often replaced tribal priests in the temples of the towns devoted to the goddesses or, as in the case of the Kalika temple in Jeypore, they tend to downplay tribal participation in the temple rituals.

One aspect of the brotherhood stories that is missing at the level of the rituals is the demeaning representation of the tribal subjects as savage, demonic, ugly and cannibalistic. The Dasara rituals seem to pertain more to the subaltern message of the Dom Raja stories, with a positive evaluation of the forest and a massive tribal presence in the capital, which regularly takes the form of effervescent assemblies, ferocious play and ritualized violence. As mentioned, Sahu estimated that 500 Dongria had come to celebrate the Juro festival in Bissamcuttack, which had a population of less than 2,000 in the 1940s, and the Dongria were probably not the only tribal participants during Dasara. In Jeypore, the population actually doubled on the occasion of Dasara at the end of the nineteenth century. According to missionaries residing in the town, 12,000–14,000 people gathered in Jeypore during

Dasara, in a town of about 6,600 inhabitants at the time (Waak 1994 et al., 220; Francis 1907, 261). While I argued for a religious understanding of the play involved in the Dasara festival, in contrast to Alfred Gell, the mythical rebellion against the wicked king and his downfall may well have been on the minds of both the king and the tribal participants during Dasara. The religious and the political certainly implicate each other here.

If the pattern that emerges from the Dasara performances in Bastar and Jeypore is taken to be distinctive, it is certainly not unique on a pan-Indian level as far as its elements are concerned. "Tribal" participation in Hindu rituals of sovereignty and thereby the positive, albeit ambivalent, relationship between forest (*bana*) and civilized realm (*kshetra*) are a widespread feature in India (Sontheimer 1994). The textual descriptions of Navaratra and Durgotsava, discussed in Kane's (1974) *History of the Dharmasastras*, for instance, reveal a number of salient features in this regard. Among them are the construction of a clay altar for the sowing of seeds of barley and wheat and the superior status of human sacrifices that would satisfy the goddess for 1,000 years (1974, 167, 183). Particularly noteworthy is the "tribal festival" (Sabarotsava) on the tenth day of the proceedings. The worshippers should then indulge in "actions usually associated with the sabaras (i.e. aboriginal tribes like the Bhils &c.)" (1974, 176). While sacrifice is conspicuously absent from that context (although amply present in the preceding days), the dimension of play, as described above, is central. "In the manner of the sabaras," people should "express ecstasy," "make merry," throw "dust and mud," cover their bodies in "mire" using obscene language and engage in "revelry" and "dances, songs and music" (1974, 17677). Moreover, the goddess requires that participants reciprocally abuse and curse one another. Exceptional, out of the ordinary, but also auspicious behavior thus characterizes the "tribal festival" that is part of Navaratra, as depicted in the classical Hindu texts discussed by Kane.

During the seventeenth and eighteenth centuries, local communities in the Khurda kingdom also depended on the participation of the nearby tribal groups during their celebration of Durga Puja and Dasara. As described by Akio Tanabe (Tanabe 2003), only through the participation of Kond and Sora ritual specialists, who first embody the goddess Ramachandi, can the chief (locally representing the sovereignty of the king of Khurda) and the Brahmans deal with the thus mediated "primordial power" (*adi shakti*) of the goddess (Tanabe 2003, 121). In fact, the chief had to temporarily submit to the power of the goddess mediated by the tribal specialist and only regained his status after the performance of the "royal sacrifice," during which the tribal medium drank the blood flowing from the victim's body (a goat) (Tanabe 2003, 122f).

The festivals of Jagannath in Puri are another example of the inclusion of "tribal" elements in Hindu rituals. The absence of tribal participation in the Dasara rituals in Puri is conspicuous, as the Jagannath cult has a very explicit "tribal connection" and a group of "tribal" temple servants (the Daita) play a crucial role in the most important festival of the town – the "renewal of the divine bodies" or Nabakalebara (Eschmann et al. 1978; Hardenberg 2011; Marglin 1985, 244f, 263f). As Jagannath is considered as universal sovereign and the king of Puri his human representation, Nabakalebara, like Dasara, is also a ritual renewal of kingship. There are a number of specific features that make the Nabakalebara (and the associated Car Festival) and Dasara similar, beyond the general theme of the regeneration of kingship. One aspect concerns the identification of Daita and the king in the songs and performances of the Davadasi (female temple dancers). The temporary suspension of royal sovereignty – when the king becomes a sweeper – is another common theme of both festivals.

Finally, while the Dasara celebrations in Puri, as described by Marglin and Hardenberg, lack public participation and play, the same cannot be said of the Car Festival, which occurs annually after the "illness" of the deities and is celebrated with special vigor in those years when the divine bodies have just been renewed. The chariots on which the deities are seated along with hundreds of Brahmans and Daita are pulled by the effervescent crowd, to which the chariot caller shouts obscenities that he would be unwilling to repeat in an ordinary context (Marglin 1985, 273f). As is well known – and similar to the former Dasara proceedings in Bastar, where buffaloes were formerly thrown in front of the chariots to be crushed to death – humans earlier also offered themselves up and jumped in front of the wheels of the chariots in Puri to seek immediate liberation.

Looking at the ritual function and the representation of the Daita, similarities with the tribal context are obvious. It is well known that Jagannath is considered to have originally been a tribal deity, represented by a stone in the forest, and was appropriated by the king and transformed into the wooden images that still exist today. Perhaps not unlike the brotherhood connection between king and subjects in the tribal myths, the Daita are also considered to be relatives of the god-king and thus, indirectly, also of the king of Puri (Marglin 1985, 247). Their ritual performance also seems to be similar to the sacrificial role of the tribes in the former Jeypore kingdom, as they ritually kill and thereby regenerate the deities. In one myth, the tribal ancestor killed Krishna in the form of a cow and in the Nabakalebara – as "unscrupulous servants" of the king – they kill the gods to renew their bodies (Hardenberg 2011, 23, 27). Because of their physical proximity and kinship connection they are considered the "body servants" of the gods. First, they help find the trees that will become the new divine bodies, then they fashion the skeleton of the gods and transfer the life essence from the old to the new bodies. Perhaps reminiscent of the Dongria buffalo sacrifice in the *juro* style, they then "hack the old images to pieces and carry them to the burial ground (. . .). There they dig a very deep hole and throw the pieces in it" (Marglin 1985, 265). As kin, they subsequently mourn for ten days, before they put on the new "flesh" of the gods, in the form several layers of different substances.

Still, the Nabakalebara and the Daita also differ from the Dasara in the jungle kingdoms and the tribal participation in the latter in several respects. No "real tribals" (Marglin 1985, 247) are involved in the Nabakalebara. As Marglin remarks, the Daita are indistinguishable from the other Hindus who participate in the festival and, before 1948, were not allowed to enter the Jagannath temple (thus their participation in the festival was restricted). Moreover, the representation of the Daita (e.g., by other temple servants such as the Devadasi) is largely dominated by their renown for impurity and inauspiciousness in connection to the death of the old images, even though they do bring about the renewal and are, as such, also associated with auspiciousness. As in the brotherhood stories, these "tribals" are associated with demons (*daitya*), and Marglin makes a direct connection in this regard with the representations of tribal Nishada in the story of King Vena (1985, 45f). Accordingly, the Daita are excluded from the daily worship of the deities that they normally may not touch. After their necessary work with the bodies during the festival, both images and temple must be purified. It is thus evident that Hindu ideas of purity and pollution (and (in)auspiciousness) largely define the status of the Daita and the limits of their inclusion and participation in the festival.

Finally, and in relation to my last remark, the role of the Daita differs from the status of the tribal participants in Jeypore and Bastar, as the Daita are the encompassed element throughout the festival. They touch the trees with a silver axe, while the Brahmans use a golden axe, and they renew the divine bodies, while the Brahmans make the final touch and add "knowledge" to the images by painting their pupils (Marglin 1985, 273). Moreover, in the liminal period of renewing the divine bodies they are subordinate to the pure Brahmans, called Pati, who cooperate with the Daita during the renewal (Hardenberg 2001; 2011, 132f). According to Hardenberg, this testifies to the "hierarchical encompassment of the forces of the wilderness" (Hardenberg 2001, 70), which the Daita represent. This consistent asymmetry contrasts with the shifting hierarchies between tribes and king/Brahmans as well as between tribal and royal deities in the Dasara festival and other rituals, such as the installation ceremony in Keonjhar or the Konto Kuari festival of the Bhuiya of Bonai (Roy 1935). The ambiguous hierarchies, as I have argued above, signify the complementary status and function of king and tribes as co-sacrificers and co-sovereigns.

The pan-Indian representations of the king as sponsor of sacrifices and husband of the earth certainly resonate with the local ideas present in the Jeypore kingdom and the Dasara festivals in the tribal areas I have analyzed. The relevance of this aspect of fertility and generative potential may be one reason why the king is represented as sacrifier and victim at the same time and identified with an ascetic in the Dasara festivals of Bastar and Jeypore. As discussed in the second chapter, king and ascetic are closely connected with regard to the imageries of sacrifice (including war and austerities performed) and transformative heat (*tapas*). These ideas align well with the focus of Dasara, as a festival that regenerates kingship as much as the earth.

In fact, and certainly also from the tribal perspective, these two aspects of earth and sovereignty are closely associated. However, I would argue that the relationship between king and subjects takes on a specific form in the jungle kingdoms, different from the center-periphery model of kingship as outlined by Ronald Inden (2007) for instance. In the case he discusses, the king is in the center and radiates power (*tejas*) outward from there. This is based on a worldview of a hierarchical chain of being, where those at the fringes – like the tribes – are low, impure and demonic, passive receivers of their graded share of royal power. Though certainly informed by such pan-Indian ideas, the pattern that developed in Jeypore, and perhaps other jungle kingdoms as well, seems to be different. Although we cannot assume that the king and his tribal subjects shared exactly the same kind of perspective, tribal and royal representations overlap to a considerable degree, and perhaps even evolved in a kind of elective affinity.

In the Jeypore kingdom, king and tribes share the same earth nature, as becomes evident in the myths of the earth-born king, and which is confirmed in the commensal relations between king and tribes. The kings also made use of tribal labor, but the sacrificial "work" performed by the tribes was certainly also crucial for the king. What we thus have is a hierarchical opposition of macro and micro sacrificers, of the king as metaperson and powerful sacrificer on the global level, who nevertheless depends on the sacrificial sovereignty of his tribal subjects on the local level. In the Dasara festivals and the other rituals that involve tribes and king, this shifting hierarchical opposition and mutual dependence is dynamically enacted, though certainly not always without tension.

6 Rituals of Rice and Rebellion: The Ganga Festival of the Joria

Turning now to the indigenous festivals that the proverb mentions – those of the Joria, the Mali and the Gadaba – it is appropriate to start with a consideration of the agricultural history of this particular region as cereals play a vital role in each of them. In his analysis of the Lachmi Jagar (Gregory 2004, 2013, 2021; Gregory and Vaishnav 2003), Chris Gregory made a strong case for understanding oral epics and the associated rituals in Bastar against the background of the regional agricultural history and the rice cultivation cycle. He argued that the Lachmi Jagar – the "Watch of Lachmi," a song of more than 30,000 lines sung by women (*gurumai*) during the cold season – is actually a metaphor for the rice cultivation process. The associated ritual performances that last about eleven days constitute a harvest festival, and the story represents the history of agricultural intensification and the historical transformation from millet to rice cultivation that had occurred in some parts of the region. In the Lachmi Jagar, this shift is narrated in the form of two marriages of Narayan, Mahadev's (Shiva's) younger brother.

Mahadev facilitates the pregnancy of Queen Cloud (Meng) by providing her with a mango, which leads to her pregnancy and subsequently to her giving birth to Lachmi (rice). The mango was only given, however, on the condition that, should Queen Cloud conceive a girl, she should be married to Narayan. At the time, the latter was already married to the Twenty-One Queens, an allegory for millets. As it turns out, after the second marriage, the two wives did not get along, with the Twenty-One Queens giving Lachmi a hard time and driving her away, resulting in a famine. Ultimately, Narayan manages to bring her back and prosperity and domestic peace is restored. This story presents a rice-centric perspective, Gregory argues, and is only performed in those regions where rice is the dominant crop and not in those areas still dominated by millets. This is clear from the contrasting valuations of the crops: Lachmi (rice) representing wealth and prosperity, while Narayan's first millet-wife being the opposite, Alachmi, signifying poverty and barrenness.

As far as the dominant cereals are concerned, India is conventionally divided into three zones, wheat dominating in the north-west, rice in the north-east and millets in the south (see Kingwell-Banham and Fuller 2012, 86). Gregory (2004) argues that Bastar lies on the rice/millet divide and describes a rice-millet continuum where, in some sub-regions and villages, millets dominate, while in others rice is the most important crop. In yet other villages, in fact most, both cereals are cultivated to varying degrees.

The region of my main concern figures quite prominently in the scientific literature on archaeobotany, agroecology, plant biology and related sub-disciplines, somewhat in contrast to the ethnographic exploration and anthropological discussion of the area. Some scholars claim that Koraput, or the Jeypore tract as it is called in the literature, is an independent center of origin for cultivated Asian rice (*Oryza sativa*), with Mishra (2009) especially mentioning the Gadaba and Sora in this connection (see also Barik et al. 2019; Roy et al. 2017). Irrespective of this actually being the case or not, what seems to be clear is that the region is an ancient agricultural hotspot featuring great diversity of local landraces and a variety of cultivation techniques. While archaeological evidence is scarce in Odisha,[1] and in Koraput especially, with regard to agricultural origins, two Neolithic traditions have been distinguished, one being the coastal area, the other the tribal highlands (Harvey et al. 2006). Investigating agricultural origins for South Asia as a whole, Dorian Fuller (2006) identified Koraput as an important agricultural region (see map, Fuller 2006, 56).

> The historical linguistic data suggests an earlier shifting-cultivation tradition, perhaps focused on hilly areas, with a subsequent more settled agriculture associated with the South Munda subfamily (. . .). The epicentre for this agricultural evolution might be suggested to be in Southern Orissa (the Koraput region *sensu lato*)(. . .). (Fuller 2006, 48)

In their earlier comparative linguistic research on Munda languages – among them those spoken in the Koraput region, that is, those spoken by the Gadaba (Gutob), Didayi (Gta'), Bondo (Remo) and Parenga (Gorum) and Sora (Sora) – Arlene and Norman Zide came to similar conclusions:

> The data presented in this paper provides good evidence that the Proto-Mundas, presumably at least 3500 years B.P. (or earlier) at a conservative estimate, had a subsistence agriculture which produced or at least knew grain – in particular rice, two or three millets, and at least three legumes. (. . .)
>
> The Jeypore Tract in southern Orissa now is (and presumably has been for some time past) inhabited by a large number of different tribal groups, including five of the South Munda groups (. . .). The tract is crucial to the understanding of the development of rice varieties in India, where a great number of wild and cultivated varieties of rice are found. It falls within the area starting in Orissa in India and extending into Burma and beyond, where it has been suggested rice may originally have been cultivated. It is also worth pointing out that in terms of the number and diversity of rice pests and the time judged necessary by entomologists to account for the development of such a profusion of them,

---

[1] Harvey and his colleagues (Harvey et al. 2006, 24) state that "Orissa is one of the most poorly studied areas of India in terms of archaeological investigations and in particular agricultural origins."

the Jeypore Tract would qualify as a possible area of origin of proliferation (. . .). (Zide and Zide 1976, 1324, 1302)[2]

In his general overview for *The Cambridge World History of Food*, Te-Tzu Chang (2008) also mentioned the Jeypore tract as being among the "areas of remarkable varietal diversity" (2008, 138) at the global level. Chang describes the evolution of cultivation practices, from the broadcasting of rice in rain-fed fields (shifting cultivation) to bounded fields that hold rain water, to the transplantation of seedlings into irrigated fields. In this regard, Chang comments that (2008, 142): "The entire range of practices can still be seen in the Jeypore Tract and the neighboring areas (author's personal observations)."

6.1 Two Different Cultivation Systems

When my colleague from archaeobotany, René Cappers, and I visited several tribal villages – especially those of Kuvi Kond and Boro Porja – in Koraput in 2019, we also noted the immense varieties of cultivated plants and cultivation practices, from gardens to level dry fields, to hill fields where ploughing is impossible, to irrigated fields. In general, however, two distinctive systems are prevalent on the Koraput plateau. The first concerns shifting cultivation, often employed on relatively steep hill slopes (Kingwell-Banham and Fuller 2012; Patnaik 1977). Here, various millets normally dominate but they are sown in the same fields as a number of other cultivated plants, such as maize, turmeric, yams and pulses. The different Kond groups – Kuttia, Dongria, Kuvi or Desia Kond – implement this kind of system, which, accordingly, shapes their social and religious life (Hardenberg 2018a, 2018b; Jena et al. 2002; Niggemeyer 1064; Sukuma 1969). Herman Niggemeyer, for instance, writes about the Kuttia Kond of Phulbani, whom he describes as "typical millet cultivators" (Niggemeyer 1964a, 95, translation PB):

---

[2] Christoph von Fürer-Haimendorf (1943, 150) likewise considers the Gadaba to be rice cultivators since long, also employing a linguistic argument: The Gadaba "are undoubtedly expert in the cultivation of rice in mountainous country, and there is every reason to believe that the growing of wet rice is a fairly ancient element of their culture." He adds in a footnote (143, 150, fn.1): "The word for 'irrigated rice field' is in Gadaba and Bondo *liyong* and in Munda *loyong*; this suggests that the cultivation of wet rice must have been common to the peoples speaking Austroasiatic languages of the Munda branch before their dispersal into widely separated tribal groups."

Thus the jungle fields on the slopes of the mountains are in every respect primary in the thought and action of the people. They dominate the mythical ideas, their fertility is the goal of almost all cults (. . .) and ultimately also the practical activity of each tribal member is determined almost throughout the whole year daily by the work on the fields. (Niggemeyer 1964a, 94; translation PB, using DeepL Translator)[3]

The second system is no less important with regard to the cultural and religious life of the cultivators. It is different from the first, as both rice and millet are traditional staple crops, but they are cultivated in different ways. Millet crops – especially finger millet (*Eleusine coracana*) but also little millet (*Panicum sumatrense*) – are sown on dry, relatively level fields (*poda*). On such fields – though not mixed with the millet – niger seed (*Guizotia abyssinica*) and dry rice of a shorter maturation period (*poda dan*) are also sown. Wet rice is cultivated in terraced riverbeds (*bera*). These rivers originate on the plateau, with the springs often being close to the villages and the slow-flowing water enabling cultivation throughout the year. In March/April, rice is sown in nursery beds and only after the April festival (Chait Porob) is the rice transplanted to the permanent fields.[4] The water of the river runs in channels on both sides of the fields, which can be opened or closed to irrigate the fields or to dry them out. A conspicuous feature of these paddy fields is that – probably through centuries of erosion – they lie much lower than the common surface of the village and one has to climb down five meters or so to reach the rice fields below.

Like the swidden fields in the case of the Kuttia and Dongria Kond, this dual agricultural practice has fundamentally shaped the rituals and worldviews of the tribal communities. Significantly, the fields (dry field vs. river field) and the crops (millet vs. rice) are contrasted by the cultivators. Bondo,[5] Parenga, Ollar Gadaba, Gutob Gadaba and Joria, and probably others, practice this kind of dual cultivation, and I would assume that all of them contrast fields and crops, although this can be little more than an informed guess because of a lack of ethnographic data. The Gutob Gadaba, in any case, juxtapose rice and millet and classify land and cereals with regard to a conceptual distinction that

---

3 "So stehen die Dschungelfelder an den Hängen der Berge in jeder Hinsicht im Denken und Tun des Volkes an erster Stelle. Sie beherrschen die mythischen Vorstellungen, ihre Fruchtbarkeit ist das Ziel fast aller Kultfeiern (. . .) und letzten Endes wird auch die praktische Tätigkeit eines jeden Stammesangehörigen fast das ganze Jahr hindurch tagtäglich durch die Arbeit auf den Feldern bestimmt." (Niggemeyer 1964a, 94).
4 I do not discuss here the recent innovation of inserting another summer crop in the cycle of wet-rice cultivation, which is ritually invisible (Berger 2015, xvi).
5 The terracing of rice fields in the beds of the rivers has already been mentioned in a short text on the Bondo published by J.A. May in 1873 (May 1873, 238).

is ubiquitous in the whole region: that between consanguines (*bai*) and affines (*bondu*) (Berger 2015, 2018), or "brotherhood" and "otherhood," as Chris Gregory (2009) formulated it with reference to Bastar.

Finger millet, especially consumed as a thick gruel (*pej, ida*), is considered by the Gutob Gadaba to be particularly life-enhancing. People who are ill should drink it, and I have seen people close to death being fed millet gruel to strengthen them and as a last-ditch attempt to prevent death. If you do not drink millet gruel, I have been told by my Gadaba friends, your blood turns whitish. The dry fields (*poda*) on which millet is grown are considered to belong to the consanguineal village space and the millet plants are accordingly conceptualized as "children of the village." The village sacrificer distributes seeds to be sown in the dry fields to all villagers while standing on top of the shrine of the village deity (*hundi*), the local representation of the earth deity. Moreover, when the village is closed off from the outside world during the April festival (Chait Porbo) the earth may not be injured, and the consumption of millet gruel is likewise prohibited.

While the Gadaba conceptualize the dry fields as "own" or consanguineal, the paddy fields are classified as affinal "other" and the rice is brought into the village as a bride. In fact, the whole agricultural year is conceived with regard to the paddy fields as a period of courting the bride (*raibadi*). All activities related to the *bera* fields are perceived as visits to the bride-givers until, after many visits, the bride is taken home after the harvest rituals. In addition to blood and the liver, rice from these fields is a crucial ingredient for the most important kind of food for the Gadaba, sacrificial food called *tsoru* or *go'yang* (Berger 2017). While other Desia also prepare this kind of food, it seems that the Gadaba have particularly elaborated this more general feature. *Tsoru* figures in numerous contexts. It is prepared during annual village sacrifices for local deities and then creates a hierarchy between the local "earth people" (*matia*) who are eligible to share *tsoru* and "late comers" (*urpia*) who eat *lakka'*. In such contexts, *tsoru* consists of the head, blood and liver of the sacrificial animal and the rice (*potri chaul*) that is collected from all households of the village. The *lakka'* food consists of identical shares of the meat from the body of the sacrificial animal and is distributed to various groups of late comers, who have to bring their own rice. *Tsoru* is also crucial for each individual, as it transforms the ritual status of a person; it is a marker of their ritual status. Only ritually mature men – those who have been fed *tsoru* during their marriage ceremonies – are allowed to share sacrificial food at the most important village shrines. It is therefore clear that finger millet and wet rice are complementary resources for the Gadaba. In short, millet is about life (and death) and being, while rice concerns status, hierarchy and structure (Berger 2018).

While the Gadaba's conceptualization of the rice/millet distinction is thus explicit, fundamental and finds multiple expressions, I know of no other community that ritually enacts the juxtaposition of these crops as elaborately as the Joria. They devote two, ten-day festivals to rice and finger millet, respectively the Ganga Puja and the Nandi Porbo. The former is performed in January (*pus*), when the Gadaba and other Desia repair the embankments of the paddy fields. This constitutes the beginning of the *raibadi* period, the suit for the bride (rice). The festival dedicated to millet takes place in February (*mag*), when the Gadaba perform either their marriages or their Go'ter.

6.2 The Joria

The category of *porja*[6] ("subjects") created such a profound confusion in the literature that Verrier Elwin once spoke about an "ethnological *bouillabaisse*" (1954, xxxvii) and von Fürer-Haimendorf suggested that the term be abandoned in academic discourse for the same reason (1943, 161, fn. 1). Nearly all tribal communities of Koraput have at times been included in this category of "subjects" and "peasants" (*roit*). Thurston (1909b, 209f), among others, classified Parenga, Bonda and Kond in this category.[7] Later, Bell (1945) was more careful. He mentions Bondo, Dhurwa and Didayi when discussing the "Porja" but states that they would be different from the "typical Porojas that are met with round Koraput [town]" (Bell 1945, 71f), adding that the Pengo, Joria and Bareng would be the "Porojas proper" (1945, 72).

Bell's view is confirmed to some extent by K. N. Thusu (1977), who conducted ethnographic research among the Pengo around the town of Nabarangpur, some 40 kilometers north of Jeypore as the crow flies. He states that the Joria and Pengo are the two communities commonly referred to as Porja (1977, 1), which Elwin considered to be culturally near identical.[8] In the village that Thusu studied, Pengo and Joria lived side by side; they stressed, however, that they were different communities (*jati*). According to the author, the Joria considered themselves senior with regard to the Pengo, which found some acceptance among the latter. The Barenga Porja are also mentioned by Thusu (1977, 3) and Chowdhury (1963/64). The latter calls them "Bareng Jodia Porjoja" in his paper on their "marriage custom." He claims they would be "originally an

---
6 Variously written as Poroja, Parja, Praja etc.
7 See also Chowdhury (1963/63), Ramdas (1931b) and Ulaka (1976).
8 "There was nothing at all to distinguish Pengas and Jhorias," Elwin states (1954, xxxviii).

offshoot of the Gond tribe" and that one "of their main traditions states their original home to be in Bastar" (1963/64, 27).[9] The villages he visited, however, were in the vicinity of Koraput town. The connection between "Bareng" and "Jodia" may be an indication that they are the same group that I discussed in previous chapters – the section of the Joria called Bening. I visited one of their villages close to the Queens Fall near Nandapur. With regard to the Census of India, the situation is not much better now, as the data provided by the Ministry of Tribal Affairs (2013, 158 iv) does not list the Joria separately but as part of the disparate Porja category (including Boro Porja, Barong Porja, Konda Porja and others) numbering 374,628 individuals.

As Elwin noted (1954, xxxvii), it is fortunate that ethnographers have moved away from using sweeping labels such as Porja and focused on distinct communities rather than grouping them all together into such a generic category. It is also important to consider the politics of naming and identification, which probably have a long history, and not only in Central India (Subba and Wouters 2013). Bell's remark that some communities "style themselves Porojas" (1945, 71) is instructive, and various communities have probably self-identified as Porja in the past to highlight a closeness to the kings of Nandapur and Jeypore, similar to the Raja Muria around the capital of Jagdalpur (Elwin 1991b [1947]).[10]

In their social structure and religion, the Joria resemble the other Desia communities of the plateau and clearly are a part of the "Koraput Complex" as outlined by Pfeffer (1997, 2019). As such, the community is divided into totemic patrilineal descent categories (*bonso*) and status categories (*kuda*), from which local dignitaries in each village, such as the village sacrificer (*pujari*, *jani*) or village chief (*naik*), are recruited. They worship the same local deities and perform the same annual festivals as all tribes on the plateau, the April festival (Chait Porbo) being among the most prominent. Like Kond and Gond communities, the Joria used to speak a Dravidian tongue (Rousseleau 2021), but all Joria I met exclusively spoke Desia.[11]

Among the distinctive features of the Joria is the way they erect megalithic monuments for the dead, namely in a long row next to the village assembly

---

9 Also Izikowitz (1969, 130) considers the Joria to belong to the larger Gond category as he writes: "The Joria and other Gond tribes have many members" on the Koraput plateau.
10 Speaking of names, both Elwin (1991, 15f) and Grigson (1991, 44f) mention a community called Jhoria Muria in Bastar and both argue that this community has a close cultural affinity to the Hill Maria of the neighboring Abujhmar Hills; however, to the Joria of Koraput, Elwin remarks, "they bear no resemblance" (1991, 15).
11 Mahapatra (1985, 299–303) briefly discusses the Desia dialect of the Joria (Jhariya) around Koraput town.

platform (*sadar*). Their most idiosyncratic aspects, as noted above, are the twin festivals that they perform, the Ganga Puja and the Nandi Porbo.[12] These festivals are also remarkable with respect to their material culture and general ritual aesthetics. I am not aware of anything comparable or equally elaborate among the other communities of the plateau. With regard to material culture, the rituals of the Gadaba or Bondo seem to be much simpler, and the stilt dances, straw men, feather head-dresses and ritual animals that I will be describing below remind me more of the Muria, as described by Elwin (1991b).

For more details on the Joria, I can refer the reader to the work of Raphaël Rousseleau, the principal ethnographer of this community, who has published one monograph (Rousseleau 2008) and numerous articles (e.g., Rousseleau 2008, 2010b, 2012, 2021; Rousseleau and Behera 2002/2003). The Ganga and Nandi festivals are, however, only relatively briefly described in his publications (Rousseleau 2008, 160–65, 2021, 250–53). Apart from his work, no serious ethnographic fieldwork with this community has been conducted.

The two villages where we documented the Nandi and Ganga festivals, Lenjisuku and Kurubi, lie in the most western part of the Joria area, about 15 kilometers due north-west of the former royal capital of Nandapur, which is now a small and insignificant town. This is the region on the eastern side of the Goradi River – which has been part of the Kolab reservoir since the 1980s (Mishra 2002) – where Gutob Gadaba and Joria villages meet. Only a few Boro Gadaba villages are to be found on this side of the Goradi, with the Gutob Gadaba area spreading south-westward until it meets the first Bonda villages in the district of Malkangiri.

My contact with the Joria was established more than 20 years ago via a Joria man called Leukon Maji, whom I first met in the Gadaba village of Gorihanjar. As is common among the Gadaba (and probably the Desia more generally), the ritual specialist or the senior (*boro*) *dissari*, who determines important dates and times of annual village festivals, is usually recruited from a different community. Leukon Maji, skinny and with long matted hair that he usually wore in a bun, was the *boro dissari* of Gorihanjar. He invited me to his village, Kurubi, and also introduced me to the people of Lenjisuku.

Lenjisuku and Kurubi are two large and – judging from the megalithic structures – probably very old Joria villages that fit into the general pattern of Desia villages described above. In the village of Kurubi, the *kuda* groups of Boi (Cobra *bonso*) and Maji (Cobra and Tiger) are most numerous, followed by

---

[12] Some Ollar Gadaba also perform simplified versions of the Nandi festival, which they have probably adopted from the neighboring Joria (Thusu and Jha 1972, 112f).

Munduli, Sisa and Jani (all Cobra). Informants mentioned still other units of the village, thereby presumably referring either to a village clan or *kutum* (see Berger 2015).[13] In addition to these Joria groups, some fifteen households of Dombo lived in the village. These groups resided in four spatial sections (*sai*) of the village: the Mandu Sai (Maji, Boi, Jani, Munduli), Moja Sai ("middle" section, Boi, Maji, Sisa), Upore Sai ("upper" section, Karningia, Majo, Boi, Jani) and the Dombo Sai (only Dombo). Different *kuda* groups are also represented in Lenjisuku: the Mordia and Munduli (both Tiger), Jani (Cobra), who provide the village sacrificer (*jani*), Boronaik (from which the *naik* is recruited), Kirsani and Maji. The latter group was the host of the Nandi deity, but different local groups were involved in the festival, as will be seen.[14] As usual, in addition to the Joria, Dombo also lived in the village (Bear and Hawk).

What is rare and spectacular in Lenjisuku is its *sadar-hundi* construction. Commonly, these stone structures are found opposite each other in the center of Desia villages. In Lenjisuku, the *sadar* is not a continuous assemblage of vertical and horizontal stones but has more the character of a colosseum. Vertical megaliths (*sil*) create a large circle, with flat stones (*sadar*) on the inside as seating places. On one side, an entrance to the open space in the middle is formed by two vertical stones, while on the other side, two huge and very old trees delimit the space, their impressive roots having embraced the megaliths over the course of time. Close to one tree but outside the stone circle proper is another accumulation of vertical stone slabs. These are placed in commemoration of the dead, but not for everyone, I have been told, only for "senior" people.[15] More or less opposite the trees on the other side of the stone circle lies the *hundi* shrine. This is the first and only time that I saw a circular, open assembly area (sadar) that actually encompasses the shrine of the village deity. As can be imagined, during both the Nandi and Ganga festivals, this place was crucial for the ritual process.[16]

---

13 Gunjia, Katia, Morjia, Chinderi, Chendia, Petia, Karningia.

14 Whereas different *kuda* groups can commonly be recognized very clearly in the spatial setup of a village, they were dispersed to a high degree in Lenjisuku. When I followed the processions from house to house I was astonished to find Maji, Boronaik, Kirsani and Munduli to be rather mixed in the different sections of the village.

15 Also in Kurubi, next to the shrine of the earth deity an assemblage of vertical stones (*sil*) was found. As in Lenjisuku it was stressed that only for senior people megaliths would be erected in the *bur* ritual, the third sequence in the process of death rituals.

16 In Lenjisuku I documented the Nandi festival on my own in 2000. In the same year I witnessed the main day of the Ganga Puja in that village as well, this time accompanied by my wife Amrei Volkmann and two Gadaba friends, Samo Sisa and Kesebo Sisa. A year later, Amrei and I spent six days in total in Kurubi to document the Ganga Puja and to conduct interviews afterwards. We were then accompanied by my research assistant, Manto Pradhan.

Each lasting about ten days, the Ganga[17] and Nandi festivals are celebrated at the end of the agricultural year and before the beginning of the new one. In the years that a village community – often consisting of several local segments or hamlets – performs them, they are celebrated in successive months, the Ganga festival in January (*pus*) and the Nandi festival in February (*mag*). Like the Bali Jatra, which will be discussed in a subsequent chapter, both festivals are usually celebrated for three successive years, followed by an interval of two years.[18]

6.3 The Ganga Festival

Although rice is a conspicuous feature of the festival, the Ganga Porbo offers many surprises and has many different aspects. Certainly, it is about different kinds of movement. As the description of the festival will show, and as many informants' statements testify, people have to move the gods. In order to do this, they have to move themselves in different ways. As in many parts of India, the gods are moved in a procession. The gods are brought into the village, hosted and moved, "walked" or made to "roam around" (*buliba*) there for days. Two other very important forms of ritual movement are "dance" (*nat*) and "play" (*kel*). Dancing and playing make the gods move and, in turn, they make people "walk" in peculiar ways which show the deities' presence. The gods' movement through the village is important to guarantee the fertility of the paddy fields and a successful harvest for the coming year. More generally, it is crucial for the health and well-being of the people and domestic animals. In order to achieve all this, however, people must sacrifice, dance and play; they must have fun, *sarda*, to make the deity feel pleased (*kusi*).

These gods (*maphru*, *debta*, *takur* which are used synonymously), as is the case among the Desia in general, have very few special characteristics. Ganga and Nandi are most often described as elder brother and younger sister respectively, but they are also at times conceptualized as co-wives, or as king and queen. Relationships between gods are expressed among he Gadaba in similar

---

17 Most often the Joria spoke about Ganga Puja. In general Indian context *puja* means "worship," in Koraput it always includes the meaning of "sacrifice." Both Nandi and Ganga are also referred to as "festival" or *porbo*. I use both these terms in the following, that is, *puja* and *porbo*. Another name used for the festival was Ganga Budia (Ganga of the "old man/woman").
18 As regards the rhythm of the performances I have heard other statements as well, for example that Ganga and Nandi are celebrated every other year, or three years in a row followed by a gap of three years. What seems to be sure in any case, then, is that the performances are not conducted annually but with an interval.

ways. However, these features were often not articulated consistently. From the perspective of the Gadaba or Joria, little can be known about deities. Questions I asked in the field, such as whether the deities are always present at their shrines, were answered with a shrug of the shoulders or "one cannot know that" (*jani hebo nai*). Deities are distinguished by the festivals that are addressed to them, as well as by their names and the locations of their shrines. However, except for the *hundi* shrine in the center of each village, these shrines look very similar, consisting mostly of trees and stones. While, for the Gadaba, the sacrificial meat offered to the gods is the crucial form of distinction, so much so that they speak of "buffalo-eating gods" and "goat-eating gods," this aspect was not so pronounced in the Ganga and Nandi festivals.

As far as names are concerned, Ganga and Nandi evoke associations with two famous Hindu deities: Nandi refers to Shiva's bull; Ganga to the goddess and divine river whom, in the myth, Shiva caught so elegantly with his matted hair. However, apart from the fact that the Ganga festival is about paddy and that paddy fields are constructed into the river beds as described above, I could find no connection between this festival and the Hindu goddess. Also the fact that Ganga/rice commonly referred to as the elder brother of his younger sister – Nandi/millet – does at least not support the association with the Hindu river goddess. Shiva, likewise, is absent from the ritual process, and during our conversations and interviews, no Joria drew connections to these Hindu deities.

The Performers

One of the striking features of the Ganga Puja is the fact that certain Joria assume a different social identity during the festival. As soon as the deity enters the village, three groups are formed: the Ghasi, the Dom[19] and the Paik. Only the Dombo are relevant from the local perspective, as Ghasi and Paik are rarely found in any Joria or Gadaba village. Clearly, the village is not the reference of this dramatic performance but the former capital of Nandapur. Breklum missionaries, who had just established a branch in Nandapur, mention the different living quarters of the Paik, Dombo and Ghasi in one of their reports from 1911 (Waak et al. 1994, 241). Ghasi probably settled in Nandapur long ago, as

---

[19] In the context of the festival this social category was referred to as Dom or Dommon ("Dom people," *mon* being the plural suffix), although it denotes the same community as the term Dombo, which is commonly used among the Desia. It is notable that there is thus a correspondence in the use of the term Dom both in the Ganga festival and the stories about the Dom king.

part of the service infrastructure of the royal court, especially as stable grooms dealing with the king's horses (Rousseleau 2008, 219; 2010b, 48). Bell's (1945, 81) description of the Ghasi in the 1945 census of the Koraput District, however empirically inaccurate it might be, actually matches very well with their ritual representation at the Ganga festival, as will be seen: "They are grooms by profession but sections of the caste are also scavengers. The Ghasis are addicted to crime and have been notified as criminal tribe. They are also noted for being drunkards and brawlers."

In contrast to the absence of Ghasi in tribal villages of the region, Dombo are ubiquitous (see the introduction and Chapter 3). In the whole area, they perform the functions of petty traders, musicians and, formerly, weavers. The village herald (*barik*) is always recruited from this group, and together with the village headman (*naik*, the latter always being provided by the cultivators of the dominant clan), he negotiates internal and external village matters. The Dombo must have been an integral part of tribal villages in the highlands for a very long time. Even in places where no other non-cultivating communities are to be found, such as in the Niamgiri Hills inhabited by the Dongria Kond (Hardenberg 2018a), they are an integral part of the local social order. They are the only group for whom the Gadaba have a Gutob term (Goren). Even though my own experiences with the Dombo and of the interaction between the Gadaba and Dombo do not confirm this view, the Dombo have frequently been represented as outside elements in the highlands, as exploiters and money-lenders profiting from the illiteracy and "innocence" of their tribal patrons. This image is found in academic literature (Elwin 1950; Vitebsky 2017a) and is also very prominent in Mohanty's novel, *Paraja* (Mohanty 1987). A statement in the *Koraput District Gazetteer* can be taken to be representative in this regard:

> The Dombs play the role of middlemen between the tribal people and the outside exploiters. (. . .) The unscrupulous Dombs very often play tricks with the simple and innocent Khonds and Saoras and deprive them of their valuable holdings on false pretexts. (Senapati and Sahu 1966, 203)

What I can confirm is that, in the region, Dombo are regarded as cunning, and this feature is also found in their ritual representation in the context of the Ganga festival.

The Paik, finally, have a high social status and are closely connected to the king. They share these features with the Rona and both communities have been at times identified or the Paik have been considered a sub-division of the Rona (Thurston 1909c, 459). According to Thurston (1909c, 458) one meaning of Paik refers to the Sanskrit term *padatika* or *padika*, meaning "foot-soldier." He quotes another source that states: "In Cuttack the Paiks formally constituted a local militia, holding land of the Zamindars or Rajas by the tenure of military service" (1909c, 458). Thurston also quotes the Madras Census Report from 1891, which holds that Paik is rather an occupational term than referring to a caste, adding that it "used to denote the retainers of the Uriya [Oriya] Chiefs of Ganjam and Vizagapatnam. These men were granted lands on feudal tenure, and belonged to various castes" (1909c, 458). Already several decades earlier, Carmichael (1869) mentioned that the Paik are no longer as numerous in some places as they used to be, as the new colonial administration replaced them with police (some Paik apparently joined the police service according to Thurston (1909c, 458):

> Formerly they were a numerous body, but their numbers are much diminished now (. . .). Now there are very few paiks kept up as fighting men; those discharged from service have taken to trading with the coast, and to cultivating their pieces of land. The fort at Kotpad on the Bustar [Bastar] frontier always had a standing garrison of seven hundred paiks. They are gradually being disbanded since we have put Police there. (Carmichael 1869, 101)

As I mentioned in Chapter 3, the vassal king of Bissamcuttack also maintained a military reserve and was obliged to provide the Maharaja of Jeypore with Paik soldiers on demand (Nayak 1989, 180).

The *dramatis personae* of the Ganga festival, all from the Joria community, thus include the following. In Kurubi, the Ghasi are represented by seven men, the leading figure among them is the *mul ghasi*. This "main" Ghasi is not only the first among the Ghasi but also the most important figure in the whole festival. He oversees the procedures, leads the public sacrifices in the course of the processions through the village and often also acts as sacrificer himself. His junior partner among the Ghasi is the *kaswati*, with similar duties. Two other Ghasi are called *parbat* ("mountain") and *balashti* (the meaning is unclear), with unspecified tasks. A Ghasi called *jali ganja* ("long-tailed rooster") plays a one-sided frame drum (*dapu*) and another called *gora* ("horse") actually performs as a horse, the *kaswati* being the horseman. Finally, the most junior among the Ghasi is the *tjuli* (the meaning is unclear), again without specified tasks. All Ghasi dress in rags, or are said to go "naked," especially on the main day of the festival (Monday), when they do not wear shirts. Their attitude is generally supposed to be repugnant, as they beg, cheat and exhibit greedy and gluttonous behavior: "their stomachs never get full," as has been commented several times. They are treated as outcasts by others, and on the day of the stilt dance especially, they are not allowed into people's houses.

Five men act as Dom. Again, among them one pair is found, similar to the *mul ghasi/kaswati* duo, namely the *kongar* and the *seti*. The task of both is to prepare the sacrificial site with cow dung (*goboro sara*) and to draw the sacrificial patterns with rice flour at the various stops of the procession through the village. They also redistribute the heads of the sacrificial animals after "stealing" them, as some have pointed out. Another Dom is referred to as *bakiya*, which might be related to *baki* or "loan" (Gustafsson 1989, 367) and thus could signify a money-lender. He acts as sacrificer during the procession. Two Dom men are referred to as *toknia*, a term perhaps related to the word "fraud" (*tokna*, Mahapatra 1985, 225) and thus to be translated as "cheaters." They are both drummers, one of them playing a two-headed cylindrical drum (*dol*), the other a kettle drum (*tamok*). Significantly, no "real" Dombo play any music during the festival, although drumming and playing the *moiri*, an oboe-like instrument, is an otherwise necessary ingredient for Desia festivals and life-cycle rituals. Like the Ghasi, all Dom are characterized by their poor dress and repulsive behavior.

The six men who act as Paik are not internally as elaborately distinguished as the Ghasi and Dom. They wear colored turbans, long-sleeved shirts and long garments around their waists and legs (*lungi*). Even though their dress is of a higher status, their behavior is also rude – although they do not cheat and steal – as they sing filthy songs (*obodro git*) throughout the festival, like the Dom and Ghasi, apparently all three of them in competition. While the Paik are not subdivided into as many personas as the Ghasi and Dom, there is one important group also classified as Paik, the Dengudi. This name means a "high" or "long" (*deng*) "shrine" (*gudi*) and is quite suitable, as it refers to a group of stilt dancers. In contrast to Ghasi, Dom and the other Paik, who all drink heavily throughout the festival, as does almost everyone, the Dengudi carefully prepare and fast for their moment at the highpoint of the festival, when the gods make them walk on stilts during the night after the last procession, and before the deities leave the village again the next day.

For the duration of the festival, these Joria men thus change their social identity and one may ask whether there are any "Joria" involved in the festival at all. When I asked this question to the *memor*[20] of the village, he replied with "we dance" (*ame nat korlani*). While this is certainly true, it is not the whole story. On the one hand, female ritual media called *gurumai*, common among all Desia communities, participate in the festival. They should also be sober and dance in the procession. At the sacrificial stops, they squat down to communicate with the deities. Finally, the most crucial role that the Joria play as "Joria" is that of the hosts of the gods. In Kurubi, there are three representations of the Ganga deity (in Lenjisuku two, who are "brothers"): three clay pots covered with three earthen lights on top. During their stay in the village, these deities

---

[20] Elected village representative (from English "ward member").

are always hosted by the same family, for generations, as the Joria stressed. Likewise, the ritual objects, pot (*handi*) and lamp (*maloi*), are said to have been the same since the foundation of the village ("the time the village sat down," *ga bosiba somoyore*). The fact that they are said not to break, even if they are dropped on the floor, is a sign of their ascribed extraordinary status.

The three deities are ranked according to their seniority. The most senior deity is hosted by a house from the Boi group, the middle deity by a Maji house and the junior deity by a Gunjia house. The male household heads are called *domi* and they care for the gods, as well as paint, decorate and worship them. After the festival, they keep them safe in their houses until the next occasion. The *domi* do not consume millet gruel for the duration of the festival and also remain sober throughout, like their wives, the *domini*. These women must fast during the day, as it is their task to carry the gods on their heads for many hours and over several days during the procession through the village. In addition, the three *domini* each carry two miniature objects made from bamboo, a sword (*kanda*) and a shield (*poiri*). Even though the names *domi/domini* may suggest a relation to the Dom, our informants did not included them in this category. Finally, one son of each *domi/domini* house performs as *budia pila*, the "son (*pila*) of the old man/woman," that is, the deity, as the festival is also called Ganga Budia, "Ganga of the old man/woman."[21] The children accompany the procession and carry a brass plate with husked rice, a sacrificial knife and oil for the lamps on top of the pots. After a sacrificial stop during the procession, they also carry the heads of the animals (goats and sheep) on this plate, until the next sacrificial break, when *kongar* and *seti* take them for later redistribution.

These are the main characters during the Ganga Porbo. More Joria are involved in other roles, mostly in the form of various animals, as will be seen in the subsequent description of the events.

The Ritual Process

In Kurubi, the Ganga Porbo we witnessed lasted for ten days, starting on Monday, January 1, 2001 and ending on Wednesday, January 10, the day after the full moon of the month of *pus* (Dec./Jan.).[22]

---

[21] *Budi* means old woman, *buda* old man, *budia* can refer to both.
[22] We did not spend the full ten days in Kurubi as this festival overlapped with other events we wanted to document or participate in, the Bali Jatra in Komra (see Chapter 8) and the Pus Porbo in our Gadaba village of residence, Gudapada. We arrived in Kurubi on Friday, January 5 and stayed until January 9 with a brief intermittent return to Gudapada on January 7.

Table 2: Overview of Ritual Roles during the Ganga Festival

Name of ritual role	Activitiy	identified sub-roles
Domi	Hosts of the Ganga deities, prepare the deities for procession	–
Domini	Female hosts of the Ganga deities, carriers of the deities during the procession	–
Budia pila	Accompany the procession, carrying ritual paraphernalia and the heads of the sacrificed victims on a brass plate	
Ghasi	Ritual role enacted by Joria: "low-caste" men accompanying the procession; dance, sacrifice, fight the Paik	*mul ghasi* (main Ghasi), *kaswati*, *parbat* (mountain), *balashi*, *jali ganja* (long-tailed rooster), *gora* (horse), *tjuli*
Dom	Ritual role enacted by Joria: "low-caste" men accompanying the procession; fight the Paik	*kongar, seti, bakiya* (money-lender), *toknia* (2)(cheater)
Paik	Ritual role enacted by Joria: "high-caste" royal soldiers accompanying the procession; fight the Dom & Ghasi	–
Dengudi	Stilt-dancers; belonging to the Paik category; fight the Dom & Ghasi	–
Monkeys	Monkey Dance	–
Other animals (deer)	Dancing	–

As is common in the region, several settlements frequently constitute a ritual unit. Often, villages have split up in the past, with a segment of the population (mostly along *jati* or *kuda* lines) moving to a new location close to the original village. Some villages have been completely abandoned due to calamities and the various groups settled in different locations (Berger 2015, 90f). Kurubi consists of Boro Kurubi (the senior and older village) and Maliput or Mali Kurubi, where the community or gardeners (Mali) live. The shrine of the Ganga deity lies in Maliput, which I did not have the chance to visit. However, informants told me that the shrine consists of trees and stones as usual and that "nothing else" is there.

Table 3: Overview of the Main Rituals and Activities of the Ganga Festival

Day 1 (January 1, Monday):	– Domi worship (with rice and incense, no blood sacrifice) Ganga deities at their shrine in Maliput – Deities are brought into the village and into the houses of the Domi
Day 2 (January 2, Tuesday):	– Fetching of bamboo sticks: Three sets of short bamboo sticks are fetched from the village of Kantaga (about 7 km linear distance, east of Kurubi), where a "senior" Ganga shrine is located. Each of the deities will be equipped with two of those bamboo sticks. The other bamboo sticks for the Ghasi, Dom and Paik can be collected anywhere
Day 3 (January 3, Wed.):	– "Real" Dombo hand over Dom *luga* (called *bauni*) to Domini – Deities are first worshipped inside the houses of the Domi, then brought to village square to receive a collective sacrifice, a goat (*kot cheli*); followed by dancing
Day 4 (January 4, Thursd.):	*Basi porbo*, feasting, no procession
Day 5 (January 5, Fri.):	– Procession through village, ending in village square – Monkey Dance – Ritual ploughing (etc.) in front of deities in village square
Day 6 (January 6, Sat.):	– Ghasi/Dom cook in the morning – Domi prepare deities in their houses; sick people visit the Domi houses – Procession through village – Monkey Dance
Day 7 (January 7, Sun.):	– Procession to Maliput – Gods return to main village in evening, dancing in square
Day 8 (January 8, Mon.):	– Procession of deities in main village, ending in the village square – Stilt dance (Goro Boga) – Paik Play (Paik Kel/Sari Kel) – Appearance of animals (deer etc.)
Day 9 (January 9, Tue.):	Gods are returned to shrine in Maliput
Day 10 (January 10, Wed.):	Feeding of Ghasi (& Dom), ritual reintegration (*jati kiniba*)

On the first day of the ritual, the three *domi* took the pots and lamps from their houses to the Ganga shrine in Maliput and worshipped the deity with incense (*dupo*) only. After this brief act of worship, they took the deities – the pots and lamps – back into the main village and into their houses. There they were placed on low and simple platforms where the *domi* worshipped them regularly from Wednesday onward.

The activities on the second and third days (Tuesday, Wednesday) also did not involve the entire village community. On Tuesday, *domi*, Ghasi, Dom and Paik obtained their bamboo sticks, "without which the deities would not walk" (*seta no hele takur bulba nai*). Three pairs of two short bamboo sticks had to be found outside the village and were placed (two for each deity) on the platform behind the deities in the *domi's* houses. The other sticks used could also be obtained from inside the village. The Paik selected particularly long and thin ones (*lomba bari*), the Ghasi and Dom shorter ones, about one and a half meters long with curved ends. These bamboo sticks were then continually carried by Ghasi, Dom and Paik, who waved them in their dances. On the subsequent day (Wednesday), the "real" Dombo of Kurubi made their only appearance at the festival. They offered "Dom *luga*" – cloth (*luga*) woven by Dombo, which they had obtained at the weekly market – to the three *domini*, who used these cloths to carry the gods on their heads during the days of the procession, in the same way women normally use cloths on their heads to carry pots with water from the wells. On the same day, the *domi* prepared the deities for the first time (which will be described below), worshipped them in their houses and then brought them to the village assembly space, where they were placed "in the face of" (*mure*) the village deity (*hundi*).[23] Then, on behalf of the village as a whole (*matam*), the first sacrifice of a goat was performed. The next day was *basi porbo*, which means that feasting is the main activity and no rituals took place.

The Procession

The procession of the deities through the village started on Friday. Beginning after midday, it continued until after sunset, with the procession moving slowly along the paths and streets of the village, making three stops at different places, but not leaving the paths. The core of the procession consisted of the three *domini*, each

---

[23] As during the following days as well, the junior deity was brought out of the house first, the senior one last, the latter being also the last one to leave the assembly place after the conclusion of all activities.

Photo 6.1: The custodian of the Ganga deity
A material representation of the Ganga deity (an earthen pot) is prepared by the ritual actor called *domi*, in whose house the deity is kept.

carrying a deity with a lighted lamp on their head, accompanied on their left and right by the three boys, the *budia pila*, carrying the brass plates with the oil for the divine lamps, the sacrificial knives and some husked rice. The *domini* were constantly moving, their backs always kept straight, swinging sideways,

Photo 6.2: The preparation of the Ganga deity has been completed
After the material representation of the Ganga deity has been prepared in the house of the *domi*, it is seated on a bed of paddy on a special ledge just next to the entrance to the inner room of the house.

swiftly lifting one foot, which briefly touched the ground next to the other foot, then moved back to its original position, and then the other foot made the same movement. In this way, they slowly moved forward, then back again, always with bent knees. Their arms moved in the same pendulum way, hanging down in front of their bodies, holding the sword in one hand, the shield in the other. Most of the time, they were faced by the two or three *gurumai*, moving in the same way but backwards and also at times holding swords.

This steady center of the procession was surrounded and orbited by the Ghasi, Dom and Paik, all dancing individually, more or less wildly, except those beating drums. At times, it seemed the Ghasi were at the head of the procession and the Paik behind the *domini* and the deities, but a little later the order would have changed and the three groups would be dancing all together around the deities, swinging their sticks. Acoustically, along with the drums, whistling was the most prominent aspect. With their bamboo sticks in one hand, Ghasi, Dom and Paik had a finger in their mouths most of the time, whistling more or less constantly. In between the whistles, they shouted "Let's play!" (*keliba!*). One man, a Dom or Ghasi, carried a bow and arrow throughout the procession, as well as a hunting horn made from water buffalo horn, which he blew from time to time. However, it could barely be heard over all the whistling and drumming. As the procession slowly moved on in this way, other men and women joined the dancing, women often in pairs, while many stood at the sides and watched. At the times the *kaswari* rode his "horse" – the other Ghasi called *gora* – the *dapu* drum would beat particularly loud and the *kaswati* would beat his bamboo stick on the thatched roofs to acquire straw for his horse. It was said that if a roof was damaged, no owner could complain. When, due to the *domini's* movement, a light on top of one of the deities went out, the *mul ghasi* would relight it. Oil was also regularly refilled from the plates carried by the *budia pila*.

The places where the procession stopped had been decided in advance, depending on who had made a vow (*manasik*) this year to sacrifice a goat or chicken. Generally, however, a stop was made in every section (*sai*) of the village. When the procession stopped, women of the *sai* rushed forward with incense, water and rice to wash the feet of the *domini* and give them *tika* with husked rice; that is, to press rice on their feet, knees, shoulders and foreheads. Some women also gave *tika* to the deities and completed the greeting with a chin kiss (*chumei*) to the *domini*, touching the latter's chins with their right hand and moving it in the direction of their mouths.[24] While the women were thus busy greeting the deities and the *domini*, the *mul ghasi* tried to steal their brass plates, hiding them under his ragged shirt and thus forcing them to chase him.

In the meantime, *kongar* and *seti*, two Dom, were preparing the sacrificial ground, while the drumming, dancing, whistling and shouting of the others continued around them. First, the ground was prepared with a mixture of water and dung, then a row of mango branches was planted and covered with a white cloth so that a kind of low barrier was made. At the time of the sacrifice, the drums, the bamboo sticks, and the bow, arrow and hunting horn were placed behind this structure. The latter three items were considered to be the weapons of the gods and were always recovered first after the sacrifice was over. In front of the mango branches, a sacrificial pattern was drawn with rice powder, with twelve sections in two rows of six. A small heap of unhusked paddy for the three deities was formed in the back row of the pattern on which the three brass plates carried by the *budia pila* would be placed. The main sacrificer at this stop (a member of the *sai*) then took the deities from the heads of the *domini* and placed them on the paddy seats, and *kongar* and *seti* contributed to the further decoration of the sacrificial site with flowers.

---

24 For a discussion on various dimensions of greetings and "skinship" in Bastar see Chris Gregory (2011).

Before every sacrifice, the deities were first invoked by the *gurumai*. Two or three *gurumai* squatted in front of the deities, their bodies swaying to and fro, and with closed eyes they addressed the deities. Variously talking and singing, they established contact with the divine, while the other actors did not bother much about what the *gurumai* were saying or singing, which was difficult to understand anyway, as the whistling and "playing" also continued throughout. Small groups of Ghasi, Dom and Paik formed next to the squatting *gurumai*, all of them singing "filthy songs" (*obɔdro git*), together and individually. Whenever we managed to understand a line of their song, which did not happen very often, the content was quite evident, such as "My penis is dry, how should that work?" After a while, the *gurumai* got up and started to dance again, surrounded by the Ghasi, Dom and Paik, and a period of more intense "playing" started. One *gurumai* also sang parts of the Nandi song and then danced accordingly. Another *gurumai* grabbed the bamboo stick of some Ghasi and holding it between her legs pretended to ride a horse, two men around her holding the ends of the stick, dragging her to and fro, while the other Ghasi danced around her, beating their sticks on the thatched roofs to feed the horse with straw.

Then the sacrificial killing started. First, numerous chickens of any color were killed, many by the *mul ghasi*, others by the sponsors and sacrifiers (*scukar*) of the animals.[25] Then sheep and goats were sacrificed, all previously promised in the form of a vow to the deities. The *mul ghasi* was also involved in the killing of these animals, alongside the *saukar* of the animals and the *bakiya*, who is supposed to do the killing in the course of the procession.[26] All the heads were first placed on the sacrificial pattern in front of the deities and the people from the neighborhood provided food offerings (*betisong*) and beer libations (*tipali*) to the gods, bowing down in front of them. After the sacrifices, another period of intense playing started, with the *saukar* of the animals dancing enthusiastically, along with Ghasi, Dom and Paik, the *gurumai* and whoever wanted to join in, the bloody sacrificial axe being raised into the air. By this time, all of the men had also retrieved their drums, sticks and the bow, arrow and horn, such that all the equipment was available during the playing.

In the meantime, *kongar* and *seti* cleaned up the sacrificial area and placed the heads of the goats and sheep on the brass plates to be carried to the next stop by the boys and then taken by them for distribution among the Ghasi, Dom and

---

[25] Notably absent was the sacrifice of coconuts during any of these stops.
[26] As usual, chicken are beheaded with a knife that is fixed between the toes of the sacrificer who then cuts the neck holding the animal with his two hands. Goat and sheep are beheaded with axes. The bamboo sticks used for dancing were also used to fix the head of the animal and to keep it at a proper distance from the sacrificer.

Paik. The heads of the sacrificed chickens were tied to the Paik's bamboo sticks until the next stop. The sacrifiers of the neighborhood placed the deities on the heads of the *domini* again and the procession continued. Each of these stops took about one and a half hours. Thus, the *domini*, who were completely uninvolved during this time, had a chance to rest from their hours of dancing.

It was long after dusk, about 7.30 pm, when the procession reached the central assembly area of the village, where the shrine of the village deity (*hundi*) is located next to the *sadar*. After some further play, the deities were

Photo 6.3: Taking the Ganga deity out of the house
The Ganga deity is taken out of the house of a *domi* to be carried by their wives (*domini*) in procession through the village. Note the garlands of paddy under which the man carrying the deity is passing.

put down on the ground between the *sadar* and *hundi* on one side and a concrete village shop (*dokan*) on the other. At this time, the candles on top of the deities provided the only light, dimly illuminating the area. Then, all of the villagers retreated into their houses to eat and the *domini* had their first meal of the day. Ghasi, Dom and Paik, the former two separate from the latter, received food from the village to cook on their own, and thus did not eat in their houses.

Photo 6.4: The carriers of the Ganga deities
The three women (*domini*) who carry the Ganga deities in a procession through the village await the third embodiment of the deity (an earthen pot) to be brought out of the house. They are flanked at their sides by two boys (*budia pila*, the third will soon be joining, together with the third representation of the deity) who carry ritual equipment and (later) also the heads of the sacrificed animals. The *domini* carry the deities on their heads on a piece of folded "Dom cloth" and hold swords and shields made from bamboo.

The Monkey Dance

After their meals, the villagers again gathered in the central assembly area in anticipation of the "monkey dance" (Monkoro Nat). Ghasi, Dom and Paik were again singing their dirty songs; men and women, more or less drunk, danced in front of the deities. The Dom and Ghasi drummers sat next to the gods close to a fire, where they tightened the skins of their drums from time to time. While in some other villages I had encountered electric light and music played from tapes (both run with batteries) predominating over the drumming, in Kurubi and Lenjisuku this was not the case. The lights on top of the deities and the fires lit here and there were the only source of illumination and also gave the nightly performances a particular atmosphere, as silhouettes of people moved and danced in and out of the shadows and into the flickering light of the fires. We were able to capture a little of this atmosphere by filming with an infrared device.

The "monkeys" were adults and children dressed in straw. Both male and female, young and old were allowed to participate, although from what I could see, most monkeys were performed by men and boys. Arms, legs, body and head were all completely covered with straw and a long straw tail was attached to the

Photo 6.5: Procession of Ganga deities through the village
The Ganga deities are carried in procession through the village on the heads of the *domini*. They are surrounded by Dom, Ghasi and Paik who carry bamboo sticks, and other dancing women.

Photo 6.6: A sacrificial stop has been prepared
The sacrificial site has been prepared, awaiting the procession of the Ganga deities to arrive. The three representations of the deities will soon be seated on the heaps of paddy and next to them the three brass plates that are carried by the *budia pila*.

back. There were two kinds of monkeys, one neutral in terms of gender, in any case without explicit sexual characteristics, while many others had huge straw phalluses attached in front. First, two little monkeys appeared, each dancing on its own, but pushing each other from time to time. They bowed down before the deities and then lay completely flat in front of them. Both moved backwards, still lying flat on their fronts, then one got up and moved behind the other, imitating copulation with his phallus. A small undisguised boy took the chance to beat both of them with a straw broom. Both monkeys then got up, waving their phalluses around, soon being joined by more big and small monkeys, many of whom first went to greet the deities. When one little monkey swung his phallus too provocatively in the face of the deities, a non-monkey adult chased him away. In contrast to the dance of the *domini*, there was no apparent choreography prescribed here, though there was certainly a behavioral pattern. The monkeys would tiptoe behind other monkeys who were not paying attention, who they then grabbed and pretended to copulate with. Inattentive non-monkey onlookers were also captured and "screwed." A *gurumai* was also dancing with one monkey, walking behind him in long leaps, with the monkeys tiptoeing away from her.

Photo 6.7: Invocation of the Ganga deities by the *gurumai*

As the dance went on, some monkeys dropped out, for example, because their straw-heads had been ripped off by someone and thrown into the fire, while others arrived, perhaps six to eight dancing at a time. Each of them looked out for victims, and grown-up monkeys also grabbed smaller ones. Then the monkeys found new promising prey. On the *sadar* and around it and even inside the low stone wall surrounding the inner shrine of the village deity (*hundi*), a large group of girls had assembled, shrieking and giggling as they watched the monkeys' performance. The little monkeys were dancing in front of the girls when, suddenly, but probably anticipated by the girls, one of them rushed toward the girls, who fled chuckling in all directions or huddled together. The little monkeys did not chase them but were content to stand triumphantly in front of the *sadar* swinging their phalluses. When the girls who had fled gradually came back, it was an adult monkey who actually broke into the lines of the girls, grabbed and captured one, dragging her to the village shop next to the deities. After this example, the smaller monkeys also dared not only to threaten but actually seize the girls, and after a skirmish, one of them managed to capture another girl. This continued for a while, until all the monkeys, in a joint assault, rushed toward the *hundi* and all of the girls fled for good. People then continued dancing and drinking, while the Ghasi, Dom and Paik were invited to have food and drink by those houses that had sacrificed a goat or sheep on the day; as we know, their stomachs never get full.

It was late at night when another ritual episode occurred, which we unfortunately missed; the ritual initiation of agricultural activities. From the first day of the festival, all agricultural activities had been prohibited; now, at the time appointed by the astrologer and soothsayer (*dissari*), at about two o'clock in the morning, all of the agricultural activities were imitated in front of the Ganga deities. Two boys served as bullocks, and the earth was ritually plowed for the first time. Also sowing, transplanting and weeding were imitated. After this ritual, the *domi* took the gods back into their houses overnight.

Photo 6.8: Sacrifices for Ganga
The *mul ghasi* (standing, with the knife between his toes) sacrifices chicken for the Ganga deities.

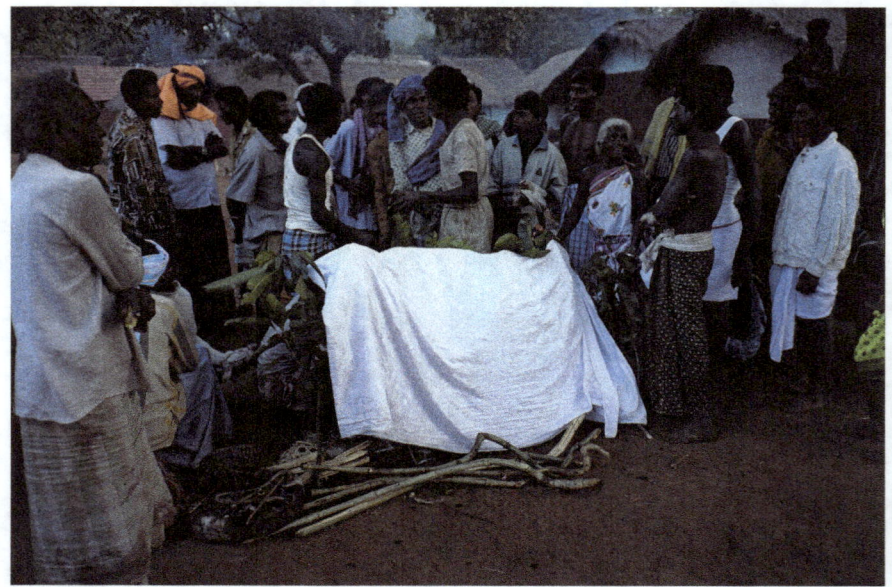

Photo 6.9: A break for the drummers and the carriers
During a sacrificial stop the ritual equipment (bamboo sticks, bamboo swords and shields, drums) are placed behind the sacrificial structure build from mango branches and covered by a piece of cloth. Note the *gurumai* with white hair standing just right of the sacrificial spot. She also played an important role in the Nandi festival in Lenjisuku, invoking the deities and accompanying the procession (photos 7.4, 7.8).

The Procession Continued

The next day, Saturday, again started slowly. In the morning, Ghasi, Dom and Paik cooked their share of the sacrificial animals from the previous day's sacrifices. If ten goats and sheep had been killed, Ghasi and Dom would receive and jointly cook six heads and six front legs (*podia*), while the Paik cooked four heads and some meat from the legs. The Ghasi then roamed through the village as peddlers. They carried useless and broken things, sold a piece of torn cloth as *sari*, demanded absurdly high rates and talked gibberish. In addition to the meals that they received from the hosts of the sacrifices and the share of the sacrificial meat they cooked themselves, they were also invited to eat and drink at the houses of the *domi*.

In the meantime, as on every day of the procession, the *domi* prepared their deities. I could witness the preparations in detail in one of the *domi* houses (see photos 6.1 and 6.2). The shrine of the deity was not in the sacred room of the

Photo 6.10: Worshipping the deities after the completion of the sacrifices

house, where the house deity (Doron Deli, the central post) is located, instead, the deity was seated on a low platform in the main room. However, this seat was just next to the passage leading to the inner room of the house and was also colored in the way all inner rooms must be painted, namely in a red earthen color. In this way, it seemed to be an extension of the inner room or, in any case, connected to it. On the platform, there were two small heaps of paddy from the last harvest, used as seats for the deity and the brass plate that the *budia pila* had been carrying. Behind these objects, the two short bamboo sticks that had been collected the previous Tuesday were leaning against the wall.

After having taken a bath himself, the *domi* lit incense, washed the pot (*handi*) and then painted it with rice powder mixed with water, thus coloring it white. Garlands with flowers[27] were tied around the pot's neck and a tiny wooden construction, an umbrella (*chatori*), was also fastened to it. While this latter item is commonly used among the Gadaba in healing rituals to fend off harmful influences, here the *domi* merely commented, "otherwise the deity will not play" (*nohele maphru kelibo nai*). The *domi* selected seven grains of husked rice and dropped them into the otherwise empty pot, which was then placed on

---

[27] White *semi* flowers and yellow *merda* ("sheep") flowers.

Photo 6.11: The Ganga deities arrive at the *sadar*
After sunset, the procession has arrived in the central assembly place and the deities are placed on the ground, seated on heaps of paddy. From there, they watch the performances of "play" and "dance" throughout the night.

its paddy seat. The small lamp was filled with oil, a new wick was added, and the lamp was then lit and placed on top of the pot. These last steps were accompanied by invocations to the deity. Then, the brass plate was washed and filled with new husked rice, and the small pot (*kondi*) containing extra oil and the sacrificial knife were placed on it, with the whole ensemble finally being seated next to the deity. In the course of the morning, it was not only the Ghasi who passed by as peddlers, but also people who were ill. They received *tika* with oil from the lamp on their foreheads, and an old man with hearing problems had oil dripped into his ear; there would be no better medicine, the *domi* explained.

In the afternoon, all deities were again taken out of the houses and the procession started in the same way as before, this time passing through other parts of the village. Only two sacrificial stops were made on this day, with the same structure as before. The *mul ghasi* again stole the brass items from the women while they greeted the deities, demanding money for their return. Before the ritual killings, the sacrifiers of the goats and sheep were invited to play, and after the last sacrificial stop, the whistling and dancing seemed to have no end. After sunset, the deities were again seated in the assembly area and soon the

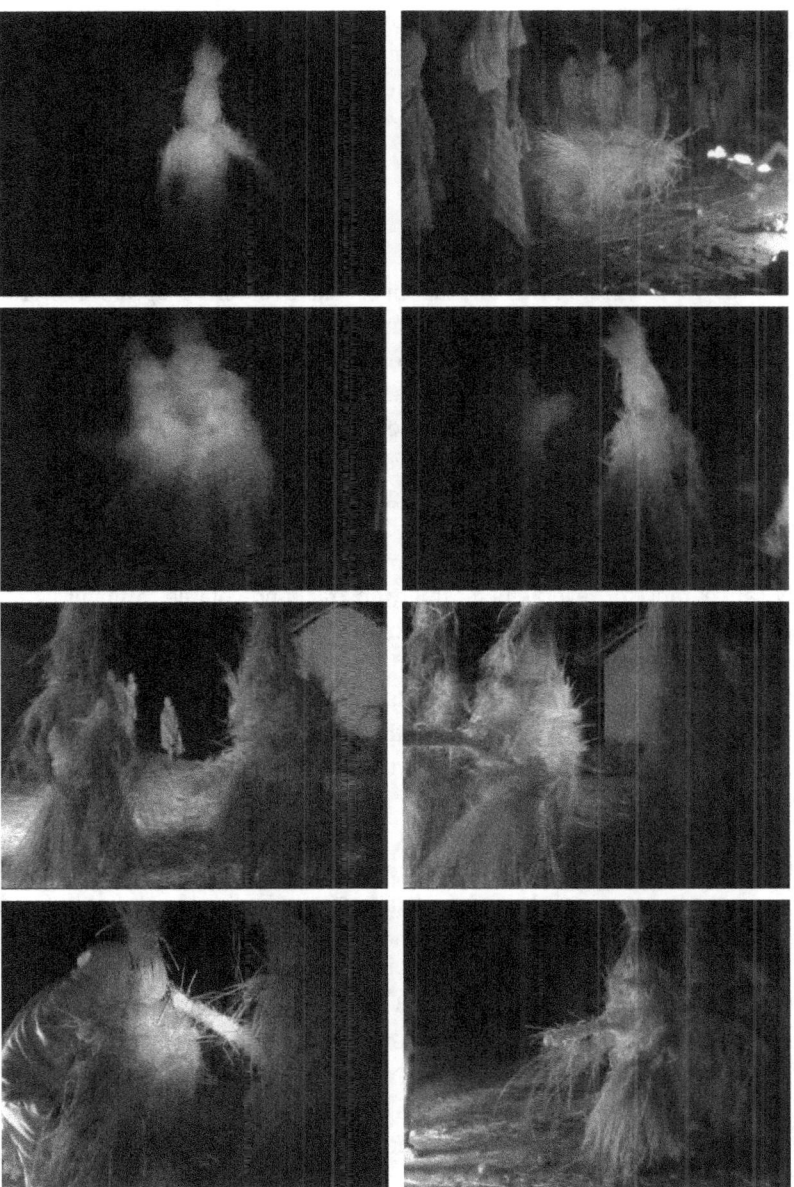

Photo 6.12: The Monkey Dance
Scenes form the Monkey Dance (Monkoro Nat). Top right: two monkeys bow down in front of the Ganga deities. In several other images one can see the monkeys swinging their straw-phalluses (stills from a film made with an infrared device, filming done by Amrei Volkmann).

monkeys made their appearance. The following day (Sunday), the procession moved through the other hamlet, called Maliput, where the gardeners (Mali) live. In the evening, the deities were returned to the main village and the night continued as it had done after the two preceding days.

The Main Day

The last day of the procession was unusual or special in several respects. The procession again started in the afternoon, but only one extensive stop was made. Afterwards, the *domini*, surrounded by all the others, slowly moved to the assembly area, where they arrived after dark. The status of the Ghasi was stressed on this day as well, their low position emphasized by the fact that none of them wore a shirt. Moreover, on this day alone, they wore a head decoration with feathers. There was no Monkey Dance in the evening, instead, a stilt dance (Goro Boga) was performed by the Dengudi, followed by a ritual fight between the Ghasi and Dom on one side against the Dengudi and other Paik. The night ended with the successive appearance of several increasingly abstract and volatile "animals."

In the afternoon, we met the Dengudi on the dry fields outside the village, where they were painting their stilts; first, white as a base color, then they added patterns in red and brown. The stilts differed in size, the highest being taller than the men themselves. All of the stilts were made from the wood of the silk cotton tree (*simli gocho*). In addition to the four sets of stilts, a wooden horse was also painted in the same way, its tail made from straw. We were asked to take care that our shadows did not fall on any of these objects.

It is the main function of the Dengudi to dance on stilts on the main day in front of the representations of the Ganga deities. Not only did they dance in front of the gods, but they also danced above the representations of the gods, their bodies becoming a "high shrine" (*deng-gudi*). As they explained it, the deities "grab" (*dorba*) them, they "inhabit" (*roko korba*) them and then they dance; if the deities are not "true" (*sot*), they fall over. A multiplicity of perspectives can already be noted in the names of the dancers (Dengudi) and of the dance (Goro Boga). While the former defines the dancers as abodes ("shrines") of the deities, the name of the dance indicates a gift to the gods, an "offering" (*bog*) of "legs/feet" (*goro*), or rather, a dance-offering. The deities are thus performers, entering the Dengudi's bodies, as well as the audience of the performance, which is a kind of offering. In sacrificial terms, the identities of sacrificer and deity are blurred or merged. Being "seated" near the village shrine, the gods watch the dance from below and they dance above at the same time. However, not only the gods and the Dengudi dance, everyone has to dance. As one Dengudi put it:

Photo 6.13: Preparation of the stilts
The stilt-dancers (Dengudi) are preparing their stilts in the dry fields outside of the village. In front, a man is putting the final touches on the "main horse" (*pat goria*). Like one of the "iron horses" in Lenjisuku, this horse has testicles, here represented by a fruit.

> It is the gods' law to walk-dance above like that [on the heads of the *domini*], of course [laughs]. After they danced they sit down there [near hundi]. After walking-dancing the gods will sit down.[28]
>
> When this deity (*maphru*) arrives here [at the assembly place] we all have to make fun (*sarda*), all people have to dance there then: the Ghasi dance, then Paik dance, we Dengudi dance there, everybody dances. Therefore the god [thinks]: "Oh, all people came, they brought the deer (*somor*), [unclear], all make-give fun." The god is pleased (with affection, *kusi*) and fever or sorrow won't befall [us]. When we go close to the god we make this dance according to the divine order (*niamre*).[29]

As with the other Paik, the Dengudi are all Joria, this task being passed on within families of different groups of the village. The function may pass from father to son

---

28 *Maphru niamre semti upore prokar semti bili buli nacho koruchu [on the heads of the domini] au (laughs). Setebele nacho korlu seti [near hundi] bosci. Buli nachi kori se maphru bosibo.*
29 *Se maphru eti asi pohonchila to amor sobu sarda lagi jiba ochi, sobu jono nacho kariba seti au: ghasimon nachibe, paikmon nachibe, ame Dengudimon seti aka, samaste nachiba ochi. Tebe maphru puni "ha samaste lok asi, somor ani kori [unclear], sobu sarda kori deitile." Maphru kusi hei kori, amor tike jor ki duka setki poribo nai au. Maphru pakore jai kori ame se niamre nacho koribu boili.*

or from one brother to the other. Women do not assume this role. The dancers may only perform during the night of the Goro Boga, which means that there is no chance to practice this skill in advance, even if it is your first time.[30] The Dengudi fast during the day before the Goro Boga and they abstain from sexual intercourse during the week before. They dress up even more sumptuously than the other Paik, with long pointed head-dresses that have a long tail, and colorful long garments around the lower part of the body, while being bare chested. They invoke the gods (*suborna*) while holding onto long wooden poles that are fixed in the ground for this purpose, and then the deity "grabs" them and they begin to walk.

The first two Dengudi were ready, standing on their stilts, exactly at the time when the deities arrived at the assembly area after sunset. Two poles of about four meters in height had been erected in the plaza in front of the village deity and the Ganga divinities, with some six meters distance between them. Holding fast to the poles, the Dengudi watched the end of procession of the deities into the assembly area, the *domini* still dancing with the deities on their heads. Ghasi, Dom and Paik jerked their bamboo sticks into the air, whistling and shouting "Let's play" even more vigorously than during the previous days it seemed, in anticipation of the climax of the festival. The drums were beaten and the hunting horn again tried to make itself heard over the general uproar. After the gods had been seated on the ground, the Dengudi began their invocations, closing their eyes and folding their hands in front of their faces, one hand holding the bunch of peacock feathers that all the Dengudi were carrying. They then let go of the poles, first staying close to them, circumambulating the poles in an anti-clockwise direction. But soon they began traversing the assembly area in any direction, walking to the rhythm of the drums, with bells attached to their stilts ringing in the same beat.

With one arm, they waved the peacock feathers, while they needed the other to join in the whistling that was going on all around them. Often, two young girls followed the Dengudi, who were dancing in the assembly area, throwing husked rice at their stilts. Dom, Ghasi and the other Paik danced around the stilt walkers, cheering them, joined by any villager who felt so inclined. Intermittently, the Dengudi returned to the poles, an occasion to have the twine attaching the stilts to their feet and legs tightened by some of the men below. When a dancer stumbled, people on the ground would stabilize him. However, one of them lost his balance completely and was carried away to the side of the dance ground. This did not exclude a return, as in such cases the dancers were also carried back to the poles, which they used to haul themselves up and started anew.

---

30 However, we noticed that when the actual Goro Boga was over, a newcomer Dengudi was still practicing a little for the next occasion.

6.3 The Ganga Festival — 253

Photo 6.14: The stilt dance, "let's play!"
A Dengudi on stilts, being cheered at by another member of the Paik group.

After about half an hour, the dances became even more tumultuous, as the Ghasi, newly equipped, re-entered the arena that they had briefly left while the Dengudi were dancing. Four of them, all still with their feather head-dresses, now carried straw (*pial*) on long bamboo poles horizontally over their shoulders. Such tools (called *sulda*) are normally used to stack straw or the millet harvest onto wooden platforms for storage or to dry before threshing. Both ends are very sharp as they have to pierce the bundles of straw or millet. Thus, they make very good weapons as well. The *mul ghasi* again was special, as he carried two poles that crossed each other, thus carrying four bundles of straw. They entered the assembly area bellowing and shouting "Let's play," greeted by the whistling and shouting of the Paik and Dom. With their bundles swinging on their long poles, the straw carriers moved through the area in sudden, impulsive backward and forward movements, beating the bamboo sticks – which they still carried – on the ground, shouting *kelibaaa!* and whistling when not shouting. Moving quickly to and fro and spinning around, the straw bundles were whirled around, while the sharp ends of the poles protruding beyond the bundles posed a real danger to those dancing nearby and even to the many onlookers who surrounded the area, as the Ghasi paid no heed to other people's safety.

Soon after the Ghasi entered the area, they were joined by the *gora*, one of the Ghasi riding on a wooden horse called "main horse" (*pat goria*), which the Dengudi had painted in the afternoon. It now became obvious that the straw carried by the other Ghasi was meant for the horse, and here they indicated their traditional vocation as stable servants. The *pat goria* was also dancing and whirling around like the straw carriers, surrounded by dancing Paik and Dom, traversed on high by the Dengudi on their stilts. One stilt dancer resting at the pole was approached by the *mul ghasi*, who tried to squeeze through the Dengudi's stilts with everything he carried. Someone else lifted a leg of the Dengudi and all danced through this "gate."

After an hour or so, the Goro Boga was over, but there was still more to come. As an old woman standing next to us announced, "Now comes the Sari Kel," the "wrestling play." The Dengudi quickly had their stilts untied and joined the others dancing on the ground, now carrying one of their stilts as a weapon. Ghasi and Dom on the one side and Paik and Dengudi on the other, all equipped with stilts or other kinds of rods or bamboo sticks, were now dancing around each other as though in a boxing ring, keeping one end of their sticks close to the ground. Suddenly, one of the Ghasi rushed forward trying to push his rod between the legs of a Paik. The other Ghasi and Dom hurried to help him, while other Paik and Dengudi tried to ward off the attack. In the course of the melee, Ghasi and Dom managed to push this Paik to the ground, where they held him for a few moments with their sticks and rods, with cheers by the onlookers coming from all sides. Soon they let him go again and continued to dance. These fights were repeated many times, often the attacker approaching his victim on tiptoe from behind. Some attacks were averted, some were successful; the whole arena buzzing with bodies covered with sweat and earth, raising clouds of dust, cheers, shouts of *keliba!* and, of course, whistling. Afterwards, we were told that each time one party managed to throw one member of the other to the ground they would receive five Rupees, but I doubt that anyone was recording who fell and how often. After a while, the Sari Kel, also called Paik Kel, was over and there was a short pause, everybody knowing what was coming next: the deer (*somor*) would soon enter the arena.

Photo 6.15: A scene from the Paik Play
Two men from the Dengudi/Paik group manage to throw a man from the Ghasi group to the ground by using their stilts.

As with the "main horse,"[31] the "animals" that now entered the area were always constructed by the same house, all from the Joria groups. In the case of the deer, the family was in general called "deer-house" (*somor gor*). The construction consisted of a corpus of split bamboo covered with a net (*jala*), under which one person could crawl to make the deer dance. On top of the bamboo framework that represented the body and legs of the animal was a longitudinal straw bundle forming the upper part of the body from head to tail. Behind the framework hiding the dancer, between the hind legs, so to speak, a calabash dangled from the straw tail, and a bell was attached still further down the tail. On the front side, a brass pot (*mota*) represented the face, with antlers protruding from the "head," which were partly real antlers from a former hunt and partly long and bifurcated wooden branches. Torches had been tied to all the ends so that the deer appeared out of the dark with burning antlers, and came dashing among the dancers in the assembly area.

---

[31] The horse had been painted by the Dengudi but jointly constructed by Mali and Joria from the Boi group.

Encircled by Ghasi, Dom, Paik and others, the deer moved to and fro in the arena, rocking from one side to the other, quickly changing direction, as if retreating in one instant and attacking in another. The surrounding men, dancing and whistling, tried to come as close to the deer as possible, always jumping back from or diving underneath the antlers when the animal decided to attack – not unlike a *corrida*, with the difference being that the deer was not injured. When the deer managed to strike someone, sparks flew from the antlers. After a while, the deer paused, with the dancer inside most probably needing a rest. The torches that had gone out during the course of the dance were re-lit and the dance continued to endless shouts of *keliba!*, whistling and drumming. Several such breaks followed, one of which was in front of the Ganga deities, where the man inside could be seen bowing to the gods in his bamboo construction; then the dance continued again. After about three quarters of an hour, the deer disappeared from the arena, without being hunted down and killed.

Photo 6.16: Nightly performances of the Ganga festival
Top left: Dengudi perform their stilt dance; top right: whistling, the *mul ghasi* enters the arena with sharpened bamboo sticks and bundles of straw for the "horse;" bottom left: During the Paik Play two members of the Paik/Dengudi group keep a Ghasi on the ground with their stilts; bottom right: the deer swirls through the arena with lightened lamps at his antlers (stills from a film made with an infrared device, filming done by Amrei Volkmann).

After a brief pause, three other, identical animals appeared, called *tellenguni*, created and made to dance by Mali (gardeners) from the other hamlet.[32] These animals were also made from bamboo constructions, which the dancers carried around their hips, their feet and upper part of their bodies being visible. Sticks with torches also protruded from the front of these bamboo frames. The three *tellenguni* danced together for a while in the assembly area, but they were less wild and also triggered less rapturous dancing by the crowd than had the deer. Accordingly, their turn was over relatively quickly and after a while the last "animal" appeared, called *mar deuri*, made by the Boi group. Accompanied by shouts, drumming and whistling, a long bamboo pole about six meters high was carried vertically into the assembly area. A completely abstract bamboo construction had been attached at the high end. Three short horizontal bamboo sticks, each carrying three torches, were attached one above the other. After a few rounds of the arena, *mar deuri* left again, this time accompanied by all the dancers and drums. This concluded the main day, and soon afterward the deities were taken back to their houses.

Conclusion of the Festival

On the evening of the following day (Tuesday), after we had left the village in the morning in order to celebrate the January festival (Pus Porbo) with the Gadaba of Gudapada, the deities were brought back to their outside shrine by the *domi*. However, the pots and lamps were again taken to the *domi's* houses, the outside shrine remaining "empty." For the last time during this festival, the *domi* had placed seven grains of husked rice inside their pots, to be inspected on the occasion of the following Ganga festival. Should they be broken, this would be an inauspicious sign and a threat to the village as a whole, including bad harvests, illness and revengeful spirits of the dead. If they remain whole, according to the *domi* of the middle deity, "Wherever we go the path is good, our language is good, what we ask for we will be given, everything will be successful."

The festival was finally concluded with the ritual reintegration of the Ghasi[33] into the Joria community. This ritual is called *jati kiniba*, *jati* referring to the social category, the Joria tribe, *kiniba* meaning "to buy." When a person transgresses group boundaries, for example, by being beaten by a lower status person or, most

---

32 Both the name and the kind of animals they represent are unclear. Also in the interview we had later with the *mul ghasi* he did not elaborate further than saying, these animals were all "on account of the Ganga deities" (Ganga *maphru isaprei*).
33 Opinions diverged here; some said the ritual would include the Dom as well.

commonly, by living with someone from a community of lower status, the person, in the former case, or his or her family in the latter case, must sponsor a ritual that effects reintegration. For those who acted as Ghasi, this reintegration was obviously deemed necessary and, as is common in such cases, a cow was killed, sacrificial food prepared and fed to those whose status had to be regained. In this way, they "join the group" again (*jati mishaiba*) (see Berger 2015, 271f).

Comparison with Observations in Lenjisuku

In Lenjisuku, we could only document the main day of the Ganga Porbo – the last day of the procession and the stilt dance – on January 17, 2000. As the general procedure was nearly the same as in Kurubi, I will primarily discuss those aspects whereby the two occasions differed.

There were only two pots representing the Ganga deities: the "elder brother" being hosted in the group of Jani, the "younger brother" by the local Boronaik group. In the houses of these hosts, the place where the deities were seated were more elaborately decorated than in Kurubi. The pots, with their lamps on top, were seated on a small basket of paddy, similar to Kurubi, but the walls behind the gods had been painted with white dots and patterns on the earthen red color. They thus resembled the mural I will describe for the Nandi festival in the same village. In the house of the "elder deity," the wall behind also had a black bell (*gondi*) painted at the top, and a basket (*dona*) hung over the deity from the ceiling above, representing a swing for the god (see photo 7.7).[34]

While the Dengudi were painting their seven or eight pairs of stilts outside the village, the final procession was slowly moving through the settlement. The dance of the two *domini* was the same and also here they were faced by a *gurumai* most of the time. What differed was the equipment representing the "horses." Here, two men (called *ghasi gora* and *lamta gora*) carried and actually partly rode on two curved iron rods called "horse" (*gora*) or "stick of Durga" (or Durga *badi*). One of these "horses" was considered male and in fact had iron testicles, the other, lacking these, was female. As in the other village, it was stressed that these horses were necessary to make the gods walk (they would be "for walking", *chaliba pai*). The *budia*, who carried the oil for the lamps walking beside the *domini*, were adult men in Lenjisuku, not boys. In many instances, they conducted the sacrifices.

---

[34] I did not take any photographs in Lenjisuku on this occasion. First people did not want me to take photographs, later some others asked me to make pictures, but then I had decided not to take any. Of course, we never took photographs or filmed without permission.

Another difference from the procession in Kurubi was the frequency of sacrificial stops in Lenjisuku. On that day, the procession stopped thirteen times to sacrifice, with coconuts also being offered to the deities. The first stop occurred in front of the "deer house" (*somor gor*), where the half-completed bamboo construction could be seen standing in the yard. Not only were dirty songs sung, but on occasion the dancing men tried to grab each other's private parts or would hold one another suggesting copulation. The general atmosphere in Lenjisuku was also slightly different from in Kurubi. While the *domi*, *domini* and Dengudi remained sober, the other participants in Lenjisuku were much more drunk and quarrels and fights occurred regularly.

At dusk, the procession entered the inner space of the magnificent assembly "colosseum," where two poles had already been erected for the stilt dancers. As in Kurubi, as soon as the two deities were placed on a sacrificial pattern between the two huge Banyan trees, the Goro Boga began. While the Dengudi started their dance, the iron horses and the stilts that were not to be used that night (and later also those of the dancers who had stopped) were placed in front of the deities. The name for the dance, Goro Boga or "leg offering," thus found quite literal expression here. The Goro Boga itself was very similar to the one observed in Kurubi, with the exception that the dancers who did not manage to let go of the pole within a certain period of time were violently pulled from it by the crowd below. Those "failed" Dengudi had their stilts seized by the men below and had to lower themselves to the ground while holding on to the pole. Heated discussions resulted.

Another difference from Kurubi was that, in parallel to the stilt dance, sacrifices for the deities were prepared. Many people had made vows and were now waiting to sacrifice their coconuts and chickens, before a ram was killed for the village as a whole. This usual order was disrupted, however, as many were too drunk and at the same time too impatient. The men tried to crack the coconuts open by beating them on the stilts, which proved difficult and took many attempts, so that others already started to kill chickens. One man grew so impatient that he simply twisted the head of his chicken and ripped it off, then threw it on the sacrificial site. While such sacrifices are usually highly ordered, the situation was characterized by verbal and physical fights and general chaos. My two Gadaba friends, who had accompanied me, shook their heads, half in bemusement and half in disapproval (although such scenes would not be inconceivable in their village either).

After the sacrifices and the stilt dance had ended, the appearance of animated animals followed. First two "horses" entered the arena, encircled by the hooting crowd; then the deer (*somor*). While, in Kurubi, the dance with the deer was more like a bullfight or playing tag, here the animal was "hunted" and "killed," although he got up again to continue the dance. While the deer was still in the arena, constructions that looked similar to the *tellenguni* in Kurubi arrived. However, they were called *daini* and were said to suck blood.[35] After the completion of their dance, the deer chased both the *daini* and the horses out of the *sadar*. It was announced that a bear would come last, but we had to leave beforehand. The *boro dissari* from Kurubi, Leukon Maji, who had originally planned to join us from the start but was too drunk when we left for Lenjisuku in the afternoon, had finally arrived and pressed us to return to his village, where we stayed overnight.

6.4 Discussion and Interpretation

Myth and Ritual

In a unique and most remarkable way, the Joria enact the themes of rule and regeneration in their Ganga festival. Mutually engaging and partially conflating myth and ritual, they temporarily transform some of their village members into representatives of the service communities of the former Nandapur royal polity and make the King God walk through their village for days. All the while, they sing and dance, sacrifice and play for the deity, who is closely associated with paddy throughout, at a moment of the year when the cultivation cycle of this most important crop is about to begin anew.

The King God or Raja Maphru, who is represented by the earthen pots and lamps during the festival, is in my view no other than the mythical deity who is said to have been born in Nandapur, who came out of the earth there (M12, see M3, M6 and below). Moreover, he is identified with the jungle-boy who became king after he overthrew the Dom Raja (M5, M6, M14), replacing a rule of barrenness and depletion – of stealing and withholding grain – with one of fertility and plenty, with a focus on paddy. The references to the Dom Raja story discussed in Chapter 3 are conspicuous, both as far as the ritual form and paraphernalia of the deities are concerned and with reference to the behavior of Dom and Ghasi. The women (*domini*) who carry and move the gods, hold and dance with exactly those weapons with which the forest boy-cum-king was provided to fight the Dom Raja in the myths: a shield and a sword made from bamboo. The deities themselves are also armed with bamboo sticks that must be

---

35 Among the Gadaba *daini* refers to a kind of witch, a woman who sucks human blood at night (Berger 2015).

brought from the "senior" shrine in Kanaga. Likewise, the behavior of Dom and Ghasi during the festival suggests the inversion of the normal order and the prevalence of Dom rule. As such, the "main Ghasi" is the most important man of the festival and the vile and greedy stereotypical behavior of Ghasi and Dom (cheating, stealing, devouring) dominates the days of the procession. The Ghasi not only care for the horses (providing straw), according to their vocation, but also *ride* the horses, even the "main horse," when they enter the assembly area after the last procession has ended. Quite clearly, keeping the brotherhood stories and the role of climbing onto the horse in mind, the horse is a symbol of sovereignty and mounting it signifies a claim to power.

Throughout the days of procession, the subjects are divided and compete with each other, while the deities also display a dual character. The division of subjects is reflected in the continuous opposition and contrast between Dom and Ghasi on the one hand, and Paik and Dengudi on the other. Paik are high-caste soldiers of the king and, as such, legitimately wear royal insignia, such as fly whisks and turbans (one can imagine they received the latter from the king during Dasara). They compete with the Dom and Ghasi during the days of procession, especially in singing filthy songs.

Different aspects of the deities are also represented, with the pots and lamps representing the Ganga deities – a manifestation of the jungle-boy-king – but carried by the women on cloth explicitly woven by Dombo and referred to as "Dom *luga*" generally. It thus seems that, when the deities are carried in the procession and the women swing their swords and shields, the deities have a dual identity, there is a co-presence of Dom Raja and Jungle King, the latter being seated on the former. However, this co-presence of barren and fertile kingship is only maintained as long as the procession moves. As soon as the deities are taken from the heads of the women – in the houses of the *domi*, during the sacrificial stops and at the end of the day, when the deities are placed between *sadar* and *hundi* – they are placed not on Dombo cloth but on seats of paddy, once again making the connection with the jungle king/Raja Maphru and rice very clear. At these moments when the icons are worshipped and are not on the move, no connection with the Dom aspect is evident, as the Dombo cloth is absent from the place of worship and kept by the *domini*, who are not involved in the sacrifices.

The climax of the festival is clearly reached on the eighth day. After the last procession, when the deities have returned to the village shrine, the antagonism between royal soldiers and Ghasi and Dom turns into violent play before the spectator gods. Given the ritual references to the Dom Raja myth, I think it is evident that this Paik play enacts the mythical rebellion against and killing of the Dom King and the re-establishment of proper rule, which is necessary for a successful new agricultural year. This fight occurs after the gods have made the Dengudi walk on their stilts due to their divine presence. The name of the stilt dance – Goro Boga or "leg/foot offering" – may also be a reference to the Dom Raja myth. On the one hand, this name indicates that the stilt dance is regarded as an offering to the deities, which it surely is. On the other hand, it may also be understood as an allusion to the inverted form of greeting (greeting being a form of worship) by the jungle-boy, when he secretly went to the capital during Dasara to show his (dis)respect to the king. While there, he saluted the Dom Raja with his feet, a "feet worship" that enraged the Dom King and led to war. Likewise, the Goro Boga is followed by the fighting of the Paik Kel, when the stilts actually turn into weapons.

The characters of Ghasi, Paik, Dengudi and Dom are most conspicuous in the performance of the Ganga festival and there can be no doubt about the seriousness of the performance and the roles assumed. The Ghasi must actually undergo a ritual of reintegration to resume their normal status as Joria. Other Joria take on other roles. All Joria act as worshippers and participants in the play, some perform in the Monkey Dance in the evenings, which makes the connection between worship of the deities, rice (their dress) and fertility (their phalluses) entirely palpable. Monkeys do not figure in the Dom Raja myths I collected – in contrast to the nurturing deer and the protective tiger – but it may well be that they figure in other versions of the myth, as part of the forest animals surrounding the boy-king. As hosts of the deities, *domi* and *domini* seem to take on the role of the old Bening couple in the myth, who become the foster parents of the boy-king. This is also suggested by the role of the *budia pila* ("child of the old couple") that their sons assume, who accompany the procession throughout, carrying oil and the heads of the sacrificial animals.

Divine Nature, Ritual Form and Well-Being

The connection between the Dom Raja myth and the Ganga festival was not clear to me when we documented the rituals in Kurubi in January 2001, let alone a year before, when I only observed the last day of the festival in Lenjisuku, totally unprepared for what happened in front of my eyes. Even when we recorded the Dom Raja story (M5) in the Bening Porja village of Sarbati in February 2001, I failed to see the striking resemblance between the rituals and the myth. Accordingly, when we returned to Kurubi in March that year to conduct interviews with the *mul ghasi* and Dengudi, I did not ask specifically about the relationship between the myth and the rituals. As the festival was not described anywhere in the literature, I was still completely in the dark about what it might actually be about. Obviously, it was concerned with rice and somehow it dealt with kingship, but that was about all I could surmise. Accordingly, I asked questions about the relationship between the festival and kingship, having historical kings in mind, and I asked if the Paik Kel could somehow be about a war (*judho*). Even if my questions proved to be largely beside the point, in retrospect, the answers of my interlocutors proved to be instructive, because they revealed their views on the deities, as well as the ritual form and the kind of kingship they had in mind.

To my question about whether the Paik Kel is about some kind of war, the *mul ghasi* answered in the negative:

> No no, not like that [i.e. a war], I mean, the god himself is like that. God (*takur*) earlier holding this [sword and shield] came out. This is not about war. It is for the god himself. Holding this god came out; otherwise god won't walk.[36]

Asking whether the festival could be related to the earlier kings of Jeypore, he replied:

> Yes, earlier! – How many fruits (*komla*) does the earth of our land [produce], doesn't it, [from] that time there is god, isn't it? The king was born from the hollow (*kaloru*), he is god. The king was born, King God came out. We cultivator-brothers we sacrifice (perform *puja*) for him, we give-make the festival. Thus their body part [probably of the sacrificial animal] we give, isn't it? For the king we do it. Who performs his sacrifice? The brothers do it, [the] king himself gave it [i.e. the sacrifice] to us. Now this work of the God King, their sacrifice [we] give-make [and] Ganga Mother walks like this with us.[37]

Quite clearly he was not talking about the past, or kings or warfare in a historical sense. With our question, we intended to refer to a historical past (*agoru*), but he immediately switched to the levels of myth and ritual, equating the king with the earth-born king-god, who emerged from the "hollow" and is intimately connected with the fertility of the land (using the mandarin, *komla*, to refer to "fruits" in a general sense). Nandapur was not explicitly mentioned here, but it is evident that the *mul ghasi* was referring to the same sequence as the myth (e.g., M12) and to the common imagination of Nandapur as the navel-place where the King God emerged. Significantly, the *mul ghasi* also talked about the relationship between the King God and the "cultivators-brothers," namely the

---

36 *Nai nai, semti nai, boile, takur nije semti, takur ago semti dori kori baharibe. Seti judho bolia nai. Seta nije tankuro pai ochi seta. Tankur dori kori baharibe, nohele takur chalibo nai.*
37 *Ha, agoru – Jete amo desoro pritu komola naiki, setebelo to takur ochi, naiki. Roja jonmo korla kaloru seta ochi takur. Nohele, roja jonmo korla roja takur baharlani. Ame roit baimonku taku puja koribu, dei kori porbo. Hele tankoro tad debi [perhaps tad, "side of the body"] nai ki – rojo projonto korbe na. Takuro puja ke koribu? Baimor to ochonti, roja amor nije amor dei kori [a few words are unclear]. Ebe se takuro rojaro kam tankoro puja dei kori Gangama emit bulucu ame.*

Joria, who received the festival from the former, and it is their responsibility to conduct it, to make Ganga Mother walk with them in the festival.

From the perspective of the actors, the specific ritual forms – the material objects such as the bamboo swords and shields, but also the dances and play, including the fighting – are all divinely prescribed ways to properly conduct the ritual. "God himself is like that," the *mul ghasi* replied. The Dengudi also insisted that the ritual form actually conforms to the divine being and will. When I asked a Dengudi about the behavior of the Ghasi, Paik and Dom during the procession, he replied: "The way the gods (*maphru*) are, that's the way we walk [in the procession]. It's not our desire! The kind of desire the gods have, in that way we do it."[38] As a divinely inspired ritual form, the performance of the festival is conceived to be unchanging, part of *niam*, the socio-cosmic order instituted by *maphru*. Accordingly, when we asked about possible changes to the festival, the Dengudi replied: "No, we do it like that since long ago (*purberu*), (. . .) [if not] the deity (*takurani*) would harm us. What the law (*niam*) was before, this law we do now."[39]

Discussing the festival as part of *niam*, the Dengudi also stressed the efficacy of the rituals. When everything is done correctly, as one *domi* said, then everything will be fine in the village. Conversely, not performing according to *niam* entails considerable risks, as the Dengudi pointed out:

> Since long ago there exists this law (*niamta*) of moving (*buli*), this law, when we stop with it in front of its face [i.e. the deity's face] – [we are] gone. When we stop with this and don't dance and sing anymore, fever-sorrow, hands-legs [i.e. everything[40]] (. . .), all this occurs, we die today, like this it would happen. This is why we carry [the deities], they go close to the deity and they do it [i.e. dance and sing].[41]

Performing rituals according to *niam* thus guarantees general well-being, what the Gadaba describe as "good-and-evenness" (*bol soman*) and the Dongria as "goodness-correctness" (*nehi ane*). A crucial aspect of the obligatory performance, according to the Dengudi, are the movements of the gods and of the

---

38 *Semiti maphru jar prokar achi, tar prokar ame chalchu. Amoro icha nai to! Maphru jar iccha achi, tar iccha ame korchu.*
39 *Nai semti aka purberu jaha achi seta koruchu, (. . .)[if not] takurani kis kis pokaiba amku. Agore ja niamta achi se niam ebe ame koruchu.*
40 The same expression is used in invocations to deities among the Oraon: "By selling my hands and legs (i.e., my all) I have purchased sacrifices" (Roy 1928, 78).
41 *Agoru niamta ochi buli kori, tar niam, tar muho (face) samnare chirai delu –gola. Ame jodi seti chirai kori nacho gito kichi koribu nai boile, jor-duka, hato-goro, kacho (unclear)-kundia (unclear) sobu hoi kori, mori-aji emti jai hebo. Setepai ame boi kori, maphru pakore jai kori seman koruchu.*

people. As the expression "dance-song" (*nacho-gito*) makes clear, bodily movements go along with a diversity of divine sound forms – the somatic and the sonic go together.

These various forms of movement – including the procession, the Monkey Dance, the Paik play and not least the stilt dance – are the most conspicuous aspects of the festival, along with the alternative social identities of Paik, Ghasi and Dom that some Joria assume for the duration of the Ganga Puja. Although no wooden *anga* frames figure in this festival, the performances of the Ganga Puja are strikingly similar to the ritual events called "god playing" and "gods market" that Alfred Gell (1980) and Nicolas Prévôt (2014) described in Bastar (see Chapter 5). During the Ganga Puja, gods are carried and walked (*buli, chalbar*) through the village for several days, such excursions significantly being combined with the offering of sacrifices, the possession of the *gurumai* and "sound abundance," as Prévôt (2014, 240) described it. Singing, drumming, shouting and whistling are all part of the movement and the celebration of the deities. As the Dengudi put it, this form of dancing-singing is the gods' desire, not the consequence of human will. As in Bastar, the mutuality of divine embodiment enables the gods to indulge in somatic pleasures – and also in "equilibrium play" during the stilt dance –, which allows humans to directly engage with and experience their gods in various dimensions of systemic effervescence: dancing, drinking, fighting, singing or walking on stilts, or a combination of these activities. As with the rituals Gell describes, the Ganga Puja also not only concerns a few select specialists but engages the whole community. Moreover, the forms of play entail ferocious behavior, which in the case of the Ganga Puja is especially true for the Paik Kel – when Ghasi enter the arena with sharp bamboo poles, they swirl around, and a little later Paik fight Ghasi and Dom. However, this seemingly chaotic scene is also part of the ritual script (*niam*) that enables the powerful multi-sensory (somatic, sonic, etc.) immanence and instantiation of the divine. If performed well, it guarantees fertility and well-being.

Dance and Play

When talking about the different forms of movement, our Joria interlocutors used various Desia terms. They spoke of "walking" (*chalibar*) or "strolling" (*bulibar*), when they referred to the procession of the deities. At various moments during the festival, actors cheered each other, and perhaps the deities as well, by requesting or motivating "play" (*kelibar*). Some of the actions, such as the Paik Kel, are explicitly designated as "play" (*kel*), while others, such as the Monkoro Nat are explicitly called a "dance" (*nat*). My wife, Amrei Volkmann, who joined me during the last six months of my main fieldwork period between October 2000 and April 2001, was particularly interested in dance and did most of the filming of the Ganga Puja, especially of the Monkey Dance, the stilt dance and the Paik Play. In our conversations with the *mul ghasi* and the Dengudi, we tried to find out whether there is a difference between dance and play and, if so, what it would consist in. When we asked the Dengudi about the Goro Boga – whose name does not indicate whether it is considered play or dance – he answered: "The stilt dance is not playing. At the end [of the stilt dance] we do it in the form of playing. (. . .) In the Goro Boga we dance, god is true and we dance, that [Sari Kel] is different."[42] The same man said that the animals that appeared after the Paik Kel would also not be "play": "No, that is not in terms of play. God long ago asked us to perform *like that* (emphasis), since our ancestors (*ani dadi*) (. . .)."[43] Obviously, at least some of the actors conceived a difference between dance and play. However, during the Goro Boga, and also while the deer is dancing, people continuously shouted "Let's play," not "Let's dance." So, what can we make of this?

What the Dengudi seems to be suggesting is that "dance" is more directly related to the divine order (*niam*), hence unchanging, and to the deities' actual presence. However, it is quite clear, as the Dengudi himself also stated, that all the actions performed in the Ganga Porbo are perceived to be according to *niam* and instituted by the gods, as mentioned above. Also, the absence or presence of deities, for instance in the form of possession or trance, is unlikely to be the criterion for identifying an action as dance or play. Surely the deities are present during the procession and playing may also involve divine presence, certainly when we think about the "gods' play" in Bastar.

In a talk she gave at the Institute of Ethnology in Berlin more than 20 years ago, Amrei Volkmann (Volkmann 2001) discussed precisely this problem of dance and play. She had worked on how different forms of choreography are created in the work of Sascha Waltz and Pina Bausch, both famous representatives of German Bühnentanz or dance theatre (Volkmann 2003), and was intrigued by the dance performances we witnessed in Koraput. She noticed that the meaning of *nat* and *kel* differed according to context. For instance, the circle dance (*demsa*) performed by the Gadaba and other Desia was also referred to as *kel* and women invited her to join the dance, saying "Let's play *demsa*."[44]

---

42 *Se (Goro Boga) khel isapre nai seta. Lasture khel isapre koruchu (. . .) Se Goro Boga kori nacho koribata, maphru sotre amen ach koruchu, se ta olga.*
43 *Nai, seta kel isap heba nai. Maphru agore aka emti prokar korba achi aka ani-dadi (. . .).*
44 During *demsa* women (men often also join) interlock their hands on their backs, each woman holding the hand of the next but one. The circle (always anti-clockwise) grows smaller and larger, and women move backwards and forwards in different steps, depending on the

However, when the Gadaba dance for tourists – which the Gadaba of Gudapada did regularly during the dry season – they referred to the *demsa* as *nat*, as they did not play for themselves but performed for others.

Moreover, *nat* and *kel* are terms that can be used distinctively, to contrast performances, more or less irrespective of their content. In this sense, the Dengudi quoted above used these words to express the difference between Goro Boga and Paik Kel. Similarly, during the Bali Jatra that will be described in detail later, Volkmann observed that the dance inside the house with the *gurumai* and the deities was considered *nat*, in contrast to the *demsa* performed outside, which was referred to as *kel*. However, it is puzzling, according to Volkmann, that during the Goro Boga both terms seem to merge, the Dengudi performing a *nat*, while the Ghasi and others encourage them in their performance by shouting they should play. She suggested, in conclusion, that *nat* and *kel* should be seen in relational terms, depending on the viewpoint taken, which is somewhat reminiscent of Amerindian perspectivism, although both of us were unaware of Viveiros de Castro's (e.g., 1998) work at the time. Volkmann asked:

> But could the appeal "*khel*" [i.e. *keliba*!] not point to the fact that the stilt dance as the dance of the gods has the same playful character for these deities among themselves as the *demsa* has for humans? In other words, from the human perspective is the stilt dance a *nat*, distinguished from the *khel* of humans; from the perspective of the dancing gods, however, the stilt dance would be *khel* that is perceived by humans as *nat*. (Volkmann 2001, 11, translation PB, using DeepL Translator)

Thus, playful interaction of any kind – whether dancing, or fighting – among a group of actors is considered as playing (*keliba*) by the participants but is regarded as dance (*nat*) in relation to outside observers not engaged in the action. For the Monkoro Nat, this could mean that the performance is a playful interaction for the participants, hence *kel*, which it surely is, but it is performed (as part of *niam*) for the deities, who watch seated on their piles of paddy and thus it is *nat* in relation to them. All forms of movement, even the walking of the deities, could be defined as either *nat* or *kel* depending on the perspective. This is valid both for humans and deities and also supports Gell's (1980) argument about the desire of the gods to engage in embodied play. When gods enjoy themselves in human bodies, swaying, walking and dancing, it is play for them and dance for human onlookers. However, I would argue that this does not entail a complete

---

rhythm of the drums and the tune of the *moiri*. A woman in front is leading the row of dancers, holding a bunch of peacock feathers like the Dengudi during their stilt dance. Unlike the Ghasi in the Ganga Porbo, however, the women do not whistle but ululate. This *demsa* is a ubiquitous phenomenon during seasonal village festivals as well as marriages.

distinction between gods and humans comparable to the difference between Gadaba women dancing *demsa* and Western tourists; quite the contrary. Exactly because the differences between gods and humans are blurred in rituals of the Ganga festival – humans embodying deities, gods manifesting in places, bodies and material objects – humans and gods can and do play with each other. Perhaps this ambiguity and temporary merging of human-divine identity is another reason why dance and play are not always easy to distinguish.

Finally, the Ganga Puja of the Joria not only entangles a tribal village festival with the regional myth of the Dom Raja, including the showdown of the "feet-greeting" during the Dasara reception. It is also a kind of Dasara on its own terms and it is in this sense that I would interpret the name of the festival. Rather than assuming a connection with the Hindu river goddess Ganga, as Rousseleau does (2008, 160), I would suggest that Ganga Puja might refer to the famous Ganga dynasty I discussed in Chapter 4, who made the Jeypore region part of their empire under the name of Tri-Kalinga. True, the deities are at times referred to as Ganga Ma and a connection between the aquatic rice-plant and rivers is self-evident for all Desia, as they are renowned for cultivating rice in the terraced beds of the rivers. However, in contrast to the Bali Jatra, discussed below, these rivers in no way figure in the festival and the river deities are not addressed as Ganga but as Kamni in the region. Without rejecting the idea that Ganga might relate to the water-deity, I thus suggest that the famous dynasty is used here as an iconic[45] reference to kingship, marking the Ganga Puja as *royal* worship or sacrifice, just like Dasara.

The parallels between the royal festival and this "local Dasara" are many and obvious. During the festival of ten days, the village turns into a representation of the capital, with people such as Ghasi and Paik, who are not normally found in villages but who comprise sections of the royal polity of Nandapur, populating the streets. The King God moves through the "capital" for several days, the tribal cultivator-brothers resume their responsibility with regard to sacrifice and play, as was stressed by the *mul ghasi*. Thereby, they effect the presence of the deities and the transformation of divine abundance into crop abundance, rice in particular, and well-being in general.

During the royal Dasara as celebrated in Jeypore or Bastar, normal rule is suspended for nine days, while during the Ganga Puja, normal rule is inverted. It is a case of Dom rule. It is here that the royal Dasara and the Ganga festival differ, as the latter is a performative commentary on misgovernment, a topic that is not

---

[45] Whatever may have been the historical connection between the Bening and former Ganga Kings (see Chapter 4, Kornel and Gamang 2010, 189; Rousseleau 2008).

prevalent in the festivals hosted by real kings, for whom it is perhaps too risky to discuss corrupt rule and wicked sovereigns. For the Joria, as I anticipated in the conclusion to Chapter 4, the ritual rebellion against the seed-withholding Dom king is a fertility cult, an *upriceing*, so to say. Rice and rebellion against the Dom king go together, as do proper rule and regeneration.

7 Of Millet and Mounds: The Nandi Festival of the Joria

The main themes of the Ganga festival are also found in the Nandi Probo, though with different emphasis. The Nandi deity also moves in procession through the village and certain characters must be involved, with some Joria playing these roles to make the deity "walk." While the festival conspicuously focuses on millet, rice makes several appearances. Compared to the Ganga festival, there is less explicit stress on play, although the Nandi song continuously invites human and divine actors to "play" (*kel*). In particular, the song requests an "elder sister" called Earth Beauty Dust Beauty (Mati Sundori Duri Sundori) to walk through the village. Moreover, a group of young affinal males perform as a rowdy crowd throughout the festival, although their performance is not depicted as "play." Alongside dancing, singing has a more prominent place than it does in the Ganga festival. Fertility is also a key issue, as will become clear from the description that follows, in particular the fecundity of the earth itself. The most conspicuous aspect in this regard is the role of a termite mound, as the deities' bodies are made from earth and termite eggs taken from such a mound. As will be seen, the ritual and mythological figure of the Earth Beauty Dust Beauty is crucial to an understanding of the intimate and, literally, substantial connection between soil and cereal, termites and millet.

7.1 The Nandi Festival

The abode of the Nandi[1] deity was a house with a thatched roof[2] in the middle of the village of Lenjisuku, belonging to Sukro Maji. He and his brothers, a group of five, were the hosts (*saukar*) of the deity and the festival, even though the Nandi Porbo concerned the village as a whole and people from many local groups participated, taking on different functions. As is also common among other Desia communities, various ritual specialists were distinguished. The village sacrificer, called *jani* – the equivalent of the *sisa* or *pujari* among the Gadaba, also called *ga pujari* ("village sacrificer") – performed sacrifices for the shrine of the earth deity (*hundi* or *nisani*) and other shrines of the village, such as the one for Pat Kanda. In Lenjisuku, the sacrificer for the Nandi deity was

---

[1] The name of the deity was pronounced "Landi" by everyone in Lenjisuku. But as the term Nandi is generally used for this festival this pronunciation will be followed here as well. Kornel and Gumang (2010, 194) state: "Some call it Nandi and some Landi puja."
[2] It was stressed that it had to be a thatched roof, not one with tiles, for example.

different from the village *pujari* and from that of the Ganga gods. Sadu Mardia and his son performed as *pujari* for Nandi, as they do every time the festival is celebrated. Another man, Ghasi Boronaik, was recruited as *kangar*, which literally means "kidnapper" (Gustafsson 1989, 845). He accompanied the procession of the Nandi deities. It was said that his participation was crucial to make the deity move. In addition to the *gurumai*, various women participated in the procession and carried, or rather danced, the deities for a part of the way.

Table 4: Overview of the Nandi Festival.

February 11 (Fri.), 2000	**Preparing the wall-painting** – Singing and painting of mural inside the Nandi house in the evenings, completed during night of 17/18 February
February 17 (Thurs.)	**Selection and worship of termite mound, raising the deities**
February, 18 (Fri.)	**Fashioning the deities** – Fetching earth and eggs from termite mound, carried into the Nandi house by *dangri* – Making of the Nandi deities
February 19 (Sat.) (full moon)	**First day of procession** – Séance of *gurumai* – Preparation of *kangar* ("kidnapper") – Collective sacrifice inside the Nandi house – Procession through the village – Rowdy affines arrive after dark – Procession ends at *sadar* – *Dangri* takes deities to tree outside village; disposal of divine bodies
February 20 (Sun.)	**Second day of procession** – New divine bodies are made – Invoking the deities, sacrifice – Procession (not entering houses), ends at *sadar*, tag game between affines – *Dangri* takes deities to tree outside village; disposal of divine bodies
February 21 (Mon.)	**Last day of procession** – Preparation of bird replica – Sacrifice, dancing and singing inside the Nandi house – "*Dangri*" (young male, affine of hosts) is prepared – Procession: "*dangri*" carrying rice – Effervescent play: throwing of mud, beer, colors – End of procession at *sadar* – After dark: "*dangri*" takes rice to tree; all utensils left there; brass plate back to Nandi house

Singing and Painting the Murals

The festival started on Friday, February 11, 2000. During the first week, no sacrifices were performed, rather the making of elaborate wall paintings – inside and outside of the house that would be hosting the Nandi deity – was at the center of activities. Every evening during that week, songs were sung while painting the walls, with every dot being one line of a song, I was told.[3] During the night between Thursday 17 and Friday 18 February, the central wall painting was completed. In particular, the owner of the house and another member of the family, Chondoro Maji, who also created the divine bodies and the bird replica later on, did the painting with the *pujari*, using rice powder mixed with water as the only color on the red-brown wall.

The main part of the mural was above the low ledge (*pindoli*) where the deity was later to be placed, the wall facing the entrance. Above the painting, suspended from two horizontal beams of the house, hung a garland of finger millet from the last harvest. Directly below the finger millet, the sun was painted and, half a meter below this, the moon. Just underneath the moon was a simple dot representing a star. This was the first element of the painting, from which the rest originated. Chondoro Maji, one of the painters, commented that the painting was "born" there (*jonmo hela*). Most of the mural consisted of lines of simple dots representing stars and symbols painted with *siardi* leaves with five "toes" representing "feet." These "paths" crisscrossed the painting, leading in all directions; I was told they would be the "paths of the gods." As such, it seemed that one was not looking horizontally at a wall but vertically up into the firmament and the Nandi song aptly represented this sensation by referring to the mural as "sky wall." Some objects not directly belonging to the painting were hanging on the wall. There was a frame drum and flasks with oil and a small protrusion of the wall in the center of the image – above the place where the deities were later seated – held an oil lamp, which was a small shallow bowl (*maloi*) filled with *koronj* (*Pongamia pinnata*) oil. Like all other lamps in the Ganga and Nandi festivals, this one was also regularly re-filled and the oil ran from the lamp down the wall onto the deities' platform.

At the center of the mural, there was a wooden shelf, around which the paths and stars had been painted. On the top-right side of the painting, four mounds representing "temples" (*mandir*) had been depicted, but the painting did otherwise

---

[3] Kornel and Gamang (2010, 196) write in this regard: "The Gurumaies sing songs and praise the devtas (gods) of the region. They sing praises of their country, kings and deities. Each name uttered by them is written as finger tip impression on the wall with rice paste."

not continue toward the right side. On the left side, by contrast, a "path" led away from the main image, continuing along the wall to the entrance of the house. Above the path, one mound, or "temple," had been painted next to another. On the outside walls, the painting framed the entrance to the house. Inside the house, below the paths with temples that ran along the top of the walls, other images had been painted, including a man throwing an object which looked like a fishing net. On an outside wall of the house, other images had been painted, including a bird, other animals and the bow and arrow of the *kangar*. Although the Gadaba do produce paintings – for example on the occasion of the "path wedding" mentioned in an earlier chapter, in front of which the *gurumai* invokes the deities – I had never seen such an elaborate mural in a Gadaba village. The Joria mural rather reminded me of Sora wall paintings. Millet garlands had also been hung on bamboo poles (similar to the rice garlands during the Ganga Porbo) in front of the entrance to the house and yard, so one had to pass under these garlands on the way into the house and the yard.

Photo 7.1: The mural of the Nandi festival
The basket with the Nandi deities has been placed at the bottom of the wall painting (the "sky-wall") depicting sun, moon, stars and the paths of the gods. Above the mural, suspended from two wooden beams, hangs a garland of finger millet.

Photo 7.2: The Nandi house
The painted entrance of the Nandi house. Inside, one of the hosts is worshipping the deities.

Selecting the Termite Mound – Creating the Divine Bodies

On Thursday (February 17), the brothers and the *pujari* selected the termite mound (*birom*) for the Nandi Porbo. A new mound is selected for every festival. No bird droppings should be visible on the mound, but otherwise no other selection criteria were mentioned. The deity was "raised" (*maphru utaiba*) through a *puja* in front of the termite mound, the eggs inside "being born" (*jonmo hela*). An egg was offered and the top of the mound was then covered by a basket (upside-down).

I arrived on the following day (Friday 18), the day the bodies of the deities were created. While normal food had been cooked and consumed by the Maji brothers in the week before, on the evening of that day, special food was prepared in the inner room of the house.[4] There, rice with black gram (*biri*) and *chemi*[5] was prepared, along with sweet balls made from finger millet and molasses (*mandru*). Although prepared in the sacred inner room and mainly intended for the (still disembodied) deities, there were no restrictions on commensality.

Accompanied by drums, the procession from the house of the deities to the termite mound started after sunset. Beforehand, the hosts and the two Nandi *pujari* had shared liquor inside the house. As we arrived and the basket on top of the mound was removed, I noticed that the termite hill had been painted or sprinkled white on top (thus resembling the painting inside the house). An object, perhaps just a stick, was stuck inside the mound; it was referred to as "sword" (*kanda*). It had probably been inserted into the termite mound the day before, when the deity was raised. For the present ritual, a white chick had been brought along and was now, as usual, asked to pick grains of rice as a sign of its acceptance, while invoking the deity. However, the animal remained stubborn and did not pick any of the grains offered. This is generally regarded as a bad sign, and I had previously witnessed among the Gadaba violent reactions from the sacrificer to such a situation. After various people present tried their luck, Chondoro lost his patience. He smashed the chick onto the termite mound and then simply twisted off its head. The bottom of the mound was then opened with a crowbar, with the men digging deep into the mound. Earth and eggs were taken out and put into a white cloth, which was placed inside the basket (that was later used to transport the deities during the procession). A young girl from the *pujari* group (Mardia), who had fasted during the day, carried the bundle in the basket in the usual Nandi style, together with one of the Maji brothers. Both of them held the basket with both hands at either end and danced in a stooped position, the steps were the same as during the Ganga Porbo, one foot briefly joining the other and then put forward or backward, then joined by the other foot in the same way, which resulted in a pendulum movement (as can be seen on photo 7.8). As they moved away from the termite

---

4 Like any house, the house of the Nandi deity had an inner room with a sacred central pillar (Doron Deli). The seat for the Nandi was in the big room, which one enters first. Significantly, no cooking place was to be found in this room, as is usual in ordinary houses.
5 I am not sure what kind of vegetable *chemi* refers to, it could have been the white beans (*semi*) commonly consumed in the area. It was described as *sag*, which refers to leafy vegetables but also, more generally, to any accompaniment to rice. It may possibly also be the plant with a similar name, mentioned by Franco and Narasimhan (2012, 246), *chemidimulo* (*Hemidesmus indicus*).

mound, everyone started singing the Nandi song: "Walk sister, walk sister, Earth Beauty (Mati Sundori); walk sister, walk sister, Dust Beauty (Duri Sundori)." Along the way back into the village, the procession had to stop a couple of times as people greeted the two carriers with *tika* and incense. The last stop was made under the millet garland at the entrance into the yard of the deities' house; the girl then took the basket into the house and the men followed.

The singing continued inside the house while the Maji brothers prepared the deities' bodies and the basket. The latter had been placed on the platform below the central painting and was then removed. From the earth mixed with termite eggs, two cylindrical bodies were made, about 10 cm long and 4 cm wide, one by Chondoro Maji, the other by the Nandi *pujari*. Anointed with oil from the lamps, they were first decorated with three lengthwise rows of cucumber seeds. Framing the face like hair or a crown, a metal half ring was placed on one end of the figure, another little ring being placed in the center of the face as a nose ring (*mundi*), and two red pearls were added as eyes. A little stick was inserted at the other end, equal in length to the body, representing a tail. Both figures looked identical but they were distinguished nevertheless; one was called Kesa Risia and the other Mota Risia. The two entities most often invoked in the Nandi song were not these two conspicuous figures, however, but two plain, flat millet cakes (called Mati Sundori and Duri Sundori), which were first placed inside the shallow basket and then covered with a layer of finger millet grains. Then the two figures were placed on top of this layer, each thus resting on one of the millet cakes, and two small chains (*risia*) were placed across both figures, covering them like a blanket.[6] It was stressed that Mati Sundori and Duri Sundori, which could no longer be seen, were "senior" (*boro*) in relation to the visible "junior" (*sano*) figures. Nevertheless, the two figures were carefully treated, their faces and bodies being constantly anointed with castor oil (*jara tel*) using a feather. Two oil lamps were placed inside the basket and lit, one on either side of the figures, and four sticks with a thread structure on top (like a small spider web)[7] were placed in each corner of the basket. Wreaths of flowers (white *ron chemi* flowers[8]) were tied between these sticks.

---

6 All these utensils are used again every time the festival is performed.
7 These "banners" are called *siral* and the Gadaba use them to ward off bad influences during healing rituals. Such a structure was also tied to the pots representing the Ganga deities.
8 Given their form, their white and purple color and the importance of the tree in the Nandi Porbo, these flowers are most likely from the *koronj* tree (*Pongamia pinnata*).

As the deities and the basket were now complete, the drummers were instructed to play (the *dapu* and *kirdi*[9]), millet was broadcast over the low platform and the deities were placed below the painting. All other items used for the procession on the next day were also placed behind the basket: a bow and arrow to be carried by the *kangar*, the head of the arrow opened like a cone (thus different from any of the three types of arrows I knew that were used for hunting fish, birds or game); four millet balls tied into a long string, which the *kangar* also wore on the subsequent days; a kind of bamboo fan to be taken by the dancing girls; a cup of oil for the deity; a bunch of peacock feathers; a basket with another small pot with oil and a little basket with husked rice, both to be taken by the *pujari* on the following day.

The presence of the deities inside the Nandi house was assured in multiple ways.[10] The hosts said the deities had been "raised" the evening before, when the eggs were "born" inside the termite hill. The deities now also resided inside the bodies that had been made. The paintings provided "paths" for the deities, which led them from the door toward the low platform in front of the wall painting. Moreover, a device common in other contexts among the Gadaba and other communities was also used.[11] A thread led from the entrance to the house above the horizontal beams that held the ceiling, which then hung down vertically on the wall painting where the sun and moon were depicted. At times, the thread lay on the wooden plank which stuck out from the wall. However, during moments of ritual action, for example, when the *gurumai* were invoking the deities, the thread was made to hang on the platform where millet was scattered and where the basket with the deities was placed. After the completion of the deities' bodies and of all the preparations mentioned, the men sat in front of them and sang long into the night.

---

9 *Kirdi* is a small kettle drum of about 30 cm in diameter, which is tied around the waist and beaten with two sticks; *dapu* is a frame drum of about 60 cm in diameter. It is carried with one hand and beaten (with a stick) with the other.
10 Such a ritual redundancy has also been noted by Vitebsky (2017a, 94). During the stone-planting ritual the dead are invited into the house in a number of parallel ways: they are raised in the underworld, enter through the door and again ascent from below via a bamboo ladder.
11 Also among the Dongria (e.g. Hardenberg 2018a, 327) or Mali (Otten 2014, 257, 259) such threads provide avenues for the deities to enter the ritual space and ritual objects.

Photo 7.3: The Nandi deities in their basket

First Day of the Procession

The next morning began with a séance by the *gurumai* and more preparations for the first day of the procession. Surrounded by the Maji brothers and other men and women, the *gurumai* let down her hair, the usual sign of the permeability of her body, and sitting in front of the deities she started singing and swaying backwards and forwards.

Afterwards, the hosts and the *pujari* drank beer (*pendom*) together inside the house after making libations on the threshold. Subsequently, the *kangar* was dressed up by the brothers. He was one of two persons who played conspicuous roles; the other was a young man dressed up like a woman on the last day. An old and torn net was tied around the lower body of the *kangar* as a kind of waistcloth and a bright yellow turban was tied around his head, to which a metal necklace was attached. In addition, a ribbon that had four millet balls mixed with molasses (*mandru*) tied to it was wrapped around his otherwise bare chest. *Mandru* such as these are very nutritious and only slightly sweet and are carried when people travel or hunt in case they do not find food along the way. Finally, the *kangar* had millet paste smeared on his back and chest and he was given a bow and arrow that he carried throughout the procession. After completion, Chondoro proudly presented the *kangar* to me for a photograph.

Photo 7.4: A *gurumai* is invoking the Nandi deities

Before the deity was moved out of the house, it received sacrifices from the village as a whole: two coconuts, one rooster and one young ram. The two Nandi *pujari*, the Maji brothers and the *kangar* invoked the deity, the coconuts were smashed and the rooster killed, with the head being placed inside the basket next to the deities. As on the occasion of the Ganga festival a month earlier, there were many arguments. The main point of contention this time was whether the ram should be killed inside the house or in the yard. After much shouting and haggling, the ram was beheaded inside the house. Again, beer was drunk, and then men and women danced and sang inside the little house.

Photo 7.5: The "kidnapper"
One of the hosts of the festival is presenting the *kangar* (lit. "kidnapper") who is ready for the procession of the Nandi deities.

The procession through the village then started. It took around ten hours in total and included more than twenty stops, each one involving at least an offering of coconuts and the consumption of beer by the core members of the procession, if not additional sacrifices, depending on the individual vows made earlier. The Nandi song aptly describes the key-elements of the procession:

The carrying of the basket with the deities:

Hold elder sister, hold elder sister, dust basket	*Hold elder sister, hold elder sister, earth basket*

The various forms of movement, play and gathering at the meeting place (*sadar*):

Let's go elder sister, let's go elder sister gathering at the meeting place	*Roam let's go sister, let's go gathering at meeting place, play let's go*

The beating of the drums:

Beat ho, beat ho, men who beat the Nandi *drum*	*Beat brother, beat, men who beat the kirudia drum*

The features of the dance:

Leg, leg, leg, leg dust will rise *Bunch of jali peacock feather swing*	*Face, face, face, face sweat will run* *Bunch of tiki peacock feather swing*

The anointment of the deities during the procession:

Keep the oil, give the oil	*keep the turmeric, give the turmeric*

And the invitations of the deities into the houses, offering water to wash, as is done for every guest:

Wash your hands and come, Earth Beauty	*Wash your legs and come, Dust Beauty*

The procession commenced when the younger Nandi *pujari* carried the basket with the deities out of the Nandi house and – in the yard, below the millet garland – handed it over to two women. One was the white-haired *gurumai*, the other was Sukro Maji's wife, the *memor* (ward member) at the time. She was especially decorated and wore a necklace of old rupee coins, had rupee notes attached to the necklace and her hair and had a silver chain suspended from her hair bun. Several other women who later carried the basket also wore necklaces made from old rupee coins; the one I had a close look at was from 1906. The *memor* and the *gurumai* then carried the basket together, the former moving backward, the latter forward, in the way described above.

Photo 7.6: Beginning of the procession
The Nandi *pujari* has passed on the basket to two women, one of them (the *memor*) seen here. She is decorated with a necklace of old rupee coins.

Throughout the day, the procession maintained a standard composition. The basket with the deities was mostly carried by two women, with other women accompanying them on each side. In front of the women with the deities, Sukro walked as the main host, always carrying an umbrella. Ahead of him were two drummers leading the procession. Also beside the deities were the *kangar*, other Maji brothers, a man with the bunch of peacock feathers and the *pujari* carrying the oil and husked rice. Concluding the procession, behind the deities, was a row of girls and women, interlocked, dancing and singing throughout. They were in the usual *demsa* formation, their arms interlocked behind their backs; however, there were two differences: the women were not dancing in a circle and the leading woman did not carry the usual bunch of peacock feathers but a little bamboo fan. As the procession moved along, the women and girls, in particular, were singing the Nandi song.

The first destination was the open megalithic meeting place (*sadar*) that also contained the *hundi* shrine. But already on its way the procession had to halt several times as villagers greeted the deities with incense and gave *tika*

Photo 7.7: The "sister" (millet) is visiting her "brother" (rice)
Mural and sacrificial platform in the house of the elder Ganga deity. In the context of the procession, the Nandi deities visit the house of the Ganga deities. Above the mural, suspended from the ceiling, one can see the pot representing the Ganga deity and the "iron horse," next to other ritual paraphernalia.

(rice marks) to members of the procession. But otherwise the procession headed straight to and into the *sadar*, where the first real stop was made in front of the *hundi* and the second between the huge banyan trees at a place called "old-man deity" (Dokra Maphru). Shortly afterwards, the procession moved out of the *sadar* and, after another brief halt on the way, it went straight into the house of the elder Ganga deity; the "sister" is visiting her "elder brother," people commented. The *kangar* was greeted in a special way, with a white thread being tied around his left ankle. The garlands of paddy from the festival a month earlier were still hanging at the entrance to the house; however, inside, the Ganga deity was no longer seated on the low veranda but had been stored away. The pot representing the Ganga deity still hung from a cross beam directly above the mural (painted for the Ganga Puja), along with the "iron horse," the small pot for oil and the special cylindrical drum (*dol*) that is used during the Ganga festival but not during the Nandi Porbo. On the low veranda, the "brother" was now seated on a bed of millet grains. A duck (*hãso*) was sacrificed, its blood sprinkled on the veranda and smeared onto the wall painting. After the sacrifice, beer (*landa* and *pendom*) was drunk by all participants in the procession who were inside the house, including the girls.

From there, the woman of the house (the Ganga *domini*) carried the basket on her own to the house of the other, junior, Ganga deity. Also here, the mural was still in place and the other ritual items of the Ganga Puja were suspended from the ceiling. After the same procedure had been repeated (sacrifice, beer consumption, singing) the woman of the house and *domini* of the junior Ganga deity took the basket to the subsequent stop, which was the house of the *barik* (the village herald and thus a Dombo). From there, two women continued, a Dombo woman and the *gurumai*, to the house of one the Maji group – the one who had made and danced the bear during the Ganga Porbo. Some of the houses who were receiving the Nandi deities were elaborately painted as well, featuring the same "paths" with "feet" as the main mural in the Nandi house. So it went on and on, with different animals being sacrificed (e.g., a goat, a pig) and beer being consumed in every house. Accordingly, the participants were in an increasingly impaired condition. At some point, the *kangar* collapsed somewhere and was left sleeping on a veranda, with his son replacing him, although without his costume.

Long after dark, at about 8:30 pm, a crowd of affinal guests arrived, mostly young men from the village of Patraput. During the day, affinal guests (*kunia* or *gotia*) – affines being the guests par excellence – already had come, bringing measures of husked rice and beer to the houses of the hosts. Ritual friends

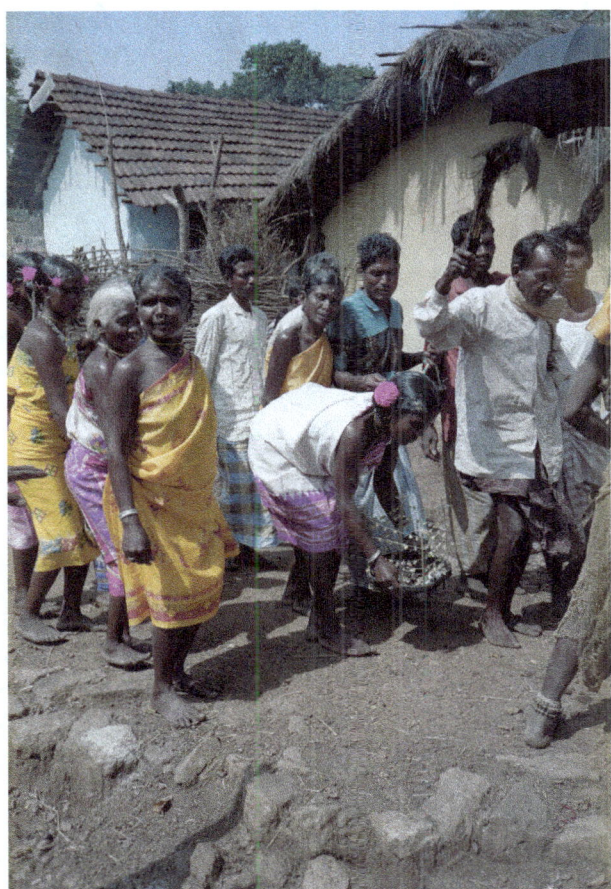

Photo 7.8: "Walk sister, walk sister, Earth Beauty; walk sister, walk sister, Dust Beauty"
The procession of the Nandi deities. Here the Ganga *domini* (host of the elder Ganga deity) is carrying the basket after the Nandi *de'ties* have visited her house.

(*moitor*) arrived as well. However, the affinal group of young men, most wearing "shirt-pant,"[12] was different from the rest. Equipped with drums, swinging sticks and shouting (not singing), they rampaged through the village. They were not referred to by any particular name, but their arrival and their behavior seemed to have been expected.

---

[12] At the time this was the local expression for people who are dressed in a "modern" way; that is, not with a waist-cloth or loin-cloth but with a "shirt" and "pants."

This affinal horde, as I call them, was already charging around in the *sadar* as the procession finally arrived there after all the preceding stops. The procession and the horde moved around each other for a while, then the latter moved on through the village, while the procession stopped in front of the closed *hundi* shrine again. Men and women sang separately in front of the Nandi deities, and

Photo 7.9: Leaving the house of the junior Ganga deity
After visiting the house of the junior Ganga deity, the Nandi deities are continuing their procession. The *domini* (female host of the Ganga deity) is carrying the basket out of her house and takes it to the next. She is followed by the *kangar* (with his bow) and the younger Nandi *pujari* (holding a container with oil). On the right a man can be seen swinging a bunch of peacock feathers. Also note the garlands of paddy from the previous Ganga festival still framing the entrance.

then a young girl took the basket. When the deities had first been brought out of the house by the young *pujari*, only married women or widows carried them from one stop to the next. Now, it was the turn of a young girl – perhaps the same one who had brought the earth and eggs from the termite mound into the village the day before – who took the deities out of the village again.

Without any further stop, she left the *sadar*, accompanied by all the others, and walked to a big *koronj* tree outside the village boundaries in between the dry fields. This leguminous tree is very important for all Desia as it produces an abundance of seeds with very high oil content. This oil (*tel*), called *koronj tel* accordingly, is used for lamps. Moreover, as mentioned above, in all likelihood, it was also this tree that provided the flowers used for the decoration of the basket containing the deities. As they arrived at the foot of the tree, the girl handed over the basket to a man from the Boronaik group. He took the deities out of the basket and removed the accompanying objects, all the rings, necklaces and pearls that had covered the divine body and face, after which he dropped the bodies made from termite earth and eggs, as well as the flat millet cakes and the grains, at the foot of the tree. The various objects, which would be used for the next embodiment of the deities, were wrapped in a cloth, put in the otherwise now empty basket and carried by the girl back to the house without a stop. Shortly after the procession had returned to the Nandi house, the wild affinal horde also arrived, in the same hooting fashion as before. They received beer from the hosts and afterwards toured the village until the morning hours.

Second Day of the Procession

The young men constituting the wild horde were also the first thing I saw the next morning, the second day of the procession. They were already squatting on the veranda and in front of Sukro's house, wrapped in blankets because of the cold, cups of heated beer in their hands. Throughout the day, they would go from house to house, being served beer and food each time. In addition to the wild horde, other affinal guests had arrived and continued to arrive over the course of the day.[13] However, they were not as numerous as expected, which was perhaps partly due to the heavy showers that had regularly poured down since the previous day – quite unusual for the time of the year. The umbrella Sukro carried as he walked in front of the deities thus also had some practical value in this situation.

---

13 From the villages of Kurubi, Hatsuku, Kesela, Paidaput and Simla.

Photo 7.10: Singing the Nandi song
The Nandi deities visit another house. While the sacrifice is going on, girls sing the Nandi song, interlocking their arms behind their back, like in the *demsa* dance.

The second thing that I noticed when I entered the Nandi house was that new bodies for the deities had been formed, which were identical to those of the previous day. They were already resting inside the basket on their platform beneath the painting. The protagonists of the first day of the procession assembled in front of the deities, and the brothers, the *pujari* and the *gurumai* jointly invoked them. The *pujari* sacrificed two white chicks, let blood drip on the deities inside the basket and then placed the victims' heads inside it. Offerings of "blood-rice" (*rokto chaul*, blood mixed with husked uncooked rice) were placed in the yard as well.

The *kangar* had recovered and was now dressed up in the same fashion as before. Subsequently, men, women and the girls danced and sang inside the Nandi house.

Shortly afterwards, the senior Nandi *pujari* carried the deities out of the house and passed the basket on to Sukro's wife, exactly as had happened the day before, and the second day of procession began. However, it was not completely identical to the previous day. There were fewer stops and the deities did not enter the houses. Seven Joria houses (Jani, Maji, Boronaik, Kirsani and Munduli) were visited, and now and then the rampaging affinal horde could be seen at different places. The *kangar* was lost on the way once more, and his son replaced him for a second time. After the visits to the individual houses had been completed, the procession moved into the *sadar* again. Without a stop in front of the *hundi*, they proceeded to the place between the banyan trees, the "old-man deity," and set down the deities. Subsequently, the deities were carried around inside the *sadar* by different women, at times leaving the *sadar* on one side and reentering on the other, the whole procession always accompanying them. A jocular scene then developed in the *sadar*, with mother's brothers (*mamu*) trying to catch and tie up their nephews (*banja*) and asking for money. Soon, this developed into a generalized tag game, which was disrupted by a heavy down pour. Most people fled to the houses closest to the assembly area for shelter, while the core of the procession remained motionless in the middle of the *sadar*, Sukro's umbrella protecting the deities, as the procession should not return to the house before sunset.

When the rain decreased in intensity, the people reappeared from the houses, and the affinal horde began to move through the village again. The procession then also continued, moving through puddles in anti-clockwise circles inside the *sadar*. With fewer people participating and drunken people falling into the mud, the procession now made a somewhat bleak impression. Round and round they went for two more hours, then the deities were put down at the place of the "old-man deity" again, between the trees. Finally, the basket was given to the young girl once more, who took the deities to the *koronj* tree outside the village, as on the previous evening. After the deities were disposed of there, the procession returned to the Nandi house and a quiet night followed, with no singing or dancing.

The Last Day of the Procession

Over the two preceding days, adult women had carried the deities on their seats of millet in the basket, while the young girl (if it actually was the same) took the basket back to the Nandi house after the divine bodies had been disposed of at the tree. On the last day, both the people and objects involved changed. A young man dressed as a young woman carried a brass plate filled with husked rice, not millet. Furthermore, a fabricated bird accompanied the procession, "flying" over it the whole time. This bird had been made by Chondoro Maji, the man who had also participated in fashioning the deities from the termite-mound earth. He made the body from a root (*keu kanda*), and he painted the face red – with vermilion (*sindur*) – and the beak black. Feathers were inserted into the body, so as to give the animal the appearance of a real flying bird. The bird was referred to as *mali chorei* or *mali chere*.[14]

Photo 7.11: "One of the hosts of the festival" presents the bird he has fashioned for the procession

The young man who was dressed up as a woman was referred to as *dangri* (the general term for unmarried girls or young women). He was an affine, Sukro's wife's brother, from the Munduli group (from the Tiger clan) of Lenjisuku. He wore a bright yellow *sari* the same color as the *kangar*'s turban, rings on his fingers, bracelets, nose rings and even artificial breasts. Desia women tie their hair in a bun behind the right ear, accordingly the young man wore a head cloth representing the hair, with a bun at the appropriate place. Flowers were attached to the "hair," like those women wear on festival days. He also had a necklace with old rupees, like those worn by the women over the previous

---

14 *Chorei* or *choroi* refers to "birds" generally, *mali* means bead, garland or necklace.

days. Moving in the same stooped way as the women had done previously, the *dangri* carried husked rice, colored yellow with turmeric, in a brass plate. A low earthenware cup filled with oil was placed in the center of the plate as a lamp (*maloi*). These lamps were omnipresent in both the Nandi and Ganga festivals.

In comparison to the two preceding days, the procession started late that Monday, with people only assembling at the Nandi house after noon. Perhaps thirty men and women, including the *kangar*, the *dangri* and the other protagonists, squeezed into the house, singing, dancing and drumming, so that the small house seemed to vibrate. A man with a string instrument (*dudunga*) typical of the Joria tried to enter but gave up, perhaps worrying about the fragility of his *dudunga*. Surrounded by the dancers, a chick and an egg were sacrificed, and then the people poured out of the house and the procession started. This time they visited the other houses of the Dombo, an area they had not visited thus far. Like the women previously, the *dangri* was now the center of the procession, Sukro held his umbrella over her head, or close to her in any case, the *kangar* was either dancing in front of or next to her and the *pujari*, carrying oil and husked rice as usual, also accompanied the procession. The bird was carried on a long bamboo

Photo 7.12: Reappearance of rice in the festival
On the last day of the festival, a male youth dressed as "young woman" (*dangri*) carries husked rice through the village.

Photo 7.13: The *sadar* of Lenjisuku
Toward the end of the festival, the procession is again approaching the village assembly place (*sadar*), a round open space delimited by megalithic stones. In the middle of the photo, above the houses, the white bird can be seen, attached to a long bamboo pole.

pole and "flew" some meters over people's heads. The affinal horde had apparently left but the procession was wild in its own way on that day.

Even during the first of two rounds, people, mainly young men, started pouring beer over other people's heads, involving young and old, men and women. They also threw earth at each other and smeared their faces with black paint. This joking continued as the procession went into the *sadar* for the first time. Without a stop, they proceeded back to the Dombo houses and to the Nandi house, finishing the first round. After having received *tika* there, they embarked on the second and final round. Without further stops, they proceeded back into the *sadar*, where beer was consumed one more time. It began to rain again, but the procession had to wait until dark, and thus they held on. Finally, after sunset, they left the *sadar* and proceeded to the *koronj* tree. The colored rice was poured on the pile of millet and earth from the previous days and the brass plate washed. The millet balls that the *kangar* had carried around his body for three days were also removed and left at the foot of the tree. The *dangri* then performed the last act of the festival and took the brass plate back to the Nandi house and placed it in front of the platform below the painting.

7.2 Discussion and Interpretation

Comparing the obvious aspects of the Nandi festival with those of the Ganga Puja, similarities and difference are apparent. Perhaps the most conspicuous contrast concerns the kind of grain at the center of each festival, rice in the former and finger millet in the latter. Like the Ganga Puja, deities entered the village space, were made to walk through the village and were invited into houses. While millet was completely absent in the Ganga Puja, the inverse situation was not the case for the Nandi festival. Remarkably, millet visited rice – the sister visited her elder brother. Moreover, at the end of the festival, we saw a return of rice.

Sacrifice, dance and play were also prominent in the Nandi festival. However, there were two related features that were markedly different, namely the elaborate wall paintings that were absent from the Ganga Puja (at least in Kurubi) and the emphasis on singing. An abundance of sound – shouting, drums, whistling, the singing of "filthy" songs – could clearly be identified in the Ganga Puja, but singing the deities into the house while painting the mural was a distinct aspect of the Nandi festival. There was also one aspect which was very prominent in the Ganga Puja but lacking in the Nandi festival. No mention was made of any king and no hierarchically ranked polity of royal soldiers and lower service castes such as the Dom or Ghasi made an appearance. Instead of a king, however, we had a queen, "queen millet." The existence of this queen was closely related to a termite mound and it is this connection between millet, termite mounds and earth that is perhaps the most striking dimension of the whole festival. The names of the two millet cakes on which the newly made Nandi deities rested, refer to the soil, the Earth Beauty (Mati Sundori) and the Dust Beauty (Duri Sundori). On a purely impressionistic level, the grains of finger millet and the laterite earth from which they grow are similar, with both having a rusty red-brown coloration and being very rich in iron.

Termites, Life and Wealth

Termites (*Isoptera*) – often wrongly identified with "ants" and frequently described as "white ants" – are ancient creatures with regard to both natural and cultural history (Irwin 1982; König 1984). A few general facts about termites and termite mounds easily illustrate why these animals are "good to think" with. Termites are "soil engineers" (Jouquet et al. 2016, 157, 159) and spend a huge amount of energy digging deep into the earth and bringing up soil from deeper layers, which they use to build impressive structures above ground. They are not only constructors but also change the organization and properties of the soil in the process. Like earthworms, which figure prominently in the cosmogonic myths of the region, termites play a key role in organic decomposition, soil formation and soil regulation (Jouquet et al. 2015). The diet of termites varies according to the family. Some feed on living plants, some on dead wood or leaves, humus or soil (Eggleton 2011, 13–14). Termites are vulnerable creatures, easy prey for predators and exposed to the effects of sunlight when above ground. Their mounds serve as fortresses against enemies, as protection against environmental challenges such as rain, drought or heat, as storage places for food and as nests for reproduction. Most of the insects live below the surface, where they build extensive networks of chambers and tunnels for ventilation, storage and defense. To reach water, the workers dig deep into the earth – up to 40 meters it has been claimed (Irwin 1982, 348) – and bring up soil that is rich in minerals, highly fertile and also at times containing particles of gold.

Next to the permanent mounds, they also build more temporary structures (called sheeting) to access food above ground – they might build, for example, a cover consisting of earth and saliva around a dead branch that keeps them hidden and protected while foraging (Jouquet et al. 2015). In the center of it all are the queen and her mate, who accompanies her throughout her long life of potentially several decades. While worker and soldier termites are sterile, the queen is a reproductive miracle and the only individual in the colony who lays eggs. After reaching full maturity, more than 30,000 eggs are produced by her hugely swollen body each day. New colonies are usually established in the rainy season, when the earth is soft. Winged alates then leave the mound and a pair finds a suitable spot to dig into the earth. There, they create a small chamber where at first workers are reproduced, who then start building the mound, which literally rises above the water in the rainy season. Colonies are regarded as one superorganism, as no individual insect has all the features of movement, defense and reproduction that are commonly associated with individual organisms. Only the collective, the "most complex colonial organism known in nature" (Eggleton 2011, 21), fulfills all the requirements.[15]

The termites I am concerned with here belong to the species *Odontotermes obesus*. They build cathedral shaped mounds that are normally one to two meters in height, but I have also seen mounds that were more than two meters high. These termites feed on plant waste material but also on weak living plants. Moreover, they are not only miners and engineers, but also cultivators. *Odontotermes*

---

15 See Eggleton 2011; Irwin 1982, Jouquet et al. 2016, 2017; König 1984; Korb 2011. See also https://www.sciencedirect.com/topics/earth-and-planetary-sciences/termite.

obesus are a species of fungus-growing termites (*Macrotermitinae*). Inside their mound, they cultivate a fungus (*Termitomyces*) they need for their external metabolism, a kind of collective stomach of the colony. Much of what they collect from outside their mound they cannot digest themselves, but the fungus can, so they place the collected food items on the fungus and eat the fungus later. Much like the human cultivators above ground – who eat the grain and keep some to sow as seeds for the next harvest – the termites keep and cultivate part of the fungus and eat the rest.[16] Both the fungus and the termites require a high level of humidity, so the termites have to make sure that there is sufficient moisture inside the mound (Jouquet et al. 2017). At least some of these natural properties of termites are well recognized by the various tribal communities of the region, who closely associate termites and their mounds with life, earth, cosmogony, the dead and, as we can see in the Nandi festival, finger millet.

Local languages clearly make the connection between termites and earth and also recognize different stages in the life-cycle of the mound and its inhabitants. In the Desia language that the Gadaba and Joria share, *birom* designates the mound and *olma* the insects. Moreover, they also specify the early stage of new termite mounds that are only one foot tall (*koari birom*[17]) and call the winged termites seen during the rainy season when they leave the mounds to found new colonies *botor kira*[18] or *butui*.[19] I am not sure if the termite "queen" is actually referred to as such, or if the Desia use the general word for worm, grub or maggot (*kira*) for her, because she actually looks like a "worm-like bag of fat" (Marais 2017, 24). However, with regard to bees, the Desia do speak of a "queen" (*rani moci*[20]), *moci* being the general term for flying insects. The Austroasiatic languages of the region explicitly make a connection between termites and earth. The Gutob of the Gadaba designates termites as *to'dur*, probably related to *tubog* or *tubo'* (earth), while in Remo – the Bondo language – they are referred to as *tobdur* (*tukka* being the inner part of the mound) (Griffiths 2008, 675, fn. 1; Bhattacharya 1968 #1152, #1497).

The capacity of termites as "soil engineers" is duly represented in cosmogonic ideas concerning the "primordial mound." John C. Irwin has argued that these conceptions are ancient, as well as widespread, and actually the "ultimate meaning" (Irwin 1982, 343) of numerous rituals he discusses, including Vedic, Hindu and tribal rituals. Various sources describe an original state of

---

16 I am grateful to Pascal Jouquet who pointed this aspect out to me and shared some of this extensive knowledge of termite mounds with me in a personal conversation and correspondence.
17 Gustafsson 1989, 132.
18 Mahapatra 1985, 253.
19 Gustafsson 1989, 384.
20 Gustafsson 1989, 457.

flood, with the termite mound emerging from the water and further "swelling" to a hill. Keeping the life-cycle of a termite colony in mind, it seems that this cosmogonic situation is repeated every year, when the flying termites leave their mounds in the rainy season to construct new mounds. In the myths, different animals are involved in this act of earth-creation, such as a primeval boar who brings up earth from the bottom of the ocean (1982, 347).

Many oral traditions of the Jeypore/Nandapur region – and also in neighboring Bastar (Gregory and Vaishnav 2003, 1–3) – deal with cosmogonic waters and the creation of the earth.[21] In local myths, different animals are involved in the the process of the cosmogonic creation of the earth. In a Didayi story, it is also a boar that helps to establish the earth, first by providing earth and then, significantly, transforming it into proper land by being sacrificed:

> When Rumrok [i.e. Maphru] wanted to make a new world he was unable to find any earth. He searched everywhere without success and it was only when he went to the boar that he found a little earth sticking to its tail. He removed it and sprinkled it on the face of the water. After a while the earth grew and grew and soon there was mud everywhere and the water began to dry up. But the mud remained damp and dirty and to harden it Rumrok killed the boar and ground its bones into powder and spread it over the world. When the mud dried it was strong and steady. (Elwin 1954, 4)

In M12, it is not a boar but a cobra and an earthworm (*ladon* or *kechua*) who provide earth and a tiger that makes it hard. Also in a Bondo story, earthworms eat and egest earth and in this way make "the soil of the whole world soft and porous" (Elwin 1954, 213).

Raphaël Rousseleau (Rousseleau 2021) provides us with a relevant variant of these cosmogonic myths that he has collected among the Joria.[22] A termite

---

21 Seen from a termite-mound-centric perspective, the beginning of the origin myth I collected among the Gutob Gadaba (M12) might also be read in an alternative way. The opening sentence is: *Nandapur kuplire jonom kori maphru, Raja Maphru, jongelre maphru jonom kori* ("At Nandapur, King God (Raja Maphru) was born in/from a hillock (*kuplire*), in the forest (*jongelre*)"). The word *kupli* means hillock, or swelling of the earth, and is translated by Burrow and Bhattacharya (1970, 201) in their work on the Pengo language, which contains many Desia words, as "mound of earth." The suffix *-re* in *kuplire* indicates that the King God emerged from within. *Kuplire* thus might mean that the King God emerged from within a small hill – possibly a reference to the location of the former throne with 32 steps (Senapati and Sahu 1966, 422) – but it cannot be ruled out either that *kuplire* here also connotes a very particular kind of "mound of earth," namely a termite mound.

22 Rousseleau's description on the Nandi festival is based on testimonies he collected in the village of Hadaput, just next to Nandapur and on more recent fieldwork conducted in the village of Sunari Guda, about 140 kilometers linear distance from the former capital (2008, 163–67; 2021).

mound, as well as rice and millet, figure prominently in this story, which also begins with a flood that drowns everything, including Bidum Dei, the "Mother of the Termite Mound." However, her son and daughter survive the flood in a boat. They are called Chulchulia/Kulkulia and San Sundari/Pila Sundari. Maphru discovers them and asks the Earthworm King (Kechua Raja) and the Llizard[23] Queen (Dendua Rani) to egest soil, which he then uses to extend the earth. A termite mound is subsequently created, in which the brother and sister settle. The story continues with the common transformation of brother and sister into spouses procreating the tribes of the region.

Especially important is an alternative conclusion to the story, which Rousseleau (2021, 253) also presents. Inside the mound, brother and sister become hungry and emerge from it. The brother sits on a pile of rice, eats rice and becomes Gangama, the sister sits on a pile of millet, eats millet and becomes the Nandi deity and Mandia Rani, the "Queen of [Finger] Millet." Obviously, this myth is highly relevant to the understanding of the Nandi festival and I will return to it later in more detail. Suffice it to say here that termite mounds in general are important with regard to the creation of the earth, and in the Joria case more specifically, they are related to the procreation of the tribes of the region – such as the Parenga, Gadaba and Joria – and to the creation of the rice and millet deities.

There is more regional ethnographic evidence that stresses the generative potential, the regenerative power of termites and their mounds, indeed connecting them with wealth, earth and life in general. This is unsurprising, given the reproductive feats of the termite queen and keeping the other facts I mentioned above in mind: that earth of the termite mound (*birom mati*) is especially rich in minerals and very fertile, that seeds are found in the storage chambers, its high humidity and its association with water. Irving (1982) further mentions that termite mounds are often linked to rituals of marriage and this is also what we see in the case of the Dongria, described by Hardenberg (2018a, 325f). The most important ritual of the marriage process among the Dongria is a ceremony called Bada. the aim of which is to invoke and invite Sita Penu Lahi Penu, the goddess of rice and wealth, and to rid the bride of evil influences (*dosa*). In the ritual, the goddess is embodied by a lump or figure made from a mixture of three kinds of soil: from a river, from a crab hole and from a termite mound. The representation of the goddess is further decorated with grains of rice and a one rupee coin, which is the "wealth" (*lahi*) that she represents and safeguards.[24]

---

23 That *dendua* refers to a lizard (generally referred to as *tendkar*) is my guess, assuming that the story refers to an amphibious animal.

24 Nanjundayya and Iyer (1931, 78f) present significant ethnographic details that complement my earlier discussion of Dasara rituals. The Ladar, an urban merchant caste of Mysore, also sow

In addition, Hardenberg (2018a, 372, fn. 67) provides us with a relevant detail in a footnote, which in fact identifies termites as the origin of all "life" (*jiu, jela*):

> An old Dongria man once explained to me the origin of the main gods in the Dongria pantheon. According to his statement, all life stems from a female deity called *ui ma*, whose name probably derives from the local word for termite, *ulama*. She created *jamaraja* and *jaura* ("*jamarani*") out of the soil.

Thus, from this perspective, even Jamarani, the first creature and "ancestral mother of all the Dongria" (Jena et al. 2002, 133), who later helps to create the sun god (see M81), would originate from a termite goddess.

The association of termites with life is not only found among the Dongria. In 2019, I had a conversation with a Joria when we visited Kuvi Kond and Boro Porja villages east of Koraput town. We talked about the Nandi festival and I learned that they celebrate it in this area as well. In order to obtain the earth for the divine figures, they shoot an arrow into the termite mound and only take the earth that the termites construct around the arrow. They then clean the earth with water so that they do not take any insects away from the mound. I told him about the practice of the Joria in Lenjisuku, where the Joria had opened the mound and deliberately took earth and eggs to create the divine bodies. As I did not remember it precisely at the time, I was thinking aloud, and wondered if they had perhaps also taken out the queen. The man was shocked to hear this and vigorously objected: "This is our life (*jibon*)," he said, "if we take out the termites, we will die."

However, in some Joria villages they apparently do take out the queen from the chamber in the context of the Nandi festival.[25] Kornel and Gamang[26] (2010, 197f) report – although it is not clear where or when they documented the

---

seeds that sprout during the ten days of Dasara. More specifically, they sow nine kinds of grains into earth taken from a termite mound. The seeds sprout into small plants in a basket in front of the goddess and are taken out on the tenth day and emptied into a well. As I will discuss below, also in the Bali Jatra the sprouting of grain during the festival is an important feature. Also with regard to this festival it has been reported that the grains are sown into earth taken from a termite mound (Ramdas 1931a, 170). Both sources wrongly speak of "ant-hills."

25 Also Rousseleau (2021, 252) describes that in the Nandi festival he documented in Sunari Guda people opened the mound to find the nest with the queen and writes: "The bigger she [the queen] is, the more auspicious it is for the coming year." He does not specify what, if anything, is further happening with the queen or what this auspiciousness refers to (e.g. to the harvest or health of the people). Given the very widespread notion of general well-being I have discussed repeatedly in this book, we may assume that this auspiciousness is also of this general kind, including crops, animals and humans.

26 Their description of the festival is quite detailed (Kornel and Gamang 2010, 195–209) and they also include a number of photographs (also of the termite queen that had been removed

festival – that after selecting the termite mound, the Joria carefully opened it and searched for the queen. After they had found it, they took it out, placed in on a clean plate with finger millet and took her to the house of the *jani*.[27] Subsequently, the ritual "raising of the gods" commenced and the divine bodies were prepared. According to the authors, these figures explicitly represented "a white ant queen replica" called "Linga," which would "look like an ant queen in shape and size" (2010, 199). However, the Joria also tried to ensure that nothing happened to the queen, who was returned to the mound and carefully placed back into her chamber the next morning. Moreover, to determine that the queen was fine, the Joria undertook a test. A small chick was put into a hole in the mound and covered with soil in such a way that the animal could breathe but not escape. The next day, the chick was examined and if it was still alive this would be the desired sign that the queen was also alive and well.

This piece of ethnographic data is certainly relevant to the interpretation of the Nandi festival, as it stresses the identity between termite queen and Nandi deities. I would argue that this practice of taking the queen out of the mound is informed by the same idea which makes it unthinkable for Joria of other villages to remove the queen: termites, and the queen in particular, represent "life." For the very same reason that the Joria man I talked to in 2019 considered it impossible to take termites away from their mound, these Joria had taken the queen into the *jani*'s house to actually and spatially connect the reproductive power of the termite queen with the new embodiments of the Nandi deities.

Termite mounds are regionally associated with "wealth" of different kinds. In her book, *Das Tor zur Unterwelt* ("The Gate to the Underworld"), in which she discusses representations and rituals of the termite mound as it appears in

---

from the mound). I do not discuss their contribution in detail here. In my view notable are the following aspects, some of which are similar to the festival as documented in Lenjisuku, some are different. First and foremost it is striking, as already mentioned, that the Joria of that village actually took the termite queen out of the mound and the figures were explicitly regarded as termite queen. The divine bodies of the Nandi deities were not left below a tree after the rituals, as in Lenjisuku, but placed into a crab hole near a river. With regard to the mural the authors also describe how the *gurumai* recited or sang names of numerous deities while the mural was made, each name being one mark with rice flour on the wall. There is a difference with regard to the main actors. They do not mention the *kangar* but three other actors. On the one hand the *tika dangri* (*tika* referring to the spot made on the forehead, *dangri* a girl or young woman), who carries the deities. While various women carry the basket with the deities in Lenjisuku, none was explicitly referred to with that name. Beside the *tika dangri*, the last day of the festival as described by Kornel and Gamang featured two ascetics (*boiragi*). On that day also a weekly market was enacted and the *jani* and *gurumai* engaged in bargaining.

27 The book also contains a picture of the termite queen in the hands of the *jani* (2010, 204).

various Indian traditions, Ditte König (1984, 69) also addressed the motif of gold found inside termite mounds. However, as the Dongria stress, "wealth" is connected to life more generally and takes on different forms, rice in particular for them, but also rupee coins. Elwin recorded myths among the Muria that make the connection between termite mounds and rupee coins explicit. It is noteworthy that both of the stories he provides us with make a crucial link between mound, money and the soul or rather life-force (*jiwa*), thus with life in general. One story has the following plot, as described to Elwin. There were two men sitting next to a blacksmith's shop. One fell asleep and the other watched as the *jiwa* of the sleeping man left his body: "Presently from the sleeper's mouth there came out his *jiwa* in the form of a lizard and went to feed. A dog saw it and chased it into an ant-hill. There it saw a pot full of rupees" (Elwin 1991b, 475). The man played a trick on his sleeping friend so that his *jiwa* initially could not find its way back into the body. However, finally, when "the sleeper awoke he told his friend what he had seen in his dreams, and they went to the ant-hill and found the rupees." The narrator ended the story by stressing that this "is a true tale of what actually occurred."

Another Muria story makes the same connection between wealth, soul and termite mound and narrates a competition between "Dream" and "Wealth," playing hide-and-seek.

> Wealth hid himself first. He took the shape of a pot of rupees and hid in an ant-hill. Dream went to a very poor boy who was lying asleep and called his soul to come out. When the *jiwa* came Dream sent it to the ant-hill. It returned, and when the boy awoke he went to the ant-hill and dug up Wealth in the shape of the pot. (Elwin 1991b, 476)

Dream had thus found Wealth with the help of the boy's *jiwa* and as Wealth in turn could not find Dream (who hid in the wind), the latter won the contest.

In the Nandi festival, references to coins and similar kinds of wealth were abundant. In colonial times, Indian rupees were made from silver (*rupa*), among other materials, such as copper (*tama*). Some of the women who carried the deities in the procession, such as Sukro's wife (photo 7.6), were adorned with necklaces of such old rupees, chains and money. Also the figures inside the basket (Kesa Risia and Mota Risia) were covered with chains (*risia*) that appeared to be made from gold and they wore nose rings. The Nandi song that accompanies the whole festival makes multiple references to these forms of wealth, to "copper coins" and "diamond rings" and to different kind of necklaces, also those (*shishirurimali*) that are said to resemble (or consist of) coins.

Further ethnographic evidence especially links termites and termite mounds to a particularly important kind of wealth, namely cereals. In a myth from the Kuttia Kond, also narrated to Elwin, a man destroys a termite mound growing on his swidden field and sticks a length of bamboo into the wrecked mound. Later, he notices that the animals have eaten the stick and is astonished by the power of the little insects. The narrator concluded: "Now we believe that ants go out from their hills and eat leaves and sticks and turn them into manure and so we have good crops. So if, when we make a new settlement, we find it infested with ants, we think it very lucky. We never kill ants" (Elwin 1954, 223). The connection between termites and manure is also made by the Joria. Rousseleau (2021, 252) reports that the Nandi goddess is also referred to (in addition to "Mother of the Termite Mound") as Mai Kotma, which he translates as "Mother of Termites." I would – alternatively and corresponding to the Kond story just mentioned – translate it as "Female (*mai*) Mother (*ma*) of Manure (*kot*)," or just "Manure Mother," as the word "female" (*mai*) is actually redundant. The Gadaba use the dung from their manure piles (*kot gadi*) exclusively for the millet fields.

The association between termites and millet is obvious in the Nandi festival, and this review of ethnographic data aims at substantiating the various connections between termites, wealth and life. Rousseleau (2021, 252) further informs us that grains of finger millet are also called "millet eggs" (*mandia onda*) and that, at the time of sowing millet, Joria sacrifice a chicken in front of a termite mound "for the success of the crops" (2021, 252), echoing the conclusion of the Kuttia story above. The Bhattra, some 40 kilometers due northwest of Jeypore, make the link between termites and millet very explicit. That termites, as do other insects, pass through different life stages and thereby totally transform their appearance, was and is certainly not lost on the tribal inhabitants of the region, who are keen observers of nature, as the Kuttia story also documents. In a Bhattra myth, millet is transformed into earth, then into termites and finally into a mound. A village chief, so the story goes, went to his swidden field with his wife and their twelve sons and their wives as well:

> They sowed rice and millet but for two years the field gave a poor harvest. The third year they only sowed millet and this time the crop was very good. They reaped it and it took six days to thresh and winnow. When it was ready, they carried it home. This took fifteen days. They got very tired: there was a little millet left and they put it on one side and went home. The pile of grain turned into earth and then into insects. These were white ants. The Chief's son went after a week to get the grain but found the heap had turned into an ant-hill. (Elwin 1954, 221)

If millet, "millet eggs"[28] – can turn into termites and termite mounds, which make the fields fertile, then surely termite eggs can turn into millet? This idea, I

---

[28] Rousseleau (2021, 252) states that termite eggs resemble grains of finger millet. However, this seems to be doubtful. It was dark when the termite mound was opened in Lenjisuku and

would argue, is certainly present in the Nandi festival, with the Nandi deities made from termite eggs and earth from the mound, resting on millet grain and millet cakes. In the case reported by Kornel and Gamang, the termite queen had actually been brought to the spot where the ritual Nandi bodies were fashioned, with the two queens side by side, producing millions of "eggs" of one sort or another.

Although neither termites and termite mounds nor finger millet are mentioned in the myth recorded among the Pengo of the Nowrangpur district (Burrow and Bhattacharya 1970, 111–22; M8), who are the immediate neighbors of the Bhattra to the east, this story provides us with a crucial insight concerning the identity of the Earth Beauty Dust Beauty (Mati Sundori Duri Sundori) and stresses the vital connection and parallelism between earth and cereals. The story is yet another version of the original incest between brother and sister, who are here called, respectively, Silaput Raja, like the King God in M5,[29] and Mai Kotma (here written "May Kodmay"), like the Mother of Termites/Manure Mother mentioned above. I will return again to this myth in the next chapter, as it prominently features the Bima, who play a crucial role in the Bali Jatra.

The Pengo consider the Bima to be the younger brothers of the earth goddess, who is called Takrani in the myth. Because the earth goddess is mistreated by the Bima, she makes the middle Bima ill and the other seven go out to search for help. They first ask a *guru*, who cannot answer their question as to why the middle Bima became ill, but tells them to go to a place called *cucunda matito rayladey jagato*.[30] While I do not know to which "place" (*jaga*) *rayladey* refers, I would translate the first term as "into the shrew-earth." *Cucunda* designates the Asian house shrew (*Suncus murnius*), a mouse-like animal that mostly feeds on insects (such as cockroaches), moves around human dwellings at night and spends the daytime in hidden corners of a house or in holes in the ground. The place the *guru* advises the Bima to visit is thus probably a subterranean one. There, the *guru* says, they would find a shaman woman (*gurumai, bejuni*) with the name of Mati Sundori Duri Sundori.

---

earth and eggs were taken out. So I cannot confirm or falsify that statement based on my own experience. In a personal correspondence, Dr. Ajay Harit, School of Environmental Sciences (Mahatma Gandhi University), replied to my question if termite eggs resemble grains of finger millet in the negative and added: "As per my experience, newly termite eggs are ovoid in shape and yellow in color and then turn into pale color and finally become white color before hatching. I did not come across any round shape of termite eggs."

29 As discussed in Chapter 4, Rousseleau (2008) argues that the forest-boy in M5 called Silputi Raja may refer to the founding king of the Nandapur dynasty.

30 Burrow and Bhattacharya (1970, 115) translate it as "to the *cucunda* ground, to the *rayladey* place."

When they reach the place, the Bima find a woman working with agricultural tools, the most common sight when one enters any Desia village. However, this woman seems to be special, as her winnowing fan is made from thatch-grass (not bamboo) and her pestle is made from straw (instead of wood). Moreover, she applies her tools not to cereals but to the earth itself. The substantial connection between grain and (termite) earth, which is so prominently made in the Nandi festival and also in the Bhattra myth, could not be stated more explicitly: she is "grinding earth (*mati*)" and "pounding dust (*duri*)." Finger millet is not explicitly mentioned here but the technique of grinding clearly indicates this cereal. The grinding stone (*jata*) that is found in all Desia houses is first and foremost used to grind finger millet for the production of the most valued millet food, the thick millet gruel (*mandia pej*) that all Desia drink at least twice a day. For all Desia it would be obvious that "grinding earth" indexes millet. A link to termites may also be discerned as the woman is processing earth, much like termites do. Moreover, engaging in such shifting significations between earth and cereal may be expected from a shamanin, whose ritual practice in particular entails transformations of her identity, the embodiment of different beings. This double relationship, complementary conception, or even identity, of earth and cereals is also highlighted by the fact that the term Mati Sundori Duri Sundori has different references. In the myth it denotes the shamanin who is processing earth and dust. In the Nandi festival the two sets of objects that represent the Nandi deities and which implicate each other are the visible termite-earth-cum-eggs made icons that resemble the termite queen and the inconspicuous and hidden millet cakes on top of which – in immediate proximity – the icons rest. But here Mati Sundori Duri Sundori refers to the millet cakes, not to the icons. The Nandi song does speak of neither termites-earth or eggs nor millet, yet it refers to both, I would argue, because the name Mati Sundori Duri Sundori encompasses and equates (termite) earth and finger millet. In fact, the Pengo distinguish a type of finger millet (*dera*) that they call "dust finger millet" (*duri derang*, *derang* being the plural form of *dera*) (Burrow and Bhattacharya 1970, 213, see also 127, 210).

There are a number of indicators that point to a close association of Mati Sundori Duri Sundori with the earth goddess. In the Nandi song (see appendix) which was sung throughout the festival, Mati Sundori Duri Sundori is constantly addressed as *noni*, as in doublet:

Noni noni noni noni Mati Sundori   *Noni noni noni noni Duli Sundori*

Noni can refer to an unmarried girl of a marriageable age (like *dangri*) but also denote an "elder sister" and the Desia women who helped me translate the song consistently chose the latter meaning. In the Pengo myth (M8), the Bima also address Mati Sundori Duri Sundori as "elder sister," just like Takrani, and it seems that *mati sundori, duri sundori* actually is the earth goddess herself, perhaps in a disguised form or representing one particular aspect of her. That Mati Sundori Duri Sundori parallels the earth goddess may not merely be inferred from her designation as "elder sister" in the myth but is also indicated by her gifts to the Bima and her actions. She not only finds the cause of the Bima's illness by means of divination (as a normal *gurumai* would) but also provides them with two sacred stones, the "cultivation stone" (*tas kal*) and the "hunting stone" (*bet kal*), which provide the knowledge and skills for cultivation and hunting. The stones have various other names, several of which refer to *darni*, who is a local representation of the earth goddess, a name also used among the Kond. It is thus the earth goddess (in the form of Mati Sundori Duri Sundori) who gives knowledge to the Bima, who are said to be the bringers of seeds and agriculture to humans, as I will discuss in the next chapter. As the epic related to the Bali Jatra festival makes clear, along with agriculture comes the obligation to sacrifice, and that is the case in the Pengo myth (M8) as well. After providing them with the cultivation and hunting stones, Mati Sundori Duri Sundori instructs the Bima on what and how to sacrifice and she actually performs the worship to the ancestors and the gods (also to Takrani) herself on their behalf. She also provides them with an assembly place (*sadar*). After all these actions, the middle Bima recovers. Finally, Mati Sundori Duri Sundori initiates the construction of a shrine (*gudi*), presumably for the worship of the earth goddess (Takrani).

In sum, in this Pengo myth (M8), it is Mati Sundori Duri Sundori – alias the earth goddess (Takrani) – who processes the earth (as cereals, millet), out of which not only cereals but also human beings emerge, humans "who have come into being piercing through the earth" (Burrow and Bhattacharya 1970, 118), providing the Bima with both the knowledge of agriculture and hunting and the proper way to propitiate the ancestors and gods. However, Takrani is unforgiving when it comes to being treated inappropriately. Even after having received all of those precious gifts from her, the Bima do not share the meat of the deer they hunted with her family, her husband, the sky god Dorom Raja[31] and their son. Furious, Takrani curses the Bima, saying "'let them eat the flesh of their own children'" and "ruined their cultivation and their hunting" (Burrow and Bhattacharya 1970, 121). The myth ends with Takrani transferring the sacrificial responsibility from the unfaithful and selfish Bima to humans, who from then on properly perform the festival and give the goddess her share.

---

31 Written "Daram Raja" by Burrow and Bhattacharya (1970, 121).

After introducing agriculture, Mati Sundori Duri Sundori notably also initiates sacrifice, not only to the gods but also to the ancestors. In the following section, the role of the dead in the pursuit of life is considered in more detail.

In this section I have been discussing the various connections between termites, life and wealth as can be derived from the ritual practice of the Nandi festival and various regional myths. A clear emphasis on soil and the parallelism between millet and earth can be discerned. However, the termite mound also signifies another kind of wealth, which I mentioned above but which was not foregrounded in ritual and myth. It is this kind of wealth that Chris Gregory (2019) described – discussing rice and millet in Bastar – as the "mother of wealth," namely water.

Termite mounds are both a location of soil creation and a place where water can be found, which they need for their fungus and for themselves. In myths of the "primordial mound" (Irvin 1982) dealing with the cosmogonic flood, termite mounds help create land out of water. However, as Pascal Jouquet pointed out to me (personal communication), the opposite is also true, termites bring up water from inside the earth. One would therefore assume that the rituals of the termite mound would have a connection to Kamni, the earth-water deities that are particularly associated with wet-rice fields, but also with other fluids coming out of the earth, such as the juice of the palm tree that is consumed as the much cherished palm wine (*salap*). However, there is very little evidence for this. In Lenjisuku, an egg was sacrificed on top of the termite mound, a kind of offering that is often provided for Kamni. However, eggs are also given to other non-human recipients and no mention of Kamni was made. Rousseleau (2021, 252) reports that millet beer and six pots of water were poured into the mound in the context of the Nandi festival he observed, but no reference to Kamni is reported. Based on what we know about the Nandi festival, I have to conclude, therefore, that explicit links to termite mounds as water sources are not made, which, of course, does not rule out the possibility that the Joria do recognize this dimension of termite mounds and, without doubt, no one needs to explain to them the relevance of water for millet as a dry field crop.

In a myth (M25) collected by Chris Gregory[32] in Bastar, the connection between termite mounds and water could not be made more explicit. The main protagonist is again Bima (here only one, not several). This time he is not the unworthy recipient of the hunting and cultivation stones as in the Pengo myth,

---

[32] Many thanks to him for sharing this unpublished ethnographic material.

but a water provider in times of a drought. Watching his grazing cattle from his seat on a termite mound, he notices smoke (probably rather "steam;" see Baghel and Kalapesi 1982, 48) emerging from a hole in the mound and assumes that there "is water in the hill." He performs austerities[33] so that the god (Bhagwan) will provide the water inside the hill. After a long time, with termites now crawling all over him, Bhagwan heeds his request and instructs Indra to let it rain and so the drought ends. Before his death, Bima instructs the villagers to worship near a termite-mound hole during the rainy season, at the time of reploughing, and since then they have performed the ritual in his name, Bhimadev Puja.

Fertility and the Dead

In regional invocations, one often hears the sentence, "the earth below, the heaven (sun/moon) above" (*tole Bosmoti, upore Dorom*), reflecting the division into earth and sky also referred to in the Pengo myth (M8) discussed above. All Desia imagine the cosmos to be divided into three worlds or layers (*pur*). The upper world (*sorogpur*) of the sun/moon deity, the middle world (*mojapur*) of humans and the underworld (*patalpur*), also variously known as the inner layer (*bitorpur*) or the domain of the King of Death (Jom Raja), *jompur*. The Gadaba do not imagine the underworld in great detail but it is clear that those who die a proper death enjoy a community life there and require things much like humans in the middle world. As such, the dead are provided with miniature looms to weave the *kisalo'*, with food and drink, schoolbooks and sandals, among other things. The Joria envision the underworld as similar but inverse and more miserable in comparison to the world of the living (Rousseleau 2008, 143). The Sora are well known for having a very intimate connection to the underworld, which they depict in great detail – also in the form of murals – and into which those men and women who become shamans have to marry (Mallebrein 2001; Guillaume-Pey 2021; Vitebsky 1993, 2017a).

The three layers of the cosmos can be connected. A number of deities are thought to be immanent to the middle world, such as manifestations of the earth goddess in the soil, or of deities in mountains, trees, water or stones. However, deities may also be explicitly invited into the middle world from

---

[33] This aspect of the myth is reminiscent of the famous Valmiki, his name deriving from a termite mound (*valmika*). He is the mythological author of the Ramayana and also has a role in the story himself. He meditates so long that termites build a mound all around and over him.

above; into the body of humans when they become possessed; into houses, paintings and objects; or through songs. One such instance was described in Chapter 3, when discussing the buffalo festival of the Dongria. In a trance, the shaman (*bejuni*) had climbed half way up a long bamboo pole to bring Niamraja down to the middle world and the village space of humans. In the marriage ritual called Bara, Dongria utilize a thread to invite Sita Penu Lahi Penu into the ritual objects. In a similar way, Joria facilitate such pathways when the divine presence is desired in the Nandi festival, doing so by drawing paintings that include pathways, or by providing threads that enable gods to move down to humans from up high. However, as I know from the Gadaba, such traffic can also be obstructed on other occasions with regard to unwelcome guests, such as vengeful spirits or thoroughly evil demons. Then, the trails are blocked, for instance, by cutting across them with knifes, urinating across a path or beating iron nails filled with "medicine" into the ground.

The water-earth goddess (Jal Kamni Patal Kamni), who is crucial for the cultivation of wet rice, is considered to be on the threshold of the middle world and the underworld. She has an obvious underworld-earth aspect (*patal*), with river water also coming from the depth of the earth and rising to the surface. As mentioned above, sago palm trees (*Caryota urens*), from which the fermented juice (*salap*) is consumed, are also closely connected with Kamni and thought to connect the underworld and the middle world, as they bring up water from below and feed humans with the juice they harvest high above.[34] Like the sago palm, with roots that reach deep into the earth and a surface structure that towers above humans, termite mounds are also considered to connect the middle world and the underworld. In search of water, the termite tunnels go deep into the earth and soil is brought up from below. Accordingly, termite mounds are widely regarded across India and throughout history as "gate to the underworld," as the title of Ditte König's book translates (1984; *Das Tor zur Unterwelt)*, which collects a wealth of data on the mythology and rituals concerning termites and their mounds in India.

Although termite mounds are not a conspicuous feature in Sora and Gadaba death rituals, these communities do make an explicit connection between crops and the dead. This will be discussed in more detail in Chapter 9. The Sora death rituals are another example of how rituals enable movement between the underworld and the world of the living. When Sora celebrate their stone-planting ritual

---

[34] I have mentioned in Chapter 3 already the Bondo story in which the incestuous founding couple, the ancestors of the twelve tribes of the region, was saved by a sago palm. Their parents had deserted the twins (brother and sister) under the tree right after their birth and the tree fed the children with water from the ocean (Elwin 1954, 185–86).

(*karja*) for a group of people who died some years before, they invite the dead into the space of the living. After raising the dead on the cremation ground, the dead are first led into the village and then enter the house of the living in several ways simultaneously. On the one hand, they enter through the door, but another avenue is also provided. A bamboo ladder is inserted into the house through the thatched roof and its base is placed into the mortar used to pound rice. In this way, the dead can climb up into the house from the underworld (Vitebsky 2017a, 81ff). The techniques and the spatial structure of Sora, Joria and also Dongria rituals are thus quite similar. While the Nandi festival of the Joria and the Dongria buffalo festival do not concern the dead but rather various deities, the aim in all cases is to bring those metapersons responsible for "wealth" and "well-being" up from or down into the middle world, as the case may be, to ensure their support by hosting them, and to discharge them at the end.

The Joria also consider crops and the dead as related, even if the connetion is not as elaborately made as among the Sora and Gadaba. In all three cases, it is not the dangerous liminal dead who are involved in wealth and well-being, but those who have established a place in the community of the dead, properly separated from the world of the living. In the *bur* ritual of the Joria, which is performed months, perhaps years after death, two stones are erected for the deceased, one flat, one upright. They are added to the row of stones at the megalithic assembly place of the village, the *sadar* (Rousseleau 2008, 138f; 2021). A year after this ritual, the dead person is included for the first time in the collective worship of the ancestors – the annual festival for the dead (Duma Porbo). The relevant social units on this occasion are the individual households, and the locations of the rituals are the vegetable gardens adjacent to the houses. Two pairs of stones are erected, representing male and female paternal ancestors of the house or the "house mother-fathers," a group into which those deceased who have in the meanwhile received their *bur* ritual are now integrated. It is at this moment, when the dead are no longer dangerous but have become benevolent ancestors, that the connection between the dead and the crops is made explicit. After the stones have been erected, the eldest male member of the house invokes the ancestors and places grains of finger millet and paddy from the new harvest on the stones, literally the embodiment of the dead of the household. Rousseleau equates this offering to a first-fruit offering of the new crops to the ancestors which thus "guarantees the protection of the next harvests and of the family from diseases" (2021, 249; see also Rousseleau 2010a, 142). Although the dead do not explicitly figure in either the Ganga Puja or the Nandi festival, they are thus considered to be guardians of the crops.

Murals and Cosmogonic Myths

In the Nandi festival the deities move from one kind of house to another. The mound is the abode of the termites and the location where the gods are raised and the eggs are "born." From there, the ritual moves into the Nandi house, where the divine bodies are fashioned. Perhaps we can speak of yet another kind of house, considering the mural as dwelling place of the gods. Without doubt, the mural is not merely a piece of art. Chondoro Maji pointed out to me the first dot of the painting where the mural was "born" and the gods inhabiting it received sacrificial blood, which was smeared at the wall.

In this respect, a comparison with the Sora wall paintings might seem obvious. The initial similarity is striking, although there are also significant differences. The Sora conceptualize their paintings explicitly as a "house," they allow the dead to dwell in the Sora's living space. "A spirit, [Verrier Elwin] was once told, sits in his picture as a fly settles on a wall" (Elwin 1955, 402). Like the Joria mural, the Sora always use rice flour mixed with water, which they apply onto a wall already coated in a red-brown earth color. While the Sora crowd their multi-storied houses with people, gods, objects, horses, bicycles – all intended, according to Elwin (1955, 437), to flatter the dead – the Joria do not depict animals or humans in the main, central part of the painting, only at the margins (both inside the house and on the outside wall). Clearly, both Sora and Joria wall paintings re-present cosmological themes. While Elwin (1955, 401) states that the Sora also provide such "houses" on various occasions and for different deities, they obviously have a focus on the underworld and on hosting their ancestors. In the case of the Joria, the upper world seems to be the dominant locus, the sun and moon (*dorom*) being in the center and the whole mural being filled with stars and footsteps that constitute paths of the gods in all directions.

Another commonality between the Sora and Joria murals is their connection to fertility, harvest and crops. The Sora paint murals on different occasions, such as to counteract an affliction caused by certain *sonums*, "spirits" of the dead. However, they particularly do so to honor the dead, who are considered to be closely related to the growth of crops (see also Mallebrein 2001, 98 & Chapter 9 below). Moreover, murals are newly painted especially in the context of harvest festivals "for improving the fertility of the crops" (Elwin 1955, 401) or the ceremonial taking of the seeds from the loft for sowing (Elwin 1955, 405). Like the Joria, the Sora create murals to assure crop abundance.

The efficacy of wall paintings in connection with vivifying sacrificial blood is well brought out in a Sora story, in which the primordial sibling pair and incestuous founding couple actually emerge from a mural. It is said that "Kittung Mahaprabhu" (Elwin 1955, 419) made the world and also a house for himself, but humans had not yet been created. Inside his house, Kittung painted a man and a woman with white earth, but he did not know how to "make them," that is, bring them to life. Therefore, he went to the sun god (Uyungsum) for advice. The latter said he should cover the drawings with leaves and after seven days cut his little finger and let blood drip on the images. Kittung did exactly what he had been told and, after nine days, the man and the woman emerged from the picture. When they had reached maturity, Kittung asked the sun god to marry them and from "them came all mankind" (Elwin 1955, 402). This story not only underlines the efficacy and generative power of murals but also associates them with the creation of the world. While in other creation stories the sibling pair finds itself in other dwellings, for instance a gourd, here they emerge from a different containment, a different "house" – the mural.

The Nandi festival also has a cosmogonic dimension and clearly is connected not only to the myth collected among the Pengo (M8) concerning the *gurumai*-goddess Earth Beauty Dust Beauty but also to the aforementioned myth documented by Raphaël Rousseleau (2021, 252f), which is yet another variant of the widespread brother-sister story. Here, the sibling pair settles in a termite mound and is then transformed into husband and wife, a procreative union, from which the tribes of the region originate. In the alternative ending of the myth presented by Rousseleau, the transformation is of a different kind, not conjugal but agricultural: after they have emerged from the termite mound, the brother turns into rice (Ganga) the sister into finger millet (Nandi).[35] Also in the Nandi festival, the deities were raised and eggs "born" inside the termite mound and then shaped in the Nandi house, just as the sister came out of the mound and turned into the Nandi goddess in the myth. But I want to highlight here the parallelism of the two instances of alterity the different versions of the myth present. Even though rice and millet, Ganga and Nandi, are rather consistently represented as brother and sister throughout the festivals (not as spouses), the myth correlates two kinds of alterity created out of consanguinity (siblingship), husband/wife (affinity) on the one hand and rice/millet on the other. Although I am not sure whether the Joria conceptualize rice and millet, river fields and dry fields, in a similar way, from a Gadaba perspective villagers would classify millet as consanguineal or "own," belonging to the village and a particular earth-locality, while rice and the river fields, by contrast, would be affinal "other," from whom the "bride"

---

[35] In this way the terms San Sundari/Pila Sundari may be understood. It could be that millet is regarded as "little beauty" (San Sundori), while the other term refers to rice. *Pila* means "children" but also "boy," which is for instance clear when Desia speak about *pila toki* meaning "boys [and] girls." This would in any case be consistent with the views of the Joria that Ganga is the elder brother of Nandi.

(rice) is taken. From a Joria point of view, the transformation of brother-sister into rice and millet may therefore also suggest such a transformation from consanguinal sameness to affinal alterity, an otherness that generally remains ambiguous (Berger 2010, 2018). What the mythical parallelism of the two transformations highlights, I would argue, is the generative potential of affinal alterity, the procreative capacity of the human and cereal couples to create different kinds of wealth. This connection between affinity and regeneration we will again encounter in the Bali Jatra and the Go'ter.

The cosmological dimension is also evident in the Nandi house itself, to which the termite earth and eggs are taken from the mound to create the new divine bodies. While in the buffalo sacrifice of the Dongria the *bejuni* bring the gods down from above with the help of a bamboo ladder, and in the *karja* ritual of the Sora, the living bring the dead up from the underworld with the same device, in the case of the Nandi festival one sees both. Eggs and earth come from the underworld below, while at the same time, gods are invited to climb down along the thread, across the mural and into the basket containing the newly made deities, the millet-eggs producing queen.

8 A Festival of "Flowers:" The Bali Jatra of the Mali

Like the Ganga and Nandi festivals of the Joria, the Bali Jatra is a festival of regeneration and well-being in the general sense. Strange as it may seem, the dominant crop in this festival is wheat (*gum*, *Triticum*), which is neither cultivated nor traditionally consumed in the area. However, the "sand procession" or "sand festival," as Bali Jatra translates literally, is not only about wheat specifically, as will be seen; yet millet is conspicuously absent in the ritual and in the accompanying oral epic. Other aspects also make the Bali Jatra different from the rituals discussed in the last two chapters. Whereas the Ganga and Nandi festivals are specific to the Joria – although their rituals have been partially adopted by adjacent communities such as the Ollar Gadaba – the Bali Jatra is much more widespread and comes in different forms (see Otten 2009). As such, it is found in Nowrangpur, Rayagada and Koraput, as well as in Bastar, and it is performed by various communities, among them the Dongria (Hardenberg 2014; Jena et al. 2002, 211), Gadaba (Ramdas 1931a, 170f), Joria, Pengo (Thusu 1977; Kornel and Gamang 2010, 218–40), Kuvi Kond (Banerjee 1969, 99), Parenga and Rona. It has also previously been hosted by the king in Jeypore. The link with kingship is quite explicit in this festival. While the king celebrated the Bali Jatra in the capital in the rainy season during the month of *osa* (August/September), preceding the Dasara festival, in other cases, it is performed in the month of *chait* (March/April) or during the cold season, starting in the month of *diali* (October/November) (Otten 2009). It is with the latter festival that I am mainly concerned here. Even though celebrated widely throughout the region, the Bali Jatra is particularly linked to the group of horticulturalists called Mali and not to a community of agriculturalists who cultivate cereals such as rice and millet, as do the Joria or Gadaba.

Tina Otten is the principal ethnographer of the Bali Jatra of Koraput[1] and my description and analysis of the festival builds on her important work, especially with regard to the Bali Jatra epic. In one of her publications (Otten 2009), she focuses in particular on the ritual procedure of the Bali Jatra, especially as she observed it the village of Lamda, which comprises a large number of Mali households. Her second publication (Otten 2014) is more concerned with the outline of the main features of the Bali Jatra epic, which is sung by female specialists – the *gurumai*.[2]

---

[1] Tina Otten also conducted research on the festival as performed in Nowrangpur.
[2] Another short publication by Tina Otten (Otten 2013) provides more photographs but no further ethnographic data or analysis.

The oral epic, which is intertwined with the ritual performance and partially enacted, is a distinctive feature of the Bali Jatra. If my arguments of the two preceding chapters are correct, then the Joria also link their festivals to myths, the Dom Raja story in the case of the Ganga Puja and the creation myths featuring a termite mound and the *gurumai*-goddess called Earth Beauty Dust Beauty in the case of the Nandi festival. The epic of the Bali Jatra, however, is of a different order. Its link with the rituals is much more explicit than in the former cases, and it is considerably more elaborate. In this and several other ways, the Bali Jatra epic of Koraput is comparable to the Lachmi Jagar of Bastar (Gregory and Vaishnav 2003; Gregory 2004), which I referred to previously.

The Bali Jatra can be divided into two ritual periods. The first comprises around 60 evening sessions of reciting the Bali Jatra epic (Otten n.d.) over a duration of several weeks, starting around the full moon in November (*diali*). Subsequently, the Bali god takes on a specific shape, namely the form of a painted clay pot that is accompanied by a winnowing fan, bow and arrow. The latter are no hunting tools but musical instruments that the *gurumai* play. The *gurumai* also initially install the deity in the Bali shrine, painting the earthen pot with white dots using a paste made from rice flour and water. The earthen pot is called Dunkul Handi, a reference, I would suggest, to the two objects accompanying it, the bow (*dun*) and the winnowing fan (*kula*). However, it is also referred to as Pat ("main") Gurumai, the goddess embodying the Bali Jatra epic (Otten 2014). The *gurumai* invite the goddess to enter the ritual objects, again by providing a "road" along which she can travel, suspending a thread from the ceiling down to the objects she will enter (Otten 2014, 257).

With the divine presence thus facilitated, the *gurumai* start reciting the epic. As Otten points out, one leading *gurumai* is usually accompanied by several others, and the specialists are joined in the Bali shrine by women and children in particular (see image Otten 2009, 35). At least one woman from every household should join each session in which the *gurumai* narrate the epic. Every evening, the attending women, each representing one household, pour a leaf-cup of husked rice into the Dunkul Handi to be distributed later among the *gurumai* (Otten n.d.). For two hours or so, the *gurumai* recite the epic nearly every evening over several weeks, accompanying the narration with the musical bow, while villagers enact certain sequences of the story inside the Bali shrine.

The second period of intense ritual activity is comparably short and lasts for about ten or twelve days, like the festivals discussed in the previous chapters. It is this phase that I will be focusing on in detail below and which I was able to partially document in the Parenga village of Komra between December 22, 2000 and January 2, 2001. As an ethnographer, my situation was the same as in the case of the Nandi and Ganga festivals. At the time, no ethnographic descriptions were available in the anthropological literature and what I observed was completely new to me. Fortunately, with more ethnographic data now available, it is possible to at least try to approach the various meanings of this complex festival, and also compare it to the other festivals discussed in this book.

In this second phase, sand is fetched from the paddies outside the village and seeds are sown at various locations – collectively, inside the Bali shrine and in each individual household – and left to germinate over the duration of this phase of the festival. A mural is painted inside the Bali shrine, in which dance, trance and sacrifice dominate the nights, along with further enactments of the epic. Ultimately, the sand is returned to the river, and the "flowers" – the sprouts that germinated for about ten days – are exchanged. Similarly to the Ganga and Nandi festivals, the Bali Jatra is performed for three years in a row, followed by an interval of three years, before the ritual cycle commences again. This rhythm in itself may be seen as a metaphor for regeneration with which these festivals are concerned.

In addition to the village *pujari*, who is involved in many sequences of the Bali Jatra, several ritual actors stand out, among them the *gurumai* and the Bima. The *gurumai* are also very prominent figures in the rituals of the Joria, described in previous chapters, as these women (few are men) communicate with the deities, often by way of trance-like séances. As ritual specialists of the Bali Jatra and custodians of the epic, the *gurumai* I am concerned with here are distinctive. According to Otten (2014, 248), these *gurumai* represent the epic as a divine form called Pat Gurumai. This goddess enables and inspires the human mediums – the Bali Jatra *gurumai* – to narrate the story in the context of the festival. These women, therefore, are much respected and have a key role and major influence on the festival as a whole. One *gurumai* usually takes the lead and is accompanied by others. During the Bali Jatra that Otten documented in the village of Lamda, the main Bali Jatra *gurumai* was a Joria woman, while, in the village of Komra where I documented the festival, both *gurumai* were Rona.

8.1 Bima: Rain, Wind and Agriculture

The ritual actors called Bima[3] are very conspicuous in the Bali Jatra. In the general sacred geography of the Desia, the god Bima is non-existent and I know of

---

3 I write the name of the local deity Bima (as do Burrow and Bhattacharya 1970), instead of Bhima, as the Desia language does not use aspiration (see Burrow and Bhattacharya 1970, 3). I write the name with "h" (thus Bhima) when referring to the pan-Indian character.

no permanent village shrine dedicated to him.⁴ However, a deity of that name does figure prominently in several regional myths and some communities also worship him in the context of specific festivals. On a pan-Indian level, Bhima is a well-known figure from the Mahabharata, the second of the Pandava brothers. Being the son of Vayu, the Vedic god of wind and storm, Bhima also displays wild features. He is a famous wrestler and a fierce (though somewhat unfair) warrior. Considering his inclination to violence, it is perhaps consistent that he married a demoness.

Ferocity, violence and deception are certainly attributes of Bima as represented in the local stories; however, his divine personality is much more multi-faceted and ambivalent. I would assume that this is so because the wind and rain he represents are potentially both vital to and deadly for agriculture, with the successful cultivation and processing of crops depending on the proper timing and intensity of rain and wind. It is this significance of Bima for agriculture that is the key theme in the tribal narratives, some of which represent him as benevolent and providing, others as dangerous and destructive.

Two Gadaba stories⁵ collected by Elwin describe Bima Raja as providing rain. One of them narrates how Bima Raja and Bima Rani created the rainy season, especially related to the queen washing herself after her menses, with humans advised by her to sow their seeds at that time (Elwin 1954, 80–81). In another story, Bima fights Indra, who is withholding rain from the world, and breaks his tank so that water falls on the earth. He also proves to be a powerful cultivator in this myth, as he tames two of Indra's wild buffaloes and makes them plough a field, a feat which also earns him Indra's daughter (Elwin 1954, 81–82). Similarly, in a Joria myth, Bima is a herder who is looking for water for his animals and finally manages to bring it down from the sky; this time, however, Indra imprisons him (Elwin 1954, 226f). Moreover, in the myth from Bastar (M25) I discussed in relation to the Nandi festival, Bima is a herder and a water provider. He discovers water in the termite mound on which he sits and through the performance of austerities he convinces the gods to provide water in the form of rain and thus end the drought.

---

4 The Pengo may be an exception. Though he provides few ethnographic details, Thusu (1977, 76f) mentions a shrine of Bima Raja, which is also called "Dharni Khamb" (1977, 77), that is associated with the Bali Jatra. According to the authors *khamp* refers to a wooden post and the deity is actually represented by such a post called Bali or Dharni Khamp (Thusu provides a drawing of post, 1977, 77), where the Bali Jatra is conducted for eight days. *Dharni* obviously refers to the earth goddess and Thusu (1977, 79) also states that "Bima/Dharni is taken to be the daughter of Mahaprabhu."
5 I have not encountered any ritual practice among the Gutob Gadaba that is related to Bima.

Bima is not only depicted as a water supplier but also as a seed provider and founder of agriculture. In a Koya story (Elwin 1954, 42), he requests golden seeds from Deur (the sky god), ploughs his field with his teeth and successfully cultivates gold. He returns half of the gold to Deur, who then spoils Bima's plan to give the other half to humankind. Another Kond story collected by Elwin (1954, 164f) in the Kalahandi District is especially instructive, as it depicts Bima and his queen as the providers of seeds in connection with human sacrifice. In this story, Bima Raja and Bima Rani live in the underworld (*jompur*). Together with their sons, they prepare two fields but have no seeds. Acting on an idea of his wife, Bima Raja kills his middle son and he "sprinkled his blood over the soil. From the boy's blood every kind of grain sprang up. Bhima Raja called a Kond and his wife and gave them the seed and through them its use spread throughout the world" (Elwin 1954, 164f).

Other stories highlight Bima's dangerous, angry, selfish and cunning attributes. Of particular relevance to my discussion of the Bali Jatra are the myths which have been collected among the Pengo and Dongria Kond, as they describe Bima's relationship to the earth goddess as well as to rice, and one of them explicitly discusses the role of Bima in connection to the Bali Jatra itself.[6] Like the Pengo, the Dongria consider Bima to be the brother of the earth goddess, who is the wife of the sun god (Dorom Raja).[7] Moreover, the Dongria specify that Bima is the mother's brother of Sita Penu Lahi Penu, the goddess of wealth and rice, who is the daughter of the sun god and the earth goddess (Hardenberg 2018a, 89; Jena et al. 2002, 144f, 161f, 210).

In one story (Jena et al. 2002, 161–63), Bima is envious of Lahi Penu, as she has been entrusted (variously by the earth goddess or the sun god) to take seeds to the human world. After having received the seeds, Lahi Penu notices half way to the human world that she has forgotten two kinds of seeds – tobacco and another plant (*bala dal*, not identified). Bima hinders her from taking these two seeds, attempting several times to withhold the seeds from her (by swallowing and hiding them), but Lahi Penu is finally able to deliver the seeds by hiding

---

[6] Bima's fierceness also comes to the fore in two Koya stories. In one of them (Elwin 1954, 87f) he is depicted as the enemy of humankind. He tried to kill the ancestral siblings of humans who were taking shelter in a gourd during the cosmogonic flood and after several attempts of shooting them with his arrows had failed, he continued to plague humankind with dangerous and heavy rains. In another Koya story Bima brings illness to humans (Elwin 1954, 53).

[7] The wife of the sun god is sometimes explicitly referred to as Dharni (as her shrine on the village level is also called)(Hardenberg 2018a, 624), sometimes she is also called Pata Dei (Jena et al 2002, 145). According to Hardenberg *pata* refers to flat stones that also represent the earth goddess in the context of the buffalo sacrifice and are considered as "mother" (2018a, 428–30).

them between her thighs. Enraged by this, Bima curses the seeds, so that the flowers of the plants would fall off (through his storm) before new seeds could ripen. However, Lahi Penu finally pacifies her uncle by promising him that he will be venerated by humans in the context of the Mandiarani festival,[8] which the Dongria actually celebrate, according to Jena et al. (2002, 203–05).[9] Among the Dongria, therefore, Bima is considered to be crucial for a successful harvest, insofar as he has the potential to destroy the crops, and not so much because he is an agent of fertility, a facet which is stressed in his rain aspect in other stories mentioned above.[10] The Dongria ascribe this procreative function to Sita Penu Lahi Penu, who seeks shelter in a piece of hollow bamboo when Bima manifests himself as a destructive storm (Hardenberg 2018a, 89).

In the Pengo creation myth (L/8) – which I discussed in the previous chapter in relation to the character of Mati Sundori Duri Sundori – the Bima (of which there are several in this story) are represented as the original receivers of the knowledge of cultivation and hunting, but they prove to be unworthy recipients. They commit various blunders and transgress ritual and social rules – they fail to

---

8 Jena et al. (2002; see also Nayak 2021, 197) describe two festivals associated with Bima. One is the Mandiarani festival, of which the authors say that it is the "grandest annual agricultural festival of the Dongria Kondh" (2002, 203). Hardenberg (2018a), on the other hand, does not mention the festival at all. Jena et al. do not provide a translation of the festival's name, which in Desia would mean "finger-millet (*mandia*)-queen (*rani*)" (finger millet is *dare* in Dongria, Hardenberg 2018a, 612). The Dongria Mandiarani festival reminds me of the Dalgada ("planting of leaves") ritual among the Gutob Gadaba, as this also is a ritual of the rainy season and especially associated with finger millet (Berger 2015, 412f). In the context of the Dongria festival in July/August all householders cut some stalks of pigeon peas, finger millet and other plants from their hill fields, when the plants have a height of about one foot. This bundle (*dalu*) they take into their houses, but eventually – after the sacrifices in the individual houses – they will be put on a wooden post that is erected for the festival next to the location of the *jakeri* and *koteiwali* stones representing the earth goddess and her husband respectively. This post is representing Bima and a buffalo is sacrificed near it in the course of the festival to guarantee a good harvest. A second post is sometimes erected as well, in front of the house of the priest (*jani*) (Jena et al. 2002, 203–5).

The second ritual associated with Bima is the "mango flower worship" (Jena et al. 2002, 210f). Bima's malevolent character is underlined here by the fact that this ritual is also meant to appease Aji Budi, the pox and measles goddess. In both cases their worship is thus intended to avert their negative influence; in case of Bima the destruction of the crops, in case of Aji Budi the growth of "crops" on people's skin. Dongria compare the shape of mango flowers to the pustules of the skin diseases.

9 Also in the myth collected by Hardenberg (2018a, 89) Lahi Penu promises Bima to request humans to perform festivals for both of them.

10 However, another Dongria story does associate Bima with the rainy season more generally, thus also acknowledges his benevolent rain-aspect (Jena et al. 2002, 144).

perform the Mango festival before hunting and do not share the meat after the hunt. As they are angry and selfish, as well as destructive ("cause ruin"), and they mistreat their elder sister, the earth goddess, she inflicts various punishments on them. Ultimately, she takes the knowledge of cultivation and hunting, as well as the accompanying rituals, away from them, making humans the new custodians of the Mango festival.[11]

The Bima also fail to appear in a more favorable light in the Pengo myth (M10) that explicitly deals with the sand festival. Erotically aroused by a girl who sings the Bali songs, the middle Bima deceives her and persuades her to leave the village, taking sand and seeds with her. With the principal girl and her seeds gone, the seeds in her village do not sprout. The Bima have thus spoiled the sand festival. Again, Takrani interferes and tells her younger brothers to take the festival down to the world of humans and to perform the festival there. In a sense, then, the Bali Jatra in Komra that I describe below is such an occasion when the Bima take the festival to the humans and conduct the festival with and for them. While the Bima of the Bali Jatra hosted by humans in Komra are no doubt powerful and wild, taking what they want, their characters are rather positive and their foundational role in human agriculture is stressed in the ritual actions, the wall painting and the epic recited by the *gurumai*.

8.2 The Bali Jatra Epic

Based on the work of Otten (2014), the plot of the epic can be summarized as follows. In the beginning of the story the world is created, in particular sand and water by the river and earth gods (Basoki, Boipari). Four creatures emerge out of the earth – who are at the same time gods, kings and the ancestors of humanity – two brothers, Shaliman Raja and Mahapatra, and two sisters, Nila Devi and Kota Devi, the latter being the daughters of seers. All are naked and subsist by gathering produce from the forest. Shaliman then marries Nila Devi, while Mahapatra marries Kota Devi; a hut is built – a simple one from branches and leaves – and a household thus established. Mahapatra then travels to his in-law's place, the seers, to invite Bima, the brother of Nila Devi and Kota Devi, to his place.[12] He

---

11 This Mango festival relates to the Chait Porbo, I would assume, a festival which is celebrated throughout Koraput and that connects *tas* (cultivation) and *bet* (hunting) with the first ritual consumption of mangos (Berger 2015).
12 In both contributions, Otten (2009, 2014) emphasizes Bima's role as Shaliman's and Mahapatra's wife's brother, or, consequently, the mother's brother of Lolit Raja and Jema. She also

returns with Bima, who brings the skills and tools of agriculture with him. With agriculture comes sacrifice and wealth. A rhino is sacrificed and a palace (called Databeli Gada) appears where the head is buried, while houses emerge where other parts of the victim's body are interred. Two children are then born to Shaliman and Nila Devi, a son, Lolit Raja, and subsequently a daughter, Jema. The marriage of Mahapatra and Kota Devi does not produce offspring. However, at the in-law's place, two girls are born, Devirani and Phulseri, who will become the friends of Jema and merge into one character (Devirani-Phulseri) in the course of the story. On his excursions, Mahapatra encounters the Tiger God (Buda Bag), who is a protector of his territory. Moreover, Mahapatra searches for a teacher for the children and finds Agniguru, who instructs Lolit Raja and Jema. The story ends with the wedding of Lolit Raja and Devirani-Phulseri (referred to as Phulseri below), a marriage that is initiated by Jema.

8.3 Interlude: Affinal Gifts and Rice

Without discussing this story in detail at this stage, one key aspect should be noted, to which I will return later – the association of affinity with regeneration. The brothers Shaliman and Mahapatra receive three affinal gifts from their mysterious in-laws, the seers, and Bima. Notably, nothing seems to flow in the other direction, which is curious given the symmetrical nature of affinal relationships in the region, as discussed in the introduction. The first affinal gifts are Bima's sisters, Nila Devi and Kota Devi, whom the two brothers marry. Bima's second gift consists of the tools for and knowledge of cultivation (the cultivation stone, so to speak), which transforms Shaliman and Mahapatra's mode of livelihood from that of gathering to an agricultural existence. This automatically requires sacrifices and fundamentally alters their whole way of life – they no longer dwell in a forest hut but in a palace. The third gift Shaliman and Mahapatra receive from their affines is a bride for their son, Lolit Raja. It is this marriage that is prominently celebrated in the Bali Jatra, and the three figures of Jema, who initiated the marriage, Lolit and Phulseri are found in the center of the mural I discuss below, being seated under the wedding canopy (*chamda*). I would argue that this marriage is so vital to the celebration of the Bali Jatra because – as in the case of the Lachmi Jagar from Bastar as discussed by Gregory – it concerns agricultural wealth, the gift of seeds, or "flower-roots"

---

notes (Otten 2009, 36), however, that in other villages he is considered to be the elder brother of Lolit Raja and Jema.

as I would literally translate Phulseri. The three affinal gifts thus provide Shaliman (and his brother) with wives (and as a result offspring), with the knowledge and tools of agriculture and with grain.

There are some indications that the seed gift of Phulseri may actually relate to rice, although this is not explicitly stated in the epic and the Bali Jatra festival prominently features the growth of wheat.[13] Otten (2014, 268) argues that the "epic seems to be clearly associated with rice," adding that there were no references to either wheat or millet in the short version she recorded. One clue that Phulseri may refer to rice concerns a metaphorical connection of "washed rice" to "blossoming flowers" that has been recorded among the Gadaba and Bondo (Elwin 1950, 147) as part of invocations to deities common among all Desia, that is, the house deity (Doron Deli) and Pat Kanda, respectively. The phrase goes *doila chaul phutla phul para hei kori*, which translates as "let [it/us] become like washed rice, blossoming flowers." Generalized well-being is at stake in both invocations, including human health, the welfare of children and cattle, agriculture and the harvest (Berger 2015, 58f). Thus, part of the invocation among the Bondo runs: "Let the crops be plentiful. Let us have no trouble. Let us be like the washed rice and the blossoming flower. O Pat Khanda Mahaprabhu, let the kingdom, earth and country be well" (Elwin 1950, 147). A very similar phrase ("Like the washed grains of rice, Like the blossoming flower") is also part of the opening verses of the Bali Jatra epic (Otten 2014, 247).

Otten also assumes a connection between Phulseri and rice, although for a different reason. She assumes that *seri* relates to *shri* as one of the names for Laksmi and therefore translates Devirani Phulseri as "goddess-queen of flower-rice" (Otten n.d.). In my view, it is rather the metaphor of a flower that signifies rice. However, obviously both views do not exclude each other; quite the contrary. The connection between rice, Laksmi and the lotus is very widespread in India (Gregory 2004; Skoda 2003). With reference to Bastar, Chris Gregory (2018) has recently discussed the complex representations of wealth and auspiciousness and aptly demonstrated the symbolic correspondence and equivalence of Laksmi (and Sita), rice, the lotus flower and the placenta. With regard to the Bali Jatra, I will also argue that "flowers" not only refer to rice but to regeneration more generally, especially to women of a marriageable age.

In addition to this metaphorical connection between the epic character of Phulseri and rice, there are also aspects of the ritual practice that clearly

---

[13] Otten (2009, 39) reports that in the context of the Bali Jatra she observed the women sowed seeds of wheat, rice, maize and beans into their baskets, adding that the seeds of wheat are considered to be of most value.

connect the Bali Jatra to rice and to the paddies. The sand in which the wheat seedlings germinate is collected in the rice fields. Before this is done, a sacrifice to Jal Kamni Patal Kamni is performed, that is, to the "water-earth deities" of the paddies and, at least in the Gadaba conceptualization, the "parents" of the "bride" (rice). The winnowing fan, which is part of the divine ensemble of clay pot, bow and arrow, is painted in the same way as I have seen it done during the wet-rice harvest among the Gadaba. A white cross is painted on the back of the fan with paint made from water and rice flour. In their Bali Jatra, the Dongria Kond – who do not sow seeds of wheat but rice, black gram and a pulse instead – worship two deities in particular. One is Bera, a male god associated with towns and the valley, rather than with the Dongria territory as such. The second deity is the goddess Bali Ma who, while being associated with Durga, when represented by a bamboo pole, she is considered to be Sita Penu Lahi Penu, that is rice (Hardenberg 2014).

Moreover, on the most important final night of the Bali Jatra, which I will describe in detail below, when all gods are invited into the temple to be embodied by the trance-dancers, the latter first receive a "rice blessing" (my term) and while dancing, they throw rice into the crowd of people sitting along the sides of the temple. This might be related to a sequence of the epic in which the Pat Gurumai, the goddess representing the epic, who descends to earth and inspires her divine counterparts to sing the epic (Otten 2014, 248), actually requests rice. In the epic, she states that she has visited the Bastar kingdom, where she was rewarded with rice, and she then announces to the Mali that she will only make their fields fertile ("visit her fields") "if she receives rice during the recitation of the epic" (Otten 2014, 272).

A final point that should be mentioned is the synchronization of the Bali Jatra with the process of the rice harvest, itself a kind of a wedding, at least among the Gadaba (Berger 2015). The wet-rice harvest may only commence after the "cooling of the earth deity" (Hundi Sitlani) in the month of November (*diali*), which entails a sacrifice for the village goddess at the time when the Bali Jatra also starts and the *gurumai* begin their recitation of the epic. The Bali Jatra thus runs parallel to this part of the agricultural cycle and completely encompasses the wet-rice harvest, including reaping the grain, threshing and bringing it into the house. The other staple crop, finger millet, is already cut before Hundi Sitlani, but threshing only commences after the completion of the wet-rice harvest and continues after the Bali Jatra is over. There thus seems to be numerous indicators that the gift of Phulseri refers to the gift of rice, a crop that has a prominent place both in the narrative of the epic and in the ritual performances.

8.4 The Bali Jatra in Komra

The Participating Communities: Parenga, Mali and Rona

The proverb linking the four festivals identifies the Bali Jatra with the Mali. As I pointed out at the beginning of this chapter, the festival is performed by a number of communities and, in the case of Komra, several groups are involved, most prominently the Mali, Parenga and Rona. I will introduce these communities briefly here before turning to the description of the festival. Even if I had wished to discuss the Mali or Parenga in more detail, I could not have done so, as the ethnographic data available is very limited.

Komra is a Parenga village in the sense that they are considered to be the first settlers and earth people (*matia*) and, accordingly, they perform the sacrifices at the village shrines and eat the senior sacrificial food (*tsoru*) with their deities. Like the Gadaba and Bondo, they are a tribal group that speaks an Austroasiatic language of the south Munda branch called Gorum (Anderson and Rau 2008). Ethnographically, this community is nearly non-existent and not even the Anthropological Survey of India bothered to conduct a study of this tribal group. Only recently a booklet on the Parenga has been published by the *Scheduled Castes and Scheduled Tribes Research and Training Institute* (Ota et al. 2018) which provides some general information but is not based on long-term research. Based on my visits to several Parenga villages, I can report that they live south of the area of the Gutob Gadaba and are less numerous than the latter. According to a recent statistical survey by the Indian government,[14] they number less than 10,000 individuals. Twenty years ago, when Gutob was still a language spoken by many, I had the impression that Gorum was a much more endangered language. Living adjacent to the Gutob Gadaba, some Parenga villages also perform the Go'ter, which will be discussed in the next chapter, and they thus engage in ritual relationships with the Gadaba that are constitutive of the Go'ter. During the Bali Jatra in Komra, the Parenga assumed various roles, especially those of the Bima and Jema. Moreover, the village *pujari* (as elsewhere, from the Sisa group) was involved in many sequences of the festival.

As far as the Mali are concerned, the ethnographic situation is not much better, with no ethnographic monograph on this community being available. Unlike the Gadaba and Parenga, the Mali are not agriculturalists but horticulturalists. They cultivate vegetables in their gardens with great skill and sell them at weekly

---

[14] Statistical Profile of Scheduled Tribes in India 2013 Ministry of Tribal Affairs, Statistics Division. Government of India. www.tribal.nic.in, p. 158 iv. See also Ota et al. (2018, 5).

markets or directly in the villages to tribal agriculturalists, often in exchange for finger millet or rice that they usually do not grow. In the general Desia hierarchy, they are granted a higher status than the agricultural communities such as the Bondo, Parenga or Gadaba; they wear the sacred thread and abstain from eating beef and pork. However, I know of no village in the region where the Mali are regarded as original settlers, and from the village perspective they are thus usually considered "late comers" by the respective earth people.

The Mali themselves also hold that they originally came from elsewhere. Otten (2014, 252) estimates that they "immigrated several centuries ago into this region [i.e. Koraput]" and that "some Mali claim that they migrated from the North as far as Kashi (Varanasi)." A Mali *dissari* explained to Ulrike Blindt (n.d.) – who stayed in a village with Mali and Kond residents (in the vicinity of the Duduma waterfall) during a student excursion by the anthropology department of the Free University of Berlin in 2000 – that the Mali originally came from Bastar (now Chhattisgarh).[15] According to the *dissari*, the word "Mali" would be derived from Mauli – a goddess we have encountered in the chapter on the Dasara – as they were the florists of her temple. He said that they had to flee Bastar, as the king used to recruit the victims for human sacrifices from among their community, and thus they came to Nandapur.

In the Koraput region, Mali are also associated with the work of temple florists and may have come to Jeypore to serve the king in that function. Senapati and Sahu (1966, 95), accordingly, claim that the word "Mali" is derived from the making of garlands (*mala*) (see also Rousseleau 2008, 82). In a Pengo story (Burrow and Bhattacharya 1970, 166–74), a Mali woman – *malni*, translated as "flower-woman" by the authors (Burrow and Bhattacharya 1970, 169) – and maker of garlands, figures prominently in an amorous relationship between a prince and a princess (leading eventually to marriage), who use the Mali woman as a go-between in their exchange of garlands. An actual historical assessment of these migrations is difficult, and the thorough embeddedness of the Mali community in Desia society at large, for instance, in terms of clanship (Pfeffer 1997), shows that they have lived in the region for a long time. In the Bali Jatra in Komra, their only task is to paint the mural inside the Bali shrine.

The Rona also say that they migrated long ago to this area to serve as militia for the king of Nandapur (Bell 1945, 82; Otten 2006, 11). As such, they are closely associated with the Paik (foot soldiers), who played a prominent part in the Ganga Puja of the Joria, discussed in the last chapter. Rono means "war"

---

15 They are known as Maraar in Bastar (Gregory 2010).

and the Rona probably received land to cultivate from former kings for their services. This may explain why they are the only group of the "non-ST" Desia (Berger 2002), who are regarded as landowners and cultivators (*roit*). As I have previously mentioned when discussing the Boirobi Puja in the village of Badigor, some Rona became powerful *mutadar* and tax collectors on behalf of the king. Today, they are found in many villages in this area and, like the Mali, they have a high status in the region and wear the sacred thread and do not consume beef or pork. Ethnographically, the situation is not as bleak as it is with regard to the Parenga and Mali, as Tina Otten (2006, 2021) did extensive fieldwork with the Rona, especially on their ideas and ritual practices concerning healing and illness. With regard to the Bali Jatra in Komra the Rona are important as they are the original hosts of the festival, which was only later adopted by the village as a whole. As such, they are involved in many of the rituals and are still regarded as the *saukar* or "hosts."

Komra Village and Bali Jatra Actors

Komra is a relatively big village – of about 300 households, I have been told – about twelve kilometers due south-west of Nandapur. The Parenga earth people belong to the Tiger clan category that is locally divided into the three status groups of Sisa, Munduli and Kirsani. Rona, Goudo (herders) and Dombo constitute a large group of late comers. Half of the Dombo community of about 80 households are Christians. As no Mali live in Komra, members of this community had been recruited from a neighboring village to paint the mural.

As in the Ganga and Nandi festivals of the Joria, various ritual roles were enacted by different people of the village, most of them easily recognizable as characters of the Bali Jatra epic. The two female *gurumai* who recited the epic (referred to as "story-song," *katani git*) were both from the Rona community. Seven Parenga men from the Munduli group acted as Bima, the most elaborately formulated and distinguished characters of the whole performance. They were ascribed particular powers and granted specific privileges. At particular moments during the ritual process they uprooted trees and were allowed to plunder the garden of any villager, without him or her being allowed to complain or ask for compensation. Once, as I was told by Ghasi Munduli, the brother of one of the Bima with whom we stayed, a man prevented a Bima from taking his vegetables from his garden and since then nothing grows there. During some of their ritual actions the Bima displayed big cigars (*pita*) and braided "sticks" made from straw called *chamta*, like sticks for drumming (Gustafsson 1989, 180). They also received the sacred thread (*pointa*), signifying high status during the course of the rituals. Although the Bima were all Munduli, being a performer is not simply a hereditary role, as the deity has to "come" to a person, who then subsequently may act as Bima.[16]

The character of Lolit Raja was also recruited from the Munduli group and performed by a young boy. Jema is a crucial character in the story, as she initiates the wedding of Lolit Raja and Phulseri. The long version of the Bali Jatra I am concerned with here is actually also called Jema Bali (Otten n.d.), which again underlines the relevance of Jema to the festival as a whole. It seems that this ritual role was open to any woman or girl of the village, with the exception of the women from the Dombo community. Although not all women performed as Jema, many women and girls of different ages assumed this role. Together with the Bima they vigorously engaged in the "trance-dance" (*baya-nat*) sessions and became possessed by the various deities that came to populate the Bali shrine during the nights. In addition, Rona and Parenga (Sisa) performed as Agniguru, and one Rona acted as Monior, probably the Shaliman of the epic. The Monior was also painted close to the three central figures – Jema, Lolit Raja and Phulseri – in the center of the mural.

Table 5: Overview of the Main Ritual Actors of the Bali Jatra

Role	Performing group	Activity
gurumai	Rona (female)	– Invoking deities, sacrificing – Custodians of the clay pot/deity – Reciting the epic – Planting seeds in the Bali shrine (*matam*) – Blessing other actors with *tika*
Bima	Parenga (male, Munduli)	– Invoking deities – "Cutting the forest," plundering gardens – Distributing sand and seeds – First stroke of wall-painting – Trance-dance
Jema	Parenga, Rona, Goudo (female)	– Trance-dance – Dancing around the "*roto*" (chariot), or Databeli fort

---

16 Ghasi Munduli's father's father, his father, and now his elder brother are performing as Bima, which suggests that the role is continued among the men of a house.

Table 5 (continued)

Role	Performing group	Activity
pujari	Parenga (male)	– Invoking deities, sacrificing
saukar	Rona (male)	– Original host, sacrifice
Lolit Raja	Parenga (male, Munduli)	– Dancing around the "roto" (chariot), or Databeli fort
Monior	Rona (male)	– Preparing the fire, "dancing" on the fire – dancing around the *"roto"* (chariot), or Databeli fort
women	all communities	– Fetching sand, sowing seeds, watering & worshipping plants – Trance-dance

Apart from the sand and seeds of wheat, the most important material objects of the Bali Jatra are the representation of the Bali deity and the Bali shrine. The *gurumai* are the custodians of the Bali deity and thus also of its material representation, the clay pot and the associated winnowing fan, bow and arrow. They painted the clay pot in a way that resembles the mural of the Joria in the context of the Nandi festival. It was sprinkled all over with white dots made from rice flour and water, and the sun and moon were also painted next to each other. The narration of the epic during the first phase of the ritual took place in the house of the Rona host, after which the deity was moved by the *gurumai* to the Bali Jatra shrine, which most participants referred to as the "temple" (*mandir*).

Until a few years before the present occasion, this shrine consisted of a small construction of bamboo and thatch that was built anew each time the Bali Jatra was performed. The government then financed the construction of a permanent concrete building consisting of one room (of about 3 by 5 meters), with an asbestos roof and two small windows with wooden shutters on the walls to the left and right of the entrance. The wall facing the entrance had a low and small concrete ledge (*pindoli*) running along its base, on which the representation of the deity was placed. It was on this wall that the mural was to be painted. A square cavity had been constructed in this low ledge to provide a place for sand and to sow the seeds of wheat. While this new construction was probably welcomed by the villagers, it had its practical disadvantages, as it did not allow the smoke from the fires that were lit inside to escape through the roof, as was previously the case. The small windows facilitated some ventilation, but often, when the room was packed with people and fires were burned inside, breathing was difficult when standing upright. I could imagine that this shortage of oxygen also had an impact on the men and women who engaged in the trance-dance.

The twelve final days of the festival which we documented[17] can be divided into four main ritual sequences: 1) Bringing the sand from the river and planting the seeds, 2) painting the mural, 3) the trance-dance in the temple, and 4) the last day, including scenes enacted from the epic, sacrifices, the return of the sand to the river and the exchange of Bali "flowers."

Table 6: Overview of the Last Phase of the Bali Jatra

December 22, 2000	(Fri.)	– Preparing the clay pot, invoking the deity – Fetching the sand, sowing the wheat seeds Break
December 29, 2000	(Fri.)	– Worship of deity – Senior Bima makes first stroke on mural
December 31, 2000	(Sun.)	– Collection of rice for guests – Mal arrive and start painting the mural
January 1, 2001	(Mon.)	– Mal complete mural – *Gurumai* narrate epic – Consecration of rice for trance-dance – Trance-dance in temple, *demsa* throughout the night
January 2, 2001	(Tue.)	– Dance of Bima and Jema continues – Monior prepares fire: "fire-walking" – Procession around the chariot (*roto*) – Bima "cut the forest" (*bon katiba*) – Clay pot to *sadar*, collective sacrifice – Procession to the river, harvesting and exchange of "flowers"

The beginning of the second phase of the festival was indicated by the propitiation of the dead (*duma*) on Friday (Dec. 22). Before all major ritual occasions or main days of a festival, the dead must receive offerings, lest angry spirits feel inclined to disturb the ritual proceedings. In the morning, individual households offered cooked rice – that was placed on leaves of the jackfruit tree – to the *duma* in front of their houses and on the paths leading out of the village.[18]

---

[17] Research in Komra was conducted on December 22, 29, 31, 2000 and January 1–2, 2001. I was accompanied by Manto Pradhan, Amrei Volkmann and at times also by Ori Sisa from Gudapada.
[18] Gadaba perform this ritual they call Duma Balo in the evening before the ritual. Moreover, they always offer crabs for the dead and exclusively for them (Berger 2015, 227).

In the afternoon, two *gurumai*, accompanied by the Bima, took the clay pot out of the temple, washed it and repainted it, in the manner mentioned, then placed it back inside in front of the main wall on the low ledge. On the wall behind the deity, one could still see the washed out remains of the former mural. Inside the temple, the Bima, *pujari* and the *gurumai* then invoked the deity and lit an oil lamp. The Bima received big cigars and straw sticks from the *gurumai* and then started dancing inside the shrine. Soon afterward, in the late afternoon, the procession to the paddies started. Accompanied by the Bima, Jema, Lolit Raja and the Dombo musicians, the *gurumai* led the procession with the village *pujari*, followed by the women of the village. The *gurumai* carried a larger basket than all the other women. According to Otten (2009, 38, 43), this basket is specifically referred to as the Jema basket (Jema Dala). The Bima also distinguished themselves from everyone else by carrying *ara*, which are hollow pieces of bamboo some 30 centimeters long, otherwise used as a dry measure.[19]

After their arrival at the river, the deities of the paddies, Jal Kamni (the water aspect) and Patal Kamni (the earth aspect) – together, usually simply referred to as Kamni – were worshipped. A small mud platform was constructed in the water between the stalks of the previously harvested rice. In addition to other paraphernalia (milk, puffed rice) that were offered, the *pujari* sacrificed an egg and a red chick, surrounded by all of the other important ritual actors. After the agreement of the deities had thus been achieved, the *ara* of the Bima and the basket of the *gurumai* were first filled with mud, then all other women quickly dispersed over the fields and hurried to fill their own baskets. The wet earth was sieved again and again, until only small red stones remained in the baskets. After all of the women had completed this task, the procession moved back into the village and to the temple. The Bima rushed ahead and gave the first proof of their extraordinary powers. Somewhere in the village they uprooted a banana tree with a stalk of fruit and placed it next to the entrance of the temple.

Inside the Bali shrine, the Bima and the *gurumai* poured the sand from their vessels onto the ground in front of the Bali deity, who had not been taken to the river. Framing the pile of sand with their *ara* and drawing ritual patterns (*bana*) with flour on top and in front of it, they then worshipped the sand, offering another egg. While this sand pile represented the village as a whole (*matam*), there were several other piles inside and outside the shrine, about fifteen in total. Like the Bima and *gurumai*, many women had poured their sand into one heap, before redistributing it later. The Bima were the first to fill their own *ara* with alternating

---

[19] The Gadaba use *ara* ritually for measuring little millet (*suen*, Panicum miliare)(Berger 2015, 421).

Photo 8.1: The Bali deity
Inside the temple, the embodiment of the Bali deity — a clay pot, winnowing fan, bow and arrow — has been prepared by the *gurumai*. The painted symbols of sun and moon can be seen on the clay pot.

layers of sand and seeds of wheat, and then they distributed small portions of sand and wheat seeds to other women, who filled their smaller baskets (*tifni*) – many of them newly made – in the same manner as the Bima. The *gurumai* prepared a special bed with sand and seeds in the cavity of the ledge right next to the Bali deity. After having completed this task, all of the women took their own baskets to their houses, where they were placed next to the central pillar of the house (Doron Deli) in the inner room. Here, the seeds were regularly worshipped and doused with turmeric water. As Parenga houses do not have windows and this inner room receives little to no light from the central door of the house, the plants virtually grow in the dark. All of the women who have fetched sand and care for the growth of the wheat seeds only eat one meal per day, in the evening, after sunset.

Photo 8.2: Distribution of seeds
One of the Bima distributes seeds from his bamboo container (*ara*) to women in front to the Bali temple.

For the following five days, while the seeds germinated, there were no other special ritual activities. After this period, people danced in the temple every evening in front of the deity and the sprouting wheat to the music of the Dombo, with some actors – especially the Bima and Jema – performing the trance-dance (*baya nat*). We returned to Komra a week later (Dec. 29), when everybody had assembled again in the Bali house. The Bima and *gurumai* first jointly worshipped the deity, then the *gurumai* started singing and worshipping one of the Bima, perhaps the most senior one, comparable to the Mul Bima – or "main" Bima – that is mentioned by Otten (2009, 37). Dancing in a trance, he then applied the first stroke of white paint over the remains of the mural from the last occasion, after which the wall would be white-washed as preparation for the new mural to be painted by the Mali. After the Bima, various women of all ages also performed the trance-dance to the rhythm of the Dombo musicians.

8.4 The Bali Jatra in Komra

Photo 8.3: Distribution of sand
Inside the Bali temple the sand that has been collected in the paddy fields is piled up, to be redistributed soon.

Painting the Mural

The Mali from the neighboring village of Kotlaput were supposed to start the mural (*chitro*) early on Sunday (Dec. 31) but they kept the people of Komra waiting. In the meantime, rice and new clay pots were collected at the assembly platform (*sadar*) for the big feast on the last day. Every household was supposed to bring one *man* (a dry measure of about 2.5 kilos) of husked rice, some chili peppers and vegetables. Some jointly brought their share as one group, for example, the Munduli collectively contributed 30 *man*. In total, ten *phuti* of rice (one *phuti* is about 60–75 kilos) were collected. Finally, about 20 Mali men arrived and started their work after we had already left the village. When we came back on the following morning (Jan. 1), the work was again under way. Several Mali were painting at the same time and directly invited me to paint something as well. I was hesitant about this invitation at first, but they insisted, asking me to contribute in the center of the image. Ultimately, I agreed and painted the head of Ganesha – for no particular reason, just assuming this would not do harm, as he is the remover of obstacles, after all – in the corner of a side wall.

332 — 8 A Festival of "Flowers:" The Bali Jatra of the Mali

Photo 8.4: Filling the baskets with earth and seeds
Outside of the Bali temple women of the village fill their baskets with sand and seeds of wheat.

The main wall – above the sprouting wheat and the Bali god – was most intensely painted and was obviously the most important. While the Mali painted this main wall, children and anyone else who so wished painted images on the other walls. The main image consisted of two nested rectangular frames with square-shaped projections in the middle of each side. These looked like the inner and outer walls of a compound. When we discussed the mural, the *gurumai* explained to me that the structure represented the temple and that all the gods painted in the interior space would later that night be called into the temple, while the others would remain outside. Above the painted temple, below the

8.4 The Bali Jatra in Komra — 333

Photo 8.5: Men from the Mali community paint the central part of the mural

Photo 8.6: The wall painting has been completed
On the small ledge below, the sprouting wheat plants can be seen next to the Bali deity.

actual roof of the Bali shrine, two large tigers were depicted facing each other, with the sun and moon next to them.

During and particularly after the completion of the wall painting, we discussed the mural not only with the *gurumai* but also with the Mali and other Parenga villagers. Not surprisingly, there were many different opinions concerning the interpretation of the images. In the center of the mural was a palanquin – signifying the royal context – carried by two people and on which three figures were seated. One Mali explained that the central figure was Jema and that those to each side would both be Lolit Raja. The leading painter among the Mali corrected this saying that the central figure would indeed be Jema and the person on the right her brother Lolit Raja, but the figure on the left would be Phulseri, Lolit's bride. This interpretation thus corresponds with the epic as documented by Otten, as Jema is the key person initiating the wedding of Lolit Raja and Devirani Phulseri. However, a *gurumai* said that there should be four figures in the center, and that Soki (perhaps Basoki) was missing. The Mali disagreed and said that the latter would be outside.

Parenga bystanders had other views and identified the figures as *hundi* (the local village shrine/deity), Vishnu or Brahma. The *gurumai* identified themselves on the bottom left of the interior realm, where there were two figures, one of them – the senior *gurumai* – carrying the Bali deity on her head. However, one *gurumai* also identified herself with a figure that other commentators insisted would be the Monior, a figure to the bottom left of the palanquin carrying a *bel* branch (*Aegle marmelos*); the thorny plant on which many of the trance-dancers would soon be sitting. The Mali also said that the figure with the *bel* branch represented the Monior, and they added that this image was painted first and thus was the starting point of the whole mural. On the basis of the epic as recorded by Otten, I would assume that Monior is Shaliman and that the scene may refer to the situation before the advent of agriculture, when the two brothers and two sisters were still naked and living in a hut made from branches and leaves.

Below the palanquin, there was an image that resembled a simple hut with a small entrance, with a bare-breasted woman to its right. Close by, there were different figures carrying plants or branches, one directly left of the "hut" under the palanquin, with a big leaf. Directly to the left of the palanquin, another figure appeared to be carrying a branch in the direction of the palanquin, and was standing next to another person close to the border of the interior realm. This figure appeared to be moving in the other direction, away from the center and pointing to another figure still further left in the alcove-like protrusion of the inner wall. This latter figure was easily identifiable as Bima, as he had a big cigar in his mouth, carried a plant (possibly a banana tree with a stalk of fruits or a plant with a sheaf of grain) over his shoulder and held a "stick" in the other hand, like the men who enacted Bima during the festival. The figure pointing toward "Bima," then, may have been Mahapatra, indicating to the other person that he is going to venture out to call Bima, as he does in the epic. These are my interpretations, however.[20] After the mural was completed, the Mali returned to their village.

Trance-Dance and Sacrifice in the Temple

With the seeds having developed into small plants and the mural completed, everything was prepared for the main night, when all the gods would be invited into the Bali shrine, as the *gurumai* had said. The gods revealed their presence by possessing the dancers, who in turn demonstrated their embodied divinity by stepping on swords or resting on thorny seats made from *bel* branches. However, a few more preparations remained. Outside the temple, stalls were built by peddlers supplying tea and sweets for the many visitors from other villages. Soon after sunset, the Rona *saukar* of the Bali Jatra suspended a rectangular decorated frame from the ceiling, which hung like a canopy directly above the clay pot representing the Bali deity and in front of the painted palanquin of the mural depicting Jema, Lolit Raja and Phulseri. While suspended from above and not supported by wooden posts, as is common, it resembled a wedding pavilion, and I would suggest that it referred to the wedding of Lolit and Phulseri and that this last night was especially related to this sequence of the epic.

All those who would soon join in the trance-dance then participated in a ritual sequence that seemed to prepare them for this task. I would describe this as a kind of rice blessing that perhaps also safeguarded them when the invited deities entered their bodies. Many women and girls with no special role in the ritual process, but who were planning to join the trance-dance later, now entered the temple – each bringing one leaf-cup of husked rice – and squatted on both sides of the room. In front of the mural, the *gurumai* recited the Bali Jatra story and next to them the other main characters and participants – Bima, Jema, Lolit Raja and the Rona *saukar* – sat in a tight circle on the ground facing each other, their hands outstretched toward the center, holding threads (*suta*) with flowers. Some of these threads were later tied like sacred threads (*pointa*) over the left shoulder and

---

20 Among the other figures that were pointed out to me were two figures on horses above the palanquin, holding swords and facing each other, the one on the right, on a black horse, being Pat Kanda, the one on the left, on a white horse, being Soro Mongola (unclear). Also Agniguru between these two horsemen, a figure emerging from flames can easily be recognized as can. the "seven sisters" or Bardani, the seven figures holding each other on the bottom right of the inner realm.

under the right arm of the participants. The Bima and Jema, especially, wore the strings in this fashion. In my view, these threads signify a temporal sacred status, a particular temporary relatedness to the divine (or demonic), which I have also observed in other contexts among the Gadaba.[21] Other women and girls wore them like necklaces or tied them around their upper arms.

One of the *gurumai* then greeted the group with the *juar* gesture (bowing with folded hands in front of the forehead) and standing outside of the tight circle of people sitting on the ground, she let one grain of husked rice fall into the hands thus outstretched. She then poured a whole leaf-cup of rice over the hands. Immediately after this, the other women and girls who were sitting on each side rushed forward pouring their own leaf-cups with rice over the outstretched hands, while also holding threads with flowers in the hand that held the leaf-cup. After all the cups had thus been poured out, the Rona *saukar* took one handful of rice and poured it into a basket, and the *gurumai* collected the remaining rice and placed it into the same basket, which was then put aside. During the trance-dance, this rice would be distributed to the dancers to throw.

The trance-dance session started at around nine o'clock in the evening, with the small temple now packed with people. On both sides of the room, men, women and children squatted on the floor, while the Dombo musicians played at the end of the room furthest from the Bali deity and mural, in a corner next to the entrance. The same scene of the trance-dance then occurred again and again, until the morning hours. A group of women and girls – around five or six at a time, some of them in the role of Jema but also others – entered the temple with coconuts and chickens as sacrificial animals, which they had promised as vows (*manasik*). The *gurumai*, the Rona *saukar* and the village *pujari* conducted the sacrifices in front of the Bali god, letting blood drip on the clay pot after each sacrificial killing. Subsequently, the women had a piece of white cloth tied around their heads,[22] some of them also wore a bamboo construction like a crown on top of this, which was decorated with flowers, perhaps signaling their role as Jema.

The Dombo started to play the drums and the *moiri* and the *gurumai* put some husked rice from the basket in each of the women's hands. The girls and women then started dancing between the crowd on either side, throwing rice in all directions, their bodies swaying to and fro. After a short time dancing in this way, a

---

21 For instance, when a child is ill, a promise is given to the attacking demon (e.g. Rau) to perform a sacrifice. Then such threads are tied around the wrist or neck of the child, which signify the relatedness to the demon or spirit at stake. When the child has recovered the thread is cut in the context of the ritual that redeems the vow (Berger 2015).

22 Also among the Gadaba I had observed earlier that *gurumai* who went in trance acted in the same way.

seat made from thorns was placed in the center of the room. This thorn seat was passed into the temple from the outside through one of the windows in a side wall, and after the performance, it was passed out of the temple through the opposite window.[23] Each of the girls and women came up to sit on the thorn seat, being assisted and partly held by two Bima standing on each side. After a woman thus sat on the thorns, an old sword – which actually looked quite blunt – was placed on top of this construction and the person then stood on it with bare feet, again being supported by the Bima. Some performers sat and stood on the thorns and sword, respectively, with caution, others with force, even jumping on the objects. Small girls were merely carried over the thorns and the sword, as they were still too young to fully perform the ritual, as the *gurumai* later said. Nevertheless, these young girls danced with much passion. At times, earthen pots were also brought in and the dancers – mostly women, but also the Bima, although no other men – sat or stood on them. The thorns and the sword inflicting no injuries on the dancers and the pots not breaking were considered to be auspicious signs of divine presence. After the sacrifices and the dance, the group of women then danced out of the temple and the next group entered. While the performance of sacrifice and

Photo 8.7: Worshippers gather inside the Bali temple for the "trance dance"

---

23 The same movement could be observed on the following day with regard to the Bima.

Photo 8.8: Distributing rice
The *gurumai* pours a leaf-cup of husked rice into the outstretched hands of the main performers during the night of "trance dance.

the trance-dance dominated inside the temple, in the space outside, predominantly young people danced the *demsa* in endless rounds.

The Final Day

Before the sand was returned in the afternoon of this last day of the festival (Tuesday, Jan. 2), a number of other ritual sequences related to the epic were performed in the morning, while more *manasik* sacrifices also took place inside the temple.

Photo 8.9: A woman is performing the "trance dance" inside the temple

Still before dawn, the first thing we observed in the morning, were the Bima and Jema dancing inside the temple and sitting on the seat of thorns once more. A little later, at around six o'clock in the morning, the Monior prepared a fire in front of the temple entrance. After it had burned down to coals and the glow had nearly disappeared, the Monior and a village *dissari* first received a blessing (*tika*) from the *gurumai* and then danced on the remains of the fire, a scene possibly related to the role of Agniguru in the epic, the teacher of Lolit Raja and Jema. The epic also narrates how the palace, called Databeli Gada, appeared at the place where the head of the sacrificed rhino had been buried. In the Bali Jatra that she observed, Otten (Otten 2014, 265) reports that on the morning of the last day the actors representing Lolit Raja, Jema and others entered an elevated hut that had been erected on wooden posts and which represented this palace. While I was told that the construction was a "chariot" (*roto*), a similar hut was erected in Komra as well, although it looked more like a tent. In front of the temple, a small elevated platform had been built, with a bamboo pole in its center and more bamboo poles at the sides, which were tied to the central one at the top. A female garment (*sari*) had been wrapped around the construction like a tarp. Shortly after the dance on the fire, the Monior, the Jema and the Bima, a woman referred to as *boro dokri* ("senior old woman") and the former *memor* (ward member, an elected office) of the village, all

Photo 8.10: Passing through the Databeli Fort
A tent-like structure has been erected in front of the temple through which several of the main actors pass.

danced out of the temple in one line and toward the platform, which they climbed onto one after the other, then circumambulated the central pole once, climbed down again and danced back into the temple. There, they received *tika* from the *gurumai*. By this time, a large crowd of villagers and their guests had assembled in the area in front of the temple, which was also bordered by the assembly platform, the *sadar*.

Shortly afterward, the Bima were again at the center of attention, as they were performing the ritual sequence called "cutting the forest" (*bon katiba*). A new seat of thorns was passed into the temple from one of the side windows, fastened onto a bier and put on the window sill on the opposite side where it was held in place by several men. One after the other, the Bima evoked the gods and climbed onto the thorn-bier, where they lay for a few moments, their bare backs resting on the sharp thorns. They then crawled out of the window and re-entered the temple through the door, where they each received *tika* from the *gurumai* and big cigars, long thorny branches and the braided straw "sticks" from the Rona *saukar*. Thus equipped, they ran out of the temple to "cut the forest." While they were rampaging through the village, further *manasik* sacrifices on behalf of visiting guests were performed inside the temple. After about half an hour, the Bima returned with branches and grass, which they left in the temple only to run off again. The next time they returned, they carried another banana tree to the temple.

The massive divine presence during the ritual can also be dangerous. Just as the Bima returned for the second time, a group of men carried a woman out of the temple, after an incident of involuntary possession. Shortly before, the woman had been found possessed and people had spat water at her in an attempt to drive the deity out. This being to no avail, the groaning and kicking woman had been taken into the temple. Sitting in front of the mural, she stared at the painting, pointing at several of the images. She then suddenly jumped to her feet and beat her head against the wall of the painting before anyone could stop her. People then seized her and tried to make her sit down again. The *pujari* then removed the decorated construction hanging from the ceiling above the clay pot. He sprinkled water on the central figures of the mural (Jema, Phulseri and Lolit Raja, according to one interpretation) and took some of the color from these images, mixed it with water and gave it to the woman to drink, which she accepted. After a while, she calmed down and was carried out of the shrine, just as the Bima returned. Her family, it was explained to me, had not provided the sacrifices they had promised, so the deity had grabbed her. In addition to demonstrating the unforgiving nature of the deities, this incident also showed that the mural was much more than just a painting. Like the wall painting of the Joria in the context of the Nandi festival, this mural was an actual manifestation of the deities it represented.

Photo 8.11: The village *pujari* inspects the stretcher with thorns for the Bima

In the afternoon, the *gurumai* removed the Bali deity – the clay pot, winnowing fan, bow and arrow – from the temple and brought it to the assembly platform of the village (*sadar*). The place was packed with people, who witnessed the final collective (*matam*) sacrifice to the goddess, presided over by the Rona *saukar*. A goat was killed, but its meat would only be distributed later. The men who had fasted would be allowed to eat the head, while the meat from the body was to be distributed to all of the houses. Along with the many visitors from other villages, all of the women from Komra arrived, proudly lifting up their Bali baskets, which they had taken out of the inner rooms of their houses. The wheat had sprouted about 20 centimeters over the

Photo 8.12: Dancing Bima
The Bima, equipped with big cigars, thorny branches and braided straw sticks.

last ten days, with the upper half of the shoots yellow because of the turmeric water that had been applied to them and the lower part pale white.

After this last sacrifice, all present moved in a long procession to the wet-rice fields outside the village. The senior *gurumai* carried the Bali deity – this time the clay pot, bow and arrow were taken along – and led the procession with the *pujari*, followed by the Bima, who carried the bamboo containers (*ara*) with their sprouts, the bamboo sticks, *chatreng* grass and other branches they had collected in the "forest" earlier. Most of them also still wore their sacred threads indicating their special status. The Bima were followed by other ritual actors, including the Dombo musicians beating the drums and all the women and men of the village. Young boys and girls lay across the path, so that this auspicious procession had to pass over them, which also involved carefully stepping on their bodies without hurting them.

When the procession reached the harvested paddy fields, all of the sacred objects were placed there and the river deities (Kamni) received their offerings again, an egg and a white chicken. The Bima were the first to take out their wheat shoots and wash the sand off their roots. All the women then dispersed over the fields, doing the same with their own plants. A few minutes later, the whole scene was buzzing with people who carried the washed wheat shoots

Photo 8.13: A demonstration of divine power
The Bima bring a banana tree to the temple, which they have uprooted somewhere in the village (also note the decorative paper-helicopter on the top right).

in their left hands and sought partners to establish or continue the "thread friendship" (*suta moitr*). To do this, two people would place a few of their wheat plants behind the ear of another person – I did not observe any restriction in terms of gender or age – who reciprocated with the same action. Both would then bow to each other to complete the transaction and confirm the bond thus established. Subsequently, people returned to their homes, hosting guests from other villages. With this sequence, the Bali Jatra in Komra ended. Three days later, when the mural inside the temple was washed off the wall, the ritual threads of the Bima were cut and the actors resumed their normal status.

8.4 The Bali Jatra in Komra — 345

Photo 8.14: Bali "flowers"
Women gather at the meeting place with their baskets of sprouting wheat.

Photo 8.15: Procession to the paddy fields to exchange "flowers"

Photo 8.16: Auspicious footsteps
On their way to the paddy fields, the Bima step on children that lie on the path.

8.5 Discussion and Interpretation: Affinity and Kingship

In my view, among the most pervasive and fundamental features of the Bali Jatra are the themes of affinity and female fertility. Georg Pfeffer (e.g., 1982, 1997, 2019) and Robert Parkin (1992) have thoroughly demonstrated that affinity in tribal Middle India is of a particular kind. Being a consequence of the ubiquitous contrast of clan brothers and marriageable others (*bai* and *bondu*), in terms of social structure affinity connects collective local units, especially villages, through the generations by the exchange of "daughter-sisters" (*ji-bouni*). As Pfeffer puts it: "normative marriage alliance between villages is a regular feature" (Pfeffer 2004, 403). These exchanges are generally symmetrical, although some communities allow reciprocation only after an interval of one or more generations (Hardenberg 2018a; Pfeffer 2004). The Gadaba and most of the other communities in Koraput,[24] regularly practice what has been

---

[24] Pfeffer (2019, 155) states that among the communities of the "Koraput Complex" only the Bondo "prohibit cross-cousin marriages."

Photo 8.17: Sacrifice for the river deities
A sacrifice is performed in the paddy fields before the Bali "flowers" are distributed.

called "cross-cousin marriage," whereby, a wife's husband's father is also her actual (or classificatory) mother's brother. These ideas of affinity – symmetrical exchange combined with an "oscillating hierarchy" (in terms of seniority) between bride-givers and bride-takers (Pfeffer 2004, 404) – also manifests in kinship terminologies.

However, these crucial features of social structure and kinship classification do not exhaust the scope of affinity as a value in the worldviews of the indigenous population. The opposition of "brotherhood" and "otherhood" (Gregory 2009, 2010), and thus of clanship and affinity, permeate and structure the lifeworld of the Desia in manifold ways. When it comes to annual village festivals involving the collective consumption of sacrificial food, the brothers belonging to the group of earth people (*matia*) claim and assert their ritual seniority by sharing the superior sacrificial food or *tsoru* (containing head and liver), while affines residing in their village are only eligible for the inferior sacrificial food (*lakka'*), prepared from the victim's body. Here, brotherhood hierarchically encompasses affinity (Berger 2015, 2018). While affines are thus subordinate in the context of annual sacrificial village rituals that stress consanguineal autochthony, affinal relationships are vital in the making of a person throughout the process of the life-cycle. The process of marriage, and the wedding rituals more specifically, are just the most obvious of those transformations of the person. As I have shown for the Gadaba (Berger 2015), affines, most notably the mother's brother (the actual maternal uncle or someone from his group) – the giver of "milk," that is, his sister – is indispensable for the development of the person in ritual terms through the feeding of sacrificial food. The sacrificial consumption of both agnatic and affinal relatedness is crucial for the ritual growth of the person. Marriage completes this process, while death rituals reverse it again.

The final death ritual among the Gadaba, to be discussed in the next chapter, has been described by Georg Pfeffer (2001, 111) as a superior form of marriage, in which, rather than affines exchanging brides, agnates transact the dead. Seen from this perspective, individuals go through a series of weddings. Common among several Desia communities are so-called "path weddings" (Berger 2015, 237–45; Otten 2010). Among the Gadaba, children who have been seriously ill temporarily engage in a close relationship with the agent of illness (e.g., the Rau demon), they are "married to" the demon for a while, until the promise of a massive sacrificial ritual is fulfilled, in which a multitude of deities are present and the relationship is severed again. Other communities, such as the Rona, celebrate "weddings" (*biba*) even more often, leading Otten (2021, 319) to remark that "highlanders may be said to lead a life of weddings." Such "weddings" thus not only institute relationships between human individuals and groups, but also involve non-human agents such as deities or demons.

The value of affinity goes further still, traversing and connecting the ontologies of humans, animals, plants and the landscape. Consanguinity and affinity as the principal modes of relatedness also inform how the Gadaba (and possibly other Desia as well) perceive land and crops. Finger millet grown on the dry fields (*poda*) around the village is considered consanguineal, as "children of the village," while rice fields constructed in the river beds are considered affinal and the rice harvest is brought into the village as a bride. Bringing in the rice is a kind of wedding, and the harvest and wedding song are one and the same. The Go'ter ritual likewise has to be understood against the background of this classification of crops and fields and the elementary opposition of brotherhood and affinity as values. As numerous creation myths of the region demonstrate, some of which I have already referred to above, the creation of affinity out of consanguinity, the transformation of the primordial siblings into spouses by divine intervention, is the very precondition of humanity. Moreover, also the mythical transformation of the siblings into rice (Ganga) and millet (Nandi) is related to this set of ideas, as I have argued at the end of the last chapter.

Affinity can thus generally be understood as encompassing modes of relatedness that are crucial for the regeneration of life and that include symbols of femininity which stress the life-giving power of women. Cows, milk, rice and flowers are among such ubiquitous symbols of female fertility, and some of these symbols are also prominent in the Bali Jatra, a festival that is dominated by women. True, the Bima are important male characters, both in the epic and in the rituals, but they are, above all, maternal uncles; they are brothers of a sister. They are the facilitators of female fertility for the reproduction of humans and crops.

In the various stories, the Bima (one or several) is consistently depicted as a mother's brother. He is the maternal uncle of Jema and Lolit in the Bali Jatra epic, of the goddess of rice and wealth (Sita Penu Lahi Penu) among the Dongria and, indirectly, also the maternal uncle of the original human siblings in the Pengo creation myth (M8). These siblings are born from the earth and thus in this sense are children of the earth goddess, the latter being Bima's (elder) sister, both in the Pengo and Dongria stories. Comparable to the Dom Raja discussed in a previous chapter, the Bima's role in the Pengo and Dongria myths is negative and selfish, they try to obstruct Lahi Penu when she wants to take the seeds to the human world; they take "flowers" – both the girl and her seeds – from the Bali Jatra performed by humans (M10). In contrast, the Bima of the Bali Jatra epic seems to be thoroughly positive and providing. As I have argued in the interlude, in the epic, Bima makes three substantial affinal gifts: that of his sisters, who marry Shaliman and Mahapatra; that of agriculture; and that of Phulseri, a metaphor for rice, as I have suggested.

The significance of women in their various roles cannot be overlooked in the festival. The *gurumai* are the custodians of the epic that they narrate and through which they represent the Bali deity, also called Pat Gurumai, according to Otten. Jema is the initiator of the wedding of Lolit and Phulseri, and in the festival the Jema play a key role as well. In fact, in some way, they seem to represent the whole festival, as it is also referred to as Jema Bali, and the main basket carried by the *gurumai* is called "Jema basket." While the Bima are also important for inviting the manifold deities into the Bali house during the sessions of the trance-dances, it is especially the women – Jema, and others without a specific role – who embody the gods and goddesses during those nights. Rather than men, all of the women of the village are vital for Bali worship, as they fetch sand from the river and let the seeds sprout inside their houses.

Many elements of the Bali Jatra have the character of a ritual "test" (*porikia*) that proves divine presence and benevolent power: sitting on thorns and standing on swords without being harmed, sitting or standing on earthen pots and not breaking them and germinating plants under adverse circumstances. All the fertile soil is washed away and the seeds have to sprout in sand, after being placed in the dark next to the central pillar of the house. Through worship and care, the women nevertheless succeed in getting the seeds to sprout, which they proudly present on the final day. The Pengo story (M10) about the sand festival also aptly demonstrates female involvement in the growth of seeds. When the principal girl becomes angry because she is unhappy with a marriage proposal, the seeds do not sprout, and when she is led away from the village by the middle Bima in a romantic but deceptive elopement, the seeds in the village stop growing. In a festival associated with former flower-makers (Mali), whose name ("sand festival") indexes the flowers to be, which narrates and enacts the wedding of a flower (Phulseri) to a king (Lolit Raja), that entails the divinely inspired growth of flowers (seeds) by flowers (women) and which ends with the exchange of flowers (seedlings), everything depends on women.[25]

In addition to the theme of affinity and female fertility, the second aspect I want to highlight here is the connection of the Bali Jatra to the king, a link which comes to the fore in different ways. One obvious feature is the sprouting of wheat over several days. This also had a prominent place in the royal Dasara proceedings in Bastar and returned in the context of the Boirobi sacrifice of the Rona of Badigor, albeit with different seeds. Furthermore, kingship becomes visible especially in the epic that is so closely related to the festival – both with regard to the mural and the ritual performances – and, finally, in the fact that a particular type of Bali Jatra has been celebrated by the former kings in Jeypore.

The epic makes it clear that the protagonists of the first generation, the divine ancestors of humans, were already kings and queens. The main transformation in

---

25 The association of postpubescent girls and women with "flowers" is very widespread, in Koraput and beyond. This becomes, for instance, evident in the context of weddings, marriage negotiations and betrothals. A Pengo story contains the following, very realistic, conversation between villagers who come to ask for a bride and the girl's party: "'Relations by marriage from Bihagura [lit. "wedding-village"], why have you come?' 'Nay, we have come to your place, that of our uncles and maternal grandfathers; there is a flower, for that reason we have come.' 'Does she suit you or not?' 'She does suit us, so we have come; we shall be able to wear the flower, so we have come.' 'Will you really be able to wear the flower?'" (Burrow and Bhattacharya 1970, 126). From his notes of his fieldwork in Bastar, Chris Gregory provided me with a section of a very similar conversation between affines in the context of a betrothal. The boy's party had come because "a flower had blossomed in the house (of the girl)" and "the scent of that flower" had reached their (the boy's) village. Then they ask if they would be "given that flower to wear." (Gregory, personal communication) But also in the context of birth the flower imagery is very much present. For instance is the placenta (and the child until the name giving ritual) referred to as "flower" (*phul*) among the Gadaba (Berger 2015) and also the Bondo word *sari* means "flower" as well as "placenta" (Bhattacharya 1968, 125 #2500). The parallelism between the lotus flower and the placenta in relation to the symbolism of Laksmi (and rice) has especially been worked out by Christ Gregory (2018) with reference to his fieldwork in Bastar in particular. "Flowers" thus refer to the regenerative powers of women generally. On fertility and "life" as a female value among the Dongria see Hardenberg (2018a, 609–14).

the mode of livelihood occurs when the Bima introduces agriculture and the foragers turn into cultivators and consequently also into sacrificers. There would be no successful cultivation without sacrifice. However, the sacrifice is of a particular kind and also accomplishes more than just a plentiful harvest. I would assume that because they are kings they require an extraordinary sacrificial victim. Given the prominence of the imagery (if not former actual practice) of human sacrifice in the region – such as the story of Bima Raja and Bima Rani sacrificing their son, which I mentioned above – it would not be inconceivable that there are versions of the epic in which not a rhino but a human being was sacrificed, as the former kings in Jeypore and Nandapur were obliged to do, as Birsa Sisa insisted. Burying the flesh of a human victim – like a seed – creates wealth.

The Kond offer the most famous example of this regenerative practice (Hardenberg 2018a, 576ff), but a Pengo story, with many parallels to a Kond myth presented by Thurston (1909a, 368–71), also clearly makes this point. In this story, a sister, who regularly cooks for her brothers, cuts herself one day and her blood falls into the food. As the brothers realize how much sweeter the food tastes, they kill her and start eating the flesh. The youngest brother, however, does not want to eat of the flesh of his sister and instead takes it away and buries it in the sand along a river, where a "flower tree" (*puy mar*) immediately springs up and produces all kinds of wealth (*dan*), including gold and silver, money, domestic animals, grain and more (Burrow and Bhattacharya 1970, 144–51).

The sacrifice of the rhino in the Bali Jatra epic also transforms the lifestyle of the two couples completely. While Shaliman Raja, his brother Mahapatra and their wives Nila Devi and Kota Devi formerly lived in huts made from branches and leaves, at the place where the rhino's head is buried a fort appears. Subsequently, they are truly recognizable as kings. The name of this fort is instructive. Otten translates Databeli Gada as "'givers-palace-fort'" (2014, 260), but the name, I would suggest, is actually a reference to the sacrificial process itself and its consequences. *Data* indeed refers to a "donor" (Gustafsson 1989, 257), a provider of sacrifices, whereas *beli* signifies the fruits of that practice. It literally means "offspring" or "increase" and is mostly related to domestic animals (Gustafsson 1989, 393). A *beli gai*, for example, is a cow that gives birth to many calves (Mahapatra 1985, 264). The Bali Jatra epic, therefore, presents us with the common theme of increaser-kings (Gonda 1956a), whose wealth – and that of their country – is the consequence of their role as sacrificers.

The increaser-kings of Jeypore also celebrated the Bali Jatra in their capital. Sahu's *The Hill Tribes of Jeypore* (1942) provides a photograph of a "Balijatra

Group,"[26] with some 40 people in the palace compound, all with headdresses and many with drums. This royal Bali Jatra was performed in the rainy season and was thus called Osa Bali, referring to the month of August/September (*osa*). It preceded the Dasara, with which it was associated, and the sprouting seeds are one obvious parallel between both festivals. Rousseleau (2008, 82) mentions that nine different kinds of seeds used to be sown in the royal Bali Jatra, which then sprouted for nine days in the palace compound in the vicinity of the shrine of Kanaka Durga. He also mentions that along with Dombo musicians the Mali also had a role in the royal Dasara, as they played the "Bali Drums," perhaps those that can be seen in the photograph.

Based on conversations with a person who actually participated in the royal Bali Jatra in the 1960s, Otten (2014) provides us with more details. Several Bali shrines used to be set up for the festival, not only inside the palace, but also at Purnagad, where the Kalkika temple is located, and at other places. The Osa Bali was and still is celebrated in villages, especially in Rona villages, which again underlines their special relationship to the king and to kingship. As far as the ritual sequence is concerned, the royal Bali Jatra seems to have been performed in much the same way as the one described in this chapter: the Bali deity was represented by a clay pot, winnowing fan, bow and arrow; the *gurumai* had a crucial role to play; and the bringing of sand and the sowing of seeds also occurred. An additional feature of the royal Bali Jatra was the dramatic performances (*natho*), perhaps of the Bali Jatra epic. In contrast to the dominance of female actors in the Bali Jatra discussed in this chapter, such staged dramas – that also had some prominence at the time of my fieldwork (Berger 2015, 393) – only featured men, also in female roles.[27] One aspect that was not mentioned in Otten's brief description of the Osa Bali are the murals, so we do not know if they were a part of the Bali Jatra shrines in Jeypore.

In my view, the most important detail of Otten's description of the Osa Bali concerns the distribution of the "sand flowers" (Bali Phul) at the end of the festival. The exchange of Bali Phul in Komra – and also in the village performances discussed by Otten (2009, 2014)[28] – took place between the participants of the festival to establish ritual friendships. As far as I could discern, this exchange occurred between anybody, irrespective of gender, age or community.

---

26 Sahu 1942, opposite of page 25; I cannot recognize many details on the poor copy at my disposal.
27 Otten (2014, 47) provides a photograph from 1960.
28 Otten states that the sprouts are given to "friends, relatives and to people one would like to be friends with" (2014, 266). In the other contribution she writes that the sand flowers are "exchanged between friends and neighbours" (2009, 41).

8.5 Discussion and Interpretation: Affinity and Kingship

The Osa Bali presents us with a variant of the transaction of sand flowers, as the sprouts had first "to be handed over to the king" (Otten 2009, 48):

> Therefore, the men proceeded to the *Dussehra* ground. The king sat on an elephant in a golden *palanquin*; his guests next to him on animals with silver *palanquins*. Among the guests, officers and functionaries, martial arts contests were performed, awards like gold or linen clothes being given to the winners. Afterwards, the *Gurumai* handed the first *bali phul* over to the king. The representatives of the villages did so as well before beginning to exchange *bali phul* amongst themselves. The king then proceeded to his palace where he exchanged *bali phul* with his friends and ministers, while the tribal people exchanged the *bali phul* among their friends and neighbours on the *Dussehra* ground. (Otten 2009, 48)

Otten's description is important in several ways. The connection between the Bali Jatra and the Dasara festival becomes apparent through the demonstrations of royal grandeur – including palanquins on elephants – as well as the performance of martial arts and, in particular, with regard to the location, the Dasara ground, which was the destination of the procession on the last day of Dasara in Jeypore. Most importantly, the "sand flower" transactions entailed a vertical and it seems an asymmetrical dimension as well, similar to paying tribute (*raja beti*) during Dasara. The *gurumai*, who were the first to hand over the "sand flowers" to the king, probably took them from the different Bali shrines where they had led the ritual proceedings over the previous nine days of the festival. They were followed by the villagers, who offered their seedlings to the king. We do not know where those seedlings came from, but I would speculate that the representatives of local communities brought them from their nearby villages to the Dasara ground, where they first presented sprouts to the king before exchanging them among themselves. On the basis of Otten's description, it seems that the king did not reciprocate this gift, as is the case when the flowers are exchanged horizontally.

Different kinds of intersections between kings and tribes have been reported to have occurred during the Dasara celebrations, as I discussed in a previous chapter. In Bastar, the tribal subjects famously abducted the king and then shared their food with him in the forest, an equalizing activity. In the context of the Jeypore Dasara, the first rice was brought from Nandapur (the Kotni Mala Hill) to be consumed by the king, but whether or not this practice included commensality among king and subjects we do not know. In all cases, tribal villagers brought their local deities to the capital, mostly in the form of flag poles (*lati*), thus performing "pole offerings" (*lati bog*). What the tribal villagers brought to Jeypore during the Osa Bali – and the *gurumai* presumably from the various shrines of the town – was the auspicious result of the festival, the visible signs of their success as sacrificers and proof that they could be certain of the divine support of their deities, who had visited their Bali houses during the trance-dances.

While the king distributed the "sand flowers" to his relatives and subordinates – perhaps flowers from the Bali shrine in his palace compound – he had first received the flower blessings of his tribal subjects. Why would this matter were it not for the fact that the king acknowledged the sacrificial sovereignty of his people and their skills in ritually navigating the flow of life?

Finally, one might ask, why is it *"Mali*'s" Bali? The connections between Dasara and the king, and the Nandi and Ganga festivals with the Joria, seem obvious enough. Although most, if not all, communities of the region celebrate Dasara in their villages, it is explicitly connected to the king and to former visits of his subjects to Jeypore to pay *raja beti*. Likewise, even if there are a few other communities such as the Ollar Gadaba that perform the Nandi festival in a limited way, the latter can be clearly identified with the Joria, and to my knowledge no community other than the Joria celebrates both festivals that belong to and refer to each other, the millet and the rice festivals. The Bali Jatra, by contrast, seems to be celebrated by many communities, and the role of the Mali in the Bali Jatra of Komra may be perceived to be marginal.

Possibly, the question of "Why Mali's Bali?" is connected to another, "Why wheat?" Despite the relevance of rice in the epic and the rituals, wheat is very prominent in the latter. As far as the seedlings are concerned, wheat seeds are considered very important, certainly in Komra, where only seeds of wheat were sown. But also in the Bali Jatra festivals documented by Otten, where the women sowed rice, maize and beans along with wheat, the latter were ascribed the most value (Otten 2009, 39). Otten is right, I think, when she considers the relevance of wheat to be related to the migration history of both the Mali and their festival (2014, 269). Like the king's Dasara, in which wheat seeds are also made to sprout, the Bali Jatra may thus be a festival that originally came from outside the region, which has been appropriated and adapted by various local communities.

The Bali Jatra of the Dongria may be a very recent example of this process. While the festival is thought of as very important by the Dongria, it has only been adopted recently, around the beginning of this millennium (Hardenberg 2014). Moreover, Hardenberg points out that, in contrast to other Dongria rituals, such as the buffalo sacrifice, the Bali Jatra links the local community with the outside world. The external connection is thus very explicit in the case of the Dongria, who have nevertheless indigenized the festival in significant ways, for example, by including a buffalo sacrifice, constructing wooden posts representing the deities in the rituals, and identifying the Bali deity with Lahi Penu, the goddess of rice and wealth.

While Mali are not particularly associated with wheat, as they do not traditionally cultivate cereals at all, they are associated with flowers and the making of garlands, and they are said to have gone to Jeypore to provide that service to the king. As such, they are "flower-people," if I may adapt the translation of "Mali" in the Pengo story provided by Burrow and Bhattacharya. It may be this association with flowers that links the Mali in the regional imagination to a festival in which "flowers" of different kinds (e.g. human and plant) are vital. That the Bali flowers are seedlings of wheat may be important with respect to identifying the historical origin of the Mali and the festival, from the perspective of the participants it may be of little relevance.

The epic and the mural, which is a visual manifestation of the narrative, are most likely among the elements that make the Bali Jatra the festival of the Mali. Although, in Komra, the epic was sung by two *gurumai* from the Rona community, the epic itself – at least in the way it was recorded by Otten – makes a clear link to the Mali, such as in the sequence mentioned when Pat Gurumai directly announces her request to the Mali to receive rice (Otten 2014, 272). In Komra, the Mali were also indispensable when it came to painting the mural. Other people, young and old, even ethnographers, could add images, but the main central wall of the mural, representing the divine characters of the epic, had to be painted by the Mali. One may thus assume that the mural and the epic, the visual as well as the sonic/discursive divine forms of the Bali Jatra, are key to identifying the Bali Jatra as the signature festival of the Mali.

Much more research needs be done to better understand the epic and the mural in order to assess variations in and commonalities of this festival within Koraput and in relation to its performance in the adjacent districts of Nowrangpur and Rayagada. At the least, the murals Otten (2009, 42) and I documented in the same region look very much alike. At the same time, in their aesthetics and materiality they seem to be quite different from other wall paintings of the region. They stand in contrast, for example, with the Joria mural of the Nandi festival or Dongria wall paintings (Hardenberg 2018a, 429, 504; Jena et al. 2002, plates XV, XXXIII), in which we find mostly abstract patterns and cosmic symbols, such as stars, sun and moon. Moreover, they also differ from the Sora wall paintings, which represent the houses of the ancestors. While the latter do include human figures, animals, bicycles and many other features, and are similar to the Bali Jatra mural in this sense, the Sora "nearly always" (Elwin 1951, 188) paint in white (rice-flour mixed in water) on a wall first painted with a red earth color. One may thus venture an informed guess that the style of the wall painting may also indicate an external origin.

9 Transformations of the Dead: The Go'ter of the Gadaba

Unlike the other festivals mentioned in the proverb, the Go'ter of the Gadaba is neither about kings, nor about gods. It is a death ritual and as such not concerned with inviting deities into the human realm to manifest in bodies, objects or wall-paintings, to play and to dance, but aims at transforming the dead (*duma*) into ancestors (*anibai*). Another feature that distinguishes the Go'ter from other festivals is that it has been, comparatively speaking, well studied. One of the most renowned ethnographers of tribal India and Nepal, Christoph von Fürer-Haimendorf, who visited the Gadaba and Bondo in April and May 1941, regarded the Go'ter as evidence that the Gadaba belong to the southernmost Indian branch of what he called the "megalithic civilization" of Southeast Asia (Fürer-Haimendorf 1943, 177). The first professional anthropologist who actually observed the ritual in 1952 – Karl Gustav Izikowitz, who, not by chance, was a specialist of mainland Southeast Asia – was reminded by the Go'ter of the *potlatch* of Northwest Coast Indians (Izikowitz 1969, 148). Indeed, the Go'ter fits squarely within the concept of a "total social fact" (Mauss 2016) and had Mauss known the ritual he would have probably discussed it in what was to become the most influential text in the history of anthropology. It was exactly this dimension of exchange that stood in the center of the analyses of Georg Pfeffer, who documented the Go'ter in the 1980s (Pfeffer 1984, 1991, 2001). My own work with the Gadaba started in 1996, with an intensive period of nearly two years of ethnographic fieldwork between 1999 and 2003 and shorter stays in the region thereafter.

The ritual not only attracted the attention of anthropologists but also of zealous reformers. Accordingly, Fürer-Haimendorf (1943, 153, fn. 2) already considered the ritual itself to be near dead because of the influential "Congress social uplift propaganda" of the time, which opposed all kinds of indigenous practices and targeted this ritual that had been designated as "barbaric", "hideous", "monstrous", "murderous" and "horrible" even in the pages of *Man in India* (Somasundaram 1949). However, despite ongoing pressure from the lowland mainstream culture (Berger 2014), early reports of the death of the ritual seem to have been exaggerated, as I was able to observe and document the Go'ter in different villages about 60 years after von Fürer-Haimendorf made the first tentative steps in understanding it. Elsewhere, I have discussed the different contributions and interpretations by Fürer-Haimendorf, Izikowitz and Pfeffer, presented a detailed description and analysis of one particular instance I observed – the Go'ter in Ponosguda to which I will return below – and discussed the Go'ter as a part of the encompassing ritual system of the Gadaba (Berger 2007, 2010, 2015, 2017).[1] In this chapter, I will especially highlight those aspects of the Go'ter that are of particular relevance when comparing it to the other festivals discussed in this book.

9.1 The Gadaba

Although the word Gadaba has also been applied to other communities, for instance, the Parenga (Gorum), it properly refers to two communities, the Gutob Gadaba and the Ollar Gadaba, the latter being regarded as "younger brothers" of the former. Gutob means "creature of the earth" (Griffiths 2008, 675) and refers to the people and their language, which is an Austroasiatic tongue of the South Munda branch.[2] The meaning of Ollar is unclear but likewise designates the people[3] and their Dravidian language.[4] In myths (M1, M12), the name Gadaba is derived from the Godavari River, their mythical place of origin.

Generally speaking, Nandapur lies in between the two Gadaba communities, the Gutob villages lying to the West, the Ollar villages to the East of the former royal capital. Numbers are difficult to verify, and the Census offers no help as it does not distinguish the Gutob from Ollar Gadaba. There may be perhaps some 20,000 Gutob Gadaba, while their junior brothers may be twice as numerous.[5] My own work – and also that of Fürer-Haimendorf, Izikowitz and Pfeffer – has focused on the Gutob Gadaba, but as far as I can say, there is little that distinguishes the communities, apart from their languages.

Go'ter is, or has been, performed by both communities, as well as by some of their neighbors, such as the Parenga and also some Dombo. Pfeffer (2001) reported that the Western Gutob villages bordering the Bondo area – some Eastern Gutob even refer to them as "Bondo-Gadaba" – have discontinued the

---

1 Next to the authors mentioned, also Das Kornel (1999, 61–72) and S.C. Pradhan (1998) have presented ethnographic data on the Go'ter. Padhi's (2011) relatively recent book does not provide new ethnography.
2 My monograph (Berger 2015) deals with the ethnography of the Gutob Gadaba in some detail. More concise overviews of their religion and society can be found elsewhere (Berger 2017, 2021). Moreover, see Goud (1991) with regard to Gutob Gadaba culture and language, Mohanty (1973/4) on ritual friendship, Pfeffer (1999) on kinship terminology and Nayak (et al. 1996) for a general description of the Gutob Gadaba in the context of development work. On the Gutob language see Griffiths (2008) and Rajan and Rajan (2001a–c).
3 See Thusu and Jha (1972), Sasikumar (1997) and Subba Rao and Patnaik (1992).
4 On the Ollari language see Bhattacharya (1957) and Bhaskararao (2019).
5 The Statistical Profile of Scheduled Tribes in India (2013, 158ii–158iv) provides the number of 84.689 Gadaba, which includes not only the Gutob and Ollar but also some 10.000 Parenga.

performance of the Go'ter, and to my knowledge no Go'ter has been performed in this Western region in recent decades. From Fürer-Haimendorf (1943), it is clear, however, that the villages of the Western region he visited – Onmail, Boro Drueil, Gadabapada, Kujam – used to celebrate the Go'ter as well. All descriptions of the ritual from the 1950s onwards refer to the Eastern Gutob villages closer to Nandapur. The reason for this decline in the Western part of the Gutob Gadaba area is unclear. It is only in this region, however, that a variant of the Go'ter is performed, the Ungon Go'ter, where rather than buffaloes, crabs (*ungon*) are tied to *simli* trees to represent the dead. Fürer-Haimendorf (1943) mentioned this ritual, and I attended such a ritual in 1999 in the village of Gutalpada. In my experience, Gutob Gadaba from the eastern villages do not perform the crab Go'ter and do not seem to take this version of the ritual too seriously.

I will now briefly mention a few aspects of Gadaba social structure that are worth knowing when approaching the Go'ter ritual. As among all Desia, the village is a crucial unit in every respect, that is, in political, economic, social and ritual terms. Ideal-typically, each Gadaba[6] village consists of one clan (*bonso*), the "earth people" (*matia*) of the place, who have the right to share sacrificial food with their local deities and who cultivate the land. Gutob Gadaba distinguish four clans or, to be more specific, unilineal totemic descent categories (*bonso*), namely Cobra, Tiger, Sun and Monkey; Ollar Gadaba feature, in addition, Fish, Cow, Hawk and Bear. Thus, we would find Cobra villages, Monkey villages and so on. In fact, all larger villages also have "late comers" (*upria*), inhabitants who arrived in the village after the earth people had already settled there. These are non-cultivating Desia communities, such as Dombo, blacksmiths or herders. However, other Gadaba may also have settled in the village of the earth people as their internal affines. In any case, as will become clear from the descriptions of inter-village relationships, generally, brides come from outside the village.

The earth people of each village segment further into four local descent groups (*kuda*) that constitute the ritual unit of the Four Brothers (*chari bai*): Sisa, Kirsani, Munduli and Boronaik. These title groups are associated with certain ritual and other roles. The village sacrificer is recruited from the Sisa group (and called *sisa* or *pujari*) and the Kirsani provide the sacrificial cook (called *kirsani* or *randari*). The *kuda* classification cuts across, so to speak, the organization of clans (*bonso*). All four *kuda* groups are found in every village, be it a Cobra or Monkey village, at least in theory. In practice, one or more of the *kuda* groups may be lacking in any particular village for demographic or historical reasons. A local group may have died out or a village may have split up along

---

6 When I speak of Gadaba in the following I am referring to the Gutob Gadaba in particular.

kuda lines. Except the title, the Sisa of one village have nothing in common with the Sisa of another. Members of the two Sisa groups may decide to intermarry, or choose not to do so; or they may engage in Go'ter exchange relationships (to be explained below), or not. In inter-village relationships, clanship is much more important. For a Cobra village, all other villages featuring earth people of different clans are potential affines and all other Cobra villages are "brothers" and thus (potential) Go'ter exchange partners.

Like all Desia villages, a Gadaba village features many sacred places, inside the village proper and in the surrounding hills. Usually, these places are only "sacred" in ritual contexts and are otherwise not given much attention. In the village center lies the shrine of the earth-deity (*hundi*) and opposite it the megalithic assembly platform (*sadar*) is found, a collection of flat and upright stones slabs. The *sadar* is the place for formal meetings to discuss village affairs, but villagers also just hang out there, sharpen their knives or axes at the stones and chat. The most important shrine outside the village is called Pat Kanda ("great sword", among other names), which is dedicated to the celestial god (Dorom) or Sun Moon deity (Sī Arke).

Again, like all tribes of the plateau, the Gadaba cultivate finger millet (*mandia, sa'mel*) and wet rice (*dan, kerong*) as their main staple crops (see Chapter 6). Millet is cultivated on the dry fields (*poda, langbo*) surrounding the village and at the foot of the hills, while wet rice is cultivated in the terraced beds of the rivers (*bera, liong*) that provide a perennial flow of water.

Alongside millet as the most important dry field crop, dry rice (*poda dan*), little millet (*suan, iri'*) and niger seed (*olsi*) are also cultivated on the dry fields. These fields are conceptually associated with the village (*ga, ungom*) as consanguineal, belonging to the brotherhood of the earth people. This aspect becomes particularly significant in the Go'ter. The third category of land is the forest-cum-hill (*dongor, bon*, there is only one word for both in Gutob, *birong*), the hills surrounding the village where, generally, rather than forest, dense scrub is found. Shifting cultivation (*podu*) plays a marginal role and is only performed by those who do not have enough land in the other two categories. In addition to cultivation of these cereals, in the rainy season, gardens (*bogicha, aro*) are kept next to the houses, where various beans, leafy vegetables and pumpkins are grown. Catching fish or crabs in the rivers and collecting tubers in the hills complements the other subsistence activities. Hunting (*bet, gu'um*) is mostly a ritual activity in the context of the Chait Porbo, the most important annual festival in the month of March/April (*chait*).

Photo 9.1: Gadaba women transplanting paddy, 1941
Photograph by Christoph von Fürer-Haimendorf, May 1941, possibly the village of Kujam (reprinted with permission; SOAS, PP MS19/6/GADA/0170)
After the festival in the month of April (Chait Porbo), Gadaba women transplant the rice seedlings in the terraced bed of a river. The large ear rings (*are sil*) that pierce the auricle and their dress (*kisalo'*) distinguished Gadaba women from all others in the region and are frequently referred to in local myths. Around the year 2000 women still wore this garment in some Gutob Gadaba villages, while it had already completely disappeared in others.

9.2 Embodiments of the Dead

The Go'ter is the fourth and final step in the lengthy process of death. Even after the first three rituals have ensured that the social aspect of the deceased person, called *duma*, is no longer dangerous or a part of the community of the living, they are still considered to linger on in and around the village and potentially to cause trouble. These *duma* still receive offerings on certain occasions, on the cremation ground and under the eaves of the houses. While the dead may receive all kinds of offerings, crabs (*kankara*, *ungon*), which are especially caught by the Gadaba in the mud embankments of the wet-rice fields, are the only animals that are exclusively sacrificed to the dead. Before most important ritual activities and festivals, crabs are sacrificed to the dead in a brief ritual called Duma Balo' (Berger 2015, 227). Presumably, crabs are iconic of the dead, as they are considered to dig tunnels into the earth and thus link the middle world (*mojapur*) of humans to the underworld (*patalpur*) of the dead.

A Parenga story (Elwin 1954, 235) narrates that humans died in the middle world:

> (. . .) but there was no path by which their ghosts could ascend to the Upper World or descend to the Lower World. So they had to remain on earth and were a nuisance to everyone. Ispur Mahaprabhu said to himself, "I must do something about this." He took a *siari* [Bauhinia vahlii] leaf and peeled off the fibres and threw them on the ground saying, "Make a path to the Upper World." The fibre turned into a spider and it spun a thread for the ghosts to climb by. Mahaprabhu picked up a *siari* seed and held it in his hand. He threw it on the ground saying, "Make a path to the Lower World." The seed turned into a crab and it dug a burrow for the ghosts to descend by.[7]

While crabs are thus crucial sacrificial animals in rituals for the dead, as they enable the latter to visit the world of humans, the *duma* are embodied in the Go'ter rituals – unless it is a crab Go'ter – by other means, notably as living water buffaloes (*por, bongtel*). As the myth above also makes clear, the dead accumulate in the realm of the living and are still considered potentially troublesome. This is also the reason the Gadaba mention as to why performing the Go'ter is necessary. However, there are also other pressures which prompt a local group to perform the ritual, as I will discuss below. The Go'ter revives the dead for one last time and provides each person who has died since the last such occasion with a new buffalo body which allows them to enjoy large quantities of food and beer for several days in the midst of their relatives, and especially in the company of women who mourn and feed the buffalo-dead. Even if the actual death of the person occurred many years before, women express their sorrow about the demise of their kin, and at certain moments in the ritual this is done dramatically, with loud wailing, talking to the dead and feeding them, beating their chests, tearing out their hair and scratching their cheeks, sometimes until they bleed.

Another kind of body is also provided in the course of the ritual, which is to be inhabited by the spirit-turned-ancestor, namely various stone slabs. Like human bodies, and also like the buffaloes in the Go'ter, the stones are washed with turmeric water and sometimes also anointed with oil (Kornel 1999). Such lithic embodiments of the dead are nothing extraordinary in tribal Central India. Vitebsky, for instance, writes with regard to the Sora: "On the day the stone is planted it is dressed in cloth, fed with liquor, rice and the blood of

---

[7] See also two myths Elwin collected among the Gadaba and Dora. The former mentions crabs as offering to a Ghost Bird (Elwin 1954, 322) and the latter also depict crabs as road-makers between the different worlds (Elwin 1954, 297).

sacrificed buffaloes, embraced, lamented and raised upright as if representing the restauration of the deceased to some kind of life" (Vitebsky 2013, 120). Similarly, among the Joria, Rousseleau (2021) observes that the erected stones are dressed and provided for with food, drink and cigarettes, concluding, "the latter [standing stone] is now treated as the true body of the deceased, and some elderly women hug it with their arms" (Rousseleau 2021, 248). Compared to such elaborate treatments, the Gadaba pay relatively little attention to the stone bodies of their deceased, most likely, because the buffalo-dead receive most of the ritual care. Among the Gadaba (same with the Joria), these lithic ancestor-bodies come in pairs, an upright stone (*sil*) is erected and a flat stone (*sadar*) is placed at its base. When the *duma* have finally left the village in the form of buffaloes, these ancestor-stones remain. This replacement also effects a collectivization of the individual dead, who merge with the undifferentiated category of ancestors.

While the buffaloes leave the village to be killed and the stones remain immobile and unchanging as part of megalithic assemblages (apart from the number of stones increasing over time), another material representation of the dead grows and blossoms exactly during the time of the year when the Go'ter is celebrated. Branches of *simli* (silk cotton tree, *Bombax malabarica* or *Bombax ceiba*) and *palda* (*Erythrina variegate*) trees are cut and planted in the earth next to the stones and the buffaloes are tied to them. While I did not pay sufficient attention to this aspect at the time of my fieldwork, several ethnographers[8] have reported that the number of branches has to match the number of buffaloes, which means that, like the animals, the branches actually represent or are at least closely associated with each individual dead.

The Go'ter ritual thus features three very different kinds of bodies: an animal body that is killed, eaten and digested; a stone body that is erected and eternally present but unchanging; and a plant body that grows and blossoms with big bright red flowers every year at the time of this crucial transformation. Not always, but often, the planted branches strike roots and grow into trees, sometimes even embracing and lifting up the stones at their base. In contrast to the disappearing (buffaloes) or permanently present bodies (stones), the branches/trees are a vivid representation of death and regeneration. Indeed, the dead do return. While the social aspect of the dead (*duma*) is gone and transformed into ancestors, the life-force (*jibon*) is reborn and reappears after an interval, similar to the

---

8 Fürer-Haimendorf (1943, 156), Izikowitz (1969, 137), Thusu and Jha (1972, 100). With regard to the external dry-field platform I can confirm that in Ponosguda too the number of branches matched the number of the buffaloes (13). My photographs or notes do not allow any conclusive comment with regard to the village platform.

flowers of the trees. The flowers blossom every year, a life-force seeks a new human body within a few weeks or months after the death of its former host to be reborn in the alternate generation (e.g., a grandfather in one of his grandchildren). However, as will be seen, the dead return in more than one way.

A Gadaba story narrates how these trees came to be associated with the Go'ter ritual. The Gadaba had earlier erected stones for the dead and sacrificed buffaloes, so the story goes, however:

> (. . .) they [the Gadaba] did not also plant trees for them [the dead]. There was a certain shaman, whose wife was a shamanin. The shaman died first and then his widow. The villagers buried them side by side. A year later they erected stones for them, sacrificing a buffalo for the shaman and a she-buffalo for the shamanin. They put the two heads of the buffaloes by the stones and danced before them all night long. In the morning they found that a *simli* tree had grown from the buffalo's head and a *palda* tree had grown from the she-buffalo's. Ever since we have planted these trees beside the menhir stones. This causes the ghosts to die and then they give us no more trouble. For the ghost comes into the buffalo and when we kill the buffalo we kill the ghost. (. . .) (Elwin 1954, 123f)

This story makes a number of important points. It argues that the Go'ter is necessary for the ultimate transformation of the dead because, when people kill the buffalo, they also kill the dead. This echoes what Gadaba had told Izikowitz: that after the Go'ter, the *duma* are "finally dead" (Izikowitz 1969, 141). The most explicit aim of the ritual is thus to get rid of the liminal dead and to transform them into ancestors, to turn buffalo-dead into ancestor-stones. Significantly, the story makes clear that life emerges out of death, a plant emerges from the buffalo head. Moreover, it makes an existential connection between the deceased human person, the buffalo and the plant, to the degree that, like the buffalo, the plants are also distinguished with regard to the sex of the dead.

The link between the trees and the dead also becomes evident in ritual actions. In the case of the Go'ter in the village of Ponosguda – which we documented in detail in 2001 –, about two weeks before the main day of the Go'ter, the dead persons who were to receive a new buffalo body later were ritually "raised" (*duma utaibar*) by the hosts of the ritual. This is a precarious moment and a specialist (*go'ter dissari*) presided over the ritual. The names of the dead were invoked, literally "filled in" (*pokaiba*), and the dead thus activated. As soon as this had happened, drums were beaten.[9] While the hosts had now raised the dead, they also wanted to make sure that no other uninvited guests –

---

[9] This is one of the conspicuous features of the Go'ter that has been remarked upon by all ethnographers. Significantly, it is not (only) the Dombo musicians who play the drums, but the Gadaba themselves and repairing the drums is one of the first things that is done when a Go'ter is planned.

stray *duma* from some other village or those vengeful spirits who had died a bad death – felt attracted. Therefore, iron nails with "medicine" were beaten into the ground at various places, and later, before dawn, the most dangerous agent of disaster, the Rau demon, was appeased by a sacrifice. Immediately after the dead had been raised, the *dissari* fetched two pairs of branches from the *simli* and *palda* trees, which were formally received and greeted at the house by the widow of the most respected and influential person among the deceased (Ranju Kirsani). After the *rau* sacrifice, one pair of branches each was planted as "posts" (*munda*) at the two main locations of ritual activity, that is, at two different megalithic structures.

I have called these megalithic assemblages "platforms" in earlier publications and I will also use the term in the following. However, they are not elevated structures but rows of flat and upright stones referred to as *munda*, thus "posts." The trees that have developed out of the branches planted there on former occasions of the Go'ter are part of these structures. Two categories of such locations are distinguished. The first is the "village" platform (*ga munda* or *ungom munda*). There are usually several of these in a village, depending on who is hosting the ritual. Often, the hosts of a Go'ter belong to the same local descent group (*kuda*). For instance, when all Sisa of a village decide to perform the ritual, this would then occur at a collection of stones on their side of the village. Other local descent groups of the village have their own stone platforms. Alternatively, a whole village may decide to perform Go'ter, or just one of its sections (*kuda*) or sub-sections (*kutum*). Also, an individual house may decide to perform the ritual – which is then called Sudi Go'ter – as its members do not want to wait any longer for the other members of their *kutum* or *kuda* group to make a decision about whether or not to conduct the ritual. Thus, the number of platforms in a village depends on which level of the social structure the Go'ter has previously been performed.

The second kind of platform is the "dry-field" platform (*poda munda, langbo munda*), which is also called *go'ter munda*. As the name "dry-field" suggests, this megalithic assemblage lies outside the confines of the village proper, in the middle of the dry fields. Its designation as *go'ter munda* is also instructive, as it indicates that certain actions are performed at this location, to be discussed further below. There may only be one dry-field platform, or there may be several, again, based on the composition of the village along local descent lines. In Ponosguda, after raising the dead and the sacrifice to Rau, the *dissari* and the hosts planted a pair of *simli* and *palda* branches at the village platform of the hosts and outside the village at their dry-field platform.

There is yet another place where stone slabs are erected; this is the central assembly platform (*sadar*) of the village, which also consists of flat and upright stones.¹⁰ However, this megalithic assemblage is circular and sometimes elevated toward the center. I have been told by the Gadaba of Gudapada, my resident village, that only when the Sisa of a village perform the Go'ter one pair of stones is added to the *sadar*. The local descent group of sacrificers (called Sisa or Pujari) is considered to be the most senior segment of the Four Brothers of a village, and thus – like the village sacrificer during festivals – they represent the village as a whole. This means, rather theoretically, that roughly every generation a pair of stones is added. Indeed, Izikowitz (1969, 131, fn. 4) considered that the age of a village could be determined in this way, as he assumed that all of the stones would be remains of former Go'ter performances. I doubt, however, that all of the stones of the *sadar* are placed there in the context of Go'ter celebrations. As soon as a new village is founded, a shrine (*hundi*) for the local earth deity is constructed and, opposite it, the *sadar*, unconnected with the performance of a Go'ter. Also, other Desia who do not perform Go'ter at all have such meeting places. Nevertheless, for the Gadaba, the *sadar* is also associated with the Go'ter, at least in some villages, and in such cases the *sadar* unites all ancestors and is the collective representation of all generations of ancestors since the foundation of the village.¹¹

While Fürer-Haimendorf (1943, 151) is right when he states that the Gadaba are "intensely democratic," this does not mean that they do not acknowledge differences in status. This is also the case among the dead who have been raised, as one person stands out and his or her buffalo is referred to as *kutti bongtel*. It is not entirely clear what *kutti* refers to. Like all the indigenous terms discussed in this and the other chapters, this one has also been spelt in different ways by anthropologists. While Pfeffer (1991, 75) also refers to the *kutti*-buffalo, Kornel (1999, 84) spells it "Khunti" and speaks of the "Lead Buffalo." I would suggest that the word actually may relate to a wooden "post" or a "stump" (*kunt*). This would make sense insofar as it is this buffalo that is first tied to one of the *simli* branches at the village platform. The precedence of this buffalo is also made explicit in other ways. This animal is purchased first and is formally received in the village (Kornel 1999; Pfeffer 1991). It is also the first animal which is later transformed into a deceased buffalo-person by feeding it with "first rice" (*sig bat*). But who among the dead is eligible to become the *kutti bongtel*? Izikowitz (1969, 135f) mentions that this buffalo, which was described to him as *raja bongtel*, contained the *duma* of

---

10 See also Fürer-Haimendorf (1943, 154, 156).
11 In their megalithic rituals, the Bondo also erect stones at the village platform (*sadar*), which they call *sindibor*. During their final death ritual (Gunom) a dolmen is erected for a specific deceased person, however this structure of stones and *simli* trees also commemorates the dead of a whole generation, all those who have died since a dolmen was last erected in the village (Elwin 1950, 219f). In that context a stone is also erected at the *sindibor* (1950, 225).

the "chief"[12] of the village section (Kirsani in this case); Pfeffer (1991, 75), by contrast, writes that this buffalo is dedicated to the most "deserving" among the dead. It could, of course, be the case that there is some flexibility as to which one of the deceased this privilege is granted. On the basis of my data, it is the most "senior" (*boro, moro*) person among the *duma* for whom the ritual is performed, that is, the eldest among the deceased.

In Ponosguda, the most respected and influential of the deceased was Ranju Kirsani, and even the whole neighborhood was referred to as "Ranju neighborhood" (Ranju *sai*). Ranju's prestige was also made explicit, as it was his widow who welcomed the first *simli* branches that had been cut at her house. However, as he was not the eldest among the deceased, his son could not claim the *kutti bongtel* for him and an elder brother of Ranju had that honor. Komlu's son, nevertheless, marked the standing and influence of his father by buying two buffaloes for the deceased and later insisted that they should not be separated. In my interpretation, therefore, seniority is also the structuring principle here. We can compare the *kutti bongtel* to the village sacrificer. The latter is recruited from within the most senior segment of the Four Brothers, the Sisa, and acts on behalf of the village as a whole. Moreover, his senior status is articulated in the precedence of his actions. He sacrifices first, followed by all the other households; he ploughs first, followed by all the other men ploughing their fields; and during sacrificial commensality, he starts eating first. In the same way, precedence is granted for the *kutti* buffalo and, I would suggest, this animal-person also represents the totality of the buffalo-dead during the ritual.

After this introduction to the different embodiments of the dead, let me briefly summarize the process leading up to the main day of the ritual, the "*go'ter* day." Normally, months before this main day, around harvest time in November (*diali*), the decision is made by a group of brothers to celebrate the Go'ter in the month of *mag* (January/February). The number of households involved and, accordingly, the number of buffaloes provided, can vary considerably. In Ponosguda, thirteen buffaloes were bought, while in Gudapada, where the go´ter was performed about three years before my arrival in 1999, about 40 buffaloes had been given away. However, Pfeffer (1991) documented that more than 100 buffaloes had been provided in the village of Gorihanjar. The buffaloes are purchased in neighboring villages or at

---

12 It is not clear what indigenous term is that Izikowitz translates as "chief." Gadaba formally acknowledge village chiefs (*naik*) who do not have actual power over people and are rather petty-chiefs. I have never heard that a *kutti bongtel* is given for such a village headman. Elsewhere in his article Izikowitz speaks of "Morolok," "those who are rich" and can perform the Go'ter (1969, 133). *Moro* is Gutob for "senior," thus, "senior person." Possibly this is also the word that he translated as chief. Most likely the "chief of the Kirsani families," was its most senior member.

Photo 9.2: Mourning the buffalo-dead
As part of the Go'ter ritual, the buffalo-dead have been dressed and are lined-up at the village platform, fed and mourned by the women (Parenga village of Budliput, 1999).

weekly markets, then the dead are raised and, a week or more later, the *duma* are made to inhabit their new host bodies. This is done by feeding them "first rice" (*sig bat*).[13] Once the dead have assumed their new bodies, drums are beaten continuously and endless rounds of feeding the buffaloes start. They are tied to the village platform during the day but are taken to the individual houses for the night. In this way the hosts of the Go'ter select the buffaloes and transform them into the "living dead" to feast them. However, who takes them away in the end and who brings the stone slabs that are erected at the different megalithic platforms?

9.3 Exchanges and Replacements

The Go'ter is part of a general system of circulation and various "chains of transformations" (de Coppet 1981, 178). This encompasses the human life-cycle, the annual cycle with its sacrificial rituals that are synchronized with the

---

[13] The importance of eating and feeding for the transformation of ritual status among the Gadaba I have extensively discussed elsewhere (e.g. Berger 2007, 2015, 2017).

Photo 9.3: Line-up for feasting
Feeding of the buffaloes at the village platform (Gutob Gadaba village of Ponosguda, 2001).

cultivation of domesticated plants and the healing rituals that are concerned with unilateral violent consumption and relationships gone wrong (Berger 2015, 2017). All these domains include relationships and transactions among the living and the dead, gods and demons, and connect different units of the social structure in manifold ways. When separately discussing the exchanges that occur during the Go'ter, this general picture should be kept in mind.

In the previous section, I discussed the different embodiments of the dead and the motivation of the hosts to be finally relieved of the liminal *duma* and transform them into ancestors. This might be glossed as the "religious" dimension of the ritual. The exchanges, then, can be regarded as the social and economic sides of the Go'ter. Of course, putting it this way is doing violence to the local perspective. For the Gadaba, it would be meaningless to distinguish social, economic and religious aspects of the Go'ter and, thus, dissecting the ritual was also not the way I previously analyzed and understood it. However, these dimensions can be highlighted here to point out the social and economic features of the Go'ter. The ritual indeed is a total social fact, as I have mentioned before, and a multitude of relationships become manifest and unfold in the process of its performance.

Photo 9.4: Women feed the buffalo-dead at the village platform (Ponosguda, 2001)

Each village and each local descent group of a village is embedded in numerous ritual relationships. The buffalo-dead that have been raised by the hosts in their village are taken by external brothers; that is, by local descent groups (*kuda*, *kutum*) of other villages that belong to the same clan (*bonso*). In larger villages, such relationships of exchange may also exist among the Four Brothers themselves, for instance, between the local descent groups of Kirsani and Sisa. As a rule, however, such relationships within the village are "junior" and less valued than relationships of the same nature between villages. It is inconceivable that the buffalo-dead are given away to affines, in the same way as it is unthinkable and a severe transgression (*umrang*) to marry within the clan category. While the buffaloes are given to brothers – which is why Pfeffer (1991) called this intra-agnatic "soul" exchange – the buffaloes are nevertheless given to others of some kind, namely to brothers of a different village.[14]

Gadaba distinguish different kinds of relationships that permanently connect agnatic local groups, and which are involved in the exchange of buffalo-dead in the context of the Go'ter.[15] One of them, the "sacrificial-food-brothers" (*tsorubai*), is also important in many ritual contexts other than the Go'ter. The second is constituted by a bond of friendship between two groups of "brothers" (the *bai moitor*). The most important category of buffalo-takers in the Go'ter, however, are the *panjabai* (the meaning of *panja* is unclear), who exclusively figure in this context. Normally, they receive the majority of the buffalo-dead and take them to their village. To convey an impression of the density of agnatic relationships, we may briefly consider the case of Gudapada, the village that I know best. The Sisa of the village have three external *panjabai* relations, the Kirsani four, and the small Munduli group only one. In addition, the Sisa have two external *tsorubai* relationships, the Kirsani one. Moreover, there are four relationships of this kind between different local groups within the village (significantly, including the Dombo). In Gudapada, only the Sisa have external *bai moitor*. This makes sixteen relationships in total. Along with the earth people, who belong to the Cobra clan category, three Gadaba late comers live in Gudapada, who are internal affines of the earth people. They have their own agnatic exchange relations with local groups elsewhere.

Although the buffalo-dead are exchanged along these agnatic lines, there are also other relationships that are important in the Go'ter. Each local group has affinal connections to numerous villages (and sub-groups of those villages) with which "daughter-sisters" (*ji bouni*) are exchanged. Besides women for marriage, these groups give and take cattle as the most typical affinal gift, including in the

---

14 More specifically, the buffaloes are given to brothers belonging to a different "village clan." I have introduced this term to denote a particular territorial aspect of the Gadaba clan system. Among the Kond (both Kuttia and Dongria) a clan is associated with a certain territory and villages of that clan are not usually found elsewhere. Among the Gadaba, Cobra, Tiger, Sun and Monkey villages are dispersed over the whole area the Gutob Gadaba inhabit and in this sense they do not have territorial clans. However, within each clan category specific villages are recognized that have a distinctive, territorial-cum-clan identity (Berger 2015, 102–8).
15 I discussed the different relationships in detail elsewhere (Berger 2015; 2017).

context of the Go'ter. Finally, the most sacred form of relatedness between two groups surprisingly transcends the classification of agnates (*bai*) versus affines (*bondu*). These "liver-friends" (*koloj moitor*) neither exchange buffaloes nor brides but receive gifts of meat on certain occasions. In summary, every village sits like a spider in a dense and extensive web of ritual relations. When a Go'ter is celebrated, all these relationships are activated and come to life, with gifts of various kinds – buffaloes, cattle, goats, meat, stone slabs, beer, rice and other kinds of wealth – flowing along these various pathways.[16]

Performing a Go'ter thus not only means to transform the dead but to meet the expectations of all the relationships involved. Accordingly, potential hosts are very careful about if and when to announce a Go'ter and rumors of Go'ter-to-be-performed abound. A local agnatic group is not only under pressure to perform the ritual because the number of the dead increases over time, but also because agnatic exchange partners who have previously given buffaloes become increasingly impatient and demand reciprocation. To finally perform the Go'ter is a liberation in a double sense, as the hosts not only get rid of the dead but also turn the tide from being debtors to being creditors. The Go'ter is an opportunity for renown, with the risk of facing shame (*laj, opoman*). In economic, social and ritual terms, it is a tremendous task. When the ritual specialist wanted to postpone the date of the Go'ter day in Ponosguda, Ranju's widow objected by saying: "We have a mountain on our heads." She wanted to be done with it.

After the buffaloes have been transformed into the living dead by feeding them with "first rice," rounds of feasting the dead follow. Increasingly, guests from outside, mostly affines, arrive in the village and their women also honor the dead by providing them with food, millet beer and consoling words. Internal buffalo-takers – those groups also residing in the host's village – may already erect stones at the two platforms, but the external and most important groups of buffalo-takers only arrive on the evening before the main day. The stones to be planted have already been selected by the external agnates and have usually been brought close to the hosting village to be picked up when they enter the hosts' village.

The atmosphere is tense and full of anticipation the evening before the main day. The buffaloes are tied to the internal village platform and the arrival of the external clan brothers is expected. When they finally arrive after dark, they do so in a martial manner, beating drums and shouting, whistling and swinging long sticks. They carry the stone slabs into the village and erect them at the village platform. During the nightly hours that follow, the men from the

---

[16] For a visual impression of the density of relationships see Berger (2015, 188f) and Baliarsingh and Nayak (1996).

buffalo-taking groups dance in front of the buffalo-dead, shouting and whistling triumphantly, slapping the buffaloes on the back and snatching the food and beer meant for the buffaloes to consume it themselves.

At about three o'clock in the morning the mood abruptly changes, when the hosts call representatives from each group into one of their houses to announce which group is receiving how many buffaloes. All of a sudden, the external buffalo-takers seem totally sober and display a bargaining spirit. The length of these discussions depends on the resoluteness of the hosts and the stubbornness of the buffalo-takers. In the end, each group receives a number of small leaf packages with husked rice, representing the number of buffaloes they are going to receive. In addition to this official distribution, old scores are settled secretly and beforehand. As the number of people who have died in the hosting group is unlikely to match the number of buffaloes they must reciprocate to their different creditors, extra buffaloes are often given, which are not tied to the platforms. All kinds of scenarios are possible. Hosts may not be able to pay off all their debts and may put creditors off and pledge to pay parts of the debt later. They may fulfill all their debt (*run*) or may give extra buffaloes as credit (*udar*) and future investment. After the formal

Photo 9.5: Bringing the stones
The junior "sacrificial-food-brothers" (*tsorubai*; the Maji group from the same village) of the hosts bring a pair of stones for the village platform. On their way they have been smeared with color and dung.

distribution, the external agnates receive raw meat, husked rice and all kinds of other things (called *jur bat*, "tearing rice") to look after themselves in the coming hours, while the hosts prepare for the final farewell.

The buffalo-dead are then taken from the village platform back to the individual houses, where they are washed with turmeric water and dressed according to the sex of the deceased; a waist cloth (*lungi*) for a male and a *sari* for a female, or a blanket (*chador*) for either of them. Moreover, personal objects are tied around the neck and to the horns of the animals. This can be anything from sandals to pots or plates, a school book or a miniature loom, a necklace or bracelets, artificial hair that women use to enlarge their buns, mirrors, combs,

Photo 9.6: Planting the stones
The stone slaps of the *tsorubai* are erected at the village platform (Ponosguda, 2001).

a knife or sickle. While the dead are thus equipped and prepared by their family members for their journey to the underworld, the external agnates have their meals of "tearing rice" and in the meanwhile may also erect *simli* and *palda* branches and stone slabs at the external platform. Late in the morning, the buffalo-dead are led out of the village in a procession and tied to the external platform in the dry fields, where they are mourned for the last time by the women. It might be assumed that this would be the end of the ritual, as the external brothers have brought the stones to replace the liminal dead with permanent ancestors. It might be expected they would now untie the animals assigned to them and take them back to their own villages to kill, cook and eat, so that the *duma* are "finally dead." However, that part which gives the ritual its name and for which crowds of people assemble around noon at the dry-field platform is yet to come: the arrival of affinal buffaloes.

Photo 9.7: Celebrating life
After the stones have been erected at the village platform by the *tsorubai*, boisterous dancing and whistling follows (Ponosguda 2001).

Photo 9.8: The "dry-field platform"
In the morning of the main day, a fence-like structure of *simli* and *palda* trees has been erected by the *panjabai* and *tsorubai* of the hosts, and one pair of stones has been planted (Ponosguda 2001).

9.4 Go'ter in the Dry Fields

From the local point of view, "affinal buffalo" is generally an oxymoron. Agnates exchange the buffalo-dead and stone slabs; affines exchange brides in marriage and give and take cattle on various occasions. However, there is a truly significant exception. In addition to the two special categories of buffaloes mentioned – the buffalo for Rau and the *kutti* buffalo, both selected from among the buffaloes provided by the hosts – the category of *purani* designates those buffaloes brought by the hosts' affines from other villages. The number of *purani* buffaloes that are brought to the dry-field platform on the main day of the Go'ter is not predetermined. In the case of the Go'ter in Ponosguda, only one *purani* was brought by their affines from Gudapada, my host village. However, various affines can decide to provide a *purani* and in addition to the number of buffaloes given by the hosts, the number of *purani* buffaloes brought by the affines indicates the grandeur of the occasion and the renown of the people involved.

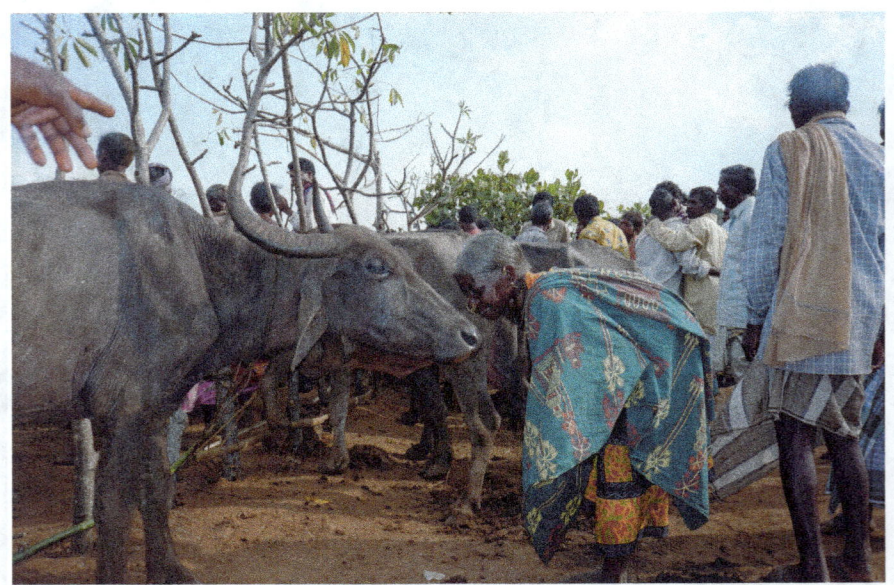

Photo 9.9: Final farewell
At the external dry-field platform a woman mourns the dead person (Budliput 1999).

Without *purani* buffaloes, a Go'ter is lacking "fun" (*sarda*) and "beauty" (*sundoro*) it is said, which is not merely an aesthetic statement but also entails a moral assessment. Such a situation should not occur. When affines decide to give a *purani*, they perform the same ritual steps in their own village as the Go'ter hosts conduct in theirs; that is, affines buy a buffalo, repair and beat drums, raise the dead person, transfer him or her into the animal, dress the animal according to age and gender and, on the main day, take the buffalo-dead to the village of the Go'ter hosts. However, the affines do not go on their own. The *purani* delegation includes the external agnates (*tsorubai*, *panjabai*) of the *purani*-giving affines; thus, local groups from yet other villages. Taking the buffalo into their midst, the *purani* delegation proceeds at a trot until it reaches the Go'ter hosting village. The gift of the *purani* thus results in a significant increase in the number of local groups that are involved in a Go'ter celebration.

Given the challenges to researching a ritual of this complexity, as the first anthropologist to actually document it, Izikowitz did a very admirable job. He understood that the killing of the *purani* buffaloes was connected to agriculture, but he could not identify who the *purani*-givers were, nor was he aware of the name of these buffaloes or that the affines come with their own *panjabai* (or *tsorubai*). It

Photo 9.10: Equipment for the underworld
At the dry-field platform: This buffalo-dead has been dressed with a *lungi* and equipped with a comb, cloth, sickle, brass pot and other objects to take to the underworld. A woman mourns the deceased (Ponosguda 2001).

was Georg Pfeffer (1991, 2001) who first identified these dimensions of the ritual. Hence, toward the end of his contribution, Izikowitz writes (Izikowitz 1969, 147):

> Perhaps the most difficult thing to explain is why certain people bring buffaloes which are later torn to pieces by the crowd. One thing has already mentioned, that is, that the buffaloes' entrails are credited with great power and that they increase the fertility of the fields.

It is crucial that the *purani* is given not only by "certain people" but by affines, as I will further discuss below. One can also be a bit more specific with regard to "the crowd." Neither the hosts nor the *purani*-bringing affines are normally involved in the killing, but everyone else can join in, especially the external agnatic relations of the hosts, as well as those of the *purani*-givers. Moreover, the location is also highly significant, as are the effervescent style and violent form of the whole procedure, which are not epiphenomena but essential elements of the ritual. No other ethnographer has described this scene in more detail with regard to a specific occasion of a Go'ter than Izikowitz, which is why I will quote him at some length below.

Photo 9.11: The *purani* delegation approaches the Go'ter village
The delegation of the *purani* bringers from Gudapada approaches the village hosting the Go'ter. A few hundred meters ahead a crowd has already gathered around the buffalo-dead at the dry-field platform (Ponosguda 2001; photograph by Amrei Volkmann).

Izikowitz describes a Go'ter in Kamarguda in January 1952. Kamarguda is located next to my host village of Gudapada. The Sisa of Kamarguda are the *panjabai* of one Kirsani[17] group in Gudapada, while another Kirsani group of Gudapada are the *panjabai* of the Munduli of Kamarguda. All groups belong to the Cobra clan category. Alongside Sisa and Munduli, Kamarguda also features a Kirsani group (also Cobra), whose *panjabai* are to be found in the village of Alangpada. The villagers of Sonkai, which Izikowitz mentions in the quote below, are the affines of Kamarguda and, hence, bring a *purani* buffalo. We join the Go'ter in Kamarguda at the moment of the main day, after the host's buffaloes have already been tied to the external platform.

---

17 Going through my notes again, I now realize that the diagram presenting the agnatic relationships of the earth people of Gudapada (2015, 188) does not show this *panjabai* relationship, namely of the Kodomguria Kirsani of Gudapada with the Sisa of Kamarguda.

Photo 9.12: The arrival of the *purani* buffalo
The *purani* bringers from Gudapada rush into the village of the Go'ter hosts, now accompanied by the hosts' *panjabai* and *tsorubai*. The *purani* is greeted at the house of the deceased, then the buffalo is immediately led out to the dry-field platform to be killed (Ponosguda 2001).

Within the village and just outside it tremendous crowds of people had now gathered. It seemed as if the people of the whole territory had come to witness the spectacle, and one could now feel an intense excitement in the air. The men were naked except for a breech cloth which had been drawn tight around the hips and between the legs. The breech cloth was as short as possible, as to not hinder movement. The men stood in groups and waited for what was going to happen, looking like fighters or athletes ready for contest. It was clear that they now waited impatiently for the climax of the drama. But they could concentrate and control their feelings.

Suddenly there could be heard music and whistling, screams and yells from the hills round about. From different directions came processions of men, armed with axes, knives and spears, and every kind of weapon they could get. They came towards the village like troops to an accompaniment of music. Those who first arrived at the village were the people from Sankai, who turned out in great numbers. They all carried weapons which they waved in the air as the danced. As soon as they came within the boundaries of the village they had to surrender all the dangerous weapons to an especially appointed policeman, a man who was considered to be sober and responsible. But this was, as far as I could understand, an exception. There was some fear of bloodshed and fighting on such occasions; thus as a substitute for their weapons the men were given long sticks or clubs with which they later danced.

When the Sankai people came in leading a buffalo, they brought it to the Kirsani's house for display. As soon as that was done, they led the buffalo out of the village. The custom is that the buffaloes contributed by relatives and friends are to be taken outside the village on the last day and torn to pieces. But, instead of turning it over to the waiting crowd, the Sankai people [perhaps their external agnates] ran off with the buffalo toward their own village. The situation was that the Kirsani had once borrowed a buffalo from the Sankai, so the Sankai gave this buffalo as a present but then took it back at once as payment for the debt.

But the Alungpada people [panjabai of the Kirsani hosts] would not stand for this, and soon there was a terrible quarrel which turned into a real fight. The Alungpada and Sankai men beat each other with clubs, and the women screamed and tried to separate them. Some of the women hung on to the clubs to prevent the men from using them. The fight got hotter. Several men were struck on the head and the blood ran in streams. This episode lasted a long time, but it was not the end of the drama.

One troop after another marched in to the accompaniment of drums and shawms. People came from several villages leading one or more buffaloes, first to the Kirsani's house, then to the Pujari's [Sisa]. Those who brought several buffaloes sometimes took one back, in this way taking care of an old debt. One person gave the Gotr families several buffaloes, but took back the number that was owed. At once, certain Gotr men ran off beyond the village with the remaining buffaloes, usually stopping in the shade of a tree. All the men followed and it did not take long for them to knock a buffalo to the ground and throw themselves over it. Soon there was a tangled mass of fighting men all over the buffalo, and each one tried to tear out the animal's entrails with his bare hands. Some crawled over the pile of men and others tried to wedge themselves underneath. Those who got hold of a piece stuck it inside their belts.

There was a stench of entrails, excrement, and blood, and everyone was more or less covered with the same. It was impossible to say whether the men were drunk or simply intoxicated with emotion. There was battle in the air. People quarreled, and the fighters had constantly to be separated. Outside the village an enormous crowd had gathered. Men, women, and children from the whole region had come to see the brutal spectacle, and some women had set up stands with food and drink for the hungry and the thirsty. It was like a big market, and everyone was festively dressed. But the atmosphere was charged in the extreme, and the excitement increased every time a new buffalo was thrown down and torn to pieces by the wild mob. Each one wanted to assure himself of a bit of the entrails for it is in the entrails that the buffalo's enormous strength resides, according to the Gadaba. The men explained that the piece they succeeded in grabbing they would later bury in their fields, thus ensuring a good harvest. No less than twelve buffaloes were torn to bits within a few hours (. . .). (1969, 139–41)

These important observations – which correspond to the descriptions of the other ethnographers of the Go'ter, including myself – contain all the elements I will focus on in my subsequent discussion: the role of the affines, the link between the dead and the growth of crops and, finally, the violence and effervescence of the ritual. However, before I commence this discussion, I want to briefly outline how the ritual ends.

Any man not from the groups of affinal *purani*-bringers or Go'ter hosts can try to tear out part of the intestines from the *purani* buffaloes, but the external buffalo-takers (usually the *panjabai*) of the hosts and of the affinal *purani*-providers claim the animals once they are dead. While Izikowitz's description makes clear that there is a certain amount of expected unpredictability in the ritual process, the *panjabai* of the affines have the right to claim the front half of a *purani*, while the *panjabai* of the sponsors take the rear half. Members of these two parties thus may try to prevent the crowd from taking away more than the entrails and the tongue, such as the valued vital organs. In the case of the Go'ter in Ponosguda that I documented, one man at some point jumped on top of the front half that his group had the right to claim and tried to keep other people away from the buffalo; he was of the opinion that the crowd had already taken enough of the intestines. The body of the buffalo was then cut in half with an axe and taken away by the respective groups. Throughout the killing of the *purani* buffaloes, the hosts' buffaloes remain tied to the dry-field platform.

One buffalo-dead has to be killed right at the platform as a "post sacrifice" (Munda Puja).[18] This may be the *kutti*-buffalo or the Rau buffalo provided by the hosts, but it might also be one of the *purani* buffaloes. From the perspective of the Go'ter hosts and their external agnates, the latter option would be preferable as the buffaloes available for transaction would not be reduced and the *purani* would be killed anyway. In this way, the hosts can give one more buffalo and possibly increase their account as creditors, while their external agnates receive one more buffalo. This was the case in Ponosguda, where the only *purani* that was brought, was formally received at the house and then killed at the dry-field platform. However, things do not always proceed in such an orderly manner, and plans are complicated by the dynamics of the situation.

For example, as Izikowitz's description makes clear, it is difficult to predict where the *purani* buffaloes will be killed by the crowd. Even if agreements have been made beforehand that a certain *purani* will be offered at the platform, someone may thwart this plan. Moreover, sometimes *purani* buffaloes are not killed at all but taken away alive. These are then called "complete" or "whole" buffaloes (*gula por*). As with the exchanges concerning the buffaloes of the hosts, all kinds of pre-arrangements can be made with regard to the *purani*. Izikowitz presents one such case with regard to the *purani* from Sonkai. However,

---

18 Various observers of the ritual and Gadaba and Parenga themselves especially mention the killing of one of the hosts' buffaloes at the dry-field platform. I have been told that the Munda Puja is obligatory and also in the conversation about the Go'ter recorded by Mahapatra (1985, 147), the Parenga informant states that one buffalo is offered at the platform, as "post offering" (Munda Bog). Pfeffer (2001, 118) and Pradhan (1998, 301) mention that the *kutti*-buffalo is killed at the platform and Kornel (1999, 68) observes that one of the hosts' buffaloes was untied to be killed at the platform as Munda Puja or Rahu Puja.

if a *purani* is supposed to be led away alive, the rights of the hosts' external agnates to receive the rear part of the animal have to be taken into account. If this does not happen, then fights are likely to occur. This may have been the situation in Kamarguda, where the hosts' *panjabai* (from Alangpada) violently protested against the *purani* from Sonkai being led way alive. Even if deals have been made with all parties involved, the situation may still develop in unexpected ways and not everyone may be informed or care about such agreements. Finally, it is possible that no *purani* is brought at all, and then one of the hosts' animals has to be killed at the dry-field platform. In any case, and also in the context of the Munda Puja, the animal is killed in the "tearing" style.

Once all of the *purani* buffaloes have arrived and been killed, all external agnates quickly untie the buffaloes that have been assigned to them and take them back to their villages. In subsequent weeks, the animals will be killed and eaten in follow-up feasts, but they may not be used again for ploughing the fields. The spectators then disperse, but many outside guests remain in the village and are invited to countless rounds of beer, liquor and food.

The next and final day sees two quite contrasting scenes. In the morning, both external buffalo-takers (some have returned to the hosts' village, some have stayed there overnight) and affines are provided with pots of hot water by the hosts. Soon a mud fight develops, at the end of which people (sometimes mutually) wash themselves and receive new clothes from the hosts. This scene of joking is followed by a highly formal sequence in which buffalo-takers and the bringers of *purani* buffaloes are honored with brass objects, a small pot (*mota*) and a plate (*tali*), together referred to as *moali*. In the case of Ponosguda, long negotiations followed between the Go'ter host and the *purani*-bringers, as the latter were not satisfied with what they were offered. Another significant detail has to be explained to appreciate this situation.

While all *purani* are provided by affines, there are two kinds of *purani* buffaloes. All affines can bring *purani* "as guests" (*got isap*), and such *purani* are later reciprocated when the guests become the hosts of a Go'ter. Only the mother's brothers (*mamu*) of the deceased persons for whom the Go'ter is celebrated have the right to bring a *purani* "as mother's brothers" (*mamu isap*), which cannot be reciprocated with a buffalo on a later occasion but only with valuables, for which *moali* stands. Under normal circumstances, the mother's brother of a deceased person would already have died long before, but his son or grandson or someone from his local descent group can assume the role of the *mamu*. As I see it, a mother's brother thus makes two successive gifts. First, he gives his sister in marriage and, second, he takes his sister's son or daughter (in the form of a buffalo) to the village of the Go'ter hosts (and former bride takers) to be killed in the fields. As I have argued before, he thus makes two complementary gifts of fecundity, one for human reproduction and one for cereal regeneration (Berger 2010, 2015, 2018). After all the *moali* negotiations have been concluded, the Go'ter ends and everyone returns home.

9.5 Discussion and Interpretation: Death and Regeneration

The Go'ter makes the dead return in different ways, albeit transformed. To the outside observer, the more obvious transformations are the revival of the deceased in the bodies of buffaloes and their replacement by stone slabs, which both marks and accomplishes the transition from deceased (*duma*) to ancestor (*anibai*). Beyond this, the Go'ter brings about the regeneration of the dry fields and finger millets in particular, the most important cereals that are grown on this category of fields. In order to realize this, two elements seem to be vital, violence and affinal involvement.

Tearing

During the Go'ter, buffaloes are killed in a way that is unique to this particular ritual.[19] Gadaba sacrifice animals in different ways: victims may be killed with a stroke on the head with the blunt or sharp side of an axe, and most often they are decapitated. In no other context is the belly of an animal cut open and the entrails torn out of the animal while, and this is important, it is still alive.[20] That this practice is key can be inferred from the ritual structure that makes this action the climax of the ritual and is reflected in the number of people in attendance. Another indicator is the term with which this practice is described. Already Fürer-Haimendorf (1943, 156) noted that this day is called *jur*, meaning "tearing to pieces day." However, *jur* not only means "to tear" but also "to plunder" and "to loot" as well as "to grow" and "to ripen" (Gustafsson 1989, 198; Mahapatra 1985, 224). It thus seems that, like the ritual action itself, the semantics of the word already encompasses both destruction and violence as well as nurture and increase.

---

19 Fürer-Haimendorf (1943, 170) reports that in the context of Bondo weddings a buffalo is killed in the same manner, though not during the final death ritual (Gunom).
20 That the entrails are torn out of the living animal is mentioned by several ethnographers (Fürer-Haimendorf 1943, 157; Pfeffer 2001, 117). Also when Gadaba behead victims it is seen to it that the head it quickly put down at the ritually demarcated place for offerings to the deity, as the life of the animal should depart there. It is the "vital" part of the offering.

However, *jur* not only refers to the particular day, but is iconic of the ritual as a whole. While anthropologists have differently spelt the name of the ritual[21] – Pfeffer (1991) assuming that the term referred to the Sanskrit word for "lineage" (*gotra*) – linguists[22] write the Gutob word "*go'ter,*" which translates as "to cut" (*go'*) and "to distribute" or to "divide" (*ter*) (cf. Rajan and Rajan 2001a, 53). Accordingly, Gadaba call the day that the "tearing" takes place either *jur din* or *go'ter din*, which both roughly translate as "tearing day."

While the name of the ritual thus refers to the killing of the *purani* buffaloes, the designations of the external megalithic platform further establish the link between the stones, the tearing and the dry fields. The internal platform is unanimously called "village posts" (*ga* or *ungom munda*) but the external platform is called "dry-field posts" (*poda munda*[23]), "tearing posts" (*go'ter munda*[24]) or "tearing [in the] dry fields" (*go'ter langbo*[25]). What these different names – which are used interchangeably – establish, is the intimate connection between the tearing of the buffaloes, the dry fields and the megalithic manifestations of the ancestors.

The ritual actions in the dry fields amount to human sacrifices or ritualized acts of homicide. After all, the *purani* buffaloes that are brought by the affines embody the living dead, as do the buffaloes provided by the hosts. The Gadaba are not concerned by the fact that one deceased person may be present in more than one buffalo. As we have seen, Komlu gave two buffaloes for his father and Ranju's *duma* was also raised and transferred into the *purani* buffalo that was brought by his affines from Gudapada. All buffaloes thus represent the dead in the same way, and are fed and mourned. However, in particular, it is the *purani* buffaloes that are killed in this particular manner, as by default all of these buffaloes are subject to "tearing." However, other buffaloes, such as the one offered to Rau or the one selected for the Munda Puja can also meet the same end. The link between the ritual killings of quasi-humans, the burial of the meat and the fertility of the earth immediately suggests a link with the Meria sacrifice of the Kond (Hardenberg 2018a; Niggemeyer 1964a), an association that was not lost on Izikowitz either (1969, 147). Certainly, we are dealing with the same sacrificial logic – which we encountered repeatedly above – that connects human sacrifice with the regeneration of crops. As is well known, the Kond were forced to abandon human sacrifices and to replace them with buffaloes that they

---

21 "Gota" (Fürer-Haimendorf 1943, 156), "gotr" (Izikowitz 1969; Pfeffer 2001, 99), "gotar" (Pradhan 1998).
22 Griffiths (2008, 671; 2010); Rajan and Rajan (2001a, 48).
23 Kornel (1999, 66).
24 Fürer-Haimendorf (1943, 156); Kornel (1999, 66).
25 Izikowitz (1969, 137).

offered to the earth goddess. As far as the Gadaba are concerned, there is no evidence of actual human sacrifices in the past. Today, the buffaloes of the Gadaba more explicitly represent human beings than do the buffaloes of the Kond, who are not dressed or addressed as humans.

The Dead and Grain

What differentiates the buffalo sacrifices of the Kond and those of the Go'ter is the latter's link to the dead, which is lacking in the former case. As discussed above, the Gadaba explicitly link the killing of the *purani* to those fields in which dry rice, niger seed, little millet and, most importantly, finger millet are cultivated. Even if, according to my interlocutors, the intestines are not (or no longer) buried in the fields[26] but eaten by those who manage to grab them, the killing as such takes place in those fields and it is there that all the blood of the buffaloes seeps into the earth; blood that "enlivens" (*bonchiba, bonchaiba*) what it touches in ritual contexts. The obligation to kill one buffalo at the dry-field platform as a "post sacrifice" in particular, shows that bloodshed at this location is crucial. The hosts' buffaloes cannot simply be tied to the platform and subsequently be taken away by their external agnates; one buffalo has to be "torn" in the fields. As mentioned above, dry fields are conceptualized by the Gadaba as "own" and consanguineal, in contrast to the affinal wet-rice fields. Dry fields belong to the village – with seeds for those fields being distributed during the April festival by the village sacrificer, standing on top of the shrine of the local earth goddess (*hundi*) – and some of the former inhabitants of the village meet their end by being ritually killed on those fields.

The connection between dry fields and the dead also becomes explicit at other times of the year. When the millet plants grow during the rainy season, they are described as "children of the village." In fact, these plants are at the center of a ritual that turns them into persons, in a similar way to human beings, a ritual called Ending Impurity (Sutok Sorani). For humans, this ritual – conducted about seven days after birth – marks the first major transformation from being a "flower" (*phul*; thus, having the pre-person status of umbilical

---

[26] Pfeffer (1991, 80) and Izkowitz (1969, 141) explicitly write that the intestines are buried in the fields, Fürer-Haimendorf (1943, 157) states that they are taken away and eaten later. Thusu and Jha (1972, 101) do not specify what is happening to the intestines and just state that "the Gotar will bring good crops in their [the hosts'] fields." I could not observe what was actually happening with the entrails but have been told that they are eaten along with beer or liquor by men, women and children.

cord and placenta) to becoming a human person. During this ritual, the infant symbolically receives sacrificial food for the first time and is also given his or her name. If the child subsequently dies, he or she is eligible for the funeral rituals; if a newborn dies before the ritual is conducted, the "flower" is buried behind the house, in the same pit as the placenta and umbilical cord. Being a person with a name also means being vulnerable to sorcery attacks and respective measures have to be taken.

As is common, the village sacrificer first conducts the ritual for the village millet plants as a whole. He goes to a millet field and buries "medicine" that is supposed to protect the young plants against sorcery attacks and the evil eye. Within a week, all households perform the ritual, which is then explicitly called the Finger Millet Ritual (Mandia Biru). Men go to their millet fields and take measures to protect the plants. Moreover, they tie one crab to a stalk of millet and set another one free. Then they offer a kind of millet cake or bread (*mandru*) – the same kind that was used in the Nandi festival – to the dead, both to the dangerous ones (*duma daini*) and to the benevolent ones, the "mothers-fathers" (*mata pita*). The dead and the dry field crops – millet in particular – are thus closely connected, not only in the sense that the dead protect the crops, but that they seem to inhabit them, share in their nature. The bloody tearing of the dead on the dry field is a crucial moment of this ontological transition. While the Gadaba accomplish this transformation of the dead in an idiosyncratic manner, the general idea is more common in the region.

In a previous chapter, I mentioned how the Joria envision the dead and their crops to be related and this is also the case with the neighbors of the Gutob Gadaba to their West, the Bondo.[27] Although, according to Elwin's interpretation, the Bondo conceive the influence of the dead on the crops to be mainly negative (Elwin 1950, 222–27), the data presented by Fürer-Haimendorf demonstrates that the dead also have the capacity to enhance the harvest, not only destroy it.[28] The final death ritual of the Bondo – the Gunom ceremony, during which, as in the Go'ter, stones are erected and *simli* branches planted –

---

[27] Elwin states that the Gunom is one of the ceremonies that is intend to increase the fertility of the fields. However, he regards its "deeper aim" to be of a psychological nature, namely (with a reference to Freud) to overcome melancholia (1950, 219).

[28] Elwin claims the same for the Sora (1955, 301f). Various myths describe transformations between plants and (dead) humans, which might suggest that "it would not be impossible for the Saora mind to conceive of the dead as in some way entering into the soil or the growing plants and acting as some kind of fertilizer (. . .)" (Elwin 1955, 302). This is the view of J.H. Hutton who also visited the Sora area and assumed that "the Guar ceremony marks the transition of the soul into the crop which along with with the previous dead it probably helps to fertilize" (Hutton in Elwin 1955, 302). Still, Elwin assumes that the influence of the dead is

is especially considered to have a positive influence on the crops. As Fürer-Haimendorf (1943, 169) writes:

> Several Bondos told me expressively that the *Gunom* ceremony is performed in order to get good crops; one man, who had erected a dolmen for his father, put it in these words: 'It is only with the help of the *sairem* [spirits of the dead] that our crops thrive, without their blessing the young blades would wither away.'

Thanks to the in-depth ethnography of Piers Vitebsky, the ideas and practices of the Sora are much better researched than are those of the Bondo. What the Gɔ'ter represents for the Gadaba and the Gunom for the Bondo is the Guar for the Sora, which literally means "stone-planting." Some villages celebrate this phase of the death rituals together with a ritual called Karja, which is the annual festival for the dead and, significantly, at the same time a harvest-commemoration (Vitebsky 1993, 22; Elwin 1955, 358). Like the Gadaba, the Sora rituals aim to transform the deceased persons from dangerous liminal beings (the experience or consciousness aspect or "soul," *puradan*) to benevolent ancestors (*sonum*). While Gadaba and Bondo also speak to their dead in the context of the death rituals – the Bondo do so via humans called "fathers of the dead" (*sairem-ba*) that temporarily represent the deceased during the Gunom ritual (Elwin 1950, 224; Fürer-Haimendorf 1943, 169), and the Gadaba speak to the buffaloes – the Sora have vastly elaborated this discursive dimension in their death rituals, in which the dialogues with the dead are, or used to be,[29] crucial and frequent. Moreover, the Sora also erect stones for the dead, sacrifice buffaloes and also "eat" the dead. Grain is collected from every household that participates in the death ritual and ground into flour, from which either a "lump" or a human figure is formed. This representation, the "soul" of the patrilineal ancestors, is then consumed by the men of the households, an ingestion Vitebsky describes as "cannibalism" (1993, 228). The dead are not only consumed in this way, however, but they continuously nourish the living. Vitebsky speaks of a "web of mutual dependence" (1993, 53):

> Sonums are nourished by soul, whether of the living humans whom they 'eat' when they attack them or of the domestic animals, grain and alcohol offered to them during sacrifices as a substitute (*apanadu*) for a sick patient. Living Sora are in turn also nourished by soul. This is not the soul of sacrificed animals (. . .). Rather, it is the soul of grain. Something of the consciousness of their ancestors is infused back into the grain grown by their descendants on the land which those ancestors used to cultivate. (Vitebsky 1993, 53)

---

mainly considered to be negative, not nurturing. The data presented by Vitebsky discussed below contradicts this view.

29 In his recent book, Piers Vitebsky (2017a) describes in detail how the Sora he knew since the 1970s have abandoned their animist religion and embraced Christianity in particular.

After death, a person has multiple and possibly fractured trajectories. The dead inhabit different aspects of the landscape, one of which is the "earth site" and, in this case, there is an especially clear connection between them and the crops their descendants cultivate and eat:

> A person who is 'in' an Earth site is also the 'soul' (*puradan*) of all the grain which grows out of that Earth. That person enters (*gan-*) his descendants house every time a harvest is taken in from the threshing flour and stored in the loft. Like previous Ancestors, then, Jamano [one deceased person] has now 'become' (*gadil-*) the grain of his descendants. This grain will be pounded in the mortar, cooked on the hearth and swallowed daily in each of their houses. (Vitebsky 1993, 141)

These ideas also become manifest in the dialogues the living have with the dead via shamans and in the songs the ancestor-men sing during the rituals, impersonating the dead. On behalf of the deceased called Jamano they sang:

> I have become lineage food   I have become branch food
> I have become lineage grain   I have become branch grain
> I have become Underworld-journey rice   I have become straight-path rice
>   (Vitebsky 1993, 141)

Having become grain, the dead still want their share of sacrificial offerings or of the grain, as another deceased, Indupur, made clear in one of the dialogues. His niece, Sandi (not present during the dialogue; the person called Sindi that appears in the dialogue is another woman), performed the stone-planting for him and thus inherited his land. Nevertheless, in the conversation, he showed his dissatisfaction, while other living persons present rebuked him.

> *Indupur: No, I don't call her mean, it's because she* [PB: Sandi] *lives on my grain* [upsurge of voices], *I'm angry because she didn't give me a share.*
>
> Rungkudi: She gave you a harvest-commemoration she gave you a stone planting she gave you sacrifices she gave you everything.
>
> Sindi: And what's more you come and take some grain away: – I've seen you in dreams, you come and scoop it up with your hands – we see it all in dreams.
>
> *Indupur: Sindi! As for the millet I don't claim that's my work I don't claim that's my labour. Hey sisters hey children, that's Sandi's mother's work (. . .) I don't claim that. But as for that other grain, give me some of that –* (Vitebsky 1993, 161)

Such a vital but also strained and precarious reciprocity between the living and the dead is also recognized by the Gadaba. Unlike the Sora, they do not verbally articulate this idea so elaborately, although the dead do speak to the living and

9.5 Discussion and Interpretation: Death and Regeneration

also formulate accusations and demands when they take possession of someone – usually shortly after someone has died. However, I think it can be inferred from the ritual actions of the living with regard to the dead, which speak clearly and loudly.

Humans fear the recently dead and try to appease them with food, liquor and sacrifices. After death, the deceased person moves along different trajectories. The life-force is reborn in another human being and the social aspect of the dead (*duma*) is more or less inactive after the third stage in the ritual process (*bur*). Still, the living acknowledge their existence during festivals, when they provide offerings for their deceased kin at their houses, on the cremation ground and in their millet fields. In the Sora dialogue, Indupur requested his share from the field that used to be his. In a similar vein, a Gadaba householder shares millet with the *duma* during the Millet Ritual, scattering crumbs of millet bread across the field while carefully walking between the young millet plants – at the time of the year when they become "persons" – requesting the dead to eat. Sharing millet with the *duma*, he hopes, will lead to an abundant harvest.

The Go'ter is the decisive transforming ritual that does many things at the same time. It enables the dead to inhabit new bodies and to return to their family for a while, being honored and provided for by the living (with food and drink, clothes, objects to take to the underworld). As we have seen, however, the *duma* are not only fed but also ultimately eaten in a cannibalistic act performed by external agnates of the deceased. They do this job without much fuss and without further rituals, killing the animals in their own villages quickly and efficiently, as one would do for a feast. The benevolent megalithic presence of the ancestors is ensured in the village opposite the shrine of the earth deity and in the dry fields. The dead who are killed during the "post sacrifice" and/or embodied by a *purani*[30] meet an alternative end, with the explicit result being that their life-force vitalizes the dry fields. Entrails and blood transfer fecundity to those consanguineal fields where millet seeds will soon be sown and later harvested and eaten, but also shared with the dead.

---

30 Although my interlocutors could not explain what the term *purani* means and why the buffaloes are called like that, it may be worth mentioning the different meanings of the word as presented by Gustafsson (1989, 325). Like the word for tearing (*jur*), which also entails an association with both destruction and growth, also the term *purani* carries different meanings. In an economic transaction *purani* is the money that is payed to match the exchange of goods, to pay the difference. With regard to discourse *purani* means "misleading" talk. Ecologically, it refers to alluvial soils, to silt that is accumulated by flowing water.

As is common in animist ontologies,[31] the trajectories of Gadaba personhood traverse different modes of being, different exteriorities or bodies: from the living human body to the disembodied spirit that may occasionally take on the form of wind, re-embodied buffalo-dead, ancestor-branches and ancestor-stones to the millet plants of the dry fields. However, the transformations do not end there. They come full circle. As I have discussed in detail elsewhere (Berger 2018), the two staple cereals of the Gadaba – finger millet and wet rice – are "resources" of different kinds. They are two complementary aspects of Gadaba grainhood. Rice concerns the ritual status of a person and creates structure and distinctions that are frequently formulated through the opposition of junior and senior. Finger millet, by contrast, which is ritually much less prominent or conspicuous, is not about structure, but about life (*jibon*) and being. Almost the first thing a newborn baby comes into contact with after leaving its mother's womb is finger millet, when the midwife rubs the entire body of the infant with millet flour. Later in life, if someone is weak, it is said that he or she is not consuming sufficient millet gruel and so their blood has become watery or whitish. Accordingly, in an attempt to prevent an approaching death, a dying person is fed millet gruel as a desperate final attempt at recovery. The life of those killed on the dry fields during the Go'ter enhances the life of the living. Animated by the consanguineal blood of the mothers and fathers who are killed in the fields, finger millet nourishes the life of their living descendants.

The transformations of human life and millet life are thus confined to the brotherhood, to the village and to the consanguineal fields pertaining to it. By contrast, wet rice is purely conceptualized as affinal, and the dead of the village have nothing to do with the growth of this cereal (unlike the Sora). The river-earth deities of the paddies (Kamni) are the providers of rice – their daughter – which they give to humans in exchange for sacrificial offerings. The affinal component in the millet cultivation cycle is less obvious but no less vital. Affines not only provide a village with "daughter-sisters" to marry and thus guarantee human reproduction, but they also provide *purani* buffaloes and thus enable the "tearing" on the dry fields and the life-enhancing bloodshed. In the Bali Jatra story discussed in the previous chapter, the affinal Bima give three kinds of gifts, if my interpretation is correct: brides, tools and knowledge of agriculture and rice. In the context of the Go'ter, the generative and life-giving value of affinal relationships comes to the fore in matrimonial exchanges and

---

31 See Arhem and Springer (2016); Descola (2013); Hardenberg (2021); Sahlins (2014), Vitebsky (2017b).

in their role in the reproduction of millet, which, significantly, entails a marked element of ritual ferocity.

Ritual Ferocity

Izikowitz's description of the "tearing day" vividly depicts its violence and ferocity. These actions are evidently intrinsic to the ritual and thus an example of what I have called "systemic effervescence" (Berger 2016a). All ethnographers have witnessed the same scenes, usually from a safe distance. When Gadaba talk about the Go'ter, they never leave out this dimension. My friend Ori regularly recalled a scene in which he was the first to grab the tongue of a *purani* – which is also credited with special generative and wealth-creating power – before all the other men struggling and fighting around the buffalo, and he would not let go of it no matter how much he was shoved around: "these motherfuckers would have to cut off my hand [to get the tongue]," he commented. Similar indigenous statements that demonstrate the fierceness of the situation have been documented. One of them is provided by Mahapatra (1985, 147), recorded in the 1960s, and narrated by Aita Killo, a Parenga from the village of Konchona: "With sticks in hand, they [actors involved in the 'tearing'] never care whether the head gets struck, skin gets scratched, leg or hand gets fractured." Richard DeArmond also collected an indigenous account of the Go'ter around the same time, which was only later published by Arlo Griffiths: "They [Gadaba men] leave for the *Go'ter* [dry] field, carrying wooden-sticks etc., hatches etc., swords. (. . .) Being drunk, they get into a lot of fighting, killing" (Griffiths 2010, 290).

The Go'ter is one further example of generative effervescent events that I have described in previous chapters. Some readers may have already noted that the term for the sacrificial practice of the Dongria in the context of Dasara in Bissamcuttack, allegedly "one of the worst centres of human sacrifice" up to 1854, according to Sahu (1942, 178), is the same as the one for the killing of the *purani*. Both are referred to as "tearing" or "snatching" (*jur, juro*) and give the whole performance its name: "Juro Festival" or Go'ter. Although the manner of killing is different – the Dongria hack the animal to pieces with their axes and strike it anywhere they can, the Gadaba slice the belly open and tear out the intestines – the "tearing" away of bits of the animal while it is still alive is the same. Moreover, the Gadaba also demonstrate two dimensions of violence, toward the animal and among the living, which really amount to two sides of the same coin.

Excessive alcohol consumption is also a common, necessary and conspicuous feature of the *juro* practices of both Dongria and Gadaba.[32] Izikowitz writes that he was not sure if the Gadaba men were "drunk or simply intoxicated with emotion;" I would say, usually, they are both. The word "intoxication" creates false associations, however, as it suggests harmful and deadly, thus toxic, consequences. From the local perspective, alcohol consumption is empowering and transformative, even though the downsides of excessive consumption are also recognized (Berger 2020). Ritual specialists drink liquor before they head to the cremation ground to deal with a revengeful spirit, or they spit liquor in the face of a possessed person to drive an unwanted *duma* out of the body. Alcohol is a powerful and enabling substance and it creates the pleasures of vertigo, as Alfred Gell (1980) discusses, which is why deities and the dead also desire it. Alcohol consumption may be a catalyst for experiences of trance and possession, thus of merging the worlds of humans, deities and the dead. In contrast to the "play" of the Ganga festival, the Go'ter does not aim at inviting gods into the realm of the living, and thereby sharing in divine power. Instead, the Go'ter creates a liminal space in which humans and the dead meet, and alcohol has an important function in facilitating this merging. We may recall here Nicolas Prévôt's (2014, 243) observations that, in the ritual context of the God Market in Bastar, drunken men represent the dead and the ancestors. In the Go'ter, it seems that the external takers of the buffaloes especially – above all, the *panjabai* – are closely associated with the liminal dead. Ultimately, they are the ones who are going to ingest them. However, even during the Go'ter they endlessly dance in front of the buffaloes and share their food and drink. They not only eat the dead but are also their commensals.

While it may be regarded as a nuisance by development workers or police who are sent to "control" these events, alcohol consumption and ritualized ferocity are vital in bringing about the regeneration at which the Go'ter aims. Drinking and violence are as generalized as the desired procreative results. Everyone drinks and all men (except the hosts and the *purani*-bringing affines) may "plunder" the buffalo and engage in the rowdy game. While the killing of the buffalo-dead at and around the *go'ter langbo* ("tearing [at the] dry field") is especially related to the regeneration of those fields, and finger millet in particular, the intended outcome is all kinds of "wealth." So, it is said that whoever manages to cut off or get hold of the *purani's* tongue will have plenty, for instance

---

32 Notably, among the festivals discussed in this book, the Bali Jatra stands out as far as alcohol consumption and ritualized ferocity is concerned. This is unsurprising as it is the signature festival of the Mali who normally neither drink beer (*pendom*) or liquor (*mod*).

plenty of money, if he happens to engage in trade. I have remarked on this generalized idea of wealth repeatedly in earlier chapters; moreover, in the context of the final death ritual (Gunom) of the Bondo it also becomes very explicit. After the stones have been erected on the evening before the main day, the dead are offered millet beer and rice and are addressed with invocations such as:

> Our millets, give (that they may thrive); we have carried (this stone) and are to perform a ceremony for you, Sukro [name of the deceased]; our children, may they be plentiful, our crops may they be plentiful, millets, oxen, buffaloes, goats, dogs, chickens, birds, men, millets, children, may they all be plentiful. (Fürer-Haimendorf 1943, 168)

As I have previously argued with regard to the *juro* of the Dongria, the violent taking of life, the killing of the *purani* buffalo-dead and the risking of life and the bloodshed of the men involved are regenerative practices. They are as important to ensuring that the desired results are attained as are the offerings to the dead. The play with and risk of life amounts to a conquest of death. Pfeffer (2001) also understood the Go'ter in these terms, as a triumph over death. Obviously, this is not an individual achievement and people continue to become ill and die. Yet, as a whole, to put it in a somewhat Durkheimian way, society thinks of itself as being in charge of death and, if not actually controlling the flow of life, at least capable of navigating its course.

It is here that the Go'ter of the Gadaba resonates with the Dasara of the king. We may recall Sarkar (2020, 341), arguing that Navaratra "became an enactment of her [Durga's] triumph over death. The buffalo, a *vahana* [vehicle] of Yama, was a symbol of death. Durga's slaying the buffalo symbolized both her mastery over and her association with death and danger." The Go'ter is not about Durga, or any other deity for that matter, but it is about buffaloes representing the dead and being killed in a violent quest for life.[33] Could it be that this parallel also did not escape the former rulers of Nandapur? Is it inconceivable that the king may have even formally sponsored Go'ter celebrations? We do know that the king or representatives of the colonial state (the "Jeypore Samasthanam", Sahu 1942, 179) did provide the buffaloes for the *juro* sacrifices performed by the Dongria in the context of Dasara in Bissamcuttack; thus ceremonies that are designated by the same name as the final Gadaba death ritual, only in Desia, not in Gutob. If the king had provided a buffalo for the Go'ter to be "torn" to pieces by his subjects, which one would he have chosen?

---

[33] Roland Hardenberg also pointed out to me (personal communication) that the ferocity we encounter in the Go'ter (and in some forms of "play" in Bastar) is not so unlike Durga's fierceness, which is essential to slay the demon and to conquer death. Thus, both in the embodied forms of feriocity as well as in their purpose similarities may be discerned.

Along with the unspecified numbers of affinal *purani* buffaloes that can be killed anywhere, whether near to or further from the external platform, the ritual stipulates the killing of one buffalo as a "post sacrifice" (Munda Puja) at the dry-field platform. The buffalo killed there may be the one dedicated to the Rau demon, one of the affinal *purani* buffaloes, or it may be the buffalo representing the most senior among the deceased, the *kutti bongtel*, which I translated as "post buffalo" and to which Izikowitz's (1969, 136) interlocutors referred to as the "king's buffalo" (*raja bongtel*). Gadaba relational logic would identify this senior buffalo-dead with all the buffaloes given in a particular Go'ter ritual.

I do not think that the Gadaba of Kamarguda had the king of Nandapur as a sacrificial sponsor in mind, but were using the term *raja* to signify the superior status of this particular buffalo-dead, his seniority. Nevertheless, one could imagine that if the king used to be a sponsor of the Go'ter, he would probably have chosen the animal which embodied the most senior of the deceased. As a metasacrificer among subaltern sacrificial sovereigns, he would probably have embraced the idea that his buffalo represented all others *pars pro toto*. Of course, it is unlikely that we will ever know.

There is another side to the ritual ferocity that the former kings probably appreciated less; the Go'ter can also be read as an "art of not being governed" (Scott 2009). This takes us back to Alfred Gell's (1997) reading of the Dasara rituals and tribal rebellions in Bastar, anticipating some of Scott's main arguments. In my analysis of Dasara, I stated that Gell overlooked, or in any case did not sufficiently consider, the religious dimensions of the scenes of unruly collective effervescence, the dimension which I have just outlined above with regard to the Go'ter. Conversely, I think it is apt to reflect on the potential political impact the Go'ter may have had. To recapitulate briefly, Gell argued that the tribes of Bastar maintained a relatively high degree of autonomy and a particularly close and undisturbed relationship to "their king" by, on the one hand, exalting him during Dasara and resorting to rebellion when anyone dared to interfere. On the other hand, the tribal subjects displayed a self-image of wildness which suggested to the ruler that it would be better to leave them alone. Pouring into Jagdalpur during Dasara, armed and in huge numbers, they would demonstrate their "political muscle" (1997, 436).

Just as Gell described the tribals populating the streets of Jagdalpur during Dasara as "armed (. . .) and in a very excitable condition" (1997, 436), the same can certainly be said of the various groups that fight over the intestines of the *purani* buffaloes in this "bloody carnival," as Somasundaram (1949, 41) labeled the Go'ter. If we assume that the Go'ter was performed at the time of the kings of Nandapur – and there is very little reason to doubt it, as the proverb explicitly makes this connection – we may also suppose that the massive display of fierceness and readiness for violence at the doorsteps of the capital may have made an impression on the ruler. Read in this way, the signature ritual of the king indexed his status as sacrificial metaperson and sovereign, while the Go'ter ritual would have had two different meanings. First, it established their claim, as "earth creatures" (Gutob), to be the sacrificial sovereigns managing the flow of life and demonstrating their ritual power to turn death into life. In this sense, *raja* and *porja* would have joined forces in the common and complementary pursuit of regeneration. Beyond this and second, the "tearing" ritual also communicated, like tribal performances during Dasara in Bastar, that the Gadaba were too wild to be ruled. Whatever may have been the political reality – and some Gadaba are known to have been palanquin bearers for the king and his retinue, not by definition a revolutionary occupation – this message would have been forcefully expressed before a huge crowd.

This massive presence of the local population is one element that none of the commentators on the Go'ter has failed to notice. I have often been told that "the world" (*dunia*) is attending the Go'ter, as was Pfeffer (2001, 111). Moreover, a Gutob Gadaba informant, Duaru, from the village of Tikrapada, told Richard DeArmond: "People from very far off drink beer and wine [liquor], and come to see the *Go'ter*. Ronas, Cowherds, Gardeners, Potters, Gorens (that is the 'cut-caste' Dombos), all communities meet" (Griffiths 2010, 290). This has also been observed among the Ollar Gadaba on the other side of Nandapur, so to speak, and as Thusu and Jha (1972, 99) write: "It is said that whenever Gatar is performed a large gathering coming from various groups of castes and tribes of the neighbouring areas, [sic] is expected to mark the occasion by their presence at the ceremony." Izikowitz (1969, 139) felt that "people of the whole territory had come to witness the spectacle" and Pfeffer (2001, 118) estimated the number of spectators on the final day to be up to 10,000. Certainly, the massive presence of people added to the grandeur of the ritual and also to the renown of the Go'ter hosts and of the successful hunters of entrails and tongues, some of whom achieved the status of "heroes" (Thusu and Jha 1972, 101). In addition, "the world" testified to the proverbial fierceness of the Gadaba, which was therefore regularly reestablished in the collective imagination of the region, including that of the king. This aspect did not change much after independence. Thus, Duaru (Griffiths 2010, 291) noted: "The police are also there", adding, "Being drunk, they [the people/Gadaba] do not pay heed to the words of the police."

10 Conclusion: Navigating Life

Hung over and exhausted, but happy, the hosts of the festival rest on the covered verandas of their houses, together with the remaining visitors, who will return to their own villages later today, perhaps only tomorrow. Some are lying asleep, some doze, some squat, holding pots of heated beer in their hands, talking quietly about the events of the past days. The work has been done and done properly, according to the divine order. One cannot know much about the gods but for sure they have their moods and their expectations. As Birsa Sisa from Gudapada says, if you don't give them food they will get angry. They are just like humans, he points out, mimicking a dialogue between disappointed and unsatisfied deities.

> So, I [Birsa] drink liquor, I eat meat, good. If someone calls [invites] me and only gives me liquor and no meat, will I be a little sad (*mon duk*) then, or not? – a bit angry (*ragi*)(. . .). I won't tell you, but I'll be a bit angry, no? (. . .) All the gods are angry now, no? Listen. What I've just said, this one [god] is in a rather bad mood (*mon korap lagla*), that one is also feeling bad. They [the gods] mingle, (. . .) here [is one], and here there will be another two people (*lok*) [gods], they say, "Why have you become a little sad? Is your body feeling somewhat bad?" They say that. – "No, no, we're in a very bad mood on account of someone. Such and such offerings (*debaku*) were [earlier] given to us, [now] the sons-of-bitches don't give anything, these motherfuckers (. . .)." – "Ha! Things are going badly for me, too, I'll also join [you]," you know? Four, five people [gods] get together join them, no? They all mingle, big, small, they all mingle.[1]

Yet, the festival has been performed well. The gods were called into the village, into the shrine, into the houses. They walked through the village; they were offered blood and liquor and meat; they were properly hosted. They were present in many ways: in the posts that were decorated, in the figures that were fashioned, in the mural that was painted, in the music that was played and the songs that were sung, in the human bodies during the trance-dance and the stilt dance. The gods played and humans played as well; they had fun. The test was performed and the *gurumai* confirmed that all had been done well, the gifts were well received, the gods were pleased. They enjoyed themselves and they will watch over humans with affection; fever-sorrow will not seize them. Well-being is now assured, for the children and daughters, cattle and sons, cultivation and harvest; everything will be good and disasters won't strike. And how many people came! The world was present! There was plenty of everything,

---

[1] For the original Desia see Berger (2015, 113–14).

10 Conclusion: Navigating Life — 397

beer and liquor, rice and meat. Everything was right and beautiful. The hosts now have a name; there is no mention of shame.

***

Despite their diversity, the subaltern festivals discussed in this book have this in common. They provide occasions when humans, deities and the dead – metapersons of different kinds – meet and mingle, engaging in the most intimate interactions. Even under ordinary circumstances, the gods and the dead are not necessarily far away, they are immanent in many features of the landscape, in trees, stones or water, in the earth itself, and in human dwellings made out of earth. Humans may at times be involuntarily drawn into close contact with such metapersons, for instance in cases of illness, possession or a transgression. However, the festivals – being specifically located in space and time; the moon itself being a manifestation of the sky god, providing the rhythm of the festivals – enable encounters of a different quality. It is as if the festivals bring about a different state of aggregation of the beings involved. Identities that are normally relatively stable come to merge and shift, human and divine beings acquire new properties, new boundaries, new bodies. In this state of ritual aggregation, identities are more volatile: Joria temporarily become Dombo, Ghasi or Paik; the dead – brought back into the midst of living human society – receive new external forms, buffalo bodies, branch bodies and stone bodies; gods climb down from the upper world to inhabit wall paintings, winnowing fans or clay pots; they become embodied in termite mounds, millet grains or sprouting wheat.

Ritual, Rappaport (1979, 200; 1999, 155–68) states, entails a "paradigm of creation," reuniting substance and form, as in cosmogonic myths that narrate how the world was created and shaped. However, unlike his emphasis on language as transformative action, "that which transforms" (1999, 156) in the highly (re)generative festivals discussed here is not so much speech but sacrifice. Certainly, invocations are also crucial, demanding the attention of the gods, inviting the dead, showing deference or formulating requests. Moreover, one could say that the Joria actually sing their mural into existence as much as they paint it during the Nandi festival. However, ultimately it is the flow of blood that transforms and enlivens; that enables the shifting of identities, the dynamics of interiorities and bodies that are so crucial in these festivals; the transfer of life, as Hocart (1970, 33) would say.

Such a flow of life is possible given the premise that the various forms of beings do not possess completely different interiorities (see Harderberg 2021). The dead are humans anyway and for their last journey to the underworld Gadaba equip them with objects of daily use, such as would be required by humans in the middle world. Through the killing of the affinal *purani* buffalo on the dry fields during the Go'ter, the life of a living deceased person is transferred to the earth, out of which millet plants will soon grow; these plants that are considered "children of the village" and they sustain the life of humans. Humans and certain plants have a very intimate relationship. Humans grow cereals – the knowledge of cultivation often said to be of divine origin, such as the "cultivation stone" in the Pengo myth – which not only entails ploughing, sowing and weeding but also performing life-cycle rituals for finger millet and rice. Conversely, while one cannot really say that plants "cultivate" humans, millet and rice make humans live and grow into ritually complete persons. Human grainhood and plant personhood condition each other in this animist cosmos.

Gods manifest in specific places, in rivers or mountains, wooden pillars or stones but the everyday whereabouts of deities is hard to fathom. In the context of rituals, they actually inhabit these places and receive offerings. In their emotional make-up, and as far as their desires are concerned, the gods do not seem to be so different from humans, they are also "people" (*lok*). They demand liquor, meat and blood, they are happy, angry or sad, they even swear like humans, those beings they have created. Gadaba call themselves "earth creatures" (Gutob) and a Pengo myth (M8) specifies that humans "came into being by piercing through the earth, [. . .] have been born splitting the earth" (Burrow and Bhattacharya 1970, 118). Also the Dongria consider themselves as "children of the earth" (Hardenberg 2018a, 622). In mythical times they emerged from the earth, after which they have received rules and knowledge and assumed their primary responsibility, performing sacrifices for their earth mother, who gives her daughter (Lahi Penu, the "wealth" of the harvest) in return. Gods themselves, it is often said, are earth-born. Dongria myths narrate how the sky god emerged out of the earth, while the Desia around Nandapur – Gadaba, Joria and others – consider the King God (Raja Maphru) to have appeared out of the earth in this "navel place;" out of a hillock or some kind of mound or a hollow. Gods, humans, the dead, animals and plants are certainly not identical, but they share being, which enables the circulation of life, for instance, between termite earth/eggs and millet seeds; transpositions exemplified in the mythical grinding of earth and pounding of dust by the *gurumai*-goddess called Earth Beauty Dust Beauty and enabled by the contextual properties of ritual aggregation.

One thing that gods lack is a physical form comparable to human bodies, with which they can move, feast and enjoy themselves. In conjunction with the sacrificial circulation of life through blood, this seems to be another vital element in the festivals discussed: gods want to play. Accordingly, they temporarily dwell in human bodies and play themselves or they are carried by dancing and swaying human bodies, such as by the Joria women who dance with the Ganga and Nandi deities, moving through the village for several days. This divine play entails the transient merging of divine and human worlds, including various forms of effervescent dislocations, temporarily shifting different forms of being. Abundance (sensory, somatic, sonic) and ritual ferocity are among those aspects that both enable and signify divine presence, dislocation and fusion.

Often, the ritual movement of human and divine bodies entails a high degree of speed and rapid acceleration, as if the spatial suffusion with godly power (*shakti*) is a function of motion, a kind of divine kinetic energy. Dance and play are aesthetic, sensational forms (Meyer 2012, 160) through which the divine is manifested and experienced. As Alfred Gell (1980) pointed out in relation to Bastar, from the local perspective, this goes both ways, gods indulging in equilibrium play and humans experiencing and sharing in divine presence. The ferocity of ritual and ritualized play, including fighting and killing that we repeatedly encountered in the festivals – both with regard to the killing of animals and between humans – is a vital dimension of these aesthetic forms and embodied practices of dislocation. The kinetic dynamics are a demonstration, a realization, at times an appropriation, of power, not in a political but in a ritual sense (or, perhaps, as a special kind of ritual biopolitics); they are means of navigating life and, conversely, ritual attempts of defying death.

The proverb *Raja Dasara, Joria Nandi, Mali Bali, Gadaba Go'ter*, as I have argued in this book, identifies a sacrificial polity, where ruling means facilitating the flow of life. As Hocart writes (1970, 33, 36), man "has come to think he can *control* that coming and going [of life]. He has worked out a technique to the end of controlling it," namely "ritual (. . .), a co-operation for life." I would not go so far as to say that the proverbial protagonists would claim to "control" the flow of life, at least no more than a sailor would claim to be able to control the sea or a pilot the sky; but they strive to master life, to navigate it. Accordingly, the aphorism assigns signature festivals to its characters, delineating their share in the joint quest – the younger brother who becomes king and the elder brothers who become subjects. The responsibility to perform these festivals is frequently stressed, for instance, in the ending of a local myth (M2), which states: "The younger brother became king (*raja*), the elder brother became subject (*porja*). The descendants of the elder brother were the Gadaba Porja. The king started with the Dasara festival, the Gadaba Porja started the Go'ter. The king sacrifices humans during Dasara, Gadaba sacrifice the buffaloes. The Joria do the Nandi." Each one assumes a specific sacrificial role that not only becomes a distinctive mark of their collective identity, but a sacrificial contribution to the whole. The leading performer of the Ganga festival of the Joria – the twin festival of the Nandi left unmentioned in the proverb, the rice-brother of the millet-sister – also clearly articulated this ritual obligation: it is the King God who gave the festival to the Joria and it is the cultivator-brothers who perform the sacrifice and make the deity walk. "Who performs his sacrifice?"

he asked rhetorically, "the brothers do it." Likewise, in the Pengo story (M10), the earth goddess told her brothers, the Bima, to take the Bali Jatra to the world of humans and perform it there and, similarly, the gods stipulated that the humans should be the custodians of the Mango festival (M8). The consequences of the failure or refusal to live up to these ritual obligations are also clearly outlined. As Birsa Sisa stated, when the kings of Nandapur and Jeypore stopped sacrificing sheep, buffaloes and human beings, illnesses – the opposite of well-being – broke out all over the world. Thus, a wicked Dom King who obstructs regeneration is fought and overthrown in the Ganga festival as in the myth.

Human sacrifice, the paradigmatic and most powerful form of sacrifice, of which all sacrificial offerings are substitutions in some way, has been a recurrent theme throughout this book. It figures in myths and is depicted in wall paintings, it is and has been performed in rituals and is a topic of conversation, even if those comments are only whispered.[2] In all instances, human sacrifice is linked to renewal, growth and wealth in the most general sense. Kings, especially, are said to have performed human sacrifices in the past, such as the kings of Nandapur/Jeypore or the That Raja of Bissamcuttack. It figured prominently in the Dasara festivals of the kings. In Bastar, the ascetic stand-in for the king was symbolically sacrificed after a period of nine days of quasi-death, which was synchronized with the germination and growth of wheat. The association between the ascetic and human sacrifice has also been documented in Jeypore. Human sacrifice figures prominently in many tribal myths. Macpherson presented a local account that narrates how the ancestors of the Kond "at first knew only the form of worship necessary for themselves, not that necessary for the whole world" (Macpherson 1865, 122), which emphasizes the general responsibility involved. The *jani* then received direct instructions from the earth goddess about how to perform the human sacrifice and she predicted: "Then see how many children will be born to you, how much game will be yours, what crops, how few will die. All things will become right" (Macpherson 1865, 123; see Hardenberg 2018a, 606). The Kond are obviously the most famous case, but such ideas are very widespread in the region. As a consequence of human sacrifice, a Pengo myth relates how a "flower tree" sprang up, bearing wealth of all kinds, such as money, gold and silver, domestic animals and grain (Burrow and Bhattacharya 1970, 144–51), while in a Parenga story, water and rain are the result, and plantain trees in another Joria narrative (Elwin 1954, 269f, 142f, M16).

---

[2] Statements about human sacrifices are not always articulated in a whisper. In 2000, when Georg Pfeffer and Roland Hardenberg visited the place in Phulbani District where all Kond are said to have emerged from the earth, they were told that an old man and a child would have been sacrificed there three weeks before (Hardenberg 2018a, 430 fn. 14).

I am not dealing here with the question of whether human sacrifice used to be actually performed or if it was and is "merely symbolic." That does not mean that I consider the difference between imagination and fact to be irrelevant; without doubt it mattered to the ascetic stand-in of the king during Dasara that he was signifying the sacrificial victim and had to disappear but was not actually killed. However, what Sahlins (1983, 88) said about cannibalism is certainly also the case here; if human sacrifices have been performed in the past, they certainly were symbolic at the same time; or, as Geertz wrote: "The real is as imagined as the imaginary" (1980, 136). The Gɔ'ter of the Gadaba may be a case in point. Of all the subaltern festivals of the proverb discussed here, it most explicitly entails the killing of humans, albeit revived dead.[3] The social person of the deceased, the interiority of former humans, is then newly contained in buffalo bodies. When documenting the Go'ter in the village of Ponosguda in 2001, I was led by one of the hosts along the row of buffaloes that were tied to the village platform. He introduced each of his relatives to me, patting the backs of the animals as he explained their kinship relationship. These impressive animals were very real and though their imagined identity as deceased persons brought back to life might be contested and was, perhaps, not in the same way real to me as it was for the participants, it was certainly a social fact with real-life consequences, again both imagined and real. This imagination influenced human behavior, affected relationships between local groups and facilitated the regeneration of finger millet.

On this note, on such occasions when the question of whether certain human practices – such as cannibalism or human sacrifice – could have actually happened was posed, my teacher Georg Pfeffer used to quote Christian Morgenstern's poem *Die unmögliche Tatsache* (*The Impossible Fact*), which ends with the verse: "Und er kommt zu dem Ergebnis: Nur ein Traum war das Erlebnis. Weil, so schließt er messerscharf, nicht sein *kann*, was nicht sein *darf*" (1983, 84–85).[4]

The proverb outlines a sacrificial division of labor in a kingdom in which sacrifice was definitely "a fundamental relation of production" (Sahlins 2017, 53; see Berger 2015, 444–74; Hardenberg 2016). Whatever else may have characterized the historical reality of the Nandapur/Jeypore kingdom, it definitely

---

3 Some Gadaba would say that the killing of the *purani* actually is not a sacrifice, as it does not entail certain elements, such as an invocation to the recipient.
4 Which translates as: "And he comes to the conclusion: His mishap was an illusion, for, he reasons pointedly, that which must not, can not be." Translated by: Max E Knight (from: https://fromtroublesofthisworld.wordpress.com/2013/06/09/the-impossible-fact-by-christian-otto-josef-wolfgang-morgenstern/) .

constituted a "cosmic polity" in the sense recently described by Graeber and Sahlins:

> Human societies are hierarchically encompassed – typically above, below, and on earth – in a cosmic polity populated by beings of human attributes and metahuman powers who govern the people's fate. In the form of gods, ancestors, ghosts, demons, species-masters, and the animistic beings embodied in the creatures and features of nature, these metapersons are endowed with far-reaching powers of human life and death, which, together with their control of the conditions of the cosmos, make them the all-round arbiters of human welfare and illfare. Even many loosely structured hunting and gathering peoples are thus subordinated to beings on the order of gods ruling over great territorial domains and the whole of the human population. There are kingly beings in heaven even where there are no chiefs on earth. (Graeber and Sahlins 2017, 2)

Indeed, the local cosmos features many metapersons that are framed in royal terms, first of all the sky god with his various names: the King God (Raja Maphru); the king of order/goodwill (Dorom Raja, Dharmu Raja), who appointed the king of divine rules (Niamraja) for the Dongria, residing in their Niamgiri Hills, and who instituted the cosmic law (*niam*) that stipulates the performance of sacrifices and festivals and thus the flow of life. Below ground, the king of death (Jom Raja, in the case of the Dongria a queen, not a king, Jamarani) rules, taking and providing the bodies that humans temporarily inhabit. The hills are controlled by the herder of the forest (Bon Goudo), who watches over game and permits human hunting. Also, among the many names of the earth goddess are those that stress her ruling capacity. As ruling queen (Takurani) she controls everything that grows from the earth. These and other metapersons certainly "govern the people's fate," but as subaltern sovereigns the tribal subjects, as sacrificers, not only influence the relations of production but also share in divine power and thus also have a means of coercion. This becomes particularly evident in the domain of the ritual system concerned with "devouring," that is, averting evil influences. In this context, the dictum is "appeal to the gods, bind the demon" (*depta mangibo, rau bandibo*); or a healer might confront an attack by a metaperson with a line from a spell that inverts the status of hunter and prey: "you're the goat, I am the tiger" (*tui cheli mui bag*). As sacrificers, they are thus not completely powerless victims but potent agents in their own terms within this cosmic polity.

The societies I have described in this book certainly do not represent the type of "loosely structured hunting and gathering peoples" Graeber and Sahlins mention. Neither did they have "chiefs on earth" to speak of as political power was not vested in any tribal office. Nevertheless, alongside all their divine royals they did have a human king. Regardless of what the king may have thought about himself, his subjects saw in their younger brother first of all a co-sacrificer;

a meta-sacrificer whose Dasara festival brought together all the communities of the region, ritually constituting the ritual polity as a totality which otherwise operated on village level or, at best on the level of ritual village confederations. This king, who sponsored sacrifices and who could domesticate the fiercest goddess, thus performed on the global scale what his subjects performed locally: navigating life through sacrifice. Did they perceive him as a god in the same way that they conceived of their deities as kings? That is difficult to say. Perhaps the situation was more akin to Vedic times, when, as Daud Ali (2011, 91) argues, human kings were regarded as paradigmatic sacrificers but not as gods. Perhaps in the former Nandapur/Jeypore kingdom this representation of the divine king was rather part of the king's own imagination.

Appendix 1: Glossary of local terms (including botanical names)

Abbreviations of different local languages

D	Desia
Do	Dongria
G	Gutob
Go	Gondi
H	Halbi
P	Pengo
R	Remo
S	Sora

Note: The same word may be locally pronounced in different ways (e.g. "festival:" *porbo, porob, parbo, parbu*) and spelt in yet more ways in the academic literature.

Details about references and sources can be found in the main text and in the bibliography.

age (D)	then, before, in front; also *purberu* (D)
agtu lok (D)	people of before; also *purberu lok* (D)
aiba borso (D)	next year
ani dadi (D)	forefathers, ancestors; also *anibai* (D), *mata pita* (D) ("mother-fathers")
ara (D)	bamboo container
Bada (Do)	marriage ritual
bai (D)	(D) brother; member of the same clan (*bonso*)
bai moitor (D)	ritual friends with the same clan affiliation
Bali Jatra (D)	"Sand Festival;" the signature festival of the Mali
bana (D)	sacrificial pattern drawn in a ritual context
banni (D)	name of a tree; *Prosopis cineraria* (L.) Druce
barik (D)	village herald, always recruited from the Dombo community
baya nat (D)	trance-dance
Bejuni (Do)	shaman
bel (D)	beli fruit or stone apple; *Aegle marmelos* (L.) Correa
Bening, Benek (D)	a cultivating community of Koraput; part of Desia society
bera (D)	paddy field; *liong* (G)
bet (D)	hunt, hunting; *gu'um* (G)
bet kal, tas kal (P)	"hunting stone, cultivation stone;" gift of the *gurumai*-goddess called Mati Sundori Duri Sundori in a Pengo myth
beti (D)	tribute paid to the king, also *raja beti*
bet-tas (D)	hunting and cultivation
Bima (D)	god of rain, wind and agriculture

bipod (D)	trouble, disaster
biri (D)	black gram; *Vigna mungo* (L.) Hepper
birom (D)	termite mound
birong (G)	hill, forest
bogicha (D)	vegetable garden, *aro* (G)
Boiro, Boirobi (D)	god/goddess receiving buffalo sacrifices
bol soman (D)	"good and even;" the condition of general well-being, reciprocity and balance
Bon Goudo (D)	"Herder of the Forest," a deity
bon katiba (D)	"cutting the forest;" ritual sequence in the Bali Jatra
bonchiba, bonchaiba (D)	to live, to enliven
Bondo (D)	indigenous community of Koraput; refer to themselves as Remo ("man," "human") in their own Munda language (also called Remo)
bondu (D)	affines; those with a different clan affiliation
bonso (D)	unilineal totemic descent category, clan
boro (D)	big, senior; *moro* (G)
boro dissari (D)	senior astrologer; ritual specialist
botor kira (D)	winged termites that leave the mound to found new colonies; also *butui* (D)
buliba (D)	strolling, walking
bumli jaga (D)	"navel place," place where the umbilical cord and placenta are buried; also a reference to Nandapur, where the King God is said to have emerged from the earth, a mound or a rock
bur (D)	death ritual
chamda (D)	a canopy or baldachin made from sticks and leaves above a ritual area
chari bai (D)	"four brothers;" ritual village unit constituted by the four local descent groups (*kuda*)
chitro (D)	mural, painting
dan (D)	unhusked paddy; *kerong* (G); Asian rice; *Oryza sativa* (L.)
dan (P)	wealth
dapu (D)	a frame drum
Databeli Gada (D)	"Donor-of-(sacrificial) Wealth-Fort;" palace mentioned in the Bali Jatra epic
demsa (D)	circle-dance common in Koraput
Dengudi (D)	"High-Shrine;" stilt dancers in the Ganga festival; associated with the group of Paik (foot soldiers)
Desia (D)	"of the land;" indigenous people of the region; the lingua franca spoken by these people
Dev Bajar (H)	"God's Market;" a tribal festival in Bastar
Dev Khel (H)	"play of the gods;" highpoint of the "God's Market"
Devirani Phulseri (D)	"Goddess Queen Flower Roots;" a character in the Bali Jatra epic
Dharni (Do, P)	a name of the earth goddess
dissari (D)	ritual specialist, astrologer, healer
dol (D)	cylindrical drum

Dom *luga* (D)	cloth woven by the Dombo
Dom Raja (D)	Dom King; mythical figure representing a wicked king
Dombo, Dom (D)	local Desia community of weavers, petty traders and musicians; Goren (G)
domi (D)	ritual role in the Ganga festival; the (male) hosts of the Ganga deities
domini (D)	ritual role in the Ganga festival; women who carry the Ganga deities in procession, the female hosts of the Ganga deities
Dongira Kond (D)	indigenous community inhabiting the Niamgiri Hills; refer to themselves as Kuang, "human" (Do)
Dorom (D)	the sky god; also Pat Deota, Dharamraja, Mahaprabu, Sī Arke (G)
doron deli (D)	the central pillar of a house, representing the earth goddess
Dorti Mata (D)	"Earth Mother;" one of the many names of the earth goddess; also Bosmoti, Takurani etc.
dosra (D)	the month (Oct.) in which the Dasara festival takes place
duma (D)	spirits of the recently dead
duma daini (D)	general term for potentially harmful spirits
dunia (D)	"the world"
dupo (D)	resin used as incense during rituals
duri derang (P)	"dust finger millet," a local variety of finger millet
ebe (D)	now
ebro lok (D)	people of now
ga bosilabele (D)	"time the village sat down;" time when a village was founded
ga munda (D)	"village post;" megalithic assemblage in a village; *ungom munda* (G)
Gadaba (D)	indigenous community of Koraput; part of Desia society
Ganga (D)	a) name of a deity; name of the festival for the Ganga deity celebrated by the Joria
Ghasi (D)	local caste of Nandapur, formerly stable grooms
Go'ter (G)	"tearing;" the signature ritual of the Gadaba
go'yang (G)	sacrificial food; *tsoru* (D)
Goro Boga (D)	"Leg Offering;" the stilt dance in the Ganga festival
Goudo (D)	community of herders; part of Desia society
Guar (S)	"stone-planting;" Sora death ritual
gum (D)	wheat; *Triticum*
Gunom (R)	Bondo death ritual involving the erection of megaliths
gurumai (D)	ritual specialist who communicates with deities via possession
gurumeni (Do)	assistant of a shaman (*bejuni*)
hundi (D)	shrine of the earth goddess in a village; also *nisani*
jakeri (Do)	stones who represent the earth goddess (Dharni) in a Dongira village, wife of the sky-god
Jakor (D)	deity associated with the earth among different Desia communities
Jal Kamni Patal Kamni (D)	earth-water deity
Jamarani (Do)	"Queen of Life and Death;" creator goddess of the Dongria; also Jaura Penu (Do)

jani (D, Do)	village priest of the Dongria and Joria
jibon (D)	life, life-force of living beings; *jiu, jela* (Do)
ji-bouni (D)	"daughter-sisters;" women leaving the village for marriage
jola (D)	a spring, source of water
juar (D)	gesture and expression of greeting
jur, juro (D)	"tearing," "snatching;" sacrificial practice; *go'ter* (G)
Kamar (D)	community of blacksmiths; part of Desia society
kandul (D)	pigeon pea or red gram; *Cajanus cajan* (L.) Millsp.
kangu (D)	foxtail millet; *Setaria italica* (L.) P. Beauv
Kappor Chua (D)	a sacred place in the Bondo area
Karja (S)	annual festival for the dead among the Sora
katani git (D)	"story-song," a narrative that is sung
kel (D)	"play," "playing;" *keliba* ("let's play")
kira (D)	worm, maggot
kirdi (D)	a small kettle drum
kisalo' (G)	traditional garment woven and worn by Gadaba women
Kordu Parbu (Do)	Buffalo Festival among the Dongira
koronj (D)	Pongam oil tree; *Pongamia pinnata* (L.) Pierre
koteiwali (Do)	stones in a Dongria village representing the sky-god and father of the Dongria; wife of the earth goddess
Kotni Mala (D)	a rock formation near Nandapur with marks that look like a huge mortar (*kunti* (D))
kuda (D)	a) Desia status categories (e.g. *sisa, munduli*); b) local descent groups (e.g. Sisa, Munduli); c) Dongria clans
Kumar (D)	community of potters; part of Desia society
kunia, gotia (D)	(affinal) guests
kusi (D)	affection
lakka' (G)	sacrificial food (often consisting of the body of the victim) junior to *tsoru*
lati (D)	bamboo poles that represent local deities; *lati bog* (D) "pole offering," the carrying of these poles during a festival
lok (D)	people, person (human or divine)
lungi (D)	male garment for the lower body
Mai Kotma (D)	"Mother of Termites" or "Manure Mother," one name of the Nandi deity
Mali (D)	community of horticulturalists; part of Desia society
maloi (D)	oil lamp
mamu (D)	mother's brother
man (D)	dry measure
manasik (D)	vow to perform a ritual
mandia (D)	finger millet; *dare* (Do); *dera* (P); *sa'mel* (G); *Eleusine coracana* (L.) Gaertn.
Mandia Biru (D)	Millet Ritual of the Gadaba
Mandiarani (Do)	Dongria ritual for finger millet
mandru (D)	round balls made from finger millet and molasses

manti (D)	"respect;" gift from the non-cultivating communities of a village during a festival, acknowledging the senior status of the earth people
maphru, Maphru (D)	a) general word for a god (like *debta*); b) the sky god, also Raja Maphru
matam (D)	with regard to the village as a whole (e.g. a sacrifice)
Mati Sundori Duri Sundori (D)	"Earth Beauty Dust Beauty;" one term for the Nandi goddess; a *gurumai*-goddess in a Pengo myth (M8)
matia (D)	"earth people;" original settlers of a village with a right to perform the sacrifices and to share senior sacrificial food; contrast with "late-comers" (*upria*)
memor (D)	elected village office; from English "ward member"
meria, Meria (Do)	formally human victims of the Kond sacrifice to the earth goddess; name of the festival
moali (D)	wealth that is given in the context of the Go'ter, combination of *mota* (brass pot) and *tali* (brass plate)
mod (D)	local liquor; *ili* (G)
moiri (D)	wind instrument played my Dombo musicians; *moira* designates the player of the instrument and the leader of the musical ensemble (furthermore consisting of three drums)
moitor (D)	relation of ritual friendship
mojapur (D)	the middle world
mon duk (D)	sadness
mul ghasi (D)	a ritual role in the Ganga festival; the leader of the Ghasi
munda (D)	a sacrificial post or stone in a megalithic ensemble
Munda Puja (D)	"Post Sacrifice" at the external dry-field platform during the Go'ter
mungo (D)	green gram; *Vigna radiata* (L.) R. Wilczek
muta (D)	a) ritual unit of associated villages; b) administrative unit for taxation
mutadar (D)	a person who formally collected tax within a *muta* for the king
naik (D)	village headman
Nandi (D)	a) name of a deity; b) name of the festival celebrated for the Nandi deity by the Joria
nat (D)	dance
nehi ane (Do)	"it will be good," "it will be right;" Dongria concept of encompassing well-being
niam (D)	social-cosmic order or moral law instituted by the gods
Niamgiri (D, Do)	"Mountain of Rules," or "Path of Rules;" the highest peak in the mountain range the Dongria inhabit
Nuakai (D)	Name of a festival; first consumption of certain crops or fruit
Ollar Gadaba (D)	the junior segment of the Gadaba; part of Desia society
Ollari (D)	Dravidian language spoken by the Ollar Gadaba
olma (D)	term les; *ulama* (Do); *to'dur* (G); *tobdur* (R)
olsi (D)	niger seed; *Guizotia abyssinica* (L.f.) Cass.
oso (D)	"medicine;" *sindrong* (G)

Paik Kel (D)	"Paik Play;" ritual sequence of the Ganga festival in which the Paik fight against Ghasi and Dom; also Sari Kel
Paik (D)	name of a community who previously constituted the foot-soldiers for the king
palda (D)	Indian coral tree; *Erythrina variegate* (L.)
panjabai (D)	ritual relationship between two groups among the Gadaba and Parenga; they take the buffalo-dead in the context of a Go'ter (literal meaning unclear)
Parenga (D)	indigenous community of Koraput; they call themselves Gorum in the Munda language of the same name (Gorum); part of Desia society
Pat Gurumai (D)	"Main Gurumai;" the Bali deity as manifested in the Bali Jatra epic and the ritual object of a clay pot
Pat Kanda (D)	"Main Sword;" one of the names of the sky god and the local shrine where he is worshipped
patalpur (D)	the underworld; also *jompur* (D), *bitorpur* (D)
pej (D)	gruel, commonly made from finger millet; *ida* (G)
Pen Kasana (Go)	"God Playing;" a festival of Bastar
pendom (D)	alcoholic beverage ("beer") made from finger millet and/or rice); similar to *landa* (D)
penu, pen (Do, P, Go)	general word for deity in Dravidian languages
Persa Pen (Go)	Cult of the clan god among the Gond
phul (D)	flower
pindoli (D)	small ledge at the bottom of a wall (*pinda* (D), veranda)
pipal (D)	pipal tree; or sacred fig; *Ficus religiosa* (L.)
pit kanda (D)	aerial yam; or bitter yam; *Dioscorea bulbifera* (L.)
poche (D)	after, behind
poda munda	megalitic ensemble in the dry fields; also *munda langbo* (G), Go'ter *munda* (G)
poda	dry field; *langbo* (G)
por (D)	water buffalo; *bongtel* (G)
porikia	test; an examination to confirm the success of a ritual
porja, Porja	a) subject (of a king); contrasts with *raja*; b) tribal communities of the region; c) specific indigenous community of the region also called Senior or Boro Porja
puradan (S)	"soul"
purani (G)	a category of buffaloes brought by affines to the village hosting a Go'ter
Purnagad (D)	the Old Fort in Jeypore
puy mar (P)	"flower tree;" a mythical tree producing wealth
raja beti (D)	the tribute paid to a king, especially in the context of Dasara
raja mila (Do)	"children of the king;" self-designation of the Dongria
randari (D)	sacrificial cook; recruited from the local group of Kirsani
Rani Duduma (D)	the "Queens Fall;" a waterfall near Nandapur, in the vicinity of the Kotni Mala Hill
Rau (D)	a demon, main agent of fatal disaster among the Desia
roit (D)	cultivators

Rona (D)	community of the region and part of Desia society; formerly constituting the militia of the king
sadar (D)	a) megalithic ensemble and meeting place in any Desia village; b) flat stones in a megalithic ensemble
sai (D)	village neighborhood
sairem-ba (Re)	"fathers of the dead;" ritual role during Bondo death rituals
salap (D)	a) juice from the Sago tree; b) the name of the tree; *Caryota urens* (L.)
sano (D)	"small," "junior;" also *me'en* (G)
sari (D)	female garment
sari (Re)	flower, placenta
satara bonda (Do)	ritual umbrella; small metal object that is attached to a bamboo pole in the context of the buffalo sacrifice of the Dongria
saukar (D)	the host of a ritual
Sī Arke (G)	"Sun Moon" deity; one name of the sky god among the Gadaba
siardi (D)	a creeper, Camel's foot climber; *Bauhinia vahlii* Wight & Arn.
sil (D)	erect stones in a megalithic ensemble
simli (D)	Silk cotton tree; *Bombax ceiba* (L.) (also *B. malabarica*)
sindibor (Re)	megalithic ensemble and village meeting place among the Bondo; *sadar* (D)
siraha, sirha (H)	ritual medium whose body a deity possesses
sisa	village sacrificer, recruited from the Sisa group of a village; also called *pujari* (D); similar to the *jani* among the Dongria or Joria
Sita Penu Lahi Penu (Do)	Dongria goddess of rice and wealth; also only Lahi Penu
sonum (S)	a transitory condition of a deceased person; the experience aspect of a deceased person
sorkar (D)	government
sorogpur (D)	the upper world
suan (D)	little millet; *iri'* (G); *Panicum sumatrense* Roth
Sundi	community of liquor distillers; part of Desia society
sundoro (D)	beautiful, good
suri bonda (Do)	ritual knife and umbrella; sacred objects in the context of the buffalo sacrifice of the Dongria
suta moitor (D)	"thread friends;" a form of friendship established in the Bali Jatra by exchanging sprouts
Sutok Sorani (D)	"Ending Impurity;" a ritual performed for newborn children
tamok (D)	a kettle drum
tika (D)	a form of greeting or blessing in which someone applies husked rice on the forehead (and potentially also the shoulders, knees and feet) of another person
tsoru (D)	senior sacrificial food, also *go'yang* (G)
tsorubai (D)	"sacrificial food brothers;" a ritual relationship between two groups of clan brothers
ungon (G)	crab; also *kankara* (D)
upria (D)	"late comer;" those people of the village who settled after the original inhabitants (earth people)

Appendix 2: Myths

Note: The myths taken from Verrier Elwin's *Bondo Highlander* (1950) and *Tribal Myths of Orissa* (1954) have been reproduced with permission of Oxford University Press India © Oxford University Press 1950, 1954.

M1

Gadaba, Guneipada, Koraput District, Elwin 1954, 519f; see page 70.

M2

Ollar Gadaba; near Boipariguda; recorded by Roland Hardenberg, Georg Pfeffer and M.D. Hussain; March 2, 2000.

At the river Godabari, on a Thursday under a *saj* tree [*Terminalia alata*] a female calf (*bachuri*) was born. A son and a daughter, their father had died, came to the Nandapur area. Near Nandapur they sacrificed the calf and that truned them into husband and wife. The wedding was announced by the *dissari* to the people and a canopy of wood and leaves was build where the wedding should take place. The brother took rice and gave *tika* to his sister, therby making her his wife. The woman also gave *tika* to her brother. Thus was the marriage consummated according to the rules. Afterwards all shared the calf meat. Then they danced *demsa*. They were three siblings: the brother, the sister and the calf.

The Children of the two, Lobo and Kuso were twins, two brothers. As they reached maturity their parents went away to seek spouses. For some time they did not find appropriate women. Then they came to a waterfall and saw two demonesses (*rakjasi*) who took water from the river. Lobo caught one of them, the other one fled. Lobo said: "I want to marry you," but she refused as she was a demoness and he a human (*moniso*). He took her violently to his house and his parents. There, an ear ring (*murmi*) was pierced through the ear of the demoness and she became a human being.

After 6 to 12 months the women wanted to go to her father's house together with Lobo. Kuso asked his elder brother Lobo not to eat anything in her father's house, except water and not to stay longer than two days. As Lobo and his wife arrive at her father's place, a cow was sacrificed there. These people were the

Gadaba. Lobo was the first time at his father-in-law's house since his wedding and his parents-in-law forced him to eat beef against his will.

As Lobo and his wife returned home Lobo admitted his transgression to his younger brother. He knew it already as God (Takuro) had told him about it. Lobo said: "Because of my transgression I and my wife will go away." The younger brother became king (*raja*), the elder brother became subject (*porja*). The descendants of the elder brother were the Gadaba Porja. The king started with the Dasara festival, the Gadaba Porja started the Go'ter. The king sacrifices humans during Dasara, Gadaba sacrifice the buffaloes. The Joria do the Nandi.

M3

Dombo; Onmail; recorded by Peter Berger & Manto Pradhan; May 5, 2000; transcribed and translated by Diptimaya Pradhan, Manto Pradhan and Peter Berger.

Well, an old man and an old woman, two people were living there. One son and one daughter, two children were born from them. The son and daughter lived, the old man and old woman died. After they had died, their God Bagwan, Takurani mother caught them [brother and sister]. Holding [them], [she asked] "Who are you, who are you?" – "I don't know" [brother and sister answered]. "[They] don't know" [the goddess] said and god caught [them again]. Goddess (Takurani) holding [them, asked]: "Who are you?" – "We [are] brother and sister, we [are] brother and sister." – "What shall I do?" [the goddess said to herself], "[I] have to change the world." "[I] change the world, [goddess] said. Then they [brother and sister] lost their memory. "Who are you?" [the goddess asked] – "I don't know" [one of the siblings answered], "Who are you?" [the goddess asked again] – "I don't know" [the other one answered]. "Now you brother sister stay together in one house" [Takurani said].

The two, brother sister, stayed in one house. From their womb (*pete*) twelve sons and daughters were born. Twelve sons and daughters were born, one became Gadaba, one Dom, one Ghasi, one Gorua, one Rona. Twelve children took birth from one mother. Children from the brother-sister womb. So, twelve people were born from those brother and sister. They were divided into 12 groups (*jati*), someone Mali, someone Kumbar, someone Dom, someone Gadaba, someone Ghasi, someone Gorua. Well, like this over time those two people [brother-sister] made a family. Made family, those 12 boys and girls, those are the children of that brother and sister's blood. Brother and sister made the paths for the whole world [i.e. distributed themselves]. God (Maphru) took rest (*bisram*).

They [brother and sister] set out for Nandapur. They went to Nandapur and the brother made her pregnant. After they went to Nandapur a brother went hunting. When he came back from hunting the clothes of his sister had fallen [she was naked]. From her place she saw that her brother was approaching: "How does my body look like? That is not good." So she fell into Queen-Gorge-Mother (Rani-Jol-Ma).[1] At Nandapur, into Queen-Gorge-Mother she fell, Hunting-Gorge (Bet Jola) and Queen-Gorge-Mother are there. The brother came to the place and thought: "My sister jumped and died, what shall I do?" He reached out and caught her at the hair (*chuti*). Her hair came off and became a *sum* bush (*sum buta*). As many bushes came into existence, you can now see at Kotni Mala. "Oho, what shall I do?" [the brother asked himself].

By the way of the Duduma waterfall she [the sister] came out at Pinda Jangre, Kapor Chua.[2] There she settled and her name became *bita kand*.[3] As she came out at Jangre, what did the god do? The brother thought: "So the brother shot his sister? Or where did she go? Now I cannot make any decision, she is gone, she went into the stream. Then the four big people sat down [i.e. a village meeting], some bigger, some smaller. They sat down and thought about what to do: "The queen is gone, so who shall sleep in Nandapur Kotni Mala?"

Then the king was born there. Navel-pit-king's house is in Nandapur. There you find *nal bumli* (navel pit), Kotni Mala (rocks with holes of a mortar), Bet Jola (Hunting Gorge). What did the king do there? At that time the forest cock was crowing. "What shall I do, the cock crowed, now it's morning [the king thought], where shall I go?" They went to Deulpada,[4] made a boat there and returned and settled in Nandapur. After they returned they cut all the *kunti* creepers until the next morning came. [They] went to Nandapur, Kotni Mala Bet Jola, and everything was made. "Oho, how would we do it?" They build a temple. They build the temple, made everything fine and ready and then the morning light came. Then the God (Maphru) went to where he pleases, he went to the upper world (*sorgo*) and he went to the underworld (*patal*), and he lived like that. [i.e. roaming around]

---

1 This place is mentioned in many stories and consists of a combnation of a water fall called Rani Duduma (Queen's Fall) and rocks that show the signs that resemble those of a huge mortar (*kunti*), called Kotni Mala.
2 Places in the Bonda area. Elwin (1954, 386) explains that this is a "sacred grove and spring" near Mundlipada, the main Bondo village, where Sita is supposed to have bathed." In the myth (M14) she is bathed there by Lakshman.
3 An arrow to hunt birds.
4 A Gutob Gadaba village.

"I did everything," god said, but something is missing. [So he made] Goradi, Karandi and Kisor [three rivers of the Gutob Gadaba area]. So these three people came out. "You will kill or I will kill [the sacrificial animal]?" They brought a crab.[5] Out of the crab they made curry and a sand deer (*bali somor*) and from little millet (*suen*) they cooked rice. Kisor made this. Goradi and Karandi they prepared a better and thinner type of rice (*sopur danoro bat*) and meat. They ate with great satisfaction. Goradi and Karandi asked themselves: "Shall I push him/it or will you push him/it?" Goradi and Karandi they cannot do it. Kisor has eaten crab and *suen*-rice, he pushed it (*teli dela*). When he pushed, it arrived here and Duduma [waterfall] came into existence. Thereafter Duduma cut the hill and the trees [made the deep valley] and the river flows into the Godavadi River.

Now, what did the king do? "Give us one foot of land" (*padek bumi*) they came to ask from the king. One foot [of land] they said but [they] turned the whole place into government settlement (*saharaj*). Made the settlement, one piece of land of the waterfall, they build the Power House, cut the waterfall. Now, how many great schemes (*jojona*) have been made everywhere: Sileru, Dokorake, Polu. In so many places dams were built, (. . .) [they] come up everywhere. That many, and what did the king do? "I have one piece of land," [he] said "and one piece I give." – "What shall I do with one piece, I have all the land of the world, what shall I do with one piece?" [the government said?] [King] gave one piece, [but] the government (*sorkar*) took everything now. [It] fell into the hand of the government. Alas (*are*), the king has no land, the *porja* have no peace (*santi*). The government keeps all the fields (*jumi*). Like that, all over the place the king lost [all things], the children of that womb [12 brothers and sisters] were true (*satya hela*) and the senior people too; old king lost the country (*buraila des*), the era (*jug*) of the king is gone. This is the reason, this is my story.

M4

Gadaba; told by Birsa Sisa; Gudapada; recorded and translaterd by Peter Berger (no date).

Earlier there also lived Bondo in Nandapur. One Bondo man went hunting, his sister was sitting near the river, husking rice [at Kotni Mala, Rani Duduma]. Her brother's arrow falls close to her and at that moment she recognized that she is

---

[5] Crabs are sacrificed only for the spirits of the dead (*duma*).

naked and jumps into the river. Her brother, trying to save her, can only grab her by the hair and as he pulls, the hair comes off and he holds it in his hands. The sister is taken away and only at Mudulipada, Andrahal [Bondo villages] she resurfaces. Her brother went searching for her and followed her in that direction. Her hair turned into grass. Since then all Bondo women shave their head.

M5

Bening Porja, Sarbati, told by Bisnat Sisa, recorded by Peter Berger and Manto Pradhan, Feb. 6, 2001, translated and transcribed by Manto Pradhan, Diptimaya Pradhan and Peter Berger; see page 82f.

M6

Gadaba; Gudapada; told by Gorua Kirsani; recorded by Peter Berger & Manto Pradhan; March 30, 2001; translated and transcribed by Diptimaya Pradhan, Manto Pradhan and Peter Berger. Note: The narrator frequently uses direct speech but it is often not clear who is speaking.

At the time, the Dom Raja of Nandapur lived in the house [palace], Dom Raja *digdiga baja*. Dom king lived and the Dom houses were built. "You, you have no father, Dom Raja *digdiga baja*." "The other day you are there, at the *meeting* (Engl.) place," he told [probably the Dom king speaking to his subject, see below].

This king [the boy] was born in Nandapur. He was born, but *ter ter ter*, they were crying. Old man and woman were crying because they had no children. They had no children and *ter ter ter* they were crying. "Oho," the old man and woman said, "we will remain alone. From whom we will get a stone [as part of the burial rituals] when we will die?" A child was crying, "Go!" he [the old man] said. "A child is crying," he said, and the old man and woman went. Child was crying, they brought a pan [*tai*, unclear], built a hut and lived there. They marked a path in the forest. When it got dark, the boy asked, "Where is our house, father?" – "Well, I don't know," he said. When they brought the pan [unclear] they also found a piece of cloth. "How can you not know the way to our house, you marked the path?"

Some other day, Dom Raja *digdiga baja* lived. "Another day, you come to the [Dasara] meeting you have to come," he told. "Come and bring pumpkins and such things, honey, tubers (*sar kanda*), such things you fetch and bring, or not?" he [Dom Raja] called and asked the old man and woman, the people of that country. Dom Raja asked, "will you bring it or not?" Thus the boy came and asked the old man and woman, "Will you bring it? 'Otherwise the people of your country will find you,' the Dom King said". – "How will he find us? Oi, child, what did you bring? I told you to bring different things," he [old man] said, "We don't know." "Otherwise hunt with an arrow," he said. "They will kill/beat us when they find us alone." – "We can search but what can we find?" On another day, "Go, buy and bring a stalk of bananas," he said. To the king-boy, he said, "Go, buy and bring it." And he brought a banana stalk. "Make me a shield (*chitkiri pairi*) and a bamboo sword," he told.

On another day, the boy asked "the [Dasara] meeting is going on, will you go? All people of the country come. I will come to the meeting, father." – "If you come, I will die", the father said, "I will die." [Having arrived at the palace, Dom King said] "You greet me 'Juar Maphru' with your feet?" [Boy:] "Which *raja*? Tell! I bid salute with my feet, quickly I will [sit] where you are sitting now. Now, where all the great, great people sit, the place to where all the people of the country came to, I saluted with my feet," he said. "Like this, I greeted by touching my left foot, yes, king, tell," he [boy] said. "How big are you, how big am I?" he said. From behind he kicked the wall with his feet, after that the world *baki dundad baki dundad* [collapsing sound] spun around. Earth destroyed, destroyed. "Ela Maphru, don't," he [boy?] said, and after doing *darshan* (divine vision) and lifting up Duidimali ("Milk-Creeper") Hill, lit a lamp and gave it. "Oh, the country is finished." He lit a lamp, walked around with his shield and bamboo sword and the earth was destroyed.

Maharaj, (. . .) here at Nandapur the *porja* decreased, but there you have a lot of place, your in-laws [unclear]. He offered seven coconuts, took them to Nandapur and settled down in Jeypore. "You have destroyed seven chains, you have shattered them." He took them to Jeypore. Earth destroyed, where many (*lake*, 100.000) kings reigned, so he took it to Jeypore, and below his lion-gate he sat court (Engl.). He established the court, made that country beautiful. Debi Raja (Goddess King), as they called him. Many kingoms (*raja tane*) have no Dasara. The Jeypore kingdom has Dasara, as they brought him there. The Jeypore *raja* is the only *raja* with Dasara. This Jeypore king, Debi Raja, they could see him [at Dasara].

M7

Gadaba; Ponosput Bagra told by a Gadaba woman and other villagers; January 26, 2016; recorded by Peter Berger and Tuna Takri; transcribed and translated by Tuna Takri and Peter Berger.

In the Dasara month we play the Lodi song, in the village of Palankpadar, on the mountain side. Every day she[6] came to the place where we were dancing ("playing"), "Come with me," she said. Up to the mountain, near the boulder, she took the girls. "What happened, where is she (the girl)?" The girl was not there and the goddess neither. She came every day, invisible, it was not a human but a goddess (*maphru*). Cleverly, she took [the girls]. But they [villagers] caught her, bound her and took her to the house of the king. Otherwise the whole village would have been gone, empty. They took her to Purnagarh, called the king and handed her over. But the goddess originates from here. Has she become the king's goddess, just because we handed her over to him? She comes regularly to her birthplace, she did not let go of it. Whenever she wants, she comes, long tongue sticking out from the mouth, it thunders when she comes. After the villagers have given the goddess away a severe drought struck them, our ancestors ("father mothers," *bapa ma*) died, many people died. Because they feared of being eaten by the goddess, the others left the place, came down the mountain, settled at another place, Mordipodor (Drought Place). The Goddess became angry, "Why did you let go of the place?" Again, the new village suffered from drought. We all go to her feet, we apologize. We stay at her feet [i.e. foot of the mountain] now and we have peace, in Ponosput Bagra, peace. We sacrifice a buffalo every year.

M8

The Pengo Story of Creation; summary of Burrow and Bhattacharya (1970, 111–22).

At the beginning of the world there was no proper land, the earth was soft and muddy. *Kati* and *cila* seedlings, tree and bamboo did not exist. Then elder sister (*nana*) Takrani was born in the inlet of the ocean, subsequently 12 Bimas, 7

---

[6] The narrators only spoke of *maphru*, which refers in its specific sense to the sky god (Maphru, also called Dorom etc.) and in the general sense to "deities." As the deity on the hill is (at least nowadays) specifically referred to as Durga I speak of a goddess here.

Pandits and 9 teachers were born from eggs. Bimas lived in the upper region (Bima Pati), Jamas in the lower region. Takrani was naked and wondered "How shall I live?" On black and red soil (*mati*) on the throne-place (*singasan jaga*) on lotus-earth a brother and a sister were born, the Snake Clan King and Silput Queen (Nang Bous Raja Silput Rani). Takrani discovered the humans and took care of them, taking them into her house, into the inner part, where the grain is husked, rubbing them and making them bigger. Silput Raja and May Kodmay became adults. Takrani wanted them to become husband and wife and to forget their siblingship. She sent the brother to the east and the sister to the west, but when they again met they still recognized each other as brother and sister. Takrani made them ill, inflicting hunger and thirst, which made their skin peel off. But still they recognized each other as brother and sister. Takrani then went to Bima, her brother, who managed to obtain special water in a "magic market" (*maya bajar*), which Takrani took and gave brother and sister to drink. This made brother and sister to sleep with each other. After ten years and ten days Bhatra and Pengo were born, subsequently Dom, Gaur [herders] and Bamon [Brahmans].

Takrani sowed and scattered seedlings of *kati*[7] and *cila*, tree and bamboo, but she remained hungry and went again to Bima. He became angry and full with rage and mistreated her. Takrani then made the principal Bima (Mur Bima) ill. The seven other Bimas went in search of a *guru* who could tell them why the main Bima was ill, but the *guru* could not answer their question. He said: "Go to *cucunda* ground (*matito*), *rayladey* place (*jagar*), there Luling Bejni,[8] Mati Sundri resides." The Bima went and found Luling Bejni, Mati Sundri. She holds a winnowing fan made from thatch grass (*heci vikha*) and a pestle made from straw (*musul astat*). She is "grinding earth" (*mati ruci kinata*) and "pounding dust" (*duri je kuti kinata*), having bells attached to her pestle and her winnowing fan. The Bima asked: "Are you Mati Sundri, Duri Sundri," which she confirmed. The Bima then prostrated in front of her and payed obeisance: "Come, elder sister, to our home, *gurumai*, take the winnowing fan along and perform a divination for us." She thus came with them and performed a divination ritual, finally stating: "Gods and Spirits of Bima Pati (the region of Bima) have seized you." Then she gave them two sacred stones,

---

[7] The plants called *cila* and *kati* are not identified by Burrow and Bhattacharya.
[8] *Bejni/bejuni* is a female diviner/shaman.

which have various names: *darni* stone[9] and *pat* ("main") stone, *nespel* and *pobgel*,[10] *kala darni* and *citra darni*. One is a "cultivation stone" (*tas kal*) that provides cultivation to cultivators, the other is the "hunting stone" (*bet kal*), which gives hunting to hunters. "*Katla nara, katla tuma*[11] has seized you," she said. Mati Sundri, Duri Sundri then instruced the Bima with regard to proper worship, she told them which animals to sacrifice and she actually performed sacrifices for ancestors and gods (Takrani) for them. She built an assembly platform (*sodor*) for them. Then the Bima recovered. She then initiated the building of a luxurious *gudi*,[12] with a golden post and a silver beam. And Takrani fixed a day for hunting and a day for ploughing.[13]

Dorom Raja, the husband of Takrani, wanted to see if *cila* and *kati* germs have sprouted and went to the world of humans, those who were in the bellies of Silput Raja and May Kodmay, "who came into being by piercing through the earth," who "have been born splitting the earth." He found that the seedlings which had been sown and scattered had indeed sprouted in the world of humans.

The Bima went hunting without having participated in or performed the Mango festival (*parbu*). They kill a deer (*samar*) and an antelope, which angers Takrani, their sister, who tells her husband, Dorom Raja, that her brothers "cause ruin" and hides the two stones the Bimas had previously received from Mati Sundri, Duri Sundri; the cultivation stone in a crab hole and the hunting stone in a fish hole. The Bima continue to hunt for days but encounter no more prey. However, a bird took a Mango fruit up into the air and let it drop down, where it landed on the chest of the principal Bima who shared the fruit with all others. In the course of the further hunting the principal Bima gets wounded by one of their own arrows. The other Bima consult a *gurumai* who tells them that they went hunting without performing the Mango festival and they ate the fruit without having performed it. She suggested a general assembly at the *sodor*

---

9 *Darni Kal* is a village deity in form of a stone (*kal*), which is worshipped in the month of Chait before sowing (Burrow and Bhattacharya 1970, 212).
10 A stone ritually installed in a village before building houses (Burrow and Bhattacharya 1970, 212).
11 This seems tob e a fixed expression appearing in myths, an "obscure term" according to Burrow and Bhattacharya (1970, 193). It probably is a description for Takrani; *tuma* means "gourd."
12 In Koraput *gudi* is a general word for shrine, so probably it is a shrine for Takrani.
13 Takrani thus provided the ritual structure of a festival. Possibly the first hunting and the first ploughing in the context of a festival like the Chait Porbo. This is likely as much of the remaining story is about the Mango festival. Chait Porbo is for many Desia the festival when mangos are eaten for the first time, which involves ritual hunting and ritual sowing of rice and finger millet as well as the ritual transplantation of the former (Berger 2015).

platform to discuss everything related to the festival. The Bima came from the upper world and the Jama from the lower world to the *sodor* and the proceedings of the festival were discussed: On what day to brew *panjga* beer, on what day to brew *narenj* beer. They properly planned and conducted the festival and made offerings to gods and ancestors.

The Bima then went again hunting and killed a deer (*samar*). Dorom Raja said to his son, "Don't cry, your mother's brothers (the Bima) will give a haunch to your mother and a chest to their relations." However, the Bima told Dorom Raja that his son, their nephew, did not go hunting and would thus not receive any meat. They then hid the meat and ate it secretly. Thereupon Takrani became angry and said, "Let them eat the flesh of their own children," and ruined their cultivation and hunting. Dorom Raja's son then wanted to hunt himself and asked a blacksmith to make him a special bow with twelve strings. With this bow he killed a male bison that was so big that it had to be carried with twelve sticks. It was carried to the throne and he divided the meat, the breast to his relations, the haunch to his mother, Takrani. The gods said, "We cannot stand Bima Pati (the region of the Bima)," and they took down the Mango festival to the world of humans, where they could partake in it.

M9

Parenga, Rajubidai, Koraput District, Elwin 1954, 166

When the Middle World was made, the great gods gathered together for a feast. Mother Basmoti ate so much that she was sick. Seven girls and five boys were born from her vomit.

The girls were called Dhanodai [rice], Mandiadai [finger millet], Kangudai [foxtail millet], Kosladai [little millet], Sitridai [not identified], Jonadai [mais or sorghum], Jondridai [not identified], and the boys were called Kandulmanda [pigeon pea, red gram], Jungomanda [not identified], Mungomanda [green gram], Birimanda [black gram] and Kultomanda [not identified]. The gods knowing that the girls would give every kind of rice and millet, and the boys every kind of pulse to men, were very pleased. They said, 'Don't stay with us; there will be no profit in that. Go to the Middle World, where men are, and dance before them.' The seven sisters and five brothers accordingly went to the Middle World and danced from village to village.

There was a Dom Raja who lived in Domgarh. One day he went out hunting. On the way he saw the dancers and was charmed by them. He decided to take all seven girls as his wives. He ordered his servants to arrest them and take them to his palace. The Raja threw the brothers into jail, and hid the girls in a pit near the palace. He kept them like this for many days.

Presently Dharmo Mahaprabhu and Pat Deota Mahaprabhu thought, 'Men must be very happy now that the seven sisters and five brothers are with them, and they must be getting plenty to eat. Let us go and see how they are.' They went to the Middle World, but when they asked people how they were, they were told that everything was as it had always been, nothing but grasses and leaves and a little meat to eat. So the two gods got onto a horse and rode to Domgarh and there fought against the Dom Raja's servants and killed them and cut off the Raja's head. They freed the imprisoned boys and girls and gave them to men, and after that there was plenty of grain and pulse in the world.

Domgarh was near this village, and still there is a stone head of the Raja and the pit where the girls were imprisoned. We sacrifice every year to the stone in order to get good rain.

M10

A Bima's participation in a Pengo Sand Festival; summary of Burrow and Bhattacharya (1970, 130–33).

A married couple was preparing a hill field, sowing keng [pigeon pea], rice, mandeya [finger millet] and jowar [sorghum].When the crops sprouted they mortgaged the field to a money-lender and received finger millet for it.

In that village they performed the ceremony of bringing sand after they had brewed millet beer. They brought sand to the house of the priest and sowed a flower. The grown-up girls sang the Bali song. The principal girl was angry and [consequently] the flower did not sprout. A priest (*jani*) was called in order to find out why the flowers did not sprout. As it turned out, she was angry because the villagers of Gupkal had come to propose marriage. On that day the grown-up boys began to sing, which cheered the principal girl up somewhat.

The gods of Bimangpur (Land of the Bima) went hunting and when it got dark they slept somewhere [apparently in a human settlement]. The old woman of the house told them that the Bali ceremony was going on and told them to go and sing with the others. So the Bima went and as the village girls sang to them, the middle Bima became excited. The principle girl asked the Bima from which village they came and he told her they would be from Bimangpur. The principal girl then requested a finger-ring from the Bima, who replied that if they would show their ring to her saliva would flow and if she would put it on, she would not drink gruel or water [but presumably beer and liquor]. The middle Bima performed magic, produced a ring and gave it to her. Then he persuaded her to come with them, falsely saying that in their city they would also perform the sand festival. So the principal girl went with the Bima and took the sand seeds (*bali biyanting*) with her. When she was gone the flower [in her village] did not sprout and the middle Bima became ill.

In order to find out what the matter was with the middle Bima, the elder Bima send the younger Bima to their elder sister [Takrani] to ask for help. She at first refused to help arguing that the Bima always ignored her as long as they were happy. But finally, grudgingly, she followed them and found the reason, telling the Bima: "You went to the world of humans and being drunk sang to the girls. Because you persuaded the principal grill to follow you and as she took the seed that belongs there you are ill." She told them to go to the world of humans, take seed and sand and to perform the ceremony there. The Bima said they would do it and took a *gurumai* along, who scooped out the sand and sowed the flower seeds. Then the middle brother recovered and his elder sister told her brothers to do cultivation and go hunting.

M11

Didayi, Patroputlu, Koraput District, Elwin 1954, 424f

The first people to be born were Didayis – a brother and a sister – on the bank of the Machkund river. Rumrok picked them up and put them in a wooden trough of the kind in which pigs are fed. Then he flooded the whole earth with water, but the trough floated on the surface. Soon everyone on the earth was drowned and Rurnrok made a new earth and the trough came to rest on the side of a hill. Rumrok woke the children up and said to the brother, 'Who is this girl? How is she related to you?' 'She is my sister,' replied the boy. Then Rumrok said to the girl. 'Who is this boy? How is he related to you?' 'He is my brother,' replied the girl. Three times Rumrok repeated his questions and each time he got the same reply. So he told them to go and live separately and they did so.

Rumrok then called the god Kinchak and told him to alter the appearance of the two children. Kinchak made the boy's face black and the girl's brown and spotted like a deer. Then Rumrok called the two to him and again asked them how they were related. They replied that they did not know each other. Then Rumrok asked the boy, 'Will you marry this girl?' 'If you wish it, I will,' replied the boy. Rumrok declared them man and wife and they began to live together.

In due time three sons were born to the couple and they grew up. One day the mother said to them, 'We have no vegetables to eat today. Go and get some.' The boys went into the jungle but they got no vegetables. On the other hand, they found a cow and brought it home. The eldest brother killed the cow but the youngest brother lay down in a corner of the house and said he had fever and did not want to eat anything. They tried to persuade him to take a little but he refused, so the rest of the family ate the meat and enjoyed it.

When they had finished their feast the mother told the boys to ride a horse that was tethered in the yard. The eldest brother tried to get on the horse's back but failed, and he went to the jungle for some bamboos to make a ladder. The second brother tried to mount the horse and he too failed. But the youngest brother immediately jumped upon its back and rode on it round and round the house. The boy's parents tied up his bedding and got a box ready for him and some food and put it out in the yard. Meanwhile the eldest brother returned from the jungle with a load of bamboos. When he saw that the youngest brother had already succeeded in mounting the horse, he threw the bamboos away. But the youngest brother ordered him to make one of the bamboos into a carrying-stick and load it with his bedding and box. The eldest brother did so and put the stick over his shoulder. But the youngest brother wanted to test him and told him to change the load on to his other shoulder. This he was unable to do and so the youngest brother told him to put it down on the ground. 'You don't know how to ride a horse,' he said, 'and you cannot even carry a load.' Then the youngest boy called his other brother and asked him to carry the load and to change it from one shoulder to the other and he was able to do so.

Then the parents said, 'It is our youngest boy who will be the Raja and our second boy will be his Didayi Poroja. But our eldest boy cannot do anything; he cannot carry a load or ride a horse and it is he who killed the cow, so he will be a Dom.'

M12

Gadaba, Gudapada, told by Gorua Kirsani, recorded, March 12, 2001, translated and transcribed by Peter Berger and Manto Pradhan (see Berger 2015, 194f).

At Nandapur, King God (Raja Maphru) was born in/from a hillock (*kuplire*), in the forest. He came out there, was born there. Near the place where he was born, he clapped his hands, and the entire earth (*dortoni*) bent (*piti kori*). He took earth from the mouth of a cobra (*nang*), [an] earthworm (*ladon*) [several words inaudible], clapped his hands, and threw [the earth] into the water [. . .], the earth was soft. A tiger (*druka*) took it into his mouth [or bit], stumbled, and the earth became hard.

After that, since he was alone, [God asked himself] whether there were perhaps human beings or not. "Go, search and come back," he said, and he sent a crow (*kua*) out. It saw that everything was full of water, and there were no human beings anywhere. A bottle gourd (*tumba*) with brother/sister or something was there. The bottle gourd was being tossed to and fro [in the water]. "Is there something there or not?" [the crow said to itself and returned to God] "Where should I sit?" it said [to God], "Maybe I'll sit on your head a while?" – "Tsi, tsi [expression of indignation]! What kind of a great person are you, what kind of a great person am I, where do you want to sit on my head? I'll set a post [in the earth for you]," he said. He set a red *simli* branch [in the earth]; [the crow] sat on it [and made its report]. "Where I've also been, [only] a bottle gourd was being tossed to and fro." – "Go, [. . .] pick it up it in your beak and bring it here," [God] said, [and the crow] brought it there.

"Who are you, brother and sister?," he [God] said [to two people inside the gourd]. – "We are brother and sister." – "*Are* [expression of surprise]! You should have the pox for two ages." [After that, he asked the siblings again,] "Who are you?" – "We are brother and sister." – "*Are*! The two of them simply don't understand," he said, and he imposed another two ages of the pox on them both [and then questioned them again]. "Who are you?" – "Who is she, who am I?" [the brother answered]. The two siblings moved into a house [and all the people of the earth arose from that]. [They] settled. The Godabir [Godavari] is our place of origin; our mothers and fathers were called to Nandapur by the king. All those who live in the jungle [the Gadaba] came [and] are no longer allowed [to go back] to the Godabir. We're people from the Godabir, Godaba. Twelve tribes, twelve groups arose: Rona, Kotia, Kamar, some Gasi, Goudo. That's how many children there are. [. . .] The Godabir is our place of birth; as soon as we came here, as soon as we arrived, the Twelve Brothers spread out.

M13

Joria, Sukku, Koraput District, Elwin 1954, 521f

The two brothers Deoguni and Nirguni lived on the Khutni-mala [Kotni Mala] Hill. Deoguni used to play on the flute and Nirguni on the fiddle. They were unmarried. They used to wander from hill to hill playing their flute and fiddle, but there was none to hear them but the trees and grass; they never met any human beings.

Presently the brothers began to feel the need of women. They continued to make their music but all the time they were thinking about women. One day in their wanderings they came to Godsila, a great and high mountain covered with rocks which gave it the appearance of a temple.

Deoguni said to Nirguni, 'Let us climb this mountain and see if we can see any human beings from the summit.' When they reached the top they saw far away a curl of smoke rising from the forest below them. Nirguni said to Deoguni, 'There is nothing but smoke.' Deoguni said to Nirguni, 'Let us go towards the smoke.' They went down and through the forest until they came to a great rock. They climbed it and saw two women. One of them had the teeth of a pig and ears big as winnowing-fans. She had a long nose and her hair hung down to her knees. The other woman was very pretty, like an ordinary woman.

Deoguni said, 'At last we have found women, but what is the good of that if they devour us?' Nirguni said, 'You are the elder and I will do whatever you say. If they do not devour us, we will marry them. But now let us play our instruments.' So Deoguni began to play on his flute and Nirguni on his fiddle and when they heard the sweet music all the beasts and birds of the forest began to dance. When the music entered the ears of the two women they tried to see who was making it, but all they could see was the whole forest dancing round them.

'We have never seen anything like this before,' they said, and they too began to dance and forgot all about their food and drink.

When the brothers saw that the women too were dancing, they went towards them, still playing on their instruments as they went. But the women were so absorbed in dancing that they did not notice their approach. Then Deoguni made a rope of *siari* [*siardi*] creeper and tied up the older ugly woman, piercing her ears and passing the rope through them. He tied a bit of *kudal* wood to her backside and put heavy wooden rings round her feet. But she did not even notice what they were doing to her, so absorbed was she in her dancing.

Then said Deoguni 'I am the elder and I must marry the elder woman. You shall marry the younger.' Nirguni was very pleased at that.

Dancing, dancing, the brothers brought the two women home. There they suddenly stopped their music and the women stopped dancing and at last realized that two men were with them. They were terrified and tried to run away, but the brothers held the elder woman by the ropes through her ears and the younger would not leave her.

For several days the brothers starved the two women until at last they agreed to be their wives. 'What will you eat?' asked Deoguni. 'Raw meat,' said the elder woman. They fed her on raw meat, but they gave the younger girl roots and leaves. The elder woman forced Deoguni to eat raw meat with her. 'I will not marry you unless you eat the same food,' she said.

Then the two brothers began to play their instruments again and soon twelve score boys and twelve score girls assembled and danced. But when the elder woman saw them she cried, 'Now at last here is some really good food,' and she rushed at them with her great mouth wide open. They ran for their lives and Nirguni and his wife ran too.

When they were alone, Deoguni threw his wife on the ground and cut off her great ears and knocked out her teeth. He took her with him towards the Dudma Falls and there they had many children who have become today the Gadabas and Parengas.

But from Nirguni and his wife there sprang a race of kings, and the Maharaja of Jeypore is one of their descendants.

M14

Parenga, Dumriput Koraput District, Elwin 1954, 528f

A merchant had a very lovely daughter. One day he took his daughter and bullocks to Nandpur and camped there. Rama and Lakshman Mahaprahhu were there. These two Mahaprabhus seeing the girl, were pleased and she was too. Love grew between them. Both Mahaprahhus seduced her and she conceived. After that she never went out of the camp. The two Mahaprabhus were afraid the merchant would kill them. But during his absence the girl gave birth to twins. Lakshman Mahaprabhu tore off a bit of her dress, tied them up in it and took them off to the jungle. He left the younger under a pipal tree and the elder under a sago palm. When the girl saw the children gone, she thought, 'Let me die too,' and begged the earth to open. A crack appeared and she went down. The Mahaprabhus ran to catch her. But she went down and ran, under the earth to Kappor Chua, where Lakshman caught her by her hair and pulled her up. There he bathed her and took her away.

At that time a Dom was Raja and all men honoured him. There was an old Beng Raja and Beng Rani. They had no children. They went to dig roots in the jungle. They came to the pipal tree and found the boy playing. Pleased, they took him home. When the boy grew up, Beng Raja prepared to go to the Dom Raja to pay his taxes. The boy wanted to go too. Beng Raja tried to stop him but he insisted. They reached the palace and Beng Raja saluted with his hands, and the boy with his foot: Dom Raja was very angry and wanted to kill him. The boy seeing this got his bamboo bow and arrow and killed the Dom Raja and the whole army and became Raja instead.

One day he went hunting and came to the sago palm. There he found his brother, and thought, 'I'll keep him to carry my loads.' The Raja took him home. The boy sometimes went to the jungle. The Raja thought, 'He goes mad like this because he has no wife.' He went to get him a wife.

Now after Rama and Lakshman left Kappor Chua with the girl, she bore a daughter who tried to devour her. Lakshman Mahaprabhu caught the girl and she tore his arm with her teeth. He was angry and brought *siari* [*siardi*] rope, bored holes in her two ears and tied her to two trees. He tied a great stone to her waist.

When the Raja went to find a wife for the boy, he found this girl. He freed her and took her home and married them. When they put them to sleep in the house the girl said, 'Don't let's stay here; let's go to the forest.' And they ran away. From these two were born the Gadabas and the Parengas; the Gadaba is the elder and the Parenga is the younger brother.

M15

Koya, Gumka, Koraput District, Elwin 1954, 563f

Mankind began with Dadaburka Koya. When men increased in number, they went to live, each in his own place. Dadaburka Koya and his wife grew very old.

One day Deur thought, 'Now all the castes are separate, but they have no leaders, none are great or small, and everyone does according to his own mind.' So Deur made a great horse and took it to Dadaburka Koya. At this time Dadaburka had with him two sons and two daughters. Deur said, 'Whichever of you two boys can mount and ride this horse will be Raja, the other will be Poroja.' So saying, he went away.

The elder son's name was Sukru, the younger's was Bhima. Bhima said to Sukru, 'You mount first, then I will.' Sukru tried hard, but could not get up, and he went to cut a bamboo to make a ladder: he put it against the creature's back and climbed up, but the horse threw him. Then Bhima and his young sister Lakshmi said, 'You can't ride; now let the horse alone and we brother and sister, will ride.' Sukru went away and Bhima caught the horse and Bhima and Lakshmi mounted it and the horse leapt and jumped and galloped, but could not throw them. Bhima said to Sukru, 'Put my bedding on a carrying-pole and follow me. We will go round the world and see what there is in it.' They went all round the world and at last came to the hill Mahul-lakta. Bhima said, 'We will live here,' and said to Sukru, 'You can go home.'

A great house was built and Bhima and Lakshmi became man and wife and lived there. They were now Raja-Rani and Sukru went home to be a Poroja. Bhima made Amins and guards and police. Very soon the police and Amins began to trouble the people and everyone was afraid of them.

M16

Joria, Parjamunda, Koraput District, Elwin 1954, 142f

One year long ago, during the Chait Parab Festival, the boys and girls of a certain village danced so vigorously that they fell sense-less to the ground. The villagers, in alarm, called the shaman to see what was the matter. But he was not able to do anything.

That night the shaman called on the names of all the gods and offered incense. He slept and in a dream heard a sound as of a horse galloping. He awoke and went out and saw Pat Deota sword in hand riding round the village. The shaman stood dumb with fear. But Pat Deota greeted him and said, 'I have come to your village after many years, but you have given me nothing to eat or drink. That is why your boys and girls are lying unconscious.' The shaman said, 'But what do you want? What can we give you?' Pat Deota said, 'I will eat goat's flesh on plantain leaves. Give me this and your children will recover.'

Now the shaman had a goat, but he did not know what a plantain was, so how could he give the leaves? He went to find some, and on the way he met Thakurani Mata and she asked him where he was going. Again the shaman was struck dumb with fear. But she said, 'I know all about it. But you are never going to get plantain leaves this way. You will only get them if you sacrifice your own daughter to me.' The shaman did not say a word. The goddess said, 'Don't be afraid. If you do as I say, your daughter will receive great honour and will live in the houses of Government and great Rajas and wherever there are temples.'

The shaman returned home and roused his daughter. This girl had a baby son. She immediately understood that her father was going to sacrifice her and began to laugh. The shaman was frightened, but the girl said, 'Don't be afraid. Take me quickly.'

The shaman, therefore, took his daughter to the shrine of Thakurani Mata and sacrificed her. From her blood sprang up plantain trees. The shaman picked the leaves and gave goat's meat to Pat Deota on them, and the boys and girls recovered.

Because the girl had one son and died, a plantain dies after it has given fruit once. And today since it grew from the girl's blood, the plantain is loved in temples and palaces.

M17

Bondo, Elwin 1950, 26

On Malyagiri seven brothers and seven sisters were born and came thence into these hills. When they saw the streams and forest they were pleased and built their village here. Then Pat Khanda Mahaprabhu was born at Mundlipada and revealed himself in a dream to the eldest of the brothers. At that very moment in Jeypore the Maharaja had a dream that Mahaprabhu had been born on earth and he sent his men to worship him. But when they arrived we ran away and hid in the jungle, for we were afraid that the work of looking after them would be too heavy for us. But they chased us and brought us back to the village and it was agreed that the business of looking after the village on the one hand and of entertaining officials on the other should be divided. So the eldest brother was named the Mundli and became the Naiko of Mundlipada, the chief of all; after him the Challan was appointed to help him, the Kirsani to carry the officials' baggage, the Dangra-Manjhi to see that the young men (*dangra*) brought wood and water for any visitor. Another brother became Sisa to perform the worship of Pat Khanda Mahaprabhu and yet another, the Pedda Naiko, to help the Naiko. There were no Doms in those days, so a Kantaru (in Oriya, Bariko) was appointed to take reports to the police; when the Doms came we gave this work to them.

Later, as the number of people increased, the descendants of the brother who was made Kirsani went to live in Kirsanipada, the descendants of the Challan separated to Salanpada and the Mundli people remained in their first home, Mundlipada.

M18

Gadaba, Sulapadi, Koraput District, Elwin 1954, 226

Mother Earth had a young and beautiful daughter. Many gods came to marry her, but she refused them and they had to go home disappointed. A Dom Raja heard about this and decided that he would marry her himself. He took his army and set out to take her by force. When the girl heard they were coming she ran away to a neighbouring village. An old woman was sitting there preparing castor seeds for oil. The girl went to her, and offered to help. But presently the Dom Raja came with his army searching for her. The girl jumped up and putting a lot of castor seeds in a winnowing-fan threw them towards the Raja saying, 'Go and save me.' The seeds turned into bees. They attacked the Raja and his army and quickily put them to flight.

M19

Bondo, Pinnajangar, Koraput District, Elwin 1954, 386

At first when Mahaprabhu sent Rajas, the Government, and the Sahibs to rule over mankind, people lived peacefully, because they were afraid of the police. But the animals were afraid of no one and they used to kill and eat each other.

When Mahaprabhu saw what was going on, he decided that it was because the animals had no officials to keep them in order. With the dirt of his right arm he made a red monkey which was called the Sahib monkey, and from the dirt of his left arm he made a big black-faced monkey. From the dust of his foot he made a wild dog. He appointed the red monkey as the Sahib-Raja and made its body and its buttocks red as a Sahib's face. He called the big monkey the Police, and the dog the Reserve Police. Then he called all the animals to him and said, 'Here is your Raja, your Police and your Reserve Police. If you do any mischief they will certainly punish you and the Reserve Police will shoot you.'

This is how monkeys were first made and this is why all animals fear the wild dog and when monkeys see a tiger, they chatter as their way of making a report to the police.

M20

Bondo, Elwin 1950, 26f

The twelve Bondo brothers were in a quandary. Who was to go at Dassera to take the Maharaja's tribute to Jeypore? Each said to the other, 'You go, you go,' but not one of them was willing. They decided at last to go out and find someone else, determined to send him by force if necessary. They took their bows and arrows and went across the hills. When they reached the Machkund River, they saw a Didayi woman; she had just finished bathing her little son; he was standing on the bank and she was naked in the river. When she saw the twelve brothers she was frightened and ducked under the water and was never seen again. The child began to howl and the brothers went to comfort him. They said among themselves. 'This is just what we want. Let us take him home and bring him up to carry the tribute to the Maharaja.' They did so and when he was old enough they got him a Bondo girl for wife. Then the brothers clubbed together to buy a goat and they collected rice and two rupees in cash and sent the boy with these things to Jeypore. When he returned they called him Mandhara – giver of *man*, honour – and his descendants have ever since performed this duty for the tribe.

M21

Jena et al. 2002, 136–43, see page 92

M22

Jena et al. 2002, 159–61, see page 95

M23

Bell 1945, 80

A tradition in the Agency, current among others besides the Dombs, has it that the Panos of Ghumsur in Ganjam district proved themselves so obnoxious to the people by their criminal habits that the Raja issued an order that any Pano should be killed wherever he should be found. In fear of this edict the men of the tribe scattered and some of them sought refuge in the hills of Jeypore. Soon after their arrival one of their number succeeded by a trick in inducing the Kondhs of the locality to accept him as their king. Observing that the Kondhs were in the habit of worshipping a certain *bija* tree [Pterocarpus marsupium] this man concealed himself in the tree and suddenly leapt from it when the Kondhs were performing their devotions, announcing that he had been sent to them to be their king. Simultaneously he summoned some of his fellow-refugees who had concealed themselves nearby and declared that they were his retinue. The Kondhs believed that a king had been given to them by the tree as a reward for their devotions and accepted the ruler thus sent to them. They built forts for him at a number of places, of which the remains of one near Sembliguda are still clearly visible and are known locally as the 'Domb fort'. A period of terror and anarchy followed during which the Raja and his followers came to be called 'Dumbas' or 'devils', which name was later changed to 'Domb'.

The tradition further narrates that the reign of the Domb kings was ended by a boy, who was found in a forest guarded by a cobra and a peacock and fed by a goat, and was brought up by the foster-parents who discovered him. After overthrowing the Dombs he established a kingdom at Narayanapatnam, which was later moved to Nandapur. One of the successor of this Raja had no male issue and at the bidding of the god Sarveswara, who appeared to him in a dream, married his daughter to a certain youth who had come to his kingdom, also at the direction of the gods, and from this union sprang the present family of the Rajas of Jeypore.

M24

Carmichael (1869, 75), Lieutenant J. Macdonald Smith, Jeypore, see page 58.

M25

As told by Jaidev Baghel in Halbi to Chris Gregory and Harihar Vaishnav on February 4, 1990. Transcribed by Harihar Vaishnav. Translated into English by Gregory and Harihar Vaishnav, Canberra, May 16, 1991.

This is a story of long ago. Three brothers lived in a village in the state of Bastar. The youngest brother was called Bhima. He was very fat but he had no intelligence. Everybody called him a fool. His elder brothers had to go here and there to work. Bhima was given the job of grazing the cattle. He used to take the cattle in the direction of the fields. He was in the habit of sitting on a white ant's mound whilst keeping watch. This was all he did. One time, when the rains did not come, the area became stricken with drought. Everybody cried. Everybody was very worried. Bhima, too, was worried. One day, when watching the cattle from atop his ant-hill, he saw smoke escaping from a hole in the ant-hill. "There is water in this hill," he thought. "I will demand that Bhagwan give me this water," he thought to himself and began to pray to Bhagwan from his position on top of the ant-hill.

Many days passed in this way. The white ants climbed all over his body. But he did not move from the mound. Then, up in heaven, Mahadev and

Parvati, thought about his actions. Parvati said: "Please look Bhagwan. This small boy is devoting his life to the performance of austerities." "Please listen to his prayers," she said. After Parvati said this, Mahadev Bhagwan called on King Indra and ordered him to let rain fall upon the land. The rains came at once. The people were very pleased. The next morning all the villagers went to replough their fields. They saw that Bhima was lying unconscious near the mound. White ant soil was all over his body. Everybody lifted him up. He told them of the smoke and his austerities and said: "Look, worship god every year near a white ant's hole at the side of the village in the rainy season. If you do this then good rains will come." Having said this, he died on the spot where they found him. They all said: "Look, we have been calling him stupid but he was smarter than us." "He helped us in a time of distress." They said he must be a god and worshipped him. From this day, Bhimadev puja is held along with that of Bhagwan Mahadev and Parvati near a white ant's hole at the side of a village every year during the time of reploughing. A month or so after the first seeds are sown the land is reploughed (bihda). This destroys the weeds and allows the paddy to thrive.

Appendix 3: Nandi song (*Nandi git*)

Sung by Kuji Sisa (Gadaba, Gudapada[1]). Recorded by Peter Berger in 2010, transcribed and translated by Damodar Jani, Chandrama Jani, Moti Jani (Machhra 2, Mahadeiput), Jayamanyu Relli, Sharanya Nayak and Peter Berger.

Hold elder sister, hold elder sister, dust basket *Daru noni*[2] *daru re duri sanguda*	**Hold elder sister, hold elder sister, earth basket** *Daru noni daru ta mati sanguda*
Your diamond ring copper coin *Tori ira mudi tama kaseru*[3]	**Your copper ring diamond coin** *Tori tama mudi ira kaseru*
Give me the *nandi* basket, cousin *Nandi sanguda de bere sana*	**Give me the dust basket, sister** *Duli sanguda de bere beni*
Your diamond rings I do not claim *Tori ira mudi labu ne keru*	**Your copper rings I do not claim** *Tori tama mudi labu ne keru*
I won't buy an elephant from your copper rings and roam *Tori tama mudi ati keni bagi na bulu*	**I won't buy a horse from your diamond ring, climb it and roam** *Tori ira mudi gora keni sagi na bulu*
Elder sister, elder sister, elder sister, elder sister, *biki* necklace *Noni noni noni noni biki suri mali*	**Elder sister, elder sister, elder sister, elder sister, *shishiru* necklace** *Noni noni noni noni shishiruri mali*[4]
Beat *ho*, beat *ho*, men who beat the *nandi* drum *Maru ho maru ho nondoria bala*	**Beat brother, beat, men who beat the *kirudia*[5] drum** *Maru bai maru re kirudia bala*

---

[1] Kuji Sisa, perhaps sixty-five years of age when she sung the song for me in 2010, was born and grew up in the Gutob Gadaba village of Tikrapada. As this village only lies at a distance of some four kilometers to the south of the Joria village of Kurubi it is likely that she witnessed the Joria festivals and learned the song in her youth. She is also the mother of my friend Domru Sisa, who figures prominently on the cover of the book *The Anthropology of Values* (Berger et al. 2010).

[2] *Noni* means "elder sister," which is how the local women translated it. But it also means "girl," like the word *dangri*.

[3] Gustafsson (1989, 115) writes with reference to the term *kasu*: "*one and one half paisa or the fourth of one ana (a coin in British India – the coin is no longer in use, but the unit of value is still used in verbal transaction).*"

[4] A longer necklace which looks like small coins.

[5] Possibly refers to a small kettle drum called *kirdi*.

∂ Open Access. © 2023 the author(s), published by De Gruyter. This work is licensed under the Creative Commons Attribution-NoDerivs 4.0 International License.
https://doi.org/10.1515/9783110458831-013

Appendix 3: Nandi song (*Nandi git*)

Let's go elder sister, let's go elder sister gathering at the meeting place
Ju noni ju noni saba sadure

Gathering, let's go *ho* cousin
Hurula dole ju be ho sana

Come playing, gathering at the meeting place
Keli asube saba sadure

Elder sister, elder sister, elder sister, elder sister, Earth Beauty
Noni noni noni noni Mati Sundori

Hold *ho*, hold brothers, the *nandi* basket
Daru ho daru bai nandi sanguda

Let's gather at the meeting place, playing let's go
Saba berune keli ale ju be

Neighborhood roaming let's go then, sister
Sai bulang ale ju bere beni

The sky-wall write, let's go then
Kude ankaru[6] leki ale ju be

Roaming let's go, elder sister, Singa Mali [hill] place
Buli jube noni Singa Mali dande

Sara Mali place [drawing] the wall painting
Sara Mali dande sara bichla para[7]

Roam let's go sister, let's go gathering at meeting place, play let's go
Buli jube ju beni ju kai saba berune keli ju

Gather at branch-pavilion, let's go sister
Samunda bole ju bere beni

Come roaming, gathering at the meeting place
Buli asube saba berune

Elder sister, elder sister, elder sister, elder sister, Dust Beauty
Noni noni noni noni Duli Sundori

Hold elder sister, hold cousin, the earth basket
Daru noni daru sana mati sanguda

Let's gather at the meeting place, roam then, let's go
Saba sadure buli ale ju be

Dry field roaming let's go then, cousin
Poda bulai ale ju bere sana

Wall-painting start, let's go then
Kude sintaru chini ale ju be

Rooming let's go, cousin, Sara Mali [hill] place
Buli jube sana Sara Mali[8] dande

Singa Mali place [drawing] the wall painting
Singa Mali dande singa bichla para

---

6 *Ankaru* probably derives from *akas*, the sky. During the translation the women explained, "the wall with sun and moon."

7 It was explained during the translation that *sara bichla para* would refer to painting the sun and moon. *Sara* refers also to a layer, for instance the layer of cow dung mixed with water (*goboro*) that is scattered (*bichla*) on the ground (*goboro sara*). *Para* means "like," "as if." *Sara bichla para* could thus also mean, "like scattering a layer (of some material)".

8 *Sara mali* also refers to fennel or cumin seeds (Gustafsson 1989, 489).

Nandi song

Sung by a group of women, Lenjusuku, February 21, 2000; recorded by Peter Berger, transcribed and translated by Damodar Jani, Chandrama Jani, Moti Jani (Machra 2, Mahadeiput), Jayamanyu Relli, Sharanya Nayak and Peter Berger.[9]

Let's beat, let's beat the drums *Maru be maru re maile baja*	**Let's beat, brother, basket music** *Maru bai maru re sagude baja*
Leg, leg, leg, leg dust will rise *Gore gore gore gore ruen uti jao*	**Face, face, face, face sweat will run** *Mue mue mue mue jhalu uti jao*
Bunch of *jali* peacock feather swing *Jali majuru ba marebe*	**Bunch of *tiki* peacock feather swing** *Tiki majuru ba marebe*
Do not doubt, elder sister, Earth Beauty *Aanu manu na noni Mati Sundori*	**Don't be sad, elder sister, Dust Beauty** *Bari baku na noni re Duli Sundori*
Let's go, elder sister, let's go, elder sister, gathering at the meeting place *Ju noni ju noni re saba sadure*	**Let's go, elder sister, let's go, elder sister to the meeting place** *Ju noni ju noni re naki berune*
Don't doubt, elder sister, gathering at the meeting place *Aanu manu no noni saba sadure*	**Don't be sad, elder sister, gathering at the meeting place** *Aanu manu no noni saba sadure*
A hundred greetings to Jakor [deity] *Jhakaru gudi ke sahe juharu*	**Sixty *saranu* (?) to *nisani munda* [shrine]** *Nisani munda ke sate saranu*
Keep the oil, give the oil *Sikonu rokai ke sikonu desu*	**Keep the turmeric, give the turmeric** *Hadudi rokai ke hadudi desu*
Bath with turmeric water and the earth will stick *Hadudi gadae mati lagede*	**Apply oil and the dust will stick** *Sikonu gasai duli lagede*
Play, elder sister, play get up and sit *Kelu noni kelu re uta basi*	**Play, elder sister, play get up and sit-eat** *Kelu noni kelu re uta basi kae*
Wash your hands and come, Earth Beauty *Hato doe aso ha Mati Sundori*	**Wash your legs and come, Dust Beauty** *Goru doe aso be Duli Sundori*

---

9 This song was very difficult to understand and I present here only selected lines, those that we could make sense of.

Bibliography

Ali, Daud. 2011. "Kingship." In *Brill's Encyclopedia of Hinduism*. Vol 3, *Society, Religious Specialists, Religious Traditions, Philosophy*, edited by Knut A. Jacobsen (editor-in-chief), Helene Basu, Angelika Malinar and Vasudha Narayanan, 90–96. Leiden: Brill.

Allen, Nickolas. J. 2000. *Categories and Classifications: Maussian Reflections on the Social*. New York: Berghahm.

Anderson, Gregory D.S. 2008. "Introduction to the Munda Languages." In *The Munda Languages*, edited by Gregory D.S Anderson, 1–10. London: Routledge.

Anderson, Gregory D.S., and Felix Rau. 2008. "Gorum." In *The Munda Languages*, edited by Gregory D.S Anderson, 381–433. London: Routledge.

Anderson, Robert S., and Walter Huber. 1988. *The Hour of the Fox: Tropical Forests, the World Bank, and Indigenous People in Central India*. Seattle and London: University of Washington Press.

Århem, Kaj, and Guido Sprenger. eds. 2016. *Animism in Southeast Asia*. London: Routledge.

Baghel, Jaidev. 1982. "Of 'Devis' and 'Devas' (as told to Roshan Kalapesi)." In *Shilpakar: The Craftsman*, edited by Carmen Kagal, 40–48. Bombay: Crafts Council of Western India.

Bailey, F.G. 1981. "Spiritual Merit and Morality." In *Culture and Morality: Essays in Honour of Christoph von Fürer-Haimendorf*, edited by Adrian C. Mayer, 23–41. Delhi: Oxford University Press.

Baliarsingh, R., and P.K. Nayak. 1995. "Totemic Groups, Title Groups and Other Social Groups among the Gadaba." *Adivasi* 36: 14–25.

Banerjee, Sukumar. 1969. *Ethnographic Study of the Kuvi-Kandha*. Calcutta: Anthropological Survey of India.

Barik, Jijnasa, Vajinder Kumar, Sangram K Lenka, and Debabrata Panda. 2019. "Genetic Potentiality of Lowland Indigenous *Indica* Rice (*Oryza Sativa* L.) Landraces to Anaerobic Germination Potential." *Plant Physiology Reports: Formerly Known As 'Indian Journal of Plant Physiology'* 24 (2): 249–61.

Barraud, C., and J.D.M. Platenkamp. 1990. "Rituals and the Comparison of Societies." *Bijdragen tot de taal-, land- en volkenkunde* 146: 103–23.

Basham, A.L. 1971. [1954] *The Wonder that was India: A survey of the history and culture of the Indian sub-continent before the coming of the Muslims*. Fontana: Collins.

Behera, Deepak Kumar. 2010. "Death and Death Rites: The Practice of Double Burial Among the Kunhu-speaking People of Northwest Orissa." In *The Anthropology of Values. Essays in Honour of Georg Pfeffer*, edited by Peter Berger, Ellen Kattner, Michael Prager and Roland Hardenberg, 294–316. New Delhi: Pearson Education.

Behuria, N.C. 1965. *Final Report on the Major Settlement Operations in Koraput District 1938–64*. Cuttack: Orissa Government Press.

Bell, R.C.S. 1945. *Orissa District Gazetteers: Koraput*. Cuttack: Orissa Government Press.

Berger, Peter. 2002. "The Gadaba and the 'non-ST' Desia of Koraput." In *Contemporary Society: Tribal Studies, Vol. 5*, edited by Georg Pfeffer and Deepak Kumar Behera, 57–90. New Delhi: Concept Publishing Company.

Berger, Peter. 2003. "Erdmenschen und Flussbräute. Natur, Umwelt und Gesellschaft in Orissa, Indien. " *Baessler Archiv* 51: 7–24.

Berger, Peter. 2007. "Sacrificial Food, the Person and the Gadaba Ritual System." In *Periphery and Centre. Studies in Orissan History, Religion and Anthropology*, edited by Georg Pfeffer, 199–221. New Delhi: Manohar.

Berger, Peter. 2010. "'Who are you, brother and sister?' The theme of 'own' and 'other' in the *go'ter* ritual of the Gadaba." In *The Anthropology of Values. Essays in Honour of Georg Pfeffer*, edited by Peter Berger, Ellen Kattner, Michael Prager and Roland Hardenberg, 260–287. New Delhi: Pearson Education.

Berger, Peter. 2011. "Food." In *Brill's Encyclopedia of Hinduism, Vol 3: Society, Religious Specialists, Religious Traditions, Philosophy*, edited by Knut A. Jacobsen (editor-in-chief), Helene Basu, Angelika Malinar and Vasudha Narayanan, 68–75. Leiden: Brill.

Berger, Peter. 2012. "Theory and Ethnography in the Modern Anthropology of India." *HAU: Journal of Ethnographic Theory* 2 (2): 325–57.

Berger, Peter. 2014. "Dimensions of Indigeneity in highland Odisha." *Asian Ethnology* 73 (1–2), 19–37.

Berger, Peter. 2015. *Feeding, Sharing, and Devouring: Ritual and Society in Highland Odisha, India*. Berlin and Boston: de Gruyter.

Berger, Peter. 2016a. "Death, Ritual, and Effervescence." In *Ultimate Ambiguities. Investigating Death and Liminality*, edited by Peter Berger and Justsin Kroesen, 147–183. New York: Berghahn.

Berger, Peter. 2016b. "Liminal Bodies, Liminal Food. Hindu and Tribal Death Rituals Compared." In *Ultimate Ambiguities. Investigating Death and Liminality*, edited by Peter Berger and Justsin Kroesen, 57–77. New York: Berghahn.

Berger, Peter. 2017. "Feeding, Sharing and Devouring: Alimentary Rituals and Cosmology in Highland Odisha, India." In *Highland Odisha: Life and Society Beyond the Coastal World* edited by Biswamoy Pati and Uwe Skoda, 71–106. New Delhi: Primus.

Berger, Peter. 2018. "Millet, Rice, and the Constitution of Society in Central India." *Paideuma: Journal of Cultural Anthropology* 64: 245–264.

Berger, Peter. 2020. "Rupture and Resilience of Religion: Dynamics between a Hindu Reform Movement and an Indigenous Religion." In *Godroads: Modalities of Conversion in India*, edited by Peter Berger and Sarbeswar Sahoo, 246–271. New Delhi: Cambridge University Press.

Berger, Peter. 2021. "Gadaba. Society on the Menu." In *Brill's Encyclopedia of the Religions of the Indigenous People of South Asia*, edited by Marine Carrin (editor-in-chief), Michel Boivin, Gérard Toffin, Paul Hockings, Raphaël Rousseleau, Tanka Subba and Harald Lambs-Tyche, 207–214. Leiden: Brill.

Berger, Peter, Roland Hardenberg, Ellen Kattner, and Michael Prager. eds. 2010. *The Anthropology of Values: Essays in Honour of Georg Pfeffer*. New Delhi: Pearson Education.

Berger, Peter, and Sarbeswar Sahoo. 2020. "Introduction." In *Godroads: Modalities of Conversion in India*, edited by Peter Berger and Sarbeswar Sahoo, 1–46. New Delhi: Cambridge University Press.

Berger, Peter, and Roland Hardenberg. 2021. "Obituary: Georg Pfeffer." *Contributions to Indian Sociology* 55 (1): 129–133.

Berkemer, Georg. 1993. *Little Kingdoms in Kalinga: Ideologie, Legitimation und Politik regionaler Eliten*. Stuttgart: Franz Steiner.

Berkemer, Georg. 2001. "Little Kingdom: A View from the South." In *Jagannath Revisited: Studying Society, Religion and the State in Orissa*, edited by Hermann Kulke and Burkhart Schnepel, 253–270. New Delhi: Manohar.

Berkemer, Georg. 2004. "Jaypur Parlakimedi Vizianagaram: The Southern Gajapatis." In *Text and Context in the History, Literature and Religion of Orissa*, edited by Angelika Malinar, Johannes Beltz and Heiko Frese, 93–117. New Delhi: Manohar.

Berkemer, Georg, and Margret Frenz. eds. 2003. *Sharing Sovereignty: The Little Kingdom in South Asia*. Berlin: Klaus Schwarz Verlag.

Beteille, André. 1977. "The Definition of Tribe." In *Tribe, Caste and Religion in India*, edited by Romila Thapar, 7–14. Meerut: Macmillan.

Beteille, André. 1991. "The Concept of Tribe with Special Reference to India." In *Society and Politics in India: Essays in a Comparative Perspective*, 57–78. London: Athlone Press.

Bhaskararao, Peri. 2019. "Gadaba." In *The Dravidian Languages*, edited by S. B. Steever, 406–430. London: Routledge.

Bhattacharya, Sagnik. 2020a. "Of States and Monsters: Negotiating the Self and the Other in Early Indian States." Research paper, University of Groningen, *SocArXiv*, DOI 10.31235/osf.io/64fhj.

Bhattacharya, Sagnik. 2020b. "A Tryst with the Tribes: A Comparison of State-Tribe Relations in Pre-Colonial and Colonial India." Research paper, University of Groningen, *SocArXiv*, DOI 10.31235/osf.io/smdza

Bhattacharya, Sudhibhushan. 1957. *Ollari: A Dravidian Speech*. Calcutta: Government of India Press.

Bhattacharya, Sudhibhushan. 1968. *A Bonda Dictionary*. Poona: Deccan College.

Bhukya, Bhangya. 2013. "The Subordination of the Sovereigns: Colonialism and the Gond Rajas in Central India, 1818–1948." *Modern Asian Studies* 47 (1): 288–317.

Biardeau, Madeleine. 1982. "The salvation of the king in the Mahabharata." In *Way of Life: King, Householder, Renouncer. Essays in honour of Louis Dumont*, edited by T.N. Madan, 75–97. Delhi: Motilal Banarsidass Publishers.

Biardeau, Madeleine. 1995. [1981] *Hinduism: The Anthropology of a Civilization*. Delhi: Oxford University Press.

Bird-David, Nurit. 1990. "The Giving Environment: Another Perspective on the Economic System of Gatherer-Hunters." *Current Anthropology* 31 (2): 189–96.

Bird-David, Nurit. 2004. "No Past No Present: A Critical-Nayaka Perspective on Cultural Remembering." *American Ethnologist* 31 (3): 406–21.

Birgit Meyer. 2012. "Religious sensations. Media, aesthetics and the study of contemporary religion." In *Religion, Media, and Culture: A Reader*, edited by Gordon Lynch and Jolyon P Mitchell, 159–170. London: Routledge.

Blindt, Ulrike. n.d. *Die Kategorie der Mali: Beobachtungen in einem Desiya-Dorf in Koraput, Orissa*. Unpublished field report. Free University of Berlin.

Borde, Radhika. 2021. "Inheritors and Custodians of a Sacred Kingdom." In *Brill's Encyclopedia of the Religions of the Indigenous People of South Asia*, edited by Marine Carrin (editor-in-chief), Michel Boivin, Gérard Toffin, Paul Hockings, Raphaël Rousseleau, Tanka Subba and Harald Lambs-Tyche, 202–206. Leiden: Brill.

Burghart, Richard. 1978. "Hierarchical Models of the Hindu Social System." *Man* 13 (4): 519–36.

Burrow, Thomas, and Sudhibhusan Bhattacharya. 1962. "Gadba Supplement." *Indo-Iranian Journal* 6 (1): 45–51.

Burrow, Thomas, and Sudhibhusan Bhattacharya. 1970. *The Pengo Language: Grammar, Texts, and Vocabulary*. Oxford: Clarendon Press.

Carmichael, David Freemantle. 1869. *Manual of the District of Vizagapatnam in the Madras Presidency*. Madras: Asylum Press.
Carrin, Marine. 2002. "Santal Conception of Time." In *Contemporary Society: Tribal Studies, Vol. 5*, edited by Gerog Pfeffer and Deepak Kumar Behera, 139–159. New Delhi: Concept Publishing Company.
Carrin, Marine. 2013. "Jharkhand: Alternative Citizenship in an 'Adivasi State.'" In *The Modern Anthropology of India: Ethnography, Themes and Theory*, edited by Peter Berger and Frank Heidemann, 106–120. London: Routledge.
Carrin, Marine. 2021. "General Introduction." In *Brill's Encyclopedia of the Religions of the Indigenous People of South Asia*, edited by Marine Carrin (editor-in-chief), Michel Boivin, Gérard Toffin, Paul Hockings, Raphaël Rousseleau, Tanka Subba and Harald Tambs-Lyche, 1–16. Leiden: Brill.
Carrin, Marine, and Raphaël Rousseleau. 2021. "Central India: Introduction." In *Brill's Encyclopedia of the Religions of the Indigenous People of South Asia*, edited by Marine Carrin (editor-in-chief), Michel Boivin, Gérard Toffin, Paul Hockings, Raphaël Rousseleau, Tanka Subba and Harald Lambs-Tyche, 147–162. Leiden: Brill.
Carrin, Marine (editor-in-chief), Jean Jaurès, Michel Boivin, Gérard Toffin, Paul Hockings, Raphaël Rousseleau, Tanka Subba, and Harald Tambs-Lyche. eds. 2021. *Brill's Encyclopedia of the Religions of the Indigenous People of South Asia*. Leiden: Brill.
Chang, Te-Tzu. 2008. "Rice." In *The Cambridge World History of Food*, edited by Kenneth F. Kiple and Kriemhild C. Ornelas, 132–149. Cambridge: Cambridge University Press.
Chowdhuri, Bhagirathi. 1963/64. "Marriage custom among the Bareng Jodia Poroja of Koraput." *Adivasi* 5 (1): 27–36.
Conzelmann, Elisabeth. 2010. "Tales of a Tank: The Siddh Sagar in Mandi." In *The Anthropology of Values. Essays in Honour of Georg Pfeffer*, edited by Peter Berger, Ellen Kattner, Michael Prager and Roland Hardenberg, 433–446. New Delhi: Pearson Education.
Coppet, D. de. 1981. "The Life-Giving Death." In *Mortality and Immortality: The Anthropology and Archaeology of Death*, edited by Sarah C. Humphreys and Helen King, 175–204. London: Academic Press.
Crooke, W. 1915. "The Dasahra: An Autumn Festival of the Hindus." *Folklore* 26 (1): 28–59.
Dalton, Edward Tuite. 1872. *Descriptive Ethnology of Bengal*. Calcutta: Office of the Superintendent of Government Printing.
Das, Arijit, Manob Das, and Rejaul Houqe. 2020. "Evaluating the Quality of Living (QoL) of the Households in Dandakaranya Region, India: A Well-Being Approach." *Spatial Information Research* 28 (2): 257–72.
De Heusch, Luc. 1997. "The Symbolic Mechanisms of Sacred Kingship: Rediscovering Frazer." *The Journal of the Royal Anthropological Institute* 3 (2): 213–32.
De Josselin de Jong, J.P.B. 1977. [1935] "The Malay Archipelago as a Field of Ethnological Study." In *Structural Anthropology in the Netherlands*, edited by Patrick E. de Josselin de Jong, 164–182, The Hague: Martinus Nijhoff,
De Maaker, Erik. 2016. "Ambiguous Mortal Remains, Substitute Bodies, and other Materializations of the Dead among the Garo of Northeast India." In *Ultimate Ambiguities. Investigating Death and Liminality*, edited by Peter Berger and Justin Kroesen, 15–35. New York: Berghahn.
Delcourt, Barbara. 2007. "Sovereignty." In *Encyclopedia of Governance*, edited by Mark Bevir, 911–914. Tjousand Oaks: Sage Publications.

Demmer, Ulrich. 2009. "Community-Society: Models of Social Life in Tribal India." In *Contemporary Society. Tribal Studies, Vol. VIII: Structure and Exchange in Tribal India and Beyond*, edited by Georg Pfeffer and Deepak Kumar Behera, 266–280. New Delhi: Concept Publishing.

Derrett, John D.M. 1959. "'Bhū-Bharaṇa, bhū-pālana, bhū-bhojana': An Indian Conundrum." *Bulletin of the School of Oriental and African Studies, University of London* 22 (1–3): 108–23.

Derrett, John D.M. 1976. "Rajadharma " *The Journal of Asian Studies* 35 (4): 597–609.

Descola, Philippe. 2013. *Beyond Nature and Culture*. Chicago: The University of Chicago Press.

Doniger O'Flaherty, Wendy. 1980. *The Origins of Evil in Hindu Mythology*. Berkeley: University of California Press.

Dumont, Louis. 1980. [1966] *Homo Hierarchicus. The Caste System and its Implications*. Chicago: The University of Chicago Press.

Dumont, Louis. 2013. [1980]. "On Value: The Radcliffe-Brown Lecture in Social Anthropology, 1980." *Hau: Journal of Ethnographic Theory* 3 (1): 287–315.

Eggan, Fred. 1954. "Social Anthropology and the Method of Controlled Comparison." *American Anthropologist* 56 (5): 743–63.

Eggleton, Paul. 2011. "An Introduction to Termites: Biology, Taxonomy and Functional Morphology." In *Biology of Termites: A Modern Synthesis*, edited by David Edward Bignell, Yves Roisin and Nathan Lo, 1–26 Dordrecht: Springer.

Elwin, Verrier. 1948. "Notes on the Juang." *Man in India* 28: 1–146.

Elwin, Verrier. 1950. *Bondo Highlander*. Bombay: Oxford University Press.

Elwin, Verrier. 1951. *The Tribal Art of Middle India*. Bombay: Oxford University Press.

Elwin, Verrier. 1954. *Tribal Myths of Orissa*. Bombay: Oxford University Press.

Elwin, Verrier. 1955. *The Religion of an Indian Tribe*. Bombay: Oxford University Press.

Elwin, Verrier. 1991a. [1949] *Myths of Middle India*. Madras: Oxford University Press.

Elwin, Verrier. 1991b. [1947] *The Muria and their Ghotul*. Delhi: Oxford University Press.

Eschmann, Anncharlott, Hermann Kulke, and Gaya Charan Tripathi. eds. 1978. *The Cult of Jagganath and the Regional Tradition of Orissa*. New Delhi: Manohar

Evans-Pritchard, Edward E. 1969. [1940] *The Nuer: A Description of the Modes of Livelihood and Political Institutions of a Nilotic People*. New York: Oxford University Press.

Fausto, Carlos, and Michael Heckenberger. 2007. "Introduction: Indigenous History and the Histor of the 'Indians.'" In *Time and Memory in Indigenous Amazonia*, edited by Carlos Fausto and Michael Heckenberger, 1–43. Gainesville: University of Florida.

Fischer, Eberhart, and Dinanath Pathy. 2002. "Drawings for the Renewal of Murals: Notes on Documents for Murals of the Kalika Temple near Jayapur in the Koraput District, Orissa (India)." *Artibus Asiae* 62 (1): 139-77.

Francis, W. 1907. *Madras District Gazetteers*. Vizagapatam Madras: Government Press.

Franco, F. Merlin, and D. Narasimhan. 2012. *Ethnobotany of the Kondh, Poraja, Gadaba and Bonda*. New Delhi: D.K. Printworld.

Fuller, Christopher. 1992. *The Camphor Flame. Popular Hinduism and Society in India*. Princeton: Princeton University Press.

Fuller, Dorian Q. 2006. "Agricultural Origins and Frontiers in South Asia: A Working Synthesis." *Journal of World Prehistory* 20 (2–4): 1–86.

Fürer-Haimendorf, Christoph von 1943 "Megalithic Ritual among the Gadabas and Bondos of Orissa." *Journal and Proceedings of the Royal Anthropological Society of Bengal* 9: 149–78.

Fürer-Haimendorf, Christoph von, and Elizabeth von Fürer-Haimendorf, 1979. *The Gonds of Andhra Pradesh: Tradition and Change in an Indian Tribe*. New Delhi: Vikas.

Geertz, Clifford. 1980. *Negara: The Theatre State in Nineteenth-Century Bali*. Princeton, N.J.: Princeton University Press.

Gell, Alfred. 1980. "The Gods at Play: Vertigo and Possession in Muria Religion." *Man* 15 (2): 219–48.

Gell, Alfred. 1992. T*he Anthropology of Time: Cultural Constructions of Temporal Maps and Images*. Oxford: Berg.

Gell, Alfred. 1997. "Exalting the King and Obstructing the State: A Political Interpretation of Royal Ritual in Bastar District, Central India." *The Journal of the Royal Anthropological Institute* 3 (3): 433–50.

Gell, Simeran M. 1992. *The Ghotul in Muria Society*. Chur: Harwood Academic Publishers.

Gingrich André, and Richard G. Fox. eds. 2002. *Anthropology, by Comparison*. London: Routledge.

Glasfurd, C.L.R. 1862. *Report on the Dependency of Bustar*. Calcutta: Government of India, Foreign Department.

Gonda, Jan. 1956a. "Ancient Indian Kingship from the Religious Point of View." *Numen* 3 (1): 36–71.

Gonda, Jan. 1956b. "Ancient Indian Kingship from the Religious Point of View (Continued)." *Numen* 3 (2): 122–55.

Gonda, Jan. 1957a. "Ancient Indian Kingship from the Religious Point of View (Continued)." *Numen* 4 (1): 24–58.

Gonda, Jan. 1957b. "Ancient Indian Kingship from the Religious Point of View." *Numen* 4 (1): 127–64.

Goud, Dhukhishyam. 1991. *Gadaba*. Bhubaneswar: Academy of Tribal Dialects and Culture, Government of Orissa.

Graeber, David. and Marshall Sahlins. 2017. *On Kings*. Chicago: Hau Books.

Gregory, Christopher A. 1997. *Savage Money: The Anthropology and Politics of Commodity Exchange*. London: Harwood.

Gregory, Christopher A. 2004. "The Oral Epics of the Women of the Dandakaranya Plateau: A Preliminary Mapping." *Journal of Social Sciences* 8 (2): 93–104.

Gregory, Christopher A. 2009. "Brotherhood and Otherhood in Bastar: On the Social Specificity of 'Dual Organisation' in Aboriginal India." In *Contemporary Society. Tribal Studies, Vol. VIII: Structure and Exchange in Tribal India and Beyond*, edited by Georg Pfeffer and Deepak Kumar Behera, 67–82. New Delhi: Concept Publishing.

Gregory, Christopher A. 2010. "Siblingship as Value. In *The Anthropology of Values. Essays in Honour of Georg Pfeffer*, edited by Peter Berger, Ellen Kattner, Michael Prager and Roland Hardenberg, 3–18. New Delhi: Pearson Education.

Gregory, Christopher A. 2011. "Skinship: Touchability as a virtue in East-Central India." *HAU: Journal of Ethnographic Theory* 1 (1): 179–209

Gregory, Christopher A. 2013. "Chhattisgarh: At the Crossroads." In *The Modern Anthropology of India: Ethnography, Themes and Theory*, edited by Peter Berger and Frank Heidemann, 46–65. London: Routledge.

Gregory, Christopher A. 2018. "Why is the lotus the primordial symbol of wealth in India? Why is the answer obvious to a midwife but not an economist?" Lecture given at the Anthropology Seminar ANU, 28 February 2018. Unpublished.

Gregory, Christopher A. 2019. "The Values of Millet: From the Global to Some Indian Locals." Lecture given at the international workshop on "Contested Millets in Africa and Asia: Past and Present", University of Groningen, 29 March 2019. Unpublished.
Gregory, Christopher A. 2021. "Indigenous People of the Bastar Plateau. Lachmi Jagar." In *Brill's Encyclopedia of the Religions of the Indigenous People of South Asia*, edited by Marine Carrin (editor-in-chief), Michel Boivin, Gérard Toffin, Paul Hockings, Raphaël Rousseleau, Tanka Subba and Harald Lambs-Tyche, 235–243. Leiden: Brill.
Gregory, Christopher A. n.d. *Who is Danteswari? A political theology of a Divine Kingdom*. Unpublished manuscript.
Gregory, Christopher A., and Harihar Vaishnav. 2003. *Lachmi Jagar: Girimai Sukdai's Story of the Baster Rice Goddess*. Kondagaon: Kaksad Publications.
Griffiths, Arlo. 2008. "Gutob." In *The Munda Languages*, edited by Gregory D.S Anderson, 633–681. London: Routledge.
Griffiths, Arlo. 2010. "The Go'ter Ritual of the Gadabas According to Duaru from Tikrapada (1965): A Gutob Text Translated." In *The Anthropology of Values. Essays in Honour of Georg Pfeffer*, edited by Peter Berger, Ellen Kattner, Michael Prager and Roland Hardenberg, 288–293. New Delhi: Pearson Education.
Grigson, Wilfrid. 1991. [1938] *The Maria Gonds of Bastar*. New Delhi: Oxford University Press.
Guha, Ranajit. 1985. "The Career of an Anti-God in Heaven and on Earth." In *The Truth Unites: Essays in Tribute to Samar Sen*, edited by Ashok Mitra, 1–25. Calcutta: Subarnarekha.
Guha, Ranajit. 1988. "Preface." In *Selected Subaltern Studies*, edited by Ranajit Guha and Gayatri Chakravorty Spivak, 35–36. Oxford: Oxford University Press.
Guha, U., M.K.A. Siddiqui, and P.R.G. Mathur. 1970. *The Didayi. A Forgotten Tribe of Orissa*. Faridabad: Goverment of India Press.
Guillaume-Pey, Cécile. 2021. "Saora. Embodying Spirits from Paintings to Script: Ritual Change among the Saora." In *Brill's Encyclopedia of the Religions of the Indigenous People of South Asia*, edited by Marine Carrin (editor-in-chief), Michel Boivin, Gérard Toffin, Paul Hockings, Raphaël Rousseleau, Tanka Subba and Harald Lambs-Tyche, 361–370. Leiden: Brill.
Gustafsson, Uwe. 1989. *An Adiwasi Oriya-Telegu-English Dictionary*. Mysore: Central Institute of Indian Languages.
Guzy, Lidia. 2007. "'Negative Ecstasy or the Singers of the Divine': Voices from the Periphery of Mahima Dharma." In *Periphery and Centre: Studied in Orissan History, Religion and Anthropology*, edited by Georg Pfeffer, 105–30. New Delhi: Manohar.
Hacker, Katherine. 2014. "The 'possessed' body: Siraha, Swings, and Performing Difference in Bastar, Central India." In *Dialogues with Gods: Possession in Middle Indian Rituals*, edited by Tina Otten and Uwe Skoda, 191–227. Berlin: Weißensee Verlag.
Hara, Minoru. 1973. "The King as a Husband of the Earth." *Asiatische Studien: Zeitschrift der Schweizerischen Gesellschaft für Asienkunde* 27: 97–114.
Hardenberg, Roland. 2001 "The Renewal of Jagannath." In *Jagannath Revisited: Studying Society, Religion and the State in Orissa*, edited by Hermann Kulke and Burkhart Schnepel, 253–270. New Delhi: Manohar.
Hardenberg, Roland. 2008. *König ohne Reich: Rituale des Königtums in Orissa (Indien)*. Berlin: Schiler Verlag.
Hardenberg, Roland. 2010. A Reconsideration of Hinduization and the Caste-Tribe Continuum Model." In *The Anthropology of Values. Essays in Honour of Georg Pfeffer*, edited by Peter

Berger, Ellen Kattner, Michael Prager and Roland Hardenberg, 89–103. New Delhi: Pearson Education.
Hardenberg, Roland. 2011. *The Renewal of Jagannatha's Body: Ritual and Society in Coastal Orissa*. New Delhi: Manak Publications.
Hardenberg, Roland. 2014. "Bali Yatra of the Kond: A Ritual Performance and its Socio-Historical Context." In *Dialogues with Gods: Possession in Middle Indian Rituals*, edited by Tina Otten and Uwe Skoda, 277–295. Berlin: Weißensee Verlag.
Hardenberg Roland. 2016. "Beyond Economy and Religion: Resources and Socio-Cosmic Fields in Odisha, India." *Religion and Society* 7 (1): 83–96.
Hardenberg, Roland. 2017. "'Juniors', 'Exploiters', 'Brokers' and 'Shamans': A Holistic View of the Dombo Community in the Highlands of Odisha." In *Highland Odisha: Life and Society Beyond the Coastal World*, edited by Biswamoy Pati and Uwe Skoda, 135–174. New Delhi: Primus.
Hardenberg, Roland. 2018a. *Children of the Earth Goddess: Society, Marriage and Sacrifice in the Highlands of Odisha*. Berlin and Boston: De Gruyter.
Hardenberg, Roland. 2018b. "'Imperial Rice' and Subaltern Millets': Cereals as resources in Odisha (India) and beyond." *Paideuma* 64: 265–283.
Hardenberg, Roland. 2021. "Dongria Kond. Perspectivism in Tribal India." In *Brill's Encyclopedia of the Religions of the Indigenous People of South Asia*, edited by Marine Carrin (editor-in-chief), Michel Boivin, Gérard Toffin, Paul Hockings, Raphaël Rousseleau, Tanka Subba and Harald Lambs-Tyche, 183–193. Leiden: Brill.
Harvey, E.L., D.Q. Fuller, R.K. Mohanty, and B. Mohanta. 2006. "Early agriculture in Orissa: some archaeobotanical results and field observations on the Neolithic." *Man and Environment* 31 (2): 21–32.
Hausner, Sondra L. 2007. *Wandering with Sadhus: Ascetics in the Hindu Himalayas*. Bloomington: Indiana University Press.
Heckenberger, Michael. 2007. "Xinguano Heroes, Ancestors, and Others: Materializing the Past in Chiefly Bodies, Ritual Space, and Landscape." In *Time and Memory in Indigenous Amazonia*, edited by Carlos Fausto and Michael Heckenberger, 284–311. Gainesville: University of Florida.
Heesterman, Jan C. 1985. *The Inner Conflict of Tradition: Essays in Indian Ritual, Kingship, and Society*. Chicago: University of Chicago Press.
Heidemann, Frank. 2010. The Priest and the Village Headman: Dual Sovereignty in the Nilgiri Hills. In *The Anthropology of Values. Essays in Honour of Georg Pfeffer*, edited by Peter Berger, Ellen Kattner, Michael Prager and Roland Hardenberg, 104–119. New Delhi: Pearson Education.
Hertz, Robert. 1960. *Death and the Right Hand*. London: Cohen & West.
Hocart, Arthur M. 1970. [1936] *Kings and Councillors: An Essay in the Comparative Anatomy of Human Society*. Chicago: University of Chicago Press.
Holy, Ladislav. ed. 1987. *Comparative Anthropology*. Oxford: Blackwell.
Icke-Schwalbe, Lydia. 1968. "Das Pferd in Mythologie und Kult bei Adivasi-Gruppen in Zentralindien. " *Abhandlungen und Berichte des Staatlichen Museums für Völkerkunde Dresden* 28: 1–25.
Ikegame, Aya. 2013a. *Princely India Re-Imagined: A Historical Anthropology of Mysore from 1799 to the Present*. London & New York: Routledge.

Ikegame, Aya. 2013b. "Karnataka: Caste, dominance and social change in the 'Indian village.'" In *The Modern Anthropology of India: Ethnography, Themes and Theory*, edited by Peter Berger and Frank Heidemann, 121–35. London: Routledge.

Inden, Ronald. 1998. [1978] "Ritual, Authority, and Cyclic Time in Hindu Kingship." In *Kingship and Authority in South Asia*, edited by John F. Richards, 41–91. New Delhi: Oxford University Press.

Inden, Ronald. 2006. *Text & Practice: Essays on South Asian History*. New Delhi: Oxford University Press.

Irwin, John C. 1982. "The Sacred Anthill and the Cult of the Primordial Mound." *History of Religions* 21 (4): 339–60.

Izikowitz, Karl G. 1969. "The Gotr Ceremony of the Boro Gadaba." In *Primitive Views of the World*, edited by Stanley Diamond, 129–150. New York: Columbia University Press.

Jena, Mihir K., Padmini Pathi, Jagganath Dash, Kamala K. Patnaik, and Klaus Seeland. 2002. *Forest Tribes of Orissa: Lifestyle and Social Conditions of Selected Orissan Tribes. Vol. 1: The Dongaria Kondh*. New Delhi: D.K. Printworld.

Joshi, M.M. 1967. *Bastar: India's Sleeping Giant*. New Delhi: People's Publishing House

Jouquet, Pascal, Nabila Guilleux, Sreenivasulu Chintakunta, Mercedes Mendez, Sankaran Subramanian, and Rashmi Ramesh Shanbhag. 2015. "The Influence of Termites on Soil Sheeting Properties Varies Depending on the Materials on Which They Feed." *European Journal of Soil Biology* 69: 74–78.

Jouquet Pascal, Nicolas Bottinelli, Rashmi R. Shanbhag, Thomas Bourguignon, Saran Traore, and Shahid Abbas Abbasi. 2016. "Termites: The Neglected Soil Engineers of Tropical Soils." *Soil Science* 181 (3–4): 157–65.

Jouquet, Pascal, Laurent Caner, Nicolas Bottinelli, Ekta Chaudhary, Sougueh Cheik, and Jean Riotte. 2017. "Where Do South-Indian Termite Mound Soils Come from?" *Applied Soil Ecology* 117–118:190–95.

Kane, Pandurang Vaman. 1974. *History of the Dharmasastra, Vol 5, Part 1*. Poona: Bhandarkar Oriental Research Institute.

Kautilya. 1992. *The Arthashastra*. Edited, rearranged, translated and introduced b L.N. Rangarajan. New Delhi: Penguin.

Kautilya. 2013. *King, Governance, and Law in Ancient India: Kautilya's Arthasastra*. Translated by Patrick Olivelle. New York: Oxford University Press.

Kingwell-Banham, Eleanor, and Dorian Q Fuller. 2012. "Shifting Cultivators in South Asia: Expansion, Marginalisation and Specialisation Over the Long Term." *Quaternary International* 249: 84–95.

König, Ditte. 1984. *Das Tor Zur Unterwelt: Mythologie und Kult des Termitenhügels in der schriftlichen und mündlichen Tradition Indiens*. Wiesbaden: Steiner.

Korb, Judith. 2011. "Termite Mound Architecture, from Function to Construction." In *Biology of Termites: A Modern Synthesis*, edited by David Edward Bignell, Yves Roisin and Nathan Lo, 349–73. Dordrecht: Springer.

Kornel, Das. 1999. *Tribal Cultural Heritage and Cult. The Gutob Gadaba Tribe of Orissa*. Bhubaneswar: Modern Book Depot.

Kornel, Das, and Giridhar Gamang. 2010. *Lost Jaina Tribes of Trikalinga*. http://korneldas.com/portfolio-item/lost-jaina-tribes-of-trikalinga/

Kosala, K.C.P. 1981. "Die Evangelisch-Lutherische Kirche von Jeypore (Jeypore Lutheran Evangelical Church = JELC)." In *Evangelische Kirche in Indien. Auskunft und Einblicke*,

edited by Hugald Grafe, 229–238. Erlangen: Verlag der Ev. Lutherischen Mission Erlangen.
Kriti, Swarnima. 2018. "Bastaria Dussehra: A Coming Together of Deities." *Sahapedia*. https://www.sahapedia.org/bastaria-dussehra-coming-together-of-deities
Kroeber, Alfred L. 1925. *Handbook of the Indians of California*. Washington: Government Printing Office.
Kroeber, Alfred L. 1939. *Cultural and Natural Areas of Native North America*. Berkeley: University of California Press.
Kulke, Hermann. 1978a. "Royal Temple Policy and the Structure of Medieval Kingdoms." In *The Cult of Jagganath and the Regional Tradition of Orissa*, edited by Anncharlott Eschmann, Hermann Kulke and Gaya Charan Tripathi, 125–137. New Delhi: Manohar.
Kulke, Hermann. 1978b. "Early State Formation and Royal Legitimation in Tribal Areas of Eastern India." In *Aspects of Tribal Life in South Asia I: Strategy and Survival*, edited by Rupert R. Moser and Mohan K. Gautam, 29–37. Berne: University of Berne.
Kulke, Hermann. 1979. *Jagannatha-Kult und Gajapati-Königtum. Ein Beitrag zur Geschichte religiöser Legitimation Hinduistischer Herrscher*. Wiesbaden: Franz Steiner.
Kulke, Hermann. 1997. "The Early and the Imperial Kingdom: A Processual Model of Integrative State Formation in Early Medieval India." In *The State in India 1000–1700*, edited by Hermann Kulke, 233–262. New Delhi: Oxford University Press.
Kuper, Adam. 1982. *Wives for Cattle: Bridewealth and Marriage in Southern Africa*. London: Routledge & Kegan Paul.
Kuper, Adam. 2002. "Comparison and contextualization: reflections on South Africa." In *Anthropology, by Comparison*, edited by Gingrich André and Richard G. Fox, 143–166. London: Routledge.
Leach, Edmund 1977. [1961]. *Rethinking Anthropology*. London: Athlone Press.
Leach, Edmund 1991. [1976]. *Culture and Communication: The Logic by Which Symbols Are Connected*. Cambridge: Cambridge University Press.
Lévi Strauss, Claude. 1986. [1969] *The Raw and the Cooked*. Harmondsworth: Penguin.
Lotz, Barbara. 2007. "Casting a Glorious Past: Loss and Revival of the *Ol Chiki* Script." In *Time in India: Concepts and Practices*, edited by Angelika Malinar, 235–263. New Delhi: Manohar.
Macpherson, Samuel Charters. 1865. *Memorials of Service in India*. London: Murray.
Mahapatra, Khageswar. 1985. "Desia. A Tribal Oriya Dialect of Koraput Orissa." *Adivasi*, 25: 1–304.
Majumdar, Dhirendra N. 1939. "Tribal Cultures and Acculturation." *Man in India* 19 (2/3): 99–173.
Majumdar, R.C. 1996. *Outline of the History of Kalinga*. New Delhi: Asian Educational Services.
Malamoud, Charles. 1982. "On the rhetoric and semantics of *purushartha*." In *Way of Life: King, Householder, Renouncer. Essays in honour of Louis Dumont*, edited by T.N. Madan, 33–54. Delhi: Motilal Banarsidass Publishers.
Malamoud, Charles. 1996. [1989] *Cooking the World. Ritual and Thought in Ancient India*. Oxford: Oxford University Press.
Malinar, Angelika. 2007. "Introduction." In *Time in India: Concepts and Practices*, edited by Angelika Malinar, 1–21. New Delhi: Manohar.
Mallebrein, Cornelia. 1996. "Dantesvari, the Family Goddess (Kulsvamini) of the Rajas of Bastar, and the Dasahra-Festival of Jagdalpur." In *Wild Goddesses in India and Nepal:*

Proceedings of an International Symposium Berne and Zurich, Novermber 1994, edited by Axel Michaels, Cornelia Vogelsanger and Annette Wilke, 483–511. Bern: Peter Lang.

Mallebrein, Cornelia. 2001. "Constructing a 'House within a House': Reading the Wall-Paintings of the Lanjia Sora from Recitations." In *Jagannath Revisited: Studying Society, Religion and the State in Orissa*, edited by Hermann Kulke and Burkhard Schnepel, 93–122. New Delhi: Manohar.

Mallebrein, Cornelia. 2007. "When the Buffalo becomes a Pumpkin: Animal Sacrifice Contested." In *Periphery and Centre. Studies in Orissan History, Religion and Anthropology*, edited by Georg Pfeffer, 443–472. New Delhi: Manohar.

Malten, Thomas. n.d. *Desia Dictionary*. Unpublished compilation based on Gustafsson (1989) and Mahapatra (1985).

Marais, Eugène. 2017. [1937] *The Soul of the White Ant*. No place: A Distant Mirror.

Marglin, Frédérique Apffel. 1985. *Wives of the God-King: The Rituals of the Devadasis of Puri*. New Delhi: Oxford University Press.

Marriott, McKim, and Ronald B. Inden. 1977. "Toward an ethnosociology of South Asian caste systems." In *The New Wind: Changing Identities in South Asia*, edited by Kenneth David, 227–38. The Hague: Mouton.

Marriott, McKim. 1989. "Constructing an Indian Ethnosociology." *Contributions to Indian Sociology* 23 (1): 1–39.

Marten, J.T. 1912. *Census of India 1911. Volume X. Central Provinces and Berar. Part I – Report*. Calcutta: Superintendent Government Printing.

Mauss, Marcel. 2016. [1925] *The Gift*. Chicago: The University of Chicago Press.

May, J.A. 1873. "Notes on the Bhondas of Jaypur." *The Indian Antiquary* 2: 236–238.

McDougal, Charles Walter. 1963. *The Social Structure of the Hill Juang*. Alberqueque: The University of New Mexico.

Means, Alexander J. 2022. "Foucault, Biopolitics, and the Critique of State Reason." *Educational Philosophy and Theory*, 54 (12): 1968–1969.

Mendieta, Eduardo. 2014. "Biopolitics." In *The Cambridge Foucault Lexicon*, edited by Leonard Lawlor and John Nale 37–43. New York, NY: Cambridge University Press.

Ministry of Tribal Affairs, Statistics Division. *Statistical Profile of Scheduled Tribes in India* 2013 Government of India. www.triba..nic.in

Mishra, Smita. 2009. "Farming System in Jeypore Tract of Orissa, India." *Asian Agri-History* 13 (4): 271–92.

Mishra, Sujit Kumar. 2002. "Development, Displacement and Rehabilitation of Tribal People: A Case Study of Orissa." *Journal of Social Sciences* 6 (3): 197–208.

Mohanty, Gopinath. 1987. *Paraja*. London: Faber and Faber.

Mohanty, Indrajeet. 2013. "Jeypore – A Historical Perspective." *Odisha Review* (June): 69–71.

Mohanty, U.Ch. 1973–74. "Bond-Friendship among the Gadaba." *Man in Society* 1: 130–55.

Morgenstern, Christian. 1983. *Alle Galgenlieder*. Berlin: Aufbau-Verlag.

Moya, Ismaël. 2015. "Unavowed Value: Economy, Comparison, and Hierarchy in Dakar." *Hau: Journal of Ethnographic Theory* 5 (1): 151–72.

Mummidi, Thanuja. 2021. "Konda Reddi: The Colors and Symbols in Konda Reddis' Rituals." In *Brill's Encyclopedia of the Religions of the Indigenous People of South Asia*, edited by Marine Carrin (editor-in-chief), Miche Boivin, Gérard Toffin, Paul Hockings, Raphaël Rousseleau, Tanka Subba and Harald Lambs-Tyche, 408–417. Leiden: Brill.

Naidu, N.Y. 1975. "Dashara in Bastar: A Study of Raja Tribal Relationship." *Folklore* 17 (3): 82–86.

Nanjundayya, H.V., and R.-B.L.K. Iyer. 1931. *The Mysore Tribes and Castes, Vol. IV*. Bangalore: Mysore Government Press.

Nayak, Prasanna K. 1989. *Blood, Women and Territory. An Analysis of Clan Feuds of the Dongria Kondhs*. New Delhi: Reliance Publishing House.

Nayak, Prasanna K. 2013. "Kingly Rites in Tribal Religions: Some Reflections on Middle Indian Tribes." In *Imaging Odisha, Vol 1*, edited by Hermann Kulke, Nivedita Mohanty, Gaganendra Nath Dash and Dinanath Pathy, 311–318. Jagatsinghpur: Prafulla.

Nayak, Prasanna K. 2021. "Bearing of Religion on the Dongria Kond." In *Brill's Encyclopedia of the Religions of the Indigenous People of South Asia*, edited by Marine Carrin (editor-in-chief), Michel Boivin, Gérard Toffin, Paul Hockings, Raphaël Rousseleau, Tanka Subba and Harald Lambs-Tyche, 193–202. Leiden: Brill.

Nayak, Radhakant, Barbara M. Boal, and Nabor Soreng. 1996. *The Gadabas: A Handbook for Development*. New Delhi: Indian Social Institute.

Niggemeyer, Hermann. 1964a. *Kuttia Kond: Dschungel-Bauern in Orissa*. München: Klaus Renner Verlag.

Niggemeyer, Hermann. 1964b. "Kuttia Kond und Pano: Zur Stellung der verachteten Klassen in Indien." In *Festschrift für Ad. E. Jensen (Teil 2)*, edited by E. Haberland, M. Schusters and H. Straube, 407–12. Munich: Renner.

Novetzke, Christian Lee and Laurie Patton. 2008. "Subaltern." In Studying Hinduism: Key Concepts and Methods, edited by Sushil Mittal and Gene Thursby, 378–399. London: Routledge.

Oberdiek, Ulrich. 1991. *Kontinuität und Wandel. Die Staatliche Integration der indischen Stämme*. München: Trickster Verlag.

Ockert, Markus. 1988. *Bericht über einen zweiwöchigen Forschungsaufenthalt bei den Didayi von Kassamput (Koraput)*. Free University of Berlin. Unpublished report.

Olivelle, Patrick. 2003. "The Renouncer Tradition." In *Hinduism*, edited by Gavin Flood, 271–287. Malden: Blackwell.

Oppitz, Michael. 1975. *Notwendige Beziehungen: Abriss Der Strukturalen Anthropologie*. Frankfurt/M: Suhrkamp.

Ota, A.B., P. Patel, and B.K. Paikaray. 2018. *Parenga*. Bhubaneswar: Scheduled Castes and Scheduled Tribes Research and Training Institute.

Otten, Tina. 2000/2001. "Changing Annual Hunting Festival, Chaitra Parba: An Outsider's View." *Adivasi* 40/41: 82–91.

Otten, Tina. 2006. *Heilung durch Rituale: Vom Umgang mit Krankheit bei den Rona im Hochland Orissas*. Berlin: Lit.

Otten, Tina. 2009. "Kingship, Tribal Society and Fertility in Koraput: Different Aspects of the Ritual Bali Jatra." In *Contemporary Society. Tribal Studies, Vol. VIII: Structure and Exchange in Tribal India and Beyond*, edited by Georg Pfeffer and Deepak Kumaar Behera, 33–51. New Delhi: Concept Publishing.

Otten, Tina. 2010. "The Concept of Biba among the Rona of Highland Orissa: Wedding Rituals to ensure Health." In *The Anthropology of Values. Essays in Honour of Georg Pfeffer*, edited by Peter Berger, Ellen Kattner, Michael Prager and Roland Hardenberg, 143–161. New Delhi: Pearson Education.

Otten, Tina. 2013. "Bali Jatra: An Oral Epic and a Ritual for Well Being." In *Imaging Odisha, Vol II*, edited by ermann Kulke, Nivedita Mohanty, Gaganendra Nath Dash and Dinanath Pathy, 240–245. Jagatsinghpur: Prafulla.

Otten, Tina. 2014. "The Pat Gurumai and the Communication with Gods and Gardeners: The Epic Bali Yatra – a Preliminary Sketch." In *Dialogues with Gods: Possession in Middle Indian Rituals*, edited by Tina Otten and Uwe Skoda, 247–75. Berlin: Weißensee Verlag.

Otten, Tina. 2021. "Rona: Wedding Rituals to Reconfirm Relations with the Divine World." In *Brill's Encyclopedia of the Religions of the Indigenous People of South Asia*, edited by Marine Carrin (editor-in-chief), Michel Boivin, Gérard Toffin, Paul Hockings, Raphaël Rousseleau, Tanka Subba and Harald Lambs-Tyche, 315–323. Leiden: Brill.

Otten, Tina n.d. "Bali Jatra: oral epic and ritual of well-being and wealth in Koraput, Orissa." Unpublished Manuscript.

Otten, Tina, and Uwe Skoda. eds. 2014. *Dialogues with Gods: Possession in Middle Indian Rituals*. Berlin: Weißensee Verlag.

Padel, Felix. 2009. *Sacrificing People: Invasions of a Tribal Landscape*. New Delhi: Orient Blackswan.

Padel, Felix, and Samarendra Das. 2006. "Double Death: Aluminium's Links with Genocide." *Social Scientist* 34 (3–4): 55–81.

Padhi, Ranjana, and Nigamananda Sadangi. 2020. *Resisting Dispossession: The Odisha Story*. Singapore: Palgrave Macmillan.

Padhi, Soubhagya Ranjan. 2011. *The Gadaba Tribe of Orissa: A Study in its socio-economic transformation*. New Delhi: Abhijeet Publications.

Parasher, Aloka. 1991. *Mlecchas in early India: A Study in Attitudes toward outsiders upto AD 600*. New Delhi: Munishiram Manoharlal.

Parkin, Robert. 1992. *The Munda of Central India. An Account of their Social Organization*. Delhi: Oxford University Press.

Parry, Jonathan P. 1994. *Death in Banaras*. Cambridge: Cambridge University Press.

Patnaik, N. 1977. "Shifting Cultivation in Orissa." *Adivasi* 16 (4): 1–21.

Pfeffer, Georg. 1982. *Status and Affinity in Middle India*. Wiesbaden: Franz Steiner.

Pfeffer, Georg. 1984. "Mittelindische Megalithen als meritökonomische Kategorien." *Paideuma* 30: 231–40.

Pfeffer, Georg. 1991. "Der intra-agnatische 'Seelentausch' der Gadaba beim großen Lineageritual." In *Beiträge zur Ethnologie Mittel- und Süd-Indiens*, edited by Matthias S. Laubscher, 59–92. Munich: Anacon.

Pfeffer, Georg. 1994a. "The Dualistic Culture of the Juang." In *Religion and Society in Eastern India. Eschmann Memorial Lectures*, edited by Gaya Charan Tripathi and Hermann Kulke, 103–116. New Delhi, Manohar.

Pfeffer, Georg. 1994b. "Music in Context: Ethnography and Meaning." *Beiträge zur Musikethnologie* 30: 14–20.

Pfeffer, Georg. 1997. "The Scheduled Tribes of Middle India as a Unit: Problems of Internal and External Comparison." In *Contemporary Society. Tribal Studies, Vol. I: Structure and Process*, edited by Georg Pfeffer and Deepak Kumar Behera, 3–27. New Delhi. Concept Publishing.

Pfeffer, Georg. 1999. "Gadaba and the Bondo Kinship Vocabularies versus Marriage, Descent and Production." In *Contemporary Society. Tribal Studies, Vol. IV: Social Realities*, edited by Deepak Kumar Behera and Georg Pfeffer, 17–46. New Delhi. Concept Publishing.

Pfeffer, Georg. 2001. "A Ritual of Revival among the Gadaba of Koraput." In *Jagannath Revisited: Studying Society, Religion and the State in Orissa*, edited by Hermann Kulke and Burkhard Schnepel, 123–48. New Delhi: Manohar.

Pfeffer, Georg. 2002. "Debating the Tribe." Unpublished Manuscript.

Pfeffer, Georg. 2003 *Hunters, Tribes, Peasants: Cultural Crisis and Comparison*. Bhubaneswar: National Institute of Social Work and Social Sciences.

Pfeffer, Georg. 2004. "Order in Tribal Middle Indian 'Kinship'." *Anthropos* 99 (2): 381–409.

Pfeffer, Georg. 2009. "Orissan Tribal Socieites: Commonalities and Variations." In *Contemporary Society. Tribal Studies, Vol. VIII: Structure and Exchange in Tribal India and Beyond*, edited by Georg Pfeffer and Deepak Kumar Behera, 232–256. New Delhi: Concept Publishing.

Pfeffer, Georg. 2014. "Ethnographies of States and Tribes in Highland Odisha." *Asian Ethnology* 73 (1–2): 259–79.

Pfeffer, Georg. 2016. *Verwandtschaft als Verfassung: Unbürokratische Muster öffentlicher Ordnung*. Badan-Badan: Nomos.

Pfeffer, Georg. 2019. *Lewis Henry Morgan's Comparisons: Reassessing Terminology, Anarchy and Worldview in Indigenous Societies of America, Australia and Highland Middle India*. New York: Berghahn.

Pradhan, S. C. 1998. "Gotar Ceremony among the Gadabas of Orissa." *Man in India* 78: 297–303.

Prévôt, Nicolas. 2014. "Music, Spirits & Spirit in Bastar, Central India." In *Dialogues with Gods: Possession in Middle Indian Rituals*, edited by Tina Otten and Uwe Skoda, 229–246. Berlin: Weißensee Verlag.

Rajan, F. Herold, and Jamuna Rajan. 2001a. *Gutob-Gadaba Phonemic Summary*. Lamtaput (Orissa): Asha Kiran Society.

Rajan, F. Herold, and Jamuna Rajan. 2001b. *Gutob-Gadaba Language Learner's Guide*. Lamtaput (Orissa): Asha Kiran Society.

Rajan, Jamuna, and F. Herold Rajan. 2001c. *Grammar Write-Up of Gutob-Gadaba*. Lamtaput (Orissa): Asha Kiran Society.

Ramdas, G. 1931a. "The Gadabas." *Man in India* 11: 160–173.

Ramdas, G. 1931b. "Porajas." *Man in India* 11: 243–258.

Rao, C. Hayavadana. 1936. *The Dasara in Mysore: Its Origin and Significance*. Bangalore: The Bangalore Press.

Rappaport, Roy A. 1979. "The Obvious Aspects of Ritual." In *Ecology, Meaning, and Religion*, 173–221. Berkeley: North Atlantic Books.

Rappaport, Roy A. 1999. *Ritual and Religion in the Making of Humanity*. Cambridge: Cambridge University Press.

Rath, Paresh. 2014. *Glimpses of Jeypore Dasahara*. Jeypore: Jeypore Sahitya Parishad.

Reichel, Eva. 2009. *Notions of Life in Death and Dying: The Dead in Tribal Middle India*. New Delhi: Manohar.

Reichel, Eva. 2017. "On Death and the Ho's Relationship with their dead." In *Highland Odisha: Life and Society Beyond the Coastal World*, edited by Biswamoy Pati and Uwe Skoda, 107–134. New Delhi: Primus.

Reichel, Eva. 2020. *The Ho: Living in a World of Plenty: Of Social Cohesion and Ritual Friendship on the Chota Nagpur Plateau, India*. Boston and Berlin: de Gruyter.

Robbins, Joel. 2004. *Becoming Sinners: Christianity and Moral Torment in a Papua New Guinea Society*. Berkeley: University of California Press.

Rousseleau, Raphaël. 2008. *Les créatures de Yama. Ethnohistoire d'une tribu de l'Inde (Orissa)*. Bologna: CLUEB.

Rousseleau, Raphaël. 2010a. *Die Geschöpfe Yamas. Ethnohistorie eines Stammes Indiens*. Translated from French (Rousseleau 2008) by Benedikt Pontzen, Unpublished Manuskript.

Rousseleau, Raphaël. 2010b. "The King's Elder Brother: Forest King and 'Political Imagination' in Southern Orissa." *Rivista di studi sudasiatici* 4: 39–62.

Rousseleau, Raphaël. 2012. "Village Festival and Kingdom Frame. Centre and Periphery from a Poraja Village Point of View." In *Voices from the periphery: Subalternity and Empowerment in India*, edited by Marine Carrin and Lidia Guzy, 132–154. London: Routledge.

Rousseleau, Raphaël. 2021. "Jodia Poraja. Religion, Environment, and Kingdom Memories." In *Brill's Encyclopedia of the Religions of the Indigenous People of South Asia*, edited by Marine Carrin (editor-in-chief), Michel Boivin, Gérard Toffin, Paul Hockings, Raphaël Rousseleau, Tanka Subba and Harald Lambs-Tyche, 244–253. Leiden: Brill.

Rousseleau, Raphaël, and Kabiraj Behera. 2002/3. "Scheduled Tribe and Forgotten Kings: Ethnohistory of the Joria Paraja in the erstwhile Nandapur-Jeypore Kingdom." *Adivasi* 42/43: 49–63.

Roy, P.S., A. Patnaik, G.J.N. Rao, S.S.C. Patnaik, S.S. Chaudhury, and S.G. Sharma. 2017. "Participatory and Molecular Marker Assisted Pure Line Selection for Refinement of Three Premium Rice Landraces of Koraput, India." *Agroecology and Sustainable Food Systems* 41 (2): 167–85.

Roy, Sarat Chandra. 1928. *Oraon Religion and Customs*. Ranchi: (no publisher).

Roy, Sarat Chandra. 1935. *The Hill Bhuiyas of Orissa. With comparative notes on the Plains Bhuiyas*. Ranchi: Man in India Office.

Rubel, Paula G., and Abraham Rosman 1978. *Your Own Pigs You May Not Eat: A Comparative Study of New Guinea Societies*. Chicago: University of Chicago Press.

Sahlins, Marshall D. 1963. "Poor Man, Rich Man, Big-Man, Chief: Political Types in Melanesia and Polynesia." *Comparative Studies in Society and History* 5 (3): 285–303.

Sahlins, Marshall D. 1965. "On the Sociology of Primitive Exchange." In *The Relevance of Models for Social Anthropology*, edited by Michael Banton, 139–236. London: Tavistock.

Sahlins, Marshall D. 1968. *Tribesmen*. Englewood Cliffs: Prentice-Hall.

Sahlins, Marshall D. 1983. "Raw Women, Cooked Men, and other 'Great Things' of the Fiji Islands." In *The Ethnography of Cannibalism*, edited by Paula Brown and Donald F. Tuzin, 72–93. Washington, D.C.: Society for Psychological Anthropology.

Sahlins, Marshall. 1985. *Islands of History*. Chicago: University of Chicago Press.

Sahlins, Marshall D. 2005 [1992] "The Economics of Develop-man in the Pacific." In *The Making of Global and Local Modernities in Melanesia. Humiliation, Transformation and the nature of Cultural Change*, edited by Joel Robbins and Holly Wardlow, 23–42. Aldershot: Ashgate.

Sahlins, Marshall D. 2014. "On the ontological scheme of beyond nature and culture." *HAU· Journal of Ethnographic Theory* 4(1):281–290

Sahlins, Marshall D. 2017. "The Original Political Society." In *On Kings*, edited by David Graeber, and Marshall D. Sahlins, 23–64. Chicago: Hau Books.

Sahu, Lakshmī Nārāyaṇa. 1942. *The Hill Tribes of Jeypore*. Cuttack: Orissa Mission Press.

Salah, Trish. 2014. "Subaltern." *Transgender Studies Quarterly* 1 (1–2): 200–04.

Sarkar, Amitabha, and Samira Dasgupta. 1996. *Spectrum of Tribal Bastar*. New Delhi: Agam Kala Prakashan.

Sarkar, Bihani. 2020. "Toward a History of the Navarātra, the Autumnal Festival of the Goddess". In *Śaivism And the Tantric Traditions: Essays in Honour of Alexis G.j.s. Sanderson*, edited by Dominic Goodall, Shaman Hatley, Harunaga Isaacson and Srilata Raman, 321–345. Leiden: Brill.

Sasikumar, M. 1997. "Gadaba (Ollari)" In *The Encyclopedia of Dravidian Tribes*, edited by T. M. Menon and M. Sasikumar, 70–78. Thiruvananthapuram: The International School of Dravidian Linguistics.

Sax, William Sturman. 2002. *Dancing the Self: Personhood and Performance in the Pāṇḍav Līlā of Garhwal*. Oxford: Oxford University Press.

Schäfer, Sophia Margarethe. Forthcoming. "Claiming Traditional Authority. Different Interpretations of Indian Parampara." In *Dynamics of Speaking and Doing Religion*, edited by Baktygül Tulebaeva and Deepak Kumar Ojha, 35–50. Tübingen: Tübingen University Press.

Schnepel, Burkhard. 1995. "Durga and the King: Ethnohistorical Aspects of Politico-Ritual Life in a South Orissan Jungle Kingdom." *The Journal of the Royal Anthropological Institute* 1 (1): 145–66.

Schnepel, Burkhard. 2002. *The Jungle Kings. Ethnohistorical Aspects of Politics and Ritual in Orissa*. New Delhi: Manohar.

Schnepel, Burkhard. 2005. "Kings and Tribes in East India: The Internal Political Dimension." In *The Character of Kingship*, edited by Declan Quigley, 187–207. Oxford: Berg.

Schnepel, Burkhard. 2014. "Contact Zone: Ethnohistorical Notes on the Relationship between Kings and Tribes in Middle India." *Asian Ethnology* 73 (1–2): 233–57.

Schulte-Droesch, Lea. 2018. *Making Place through Ritual: Land, Environment and Region among the Santal of Central India*. Boston and Berlin: de Gruyter.

Scialpi, Fabio. 1986. "The Feast of Dasarā in the City of Mysore." *East and West* 36 (1–3): 105–36

Scott, James C. 2009 *The Art of Not Being Governed: An Anarchist History of Upland Southeast Asia*. New Haven: Yale University Press.

Senapati, Nilamani, and Nabin Kumar Sahu. 1966. *Orissa District Gazetteers: Koraput*. Cuttack: Orissa Government Press.

Shah, K.J. 1982. "Of artha and the Arthashastra." In *Way of Life: King, Householder, Renouncer. Essays in honour of Louis Dumont*, edited by T.N. Madan, 55–73. Delhi: Motilal Banarsidass Publishers.

Shortt, John. 1868. "A Contribution to the Ethnology of Jeypore." *Transactions of the Ethnological Society of London* 6: 264–364.

Shulman, David Dean. 1989. *The King and the Clown in South Indian Myth and Poetry*. Princeton, N.J.: Princeton University Press.

Simmons, Caleb. 2018. "The King and the Yadu Line: Performing Lineage through Dasara in Nineteenth-Century Mysore." In *Nine Nights of the Goddess: The Navarātri Festival in South Asia*, edited by Caleb Simmons, Moumita Sen and Hillary Rodrigues, 63–82. Albany: State University of New York Press.

Simmons, Caleb, Moumita Sen, and Hillary Rodrigues. eds. 2018. *Nine Nights of the Goddess: The Navarātri Festival in South Asia*. Albany: State University of New York Press.

Singh Deo, Kumar Bidyadhan. 1939. *Nandapur: A Forsaken Kingdom*. Cuttack: Utkal Sahitya Press.

Sinha, Surajit. 1997. [1962] "State Formation and Rajput Myth in Trinal Central India." In *The State in India 1000–1700*, edited by Hermann Kulke, 304–342. New Delhi: Oxford University Press.

Skoda, Uwe. 2003. "Goddess Laksmi and her symbolic dimensions on a tribal frontier." *Baessler-Archiv* 51: 25–44.

Skoda, Uwe. 2005. *The Aghria: A Peasant Caste Caste on a Tribal Frontier.* New Delhi: Manohar.
Skoda, Uwe. 2008. "'Coming Out' of the Palace: The Bamra Royal Family and the Performance of Power during the Elections 2004." In *Power Plays: Politics, Rituals, Performances in South Asia*, edited by Lydia Guzy and Uwe Skoda, 179–204. Berlin: Weißensee Verlag.
Skoda, Uwe. 2012. "Texts, Centres and Authorities: The History of the Royal Family of Bonai." In *Voices from the periphery: Subalternity and Empowerment in India*, edited by Marine Carrin and Lidia Guzy, 103–131. London: Routledge.
Skoda, Uwe. 2015. "Rajas, Adibasis and their Goddess(es): Dasara Rituals and a Sacrificial Polity in a Former Feudatory State in Odisha." *Internationales Asienforum* 46 (1–2): 81–101.
Skoda, Uwe, and Tina Otten. 2013. "Odisha: Rajas and Prajas in a multi-segmented society." In *The Modern Anthropology of India: Ethnography, Themes and Theory*, edited by Peter Berger and Frank Heidemann, 208–226. London: Routledge.
Smith, Brian K. 1990. "Eaters, Food, and Social Hierarchy in Ancient India: A Dietary Guide to a Revolution of Values." *Journal of the American Academy of Religion* Lviii (2): 177–206.
Somasundaram, A. M. 1949. "A Note on the Gadabas of Koraput District." *Man in India* 29: 36–45.
Sontheimer, Günther-Dietz. 1994. "The Vana and the Ksetra: The Tribal Background of Some Famous Cults." In *Religion and Society in Eastern India*, edited by Gaya Charan Tripathi and Hermann Kulke, 117–164. New Delhi: Manohar.
Sopher, David Edward. ed. 1980. *An Exploration of India: Geographical Perspectives on Society and Culture.* Ithaca, N.Y.: Cornell University Press.
Spate, O.H.K. 1960. *India and Pakistan: A general and regional geography.* London: Methuen & Co.
Stanley, William. 1996. "Machkund, Upper Kolab and Nalco Projects in Koraput District, Orissa." Economic and Political Weekly 31 (24): 1533–1538.
Steever, Sanford B. ed. 2019. *The Dravidian languages* (2nd ed.). London: Routledge.
Stein, Burton. 1983. "Mahanavami: Medieval and Modern Kingly Ritual in South India." In *Essays on Gupta Culture*, edited by Bardwell L. Smith, 67–90. Delhi: Motilal Banarsidass.
Strümpell Christian. 2008. "'We work together, we eat together': Conviviality and modernity in a company settlement in south Orissa." *Contributions to Indian Sociology* 42 (3): 351–81.
Subba Rao, V., and D.R. Patnaik. 1992. *Gadaba: The Language and the People.* Amaravathi: Papayaradhya Sahiti Kendram.
Subba, Tanka B., and Jelle P. Wouters. 2013. "North-East India: Ethnography and Politics of Identity." In *The Modern Anthropology of India: Ethnography, Themes and Theory*, edited by Peter Berger and Frank Heidemann, 193–207. London: Routledge.
Sundar, Nandini. 2001. "Debating Dussehra and Reinterpreting Rebellion in Bastar District, Central India." *The Journal of the Royal Anthropological Institute* 7 (1): 19–35.
Sundar, Nandini. 2007. *Subalterns and Sovereigns: An Anthropological History of Bastar, 1854–1996.* New Delhi: Oxford University Press.
Suryanarayan, M. 2009. "The segmentary Lineage system among the Saoras of Andhra Pradesh." In *Contemporary Society. Tribal Studies, Vol. VIII: Structure and Exchange in Tribal India and Beyond*, edited by Georg Pfeffer and Deepak Kumar Behera, 185–203. New Delhi: Concept Publishing.
Tambiah, Stanley J. 1985. *Culture, Thought and Social Action.* Cambridge: Harvard University Press.

Tanabe, Akio. 2003. "The Sacrificer State and Sacrificial Community: Kingship in Early Modern Khurda, Orissa, Seen Through a Local Ritual." In *Sharing Sovereignty: The Little Kingdom in South Asia*, edited by Georg Berkemer and Margret Frenz, 115–135. Berlin: Klaus Schwarz Verlag.

Thapar, Romila. 1971. "The Image of the Barbarian in Early India." *Comparative Studies in Society and History* 13 (4): 408–436.

The Laws of Manu 1991, translated by Wendy Doniger and Brian K. Smith. London: Penguin.

Thurston, Edgar. 1909a. *Castes and Tribes of Southern India, Vol. III*. Madras: Government Press.

Thurston, Edgar. 1909b. *Castes and Tribes of Southern India, Vol. VI*. Madras: Government Press.

Thurston, Edgar. 1909c. *Castes and Tribes of Southern India, Vol. V*. Madras: Government Press.

Thusu, Kidar Nath. 1968. *The Dhurwa of Bastar*. Calcutta: Anthropological Survey of India.

Thusu, Kidar Nath. 1977. *The Pengo Porajas of Koraput. An Ethnographic Survey*. Calcutta. Anthropological Survey of India.

Thusu, Kidar Nath, and Makhan Jha. 1972. *Ollar Gadba of Koraput*. Calcutta: Anthropological Survey of India.

Ulaka, Rama Chandra. 1976. "The Social Life of the Paraja." *Adivasi* 17 (2): 21–32.

Vadivelu, A. 1915. *The Ruling Chiefs, Nobles and Zamindars of India*. Madras: G.C. Loganadham.

Vitebsky, Piers. 1993. *Dialogues with the Dead: The Discussion of Mortality among the Sora of Eastern India*. Cambridge: Cambridge University Press.

Vitebsky, Piers. 2013. "Stones, Shamans and Pastors: Pagan and Baptist Temporalities of Death in Tribal India." In *Taming Time, Timing Death: Social Technologies and Ritual*, edited by Dorthe Refslund Christensen and Rane Willerslev, 119–136. Farnham: Ashgate.

Vitebsky, Piers. 2017a. *Living without the dead: loss and redemption in a jungle cosmos*. Chicago: The University of Chicago Press.

Vitebsky, Piers. 2017b. "The Sora 'tribe': animist, Hindu, Christian. Online supplement to Vitebsky (2017a)." http://www.press.uchicago.edu/sites/Vitebsky

Viveiros de Castro, Eduardo. 1998. "Cosmological Deixis and Amerindian Perspectivism." *Journal of the Royal Anthropological Institute* 4 (3): 469–88.

Volkmann, Amrei. 2001. "Tanz und Spiel mit den Göttern: Die Ganga Puja der Joria im Koraput Distrikt." Paper presented in the Institute of Ethnology, Free University of Berlin (November 2001). Unpublished Manuscript.

Volkmann, Amrei. 2003. "Körper und choreographisches Verfahren im Tanztheater von Pina Bausch und Sasha Waltz." In *Modelle künstlerischer Produktion*, edited by Friedrich Weltzien and Amrei Volkmann, 91–98. Berlin: Reimer Verlag.

Vora, Rajendra, and Anne Feldhaus. eds. 2006. *Region, Culture, and Politics in India*. New Delhi: Manohar.

Vyasulu, V. 1985. "Underdeveloping Koraput." *South Asian Anthropologist* 6: 63–71.

Waak, Otto, Alfred Bruhn, Anthon Asha, and S.C. Sekhoro Mohoriya. 1994. *Indische Kirche und Indien-Mission, Teil 1*. Erlangen: Verlag der Ev.-Luth. Mission.

Wadley, Susan. 1977. "Power in Hindu Ideology and Practice." In *The New Wind: Changing Identities in South Asia*, edited by David Kenneth, 133–157. The Hague: Mouton Publishers.

Weisgrau, Maxine. 2013. "Rajasthan: Anthropological perspectives on tribal identity." In *The Modern Anthropology of India: Ethnography, Themes and Theory*, edited by Peter Berger and Frank Heidemann, 224–259. London: Routledge.

Wolf, Eric Robert. 1966. *Peasants*. Englewood Cliffs, N.J.: Prentice Hall.

Woodburn, James. 1982. "Egalitarian Societies." *Man* 17 (3): 431–51.

Zide, Arlene R. K, and Norman H. Zide. 1976. "Proto-Munda Cultural Vocabulary: Evidence for Early Agriculture." *Oceanic Linguistics Special Publications* 13: 1295–1334.

List of Tables

Table 1   Comparison of "Brotherhood" and Dom Raja Stories —— 89
Table 2   Overview of Ritual Roles during the Ganga Festival —— 233
Table 3   Overview of the Main Rituals and Activities of the Ganga Festival —— 234
Table 4   Overview of the Nandi Festival —— 271
Table 5   Overview of the Main Ritual Actors of the Bali Jatra —— 325
Table 6   Overview of the Last Phase of the Bali Jatra —— 327

List of Maps

Map 1 Odisha in Central India —— 6
Map 2 The Eastern Ghats and the Bastar Plateau —— 7
Map 3 The Nandapur/Jeypore Region —— 8

List of Photos

Photo 6.1	The custodian of the Ganga deity	236
Photo 6.2	The preparation of the Ganga deity has been completed	237
Photo 6.3	Taking the Ganga deity out of the house	240
Photo 6.4	The carriers of the Ganga deities	241
Photo 6.5	Procession of Ganga deities through the village	242
Photo 6.6	A sacrificial stop has been prepared	243
Photo 6.7	Invocation of the Ganga deities by the *gurumai*	244
Photo 6.8	Sacrifices for Ganga	245
Photo 6.9	A break for the drummers and the carriers	246
Photo 6.10	Worshipping the deities after the completion of the sacrifices	247
Photo 6.11	The Ganga deities arrive at the *sadar*	248
Photo 6.12	The Monkey Dance	249
Photo 6.13	Preparation of the stilts	251
Photo 6.14	The stilt dance, "let's play!"	253
Photo 6.15	A scene from the Park Play	255
Photo 6.16	Nightly performances of the Ganga festival	256
Photo 7.1	The mural of the Nandi festival	273
Photo 7.2	The Nandi house	274
Photo 7.3	The Nandi deities in their basket	278
Photo 7.4	A *gurumai* is invoking the Nandi deities	279
Photo 7.5	The "kidnapper"	280
Photo 7.6	Beginning of the procession	282
Photo 7.7	The "sister" (millet) is visiting her "brother" (rice)	283
Photo 7.8	"Walk sister, walk sister, Earth Beauty; walk sister, walk sister, Dust Beauty"	285
Photo 7.9	Leaving the house of the junior Ganga deity	286
Photo 7.10	Singing the Nandi song	288
Photo 7.11	Chondoro Maji presents the bird he has fashioned for the procession	290
Photo 7.12	Reappearance of rice in the festival	291
Photo 7.13	The *sadar* of Lenjisuku	292
Photo 8.1	The Bali deity	329
Photo 8.2	Distribution of seeds	330
Photo 8.3	Distribution of sand	331
Photo 8.4	Filling the baskets with earth and seeds	332
Photo 8.5	Men from the Mali community paint the central part of the mural	333
Photo 8.6	The wall painting has been completed	333
Photo 8.7	Worshippers gather inside the Bali temple for the "trance dance"	337
Photo 8.8	Distributing rice	338
Photo 8.9	A woman is performing the "trance dance" inside the temple	339
Photo 8.10	Passing through the Databeli Fort	340
Photo 8.11	The village *pujari* inspects the stretcher with thorns for the Bima	342
Photo 8.12	Dancing Bima	343
Photo 8.13	A demonstration of divine power	344

Open Access. © 2023 the author(s), published by De Gruyter. This work is licensed under the Creative Commons Attribution-NoDerivs 4.0 International License.
https://doi.org/10.1515/9783110458831-017

Photo 8.14	Bali "flowers" —— 345	
Photo 8.15	Procession to the paddy fields to exchange "flowers" —— 345	
Photo 8.16	Auspicious footsteps —— 346	
Photo 8.17	Sacrifice for the river deities —— 347	
Photo 9.1	Gadaba women transplanting paddy, 1941 —— 360	
Photo 9.2	Mourning the buffalo-dead —— 367	
Photo 9.3	Line-up for feasting —— 368	
Photo 9.4	Women feed the buffalo-dead at the village platform (Ponosguda, 2001) —— 369	
Photo 9.5	Bringing the stones —— 372	
Photo 9.6	Planting the stones —— 373	
Photo 9.7	Celebrating life —— 374	
Photo 9.8	The "dry-field platform" —— 375	
Photo 9.9	Final farewell —— 376	
Photo 9.10	Equipment for the underworld —— 377	
Photo 9.11	The *purani* delegation approaches the Go'ter village —— 378	
Photo 9.12	The arrival of the *purani* buffalo —— 379	

Index

Adivasi 14, 16, 65, 75, 77, 92, 94, 137
affines/affinity 10–12, 16, 21, 23, 24, 37–39, 136–137, 147, 150, 217, 222, 270, 284–292, 310–311, 346–350, 370, 374–383, 390, 394, 397
– in myths 23, 58, 69, 71–74, 85, 87, 89, 104, 111, 218, 318–321
agnates/agnation (brotherhood) see clan 24, 39, 97, 100, 104, 132, 147, 213, 263, 347–348, 369–378, 380–382, 385, 389
– and social structure 11–12, 15, 22, 33, 129, 150, 159, 222, 347, 357–359, 365–366
– in myths 23, 32, 58, 69–78, 85, 87–89, 94, 95, 102, 104–105, 189
agriculture/cultivation 114, 145, 163, 165–166, 170–171, 180, 183, 189–190, 191, 195, 197, 207–208, 210–211, 214, 234, 237, 240, 247, 260, 269, 270, 273, 276, 283, 291, 301, 308, 353, 354–355, 360, 396
– agricultural cycle 116, 192, 245, 321, 260, 390, 367–368
– regional history of 218–220
– Bima and 314–318
– rice cultivation cycle 116, 145, 218
– different regional cultivation systems 220–223, 359
– shifting cultivation 220–221, 359
– knowledge of cultivation 37, 96, 304, 317–318, 319, 398
– as related to sacrifice 350
– and hunting 75, 318
– human grainhood/plant personhood 367–368, 385–390, 397–398
– and (human) sacrifice 80–81, 103, 263–264, 384
– in myth 83, 86–87, 94, 95, 218, 297, 301, 302–305, 310–311, 318–320
– and termites 300–301
– and murals 309
– and the Bali Jatra in Komra 327–346
– and Go'ter 364, 380, 384, 389–393
– and Gunom 386–387

– and Guar 387–388
ancestors 15, 21–26, 38, 72, 175, 304–307, 318, 350, 354–383, 387
Austroasiatic languages 12, 220, 295, 322, 357

Bali Jatra 19, 29, 37–39, 190, 208, 298, 312–355, 390, 392
Bastar 13, 19, 34, 117, 121, 129, 130, 133, 147, 158, 159–177, 188–191, 207, 212, 214, 218, 224, 320, 353, 394, 400
Bening/Benek (ethnic group) 32–33, 82–83, 114–116, 145, 180, 224, 262, 268
Bhattra (ethnic group) 59, 301–303
Bhuiya (ethnic group) 20, 33–34, 64, 131–133, 136–143, 148–150, 157–158, 212
– Konto Kuari festival 140–143, 149, 212, 216
Biardeau, Madeleine. 49
Bima 37, 302, 304, 314–319, 328, 334, 349
Bird-Davic, Nurit 16, 26
Bondo/Remo (ethnic group and language) 5, 66–67, 76, 77, 79, 80, 88, 103, 142, 219, 220–221, 223, 295, 296, 307, 320, 346, 350, 356–357, 365, 383, 386–387, 393
Boro Porja (ethnic group) 220, 224, 298

Carrin, Marine 21, 27
Central India 29, 127, 148
– Tribal Central India as a Culture Area 8–14, 24, 39, 150, 158–159, 361
Christianity 28–29, 387
Clan/clanship 10, 12, 23, 94, 96–100, 107, 129, 347
– brotherhood 15, 22, 38, 101, 129, 132, 347
– village clan 226, 370
– clan territory/territorial clan 96, 97, 99, 124, 132, 150, 184, 212
comparative analysis 9–13, 15–17, 213

dance (*nat*) 227
– vs play (*kel*) 265–268
– trance-dance 325, 331, 335–338
– monkey dance 242–245, 249

Open Access. © 2023 the author(s), published by De Gruyter. This work is licensed under the Creative Commons Attribution-NoDerivs 4.0 International License.
https://doi.org/10.1515/9783110458831-018

Dasara 1, 17, 29, 30, 34–35, 61, 79, 100, 117, 122–123, 353
– Gell's analysis of Dasara 130–131, 394–395
– integrative function of Dasara 151, 156–157, 212, 403
– myths and Dasara rituals 213–214
– Dasara and fertility 217
death/the dead
– and grain 306–308, 385–391
– death rituals 15–16, 25, 38, 348, 387, 393
– Gadaba conception of death 23–24
– sacrificial death and regeneration 34, 156, 171, 172, 395
– temporal death 209, 211
– king's death 53
– as related to fertility of earth 306–308, 388, 400
– navigating life/death 393, 399
Demmer, Ulrich 16
Derret, John 50–53, 58
descent 10, 12, 23, 224, 358, 369
Descola, Philippe 105
Desia (ethnic group) 102, 270, 287, 290, 303, 358
– non-ST Desia 13, 324
– of Koraput 27–28
– sacred geography 314, 359
– Desia hierarchy 323
– lifeworld 347
Didayi/Gta'(ethnic group/language) 18, 72, 73, 192, 219, 223
Dom Raja 32, 33, 79, 81–90, 104–105, 116, 145, 213, 260, 268, 313
Dombo/Dom 11, 13, 18, 28, 73, 89, 91, 113, 229, 324, 358
Doniger Wendy 53–54
Dongria Kond (ethnic group) 11–13, 90–100, 101–105, 107, 117, 122–125, 135, 183–187, 188, 197–199, 206–208, 297–298, 316–317, 354
Dravidian languages 12, 24, 224, 357
Dumont, Louis 149

Eastern Ghats 4–5, 71, 110, 144
effervescence 19, 26, 30, 130, 167, 173, 189, 190, 207, 213, 377, 394

– systemic collective effervescence 176, 265, 391
– effervescent dislocation 176, 399
Elwin, Verrier 59, 66–70, 77, 81, 88, 91, 103, 192, 223–225, 300–301, 309–310, 315, 361, 386–387
embodiments 304
– of the dead 39, 308, 360–368
– of deities 241, 287, 299, 328
Evans-Pritchard, Edward Evan 23
exchange 11, 15, 16, 23–24, 346–350, 348, 353, 359, 366, 367–373, 375–383

Fischer, Eberhard 202–204
Fuller, Chris 15, 50
Fürer-Haimendorf Christoph von 129, 147, 220, 223, 356, 365

Gadaba (ethnic group) 12–13, 15, 20–29, 65–68, 69–71, 76, 102–104, 151, 180, 192–193, 193–197, 199–206, 220–223, 356–395
Ganga Festival 2–3, 25, 36, 218–269, 293, 310
Gell, Simeran 120–121, 128, 146–147
Gell, Alfred 130, 147, 170, 172–177, 267, 394
Ghasi (ethnic group) 228–229, 261
Guha, Ranajit 1, 78, 105
Go'ter 26, 38–39, 133, 190, 348, 356–395
Godavari 5, 23, 75, 357, 462
Gond 70, 129, 158
– Gond Complex 11, 13
– Maria Gond 70, 72, 167–168, 224
– Muria Gond 106, 107, 121, 165, 167–168, 174–177, 224–225, 300
Goudo (ethnic group) 13, 18, 64, 77
Gregory, Chris 158, 160, 161, 218, 222, 305, 319, 320, 350
Guar 386–387
Gunom 365, 386–387, 393
Gutob (language, ethnic group) 12, 13, 132, 150, 205, 357, see Gadaba

Hardenberg, Roland 11, 91, 97–100, 123, 184, 186, 191, 197–198, 209, 215–216, 297–298, 316–317, 354, 393, 400

Heckenberger, Michael 20
hierarchy 18, 44–48, 73, 94, 101, 105–106, 216, 217
– hierarchical opposition 149, 217
– oscillating hierarchy 11, 347
Hindu
– religion/society vs. tribal religion/society 10, 14–15, 105–107, 121, 128, 133–136, 147–148, 212–217
– ideas of kingship 30, 43–63, 105
– cultural hegemony of Hindu kingship 123–127
– influence on tribal society 77
– empires 208–212
Hinduism 15, 45, 50, 58
Hinduization 121, 125, 126, 133, 201
Ho (ethnic group) 8, 11, 12
Hocart, Arthur M. 102, 126, 399
hunting 32, 37, 48, 304, 317, 359, 402
– gathering-hunting 16, 150, 402

Inden Ronald 35, 51, 53–55, 59–63, 212, 217
Indrawati 5
Irwin, John C. 295
Izikowitz 3, 224, 356, 363, 365–380, 384, 392, 395

Jeypore 4–5, 27 (see Nancapur)
– Dasara in 67–68, 177–180, 213, 353–354, in comparison to Bastar 187–191
– history of kings 108–119
– Juro Festival Bissamcuttack 183–187
– tribal villages close to 199–206
– region an agriculture 219–220
Jong, Josslelin de 9
Joria (ethnic group) 223–227, 199–208, see Ganga and Nandi Festivals
Juang (ethnic group) 24, 106, 119, 120–123, 143
jungle kingdoms 108, 157–159, 187–191, 212–217

Karja 308, 311, 387
Kond (ethnic group) 12 (see Dongria Kond)
– Kuttia Kond 27, 77, 220–221, 300–301, 370
– Kuvi Kond 192, 220, 298, 312

– Kond Complex 11
– Meria 96, 139, 208, 384
Koraput 4–5, 13, 28, 29, 30, 79, 109, 119, 122, 126, 144, 181, 219, 323, 346, 355
– Koraput Complex 12, 224, 346
Kotni Mala Hill 33, 67, 75, 84–85, 114–115, 145, 180–181, 183, 415, 416, 426
Koya (ethnic group) 12, 16, 58, 74, 120, 316, 429
Kroeber, Alfred 9
Kulke, Hermann 108–110, 125, 128, 133–134, 146–147

Machkund 5, 75
Mahima Dharma/Olek Dormo 29
Malamoud, Charles 46–48, 52
Mali (ethnic group) 13, 233, 250, 255, 257, 277, 312–355
Mallebrein, Cornelia 161, 163, 165–168, 171, 172
Marglin, Frédérique Apffel 209–210, 215–216
McDougal, Charles 106, 120–123, 143, 147, 150
millet 212, 222, 348 (see finger millet)
– millet gruel 70–71, 222, 232
– millet beer 185, 371
– in myths 86, 296, 301, 416, 422, 423
– millet cultivation 217–218, 220–222, 359
– vs rice 222–223, 228, 283, 390
– little millet 328, 359, 385, 416
finger millet
– and ritual 26, 191, 192, 310, 317, 385–386, 389
– in the Nandi Festival 270–311
– as Nandi 228
– and termites 274–278, 295, 299, 301–305
– and animist ontologies 390, 397–398
– and Go'ter 391–392
missionaries 29
– Breklum mission 28, 119
Munda (ethnic group) 11, 219
Munda languages 12, 219, 220, 322
murals 202–203, 272, 309–310, 355
myths 68–69

– brotherhood stories 32, 69–78, 89, 94, 101, 105–107, 140, 213
– Dom Raja stories 32, 79–89, 94, 101, 104, 116, 140
– tribal myths 19, 68, 78, 213, 400
– of Dongria Kond 91–96
– King Vena 31, 53–56, 58–59
– Bali Jatra epic 312–313, 318, 349, 351, 352
– Lachmi Jagar 218

Nandapur (see Jeypore) 4–5, 13, 28, 33, 66–68, 85, 110–112, 116–118, 144, 150, 177, 180, 189, 263, 393, 400–401
– Dasara in 180–183
– history of kings 108–119
Nandi Festival 29, 223, 270–311
Nayak, Prasanna K. 123–125, 143, 183–184, 186–187, 357

Odisha 4, 6, 8, 219
Ollar Gadaba 13, 66, 72, 84, 114, 180, 192, 204, 221, 225, 312, 357, 395
Ollari (language) 12–13, 357
Otten, Tina 4, 177, 312–314, 318–321, 323, 324, 328, 330, 334, 339, 348–349, 351, 352–355

Paik (ethnic group) 36, 93, 103, 118, 124, 135, 186, 228–269
– Paik (Sari) Play 254–255
Parasher, Aloka 55–57
Parenga/Gorum (ethnic group) 66, 70, 72, 74–75, 77, 80, 86–88, 219, 221, 313, 322, 324–346, 357, 361, 367, 381, 391, 400
Parkin, Robert 12, 24, 346
Parry, Jonathan P. 46, 52
Pengo (ethnic group/language) 37, 64, 72, 223, 302, 303, 316, 349
Pfeffer Georg 2, 10–13, 16, 158, 192, 224, 346–348, 356–357, 365–367, 370, 377, 381, 384, 385, 393, 395, 400, 401
play 30, 191, 228, 224, 265–266, 265–270
Porja (ethnic group) 15, 220, 223–224, 298
Prévôt, Nicolas 161, 175–176, 190, 265, 392

raja/porja (relationship) 1–2, 15, 17, 43, 64–68, 101–107, 144–151, 189, 206, 213
– in tribal myths 69–90, 91–96
– Dongria Kond buffalo sacrifice 96–100
– history of 108–119
– models of 119–137
– as co-sacrificers 1, 107, 137–144, 149, 157, 172–173, 216, 395, 399–400, 402–403
Rani Duduma 33, 75, 114, 180, 415, 416
rebellion 19, 33, 78, 87, 89, 105, 116, 120, 145, 269
– Santal rebellion 27
– tribal rebellions 120, 130, 394
– mythical rebellions 19, 82–90, 105, 112–115
– enacted in ritual 145, 254–255, 261–262, 269
Rice (see agriculture)
– cultivation 218–222, 359–360
– and ritual 114, 145, 261–262, 283, 289–291, 319–321, 335–338, 365, 367, 371, 374
– as wealth and life 93, 102
– and rebellion 116, 145, 269
– Lachmi Jagar 218
– valuations of rice (and millet) 222–223, 348–350, 390
– Ganga deity as rice 228
– and the dead 388
ritual
– ritual aggregation 25, 101, 106, 397–398
– signature rituals 1, 4, 19, 37, 205, 355, 395, 399
– ritual ferocity 173–174, 177, 183–186, 188–190, 391–395, 399
– ritual (sacrificial) polity 1, 2, 17, 19, 100, 142, 399, 403
– ritual temporality 25–26, 162–163
– ritual (socio-cosmic) order/*niam* 2, 21–22, 25–26, 30, 36, 67, 70, 78, 79, 91, 96, 102, 104, 264–267, 402
Rona (ethnic group) 13–14, 18, 139, 197, 207, 229, 323–324, 352
Rousseleau, Raphaël 4, 33, 58–59, 75, 82, 84, 113–115, 119, 123, 125–127, 144–146,

148, 178–183, 225, 268, 296–298, 301–302, 305, 308, 310, 352, 362
Roy, Sarat Chandra 140–143, 149, 157–158

Sacrifice
– sacrificial polity 1, 2, 17, 399
– sacrificial sovereignty 2, 30, 103, 147, 149, 354, 395
– king as sacrificer 17, 21, 30, 45, 48–49, 51–53, 61, 67–68, 79, 81, 100, 102, 105, 137, 155, 171, 217, 399
– tribes and king as co-sacrificers 1 17–19, 102, 104, 107, 137–144, 148–150, 157–158, 172–173, 183–187, 188, 207, 212, 216–217, 263, 354, 395, 399–400, 402–403
– human sacrifice 28, 30, 39, 67–68, 79, 80, 135–137, 163–164, 165, 170, 177–178, 182, 187–188, 190, 203, 205, 208, 211, 214, 316, 351, 384, 391, 399, 400–401
– in myths 92–95, 160–161, 304–305, 316, 319, 351, 413–414, 416, 419, 421, 423, 430
Sahlins, Marshall D. 2, 22–23, 78, 105, 150, 401, (and Graeber) 402
Sahu, Lakshmi Narayan 180, 183–186, 189, 191, 213, 391
Santal (ethnic group) 27
Sarkar, Bihani 155, 393
Sax, William 50, 52
Schnepel, Burkhart 33, 108, 110, 112–113, 115, 117, 119, 124, 128, 134–139, 144, 147–148, 183, 185–186
Sinha, Surajit 127–129, 136, 146, 143, 157–158

Skoda, Uwe 130–133, 136, 140, 146, 148, 157–158
Sora (ethnic group) 7–8, 11–13, 22, 25–26, 29, 134, 306–309, 311, 355, 361, 386–390
Stein, Burton 35, 155–156, 187
Strümpell, Christian 7
subaltern sovereignty 1, 18–19, 31, 102, 107, 116, 132, 137–139, 148–150, 168, 190, 402
Sundar, Nandini 133, 161–162, 167, 173

termites
– general properties of 293–295
– local knowledge/terms of 295
– in the Nandi Festival 271, 274–277, 287, 290, 298–299, 303
– in myths 297, 300, 301, 304, 306
– and agriculture 300–301, 304
– and wealth/life 297–299, 300, 305–306
Thapar, Romila 55–58
Thusu, K.N. 64–65, 223, 315
time
– historicity vs temporality 20
– local conceptualizations of 20–26
– changes in conceptualization of 26–29
– and ritual 162–163

Vitebsky, Piers 12, 22–23, 90, 176, 277, 361–362, 387–388
Volkmann, Amrei 3, 226, 265–267, 327

wheat 165–166, 171–173, 190, 208, 214, 218, 312, 320–321, 326–327, 329–330, 332–333, 342–345, 350, 354–355

www.ingramcontent.com/pod-product-compliance
Lightning Source LLC
Chambersburg PA
CBHW051533230426
43669CB00015B/2586